Seven Ages of Paris

ALISTAIR HORNE is the author of many bestselling books, including *The Price of Glory*, *Small Earthquake in Chile* and *How Far From Austerlitz?: Napoleon, 1805–1815*, as well as the authorized two-volume biography of Harold Macmillan. He was knighted in 2003 for services to Franco-British relations.

Back into Power

The Land is Bright

Canada and the Canadians

The Price of Glory: Verdun 1916

The Fall of Paris: The Siege and the Commune 1870–71

To Lose a Battle: France 1940

The Terrible Year: The Paris Commune 1871

Death of a Generation

Small Earthquake in Chile

Napoleon: Master of Europe 1805–1807

The French Army and Politics 1870–1970

A Savage War of Peace: Algeria 1954–1962

Macmillan: 1894–1956

Macmillan: 1957–1986

A Bundle from Britain

How Far From Austerlitz?: Napoleon, 1805–1815

The Lonely Leader: Monty 1944–45
(with David Montgomery)

Telling Lives
(editor)

ALISTAIR HORNE

Seven Ages of Paris

PAN BOOKS

First published 2002 by Macmillan

This edition first published 2017 by Pan Books
an imprint of Pan Macmillan
20 New Wharf Road, London N1 9RR
Associated companies throughout the world
www.panmacmillan.com

ISBN 978-1-5098-8925-9

19 18

A CIP catalogue record for this book is available from
the British Library.

Typeset by SetSystems Ltd, Saffron Waldon, Essex
Printed and bound by CPI Group (UK) Ltd, Croydon, CR0 4YY

Visit **www.panmacmillan.com** to read more about all our books and to buy
them. You will also find features, author interviews and news of any author
events, and you can sign up for e-newsletters so that you're always first to hear
about our new releases.

FOR NICKY

Good friend, and ally, of many years;

best of publishers for nearly forty

Contents

List of Illustrations

SECTION TWO

SECTION THREE

MAPS

Foreword

BY MAURICE DRUON

Over and above their rivalries and their ententes, for nearly a thousand years France and England have exercised upon each other a reciprocal attraction, almost a fascination. The evolution of their history, institutions and literature has been, for leading intellectuals of the two countries, a constant object of contemplation, of study and – if one may say so – of delight. For our generation Alistair Horne stands in the first rank of this elite.

Among the twenty-odd books which (apart from the official biography of Harold Macmillan) have established his fame, a large part such as *How Far from Austerlitz?: Napoleon, 1805–1815*; *The Terrible Year: The Paris Commune 1871*; *The Price of Glory: Verdun 1916* and *A Savage War of Peace: Algeria 1954–1962* have had as their subjects episodes of French history. Alistair Horne has no need to be introduced to the public. His renown precedes him.

In doing me the honour of asking me to write a foreword to *Seven Ages of Paris*, he wanted (I felt) only to offer me the opportunity to express once more the gratitude that I cherish, since the commitments of my youth, towards Great Britain and the heroic city of London, which were, during the worst ordeals of the last century, the ultimate refuge of our honour and the citadel of our liberty. It requires, however, no effort at all from me to express my admiration for the substantial book of which I have had the advantage of being one of the first readers. It will remain, I believe, Horne's most outstanding work.

Devoting many years to its preparation, he has poured into it all the knowledge acquired through his earlier works. He has consulted every possible source, not only French and English, but European and even American. He has brought to light accounts that have generally been ignored, and that are often out of the ordinary. His researches demanded innumerable visits to Paris, where – a tireless walker – he has endeavoured to tread upon the very soil that bears the footprints of the personalities he describes, and where there occurred the events which he narrates. Not a single century holds any secrets from him.

In retracing the history of Paris, from its most distant origins, Roman as well as Gallic, he offers us, in effect, a new history of France herself – a personalized history, and one that is very captivating to read. For Alistair Horne is a storyteller as well as a historian. When he writes history, he tells us a story – superbly and dramatically. He has perfectly grasped the wavelike continuum in France's destiny, which travels incessantly from the heights to the depths, because – though the French have always jibbed at reform – they have repeatedly been ready to throw themselves into adventures and revolutions. It required supermen to make France's destiny go forward, or to be masters of it.

With every sound intuition, Horne dates the first great epoch of Paris from the reign of Philippe Auguste. Precocious genius in the art of power and a formidable medieval strategist, Philippe Auguste was obsessed by the unity of the territory. In order to govern his kingdom firmly, he needed a vast, active and powerful capital which was solidly fortified. The same necessity imposed itself on his grandson, Saint Louis, himself obsessed by the unity of law, and upon Saint Louis' own grandson, Philippe le Bel, who devoted his efforts towards the unity of the state. Those three rulers invented the nation, with its irreversible characteristics, and that centralization – based on Paris – which still marks France.

Allying his dedication to truth with a sense of the epic, it is at the pace of a cavalcade that Alistair Horne makes us journey through the centuries leading from the Middle Ages to the Renaissance. From then on he wanders at a more leisurely speed. He is an apostle of factual history. He leaves it to others to embark on *a priori* theories or on the drawing of abstract sociological conclusions. He just tells it as it was.

I am glad that he has his likes, and expresses them, as he expresses his antipathies. Without a little passion, history is cold, history is dead. Of all the French monarchs, it is Henri IV, visibly, who wins his favour. This courageous warrior, this skilful diplomat, this peacemaker, this dedicated philanderer, who lacked neither cunning nor generosity, appeals to him. In contrast, Louis XIV, thinking constantly of *la Gloire*, this quintessence of an autocrat, irritates him. Horne reproaches him, not without reason, for having prepared the collapse of his dynasty through his abandoning Paris for Versailles. He has difficulty in disguising a certain contempt for Louis XV and for the unfortunate, inadequate Louis XVI.

When Bonaparte appears, it is by means of a long flashback that the author relates the events of the Revolution, and paints for us the state of squalor and dilapidation in which the Terror had left Paris – with its stinking and muddy streets, façades demolished, a city in terrible misery. He observes, amused, the removal of moral constraints during the Directory, before Napoleon arrived to reconstruct the state – and then the capital. But when this conqueror who was both a lawgiver and a builder, having overthrown Europe, falls victim to the immoderation of his dreams, he leaves behind him a Paris that is one immense construction site.

Horne alternates the art of synthesis with that of detail. If he pauses near the bed of Mme Récamier, it is not only to contemplate Chateaubriand sporting poses which he liked to strike, but to remind us that there was also an old M. Récamier, the great banker who was responsible for a resounding bankruptcy, and who yet managed to recoup his fortunes. When he crosses the Pont d'Iéna, it is to remind us how the English soldiers Wellington posted there, in 1815, prevented Blücher from destroying the structure the name of which he regarded as an insult to Prussia.

Horne is everywhere and knows everything. When he stops at a crossing, he sees there the coup which was carried out under Louis-Philippe. Or he sees the old streets and the patrician houses destroyed by Haussmann in order to open up the *grands boulevards* which changed the face of Paris during the prosperous reign of Napoleon III – who built so much yet ended so tragically.

He knows the numbers of cholera victims, during each epidemic, and the numbers of prostitutes, and the numbers of thieves, just as he knows the price of rats, and of the cat meat sold in the butchers' shops during the terrible siege of 1870. (Yet he also notes how cellars remained full – for, although the population lacked everything else, Paris never went short of wine!)

The descriptions of Paris before and after the two great wars of the twentieth century, separated by a 'Phoney Peace', are given fully and judiciously. Among the fragments of courage which illuminate the work, not the least is that recalled by the great victory parade of 1919 – a cortège not only of heroism, but also of illusions.

Nothing escapes his paintbrush which depicts men and things in their proper chiaroscuro, and which brings alive once more fashions and those who created them, ideas and those who launched them, the arts and those who gained fame therein, political battles and those who failed or triumphed.

It was an English writer, Charles Morgan, greatly admired in my youth but now perhaps unfairly forgotten, who wrote, 'France is an idea necessary for civilization.' Alistair Horne evokes this idea when he makes us relive the Occupation, with an accuracy to which my own recollections can testify – but also with manifest emotion. A cruel shadow descended on Paris when Nazi troops marched down a deserted Champs-Elysées. Terrible food shortages, heating non-existent, empty shops but full theatres, shoes with wooden soles that clattered on the pavements in the haste of getting home before the curfew, brutal round-ups, black market and clandestine operations – here were four years of humiliation, of privation, fear and denunciations, but also of heroism. If Horne underlines the exploits of the Resistance, he also hesitates before condemning the cowardice of the collaboration. 'How can we judge?' he says. 'It never happened to us. What would we have done in their place?'

That 'certaine idée de la France' found refuge in London, with de Gaulle. The light returned to Paris in the exalted but also troubled hours of the Liberation. Intellectually as much of a Gaullist as an Englishman can be, Alistair Horne cannot quite resist the strange seduction which the Man-of-18-June exercises upon all those who study him: this arrogant visionary, this uncompromising prophet, this acclaimed solitary, this authoritarian tactician, the last of the great French monarchs, who, like the first, united in his person nation, law and state. Once again it was Paris, through a new bout of fever in 1968, the least bloody but also the most disturbing of her history, which darkened and abbreviated the end of de Gaulle's reign.

Yes, I have taken enormous pleasure in rereading the history of my country, rejuvenated by the eye of a Briton. Having admired the elegant and fluid style of Alistair Horne, I wager that this book will go into many translations. For all those lovers of Paris so numerous throughout the world, it will provide a generous source of reference, an exciting travelling companion – and, in the evening of life, a lullaby of nostalgia. *Seven Ages of Paris* is, in itself, a monument.

MAURICE DRUON,
Académie Française, KBE

Preface

WHEREAS LONDON, through the ages, has always betrayed clearly male orientations, and New York has a certain ambivalence, has any sensible person ever doubted that Paris is fundamentally a woman? It was thus that I first conceived this book – not as any arrogant attempt to write an all-embracing history of Paris, but rather as a series of linked biographical essays, depicting seven ages (capriciously selected at the whim of the author) in the long, exciting life of a sexy and beautiful, but also turbulent, troublesome and sometimes excessively violent woman.

Not only is she herself all woman, but in every age Paris seems to throw up from within an extraordinary range of fascinating, powerful and often dangerous women who leave their mark on the city. They may be seen to begin with tragic Héloïse; Henry James properly dubbed her 'a Frenchwoman to the last millimetre of her shadow ... worth at least a dozen Abelards', and though she spent most of a long, sad life banished far from Paris, she always seemed to me equally a *Parisienne* to 'the last millimetre'. Then there is Eleanor of Aquitaine, and Henri IV's passionate and violent Reine Margot. The reign of Louis XIV educes the bossily pious Mme de Maintenon, counterparted by her outrageous and rather more attractive – and unlikely – friend, the courtesan Ninon de Lenclos. The age of Napoleon has, of course, Josephine – and many others with walk-on (generally boudoir) parts; similarly with Louis Napoleon, beginning with the frigid Empress Eugénie and ending with the fiery 'Red Virgin', Louise Michel, whose *pétroleuses* did their best to burn down Paris in the last days of the Commune. A happier age, briefly, of the Belle Epoque brings Sarah Bernhardt across the boards and culminates with Colette traversing – and surviving – two appalling world wars. The few bright moments of the 'Phoney Peace' of 1919–39 are illuminated by great vedettes like Josephine Baker, who became as much a *Parisienne* as any of them. And finally we have the post-1945 age of Piaf and Sagan, Simone de Beauvoir and Coco Chanel – all of them women who to some degree dominated the Paris that nurtured them.

The great Richard Cobb, late of Oxford, England's foremost connoisseur of Paris, in moments of exasperation was given to exclaim, 'Wonderful country, France ... pity about the French!' Of course he didn't really mean it, and it was far too all-embracing an insult. Occasionally, on a soaking-wet day when there is no parking and the concierge turns his back on me, I have felt, more specifically, 'Pity about the Parisians.' Then they will do something utterly disarming, generous to a fault. At least, neither Paris nor the *Parisiens* can ever be boring. I hesitate to appear to misprize my native city, but how can the history of dear, sedate old London town possibly compare to Paris for sheer excitement? (Of course, one can sometimes have perhaps too much excitement.) Against several revolutions, including one rather big one, several sieges, several occupations, what has mild-mannered London to offer but one regicide, a plague and a fire? A city without walls, protected by the Channel instead of only the gentle Seine, never threatened with starvation or besieged by an enemy – at least until Hitler came knocking at our door? And, against the great builders and city-planners from Philippe Auguste to Haussmann, of whom can London boast? A Wren or two. Then, where were our Impressionists during the Belle Epoque?

Perhaps fortunately for us sleepy Londoners, we have never known the violent changes of mood that have worked on Parisian adrenalin – for instance, Napoleon's triumphal return from Tilsit, as Conqueror of Europe in 1807, followed only seven years later by Russian Cossacks camping in the Champs-Elysées; the dazzle of the Second Empire of 1867, followed by the horrors of the Commune of 1871; the Belle Epoque by the drama of the Marne of 1914; the catastrophe of 1940 by the rhapsody of the Liberation four years later.

On top of Paris's immortal beauty, her swift changes of mood never cease to fascinate me. Because of the chances of geography and history, she has always been a microcosm of the nation's life, perhaps more so than any other capital in the world. In the course of work on nine books on French history, over three decades (sometimes a love–hate relationship), I found the scene repeatedly darting back to the capital, telling me things, little details, I didn't know. So I kept a 'discard box', much as Churchill is said to have done in the Second World War – a kind of scrapbook, which is the origin of this book.

Like a hauntingly alluring, and exacting, mistress Paris has never quite left me. The choice of her seven ages is highly idiosyncratic; some of the leading actors, like Henri IV, I came to venerate; Louis XIV to dislike even more than I did already; about Napoleon I had written a certain amount already, yet his role in the development of Paris turned into a new voyage of discovery; de Gaulle I found myself reappraising and admiring more than I had in those contentious days of the 1960s when he was such a thorn in the side of *les Anglo-Saxons*. At times, in order to set each age in its right framework, I found myself almost composing a history of Paris from Julius Caesar onwards – even a history of France. The four and a half years of writing were wonderfully self-educative. My selection of the seven ages, is, as I cautioned earlier, idiosyncratic, personal – and prejudiced. For instance, students of the Great Revolution may justly complain that I have foreshortened the terrible years from 1789 onwards. Yes, but so much has been written – especially since the *bicentenaire* of 1989 – what is there that is new? And anyhow, as far as Paris was concerned, it was such a destructive, life-denying, wretched time. Again, I may be asked why I chose 1969 as my cut-off date. What about the Paris of François Mitterrand, that most adroit of modern French politicians, and as intriguing a subject for biography in his own right? In defence, I turn to Mao's Prime Minister Chou En-lai, who, when asked for his view on the Great Revolution, gave the immortal response, 'It may be too early to tell.'

*

Many people have helped and encouraged me during the years spent preparing and writing this book. In particular I wish to express my thanks to Sir Michael and Lady Jay, for help and hospitality at the British Embassy in Paris, and to Christine Warren, former Assistant Comptroller in the Embassy; to Ambassador and Mrs Evan Galbraith, at the US Embassy in Paris; to Mme Bennett of the Mairie de Paris, M. Herrault of the Hôtel Matignon, M. Denoix de Saint Marc of the Conseil d'Etat; M. Maurice Druon KBE, former Secrétaire Perpetuel (not least for his most generous Foreword, and M. Laurent Personne of the Académie Française; M. Guy de Rothschild and Mme Kolesnikoff, Hôtel Lambert; Mme Le Lieur, Hôtel de Sens; Mme Garnier-Ahlberg, Hôtel Sully; M. Luc Forlivesi, Archives Nationales; M. Alfred Fierro of the Bibliothèque Historique de la Ville de Paris, and the helpful staff of the Musée Carnavalet. I owe appreciation to kind friends in Paris who have helped me with various points of research, notably Mrs Jake Eberts and Mrs Gaby Steers.

I owe an almost career-long debt to my oldest French friends, S. E. Francis Huré and his late wife Jacqueline, heroine of the Resistance, who, in the 1950s, first made me think – with affection – about France, and especially about Paris.

In England I am indebted, as always, to the London Library, to the Cambridge University Library and the Seeley Library; to my college, Jesus College Cambridge, for offering me a sanctuary from time to time. Mr Tony Nuspl (now of the University of Saskatchewan) carried out invaluable research for me on the three earliest Ages, while taking his PhD at Cambridge, and to him I am greatly beholden. My former colleague on the Franco-British Council, Professor Douglas Johnson, gave me helpful advice at various stages. I am indebted to *Military History Quarterly* for allowing me to draw on various articles I wrote for them; and also to *Time Out* for permission to use sections of my article 'History in Marble', from their excellent *Paris Walks* (London, 1999). Ms Josine Meijer did the picture research, with skill and diligence, aided in Paris by Kate Lewin; while, over several years, Mrs Michael Robjohn worked stoically on research, filing and secretarial work, and keeping the author on the rails – I am most grateful to her. In a special category, I owe much gratitude to Mr Peter James for his incomparable excellence as an editor: this book, our fifth together, longer and more complex than any of the others, came to require immense labour from him. Any surviving mistakes are, most emphatically, mine alone.

On a personal and purely selfish note of gratitude, I would like to acknowledge my own extraordinary good fortune in having lived some of Age Seven in Paris, the good and the great times, and the bad times – over a period of some five decades.

ALISTAIR HORNE
Turville, May 2002

A Note on Money

Pre-revolutionary French currency is difficult to convert into modern values. At various times in French history different *monnaie* was used, the value of which could be arbitrarily changed. The écu, for example, might be worth three or six livres, depending on the date. Struck at the time of Louis XI and Charles VIII in the effigy of the king, it was worth five francs. Then there was the pistole, notionally worth ten livres. The livre itself, divided into sous and deniers and for long the standard measure of currency, originally equalled a certain weight of silver, but this was progressively reduced in value from the days of Charlemagne onwards. (In today's terms the livre in the time of Louis XIV might be worth somewhere between eighty pence and £2, though some experts have recently put it as high as US$40. Such a discrepancy illustrates just how hard it is to establish a sensible relativity.)

To complicate matters further, the livre tournois (meaning struck in Tours) was worth one-fifth less than the livre parisis (struck in Paris). Named after Louis XIII in 1640 (and struck by a Superintendent Bullion), there was the louis d'or equalling ten francs; later it became worth twenty-four francs and – later still – was replaced by twenty-franc pieces. In 1720 its official rate was fifty-four livres; after the John Law bubble burst, it fell to thirty-nine. The franc itself was introduced by King Jean le Bon in 1360, in the midst of the Hundred Years War (and a time of runaway inflation), as an update of the écu; it was superseded in turn, and disappeared for over 200 years. At last, under the Revolution the franc became the official currency, decimalized to contain 100 centimes. With the advent of Bonaparte, a napoléon was issued, worth thirty francs; it had a short life. Devalued many times, sometimes coined in light (and worthless) aluminium pieces, under de Gaulle the franc was restored as the nouveau or 'heavy' franc, worth 100 old francs. It was to disappear, after six-and-a-half centuries, swallowed up by the euro, in 2002.

INTRODUCTION

From Caesar to Abelard

Get down on your knees and pray! I know it, I see it. The Huns
will not come.

Sainte Geneviève, in AD 451

ORIGINS

Mythomanes of Paris (of which there are many), seeking to imbue the
city's past with even more glamour than is already its due, claim that its
progenitor was that Paris of legend, son of Priam, who so upset three
competitive goddesses and whose passion for Helen launched one of
the longest wars in history. Philippe Auguste, his poets and his historians
were especially partial to the Trojan Connection: a 'Catalogue' or family
tree dating from the latter years of Philippe's reign is captioned, 'These
are the names of the kings of the Franks who came from Troy.' (Hence,
in a direct line, derived the Phrygian caps of ancient Troy, sported by
those terrifying maenads of the Great Revolution, the *tricoteuses*.) Others
dedicated to discovering the earliest origins of Paris, marginally less
romantic, reckon its true founder – in purely archaeological terms – to
have been a tiny mollusc in some dark Jurassic Age called a nummulite.
This provides a link to Venus, goddess of love, also born out of a shell –
a myth celebrated on the Renaissance Fontaine des Innocents close to
where Henri IV met his assassin. Other early *Parisiens* (in the Neolithic
Age) were less feminine – giant, mammoth-like elephants who lumbered
down from their habitat on the slopes of Belleville and what is now Père
Lachaise Cemetery, to slurp from the (still pure) waters of the Seine.

The less starry-eyed trace the true origins of Paris back to the
Romans, who under the leadership of Julius Caesar had conquered Gaul

in the first century BC. In AD 358, the twenty-five-year-old Emperor Julian
found Lutetia (as the Roman colony on the Île de la Cité was called),
with its vineyards, figs and gentle climate, so thoroughly agreeable that
he refused a summons to lead legions to the Middle East. 'My dear
Lutetia,' he wrote. 'It occupies an island in the middle of the river;
wooden bridges link it to the two banks. The river rarely rises or falls; as
it is in summer, so it is in winter; the water is pleasant to drink, for it is
very pure and agreeable to the eye.' Julian sojourned there three years,
thus in effect making Paris *de facto* capital of the Western Empire,
counterpart of Constantinople in the East. Indeed he proclaimed himself
emperor on the Île de la Cité. (The next such ceremony was to be
Napoleon Bonaparte's in 1804.) The Roman tradition became dear to
later rulers of 'Lutèce'. In his godlike splendour, the Roi Soleil would tap
into it, content to see himself portrayed as Hercules on the Porte Saint-
Martin. The Great Revolution and its heirs reinvented such artefacts as
consuls and senators, tribunes and togas. Napoleon I emulated Trajan's
Column to proclaim his victories over his Russian and Austrian foes at
Austerlitz in the Place Vendôme. Napoleon III reverently clad the statue
of his great uncle atop it in a toga, and, when things were going badly
for him in 1869, went to pay homage to the Roman ruins of Lutetia. A
less pleasant legacy dating from Roman days was the entertainment of
roasting stray cats alive, on the ill-omened Place de Grève, which
continued until Louis XIV ended it in the seventeenth century.

It was not only the gentle allure of muddy Lutetia, its vineyards and
the 'clear and limpid' waters of the Seine that attracted the Romans.
From earliest days the navigable Seine and the north–south axis which
intersected it at the Île de la Cité formed one of Europe's most important
crossroads. The island itself constituted a natural fortress, all but unassailable – except when unprincipled barbarians like the Norsemen took
it from the rear by floating down from upstream, whence the wine,
wheat and timber from Burgundy normally came. In the ages before
road or rail transport, the Seine – in marked contrast to the estuarial,
shallow and narrow Thames – was an ideal river for major commerce.
Its broad and deep currents were not too swift, and hard turf or stone
lined most of its banks. Early descriptions of Paris comment on the
extraordinary capacities of the waters of the Seine to support heavy
loads. Together with its tributaries, the Oise and the Marne, the Seine
linked up most of northern France and reached out southwards and
eastwards, up to Montargis, Auxerre, Troyes and numerous lesser towns.
It enabled Paris to dominate commerce in the north, making her a

natural capital for trade early in the Middle Ages, never to lose this primacy. Meanwhile nearby stone quarries enabled her rulers to float down vast quantities of building material to construct her walls and fortifications.

By the end of the first century AD, Christianity had arrived in Paris, followed shortly thereafter by the first martyrs. Dionysius, or Denis, came from Rome and was probably Greek. Aged ninety, he was arrested for denying the divinity of the Emperor, imprisoned on what is now the Quai aux Fleurs, close to the modern Préfecture de Police, and then dragged up the Roman highway that still bears his name northwards from the Seine. On top of a hill overlooking the city where stood a temple to Mercury, he and two supporters were decapitated. According to legend, he picked up his head with its long white beard, washed it in a nearby stream, and continued walking for 'six thousand paces'. The spot where he finally dropped and was buried became a holy place. Eventually the cathedral of Saint-Denis was built on its site, subsequently to become the burial place of French kings from Dagobert onwards. His place of execution became the 'Mons Martyrum' – or Montmartre; and the city annals chalked up their first revolutionary martyr as well as their first bishop.

With the death of the benevolent Julian and the collapse of Roman power after the best part of six centuries, various 'barbarians', pushed westwards by some unrecorded pressure in Central Asia, came trampling in from the east – Vandals, Franks, Avars and Huns. The Île de France – one of the most ancient provinces of France, formed by the rivers Seine, Marne, Ourcq, Aisne and Oise – even then presented an enticing land of milk and honey, and Paris trembled. In 451, the worst of the lot, the Huns under their fearsome leader Attila, crossed the Rhine heading westwards. At Cologne they were reported to have massacred 11,000 virgins. Parisians prepared for a mass exodus, piling their belongings on to wagons with solid wooden wheels. But a fifteen-year-old orphan girl called Geneviève, who had come close to fasting to death in her convent – like another French teenager nearly a thousand years later – had a vision. She exhorted the populace not to leave, telling them, 'Get down on your knees and pray! I know it, I see it. The Huns will not come.' She was proved right. Unlike Hitler, they stayed away, eventually to be driven back across the Rhine. Contemporary wits explained Geneviève's 'miracle' by suggesting that there were not 10,000 virgins in Paris to make it worth Attila's while. A more likely explanation was that Attila had opted to head for Orléans to deal with his Visigoth foes there.

Whatever the reasons behind Attila's deviation, Geneviève's intercession was rated a miracle. Less successfully she later led the Parisians against the barbarian and pagan Franks. Embodying the spirit of resistance, and living to the ripe old age of ninety, she helped convert the conquering Frankish king Clovis, and became the patron saint of Paris. Her bones rested in the Panthéon, until scattered by the revolutionaries of 1789. Slender and austere in its elongation, her 1920s statue stands imposingly on the Left Bank's Pont de la Tournelle, close to the area associated with her – christened Mont Sainte-Geneviève in her honour and eventually to embrace the Sorbonne. At various desperate moments in subsequent Paris history, when fresh barbarian hordes emerged from the east, mass supplications were made to Sainte Geneviève calling for her renewed intercession to save the city – with varying degrees of success.

MEROVINGIANS, CAROLINGIANS AND CAPETIANS

A dynasty of Frankish rulers, most of them louts, their name appropriately derived from the Latin for 'ferocious', now entered the scene. Pushing in from the east and devastating the Gaul lands as they went, they came to be known as the Merovingians. Clovis, with his bride Clotilde, father Childeric and sons Clotaire and Childebert, moved into Paris from Clovis's temporary capital at Rheims. As the Merovingians wrangled and split among themselves, there followed two and a half dark centuries of chaos and internecine savagery for Paris – its name now changed permanently from Lutetia. Clovis managed to kill off most of his family; after each killing he built a church in contrition. He was a great church-builder.

They were not gentle or nice people, these Frankish forebears of the modern-day Parisian, but at least, under Clovis, the notion of Paris as a capital city first became accepted, because that was where he had his palace. His descendant Dagobert (629–39), on his interment (he died of dysentery, aged only thirty-six) at Saint-Denis, established the tradition of burial there for subsequent kings of France. But during these dark years the country found itself fragmented, and refragmented, among short-lived nations with strangely Orwellian names such as Neustria and

Austrasia. Constant warring meant that rulers spent little time in Paris, which remained an unhygienic settlement of rude wooden huts, incendiarized at regular intervals.

In the eighth century, a new threat distracted and menaced Paris, this time from the south, in the form of the Saracens. Their progress was halted at Poitiers (732) by Charles Martel, but to raise funds for his campaigns he had to sack the abbeys and churches of Paris (his chosen capital was Teutonic Metz). A special deal between Martel's successor, Pépin (founder of the Carolingian dynasty), and a beleaguered Pope was to be of historic importance for both Paris and France. In exchange for being anointed and crowned in the basilica of Saint-Denis in July 754 by Pope Stephen, Pépin guaranteed to restore him to Rome. Henceforth Pépin saw himself entitled to wield the Sword of God, consequently inaugurating a special relationship whereby various French rulers through the ages, down to Napoleon and his imperial nephew, could claim prerogatives to intervene in Vatican affairs.

The closing years of the century saw the arrival of Pépin's son Charlemagne, a rather less attractive character than his portraits and subsequent canonization would suggest. Crowned Holy Roman Emperor in 800 by Pope Leo III, who anointed him as 'his excellent son', Charlemagne fought forty-seven campaigns in as many years; his great (though short-lived) empire extended from the Pyrenees to the Elbe, but he ran it all from Aix-la-Chapelle (Aachen), not from Paris. Once again Paris had an absentee ruler who did nothing for her, and she was not even mentioned in his last will and testament. Nevertheless, subsequent city elders (somewhat surprisingly) were to erect a statue to him in front of Notre-Dame. Charlemagne's son, the first of eighteen kings named Louis, in fee to the papacy and under the thumb of his second wife, let it all go, allowing the empire to end up, by the turn of the century, dismembered into seven parts.

Meanwhile, as the Carolingians wrangled, and all Europe sank into a kind of lethargy, in the ninth century a new warrior race emerged from the north. The Norsemen, and their kinsmen the Danes, surged out of bleak Scandinavia to invade the British Isles and Russia as far as Kiev, and even reached Constantinople. In 845, it was the turn of Paris, when 120 longboats, decorated like terrifying black sea-dragons and bearing thirty pairs of oars, attacked the city (unexpectedly) from upstream. Once again the population fled, and the Norsemen carried off tons of booty, including the magnificent bronze roof of Saint-Germain-le-Doré. Defenceless Paris was attacked again in 852 and 856, when more churches lost their roofs, and yet again in 858, in 861 and in 865. As in the time of Attila, Paris shrank back into the original ten hectares of the Île de la Cité. The wooden walls of Roman days were hastily reconstructed, while to defend its two bridges – the Grand Pont connecting it to the Right Bank and the Petit Pont to the Left – two wooden towers were erected, called *châtelets*, or 'little castles'.

In 885, when Charlemagne's imperial structure had all but disintegrated and the throne of France was to all intents vacant, there came the city's worst tribulation. Setting forth from England, a force of Norsemen under the command of Siegfried captured Rouen and headed on up the Seine. Fourteen hundred boats reached Paris, conveying a formidable force of some 30,000 hirsute warriors. Led by a heroic Comte de Paris, Eudes, who was to prove himself France's *homme fort*, Paris refused to surrender – the first time that any city had resisted the terrible Norsemen. Paris was besieged for ten grim months, but at last, after some highly dubious negotiations, Siegfried was bribed with 700 livres of silver and allowed a free passage, both ways, to carry the war upstream to Burgundy, and leave Paris in peace. Siegfried then repeated the procedure, 'subjecting unhappy Burgundy to the worst winter it had ever known'. Not surprisingly, the episode was to lead to centuries of instinctive mistrust and hatred of Paris by the Burgundians, culminating during the Hundred Years War in their alliance with the English.

In 911, the Norsemen were bought off definitively by giving them the duchy of Normandy, which they had in fact already been occupying for a number of years. Thereby the dread pirates acquired a territorial base, a certain respectability and a religion. For the next century the superabundant energies of these new Normans, under Duke Rollo, were directed notably against the British Isles, culminating in the overthrow of King Harold at Hastings in 1066. In France, there followed more years of anarchy, chaos and exhaustion, until the turbulent tenth century approached its end with Louis V dying devoid of heirs, thus ringing down the curtain on the Carolingian dynasty. Now a great-nephew of Eudes, Hugues Capet – a true Frenchman, or at least a man with a French-sounding name – opens the new millennium for France. In 987 he was duly elected king by assembled French barons. A month later he was crowned in Rheims Cathedral, thereby establishing a fresh precedent, like Dagobert's interment at Saint-Denis. As the energetic Normans swarmed across the English Channel and then began to reorganize the sleepy and backward Saxon England they had conquered, so a new threat to France was about to take shape – a threat that, from time to time, was to appear more immediate, and would certainly endure for longer, than any since the Romans of Julius Caesar. When the millennium dawned, the vulnerable new France ruled over by the Capetians consisted of no more than the diminutive domain called the Île de France, with Paris at its centre, surrounded by the hostile states of Burgundy, Flanders, Normandy, Aquitaine and Lorraine. She was poor, her vassals powerful and her rulers inhibited by linguistic anarchy wherein few spoke a common language; and she was heavily dependent on the support of the Church. But by 1328, when the Capetian dynasty had run its course, the Kingdom of France had become the most united and potent in Western Europe.

Little is known of Hugues Capet (the surname came as a sobriquet because of the abbeys whose *cappa* he wore). He seems to have been a timid and anomalous character who achieved little of distinction before dying of smallpox after a reign that lasted only nine years. His heir, accorded the nickname of Robert le Pieux, became the first ruler almost since the Romans to bother seriously about the reconstruction of Paris. His most memorable act was to restore the Palais de la Cité, which had stood on Roman foundations for a thousand years and was now showing signs of dilapidation, but he also set about rebuilding the Paris abbeys of Saint-Germain-des-Prés and Saint-Germain-l'Auxerrois, which had lain in ruins ever since the Norse raids and the First Siege of Paris.

Yet Paris remained the unimpressive capital of an unimportant state. The queen of Henri I (1031–60), Anne of Kiev, coming from a supposedly backward country, was not taken by her husband's domain; nose in air, she wrote to her father, Yaroslav the Great, complaining that it was 'a barbarous country where the houses were gloomy, the churches ugly and the customs revolting'.

Then, after several more dim Capetian kings, there arrived the first of the significant rulers of the dynasty, Louis VI, Le Gros.

SUGER AND THE TWELFTH-CENTURY RENAISSANCE

The three decades spanned by Louis VI's reign (1108–37) represent an important turning point, not just in the artistic development of Paris, but in the cultural history of the West as a whole. Until one considers the dates, it is hard to grasp that what is known – with considerable justification – as the twelfth-century Renaissance, a true window of bright light in the Middle Ages, took place over a century before Giotto and Dante were even thought of, its landmarks and symbols the soaring gothic glories of numerous cathedrals. Originating supposedly in the East, it was in France (and especially in the nuclear Île de France) that the innovation of gothic religious architecture found its most fertile ground and its inspiration. Close to the heart of it was a most remarkable Parisian – Abbé Suger.

Abbot of Saint-Denis for thirty years until his death in 1151, Suger was the first in a long line of able and enlightened ministers to the kings of France – a diplomat, a statesman and a businessman, outstanding for his architectural good taste, as well as being a churchman who built (or rather rebuilt) the magnificent basilica of Saint-Denis. But Suger was also an author, who took it upon himself to write a chronicle of his sovereign. His *Life* is full of wars and rumours of wars, including the first of the long-running contests against the new foe, the Norman English. In 1124 the French and their allies under Louis defeated a coalition of Henry I of England and the Holy Roman Emperor, at Rheims. More important, however, from the point of view of France – and Paris – was Louis' successful struggle against the feudal lords of France, which lasted through most of his reign. Rather late in life, Louis le Gros married an admirable and extremely plain woman who provided stability and bore him nine children, thus assuring the future of the dynasty. Skilfully he arranged – just before his death – the marriage of his infant son Louis to Eleanor of Aquitaine. It was not to be a happy alliance, bringing with it much future trouble; but it achieved without a blow reunification with the great Duchy to the south-west – and a period of relative tranquillity for the Île de France, and Paris.

In marked contrast to his sovereign, the Abbot of Saint-Denis was a monk of very modest stature, thin, sickly and in poor health, yet with immense energy, and he was to prove of considerably greater historical importance than either of the two kings he so faithfully served. Suger was both product and epitome of the twelfth-century Renaissance, as well as being a profound influence in the aesthetic development of France and of Paris. In that all too brief passage of enlightenment between the Dark Ages and the purging of heresy in the later Middle Ages, the best and brightest arbiters of Church thought had little difficulty in squaring love of God with love of worldly beauty and of the sensuous world. Suger himself could be quite unashamed in his passion for exotic stained glass, and for the hoard of gold, jewellery and other *objets d'art* which he crammed into the treasury at his beloved Saint-Denis, but he was confident that there was a pragmatic excuse for church embellishment: if the common people (that is, the illiterate) could not grasp the Scriptures, then they could best be taught them through the medium of pictures, or stories carved in stone. Here was a substantial advance in medieval Christianity over the fundamental Muslim approach which allowed of no representation of the human figure.

'In the Middle Ages,' wrote Victor Hugo, 'human genius had no important thought which it did not write down in stone.' In 1132, so it is recorded, the gothic style with its soaring spires, lofty rib vaults and pointed arches, took root in France when Suger decided he had to rebuild, on a vastly expanded scale, the ancient romanesque abbey at Saint-Denis. Several times during his stewardship there had been distressing scenes on feast days, when the dense crowds had led to the faithful being trampled to death in the crush. There were even occasions when monks showing off the reliquaries had been forced to escape through windows to save them. Suger's great new basilica was consecrated no more than a dozen years after it had been conceived – an extraordinary achievement. No expense was spared in the richness of its decoration. It must surely be seen as a true testimony to the spirit of the age that, with such crude tools, simple measuring devices and rudimentary mathematics handed down from Euclid and Pythagoras, the architects and masons of Suger could create these lasting miracles of construction. 'Who was the sublime madman', was the rhetorical question of Vauban, Louis XIV's great military architect, 'who dared launch such a monument into the air?' as he contemplated the massive central tower of Coutances Cathedral (1220–50) that seems to float in the sky. Soon after the consecration of Saint-Denis, Suger's architect transported his know-how to Chartres where, though it would be many years in completion, the finest of all the jewels of Latin Christendom was constructed. The great cathedrals of Sens, Laon, Bourges, Rheims and England's Canterbury all owed something to the delicate little Abbot of Saint-Denis.

SULLY AND NOTRE-DAME

Finally, and most important, there was Paris's own mighty Notre-Dame, begun in 1163 under the genius of Maurice de Sully, who started life as the simple son of a peasant from the Loire. Notre-Dame replaced on the Île de la Cité the ancient sixth-century church, itself built upon the foundations of a Roman Temple of Jupiter, which – like Saint-Denis – had become too small for its congregation. Paris badly needed a great cathedral as a religious focus that would provide tone and gravitas previously lacking in the city. Only a few years before there had been an unseemly affray in Sainte-Geneviève as Pope Eugenius III, in Paris to bless the departure of the Second Crusade, celebrated Mass there. In honour of the occasion, the canons of the church had spread a resplendent silk carpet before the altar, but when the service was over the Vatican retinue folded it up to take it away with them. A lively altercation ensued between the Italian and the Parisian priests, ending disgracefully in an exchange of blows inside the church. During the rumpus, the sacred carpet was torn in two. Candelabra were seized and used as weapons; the King, Louis VII, trying to separate the combatants, was himself struck in the face.

In the popular concept of the early Middle Ages, a church was likened to a ship steering for harbour, and what could be more appropriate than Notre-Dame's extraordinarily dominant position on the Seine, athwart the stern of the Île de la Cité, shaped so much like a ship? Indeed, such was to become the city's coat of arms, with the singularly appropriate motto *Fluctuat nec mergitur* (She is tossed on the waves but is not overwhelmed). Construction work in the narrow streets of medieval Paris proved an immense undertaking. Masons had to haul the stone from quarries far from the city; while a new street, Rue Neuve-Notre-Dame, was pushed through to enable materials to be brought up to the building site from quarries upstream on the Seine. Pope Alexander III blessed the foundation stone, while Thomas à Becket was among those to watch its construction before returning to be murdered in his own Canterbury Cathedral. Even though he served thirty-six years as Bishop of Notre-Dame, Sully was not fortunate enough to see either the mighty portico or the two massive towers of his cathedral: it was two centuries before the work was entirely complete. But Sully did survive to baptize, in the chapel of the nearby Palais de la Cité, the grandson of Louis VI, Philippe Dieudonné Auguste, born two years after the start of building on Notre-Dame, and the king who in turn would give Paris a real start in the world.

As in Roman days, under Sully the *parvis de Notre-Dame* became the true centre of Paris, the heart of France, with all distances of main roads measured from a bronze plaque set in the middle of it. From the cathedral's seminaries, in the course of the thirteenth and fourteenth centuries alone, came no fewer than six popes. But the reputation of Sully's monumental edifice has fluctuated hugely over the ages. Two centuries after its inception, streets neighbouring it were designated by the *prévôt* (provost) of Paris as an area for prostitutes, the warren of mean hovels becoming a bastion of vice, bawds, whores and ponces. Other great religious structures like Saint-Denis, Rheims and Louis IX's magical Sainte-Chapelle took over many of its functions. The cathedral itself suffered centuries of neglect and dilapidation, and the revolutionaries of 1789 in their wild orgy of republicanism threatened to raze it to the ground. Napoleon Bonaparte restored it so that he could be crowned emperor amid its ancient symbolism, in December 1804, but its ravaged, dead walls had to be draped with hangings and baldachins to provide the required sumptuousness. Six years later he would marry Josephine's successor, Marie Louise of Austria, there. Two decades later Victor Hugo lent Sully's twelfth-century handiwork new romantic life in his creation of the figures of Quasimodo and the hapless Esmeralda in his great eponymous novel.

Most of what one sees of Notre-Dame today, however, is the legacy of the nineteenth-century gothic medieval restorer – or vandal, depending on the point of view – Viollet-le-Duc, creator of the walled city of Carcassonne that is so romantically exciting when seen from a distance, so phoney close up. Even the twenty-eight Kings of Judah on the great western façade, destroyed by revolutionary zealots, are reproductions of Sully's originals. Then, seven years after Viollet completed his work, Notre-Dame was threatened once again with destruction, this time by the Commune in 1871, when pews were actually piled up in the centre of the nave and soaked with petroleum. In 1944 it was Hitler's turn to threaten it. Notre-Dame, however, was to outlive them all.

At the same time that he was building Notre-Dame, Sully launched the construction of the neighbouring Hôtel Dieu, the oldest hospital in Paris – and for centuries the only one – built on the foundations of an older hospital probably destroyed by the Norsemen. (Its name, still surviving, was given it by Philippe Auguste.) Sully left orders that every canon of Notre-Dame should bequeath a bed to the Hôtel Dieu on his death – a helpful contribution in an age when five patients often shared one bed. Under his administration, for the first time patients were segregated according to sex and illness. The Hôtel Dieu enjoyed royal patronage, and when Philippe Auguste set forth on the Crusades, he generously supplied extra bedding by offering it the straw of the stables his horses had vacated.

ABELARD FOUNDS A UNIVERSITY

To Paris, Suger and his king brought a new vitality, while in turn Louis VI came to mean more to her citizens than any of his Capetian predecessors. In terms of non-religious architecture, he replaced the wooden Grand Châtelet on the Right Bank with a robust stone tower, and under its protective shadow there grew up a whole district dedicated to commerce and provisions which later became Les Halles (see Chapter 2). Like Louis le Gros himself, Paris grew fat and prosperous, swallowing up villages so that only their steeples indicated where they had once been. On the Left Bank, sacked by the Norsemen, marshes were drained for new settlements, while monks canalized the stream of the Bièvre (where a future ruler of France, François Mitterrand, was to have his private residence) and wealthy merchants began to build their houses there.

This same Left Bank during the reign of Louis le Gros saw the beginnings of a famous academic centre under the tutelage of one Pierre Abelard, later to become known as the Sorbonne. This redoubtable figure, a true Renaissance man, years if not centuries ahead of his time, was to enact with Héloïse one of the world's great tragic love stories, as well as to introduce a new word into the French vocabulary, *abelardiser* (to castrate). But it is as a revolutionary teacher who was to found the great University that Abelard is central to the development of Paris.

Born near Nantes in 1079, the son of a minor noble, Abelard chose to pursue the studious life, wandering from one school to another in the fashion of the age. When he was about twenty he was drawn to the Cathedral School of Paris by the fame of the much respected William of

Champeaux, and here he shocked his fellows by presuming to question the principles of his teacher (there was always a certain unappealing arrogance in Abelard). After further stormy wanderings, in which he narrowly escaped being branded with heresy, he set up in Paris as a teacher in about 1114. A few years later he came to lodge in the house of one Canon Fulbert, as tutor to Fulbert's niece Héloïse (who was already, precociously, a young woman of considerable learning) – she aged seventeen, he thirty-eight.

There ensued the greatest story of romantic love perhaps ever to have come out of Paris, and a remarkably well documented one. Abelard was not discreet, and – in his passion – neglected his students. Héloïse had a baby, given the egregious name of Astralabe (though we never hear of him again, in the archives or in any of the lovers' letters) and sent off to Brittany to be brought up by Abelard's sister. Abelard insisted on doing the decent thing and marrying his love – but shamefully tried to keep it secret. 'In marrying, I was destroying myself; I was casting a slur upon my own honour,' he wrote in retrospect, and with a certain lack of grace. Héloïse, a thoroughly modern woman and ever the greater realist of the two, resisted – but in vain – on the ground that marriage would terminate Abelard's brilliant career within the Church. Despite the marriage, the uncle Fulbert – outraged by this slight on the honour of his house – sought a hideous vengeance. In the dark of night, he treacherously had Abelard castrated. Héloïse, distraught, took the veil, eventually to become abbess of the Paraclete Convent at Nogent-sur-Seine given her by Abelard. Her eloquent and agonizing letters make it plain that, to the very end, she would have put her love for Abelard before love of God, a judgement verging on the heretical, that surely would have brought her to the stake a hundred years later.

In contrast to Héloïse, Abelard at once accepted the disaster that had befallen him as due punishment requiring total expiation, and through impotence he flowered mightily in intellectual output – albeit in unorthodox thinking which, had it been a less liberal age than the twelfth century, would most probably have led him, too, to the stake. He began by becoming a monk at Saint-Denis, then went as abbot to a hermitage in Brittany where the coarse and ungodly bawdiness of the monks made him utterly miserable. In 1121, he was condemned for heresy at the Council of Soissons for his *Theologia* and achieved the undying enmity of the ascetic Saint Bernard of Clairvaux. Around 1133, he returned to Paris as master at Mont Sainte-Geneviève, and it was here that he began the most brilliant phase of his life as a teacher, and founder of the University of Paris. Seven years later he was accused of heresy by the implacable Saint Bernard at the Council of Sens, and died in 1142 at the priory of Saint-Marcel near Châlons-sur-Marne while on his way to make a personal appeal in Rome to Pope Innocent II. When Héloïse died in 1164, the two bodies were laid in the same coffin at her convent. Finally, 650 years later, in a romantically inclined nineteenth-century France, the two lovers were reunited in a common grave at the fashionable Père Lachaise Cemetery in the unfashionable east end of Paris, under a suitably gothic canopy of stone.

As a teacher, Abelard's intellectual fame rests on his introduction of logic and rationalism into the discussion of theology, dispelling for the first time some of the mystical tenets that had hitherto held sway. He was writing in an era when the classical rationalism of Plato and Aristotle was just being rediscovered. By employing dialectics as a means to this end, Abelard's methods were as controversial as the body of his thought, for it was unheard of for a teacher to encourage his students to argue with him. 'By doubting we come to enquiry, and by enquiring we pursue the truth,' was his famous credo. Perhaps in reaction to the hostility directed against him, Abelard and his small band of scholars migrated from the Île de la Cité to the Left Bank, at the foot of Mont Sainte-Geneviève, an area ever since known as the Latin Quarter – because of the prevalence of Latin spoken there. They set up in what later became known as the Rue de Fouarre, Street of Straw, so named because of the straw-covered rooms where the students sat (it still exists today, just over from the Pont au Double). From then on it came to be said that Paris 'learned to think' on the Left Bank.

Through Abelard, in pedagogical terms the twelfth century became the age of dialectics; and, through the focal point his teaching provided, inevitably Paris's first university grew around it. Though modelling itself on northern Italy's Bologna, Europe's oldest university, this forerunner of the Sorbonne started off life as a guild – or, in effect, and which was to be of considerable consequence in the later, stormy eras of the Sorbonne, not least in 1968, a trades union.

LOUIS VII INHERITS SUGER

Under the administrative genius of Suger the city's first centralized administration was set up; so too were its professional guilds, the earliest being the ancient company of water merchants – appropriately enough given the transcending importance of the Seine. They were followed by the mercers and the butchers. Yet in many aspects Paris remained a collection of villages, with pigs roaming muddy streets. One such 'diabolic' boar caused the death of Louis VI's first-born heir Prince Philippe, when his horse shied and threw him near Saint-Gervais. There followed the great political coup of the fat King: the marriage of his new heir Prince Louis to Eleanor of Aquitaine. But on his return from the wedding in Bordeaux, Louis VI was stricken with dysentery, dying in 1137 in his Palais de la Cité – on a carpet over which he supposedly had had ashes laid in the form of a cross. He was only fifty-six, but his final achievement profoundly affected the destiny of France.

Just as the English Plantagenets, by way of wreaking England's revenge on the mainland of France, were establishing a firm foothold in Normandy, Louis VII inherited from his father a united kingdom, at peace with itself and abroad, sound finances and, above all, Abbé Suger. But, unfortunately for France, he inherited little of his father's strength of character. Jealously in love, he immediately fell under the spell of his bride Eleanor, a formidable woman, intelligent and well read, coquettish and highly sexed, perhaps the outstanding personality of her age. Louis' religious policy seems to have been dictated by Eleanor, which led to a falling out with the Pope and excommunication. To gain reconciliation with Rome, he ill-advisedly set forth on a crusade – the conventional wisdom of those days. Afraid (because of her amorous propensities) to leave her alone in Paris, he took Eleanor with him. It proved a huge mistake. By the end of a journey plagued by heat and hunger, as well as by danger at the hands of the enemy, Eleanor had come to detest her weak husband. In Syria she fell into the arms of a youthful uncle, Raymond of Aquitaine, Prince of Antioch. When Louis pressed on to besiege Jerusalem, Eleanor was also rumoured to have bestowed her favours there on a virile Moorish slave. Meanwhile Louis suffered a serious military defeat.

At home Suger, appointed regent, administered the kingdom with remarkable skill, but, to maintain the roofs of Paris in good repair, he was forced to dip into his own considerable wealth, as well as ransacking the coffers of Saint-Denis. There was a threat of revolt by the King's younger brother, the Comte de Dreux, which Suger managed to stifle; but, now a frail old man, he wrote urging Louis to return post-haste. The King returned, together with Eleanor, pregnant with a child that was not his. Suger reported that 'we have seen to it that your houses and palaces are in good order'. Two years later he died – having given Louis one last piece of advice: don't divorce Eleanor, but put the interests of the kingdom above your own marital grievances. Shortly after Suger's death, however, in 1152 Louis obtained an annulment from the Pope on the ground that he and Eleanor were too closely related. Two years later, a free Eleanor married Henry Plantagenet, the future Henry II of England, a potent and ruthless warlord many years younger than herself. She was to live to be eighty-two, and to give Henry not only a number of illustrious sons but, more important, Aquitaine, or suzerainty over half of the territory that Louis le Gros had bequeathed France. With it came a *casus belli* for what French historians call the 'first' Hundred Years War.

Hardly was Suger cold in the grave than all the political achievements of Louis le Gros began to fall apart. Within ten years of Suger's death, Louis VII had been defeated in battle by his rival for Eleanor, and had lost Brittany and Toulouse as well. By the end of his forty-three-year reign he had managed to reduce France geographically to what she had been in the time of the first Capetians, throwing to the winds – or, rather, to his rival in love – his father's legacy of rich Aquitaine.

Louis had two daughters, supposedly, by Eleanor – but no heir. He remarried, but his second wife died childless. His third wife, Alix of Champagne, in 1165 finally produced a son who – fifteen years later – was to become Philippe II. Consciously mirroring the Roman emperor who gave his name to the month, he was named Auguste because he had been born in August. As well as the crown of France, to young Philippe Auguste was also bequeathed as a legacy the priceless foundation work of Suger, of the twelfth-century Renaissance, which would come to be seen as a true golden age for France, and for Paris.

AGE ONE: 1180–1314

PHILIPPE AUGUSTE

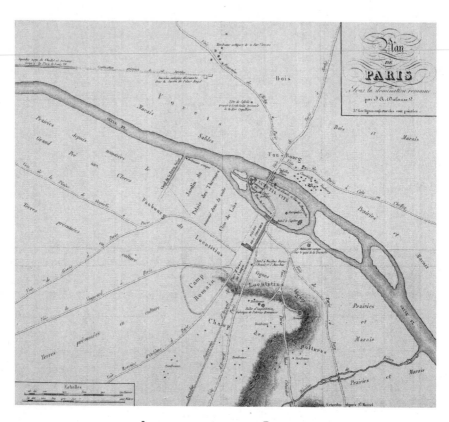

LUTETIA, UNDER THE ROMANS

1

Sunday at Bouvines

I only wish this pile of stones could be silver, gold or diamonds ... the more precious the materials of this castle, the greater pleasure I will have in possessing it when it falls into my hands.

Prince Philippe (later King Philippe Auguste), aged nine, in 1174

THE BUILD-UP

Some important battles in history have a surreptitious way of crystallizing what has gone before, as well as putting down a kind of marker for what is about to occur. They can also affect the pattern of events far beyond the battlefield itself. It is perhaps what makes historians call them 'decisive'. Bouvines, fought on 27 July 1214, was one of those. It was won by France against a powerful coalition of foes headed by King John of England, on a Sunday. This in itself was unusual, for in those days of religious correctness knights and kings on the whole observed the sabbath as far as battle was concerned. Bouvines was, moreover, to set the future shape not only of France but of Britain, too – and it would be fundamental to the development of the capital city Paris was to become. Some fifteen kilometres equidistant from the present-day cities of Tournai (in Belgium) and France's Lille, Bouvines lies in soggy Flanders, site of the terrible battlefields where the destiny of France was to be played out exactly seven centuries later, 200 kilometres north-east of Paris.

When France's King Philippe Auguste arrived on the throne in 1180,* aged fifteen, he inherited a tiny state, a fraction the size of Plantagenet

---

* He had been joint king for the last year of his father's life.

England and its European dependencies, land-locked and surrounded by powerful rivals. How then did he come to find himself fighting – and winning – such a key battle in so unpromising a corner of Europe?

The then King of England, Henry II, was an imposing, authoritarian ruler who, at least in the early stages of his reign, seemed to have everything going for him. His French father, the Plantagenet Duc d'Anjou, brought him the rich territories of Anjou and Normandy; and he acquired England through his father's marriage to the unhappy Matilda, heiress to William the Conqueror's son Henry I. Between Matilda and her cousin King Stephen, England had been reduced to anarchy and, by the time Henry Plantagenet came to the throne in 1154 at the age of twenty-one, was only too ready for the smack of strong rule. In short order, Henry found himself reigning unchallenged from the Cheviots to the Pyrenees, his short-lived Angevin Empire looming over the diminutive plot that was Louis VII's France. With conspicuous cunning, Henry set about the encirclement of that plot by a network of alliances, and at times during his reign it looked as if the best the Capetians could expect would be to become vassals of the Angevin Empire controlled from Westminster and Rouen. Yet the murder in 1170 of Archbishop Thomas à Becket – apparently invoked if not actually ordered by the King – turned things upside down. The 'turbulent priest' became an instant international martyr, and a saint. Henry could wear a horsehair shirt and have himself flogged in Avranches Cathedral by way of atonement, yet his image, and his power, would never quite recover from this particular bloodstain. Louis, France and Paris were saved.

Storing up trouble for himself and the Angevin Empire, the increasingly unpopular Henry now carried out a Lear-like break-up of his territories between his sons, Henry the Young (aged fifteen in 1170), Richard (the future Coeur de Lion, aged twelve) and Geoffrey (eleven). John, born only in 1167, was left out of the carve-up – thus to be known henceforth in France as 'Jean-Sans-Terre'. As Lear discovered, this was to prove folly in the extreme. Prince Henry, though already crowned in anticipation in 1170 and strategically married to the daughter of Louis VII, was treated by his father-in-law as if he were already king, but in fact was never to succeed – dying in 1183. In 1173, a general insurrection, the product of widespread popular discontent, broke out against Henry. With his customary vigour, however, over a period of two years he crushed one by one all the coalitions mounted against him.

Meanwhile in 1176 the worst flood of the Seine in memory swept away both bridges, carried off mills, houses and livestock on the crumbling banks, and came close to engulfing the whole city. Attempting a form of flood control untried in modern times, Louis and his entire court and every undrowned monk and priest, headed by the Bishop of Paris, went in procession to the edge of the swirling waters. Holding aloft a nail from the True Cross, the Bishop prayed: 'In this song of the Holy Passion, may the waters return to their bed and this miserable people be protected!' The rain stopped, and the waters ebbed just in time.

The uprising of 1173 had demonstrated the fundamental Achilles heel of Henry's empire – the divisiveness of his quarrelsome sons, greedy for territory and glory. Their future adversary Philippe, heir to the ageing Louis, saw it. Aged only nine, standing before Henry's seemingly unassailable fortress at Gisors, and showing his future mettle, he is said to have remarked to his entourage, 'I only wish this pile of stones could be silver, gold or diamonds ... the more precious the materials of this castle, the greater pleasure I will have in possessing it when it falls into my hands.' He would have to wait the best part of a generation.

In 1180 Louis VII died, and Philippe Auguste succeeded him, aged only fifteen. As he grew into the job, Philippe earned a reputation for being *rusé comme un renard* (cunning as a fox). The only existing contemporary pen-portrait of him describes him as:

> a handsome, strapping fellow, bald but with a cheerful face of ruddy complexion, and a temperament much inclined towards good-living, wine and women. He was generous to his friends, stingy towards those who displeased him, well versed in the art of stratagem, orthodox in belief, prudent and stubborn in his resolves. He made judgements with great speed and exactitude.

He was keen to seek the counsel of intelligent men of humble birth, notably Brother Guérin, Bishop of Senlis, and Barthélemy de Roye, and he restricted his advisers at court to a very small circle. He was to give the French monarchy (in the words of the historian André Maurois) 'the three instruments of rule which it lacked: tractable officials, money and soldiers'. He was also to be one of the first true lovers of the city of Paris.

France was soon at war again. By the facts of life of the twelfth century, this signified skirmishes interrupted by frequent truces, but without any grand battle – until Bouvines in 1214. By the fifth year of his reign, through a combination of skilful campaigning in Picardy and the dowry of his first queen, Isabelle of Hainault, the young Philippe had managed to expand his kingdom substantially northwards and southwards, including the key city of Amiens. Almost immediately, he found himself at war with the mighty Henry. It seemed like David taking on Goliath, but Philippe was cunning in his strategy of isolating the old King by forming alliances with his sons, first Geoffrey, then Richard (Prince Henry having died barely three years after his father-in-law Louis) – and also with Barbarossa, the German Emperor.

Henry, stricken by rheumatism and a painful fistula, was already old beyond his years. At the beginning of 1188, Philippe, having split the Angevin Empire and doubled his forces through his alliance with Richard, was poised to move into Henry's Normandy. Then suddenly news came from the Middle East that the Saracen, Saladin, had taken Jerusalem and was threatening Antioch. The Pope, Clement III, commanded the Christian kings to cease fighting each other and embark on a fresh crusade (the Third). But before they could set out, Henry had died, on 7 July 1189, in the chapel of his French château of Chinon, to be buried in his Abbey of Fontevrault. On the 20th, Richard was crowned duke of Normandy in Rouen, and king of England in London on 3 September. He and Philippe Auguste then departed, as allies and close friends, for the Holy Land.

Despite the romanticized portrait of him given in British Victorian history books, Richard Coeur de Lion was something of a brute. He was arrogant and quarrelsome, with a habit of sowing hatred and rancour around him. At home (which he rashly left in the treacherous and incompetent hands of his brother, Jean-Sans-Terre) he was accepted as a neglectful, popular absentee ruler, as befitting the repute of a knight errant. In contrast, Philippe left his kingdom well organized and in good hands, as set down in a famous document, the *Testament of 1190*. Among other things, this provided for the construction of a continuous fortified wall or *enceinte* girdling Paris, making her impregnable to any enemy assailant for the first time in her history. It was just as well, because he and his friend Richard (their intimacy had evidently extended, in the innocent way of the Middle Ages, to sharing a bed in Paris) were soon to become the most bitter enemies. Reaching Genoa together, the two leaders first fell out over the number of ships each was to provide for crossing the Mediterranean. In Sicily there were English charges of bad faith against Philippe, accused of conniving in the destruction of Richard's army. Finally arriving in the Holy Land, the two kings managed to tip the balance in the terrible Siege of Acre, already under attack for two years. But by the time of its capitulation in July 1191, intrigues plus the stresses of a grim campaign had seriously undermined the Anglo-French entente. To the enduring fury of Richard, Philippe now decided to break off from the Third Crusade and head for home. The Count of Flanders had died during the Siege, and Philippe had his eyes on the Count's possessions in Artois and Vermandois.

Richard, on the other hand, in the story so well known to generations of English schoolchildren, during his journey home fell foul of the German Emperor Henry VI, who kept him locked up for many long months in the Danube fortress of Dürrenstein, pending payment of ransom. Unfounded rumours ran round Paris that Richard had tried to poison Philippe at Acre, and even to have him assassinated in his own capital on his return. Rashly, and acting in deplorably bad faith with Richard's evil brother John, Philippe endeavoured to bribe the Emperor with a substantial sum to continue to keep Richard under lock and key. The Emperor Henry thoughtfully revealed all to Richard, who finally reached London in March 1194. Immediately he launched a fresh war against his former friend. It was to last five years, with a continuity and intensity rare in the twelfth century.

Much of the English King's fighting on French soil was carried out by a particularly brutal mercenary, Mercadier, who moved with utmost speed and ruthlessness from one province to another. No quarter was given, with both sides issuing orders to blind or drown prisoners-of-war. Predictably, John switched sides as soon as his brother set foot in Normandy and surrendered Evreux, having first massacred all his French allies there. On 3 July 1194, Philippe Auguste suffered his most humiliating defeat, at Fréteval in the Vendôme, losing his baggage train, his treasury and the national archives. To bottle Philippe up in Paris and to prevent him ever again threatening Normandy, Richard constructed an unassailable fortress at Château Gaillard on a key bend in the Seine, still a most imposing castle commanding the approaches to Paris. Defeat followed defeat for Philippe. Swayed by Richard's superior diplomatic skill, the Emperor Henry also joined in against Philippe, announcing his intention of annexing the right bank of the Rhône.

By the end of 1198, it looked as if France would be sliced up once again and become a fiefdom of either Richard or the Emperor. Once again, intervention from afar saved the day. After news had come from Spain that the Moors were threatening a new invasion, the new Pope, Innocent III, applied irresistible pressure to the combatants to reach a truce. The results were extremely tough on Philippe, obliging him to forfeit all of Normandy save the citadel of Gisors – on which as a nine-year-old he had first set eyes – and with it he in effect lost all the fruits of his campaigning over the previous ten years. Had he died at this point, he would have been remembered with scorn as a historical nobody, and it seemed it would be only a matter of time before Richard renewed the war, with a final drive on Paris.

Then the two sides' fortunes were abruptly reversed. While besieging a rebel fortress in Limousin with the dread Mercadier on 26 March 1199, Richard was wounded in the left shoulder by a bolt from a crossbow. Gangrene set in, and the warrior-king soon died. All the defenders of the besieged city were hanged, but – just before he died – Richard with a last chivalrous gesture requested that his assailant be spared and given a sum of money. The moment he was dead, however, Mercadier had the sharpshooter flayed alive and impaled. 'King Richard is dead, and a thousand years have passed since there died a man whose loss was so great,' sang the troubadours. In Paris, Philippe Auguste no doubt heaved a sigh of relief. Now there would be only weak, evil and hated Jean-Sans-Terre to deal with.

THE PAPAL ROLE

All through Capetian France's struggles against the Plantagenets, Louis VII and his son had to contend with a powerful, and often unpredictable, player on the sidelines. Stalin's sneering question to Churchill during the Second World War – 'How many divisions has the Pope?' – would have been answered in the twelfth century with 'a great many'. At the wave of the papal crucifix, or with the despatch of a legate, each pope could summon up armies and nations to bring pressure to bear on miscreant rulers. In the Middle Ages, thoughts of death and eternal damnation were uppermost in all people's minds. Upon the spiritual state of grace at the moment of death depended happiness, or misery, for the whole of eternity. Though by the later Middle Ages views on the afterlife had lost some of their certainty, in the twelfth century notions of Purgatory were little considered; it was a straight choice between the Bosom of Abraham and the Cauldron of Hell. Such was the dread of eternal damnation, such the dread of excommunication or an 'interdict' upon a whole nation, that the mere threat could reverse policies or even overturn thrones. Perhaps never again would the power and influence of the Pope be greater.

Manipulating and conspiring on the international scene, some pontiffs resembled a Metternich or a Bismarck of their times. The Pope at the time of Philippe's accession was Alexander III, a vigorous reformer who strongly supported Becket's stand against royal encroachment on Church matters, and who did much to consolidate papal authority throughout Europe. Several popes later came Innocent III – there was a certain irony in the name – who had his finger on every pulse within the Church, and influence everywhere in the Christian world. With their authority challenged by the hostility of the Hohenstaufen Holy Roman emperors and by an array of four imperial anti-popes, these medieval pontiffs found themselves constrained to juggle alliances with England and France with often bewildering rapidity – as has already been seen.

Philippe's father had fallen into (temporary) papal displeasure through his divorcing Eleanor, but it was nothing compared to the trouble that overtook Philippe himself. His first wife, Isabelle of Hainault, who had brought him Artois, died aged only nineteen. In 1193 he entered into another politically adroit union with Ingeborg of Denmark, a pretty girl of eighteen. But no sooner had the unfortunate Ingeborg arrived in France than Philippe mysteriously seemed seized of a total and irremediable aversion to her. He tried to persuade King Knut to have her back; the King refused, and complained to the Vatican. Philippe divorced Ingeborg, who – after a spell in prison – was placed in a French convent, and three years later he bigamously married a Bavarian princess, Agnes of Merano.

One of the first acts of Innocent III was to declare in 1198, 'The Holy See cannot abandon persecuted women without defending them.' He ordered the divorce annulled and a remarriage, under threat of personal excommunication of the King and Agnes, and of an interdict on the whole kingdom of France. The interdict was enforced in that year, to the deep distress of Philippe's subjects. Finally, after nine months of resistance, during which time Philippe Auguste had actually gone so far as to give the Papal Legate his papers to leave the country, he submitted on all counts. Ingeborg was reinstated and Agnes chased off, and in September 1200 the interdict was lifted – with Innocent III going so far in the pursuit of reconciliation as to legitimize Agnes's children.

To his discredit, however, Philippe Auguste was being rather less than honest. He sequestered Ingeborg, first in a château in the Forest of

Rambouillet, then under house-arrest at Etampes, while Agnes remained in France, set up by Philippe in a château nearer to Paris. A solution seemed to be presented by the death of Agnes in 1201. Nevertheless, for several years of interminable negotiations between King and Pope, the unfortunate Ingeborg was kept in this wretched state. France and the Vatican came close to rupture once again; but, politically, they needed each other. Then, suddenly, in 1212, Philippe announced that he was going to take Ingeborg back as his queen, if not as his wife. There was relief in the Vatican, and great celebrations in Paris and in the nation at large. But, as usual with Philippe Auguste, the considerations were purely political. He had decided to administer the *coup de grâce* to King John and to invade England, and for that he needed the support of Ingeborg's brother, the King of Denmark, and – above all – of the Pope.

The distasteful story of Ingeborg illustrated just how far the power of the Capetian monarchy had reached under Philippe Auguste, to the point where he could openly defy and outmanoeuvre that most powerful pontiff, Innocent III, over a period of many years when all the faults were manifestly on his side. It also demonstrated the single-minded stubbornness of his character, and the fear that he was able to inspire.

By 1213, King John had fallen into every trap laid for him by Philippe, political and military. By refusing to heed a summons to attend a court of adjudication in Paris, in his capacity as Duc d'Aquitaine, he gave Philippe a pretext to declare his fiefdoms forfeit and to renew war against him. By his cruelties John had progressively alienated the sympathies of his subjects in France, and Philippe had already taken from him Rouen, the Angevin capital in France, followed by the whole of Normandy – which meant the end of Henry II's short-lived Angevin Empire. It looked as if Philippe had all the chips: the Pope, the Danish fleet and the Emperor, and he had also seized from John Touraine, Brittany, Maine and Anjou. In 1213 John fell foul of Innocent III for rejecting Stephen Langton as archbishop of Canterbury, and was placed under an interdict, with Philippe openly invited to invade, to remove John's crown and place it on the head 'of someone who would be worthy'. Philippe had a candidate – his son and heir Louis – and had already been at work subverting the Welsh and Irish against John as well as some of the English barons. According to a French chronicler, he awoke one morning exclaiming, 'God, why am I waiting when I should just go out and conquer the English?' In fact, his preparations had been carefully laid. In the only serious attempt at invasion between William the Conqueror and Napoleon, a fleet of 1,500 sails and an immense army were assembled in the Channel ports in May 1213.

Then, just as Philippe was about to embark on this tremendous enterprise, two weeks later came the devastating news that Innocent – perhaps still mistrusting the wayward King, and eager to show his claws – had reversed his policy yet again, and had become reconciled to a humbled John, who was now ready to comply with all the Pope's demands. Philippe was ordered to pull back.

THE *BELLUM*

For a spell, the skies looked dark for Philippe yet again. At the beginning of July 1214 John himself attacked in Aquitaine, threatening Philippe from the south-west and drawing Prince Louis down to meet him in Anjou, while his allies (including John's nephew Otto IV of Brunswick, the Holy Roman Emperor) launched their main effort in Flanders. Aged twenty-six, the future Louis VIII, based on Chinon, managed to defeat John and an army three times the size of his own at Roche-au-Moine, close to Angers. Philippe was gratified by his heir's success, but the main threat to France lay in the north on the plain of Flanders, close to Lille, where Otto and his allies had concentrated a force of 80,000 men and 1,500 knights – a massive army for those days – ready to advance southwards on Paris. Philippe could muster no more than 25,000 men, of whom 500 were *chevaliers*. His infantry included, for the first time, a substantial body of bourgeois *Communes*, regarded as a great novelty, who were to play a role of historic significance.

In the twelfth century, military operations were divided into two kinds, *guerra* and *bellum*. *Guerra* was normal warfare usually fought around castles, for immediate goals and with inconclusive results. In contrast, a *bellum* sought to obtain a definitive decision with important objectives. As a wager of total victory or loss, it was regarded as a judgement of God. France had not risked a proper *bellum* against her adversaries since 1119, a hundred years previously, when Philippe's grandfather Louis VI had been decisively defeated by Henry I of England at Brémule. Now, as the rival forces manoeuvred into position in

Flanders, both Philippe and Otto decided to risk all on one throw, to fight a true pitched battle, and opted for a *bellum*.

The news reaching Otto's camp of John's defeat at Roche-au-Moine, coupled with the realization that he could not expect his intervention in the battle, must have been demoralizing. But by now events had acquired their own momentum. Philippe was heading for Lille along the road that traversed the Marcq at the key bridge of the hamlet of Bouvines, when he was intercepted by the vanguard of Otto's army. The bridge lay in a position of prime geographic importance, the only crossing point in a swampy area, and the meeting point of French, Flemish and imperial territories. The high ground on either side offered good hard-going for cavalry. But an important consideration caused both kings to hesitate before facing battle: it was then 27 July, a Sunday, on which Christians were forbidden to fight.

When the French rearguard spotted the allies in full battle array, Brother Guérin, Bishop-elect of Senlis, proposed that the King draw up his lines to meet the enemy. He was outvoted by the rest of the counsellors, who thought that the allies were moving on to Tournai and would not fight on a Sunday. The good sense behind Guérin's judgement was confirmed, however, when the French rearguard reported fierce attacks. The final decision to engage the imperial forces was supposedly taken while Philippe was resting, exhausted by the heat, with his armour off, under the shade of an ash tree. In short order, the King performed the requisite rituals to consecrate the forthcoming encounter as a true *bellum*.

It was the *canicule*, or dog-days of summer, and 27 July was a day of intense heat, dreadful for knights in heavy armour, fighting half blinded by the sweat cascading down inside their helmets, with a heavy dust kicked up by the thousands of horses. The course of the battle evolved in three sectors, with the French right wing being the first to engage, then the centre, and finally the left, Bishop Guérin beginning the action on the right with a sally by mounted sergeants from the Abbey of Saint-Médard – his success in this part of the battlefield preserving Philippe's main army from the serious danger of being turned and pushed back into the swamps of the Marcq. In the centre, however, during one cavalry mêlée, which fully occupied the French knights, the imperial sergeants were able to break through the lines of the *Communes* foot-soldiers drawn up in formation in front of the King. Striking back at them, Philippe became briefly separated from his bodyguard and was unhorsed by the enemy infantry using long hooks. Hurling themselves on the helpless King, Otto's men tried in vain to find a chink in his coat-of-mail through which to thrust a fatal dagger. In these brief seconds the whole history of France hung in the balance. However, his heavy armour and a quick response from the knights of the King's household, who threw themselves down protectively upon him, saved Philippe's life. They gave him a fresh horse and conducted him to safety.

The imperial attack was matched by a French counterattack that equally imperilled Emperor Otto's life. In the end, four imperial knights succeeded in conveying the Emperor to safety, although they themselves were captured. Otto now galloped off the battlefield, hardly stopping until he had reached his base camp at Valenciennes, thirty kilometres away. The battered imperial insignia, with Otto's fear-inducing great eagle mounted above a dragon and borne on a four-wheeled chariot, were however triumphantly presented to King Philippe, and then transported to Paris along with captives and booty.

Guérin, whose victories on the right wing had enabled him to pass to the left, helped achieve success there too. By five o'clock, the fighting was all but over, having lasted no more than a few hours. Philippe's triumph was complete. The military leader of the coalition were incarcerated, some at Philippe's newly built tower of the Louvre outside his city-walls, thus effectively dissolving John's coalition against his French rival.

The victory at Bouvines prompted waves of spontaneous rejoicing throughout the realm: the populace danced, the clergy chanted, and bells were rung. Flowers and branches festooned churches and houses and carpeted the streets of towns and villages. Peasants and harvesters shouldered their scythes and rakes, leaving ripened crops, and rushed instead to see the captives led to Paris in chains, and to join the townsmen and grandees in greeting the King. Bishop Guérin headed the procession into Paris, singing canticles and hymns, as the King walked behind.

At various crises in French history, propagandists would dust off the victory of Bouvines and recycle it as a touchstone of national faith. At the time of Louis-Philippe's bourgeois monarchy in 1840, Bouvines would be trotted out as the first true victory of king and 'people'. In the run-up to the First World War, it would be evoked as a glorious feat of French over German arms. Since 1945, if it is referred to at all, it is chiefly as a victory over *les Anglo-Saxons*. Though it hardly rates in English history books as a decisive battle, Bouvines was an outstanding victory. In purely military terms, it represented a triumph of mobility and superior morale.

Philippe was now forty-nine, with another nine years left to reign. For him, in Paris, victory at Bouvines meant a remarkable reconciliation between the three orders of King, Church and nobles. Never before had a French monarch been so secure on his throne, or France so secure in Europe. Philippe Auguste found himself master of France, and France in the first rank among European states. He had fought, and won, the first truly national war in French history. Bouvines was a kind of Valmy of the Middle Ages, a victory not only of the King and his knights, but of the King and the common people. With it the French first became conscious of being a nation – and Paris of being a capital, increasingly the administrative heart of that nation.

2

Capital City

The two nations set off in different directions. England headed towards liberty, France towards absolutism.

Ernest Lavisse, *Histoire de France*, III, p. 202

THE GREAT WALL

Unforeseen – and unforeseeable – at the time, the consequences of *le dimanche de Bouvines* in July 1214 were immense: for both France and England, for the future shape of Europe and, not least, for the city of Paris. Enraged by the lost battle and exasperated by all the past wickedness of their own king, now truly Jean-Sans-Terre, the English barons rose up and forced him to sign the Magna Carta at Runnymede in April the following year. And in a treaty once more imposed by the Pope, John agreed at Chinon to pay reparations and implicitly to accept the French conquests in Anjou, Brittany and Poitou. In marked contrast, for the last nine years of his life Philippe himself was to fight no more battles. Instead he concentrated his prodigious energies on reasserting the power of his personal rule, reforming his government and reconstructing his capital. The conduct of war, now on the peripheries of his hugely expanded domain, he left to his son and heir Louis, who was able to act with a remarkable degree of independence.

In May 1216 the future Louis VIII, invited to be king of England by a faction of disaffected English nobles, actually landed with an army some 15,000 strong on the Isle of Thanet. For a moment it looked as if the English crown would indeed pass to Capetian France. Then, in one more of those unexpected reversals of history, in October John suddenly died of the famous surfeit of lampreys. His death, which took place at the same time as that of the all-powerful Innocent III, provoked a sudden wave of patriotic loyalty to his heir, the innocent nine-year-old Henry. Louis was forced to leave the country through the hostility of the bishops and populace, and on his way back home in August of 1217 his fleet was almost totally destroyed off Calais in one of the first decisive victories of English naval power.

Now, for at least as long as Philippe lived, there would be no further threat from an impoverished and enfeebled Plantagenet England. Once vast, its mainland empire was reduced to Gascony and the port of Bordeaux. Severed for ever was the old, intimate connection with nearby Normandy. At the same time as Philippe had been countering the external menaces that faced him from his accession, he had with similar vigour, adroitness and sense of purpose been subordinating the recalcitrant barons of France. Four and a half centuries before his successor Louis XIV actually said it, the principle of *L'état c'est moi* was foreordained by Philippe Auguste. Historians are generally agreed that Bouvines was a turning point for both countries, fundamentally shaping the destinies of each. Says Ernest Lavisse, 'The two nations set off in different directions. England headed towards liberty, France towards absolutism.'

When the terrible Algerian War, which tore France apart for eight years, ended in 1962, President de Gaulle remarked, with massive relief, 'France was now free to look at France.' After Bouvines, it could equally well be said that Paris was free to look at Paris. What she saw was the beginnings of a most imposing capital, where Philippe had built well on the foundations laid by his father and grandfather. He had also most impressively – and literally – built his own foundations.

Before Philippe, travellers approaching Paris would have seen from the vineyarded hill of Montmartre a turreted city surrounded by a wooden palisade which protected the Right Bank, much as it had done since the days of the Norse invasions. Philippe Auguste changed all that. Appreciating the vulnerability of his capital, key to his whole small realm, he set about making it impregnable with a 'continuous wall, well provided with towers and fortified gates, other royal cities to be protected similarly'. Initially this medieval Maginot Line protected only the Right Bank, enclosing many meadows and marshes hitherto lying outside the city confines, but as Otto's hostile coalition of Germans and Flemings began to threaten Paris from the east and south, from 1210 onwards the Left Bank – then largely an area of orchards and vineyards – also came to be embraced within Philippe's great system of ramparts.

Whereas the old wooden stockade, dating back in places to Roman times and which had withstood the Norsemen, enclosed a meagre ten hectares comprising mainly the ancient settlement and seat of government on the Île de la Cité, under Philippe this was expanded to 250. It began on the Right Bank near the present-day Pont des Arts, then passed through the future rectangle occupied by the Louvre, cut across the Rue Saint-Honoré, then swung eastwards by the Portes Saint-Denis and Saint-Martin, the ancient entrances to the city. It then curved southeastwards, embracing much of the marshland of the Marais, to intersect with the Rue des Francs Bourgeois just west of where Henri IV would four centuries later lay out what was to become known as the Place des Vosges, ending at a riparian tower on the Quai des Célestins. Crossing the Seine via the eastern tip of the sandbar that was to become the Île Saint-Louis, it began again on the Left Bank at the Quai de la Tournelle, ran inside the old moat of the Rue des Fossés Saint-Bernard, then turned west to enclose the Abbey of Sainte-Geneviève. It traversed the present-day Boulevard Saint-Germain (but leaving the prosperous abbey and Saint-Sulpice just outside to the west), then terminated once more on the river at the Tour de Nesle, which once stood on the site of the present Institut de France and which was to achieve infamy under the reign of Philippe le Bel a hundred years later.

Completed just before Bouvines (by which time the immediate threat of attack had passed, not to be revived until the Hundred Years War), the Great Wall of Philippe Auguste took the best part of twenty years to construct. Despite his preoccupation with external warfare, Philippe was very closely involved in the planning of it. He personally supervised construction details, specifying that the wall should be no less than three metres thick at ground level, and two and a half metres thick at a height of six metres; it was to have thirty-three towers north of the Seine and thirty-four to the south, each carefully rounded so as to deflect cannonballs, and two dozen fortified gates. Overall it would have been some ten metres high. Philippe's engineers built extremely well, and to this day you can still find sections of immensely rugged masonry in various parts of the old city. An imposing stretch lies off the Rue Clovis, now set within the grim edifice of the new Sorbonne; the best part of a tower stands encompassed within a building close to the Procope, Paris's oldest restaurant, in the Cour du Commerce Saint-

André. On the Right Bank, you can find a section in a *lycée* near the Hôtel de Sens, another close to the Musée Carnavalet on Rue des Francs Bourgeois.

THE LOUVRE AND LES HALLES

To guard the approaches to Paris from where the Norsemen had come in the ninth century, Philippe stretched a thick chain across the Seine, supported on boats, and another at the eastern approaches to the city. Just outside his new wall, he built a powerful, squat and square *donjon*, flanked with turrets, just across the river from the Tour de Nesle. In the centre of it was a great tower, forty-five metres in circumference and thirty metres high – though, because of the thickness of its walls, it probably afforded an internal diameter of no more than eight metres across. It acquired the name of the Louvre, possibly derived from *louve*, or female wolf, because it was used as a hunting box, but more probably from the archaic word *louver* or blockhouse, or even, quite simply, from *l'oeuvre*, the work. The first stone of the Louvre was laid in 1202, and it was originally designed as a major stronghold (though it never came to be used as such) and a treasury. Not a palace to be lived in, it was only in the reign of Charles V (1364–80) that the Louvre, with windows struck through Philippe's grimly functional arrow-slits and with fancifully decorative pointed roofs superimposed, became a palace fit for a king. Philippe Auguste, like his ancestors, continued to reside on the Île de la Cité.

In addition to the Louvre there were, now inside the *enceinte*, the two defensive towers of the Grand and Petit Châtelet guarding the bridges that linked the Île de la Cité with both banks of the Seine. The Grand Châtelet, founded on a wooden guard tower built in 870 to ward off the Norsemen, was converted by Louis VI, Philippe's grandfather, into a considerable fortress. Now Philippe's wall rendered its original role obsolete, so instead it became the office of the *prévôt* (the acting governor of Paris, the representative of royal authority), and later the most sinister of all its prisons, its thick walls muffling the cries of the tortured. In his epic in praise of the King, *Philippidos*, Guillaume le Breton, poet laureate of the time, draws various parallels with the walls of Troy. But such fortifications were only the tip of the iceberg of Philippe's construction work in Paris.

When he was just twenty years old (as the story goes), Philippe went to the window of his palace on the Île de la Cité to admire the Seine, but the stench that greeted him as a heavy wagon stirred up the mud on the street outside made him reel back. Pigs had been banned from Paris ever since the Crown Prince, Philippe's uncle, had been killed by one frightening his horse – but the law had proved all but unenforceable. In a medieval Europe accustomed to evil-smelling streets, Paris had prize-winning qualities that were to endure through the ages. The streets were simply open sewers, hence the names given to some of them: Rues Merderelle, Tire-pet, Fosse-aux-Chieurs and so on. Each rainfall turned them to a mud enriched by the droppings of horses and domestic animals, the waste from the tanneries and butcheries, and of the residents themselves in their houses innocent of any plumbing; and there were the forbidden swine to root through it and churn it all up. Thus, as a consequence of his shock on opening the window on the Quai de l'Horloge, young Philippe ordered all streets to be paved. A start, a slow start, was made during his reign – beginning, understandably, with the streets adjacent to the Palais de la Cité. Gradually main thoroughfares like the Rues Saint-Martin and Saint-Jacques, Saint-Antoine and Saint-Honoré, became the first to be cobbled, or rather paved with flagstones.

Within the protective walls Philippe had erected, Paris for the first time was now able to build in peace for the centuries to come. His achievements were remarkable. The rebuilding of the great cathedral of Notre-Dame begun by Bishop Sully under Philippe's father in 1163 was completed. Sainte-Geneviève was rebuilt too, while the districts of Saint-Honoré, Saint-Pierre (which became Saints-Pères) and Les Mathurins – all named after the churches or monasteries founded in them – came into being. Three new hospitals were constructed, including the Sainte-Catherine on the Rue Saint-Denis founded for women in 1184. To replace the waters of the Seine, already partially polluted, a catchment for fresh water was created from springs up on the heights of Belleville outside the city, and new aqueducts, the first since the Roman era, and numerous fountains, were built (one, on the corner of Rue Saint-Martin, was to provide the citizens of Paris with drinking water for seven centuries).

One of Philippe's most lasting contributions to Paris was the creation of Les Halles, which Emile Zola was to dub 'the belly of Paris'. All through the history of the city, down to the present era, the distribution of food has presented a fundamental headache, with cheap foodstuffs arriving in the city from underpaid producers, to reach the consumers at vastly inflated prices – due to the demands of the middlemen, in turn caused by the anarchy of the city's narrow medieval street system. Adjacent to the unsavoury Grand Châtelet on the Right Bank was the Grève, a gravelly sandbar on which there were no buildings, except for water-mills for grain, and where there piled up shipments of all kinds of goods – hay, grain, wood, wine, fish, coal, salt and hides – conveyed up and down the Seine. It was to become a sombre place of public executions, but by the time of Philippe Auguste there had accumulated around it through the ages a malodorous anarchy of miscellaneous trades. Probably the most polluting were the tanners, who gave the Quai de la Mégisserie that runs past the site of the Grand Châtelet its present name. Other streets long since disappeared revealed the business conducted there: Rues de la Grande Boucherie, la Tuerie (slaughterhouse), Pied de Boeuf, Pierre à Poisson and de l'Ecorcherie (knacker's yard), as well as the Val d'Amour and Pute-y-Muce (whore in hiding). The noise and smells around this area in medieval Paris must have been unspeakable. Adding to the concentration of commerce and merchandising was the fact that the great north–south axes of Rues Saint-Denis, Saint-Martin and – across on the Left Bank – Saint-Jacques, and that to the east and west of Rue Saint-Antoine, all funnelled into the narrow streets around the Grève.

To relieve the pressure, in the early part of the twelfth century Louis le Gros had set up a primitive market on some marshy fields, Les Champeaux, which became known in perpetuity as Les Halles (apparently originating from the expression *pour ce que chacun y allait*). In 1183 Philippe Auguste had them replaced with two permanent stone buildings designed to protect both goods and vendors from bad weather and from robbery. Although the topography of Paris in the twelfth century is not clear, Les Champeaux were known to have been located on a little mound. As such, the site was protected from the inundations which periodically occurred in the marshy area situated to the north-west. It seems likely that the site also provided a link with Montmartre to the north.

Under Philippe Auguste, the market entered an era of growth. In 1181, the King incorporated into Les Champeaux the Saint-Ladre or Saint-Lazare fair which was held outside the city limits, probably between the Saint-Laurent church and the Saint-Lazare leper house (that is, at the present-day intersection of Rue du Faubourg Saint-Denis and the Boulevard Magenta). The following year, according to some sources, the market was further enlarged by the confiscation and demolition of houses owned by Jews. Philippe, in contrast to his father, was to earn a bad reputation in his dealings with the Jews and their property.

Economic conditions in the twelfth and thirteenth centuries were favourable to the growth of trade, not only in France but in Europe generally. By the creation of new roads, by the development of new needs, by the maintenance of relative peace, commercial relations by land and by water could extend internationally. But there were still problems, since a lone merchant couldn't hope to succeed by throwing himself into some far-off trade adventure. Thus an individual's first care was to place himself under the protection of someone stronger. Everywhere merchants encountered depredation, protectionist land magnates, fiscal barriers and tolls. To begin negotiations allowing the purchase of distant goods, to guarantee the transport in security of the goods and their sale on the market, merchants had to form themselves into companies and assemble together in approved places and at certain times of the year. Hence, it was only to be expected that Paris, capital of a kingdom and a European city by virtue of her university, should have become a large commercial centre, especially with a well-placed site on the Right Bank available for such use. In establishing Les Halles, Philippe struck a blow for Paris as a major trading centre of Europe. Down through the ages, through repeated rebuilding and expansion, the market continued on Philippe's original site, with the surrounding area retaining much of its original flavour – until Presidents de Gaulle and Pompidou evacuated the whole congested complex out to Rungis, on the way to Orly Airport, in the 1960s.

THE UNIVERSITY

Over the years from Abelard to Philippe Auguste, the University of Paris had grown up to become a significant force in the land, along with the monarchy, the nobility and the Church. From earliest days, its students had keenly and liberally involved themselves in city life, outside the walls of Academe – so much so that in the south transept of Notre-Dame a series of reliefs shows scenes from student life, as well as depicting a medieval seminar in progress (though they are listening closely, the participants appear to be taking no notes). In 1200 the new century began with a brawl between town and gown in Paris, grave enough for the King, Philippe Auguste, himself to get involved. An account given by the English chronicler Roger of Howden describes how a band of German students wrecked a tavern and severely beat the owner. In a punitive raid, Thomas, the royal *prévôt* of Paris, attacked the Germans' hostel with urban militia; as a result some Parisian students from the University were killed.

Outraged by this incident, the University's professors joined their students in demanding redress and suspended teaching, threatening to leave Paris in a body. Here, as in later centuries, the most potent weapon in the armoury of both students and masters was to strike – or, in medieval terms, to order 'a cessation of lectures'. It caused Philippe to fear that the students might boycott his city and even migrate to Plantagenet England. At the same time he had another, more personal motive for appeasing the University. His dispute with the Pope was still running, and his lands were still under interdict, so he was keen to win over Paris churchmen (under whose aegis the University existed) for their support in the royal cause. Accordingly, in July 1200, under power- ful pressure, Philippe issued a charter (the University's first) that was highly beneficial to the students. To punish the *prévôt*, the King pro- posed that Thomas be imprisoned for life unless he chose to submit to trial by ordeal. If he failed it, he was to be executed; if he passed it, he was nonetheless forever prohibited from holding the office of *prévôt* or *bailli* (bailiff – see below) and from returning to Paris. He survived the ordeal and went into exile. Similar measures were taken against his henchmen.

Constituting a substantial segment of the city's population by this time, these scholars enjoyed clerical privileges that exempted them from normal jurisdiction. Ecclesiastical courts had formulated two sets of privileges to protect the clergy. The first was the *privilegium canonis*, under which the clergy were considered sacred personages. Any phys- ical violence against them was therefore sacrilege, and punishable by immediate excommunication, for which absolution could be obtained only by arduous penance. Under the second, the *privilegium fori*, the clergy were exempt from the secular courts and subject exclusively to ecclesiastical jurisdiction. In Paris, because of the concentration of scholars, the problem of repressing clerical crime was more acute than anywhere else.

Yet, having avenged the students' honour by punishing Thomas, the King promised to reinforce the *privilegium canonis* by commissioning the agents of royal justice to protect clerics from all such assaults by laymen. If the townsmen saw any layman assaulting a student in Paris, except in self-defence, they were required to arrest the offender, hand him over to royal justice and give evidence against him. Finally, Philippe commanded his officers:

> neither to arrest clerics accused of crimes nor to seize their chattels without serious cause. If arrest was deemed necessary, the cleric was to be delivered immediately to an ecclesiastical court, which would attempt to satisfy the king and the injured party.

Particular care was to be exercised to avoid physical injury to the students unless they resisted arrest. All complaints of violence were to be investigated by inquest. Both the *prévôt* and the people of Paris were required to observe these measures under oath. Philippe's statute thus went to exceptional lengths in giving the University vital concessions and privileges which it would strive to safeguard over the ages.

The students and their masters thereby received virtual immunity from royal justice, which was greatly to exacerbate the headaches the *prévôt* had in maintaining order in the city. Their protected status encouraged aggressive behaviour among the scholars, who became renowned for their brawling and rioting, as well as for committing more violent crimes. By 1221, the Bishop of Paris, under whose edicts they came, excommunicated all students carrying arms. Two years later (the year of Philippe's death) the hatred of town for gown reached a peak when the Paris citizenry fought a pitched battle against the students during which 320 were killed and their bodies thrown into the Seine.

DESPOILING THE JEWS

How did Philippe Auguste manage to raise money for all his vast urban projects in Paris, defensive and peaceful? As well as being a highly talented fund-raiser, Philippe seems to have been a most astute financial manager. While his father Louis VII had – according to the chroniclers – only 19,000 livres' spending money per month, by Philippe's death in 1223 his son Louis VIII could reckon on a sum of 1,200 daily, or nearly twice as much. When it came to financing his ambitious fortifications, not only of Paris but of most of his important cities like Orléans, Laon and Péronne, Philippe was greatly aided by a most efficient and modern-minded system of standardization. Whereas in 1197–8, Coeur de Lion had spent 34,000 livres on the construction of his vast fortress of Château Gaillard alone, Philippe's total programme (before his conquest of Normandy) cost no more than 40,000, while the whole of the Left Bank stretch of *enceinte* wall came to no more than 7,020 livres. He kept his economy under tight control, was meticulous in exacting taxes from his vassals, as from the wealthy clergy, while as his banker he employed the Templars, expert in augmenting their fortunes – which was to be their downfall a century later, under another Philippe. He turned a blind eye to Simon de Montfort's brutal crusade against the Albigensians of south-west France, of whom he disapproved, but readily accepted the spoils into his exchequer. One of his main sources of income, however, derived from the Jewish community of Paris.

From Philippe Auguste to Philippe Pétain, and beyond, treatment of the Jews in Paris, indeed in northern France as a whole, was never conspicuous for its generosity. But this was true of most of medieval Europe. There were the relatively good periods, and the very bad. To his shame, the reign of Philippe Auguste belonged categorically to the latter. In French Jewish lore, he came to be known as 'that wicked King'. Under Louis VII, the Jews had been relatively well treated, their synagogues protected, and they had prospered. By the end of Louis' long reign their small community had come to own nearly half of all private property in the city, with large numbers of the citizenry in their debt. But before his father was even cold in the grave Philippe, still barely fifteen and probably acting under pressure from the establishment, in 1180 issued orders for the Jews under royal protection in Paris to be arrested in their synagogues, imprisoned and condemned to purchase their freedom through surrender of all their gold and silver and precious vestments. Though not in fact initiated as religious persecution, it was a cynically skilful ploy for getting on his side both the Church and the great mass of wealthy Parisian debtors. Above all, it granted Philippe the immense sum of 31,500 livres, which he needed both for building the walls of Paris and Les Halles, and for equipping his army to defeat the Plantagenets. Two years later, he followed up with a decree expelling the Jews from France and confiscating the totality of their wealth. Debts were wiped out – except for a fifth which the royal coffers appropriated.

Altogether the value of Philippe's first depredations against Paris

Jewry was equivalent to roughly one and a half times what his government might expect to raise in normal predictable revenue for an entire year. This was not, however, a formula found acceptable to all of his neighbouring vassals, and in 1198 he relented partially – and then kept changing his mind at varying intervals, with the cruellest of consequences. Perhaps only a couple of thousand Jews, out of a total population of some 60,000 to 100,000, were involved, but the expulsions brought to an end the ancient *Juiverie* on the Île de la Cité, and their synagogue was converted by Bishop Sully, creator of Notre-Dame, into the Church of the Madeleine. When the Jews returned, they settled predominantly in the Marais area of what was to become the 4th arrondissement (which still retains most of the traditional Jewish shops and restaurants of Paris). But, once again, the Jews were expelled from the whole of France, their property confiscated, under Philippe le Bel a century later. In many ways, the policy of Philippe Auguste, with its frequent vacillations, was harsher than that of his successor, insofar as it provoked crude anti-Semitism with the native Parisians attacking the Jews as blameworthy for any disadvantageous change in the tax laws.

LAW AND ORDER

Ruthless and absolute monarch as he was, there is no question but that Philippe Auguste had the interests of Paris very high among his priorities – if not top, after Bouvines. Though his father had first established the city as France's permanent seat of government, it was Philippe who truly loved her, and he was the first ruler to make her – secure within her new walls – a *caput*, his administrative capital. Records (remarkably complete, considering the distance of the times and the fact that the national archives had been lost at the Battle of Fréteval) show that, despite his many absences in battle, 31 per cent of all Philippe's royal *actes* from the Curia Regis had a dateline of Paris, thereby indicating his residence there. In the remaining decade of his life after Bouvines, consequent to the peace and stability that the victory over John and his allies had given, he spent most of his days in the city, planning, reorganizing it – and building.

In terms of administration, though he had ruthlessly crushed and brought to heel his rural nobles, and absolute ruler though he was, in Paris he introduced an astonishing degree of devolution – or what, in those days, would have passed for the beginnings of democratic rights. Under Louis VII, the Paris merchants had thrived, but it was Philippe who first gave the bourgeois classes, the Latin *burgenses nostri*, their official standing. It was he who, in his extraordinary *Testament of 1190*, had handed over the affairs of Paris to six eminent bourgeois while he went off to the Crusades; and it was under him that the Paris water merchants, also members of the bourgeoisie, were granted virtual control of river traffic on the Seine (in itself a measure of the prime importance of the river in the life of the city). In the Hôtel de Ville on the Right Bank, east of the Louvre, it was Philippe too who instituted the *parloir aux bourgeois*, the first seat of a Parisian municipal administration.

Parisian law and order, too, received its impetus from Philippe. Just before embarking on the Third Crusade, in an ordinance of 1190 he had created the system of *baillis* (or bailiffs), placed directly under the royal government. Drawn from the bourgeoisie, a useful counterweight to the landed seigneury, they were responsible for the dispensation of justice – and also for checking up on any excesses committed by the *prévôts*. Fearful of assassination by an agent of Coeur de Lion, in the course of his struggles against the Plantagenets Philippe formed the habit of going around the city with an escort of guards armed with truncheons, rude predecessors of the modern gendarmerie and riot police. In marked contrast to the authoritarian Henry Plantagenet, bitterly struggling with the Church to wrest judicial rights from it (and perhaps in reaction against the martyrdom of Becket), Philippe was generally meticulous in allowing the clergy to preserve these prerogatives. Unusual was a case, in 1210, concerning a group of heretics condemned at the councils of Sens and Paris. These members of the clergy were degraded, handed over to the King's court and burned in the fields of Les Champeaux.

Evidence about the kinds of punishment imposed by the authorities seems to be scanty for the reign of Philippe Auguste itself, but they were a great deal less draconian and ingenious in their cruelty than a century later, under Philippe le Bel, when horrible refinements of torture became current. But if one relies on sources dating from around 1400, it is possible to infer that in early-thirteenth-century Paris the crimes of treason, homicide and rape were punished by dragging the culprit through the streets and then hanging him. Arson and theft of property also merited hanging; heresy and sodomy earned the stake; currency forgers were thrown into boiling water. The lesser offences, principally the infliction of blows and injuries where blood was shed, recorded in the registers under the heading 'little blood' (*sang menu*), were for a long time covered by the law of retaliation, although eventually they became liable only to fines, imprisonment and penalties corresponding to the harm caused. Frankish customary tradition applied a whole range of penalties against theft, not just the death penalty. Under the jurisprudence of Charlemagne, theft was liable to penalties ranging from the loss of an eye to the gallows, and this custom lasted at least until the reign of Saint Louis. Corporal punishment, such as hanging, whipping, branding and loss of a limb, were designed to be deterrents.

Ecclesiastical judges could condemn to death too. One Jean Hardi died at the stake for having sexual relations with a Jewess, which was held to be contrary to nature. Men were usually killed by hanging, women by whipping. Suicide was also considered a crime, so the suicide's cadaver would be hanged. Non-capital corporal punishments pronounced in the name of the bishop – for example, the mutilation of an ear or branding by hot iron – were carried out at the Croix-du-Tirouer, in the Rue Saint-Honoré at the top of the Rue l'Arbre-Sec.

In addition to the royal and episcopal justice, there were judicial organs of seigneurial jurisdictions in Paris; their sergeants kept an eye on petty, daily offences like insults, altercations, brawls and games of chance. Justices in Paris exercised their rights using pillories, with petty criminals subjected to ridicule by the crowd in the square before the church. At Saint-Germain-des-Prés there was a pillory at the crossroads of the present-day Rue de Bucy and the Boulevard Saint-Germain. At night, since fear of evil spirits and wrongdoers alike was greater under cover of darkness, the magistrates paid particular attention to security. The hour of curfew having been fixed by decree, the town clock would impose silence, the taverns would shut and house doors would close as the night watch began its round. The night guard (*le guet*) was the responsibility of the guilds, whose members were expected to volunteer by turns so that a full complement of sixty burgesses each night was available to make the rounds or stand at assigned posts. (Later, by 1364, the town watch was supported by the royal guard, consisting of a company of twenty mounted sergeants and several dozen armed foot-soldiers.) Patrolling the city was never a professional job in medieval Paris: it relied instead on the ties of family, work and neighbourhood, and on the authority of heads of families, guilds and volunteers in the militia.

There were haunts of poverty and shame on Philippe Auguste's map of Paris. The basic principle of medieval regulation in this regard was to designate certain areas for prostitution and limit vice strictly to them. Thus in London prostitutes were assigned two sites; in Venice they were confined to the Castellato, at the centre of the Rialto; in Amiens they were obliged to spend both night and day in the Rue des Filles, but this street proved to be too small and the district was enlarged. The aim of this sort of social hygiene was to locate these places well away from seigneurial residences, in poor districts, often along the river. The sites where vice could be practised in Paris (notably in close proximity to Notre-Dame) were in fact not fixed by Philippe Auguste, but by his grandson, the saintly Louis IX. Tradition attributes to this pious monarch the designation of eight streets where the 'common ribalds' could ply their trade, though ordinances of 1254 and 1256 laid down that prostitutes should be driven out of town.

DRESS, SONG AND LOVE

In a world where comforts shared by all classes were few, degree showed itself to a large extent in apparel. In bed at night, all wore nothing – men and women, rich and poor. By day, a baron could be spotted in cold weather by his fur-lined *pellice*. Men of all ranks wore *braies*, the full, pleated breeches favoured by the Gauls, while the affluent also wore long stockings, or *chauces*, often in brilliant colours and of rich materials such as silk or cotton (imported from Africa, therefore of even greater rarity). Above would be worn a pleated doublet with full but short sleeves revealing the tight-fitting *chainse* shirt (handsomely embroidered in the case of the wealthy). Instead of a *braie* women who could afford it wore a long linen *chainse* trailing to the ground. Elegant women wore clothes of brilliant hue – for example, a purple mantle fastened by a gold pin at the breast, and a high wimple. Hair was parted in the middle, with two long plaits dropping down as far as possible. For men, shaving was no easy matter – performed with an instrument like a carving knife, painful on a virile stubble.

To palliate the hardship of medieval life, entertainment was of the highest priority. Parisians of all ranks loved a party, especially a good wedding feast, where minstrels would perform. The principal instrument of the visiting *jongleur* would be a *viele*, a flat-bottomed fiddle, vaguely triangular, with three strings worked by a concave bow that was a little awkward to handle. The music of the times was, it seems, seldom in unison. The *jongleur* would first of all strike a note on his *viele*, and then chant; the much loved, heroic *Chanson de Roland* could take as long as five hours to perform. With his wide knowledge of Jerusalem, the Siege of Antioch, of Arabs and Babylonians, drawn from the Crusades, and his tales of heroes who would give up all in the cause of the Faith, the well-travelled *jongleur* was a much sought-after figure. Though the *chansons de geste* such as *Roland*, with their attachment to a chivalry that was heroic to the point of suicide and absurdity, were arguably to help France lose the Battle of Crécy in the next century, they now kindled in Parisians for the first time a patriotic feeling of intense love for *la douce France* – principally identified with the immediately surrounding Île de France.

Out of these *chansons* grew another form of literature of great importance, centred on women and dealing with courtly love. In this early development of feminism in France, the Crusades played a signifi-cant role: because of the lengthy absence of the lord, the lady gained more power. Here Eleanor of Aquitaine was perhaps a role model, as well as importing to rude Paris the 'courtly' manners of the south. Beginning a long tradition, great ladies took to having lovers, in addition to their lawful spouses. Whereas in the more northerly clime of England the courtly lover of Malory and the Round Table tended to platonic adoration from afar, the Parisian woman already expected – and received – more earthly devotion. Nevertheless, as André Maurois points out, such *chansons* contributed to a 'discipline of customs and manners which was a great step forward to civilization'. With it came the ascend-ant influence of the Parisian woman, and also the importance attached to love – and with it humour and satire.

THE KING DIES

The last years of Philippe Auguste's reign were marred by a campaign in south-west France of appalling savagery against fellow Christians: the Albigensian Crusade. Whatever the actual heresy adopted by the unfortunate Albigensians, or Cathars (it was called Manichaeism), they were charged with enormous outrages such as institutionalized sodomy. The tolerance that had characterized Abelard's twelfth century was fast evaporating, and charges of heresy, and the Inquisition, lay just around the corner, with the most baleful influences on France – and Paris. There were also thinly disguised territorial motives in the Albigensian Crusade, and, as with all religious civil wars, it was prosecuted with ruthless ferocity. Whole areas of Languedoc were laid waste by the awful Simon de Montfort. Whipped on by the Papal Legate, Arnaud Amalric, with the alleged exhortation 'Kill them all. God will recognize his own', the brutal massacre of the inhabitants of Béziers, where 7,000 men, women and children were herded into the Church of the Madeleine and slaughtered, is remembered to this day. The war in Languedoc was to drag on wretchedly for decades. Urged on by the Pope, Philippe pursued it with reluctance, but it remained a blot on the closing years of his reign and distracted him from his plans for Paris.

In September 1222, when the Albigensian affair had taken a turn for the worse, Philippe was laid low with a fever which plagued him for the next nine months. Recognizing that death was near, he bequeathed his jewellery to Saint-Denis, and the substantial sum of 50,000 livres as compensation for citizens whom he had wrongfully condemned or who had been victims of his 'extortions'. In July 1223, he was in the Eure, heading for a conference in Paris on the latest papal agenda for a crusade, when his condition deteriorated. On the 11th he was duly bled, and the following day he insisted that he had to die in Paris, but he had only reached Mantes on the 14th when death claimed him. He was buried the next day in his beloved Saint-Denis, having passed on a request to his successor to 'offer justice to his people, and above all to protect the poor and humble from the insolence of the proud'.

With his death, Paris in particular mourned a great ruler. The virtual founder of France, who had established a powerful country, Philippe

Auguste left a capital for the first time secure enough within the mighty walls he had built around it to develop, thrive and expand. Paris had at last become the definitive administrative centre of France, as well as Europe's capital of learning. With a population in Abelard's time of 100,000 (the largest in Western Europe, but still tiny compared with the one million of contemporary Constantinople), it was now approaching the 200,000 mark. And the great gothic cathedrals that Philippe and his father left behind them were only the first instalments of a historic grandeur.

3

The Templars' Curse

Pope Clement, iniquitous judge and cruel executioner, I adjure you to appear in forty days' time before God's tribunal. And you, King of France, will not live to see the end of this year, and Heaven's retribution will strike down your accomplices and destroy your posterity.

Jacques de Molay, in 1314

SAINT LOUIS

Louis VIII, nicknamed 'Le Lion', was the first Capetian monarch not to be designated king in advance during the lifetime of his father – a symbol of how strong Philippe Auguste had left the dynasty. Louis was thirty-six, but died of dysentery three years later (though the circumstances excited suspicion) while at the incessant wars in the south-west, at Montpensier. Keeping on his father's ministers, such as Bishop Guérin the hero of Bouvines, and maintaining all his policies, Louis VIII's short reign was but a continuation of Philippe's. At his death, his son Louis IX was only twelve years old. So authority remained vested in his mother, Blanche of Castile, the Regent, who also took over the same ministers and policies. There were troubles with Philippe Hurepel, the legitimized son of Philippe Auguste and Agnes of Merano, abetted by Henry III of England; but Hurepel died in 1234, and Louis IX enjoyed a relatively tranquil and successful forty-four years on the throne.

Coming to the throne in 1226, Louis IX – 'Saint Louis' (he was canonized in 1297 by Pope Boniface VIII, notably for his crusading zeal, but also perhaps partly to propitiate the French, who were then closing in on Rome under Philippe le Bel) – was to consolidate much of the work of Philippe Auguste both in France and in Paris. When he took over the reins from his mother he is reputed immediately to have impressed his less pious contemporaries by the purity of his soul. He seems to have been a strange, complex man, terrified by his dominant mother and her threats of the devil into wearing a hairshirt by day and, at night, performing fifty genuflections and reciting as many Ave Marias before going to bed. In Maurice Druon's summation, 'He was one of the great neurotics of history. Had he not inclined to saintliness he might have been a monster. Neros are made of the same fibre.'

Certainly, with his passion for crusading he would seem in the eyes of today's historians rather less than deserving of sainthood. But he brought to the Capetian dynasty a morality which would die with him. In geopolitical terms, he routed Henry III's English at Saintes in 1242, then concluded a (brief) peace with England. During his reign the unfortunate Albigensians were finished off (1229), and Languedoc became assimilated into France, and, through his marriage in 1234 to Margaret of Provence (another powerful woman), he acquired for France a claim to one of the richest and largest of her neighbours to the south. By the Treaty of Paris of 1259 Normandy, Anjou, Maine and Poitou were attached to the French Crown, bestowing on Louis considerable prestige in Europe.

Louis was very tall and thin, his figure described as being 'bowed by fasting and mortification'. Some of his earthy contemporaries were not impressed by his excessive piety, which extended to washing the feet of his nobles, and on occasion they jeered at him for being a 'king of priests' rather than of France. Inflexible in his beliefs, he installed the Inquisition in France, with all the misery which that was to bring, and turned his back on the liberalism of the twelfth century.

In 1248, channelling his piety into crusading zeal, Louis embarked on the Seventh Crusade, against the wishes of the Pope and against the judgement of his counsellors. In a remarkable display of the French monarchy's new solidity, he also took with him Queen Margaret and two of his brothers, leaving his mother, Blanche of Castile, once more in charge in Paris. The aim of the Crusade was to liberate the Holy Land from the Sultan of Egypt, but – as usual – things went wrong and by 1250 Louis, stricken with typhus, was a prisoner of the Sultan at El Mansura after a catastrophic massacre of his forces. With great difficulty the King raised his own heavy ransom with recourse to the affluent Knights Templar, though at first they had refused. He then opened negotiations with the Muslims for the delivery of Jerusalem – which might well have succeeded but for the arrival of news of the death of the Regent, his mother Blanche.

Hastening home to Paris, he found a sea of internal troubles arisen in his absence, including a bizarre peasant uprising known as the revolt of the *pastoureaux*. Their origins obscure, their alleged goal was to deliver the King from imprisonment, and they wandered in bedraggled, penniless bands from village to village in the northern provinces, finally descending on Paris as a horde incremented by thieves, vagabonds, gypsies and tarts. Initially they found much sympathy in a populace now fed up with crusading and with a Church grown fat on privilege and corruption. Estimated at 60,000 strong they killed several priests, threw others into the Seine, wounded a large number and indulged in various acts of apostasy. Eventually their assaults extended to the propertied nobility and the Jews. Driven out of Paris by a populace that swiftly tired of them, the *pastoureaux* then moved on to cause trouble in Rouen and Orléans. On the King's return, they were mercilessly hunted down and hanged as far away as Aigues Mortes, the great embarkation port created by the Crusaders at the mouth of the Rhône. This anti-clerical *jacquerie*, like other similar movements in medieval France, left behind no legacy.

Back in Paris, Louis continued the work of consolidating and building on the institutions created by Philippe Auguste. He was the first to realize that such a complex organism as that which his grandfather had created could not be administered like private family property. Under him, the various organs of state in Paris began to split like amoebas, giving rise to the Grand Conseil, in charge of political matters, the Chambre des Comptes, and the Parlement. (The last had nothing whatever in common with the Parliament of England, created about the same time. It was not a representative assembly but in fact filled the role of the supreme court of appeal in the kingdom.) The royal *baillis*, administrators and tax collectors, were made subject to audit by *enquêteurs*. Louis also created the national archives (the first records of which had been destroyed, as we have seen, at the Battle of Fréteval in 1194), in which were preserved all royal acts, treaties, title deeds and judgements. It also first housed the priceless collection of illuminated manuscripts, such as those of Denis the Areopagite which show in marvellous detail life in medieval Paris, eventually to find their way into the Bibliothèque Nationale. In addition Louis founded Paris's first hospital for the blind, the Vingt-Quinze, which could offer shelter to 300, and a home for prostitutes, the Filles-Dieu. Throughout his reign finances were healthy, with receipts exceeding expenditure. His organization of resources was such that from Paris he could despatch food to any part of the country that was famine-stricken. The burden of taxation imposed under Philippe Auguste was alleviated, a new middle class came into being in Paris, and, by the end of his reign, the country as a whole had never known such material prosperity.

In 1259 Louis signed a conclusive peace, the Treaty of Paris, with Henry III, designed to bring to an end the age-old struggle with England. National-minded Frenchmen, especially in retrospect, found it hard to comprehend why – negotiating from a position of strength – Louis gave so much away to the defeated, in the shape of territories like Gascony and Guienne in the south-west. Some have claimed that it led to the Hundred Years War. Nevertheless, it was an act of astonishing, modern-minded moderation, and gave the fair-minded King a reputation as a mediator to whom all Europe would resort in his lifetime – including even Henry III when in dispute with his own barons. 'Never had a united Christendom come closer to realization,' comments André Maurois.

Louis' reign also saw a new flowering of thought. Aristotle was rediscovered, and philosophy attained a fresh significance; literature flourished with such works as the *Roman de la Rose* and its anatomy of courtly love; and the great gothic cathedrals, such as Notre-Dame, were completed. The piety of Saint Louis was also to bequeath to Paris one of its greatest jewels, the Sainte-Chapelle. In 1239, Louis acquired the purported 'Crown of Thorns' from the Emperor of Constantinople, Baudouin II. A wily oriental, Baudouin knew a good thing when he saw it coming and charged the King an outrageously high price (more than four times what the whole chapel was to cost). The acquisition of this most priceless relic placed France firmly in the forefront of Christendom. To house it, and further relics subsequently acquired on the Crusades, in 1242 Louis began building the Sainte-Chapelle, completed in the record time of six years.

There it sits to this day, having survived wars and revolutions, protected within the confines of the largely disappeared Palais de la Cité, a miracle of filigree stonework. Dramatically it counterpoints the grimly solid, dark pessimism of the adjacent Conciergerie, with its sad, damp little court, 'for the women', dating back to the Revolution, its open washing trough and huge spikes to prevent intruders from climbing into the Palais de Justice. Inside, the lower chapel, dedicated to the Virgin, with its low ceiling painted with a star-studded sky, is darkly mysterious, its powerful external buttressing sharply contrasting with the delicacy of the ethereal upper level. Here all is open space, flooded with coloured light from its renowned thirteenth-century stained-glass windows. Atop it all, its thirty-three-metre spire (made from cedar in the nineteenth century, an exact replica of the medieval original) springs boldly sky-wards, a masterpiece of refinement visible from almost every vantage-point in Paris.

In 1257, under Saint Louis' confessor, Robert de Sorbon, the Univer-sity of Paris now gained its enduring name of the 'Sorbonne'. By the end of the thirteenth century, it had attained the constitutional form that would carry it through the rest of the Middle Ages, and a century later it had as many as forty colleges. Robert de Sorbon started off the University library with a bequest of sixty-seven volumes; thirty years later the collection numbered 1,017 titles, all painstakingly written on parchment and often exquisitely illuminated. Of these only four were in French, the remainder still in Latin.

If gown took it out on town from time to time in medieval Paris, it was perhaps not surprising. The students, aged between fifteen and thirty, had a pitiably hard life. Often their backs bore the signs of heavy beating, inflicted by less amiable masters than Abelard. Bitterly cold in winter, with only one much patched garment to their name, they would lodge:

> in a poor house with an old woman who cooks only vegetables and never prepares a sheep except on feast days. A dirty fellow waits on the table and just such a person buys the wine in the city ... After the meal, a student sits on a rickety chair and uses a light, doubtless a candle, which goes out continually and disturbs the ideas.

The next day's lectures would begin at 5 a.m. Receiving no stipend, the scholar would often have to pay extortionate rents for these meagre lodgings himself – as well as find a way of paying his master's wages, for, likewise receiving no regular salaries, each professor had the right to teach for whatever fees he could extract from such students as he could persuade to come to his lectures.

The Saint-King's pious achievements, however, could not in the end save him. Against the counsel of the Pope and his own family, helmeted in the searing heat of high summer in 1270, Louis rashly set off from Aigues Mortes on a new crusade, the Eighth. In Tunisia, his army was decimated by sun and plague at Carthage, and he himself, aged fifty-six, succumbed. There was widespread mourning across France. He left the country in unprecedented prosperity, and a moral prestige which carried inestimable weight in foreign affairs. For the next two centuries the landed gentry would clamour for a return to 'the good customs of Saint Louis'. Louis' saintly moral standards were to lead the kingdom inexorably towards an absolute monarchy, with all its attendant strengths and weaknesses. By the end of his reign, medieval France had created for herself a civilization that was identifiably entirely her own. Saint Louis left behind him a capital that was to 'change no more', for 'All the organs of public life, like those of a living body had come into existence, had found their place and, on the whole, were to retain it.'

Houses might be built and rebuilt, but Paris would remain the same, growing 'concentrically like a tree' – first of all to fill out the undeveloped areas embraced by Philippe Auguste's protective wall.

A NEW HARSHNESS

Louis' heir Philippe III – otherwise known as 'Le Hardi' – ruled for only fifteen years and indeed made little impact on Paris. He spent most of his reign away from the capital campaigning, notably in the disastrous war with Aragon. His greatest, dynastic, success was to marry his second son to Joan of Navarre, the independent kingdom down on the Pyrenees. It was Navarre which, several centuries later, was to provide France with perhaps the greatest of all her kings, Henri IV. Philippe's first son died, possibly of poisoning; so, in 1285, his second son succeeded to the throne as Philippe IV.

Mystery and controversy surround Philippe IV, who was swiftly to prove one of France's most unpleasant, indeed most disastrous kings, leaving in his wake catastrophe for the country and misery in Paris. Under him a new depth of savagery manifested itself in the life of Paris, a dark retreat from the enlightenment of Suger and Philippe Auguste. The new King was called 'Le Bel' on account of his fair but icy good looks, but few reliable personal descriptions of him survive. Like his saintly grandfather, he wore a hairshirt much of his life, but his was a ferocious kind of piety, and during his reign the Inquisition which Saint Louis had introduced into France was exploited to grim and terrible ends in Paris.

His defenders among French historians claim that Philippe further

cemented and consolidated the fundamental institutions of France, and
further extended her territories. All his revisions of the body politic –
such as the diminution of feudal powers – tended, however, only to
increase the power of the throne, advancing it further towards absolute
monarchy. In Paris, in contrast to London where the Lords and the
Commons were willing to sit together as a legislature, the three Estates
(the Clergy, the Nobility and the Third Estate or non-privileged classes)
remained separate, thereby making impossible a joint, national representation – a failing that would impede the development of democracy in
France right through to the Revolution of 1789. Systematically Philippe
applied himself to the destruction of all external and internal rivalry,
and to achieve all this he brought in hard-faced, wily lawyers from the
provinces. The first meetings of the Estates, later to become the Estates-
General, took place under Philippe, but the periodic *consultations* he
granted to them tended only to confirm legislation already promulgated
by him. In Philippe's Paris the Parlement evolved into a more stable and
responsible affair, comprising lords spiritual and temporal, meeting twice
a year for a session of two months, and acting as both a court of appeal
and an advisory council.

Trouble started with Philippe's extravagant plans, in 1298, to rebuild
the Palais de la Cité of his ancestor Philippe Auguste to more sumptuous
standards, so that it would be 'the most beautiful that anyone in France
ever saw'. It would house under one roof all the functions of administration, treasury and justice of the kingdom. It was a triumph of late
gothic art, where even the sinister vaults of the Conciergerie beneath
were works of great beauty. In a Great Hall divided by two massive
naves, under whose columns statues of past kings surveyed the scene,
would sit his Parlements and Estates. This sombre chamber, with its
Salle des Pas Perdus above, still survives today, close to Saint Louis'
ethereal Sainte-Chapelle. Even closer, possibly too close for comfort, was
one the four great defensive towers known as the Tour Bonbec, or
Blabbing Tower, so called because it was there that torture loosened
prisoners' tongues. Philippe's Palais de Justice (incorporated into the
Palais Royal, which he had vastly extended) was staffed with a costly
army of permanent salaried officials.

Philippe le Bel was never to complete his awe-inspiring Palais Royal,
or to enjoy it. Deservedly he became known as France's most spendthrift
king. Under him the cost of running France was six times as much as it
had been under Philippe Auguste less than a century earlier, even
allowing for inflation. Apart from the money poured into the new Palais,

where his predecessors had sought territorial aggrandizement by war and conquest he resorted to outright purchase. All of this led to appalling and recurrent financial difficulties, forcing Philippe to search constantly for fresh sources of revenue. He invented new taxes like the *maltôte*, a levy on corporate business, an income tax earmarked for 'the defence of the realm'; he cancelled the Crown's debts; and he ruthlessly confiscated personal treasures and fortunes. Most notoriously he introduced rampant inflation by adulterating the currency, reducing its weight in gold at the mint – the first French king to do so. Shamelessly he admitted, 'We have been forced to have these pieces coined which perhaps lacked some of the weight and alloy of those struck by our predecessors.' Under Philippe's cruel laws, private counterfeiters were subject to the hideous penalty of being boiled alive, but, as counterfeiter-supreme, the King himself was untouchable. Riots against inflation by the impoverished *commerçants* of Paris in 1307 were ruthlessly crushed, with twenty-eight offenders publicly hanged on the eve of Epiphany from elms at the four entries to the city. There would be no wider revolt.

Yet none of this was enough to fund the outpouring from the royal exchequer. He therefore turned his eyes towards the moneylenders – first of all the Lombards, who had moved up from their native northern Italy and made themselves extremely wealthy (and, consequently, unpopular), not least in funding the Crown during the early days of Philippe le Bel's reign. He next came down on the Jews. After their brutal expulsion by Philippe Auguste, Jewish communities had gradually trickled back to re-establish themselves in France. Particularly in the south they flourished, setting up admirable intellectual centres in their schools, and accruing considerable wealth. In 1288, three years after Philippe's accession, thirteen Jews of both sexes were burned at the stake in Troyes – a foretaste of what was to follow. Under instructions transmitted through his counsellor Guillaume de Nogaret, beginning in the summer of 1306 all Jews were ordered out of France, condemned as usurers, their property confiscated.

AGAINST POPES, TEMPLARS AND PRINCESSES

In his relentless quest for cash, Philippe le Bel now looked towards a source which none of his forebears had dared consider: to the Vatican and the mass of papal wealth. Since 1294, Benedetto Caetani, trained in law at Bologna to become a fiercely ambitious and arrogant pope under the name Boniface VIII, had pursued a policy of worldly intervention in the affairs of states that was as troublesome to France as Innocent III had been. In his view, every human being was subject to the Pope. For the centenary of 1300, Boniface threw a gigantic party, drawing some two million pilgrims to Italy, and hubristically appeared clad in the insignia of the Roman Empire, exclaiming, 'I am Caesar!' His ambitions brought him at once into direct conflict with Philippe, who despite his cash-flow problems nourished grandiose schemes for a new Christian empire stretching from the North Sea to the Mediterranean, controlled from Paris and embracing the papal state. From the time of Innocent III, Rome had financed crusades through taxes on the clergy; Philippe now imposed a similar tax to finance his own military operations in Gascony. Boniface riposted by preparing a bull excommunicating Philippe, a formidable document which might have resulted in the complete dismemberment of France. In Paris, on 24 June, a massive crowd assembled in the gardens of the Palais Royal to show support for the King. Priests loyal to the King were paraded, drowning out the courageous voices of traditionalists faithful to Rome.

Before Boniface's *Unum Sanctum* bull could be applied, however, French forces headed by Chancellor de Nogaret invaded the papal palace at Anagani in 1303. They mobbed the pontiff in a scene of unprecedented violence with a view to forcing his abdication. Boniface declared he would rather die, challenging Nogaret's men to kill him: 'Here is my neck, here is my head!' He never recovered, and died a month later. All Europe was shocked by this affront; Dante, though he hated Boniface, regarded it as a recrucifixion of Christ.

Though simultaneously confronted with serious military defeat at Courtrai in Flanders against Edward I of England, Philippe refused to back down. Boniface's elderly successor, Benedict XI, survived only nine months (poison in a dish of fresh figs was suspected), and there now followed one of the most grotesque periods in all papal history – what came to be known as the Babylonian Captivity of the Popes at Avignon. For eleven months the Conclave sat in deadlock, divided between pro- and anti-French factions, until at last a split in the anti-French front enabled Philippe to triumph with the election of a French pontiff, Bernard le Got, the Archbishop of Bordeaux, as Clement V. Another Bologna-trained lawyer, not even a cardinal, Clement was a shameless nepotist who made cardinals of five members of his family. Using the prevailing chaos in Italy as an excuse, he agreed to be crowned at Lyons and thereafter settled in the bishop's palace in Avignon, beginning the seventy-year exile, forerunner of the Great Schism, that was an unmitigated disaster for the Church. Never again was the papacy to know the power of an Innocent III or a Boniface, and a French king was the cause.

Clement was prepared to do most of Philippe's bidding, though he jibbed at his efforts to have his deceased enemy Boniface branded a heretic and sodomite. He did, however, open the door to Philippe's most fateful act – the dissolution of the Knights Templar. The focus shifts dramatically back to Paris, where the Knights Templars resided in their enclave of the Temple, a vast *donjon* flanked by four towers just outside the city walls to the north of the Marais. Here they lived in a splendour rivalling that of the Palais Royal. Their wealth was legendary. The order had been founded after the First Crusade, under the edict of Louis VII, with the noble function of defending the Holy Land as 'poor *chevaliers* of Christ'. It had started modestly as a confraternity near the Dome on the Rock, in 1118. Over the years, they and their rival military order, the Hospitallers, left many magnificent castles across the Levant, including the famous Krak des Chevaliers near Aleppo. They were fanatically brave in battle, and as late as the final battle for Acre in 1291 their Grand Master had been among the fallen. Recognized all over Europe by their robes of white with a red cross on the front, in 1128 the Templars had acquired a rule, supposedly dictated by the ascetic Saint Bernard of Clairvaux himself, of dedicated austerity as monk-soldiers. But over the course of the intervening two centuries loot derived from the Crusades, coupled with exceptionally skilful husbandry, had enabled the Templars to amass immense riches – and therefore power, making them almost a sovereign state in their own right.

Inevitably corruption had set in, and with it the venal envy of the outside world. Over the thirteenth century, the Templars had become *de facto* bankers to the Crown (Philippe Auguste actually kept his treasury in the Temple), rivals to the Lombards and the Jews as moneylenders. But they had incurred Saint Louis' profound displeasure when they had initially refused to raise funds to ransom him from Egypt. His grandson was mindful of this: the Capetians had long memories. The Templars' reputation for greed was widespread; so were rumours of some of their simpler vices of the flesh. For centuries after their demise the expression *boire comme un Templier* was common currency in France, while the old German word *Tempelhaus* became synonymous with a house of ill-repute. Exploiting their unpopularity, in October 1307 Philippe – through the medium of Chancellor de Nogaret – declared war on the Templars, levelling trumped-up charges of heresy, necromancy and sodomy against them, similar to those raised years earlier against the Albigensians. In the preamble to his proclamation, Philippe, employing every image, spoke of:

> a bitter thing, a deplorable thing, a thing terrible to think about, terrible to hear, detestable, execrable, abominable, inhuman, which had already echoed in our ears, not without making us shudder with a violent horror. An immense pain developed in us.

The Templars were accused, *inter alia*, of 'sacrificing to idols', of 'infecting the purity of the air' and of 'torturing Christ a second time'.

With a nod from an acquiescent Pope Clement, the Inquisition, originally designed to stamp out heresy, now in all its nastiness became the instrument for destroying these declared enemies of the temporal state. In a remarkably well-orchestrated raid, all the Templars were arrested one night and their property declared forfeit. One after the other they appeared before inquisitors, counsellors of the King and torturers, in the cellars of their own fortress, and in the presence of a throng of eager spectators. The tortures were so appalling that one Templar saw twenty-five *frères* die 'under the question'. Public burning at the stake was now the favoured ritual under the Inquisition. In one of the most deplorable episodes ever to be witnessed in Paris, 138 Templars were burned at the stake, a large number between the Bois de Vincennes and the Porte Saint-Antoine. As the flames rose, most of them retracted the 'confessions' they had made under torture – sure evidence of the unsoundness of the charges against them.

Proceedings against the Templars went on until the climax was reached in 1314. The Grand Master of the order himself, Jacques de Molay, who refused to answer charges, had been tortured and thrown into prison for seven years, together with his chief assistant Geoffroy de Charnay. In March that year they were dragged on to the *parvis* of

Notre-Dame to hear their sentence. Philippe, enraged by their prot-
estations of innocence, ordered the two Templar leaders to be immolated
that same evening. A special scaffold was set up on the Île des Juifs,
opposite the Quai des Grands Augustins, and roughly where the Vert
Galant statue of Henri IV now stands. As the flames licked around him,
Jacques de Molay is reputed to have uttered a terrible curse:

> Pope Clement, iniquitous judge and cruel executioner, I adjure you
> to appear in forty days' time before God's tribunal. And you, King
> of France, will not live to see the end of this year, and Heaven's
> retribution will strike down your accomplices and destroy your
> posterity.

Within forty days, Pope Clement V had fallen ill of an agonizingly
painful disease and died on 20 April; Chancellor de Nogaret died of
mysterious causes a short while later; Philippe le Bel died after a hunting
accident that same year, on 29 November, aged forty-six. Over the next
few years, his three sons would also be struck down, bringing to an end
the Capetian dynasty.

In that same terrible year of 1314, before Philippe le Bel reaped his
just rewards, Paris was rocked by a royal scandal. On the Left Bank, just
opposite the Louvre, stood the medieval Hôtel de Nesle, a defence tower
that had grown into a sumptuous palace. In 1308, Philippe le Bel had
acquired it and converted it into apartments for his three sons and their
families. The princes – Louis, Philippe and Charles – lived there with
their wives, respectively Marguerite (a granddaughter of Saint Louis on
her mother's side), Jeanne and her sister Blanche. Before long Marguerite
and Blanche were caught using the old medieval tower as a place of
assignation with their lovers, two dashing brothers, Philippe and Gautier
d'Aulnay, who were their gentlemen-in-waiting.

The King was merciless. Princesses Marguerite and Blanche were
rapidly found guilty of adultery. Under torture, the d'Aulnays admitted
that their liaisons had been going on for three years. They were then
skinned alive in front of an enthusiastic crowd, castrated and then
disembowelled, decapitated and their trunks hung by the armpits on a
gibbet to be devoured by birds of prey. The crowd cheered itself hoarse
as the executioner held aloft the severed genitals of the lovers – an
indication of how brutality and the worst appetites for cruelty had been
sharpened in Paris in the years between Philippe Auguste and Philippe
le Bel. All who had abetted the lovers were drowned or secretly
despatched.

Marguerite and Blanche were forced to witness the execution of their lovers. Their heads shaven like *collabos* after the Liberation of 1944, they were then condemned to solitary confinement for many months in miserable, icy conditions in Richard Coeur de Lion's old fortress of Château Gaillard. Then, when Marguerite's husband Louis, now king, decided he wanted to remarry, rather than spend time seeking an annulment he had her suffocated between two mattresses. After seven years in Château Gaillard, Blanche, divorced by her husband, was permitted to take the veil in the Convent of Maubuisson, where she lived until her death in 1326. Jeanne, who although acquitted was suspected of participating in the tower orgies, was spirited out of Paris until the scandal died down, then reunited with her forgiving husband Philippe, who had in turn become king. Rather insensitively, it would seem, he gave her the Hôtel de Nesle as her residence. The evil reputation of the Hôtel continued; stories persisted down the ages that Jeanne, watching from her window in the tower, would send for passing students and, having exhausted their virility, would then have them tied in sacks and thrown from the top of the tower to drown in the Seine below.

And so the new century began, opening for Paris on a setting as brutal and menacing as the previous century, under Philippe Auguste, had opened bright and full of hope. France was now the most populous and powerful country in Europe, while Paris – bulging out beyond the city wall – contained 300,000 souls to London's 40,000. But – in fulfilment of the Templars' curse – Philippe le Bel was to be followed by a catastrophic sequence of famines, wars and plagues, and it would take four centuries for France to recover that same level of population.

AGE TWO: 1314–1643

HENRI IV

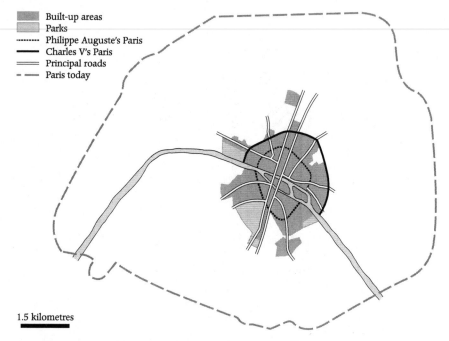

1.5 kilometres

PARIS, FROM PHILIPPE AUGUSTE TO THE ACCESSION OF HENRI IV

4

Besieged

I rule with my arse in the saddle and my gun in my fist.

Henri IV's fighting motto

THE HUNDRED YEARS WAR

When Philippe le Bel died in 1314, following the terrible curse of the Templars, and only forty-four years after the death of Saint Louis, he had so dominated his period that it seemed as if 'the heart of the kingdom had ceased to beat'. Because of his sin against the Templars, all Philippe's good works, his institutional reforms, would soon be forgotten. In the 327 years since the election of Hugues Capet, only eleven kings had reigned over France – a prodigious dynasty. Now, over the turbulent fourteen years that followed Philippe's death, there would be no fewer than three kings, all of them his sons, and none of them producing heirs who survived.

The cuckolded Louis X, Le Hutin (the Headstrong or the Quarrelsome), outlived his father by only eighteen months. Ill at ease in his unruly capital, Le Hutin – like other French kings after him – moved out of Paris to the sombre Château de Vincennes. In May 1316 he died after a brief bout of pneumonia, though rumours of his poisoning by a kinswoman, Mahaut of Artois, were never allayed; and his posthumous son John died mysteriously six months later. Theoretically, the succession should have gone to Jeanne, questionable daughter of Louis and the adulterous Marguerite, but Louis' lanky younger brother Philippe evoked the ancient Salic Law whereby the female line was precluded from the succession – an act of signal importance in the succession of future kings of France – and mounted a *coup d'état*. As Philippe V ('Le Long'), husband of the supposedly predatory Queen Jeanne, he ruled for six years, dying of tuberculosis in 1322. Then came Charles IV, who likewise lasted only six years. Having divorced the hapless Blanche, he married again but produced only three daughters, and died suddenly at Vincennes in 1328.

Thus ended the Capetian dynasty after three centuries, fulfilling in its entirety the curse of the Templars. The succession now went sideways to a cousin, Philippe of Valois, who started a new dynasty as Philippe VI. The first Valois were scornfully dubbed 'kings by chance' by contemporaries. But as he was already acting as regent, and was cousin to the three dead kings, as well as great-grandson of Saint Louis, Philippe VI's claim to the throne of France was perfectly legitimate. This, however, was not how it was seen by Philippe le Bel's only daughter Isabella, the 'She-Wolf of France', who had married the English king Edward II. Her teenaged son Edward III, king since 1327, laid claim to the French crown, and in 1337 the Hundred Years War began, with a few border skirmishes down in Guyenne.

Meanwhile, in Paris grim and chaotic times had descended once the firm hand of Philippe le Bel had been removed. In 1315, there had been a disastrous harvest, and famine settled on an unprepared city, her plight exacerbated by an improvident government. A comet passed over the city and was visible for three nights – an ill omen in the minds of Parisians. Two years later a fresh bout of irrational upheaval in the provinces sent a new wave of half-crazed *pastoureaux* flooding into Paris. Comprising an assortment of unemployed youths seeking adventure, brigands, thieves, unfrocked priests, beggars and whores, they seized the Châtelet, assaulted the *prévôt* and pillaged the Abbey of Saint-Germain-des-Prés. They swept through the country, provoking new outrages against Jewish ghettos that had survived Philippe IV's expulsion orders. At Chinon all the Jews were rounded up and thrown into one huge fiery pit; in Paris they were burned on the island that tragically bore their name at the tip of the Île de la Cité, on the site where Jacques de Molay had been immolated. Louis le Hutin, apparently seeking forgiveness of his sins (notably the murder of hapless Queen Marguerite) and to curry favour with the populace, decided to empty the prisons. As a result, crime took off; it became dangerous to venture out at night, and there were more robberies and murders than had been known for forty years. From the areas where Saint Louis had strictly confined them, prostitutes now moved into the public baths, to the point where honest men could no longer go for an innocent soak without being exposed to more insidious temptations of the flesh.

To bring order to the chaos left by Le Hutin, his successors had the gallows and scaffolds working overtime; to satisfy demand, in 1325 the famous wooden gibbet at Monfaucon was replaced by one of sixteen stone pillars over ten metres high, and joined together by heavy beams. The corpses hung there until they disintegrated. That same year a gentle spring and a brief period of commercial prosperity under Charles IV lulled Parisians into expecting happy times ahead. Then came the bitterest of harsh winters; the Seine was covered with ice and even wells froze, trees cracked in the gardens, starving birds flocked into the city, and the cold fissured the stone walls. Food prices rocketed, as did the death toll.

Yet all through this period the population of Paris was forging ahead. Spaces between houses on the Left Bank where there had once been only fields and watermeadows were now being built on. The Abbey of Saint-Germain-des-Prés was no longer an isolated entity. Already the city was beginning to press up against the protective walls of Philippe Auguste. Paris was getting overcrowded again – dangerously so, if she were to be hit by a fresh epidemic. Nevertheless, except under Charles V during a brief truce in the Hundred Years War, virtually nothing of lasting value or permanence would be built in Paris until François Premier 200 years later. Under the early Valois, Paris stagnated. Though there was little or no physical development in the city, at least some evolution was to be seen in the apparel worn by the modish. At court, men took to adorning themselves with more jewellery than their women, wearing narrow-waisted tunics so saucily short that they revealed the buttocks and shoes so pointed that they made walking difficult.

In 1340, Edward III of tiny England assumed the title of King of France, and effectively destroyed the French fleet at Sluys, off the coast of Flanders. His troops landed virtually unopposed on the Cotentin Peninsula of Normandy, just where Eisenhower's Americans would land almost exactly 600 years later. In 1346, the English longbowmen – employing the most advanced weapon in all Europe – won one of history's decisive battles against the ponderous French cavalry at Crécy on the Somme. All that Philippe Auguste had won for France at Bouvines now seemed lost. In a historic scene, recorded not least by Rodin, the burghers of Calais surrendered to Edward with halters round their necks. England was to hold this vital foothold, this arrow pointed at Paris, until the days of Elizabeth I more than two centuries later.

Edward's small armies were highly efficient and full of national spirit. Year after year his marauding bands plundered and laid waste to northern France. Ten years after the massacre at Crécy another shattering defeat was inflicted at Poitiers by Edward's son the Black Prince on an army that had not troubled to learn the lessons of the earlier débâcle. As if this were not enough, now the Black Death descended. Perhaps half the population of France was wiped out by the deadly combination of war and plague.

Preceded – so legend had it – by a portentous ball of fire in the skies over the city, the Black Death reached Paris in the summer of 1348, then moved slowly on towards Flanders and Germany. Paris herself, always vulnerable to any epidemic as a result of her overcrowding and poor sanitation, suffered far worse than the countryside or the smaller towns. Believing cats to be the source of plague, the Parisians killed off their most effective instruments for dealing with the plague-bearing rat population. The death rate reached 800 a day. The cemeteries and charnel houses were overflowing; soon there were not enough living to bury the dead, who lay rotting in their houses or even on the streets. Priests abandoned the sick and dying to shrive themselves. Those rich enough to do so, nobles and churchmen, left the city: 'Those who were left drank, fornicated or skulked in the cellars according to their inclinations.' It seemed as if life, at best, could only drag on for a few painful weeks. Paris was described as having come close to 'a complete collapse of public and private morality'. By the time the plague receded, in the winter of 1349, her population had been decimated.

During the Hundred Years War, France's struggle for national survival left little time, cash or spirit for grand building designs in the capital. By way of a reminder of the grim fourteenth century, only a handful of half-timber houses remain, in the Rue François Miron – one of which today serves as a *maison de rencontre*. The fortunes of Paris rose and fell with those of the Valois kings. The sobriquets of these pre-Renaissance rulers did not always accurately reflect their characters, or their achievements. There was Jean le Bon, who was both bad and disastrous, losing for France the Battle of Poitiers, while Charles le Fou was certainly no worse; Charles VII, 'Le Victorieux', seems not to have been, losing his capital (for a while) as a result. A praiseworthy exception to the rule was Charles V, 'Le Sage' (1364–80).

The auguries for Charles V, a small and deceptively frail man, were not encouraging. In 1356, while he was still Dauphin, his father, the ill-starred Jean le Bon, and his brother Philippe were both imprisoned in London, having been captured, most humiliatingly, at Poitiers – from which battlefield Charles himself had managed to beat a rapid retreat. Taking advantage of the King's defeat, in Paris the headstrong *prévôt*, Etienne Marcel, urged administrative reforms upon the monarchy that would today be regarded as distinctly democratic. Foreshadowing many things to come in Paris, including the events of 1789 and the Commune of 1871, Marcel held that a 'Commune of Paris' should govern the kingdom, in consultation with the King. The monarchy experienced one of its most perilous moments when, at a cabinet meeting, two of the Dauphin's principal counsellors, the marshals of Champagne and Normandy, were slaughtered before his eyes by supporters of Marcel.

But Marcel had overreached himself. Like Adolphe Thiers and the Versailles government in 1871 (or like Louis XIV and his mother, the Regent, during the Fronde), Charles decided to pull out of Paris and regroup with a view to seizing the capital by force. Around Paris the peasants, pushed over the brink by the deprivations of war, rose and made common cause with Marcel. But this *jacquerie* revolt was put down, and some 20,000 slaughtered. Etienne Marcel then committed the unthinkable, and allied himself with the occupying English. This was altogether too much for the Parisians; 'hooted at and censured', Marcel was assassinated by his own followers in July 1358. From Compiègne Charles then re-entered Paris with ease and, at once demonstrating clemency and pushing aside Marcel's constitutional reforms, ruled as an absolute but restrained monarch.

Charles now sought to secure Paris by upgrading the protective wall of Philippe Auguste, pushing it outwards to embrace the recently expanded city *faubourgs* (or suburbs) and fortifying the precincts of the Abbey of Saint-Germain. He abandoned Philippe's old palace in the smelly and claustrophobic Île de la Cité, first for the Hôtel Saint-Pol in the Marais and then, in 1368, for the fresh air and security of the Louvre. A cultured man and patron of the arts, Charles demolished Philippe's grim old bastion, replacing it with a palace that, while it remained a stronghold, was embellished with fantastical turrets, pointed spires, conical roofs with lacy ridges, crested battlements and tall gilt weather-vanes as handed down to posterity in the exquisitely illuminated fifteenth-century manuscript *Les Très Riches Heures du Duc de Berry*, compiled by the brothers Limbourg. Less militarily functional windows began to supplant the narrow arrow-slits of a city at risk. Its elegant, light-hearted fancies would have done credit to Bavaria's Schloss Neuschwannstein, and no doubt it was the Louvre of Charles V that partly inspired Mad Ludwig. Moving into it four years after he came to the throne, Charles was the first and almost the last French king to make the Louvre his principal residence. Within its safe walls he collected his ancestors' manuscripts to found the first Bibliothèque Nationale. Outside, a great rampart, running just five metres east of today's Arc du Carrousel, now marked the western limits of Paris.

Like many of his successors, Charles ran into trouble with the rowdies of the Sorbonne; he met it by closing off the Rue de la Fouarre with chains at each end. In the next reign, that of his son, the unfortunate Charles le Fou (Charles VI), the University once more earned opprobrium by supporting a collaborationist party that favoured making Henry V of England the rightful king of France, thus earning for itself the epithet 'an annexe of Oxford'.

What Charles V did for Paris, however, was not matched by either his financial or his diplomatic acumen. The Hundred Years War continued in all its horror, bringing France – and Paris – one of the most tragic periods in history. At Agincourt in 1415, as many as 10,000 French warriors fell to Henry's longbowmen, at negligible cost to the English. It was a time of bitter cold, when the wolves came into the city to keep warm. The combination of the war and the Black Death had rendered much of the rural population of France homeless and starving. Fleeing the ruined countryside, these uprooted peasants sought shelter inside Charles V's girdle of walls, where they set up a perilous no-go area in a tangle of reeking streets, establishing their own laws and terrorizing the populace. In daytime they spilled out into the rest of Paris, transmogrifying themselves into blind or limbless beggars; by night they miraculously recovered their faculties, attracting to the unsavoury area the name Cour des Miracles. In *Notre-Dame de Paris*, Victor Hugo described it as an 'immense changing-room of all the actors of this comedy that robbery, prostitution and murder play on the cobbled streets of Paris'.

Paris was now under the occupation of *les goddams* (as the English soldiery were known). From Les Tournelles, his palace in the Marais, on the present site of the resplendent Hôtel de Soubise, the Duke of Bedford, brother of Henry V and self-proclaimed Regent of France (1420–35), governed Paris – and not badly, though few Frenchmen would admit it. King without a capital, Charles VII ruled from Bourges over a divided rump of France – comparable to the area of non-occupied Vichy France from 1940. Then came Jeanne d'Arc, and by 1453 *les goddams*, now riven by a combination of weak kings and their own civil disputes

– the Wars of the Roses – had departed. With them also went the wolves. But, though the Hundred Years War was at last at an end, more wars followed, and internecine civil disputes too, with Louis XI taken prisoner in his own country, at Péronne in 1468.

RENAISSANCE STIRRINGS

By now, however, the first glimmer of a new light was beginning to illuminate Paris from the south-east, from Italy. Already during the reign of Charles VI contemporary paintings depict the mad King lying on his bed richly caparisoned in garments, the fabrics of which had made the wealth of Renaissance Florence. Liberated from the scourge north of the Channel, the Valois began to turn eager, and greedy, eyes towards Italy. Through marriages and deaths (notably of King René of Anjou and of Provence) and almost by default Louis XI made huge territorial gains, which set him among the great builders of the nation. During his reign, France acquired much of the geographical shape of the hexagon she inhabits today. Maine, Anjou and Provence, even powerful Burgundy, so long a thorn in the side of France, fell into Louis' hands virtually without a battle. He also obtained a foothold in Naples. With Naples there opened a window that would bring enormous cultural wealth to Paris, but would also lead to the undoing of many a subsequent French ruler – down to Napoleon III – seduced by the allure of Italian sun and riches. Louis XI, sometimes described as the 'strangest of all the Valois', was certainly the most restless, spending half of his twenty-two-year reign wandering, away from Paris, and dying in his château at Plessis-les-Tours.

Nevertheless, within a few years of the departure of the last English troops, France under Louis XI recovered (as she was often to do) with astonishing rapidity. Recovery was partly a result of the fertility of her soil, coupled with the industry of her peasants; but it was also spurred by what de Gaulle later mystically identified as 'une certaine idée de la France', or as André Maurois puts it 'a deep-rooted certainty that a Frenchman can only be a Frenchman'. Hand in hand with this went a fundamental, unshakeable belief in France's universal *mission civilisatrice*.

In 1461, Louis XI made his *joyeuse entrée* into Paris. As André Maurois relates:

> Upon his entry, the herald, Loyal Coeur, presented him with five noble ladies who represented the five letters of the name *Paris*, and each of them made a speech of welcome. The horses were caparisoned with cloth of gold lined with sable, with velvet lined with ermine, and with cloth of Damascus mounted with goldsmiths' work. At the fountain of Ponceau, three handsome girls took the part of the Sirens, all naked, and you could see 'their lovely breasts, round and firm, which was a very pleasant thing', and they warbled little motets.

On the Pont au Change, the bird-sellers, who had a monopoly on the Place du Châtelet (they still have it), released 200 of their wares, brilliant of plumage. But Paris benefited little during Louis' reign. Indeed he seems to have been something of a skinflint, once declaring, 'I have decided to marry my small daughter Joan to the small Duc d'Orléans, because it seems to me that the children they might have would not cost much to feed.'

Louis' son Charles VIII soon became seduced 'by the phantoms and glories of Italy', and involved himself in a lightning campaign that was so effective that it almost resembled a promenade, bringing him to the very gates of Rome. Initially, the Italians seemed to welcome the French; Charles in turn came home enthralled by Italian art, thus opening France's doors to the Renaissance. Alas, in 1498, aged only twenty-eight, the poor gangly fellow died after bashing his head on the low lintel of a door at Amboise on the Loire, the château to which he was so passionately attached. On his death, the succession went sideways, to the Orléans branch of the House of Valois. The new King, Louis XII, great-grandson of Charles V, was yet another who did not share his forebear's passion for Paris. He too was to be enticed into the maze of Italian politics and intrigue, by Pope Julius II, the builder of St Peter's and the Sistine Chapel. This warrior Pope, aroused by Machiavelli, wanted the weight of French arms as a counterbalance to his enemy, the Venetians. But as soon as Louis became too successful and occupied Milan, Julius II switched sides and sought to get rid of the French. In 1513 Louis' army was crushed at Novara, Milan was lost, and the French had to beat an indecently hasty retreat back over the Alps. Though Italy was lost, she was never forgotten. Aged fifty-three and without an heir, Louis was married a third time, to Mary, the sixteen-year-old sister of England's

Henry VIII. In an apparent effort to please his lusty young bride, the sickly Louis was said to have greatly exceeded his strength and died suddenly in the middle of the night on New Year's Day, 1515.

In France as a whole, which enjoyed a period of rare prosperity and peace at home, the reign of Louis XII was generally rated a success – though, like his predecessors, he had had little time – or money – to devote to his capital. Thus, over five reigns during the previous century and a quarter, Paris virtually stagnated. When they were not away at the wars, the later Valois concentrated their wealth and energies on the joys of *la chasse*, and on translating the marvels of the Italian Renaissance to their glorious châteaux on the Loire – Amboise, Blois, Chenonceaux, Chaumont and Azay, culminating in the modest hunting lodge of François I at Chambord, with an entire village constructed on its roof and its great spiral staircases designed to take a horse and coach.

Anything to be away from smelly, pestilential, unruly Paris!

TWO STRONG KINGS

It would be hard to imagine a greater contrast than that between the sickly and delicate Louis XII and his successor, the robust, rumbustious François Premier. Just twenty-one when he succeeded (sideways, like the heirless Louis), François was a giant of over two metres tall, with long legs and arms and massive hands and feet. In his energies, appetites and tastes, he was every inch the Renaissance king; in the magnificence of his clothes he closely resembled his contemporary, England's Henry VIII – the close-fitting doublets with the slashed sleeves, the extravagant Italian shoes and the feathered hats. He brought Benvenuto Cellini to France, and Leonardo da Vinci died in his arms. Like his two prede-cessors, as Bismarck might have said in a different context, François' 'map of Europe' lay in Italy – and so did his fate. Inheriting a country threatened on three sides – by Henry VIII across the Channel, by Emperor Maximilian beyond the Rhine, and by Ferdinand of Aragon over the Pyrenees – François decided to seize the initiative by recap-turing Milan – almost on a whim. At first things went well. At the resplendent Field of the Cloth of Gold, a forerunner of lavish state visits,

François managed to entice Henry VIII into watchful, and only temporary, neutrality. But the death of Maximilian I brought a far more redoubtable foe to the east – the Holy Roman Emperor Charles V, ruler of Habsburg Austria and King of Spain.

Thus hardly had France recovered from the Hundred Years War against England than a new challenge appeared. Spain, released from Moorish bondage and now, under Charles V, allied by marriage to the Austrian Habsburgs, confronted France on both sides, east and west. Here were the beginnings of France's ensuing four centuries of conflict with the Germanic world; by the time of François' death in 1547, it should have been clear that the enduring problem for France was no longer Italy.

Ten years into his reign, disaster struck the perhaps excessively hubristic François. His cousin, Charles de Bourbon, Constable of the Kingdom of France and thus its most powerful military leader, defected to the enemy. Suddenly it looked as if the dreadful days of the Hundred Years War might be returning, with enemy troops advancing to within fifty kilometres of Paris – as close as Kaiser Wilhelm was ever to come. Rashly crossing the Alps once again, François led his army to total defeat at Pavia in 1525, crushed by Spanish infantry, the most formidable soldiery in Europe at that time. He himself was wounded and taken prisoner – the last French ruler to be imprisoned by a foreign power until Napoleon on Elba. Paris was left all but undefended. To his mother François wrote the famous words: 'Madame, of everything there remain to me only honour and life, which are unscathed.' To many Frenchmen, however, it must have seemed as if the melancholy prediction of Louis XII was coming true: 'We busy ourselves in vain ... that big young fellow will spoil everything.'

It looked as though a resurgent, fiercely reactionary Catholic Spain, bursting with wealth plundered from the New World, was becoming master of Christendom. Meanwhile, across the Rhine an event that was soon to shake Christendom, especially France, went by almost unnoticed. In 1517, a little-known German monk called Martin Luther nailed his ninety-five theses to the door of the local church at Wittenberg, in protest against the sale of indulgences to finance the building of Saint Peter's, and against the harshness of Madrid-oriented Catholicism in general. There followed his excommunication and his courageous appearance before the dread Charles V at the Diet of Worms in 1521. Though beset by enemies, at home and abroad, François had at least succeeded in preserving the national integrity of France; but, as his foreign wars ended, so the sixteenth century's wars of religion began, leading to an epoch of terrible civil conflicts in France.

While in captivity François studied his captors' success in the New World and dreamed up his 'grand design' for France. On his release (after submitting to a draconian peace treaty) he was to found the port of Le Havre as a base for exploration and to despatch Jacques Cartier on the first of his voyages to discover Canada. Much of his energy went into hunting, and the building of vast hunting-boxes such as Chambord, precursor of Versailles. As a result of all this, on top of his unrelenting military expenditure, François' finances were constantly in a tangle, and the country heavily in debt. To offset some of this burden, François introduced bonds on the Hôtel de Ville as a principle of public debt, while money moved into the hands of a bourgeoisie seeking to merge with the nobility.

Despite his many other distractions, François I was, however, the first king since his great-great-grandfather Charles V, nearly two centuries before, to undertake serious works in Paris. Allowing the Renaissance to establish its ineffaceable imprint there, he razed Charles' fortress Louvre as well as the last structures of Philippe Auguste. Evincing Paris's new sense of security at the heart of the nation, the Louvre was no longer a bastion (after his incarceration in Madrid, François had a horror of fortresses), but an elegant and majestic palace. Designed by the architect Pierre Lescot and the sculptor Jean Goujon – 'the French Phidias' – it was to prove a masterpiece of Renaissance grace, its style borrowed from Greece and Rome but with an unmistakable Frenchness. François had had time to complete only the two south-west sections on the Cour Carrée (the palace as a whole was not finished until 1663). His son Henri II and later Henri III were to add the two lateral wings. But François had set the classical design for the future, as well as initiating the art collection that would make the Louvre the greatest gallery of paintings in the world. Legend has it that he brought its most famous canvas, the *Mona Lisa*, to Paris after the death of Leonardo in 1519.

Always forward-looking (except perhaps in warfare), François abandoned the royal palaces in the Marais to open up that quarter to development by wealthy entrepreneurs, buying up land previously belonging to the religious orders. In 1535 he founded the Collège de France, as a competitor and a corrective to the unruly Sorbonne next door. One of its specific aims was to propagate the humanistic ideals of the Italian Renaissance, and for the first time lectures were given in an enriched French language.

Among François' most portentous introductions from Italy was the daughter of a wealthy Florentine banker, Catherine de Medici, as a bride for his heir, the future Henri II. With her came Italian culture of the high Renaissance, intrigue – and the art of poison. In 1547 François died, worn out by war, hunting and sex. Notwithstanding all his absences and distractions, it was he – lending a brilliance to the French Crown unknown since Saint Louis – who truly and ineradicably established the Renaissance in Paris. The fashion and style of the times in François' France sprang from the top, from the court which followed the King wherever he went, a train of 12,000 horses, tents, baggage, tapestries, gold and silver plate, and wives, sisters and mistresses. 'A court without ladies is a springtime without roses,' he proclaimed, and later French monarchs were to follow his lead. Poetry, music, games, gallantry and revels were the order of the day in this new France, suddenly prosperous in his last years through trade with Florence and a gold-laden Spain. Whereas Louis XI (perhaps like later sovereigns of Britain) thought that 'knowledge makes for melancholy', François was genuinely a 'lover of good literature and learned men'. He was as adept in conversation about painting as about war, and it was said that 'Whoever chanced to come was received, but he must needs not be a fool or a stumbler.' It was the era of Rabelais, intoxicated with knowledge and earthiness, moving on from the courtly love songs of the troubadours, the *jongleurs* and the pious mystery plays of the Middle Ages; a time when – abandoning their prescriptions of modesty – painters could depict the King's mistress *aux seins nus.*

If the ideal of Frenchmen of the Middle Ages had been Philippe Auguste's grandson Saint Louis, among the Valois of the sixteenth century it was Machiavelli. From the Borgias' Italy, François' outrageous friend Benvenuto Cellini brought not only art but a new morality; in his world *la vie sexuelle* was free, and even murder was forgiven – if the offender was an artist. 'Virtuous young people', he boasted, 'are those who give the most thrust with the knife.' In the world of Philippe Auguste, Cellini would have rated the gallows and hell, but in the sixteenth century he was befriended by princes amused by his antics. Those men and women of the Renaissance, in France as in Italy, 'had so much animal violence that the scruples of their minds never put a check on the motions of their bodies. They were good Catholics, but they did not go abroad without a dagger in their belts.'

With the death of François, one strong king followed another. Lacking his father's charisma, Henri II was a sombre man, not over-endowed with brains, and chiefly interested in physical exercise. Wedded to a Medici, Henri II more than continued the Italianate traditions of François I, further advancing François' work on the Louvre, and with Catherine, his widow, commissioning Philibert Delorme to build a great new Renaissance Palace of the Tuileries, further west and perpendicular to the Seine. But under Catherine there also intensified an altogether more sombre aspect of the Renaissance in France – the Wars of Religion.

In 1559, under Henri II, a treaty was signed, that of Cateau-Cambrésis, one of those which laid the basis for modern France. Under it Queen Elizabeth was forced to relinquish England's last foothold on the French mainland – Calais – which, though it had surrendered the previous year, had remained a permanent threat. At the same time, France secured three fortresses that would play a key role in wars against a new enemy, Germany, in both 1870 and 1914. By this treaty France also firmly turned her back on Italy – at least until Napoleon. It was a good accommodation for France, and extensive festivities were organized in Paris to mark it and to celebrate the weddings of two royal princesses. The athletic Henri joined in by entering a jousting tournament at Les Tournelles palace, where once the Duke of Bedford had held sway and on what is now the Place des Vosges in the Marais area. But the lance of his adversary splintered and put out his eye. After ten days of agony Henri died, aged forty-one, having reigned barely twelve years. Though he had been wearing the colours of his mistress, the sixty-year-old Diane de Poitiers, his widow Catherine ordered the palace to be razed to the ground.

Henri's sufferings, however, were as nothing compared to what now overtook France in the course of the half-century that followed his death, and to which the country all but succumbed. The violent death of the second of two authoritarian and strong rulers marked an equally violent turning point in the history of both the Valois dynasty and France itself. From then on began the grim period of European struggles between Catholics and Protestants known as the Wars of Religion. Under the unrelentingly harsh Catholic fundamentalism of first Charles V, then Philip II of Spain, which throughout the sixteenth century wielded the most powerful military force in all Europe, the Inquisition was given full rein. Europe, and France, seemed destined to be torn apart by the rival factions. What now overtook France, and Paris, in the three decades from 1559 to 1590, was like an infinitely more savage Gallic version of William Shakespeare's History Plays – the disorder and savagery which follows when strong rulers give way to weak ones.

Of notable Italian lineage, Catherine de Medici was well versed in the arts of Machiavelli – and of poison. Apparently barren for the first nine years of her marriage, she went on to produce ten children, three of whom became the next kings of France – and the last of the Valois dynasty. Coming to the throne aged fifteen, her eldest son François II, who had married Mary Queen of Scots, had one of the shortest and most wretched reigns in French history (1559–60). Oppression of French Protestants reached new heights; and in 1560, after summary trials, a number of their leaders were hanged from the battlements of the beautiful Château d'Amboise – with François and Mary, reputedly, gloating over the hanged men by torchlight. A few months later, François died of meningitis; Mary Stuart returned to Britain and met her tragic end. The next King, Charles IX, was only ten. Under Catherine as regent, a confused series of civil wars broke out between Protestants – now becoming numerically threatening – and Catholics, with multiple murders of the rival leaders and massacres of their supporters.

The killings culminated in the infamous Saint Bartholomew's Eve massacre of 24 August 1572. In the atmosphere of confusion, sectarian hatred and fear that prevailed in Paris, who was actually responsible for the massacre is regarded by modern historians as uncertain. The view long held was that Charles IX, acting on his mother's advice to resolve France's dilemma by a mass purge of Protestants, gave the terrible order: 'Kill them all, so that not one will be left to reproach me for it.' Possibly the court intended only the liquidation of a few Protestant ringleaders, gathered in Paris for the wedding earlier of Henri of Navarre to Catherine's daughter Marguerite (Margot), and the Paris mob then ran amok. Some fifteen thousand were slaughtered that night, most of them in Paris, which according to witnesses 'looked like a conquered city'. Survivors, the Huguenots, began to leave France in legions. Shortly after Saint Bartholomew's Eve, Charles too died of a mysterious illness. Tuberculosis was suspected, but it has been suggested that he was poisoned by his ruthless mother. Charles' younger brother now became king as Henri III. One of France's more bizarre monarchs, on account of his effeminacy and occasional practice of appearing at official ceremonies in drag, he became known as the 'King of Sodom', surrounded as he was by a mincing entourage known as his *mignons*. It was clear that Henri, though married, would produce no heir, and a serious dynastic crisis ensued. The end of the Valois dynasty loomed. The obvious and most promising contender was a cousin twenty times removed (and also his brother-in-law by marriage), Henri of Navarre. The only trouble was that

Henri (the future Henri IV) was a Protestant. The forceful reigning Pope, Sixtus V, promptly proclaimed a virulent bull nullifying his rights to the throne of France, and gained the support of Philip II's Spain. When Elizabeth executed Mary Queen of Scots, François' widow, a new war of religion (the eighth) engulfed France – and Europe.

THE THREE HENRIS

By the 1570s, the Catholic Guise family had come to control the army, much of the Church and whole provinces of France. Paris herself was controlled by the Catholic League, created in 1576 and directed by the second, all-powerful Duc de Guise (Henri, 1550–88). The League was more dangerous than anything preceding it in Paris, insofar as it incited and mobilized the lower orders. Amid fresh internecine bloodshed, in 1588 it organized a Day of Barricades, virtually taking over the city, despite the opposition of the city's Catholic aristocracy. Henri III fled his capital; Henri de Guise was then assassinated in Catherine's bloody Château de Blois, on the orders of his namesake the King. Catherine de Medici herself died the following January. 'It is not a woman,' observed a contemporary, 'it is Royalty which has just expired.'

In August of that same year, 1589, Henri III, fleeing from his enemies, and held responsible by the Catholic 'ultras' for the death of their hero, Henri de Guise, was stabbed in the stomach (while sitting on his commode at his Château de Saint-Cloud, south-west of Paris) by a fanatical monk. With his dying breath, Henri sent for the other Henri (of Navarre) to be his successor: '*Mon frère*, I can feel clearly that it is for you to possess the right which I have worked for, to preserve for you what God has given you.' He urged his successor to embrace Catholicism.

As with Philippe Auguste before him, Henri IV's reign began with a great battle outside Paris, this time at its very portals in 1590. But it was a battle the King did not win. With a motley force of 10,000 men, he had taken off from Tours to assert his right to the throne bestowed on him by the dying Henri III. It was a fairly distant right, in that he was the nearest blood descendant along the line from the thirteenth-century Saint Louis, but he was enormously popular, especially down in Navarre.

Indeed he was an immensely attractive figure, to women and to men – despite its being said that he was disinclined to bath and smelled strongly of goat. A warm-hearted Gascon from the south-west of France, he was always in love (usually inconstant), sending his current mistress(es) passionate – and indiscreet – letters full of details of his military and political operations. As, in all probability, they had meanwhile been dumped, the scorned women tended to hand over to his enemies valuable intelligence about his intentions.

Hence, unsurprisingly, his military operations were not always blessed with success (which perhaps could be taken as one good reason why eventually, unable to win on the battlefield, he was forced to change his religion to obtain the crown of France). Nevertheless, he was personally fearless in battle. 'I rule with my arse in the saddle and my gun in my fist,' was his fighting motto. 'Rally to my white plume,' he exhorted his men on the battlefield; 'you will find it on the road to victory and honour.'

Ranged against him in Paris was the fanatical Council of Sixteen, its members determined to purge not only Protestants and their own personal enemies, those loyal to the late Henri III, but in addition those aspiring only to remain neutral. The commander of the Catholic forces, and hero of the Parisian crowds, was Charles de Lorraine, Duc de Mayenne, avenging brother of the assassinated Henri de Guise. Mayenne had an eye on the throne himself, and enjoyed the support of Philip II of Spain, the Italian Duke of Savoie – both sworn enemies of France – and the Vatican. Arbitrarily Mayenne proclaimed the aged Cardinal de Bourbon king – though he had already fallen into the hands of Henri of Navarre, his nephew.

With most of the big cities supporting the League, Henri decided to move with his troops into Normandy, where he could be sure of finding friends. From Paris Mayenne followed him, to Arques near Dieppe, boasting that he would bring Henri back in a cage. Instead, in a confused fight in the mist on 20–21 September 1589, he was roundly defeated. A triumphant Henri then headed for Paris, intending to deliver a crushing blow to the heart of the Leaguers. But surveying the vast city from the belfry of the ancient Abbey of Saint-Germain-des-Prés, he realized that the 400-year-old walls built by Philippe Auguste were too strong for the effectives available to him to contemplate a frontal assault. So on 11 November he disengaged from Paris, retiring anew to Normandy for the winter.

After four chilly months spent by both sides preparing for the spring campaigning, a new engagement was fought on 14 March 1590 at Ivry, just four days' march west of Paris. By this time Mayenne had received substantial reinforcements from Spain, Philip II justifying his first military intervention in French affairs on the ground that there was 'an imminent danger to the Holy Catholic Church'. Though his forces were outnumbered, again the day ended in a clear-cut victory for Henri – after some ferocious hand-to-hand mounted combat. Following the battle, he demonstrated a less agreeable side of the Renaissance warrior: mercenaries accused of having behaved treacherously at Arques on Mayenne's side had their throats cut without mercy, as did many French footsoldiers. Mayenne himself fled with his cavalry.

By 7 May the King was on the outskirts of Paris again, his army divided into separate corps to set up a blockade around the city. Writing to his mistress Corisande, from Chelles, he boasted:

> I am before Paris, where God will assist me. Taking the city, I will finally begin to feel the effects of the Crown. I've taken the Charenton bridge and the bridge of Saint-Maur with cannon, and hanged all that were hiding there. Yesterday, I took the outskirts of Paris, by force; the enemy lost many and we only a few . . .

He had burned all the windmills, essential for producing bread, that lay outside the city walls so that 'it must happen that within twelve days, they are either rescued or they surrender'. Henri was certain that, after Ivry, the divided Parisians would rapidly capitulate. But he was proved wrong. Paris had had ample time to improve her defences and stock the city's stores with food. After two failed attacks, the twelve days became three months. Henri now sat down to starve Paris into submission.

THE SIEGE

Historically, besieging armies tend to need a substantial majority over the invested force. To besiege this large walled city of 220,000,* now the biggest in Europe, Henri IV had only some 12,000 to 13,000 men,

---

* As a result of the Black Death and the Hundred Years War, the population had fallen from the 300,000 of 1314.

including a cavalry force of 2,000; the total rose through reinforcements to no more than 25,000 by July. Against this the Leaguers could marshal a garrison of over 50,000 men. These included 800 French *arquebusiers*, 500 Swiss footsoldiers and 1,200 elderly German *Landsknechte*, while each of the sixteen *quartiers* provided a militia of 3,000 men, well armed but not uniformly reliable. Pigaffetta, a veteran Italian captain in the entourage of the Papal Legate, Enrico Caetani, contemptuously described this force on the ramparts as resembling 'dogs that bark furiously on the threshold of a house, but never venture outside'. In addition, however, there prowled in the background the potential relieving force of Mayenne (defeated at Ivry) and the Spaniards and Italians of the redoubtable Duke of Parma in the Spanish Netherlands (present-day Belgium). After all their experience gained in the reconquest of Granada from the Moors, and their expeditions in the New World, the Spanish infantry throughout Europe had, justly, gained a reputation something akin to the Wehrmacht shock troops of 1940.

In terms of artillery, Henri's royal army was able to wheel into place no more than a handful of heavy siege cannon, and lighter culverins, or field pieces. By the end of the sixteenth century the art of siege gunnery had advanced over that of previous centuries, but not that much; moreover, as of 1590, the Huguenots were not renowned either for their artillery or for efficient handling of it. So Henri was faced with reducing Paris through starvation – as indeed the far better-equipped forces of Bismarck and Moltke were to do three centuries later.

News of the defeat at Ivry had caused a great deal of 'annoyance and astonishment' among Mayenne's supporters inside Paris. As Henri increased the pressure, a mood of bloodthirsty defiance took hold in Catholic circles, with priests taking to the streets with cries of 'Au meurtre! Au feu! Au sang! À la vengeance!' against the King. Yet there was also a dominant sense of foreboding. Poor peasants from the outlying regions whose stores had been consumed by the besiegers poured into the city. It was calculated that there was only enough food within the city for four to six weeks, and there were fears that Henri would be able to stir up an insurrection inside the city. Orders were issued – and then mistakenly rescinded – to expel refugees, the sick and other 'useless mouths' to save food. In a kind of scorched-earth strategy, houses on the perimeter that might prove useful to the besiegers were demolished; and, because there weren't enough soldiers, it was decided to make little attempt to defend the *faubourgs*.

The Paris defenders were placed under command of the twenty-two-year-old half-brother of Mayenne, the Duc de Nemours, said to be energetic and zealous, but short of experience. Then, upon a scene hardly encouraging for the Catholics, there suddenly appeared a secret weapon – in the shape of the Papal Legate, Enrico Caetani, sent by Pope Sixtus V, perhaps the most resolute of all the Counter-Reformation pontiffs. Caetani's mission was to purchase the release from Henri of Cardinal de Bourbon and to stiffen the resistance of the Parisians. Furnished with a credit note for 100,000 écus to devote to the Cardinal's freedom, he promptly spent the money on providing the besieged with arms and foodstuffs. (The Cardinal anyway died during the siege.) Caetani established his moral ascendancy by declaring in a sermon before the Sorbonne that, 'whether Catholic or not', Henri was to be excluded for ever from the throne of France.

Henri positioned two batteries of cannon on the heights of Montmartre, bombarding Paris indiscriminately, but with little effect on civilian morale. The Parisians, according to contemporary accounts, 'just laughed'. But hunger began to take hold. Donkeys began to disappear, then – as would also happen in 1870 – cats and dogs, and even rats. Rations were reduced, and one man was reported eating candle tallow; there were said to be experiments in milling bones out of the graveyards for flour, and there was more than one account of cannibalism – 'little children disguised as meat'. A mother was found to have eaten her two dead children – both supposedly interred in accordance with Catholic rites, but a thigh was discovered in an *armoire*. The maid confessed everything, after the mother's own death. As always, it was the poor who suffered most grievously, while (so it was claimed) religious establishments had stored provisions to last a year. According to Captain Pigafetta, in the wealthy districts there were shops selling game and a wide range of foods – at extortionate prices. By August, Henri had captured all the suburbs and brought his guns 'to within a stone's throw' of the ramparts. It looked as if the fall of Paris was now but a matter of time. Pacifist feelings gathered strength. The Catholics, especially the extremist leaders of the League, steeled themselves for a dreadful orgy of revenge for St Bartholomew's Eve. But Henri, with his customary shrewdness, saw that clemency would serve him best. The League, however, rejected Henri's terms, and the siege continued. Then two events of great significance took place – both of them outside Paris. First, on 27 August, the intransigent Pope Sixtus died, to be followed by more liberal pontiffs, three in just over a year; then came Clement VIII, who was radically to alter Vatican policy towards France and come to terms with Henri of Navarre. On the other side of the balance, however, and with far more immediate consequence for the starving Parisians was the news, which reached the city on 30 August, of the approach of a formidable liberating army led by the Italian Alexander Farnese, Duke of Parma, commander of Philip II's forces in the Spanish Netherlands. One of Europe's most outstanding generals, Parma had been ordered by Madrid to give up his current campaign against the Dutch and to hasten south to save Paris. At Meaux, some forty kilometres east of Paris, close to where the Kaiser was to be halted on the Marne in 1914, Parma linked up with Mayenne.

Henri made one last assault on the southern ramparts, but was repulsed by four Jesuits, a librarian and a lawyer who defended the threatened sector with pickaxes. He was now obliged to abandon the siege and defend himself against Parma and Mayenne. To a new mistress, he wrote gloomily:

> Mistress, I am writing this to you the day before a battle. The issue is in the hand of God, who has already decided what will come of it and what he deems to be expedient for his glory and for the salvation of my people. If I lose the battle, you will never see me, because I am not the kind of man to flee or to retreat. I can assure you, however, that if I die, my penultimate thought will be of you and that my last will be of God.

But, manoeuvring with more skill than Henri, Parma denied him both battle and a glorious death, and instead focused his attention on taking and securing the approaches to Paris. On 1 September a first convoy of foodstuffs reached the wretched city. By the 7th, Parma held both banks of the Marne at Lagny and was able to rush provisions down the river – that age-long lifeline of Paris.

Proud Paris was liberated, amid frenzied rejoicings. But at what a cost! Out of its pre-siege population of 220,000, as many as 40,000 to 50,000 are estimated to have died of starvation or disease. The economic life of France's capital had been seriously damaged by the most crippling siege in the history of any major European city since that of Constantinople by the Turks in the previous century. After all their suffering, the Parisians became increasingly disenchanted with the conduct of the League, and – with their habitual impatience – dismissive of its leaders.

After four months of privation, the Papal Legate Enrico Caetani could not wait to get back to Rome. One of his entourage, the Bishop of

Asti, Monsignor Panigarole, was to recall the torments of 1590: 'there was no meat, no fish, no milk, no fruit, no vegetable. I would almost say there was no sun, no sky, no air ... One thinks of the Siege of Jerusalem, one thinks of Titus and Sennacherib! It was a miracle ...'

5

'Worth a Mass'

> As soon as he was master of Paris, one saw nothing but
> stonemasons at work.
>
> The *Mercure Gallant* on Henri IV

PARIS REGAINED

Once the siege was raised in the autumn of 1590, outside Paris the war
continued fitfully, with Henri striving to isolate the capital from other
French cities. In January 1591 he made another attempt on Paris, a
Trojan-horse ruse directed at the Porte Saint-Honoré with soldiers disguised as peasants carrying sacks of flour, but they were driven off.
The League took its revenge by executing four Parisian dignitaries for
collusion, but was itself punished in turn by Mayenne, keen to maintain discipline, with the summary hanging of six of its leaders. France
had arrived at a kind of stand-off. It was clear that neither Counter-
Reformation Catholicism nor Protestantism would be acceptable to Paris.
Added to all the killings during the thirty-year series of religious wars,
the exhaustion inflicted by the siege left Parisians, anxious to free
themselves from the reactionary inflexibility of the Leaguers, in a mood
for compromise. Unable to win a clear-cut military victory, sensing the
atmosphere in the capital and taking advantage of the new, temperate
mood in the Vatican, as well as exploiting splits within the Paris League
itself, Henri decided to play his supreme card.

By the summer of 1592, he had come to understand that he would
have to abjure Calvinism if he wished to consolidate his hold on the
crown. His personal salvation concerned him hardly at all, but he
realized that he could not move too quickly or his Catholic subjects

would distrust him all the more. The following January the Estates-General of the League met in Paris, but it was not until May that Henri made the bombshell announcement that he had resolved to convert, 'having recognized and judged that it was good to do so'. Negotiations took place between the League and Henri at La Villette, with Henri still pressing for a military advantage round the capital.

Then, at Saint-Denis on Sunday, 25 July 1593, the resting place of kings of France including Dagobert, Philippe Auguste and Saint Louis, Henri of Navarre, now a vigorous forty-year-old, solemnly abjured his Protestant faith to embrace Catholicism. The previous evening, leaders of the League, apprehensive about the coup that Henri was about to achieve, ordered parish priests in the city to declare the immediate excommunication of anyone daring to take part in this 'comedy of the conversion'. Mayenne ordered the guards along the walls to shoot at anyone leaving the city during the next twenty-four hours. But these measures proved ineffective. Several hundred Parisians stole out of the city under cover of darkness to witness the ceremony at Saint-Denis. That day, crowds, estimated variously at between 10,000 and 70,000, lined the streets and the square. The royal procession progressed along a thick carpet of flowers thrown by well-wishers crying 'Vive le roi!' at every step taken by the King. Henri was dressed in symbolic white: a simple white doublet and white stockings contrasted by a black cape, black shoes and a black plumed hat. This costume was designed to represent purity and innocence, and was carefully chosen by the King to reflect his whole-hearted penitence. He bore none of the usual insignia of office, such as fleurs-de-lys or crowns. The only emblem of royal authority was his sword, a sign of the power which reinforced the significance of his conversion. As he approached the steps of the church, he relinquished even this symbol.

After he had received absolution from the Archbishop, a flock of white doves was released from the abbey's belfry, to indicate the occurrence of a 'miracle'. Then Henry IV left Saint-Denis and rode on horseback with an escort to Montmartre, where, at the martyred saint's tomb, he gave thanks to God for his conversion. There was more wild cheering as he rode through the hilly streets. From Montmartre he surveyed the rebellious capital which still defied him, as cannonades and fireworks lit up the sky in his honour. Paris, Henri is famously said to have observed that day, was 'well worth a Mass'. For all his earthy cynicism, however, Henri IV, founder of the Bourbon dynasty, was to prove one of France's greatest monarchs. With Paris longing for peace and stability, the League

was at last crumbling to pieces. There now began a steady stream of
desertions to Henri's camp, and in August 1593 a general truce was
concluded with Mayenne. The stage was set for Henri's triumph in Paris.

On 22 March 1594, having already been formally crowned in
Chartres, he entered his turbulent capital as Henri IV. There had, in
effect, been a coup, negotiated during the previous night in deepest
secrecy between the Duc de Cossé Brissac, the newly appointed
Governor of Paris – eager for a marshal's baton from a grateful ruler –
and two representatives of the Paris bourgeois *échevins*, or aldermen.
Together with the *prévôt* and a small posse of troops, Brissac seized the
Porte Saint-Denis and headed for the Louvre. There they were halted by
a guard of some twenty German *Landsknechte*, but these were dispersed,
killed or thrown into the Seine.

That was the sum of resistance. The Grand Châtelet was taken
without a shot, and at 6 a.m. Brissac was opening the gates of Paris to
Henri. It was cold and raining, but the King nonetheless removed his
ornate headdress as he began his descent along the Rue Saint-Honoré.
Promptly, and diplomatically, he went to Notre-Dame to sing a Te Deum.
The pealing of the cathedral bells was the first warning the sleepy
Leaguers received that the enemy they had so resolutely held at bay for
three years was now in their midst. Swiftly Henri's champions ran
through the city, proclaiming a general amnesty and instructing all to
wear a white scarf as a sign of loyalty.

Now properly awake, crowds poured into the street to see the King
as he left Notre-Dame to make his way to the Louvre. Previous *joyeuses
entrées* into Paris of kings newly anointed or on marriage had been
lavish affairs. At the triumphal entry of Henri II in 1549, for instance,
leading poets and artists had been hired to decorate the route of the
procession, terminating at the Palais de Justice with symbolic statuary
and triumphal arches inscribed with verses in praise of the King. The
parade had included representatives of all the city's corporations, including fifty pastry chefs, forty barrel-makers, 250 printers and 200 tailors.
A second, similar procession had been held two days later for the entry
of the Queen.

All that was in marked contrast to the simple spontaneity that now
greeted this far more historic entry of Henri of Navarre. Bravely the King
walked through the streets, jostled and greeted by the curious. Many
were surprised to find him quite human, physically normal and friendly;
the League preachers had never portrayed him that way. That afternoon
Philip II's Spanish garrison left the city in good order. They filed past,

saluting the King. To their leaders he responded, 'Recommend me to your master, but *never* come back.' The party attached to the Papal Legate had already decamped in the morning, taking with it a few Parisian parish priests who were implicated in the activities of the League. Later, the standing corporations of the city and individuals who had compromised themselves by collaboration with the League requested an audience to seek forgiveness. Henri was willing to show himself a gracious victor; no more than 140 individuals were banished from the city, and even these were allowed to rejoin Mayenne in Meaux, should they so desire. No obstacles were put in their way. There were no executions, no confiscations of property. On the other hand, as an instrument of discipline, Henri had erected a gallows near the Porte Saint-Antoine, 'to hang any person who should be found so bold as to attempt anything against the public peace'.

THE CITY IN 1594

After all the years of bitter internecine fighting, followed by the terrible deprivations of the 1590 siege, the Paris that Henri IV inherited was indeed a sad city. Nothing had been repaired, let alone built. Living conditions had become unbearable. The siege, mob violence and the continual guard duty imposed on many citizens had caused shopkeepers to shut their doors and workers to stop producing even the necessities of life. Commerce had ceased when the siege made land and river traffic impossible. One of Henri's first acts had been to order that shops be opened and work resumed.

The streets were covered with a thick slime of decayed garbage, ashes, urine and faeces (animal and human). Uncobbled, they became impassable during rains, and even where paved the holes were so deep and full of mud that horses risked breaking their legs. It was reported that only 'the most refined courtiers' were able to avoid the mud by resorting to a horse or a mule, often with their wives *en croupe*. There were only eight functional *carrosses* in the whole city. If the paving originated by Philippe Auguste was in a dreadful state, so were the bridges. Lack of funds blocked even the most essential projects.

Grandiose schemes initiated by Hugues Aubriot to provide a system

of sewers had been brought to a standstill. Sanitation in this overcrowded city was worse than it had ever been, and its very survival had
become endangered by the neglect of public fountains and streets
during the years of violence. With each year of the war, contamination
of water supplies had increased and the peril of epidemic had grown
greater. Plague was constantly in attendance, and even though the
municipal government knew the water to be contaminated it did little
to restore the fountains. Many had ceased to flow at all; conduits leaked,
flooding cellars and privies in nearby houses. For lack of water the
Parisians turned back to well and river water, both of which were
contaminated. Over the course of a decade and a half there were no
fewer than three plague epidemics; 30,000 had died in 1580, and two
years after his *entrée*, in 1596, Henri was forced to retire to Rouen after
600 had died of *la peste* in the Hôtel Dieu in one month. To the
multiplicity of street cries was added that of a much sought-after vendor
of patent rat-traps:

> La mort aux ratz aux souriz
> C'est une invention nouvelle!

The plight of the poor had become more grievous than ever. To
keep the hordes of militant beggars at bay, householders were instructed
by ordinance not to have more than one street door, and never to leave
their homes uninhabited. Many of the beggars joined murderous bands
with names such as 'Tire-Laine' and 'Mauvais Garçons'. Punishments
were correspondingly draconian; the Italian Ambassador recorded, in
1577, hangings every day in Paris, 'at every point'. Since the days of
Philippe Auguste the forms of execution had also become increasingly
ingenious and refined, suitable to every infraction. A letter to Rabelais
listed some of those meted out to religious malefactors: 'brûlez, tenaillez,
cisaillez, noyez, pendez, empalez, espaultrez, démembrez, exécutrez,
crucifiez, bouillez, escarbrouillez, découpez, fricassez, grillez, tronçon-
nez, écartelez, déhinquaindez, carbonadez, ces méchants hérétiques'.
Abandoned for a century, the brutal wheel had been brought back as an
instrument of capital torture; decapitation was reserved for the gentry.

In physical terms, the Paris Henri inherited in 1594 was encircled by
a grey stone wall two and a half kilometres in diameter, and about
sixteen kilometres in circumference. Towers built by Charles V rose up
every seventy metres. At the four points where the walls came down to
the Seine stood tall, though neglected, bastions, from which heavy iron

chains could be suspended across the river to prevent enemy ships from sailing into Paris during a siege.

Paris was still very much a medieval city, with the Île de la Cité at its heart. At the western end of the island stood the Palais, a chaotic maze of chiefly gothic buildings. Since the King and court had departed, it now housed the Parlement, the Chambre des Comptes, the Cour des Aides and the Cour des Monnaies, together constituting the highest functions of government. Louis IX's Sainte-Chapelle, built in the thirteenth century, stood in the centre, its delicate spire rising sublimely over all the surrounding buildings. Around the Palais, much as now, there scurried a population of some 4,000–5,000 magistrates, clerks, copyists and minor officials. In addition, merchants, booksellers, paper- and ink-sellers, prostitutes, singers, letter-writers and beggars, among others, daily set up shop or frequented the dozens of stalls tacked on to the buildings. The focus of all this bustle was the Grande Salle, with its marble floor, heavy columns lined with statues of French kings, and gold ceiling – a favourite meeting place for *tout Paris*.

Still connecting the Île with the Left and Right Banks were bridges crowded with overhanging wooden buildings, veritable deathtraps. In December 1596, the Pont au Meunier collapsed, depositing its 160 or more inhabitants in the Seine. The bridge had been swept away by currents many times, and earlier that year inspectors had warned house-owners that it might fall. Probably absentee landlords, they did nothing. When the bridge finally disintegrated, François Miron, the *prévôt*, installed six months previously, took charge of the rescue operations. He ordered guards placed over the wreckage to stop pillaging, and then began the task of prosecuting the guilty parties, the owners of the bridge, in an operation that might easily have set off a general riot.

On the Right Bank, the Hôtel de Ville was an unfinished palace in the French Renaissance style, but it served as the meeting place for the elected officials of the bourgeois of Paris – and for receiving members of the royal family and visiting dignitaries. The registers and the seals of Paris, and its official weights and measures, were kept there. Outside, the Place de Grève, with its sombre associations of numerous public executions, was at a much lower level than the present square (the Place de l'Hôtel de Ville) and was frequently flooded by the Seine. People living on the square profitably rented out their windows on days of public execution. Apart from the area immediately bordering on the quays, Paris eastwards from the Hôtel de Ville was mainly aristocratic. The Marais, despite its insalubrious odours, remained the most fashionable *quartier*. Its residents generally ended in the nearby Cemetery of the Innocents. Like the Place de Grève, the chapels, charnel houses with their frescoes of the Dance of Death, aroused the morbid curiosity of visitors. The worm-laden earth of the Innocents was said to be remarkable; it could *manger son cadavre en neuf jours*. When graves had to be dug again in the same spot, the bones were pulled out of the earth and stored in piles along the walls. Two or three common graves stood open at the same time, to receive the humbler citizens, or victims of plague.

On the western fringe of the Right Bank stood the Louvre. Following demolition of the *donjon* under François I, access to it was gained from the east side. This postern entrance had been built by Charles V as part of the flamboyant residence into which he had transformed the old fortress of Philippe Auguste. After crossing the drawbridge over the moat and passing under the east wing, one entered a courtyard crowded with people, carriages and horses. The gothic walls of the 'old' Louvre on the north and east sides of the courtyard contrasted sharply with those facing the Seine and the west, built by François I and Henri II in the Renaissance style. Here was a balanced façade of classical columns, windows and statues.

On the Left Bank, beyond Saint-Etienne-du-Mont, a belt of colleges and elegant houses built by judicial families formed a half-circle from the Convent of the Cordeliers on the west, which stood just inside the walls from Saint-Germain-des-Prés, to the commercial and bourgeois section of the Place Maubert. A medley of colleges and private houses stretched eastward from the Rue Saint-Jacques to the Place Maubert – described as the most bourgeois part of Paris. The families living there still behaved, talked and dressed like wealthy merchants rather than adopting the orotund courtly language characteristic of social climbers in the grander families. Meanwhile, the Place Maubert witnessed executions and occasional burnings of heretics in the sixteenth century to rival its grisly competitor across the river.

Beyond the city walls, in the city's *faubourgs*, monasteries had sprung up to gird Paris with a belt of cloisters, refectories, churches and gardens. The Abbey of Saint-Germain-des-Prés, the richest and largest of these, occupied what were to become the most fashionable parts of Paris in the eighteenth century. Founded in about 543, it had grown up under the double aegis of the Benedictine order and royal favour. The abbots were high-ranking feudal lords, usually of royal blood. The Faubourg Saint-Germain, extending from the land where the Luxembourg Palace now stands west of the Seine, to that of the Eiffel Tower, lay completely under the jurisdiction of the abbey court. The monastery contained one of the largest prisons in Paris, and was the scene of many public hangings. Standing almost alone beyond the walls in 1600, Saint-Germain still possessed all the characteristics of a medieval stronghold. Surrounded by a wide ditch, high crenellated walls, towers, drawbridges and gates, the abbey remained physically and judicially independent of Paris. Its three towers dominated the entire Left Bank. Here each year a fair was held near the monastery beginning a fortnight after Easter and lasting for at least three weeks. The main pavilion was nearly sixty metres wide. Its stone walls and high roof sheltered the principal alleys of stalls, named Normandy, Paris, Picardy, Chaudronnière, Mercière and Lingerie. The fair was a very fashionable and also a 'very wild place to go'. There Parisians showed off their new clothes, while young noblemen would gallop through on horseback, knocking over carts and displays, and picking up girls along the way. It was a favourite haunt for pickpockets and merchants selling trash. Prostitutes gathered there to prey on provincials and Parisians alike.

HENRI REBUILDS

With characteristic energy, Henri began deluging Paris with orders for repair and reconstruction. To mend the accrued dilapidations alone looked likely to take years. Every summer there was still a shortage of food, particularly bread, and a threat of *la peste*. Conditions were to grow worse between the summer of 1596 and the summer of 1605 before they got better. Even with the free labour of the religious orders, welfare costs went well beyond what the prosperous bourgeois were willing to pay. Yet Henri did not wait for the collapse of the Pont au Meunier, or even a second wooden bridge, before setting to work to build a new and dazzling Paris. 'As soon as he was master of Paris, one saw nothing but stonemasons at work,' recorded the *Mercure Français* in the year of his death. The new King was one of those born builders. Ambassadors who had known Paris in the days of the League expressed astonishment.

Building was a true passion for Henri. In some ways he was a kind of Haussmann before his time. His ambition was to clear away the cluttered medieval *quartiers*, the breeding-places of pestilence, crime and revolt, and replace them with an orderly classical elegance that his predecessors had imported from Italy – and to do so on a grand scale without precedent. In his reign of sixteen years, he did more for Paris than any other ruler, before or since. In 1600, he became the first to institute planning regulations for Paris, issuing an order requiring house-owners to obtain official confirmation of the building line before under-taking any construction or repairs. The building of timber houses was now banned, including those with a timber frame. A new style, an elegant combination of brick and stone which can be seen in the present-day Place des Vosges, became the vogue.

Within a year of his arrival, sweeping aside all obstacles and objec-tions, Henri was at work extending the Louvre with a magnificent gallery, 500 metres in length, along the Seine, the Galerie de Bord de l'Eau and the Pavillon de Flore to link up with the Tuileries Palace laid down by Catherine de Medici back in 1566. On its ground floor he set up his own school of fine and applied arts. Three years later, he was ordering completion of the Pont Neuf, a project dating back to his predecessor Henri III in 1578. This wonderfully elegant bridge that still spans the Seine across the western tip of the Île was to be Paris's first stone structure, unencumbered by houses, and robust enough to withstand the excesses of the unruly river. By 1601, Henri had finally achieved peace with his principal enemies abroad, and the far-sighted and liberal-minded Edict of Nantes in 1598 had brought about peace between the religious factions at home. On 11 March 1601, he was telling his administrators: 'now that the country is at peace, regard must be paid to the embellishment of the kingdom, and in particular to finishing the projects begun by his predecessors, namely the Pont Neuf and the [water-supply] fountains'.

But Parisians were reluctant to pay for the bridge, and infuriated the King by suggesting that the country at large be taxed for it. At one point he threatened to drop the whole project; but eventually the Pont Neuf was funded by a new tax levied on every barrel of wine brought into the city. Work on it resumed that summer. A short while later, Henri came down to inspect the work and, seeing an uncompleted arch, he took a running jump and leaped across the gap over the Seine – to the delight of the workmen and passers-by.

In 1607, Henri followed up the opening of the newly completed bridge with a visionary scheme to develop the land between it and the old Palais. He handed it over in a grant to de Harlay, First President of the Parlement, on condition that the Place Dauphine – named after his infant son – would be built. Houses of red brick with festoons of stonework (the style was borrowed from provincial architecture, and then copied again in the ensuing years in the many charming Louis XIII châteaux of the Île de France), all of a pattern, were to form a large symmetrical triangle, open at the top by the Pont and framing a vista of the Palais as its base, in the first unified piazza to be constructed in Paris. The scheme was not actually completed until five years after Henri's death, with the erection of the ebullient equestrian statue – the 'Vert Galant'* – that still dominates one of the most favoured sites in all Paris, and with the addition of the enchanting small garden that forms the tip of the Île de la Cité, like the prow of a ship. But Henri's Place Dauphine swiftly became a major commercial success, with the houses taken by diplomats and provincials pursuing lawsuits in the courts, and the arcades below filled with shops, workshops and restaurants.

Under Henri the Pont Neuf was soon pulsing with vitality, something like the Boulevard Saint-Germain in its heyday, where you could purchase a parasol, a chicken – or a tart. With music being played all along the bridge, the hubbub must have been immense, and incessant. Echoing the gay and bawdy tone set by the Vert Galant himself, in its love of life it must have been a microcosm of a city at last released from anxiety, fear and deprivation.

Henri was delighted by his first creations. In 1607 he launched an even grander scheme for the Marais, on the site of the razed Hôtel des Tournelles, scene of the tragic joust that had killed Henri II. It was to be known as Place Royale – finally Place des Vosges. Though not finished until two years after Henri's death, it remains perhaps the most lasting tribute to his reign, with its symmetrical perfection the true gem in his crown as an architect of Paris. Over the centuries it fell into terrible decay, but survived to be superbly resurrected during the 1960s, and remains one of the most magical squares in all Europe. Its construction confirmed the Marais, until the age of Louis XIV, as the fashionable residential area of Paris.

Grander still than the Place Royale was Henri's plan of 1609 to build – also in the Marais – a vast semi-circular piazza to be called the Place de France, and designed truly to put Paris on the map as an impressive modern capital, outdoing Rome's Piazza dell' Popolo in splendour. It was to be sited at the city limits to the north-east, and from it would radiate eight important, and ramrod-straight, thoroughfares each bearing the

* 'Vert Galant', or the 'Gay Blade', was the abiding Parisian nickname for Henri.

name of a French province. Thus visitors entering through its gate would be instantly impressed by the union of Paris with the provinces under Henri's flag of reconciliation. Alas for Paris, Henri's death the following year aborted the Place de France; all that remains of the concept is the dead-straight and classically handsome Rue de Turenne in the Marais.

Henri's original intent for his Place Royale was, rather than the *quartier chic* into which it evolved, to create a low-rent development which would 'house the workers whom we would attract here in the greatest possible numbers, and ... serve as a promenade for those citizens of the town who were most crowded in their houses'. One should note, however, given the hurricane that was to sweep Paris at the end of the next century, that neither Henri's town-planning nor that of his successors actually did much to alleviate the miserable housing conditions of the Parisian poor.

On top of all these vast building schemes, Henri had to find time – and money – to house his ex-Queen, the demanding Margot, and her successor, not to mention the regiments of mistresses and their royal bastards whom he continued to collect. Henri's marriage to La Reine Margot had been extraordinarily *mouvementé* and modern – certainly by sixteenth-century standards. Margot, meticulous in her personal habits and sensitive to untoward odours, had swiftly become disenchanted by Henri's slovenliness and goatlike attributes, and soon both had embarked on a string of affairs. Yet, throughout, and even after divorce, they remained curiously devoted to each other, with Margot once saving Henri's life by organizing his flight from Paris in 1576. By the time of his coronation, however, the marriage had all but broken down, and Henri was living as man and wife with Gabrielle d'Estrées. Of noble birth, as well as great beauty and high intelligence, Gabrielle represented probably the most serious attachment in the philandering life of the Vert Galant.

In 1599 Henri had decided to ask Pope Clement VIII for an annulment of his marriage to Margot to enable him to marry Gabrielle. This would have made their illegitimate son, the Duc de Vendôme, heir to the throne – not a step likely to be pleasing to the powerful Medicis. Preparations for the wedding were already under way that spring. Henri had placed a conspicuously large diamond ring on her finger, provoking Gabrielle to remark publicly and hubristically, 'Only God or the King's death can put an end to my good luck!' In the event, it was her own death which intervened.

One evening in April, while Henri was at Fontainebleau, Gabrielle was awaiting his return in one of their favourite trysting places, a little palace in the Marais in the romantically named Rue de la Cerisaie, or Street of the Cherry Orchard (which still exists). It belonged to a rather sinister figure named Sebastiano Zametti, alias Zamet, an Italian banker who also served as a kind of court jester to the King – and probably *procureur*. A gambling campanion of the King, he was owed vast sums of money by Henri as well as by many of the French nobility. Zamet was even said to have been a lover of Gabrielle. Famous for his table, that night he treated her to one of his celebrated dinners. Almost immediately Gabrielle suffered acute convulsions of the nervous system, gave birth to a still-born son, and, aged only twenty-six, died in terrible pain before Henri could reach her side the following day. It was widely believed that Zamet had slipped her one of the notorious Medici poisons.

Henri was inconsolable – for a while. But his sophisticated minister Baron de Rosny, though a lifelong Protestant, urged him to consider for dynastic purposes another Medici, Marie. Habitually amenable to Rosny's persuasion, Henri agreed. His country, impoverished by war, his building projects, his gambling and his amours badly needed Florentine money. Marie arrived in Lyons, and to her intense rage Henri insisted on bedding her in advance of the marriage ceremony on 17 December 1600. Described unkindly as 'the fat banker', the twenty-eight-year-old Marie was certainly no beauty – but the following year she produced an heir for Henri, the future Louis XIII, and then settled down to an annual pregnancy. She also added, conspicuously, to the great buildings of Paris, most notably in the shape of the superlative Luxembourg Palace, built in her widowhood and in the style of her native Florence.

All Henri's women had to be housed, or else financed to build their own sumptuous quarters. Above all, there was Margot, still entitled to call herself queen (part of the annulment deal with Henri). With typical generosity, the Vert Galant allowed her back to Paris after eighteen years' exile in Provence and gave her a stretch of land along the Seine on the Left Bank, with an unrivalled view over her childhood home in the Louvre. Here she built a magnificent mansion just behind the present Académie Française.

While work was in progress, she lodged in the handsome Hôtel de Sens in the Marais, one of Paris's last medieval buildings that still survive today. There ensued a grim tragedy, suggesting that though in her fifties Margot was by no means sexually extinct. Among her pages she had two young lovers – the Comte de Vermond, aged eighteen, and Dal de Saint-Julien, aged twenty. In a fit of jealousy Vermond shot his rival. Saint-Julien was the current favourite, and the murder drove Margot insane with rage; she had Vermond executed as she watched from a window. Depleted, *d'un seul coup*, of two young lovers, Margot quit the Hôtel de Sens for ever for the Left Bank. But her gardens, on which she lavished almost as much passion as she had upon her lovers, and which became the pride and joy of the *quartier*, soon aroused the jealousy of her successor, Queen Marie, gazing at them from the Right Bank. To trump Margot, she laid out the superb Cours de la Reine, the tree-lined *quai* 1,600 metres in length, reaching to the present-day Place de l'Alma. Her son, Louis XIII, later had to sell the property – to pay off Margot's debts.

SULLY

Indebtedness was a constant problem for Henri throughout his reign. Fortunately he had the admirable Sully to help him. But before Sully could bring order to France's derelict finances, Henri had had to put an end to strife, within and without the kingdom – something only he, with the immense moral stature he had now achieved, could do. As a first step, he succeeded, in 1595, in persuading Pope Clement VIII to lift the deadly ban of excommunication which had been placed upon him during the Siege of Paris. At a stroke the main weapon of the Catholic extremists of the Paris League was removed. In the spring of 1598, Henri signed both the Peace of Vervins, which ended the debilitating war with Spain, and the Edict of Nantes, which granted France internally at least an armistice in the Wars of Religion which had paralysed her over the past half-century. The Edict, which granted France's one million Protestants freedom of worship, rights to all state offices and other concessions, was by the standards of the time a visionary act of reconciliation and liberalism, and an important marker in the march of humanism.

To be considered truly great, a leader of men needs to be able to attract the best of talents to his side. If it was true of Napoleon, it was certainly true of Henri IV in his choice of Maximilien de Béthune, Baron de Rosny and – later – Duc de Sully to run his affairs. One of the most remarkable administrators ever produced by France, Sully had followed

Henri's flag since the age of sixteen. He was also a dedicated Protestant, so it was not until the settlements of 1598 that Henri was able to bring him forward, aged thirty-eight, as his *grand voyer*, or chief of the municipal inspectors of Paris – in effect, his finance minister. That rare combination, a soldier-financier, Sully was a man capable of extreme ruthlessness – and was strangely popular with, and acceptable to, Catholics and Protestants alike; they trusted him. He rose each morning at four, and worked till ten at night, and by 1608 he had stabilized the nation's finances, massively reducing debt and accumulating a reserve of cash in hand.

It was the time of the early scramble for colonies in the New World, but Sully saw France's map of the world lying entirely in Europe. 'Things which remain separated from our body by foreign lands or seas will only be ours at great expense and to little purpose,' was his view. Instead he performed wonders to repair the damages of war, reconstructing bridges, rebuilding roads (and lining them with trees), laying out a network of canals, draining marshes and improving afforestation, and spending more money on these areas than at any other time during the century. Modern France is greatly indebted to Sully for the ordered beauty of her countryside, as well as for the establishment of industries making carpets, tapestries and glass. In Paris he ordered new streets to be cut which would allow carriages and merchants' carts to pass. Soon, residence in a broad, straight street was to become a mark of social status.

Sully left to posterity a fine *hôtel* between the Place des Vosges and the Rue Saint-Antoine, but he was something of a puritan, opposed to the idle and pleasure-loving ways of life, and Henri's wanton extravagances were a constant worry to him. Having to squeeze Parisians to meet the gigantic costs of the King's improvements to the Louvre was bad enough, but on top of that were all the women – and his profligacy as a gambler. As age began to exact its toll, affecting at least his external aspects, and the Vert Galant remained *galant* but no longer green, Parisians – ever restless and impatient – found the image less enchanting, and now tended to see instead the cost of it all. Catholics chafed under the terms of Nantes, and the League began to raise its head again. By 1610, Henri's popularity was distinctly waning.

From 1601 to 1610, a delicate Pax Gallicana had been maintained on Henri's borders, during which time France – and Paris especially – had prospered. The King, through the voice of Sully, began to talk ominously about the 'Grand Design', whereby the continent would be ruled by a council of sixty elected members. More specifically, the Design targeted

Flanders and the Rhineland (an orientation that was to bring to ruin Henri's grandson, Louis XIV). There the death of the Duke of Jülich-Cleves had left this important principality in a power-vacuum, enticing to Spain. But, in the eyes of Parisians, there was far more to it than mere power politics. Henri had unbecomingly fallen in love with a fifteen-year-old girl, Charlotte, daughter of the Constable of France, from the powerful house of Montmorency, who had captured his imagination dancing before him in a fête as one of the nymphs of the goddess Diana. Suspicious (rightly) of the King's intentions, her fiancé, the Prince de Condé, fled with Charlotte across the border to Brussels in November 1609, escaping ahead of the King's *prévôts* by only a few hours.

Stricken, the lovelorn King wrote that, from misery, 'I am now nothing more than skin and bone. Everything displeases me; I run away from company and if I permit myself to be brought into any gathering, instead of cheering me up, it succeeds in killing me.' Shocking though it was to the French body politic, it looked as if Henri was prepared to go to war to get her back. The atmosphere in Paris particularly was tense as the war on which Henri seemed to be embarking threatened completely to redraw the map of Europe, placing France squarely in the camp of the Protestant nations. By May 1610 a powerful (and expensive) French army 50,000 strong, backed by English and Dutch troops, was poised to invade Flanders; but on the 14th of that month, on the eve of Henri going off to join his soldiers, something unimaginable occurred.

6

Regicide, Regent and Richelieu

An entire city, built with pomp, seems to have arisen miraculously from an old ditch.

Corneille, *Le Menteur*, 1643

ASSASSINATION OF HENRI IV

At 4 p.m. on 14 May 1610, Henri was travelling from the Louvre to meet
Sully at the Arsenal when his coach became stuck in congested traffic
in the narrow Rue de la Ferronnerie, close to today's Centre Pompidou.
Since his formal accession in 1593 there had been twenty-four known
plots to assassinate him, but Henri was careless of danger, perhaps
believing that destiny would protect him. Nevertheless, in recent months
he had apparently had several premonitions of his death. After going to
Mass at the Church of Saint-Roch that morning, he had met with
Marshal de Bassompierre, who had found him 'strange in his manner';
his thoughts seemed fixed on his death. Bassompierre chided him for
his uncharacteristic gloom, remarking that he was just in the prime
of life: 'Had he not the finest kingdom in the world, a beautiful wife,
a beautiful *maîtresse* and two lovely children?' It was to no avail. '*Mon
ami*,' said the King, 'I've got to leave it all!' Because of the narrowness
and congestion of the Paris streets, Henri was travelling in a small, light
phaeton with open sides. Yet that same Bassompierre had just received
from Italy a remarkable invention: a heavy coach enclosed by glass
windows, the armoured limousine of its day. Had the King been in
Bassompierre's Italian vehicle, less accessible from the street, he might
well have survived.

A thirty-two-year-old with red hair, François Ravaillac, was awaiting his opportunity. Ravaillac was a rejected monk and failed schoolteacher from Angoulême who had done time in a debtors' prison; he was also a fanatical Catholic, given to hallucinations and delusions about his role as deliverer of France and said to have declared that he would 'prefer the honour of God to all else' and that he would like to see all heretics subjected to fire and brimstone. He had come to Paris in December 1609 seeking, in vain, an audience with the King in order to tell him to banish the Protestants, or else force conversion upon them. Returning to Paris the following April, Ravaillac was appalled to learn of the preparations for war, a war against the Pope, which, in his eyes, 'meant war against God'. He stole a short kitchen knife from an inn, determined to kill the King, but changing his mind at least once.

In the Rue de la Ferronnerie, Henri's coach was blocked by a broken-down haycart in collision with a wagon laden with provisions, while another cart had collapsed under the weight of its load of barrels – a typical Parisian scene. The King's attendants dispersed to help with the carts. Ravaillac, having stalked Henri all morning, now saw his chance, leaped on to the running-board of the coach and stabbed the King three times, just as he was reading a letter. After the first blow Henri heroically murmured, 'Ce n'est rien', but Ravaillac's second blow severed his aorta, killing him instantly. The assassin made no attempt to flee, and was seized by Henri's travelling companion, the Duc d'Epernon. The King was rushed to a neighbouring apothecary, but there was no hope. His body was taken back to the Louvre, where he had been living, while overnight Paris was assured that he had only been wounded.

When the truth finally got out the next day, a horrified Paris began to look for vengeance. The tax burden and the sex scandals were forgotten; the ill-conceived expedition to Jülich swiftly put on hold. But who, apart from the madman Ravaillac, was to blame? Ravaillac, subjected to the most appalling tortures, was insistent that he had acted alone. Most of Paris refused to believe this; there was evidence that there had been several plots in hand, Henri having earned the hatred of extremists on both sides for his efforts towards religious reconciliation. Heavily under suspicion was his former mistress the Marquise de Verneuil, known to have been hoping that, upon Henri's death, her son, the bastard child of the King, would succeed. And there was always the sinister hand of Spain. A paralysing fear spread through the city that, after two decades of peace, civil war would grip the land once more. The Jesuits, for one, fearful that they would be blamed, hastened to praise the King and acquired his heart to bury in their chapel at La Flèche, on the Île de la Cité; while Huguenot leaders rushed forward to acclaim him the best king Providence had granted them.

On 27 May, still protesting that he had acted as a free agent on a divinely inspired mission, Ravaillac was put to death. Before being drawn and quartered, the fate of a regicide, on the scaffold erected at the Place de Grève, he was scalded with burning sulphur, molten lead and boiling oil and resin, his flesh then being torn by pincers. After this hors d'oeuvre of inhumanity, his arms and legs were attached to horses which then pulled in opposite directions. One of the horses 'foundered', so a zealous *chevalier* offered his mount; 'the animal was full of vigour and pulled away a thigh'. After an hour and a half of this cruelty, Ravaillac died, as the mob tried to prevent him from receiving the last rites and urged the horses to pull harder. When what remained of the regicide finally expired, 'the entire populace, no matter what their rank, hurled themselves on the body with their swords, knives, sticks or anything else to hand and began beating, hacking and tearing at it. They snatched the limbs from the executioner, savagely chopping them up and dragging the pieces through the streets.' Children made a bonfire and flung remnants of Ravaillac's body on to it. According to a witness, one woman actually ate some of the flesh. The executioner, who was supposed to have the body of the regicide reduced to ashes in order to complete the ritual as demanded by the law, could find nothing to bring his task to completion but the assassin's shirt. Seldom, even at the height of the Terror, can the Paris mob have acted with greater ferocity, a ferocity born as much of fear as of grief and vengeance. But their frenzy also attested to the powerful sentiments of loyalty to the Crown which Henri had done so much to rekindle.

The King's embalmed corpse was placed on display in the Louvre until 29 June, then conducted solemnly to Saint-Denis, where he had first made his vows as a Catholic monarch seventeen years before, and where a solemn funeral service was held on 1 July. The cortège then processed across Henri's own recently completed Pont Neuf.

THE REGENCY

Of Henri's all-too-brief reign, it would be hard to improve on André Maurois' assessment. The results may have been 'less astonishing than legend would have them', he wrote,

> but at least Henri IV and Sully gave France ten years' truce, and the country remembered it as a golden age ... 'You cannot be a Frenchman', said Henri de Rohan, 'without regretting the loss to its well-being France has suffered.' Ten generations have confirmed this judgement, and Henri IV remains, together with Charlemagne, Joan of Arc and Saint Louis, one of France's heroes. He typifies not France's mystical aspect, but its aspects of courage, good sense and gaiety.

Much loved by so many of his countrymen, Henri of Navarre was the second consecutive French king to die by the knife of a religious zealot. What would have happened in Paris if Ravaillac had proved to be Huguenot or the tool of a Protestant conspiracy instead of a lone Catholic fanatic is awful to contemplate. As it was, the city trembled for days if not weeks; throughout the country a renewal of civil war was widely predicted. Waiting in the wings, in Milan, fêted by Spanish envoys there, was the self-exiled Prince de Condé, the last would-be cuckold of the murdered King and a close prince of the blood – though he was held back by a lack of both charm and resolve. But Henri at least had planned his succession as well as he could. For all the rival claims of the mistresses, he had left a legitimate heir by Marie de Medici, Louis XIII.

The new King, however, was a child not quite nine years old; over the next hundred years, there would be three child kings in a row on the throne of France, ruling through three regents. This was a uniquely dangerous situation for a mighty country confronted by watchful enemies, both inside and outside. In the case of both Louis XIII and his son, Louis XIV, aged four when he came to the throne, the regent would be a woman, the Queen Mother. But Henri had foresight. Six months before his death he had declared to Marshal de Lesdiguières that he 'well knew that the foundation of everything in France is the prince's authority'. For that reason, he intended to establish the Dauphin 'as absolute king and to give him all the true, essential marks of royalty, to the end that there might be no one in the realm who would not have to obey him'. Here, *de facto*, was enunciated the principle of absolutism by which, for better or worse, France would be governed until the Great Revolution 180 years later – and which would be revived under Napoleon.

On the eve of setting off for the wars, Henri had taken the wise precaution of designating his queen, Marie, to act as regent in his absence, supported by a Regent's Council fifteen strong. Though she had not the authoritarian will of her predecessor, Catherine, Marie – fat, blonde and comely enough when Rubens glorified her – sensibly retained all Henri's ministers. Only the ageing Sully resigned; but he left France's coffers full. Acting judiciously to calm Protestant fears of another Saint Bartholomew's, one of her first moves was to confirm the Edict of Nantes. But the stability achieved by Henri, which was not rooted in any fundamental reforms, had been no more than a temporary truce, and as such it remained constantly at risk.

When Marie was declared regent shortly after the announcement of Henri's death, Parisians were so shocked and frightened 'that in a moment the expression of all Paris changed ... The boutiques closed; everyone began to wail and cry, with women and girls tearing their hair out.' In fact, Parisians did not rise up in revolt. Instead of running to arms, they prayed for the health and prosperity of the new King, the whole of their fury directed against the regicide. So Marie was able to lay a foundation sufficiently sound for the young Louis XIII to survive campaigns against the princes in 1619–20 and against the Huguenots in 1627–8 – and to resist the external pressures of the Thirty Years War that ravaged central Europe.

Outside Paris but within the Île de France, increasingly affluent nobles built a multitude of elegant châteaux, harbingers of Versailles – constructed like Courances in the brick-and-stone manner of Henri IV, one of the most felicitous styles of any. But within the capital few great new building projects were undertaken under the Regency. The Queen Mother contented herself with purchasing and completing her sumptuous Luxembourg Palace, summoning Rubens from Antwerp in 1621 to decorate its galleries with twenty-five vast canvases that celebrated, with magnificent flattery, the main events of her marriage and the benefits to her adopted country of the Regency. Here in the Luxembourg's wild park, the young Louis played, his dogs coursing after hare and boar where today children play tennis and watch Punch and Judy shows.

Above all, the final touches were applied to Henri's masterpiece, the Place Royale.

In 1612 the engagement was announced of the ten-year-old Dauphin to Anne of Austria, daughter of Philip III of Spain, a thoroughly dynastic arrangement. At the same time, Louis' sister Elisabeth was betrothed to Anne's brother, the future Philip IV of Spain. That April saw one of the most extravagant celebrations ever mounted in Paris, dignifying the double engagement and inaugurating the newly opened Place Royale. A mock *carrousel*, called the Château de Félicité, complete with turrets and battlements, was erected in the city centre, but this time – in response to the tragic death of Henri II and all that had followed it – there would be no jousting. Instead the Regent and her court watched from specially constructed stands as an elaborate cavalcade passed before them, thrilling some 200,000 Parisians who had gathered in the streets. As night fell, accompanied by a tremendous blast of trumpets, drums and *clairons*, and the firing of 4,000 rockets from the towers of the nearby Bastille,* the whole Château de Félicité was set alight. Two more days of celebration followed.

The great festival in the Place Royale, which so fittingly marked Henri's lasting bequest to Paris, also assured the popularity of La Reine Marie – but only temporarily. Already suspect because of her Italian background, Marie rashly handed considerable powers to her Italian favourite, a woman widely regarded as 'a swarthy and greedy sorceress' called Leonora Galigai, whom she had imported from her native Florence. Leonora was married to an affected fop, Carlo Concini, whom the Queen made Marquis d'Ancre, and a marshal of France – though he never fought a battle. The Concinis seemed to exert a curious influence over the Queen Regent, enriching themselves and picking up titles, and generally making themselves hugely unpopular. They soon became scapegoats for all the real or imagined shortcomings of the regime. Meanwhile, in October 1614 Louis had reached his majority, aged twelve, and – frail, elegant and dressed in white – had appeared before the Estates-General where the young Bishop of Luçon, by name of Richelieu, first made his mark with a speech of forceful eloquence. The boy King thanked his mother profusely for 'all the trouble' she had taken on his behalf, and declared that he wished her to continue to govern and to be obeyed.

The young King was a glum shadow of his father, substantially

---

* The Bastille had been built by Charles V in 1370 as the Castle of Saint-Antoine.

lacking his charm and panache, and so fearful of women that he was certainly no Vert Galant. He was a strange man. A lonely child, sulky, morose and shy, he grew up to be secretive, cold, hard – and capable of great cruelty. He was unsociable and a dreamer, who seemed always to be bored. When asked to pardon a condemned peer (and personal friend), he is said to have remarked, 'A king should not have the same feelings as a private man.' Like his mother he made a poor choice in favourites: Charles d'Albert de Luynes, Grand Falconer at the court. Luynes, who was twenty-three years older than Louis, was a fairly humble *petit gentilhomme* from near Aix-en-Provence, born – according to Richelieu's acid comment – of a canon from Marseilles and a chambermaid. He was good-looking and well built, and his early hold on young Louis – from 1614 onwards – derived from his expertise in riding and hunting.

In November 1615, aged thirteen, Louis was finally married to the Spanish princess Anne of Austria, now a beautiful young woman. He made a show, unusual for him, of being *joyeux et galant* during the festivities, but he is said not to have entered his wife's bed until five years after their marriage, and then only when he was led to it by Luynes. There was to be no issue of the marriage for twenty-two years. But for the advent of one of history's greatest politicians, Cardinal Richelieu, his reign would probably have been little short of a calamity for France.

The Concinis, arrogant parvenus, came increasingly to annoy Louis by cheekily parading outside his windows in the Louvre, with an escort two or three hundred strong. The situation grew intolerable. In April 1617, Louis, almost certainly egged on by his favourite, ordered the elimination of Concini. On the morning of the 24th, accompanied by a retinue of fifty, the puffed-up Marshal d'Ancre entered the Louvre through the great door facing on to Saint-Germain-l'Auxerrois. Immediately a courtier, Vitry, a former counsellor of Henri IV, supported by a few men, sprang out and, putting his hand on the right arm of Concini, announced, 'The King has commanded me to seize your person.' Concini cried out for help, but was immediately felled by a volley of pistol shots. His retinue did nothing. Meanwhile Louis and Luynes were waiting anxiously inside, ready to flee if the plot failed.

Within the very courtyard of the Louvre, Paris could chalk up another ruthless murder. The city rejoiced ferociously at the end of the hated Concini, who was suspected of complicity in the death of Henri IV and even blamed for the failure to place his statue on the Pont Neuf.

Buried after the killing at Saint-Germain-l'Auxerrois, Concini's body was later dug up, torn apart and cannibalized: 'Having torn out the heart, one mob roasted it on a charcoal brazier, and ate it with relish.' With the murder of Concini, at sixteen the unpleasant Louis had truly come of age. 'Yes, now I am king!' he declared. At court it was as if lightning had struck. Abject by definition, the courtiers rallied instantly to their new star, raising him up in the window of the palace to show him to the guard assembled in the courtyard. Marie de Medici, realizing that her innings was over, said resignedly, 'I've reigned for years, and now I expect nothing more than a crown in heaven!' She was exiled (briefly) to Blois. Her Italian best friend, Leonora Galigai, Concini's widow, was seized while trying to conceal her jewellery in a mattress, and then burned on the Place de Grève as a witch. 'What a lot of people to see a poor woman die!' she is said to have exclaimed. Richelieu, compromised by his association with Concini, went back to his diocese. Luynes was made a duke and appointed master of the royal household – in effect, master of the state. He was to prove an increasingly pernicious influence on Louis.

LOUIS XIII GROWS UP

With the double marriage, the Spanish threat to France which had so exercised Henri IV was now approaching its end. Indeed Spain, about to begin her long descent into torpor following the death of Philip II in 1598, was no longer her principal enemy. Once again the dangers were internal. Luynes, a Catholic zealot, soon found himself entangled in a campaign against the Protestants in the south-west of France. An incompetent general, in 1621 he so mishandled the siege of Montauban that it had to be abandoned after three months. Among the many casualties was Luynes himself, dead of the *fièvre pourpre*, or camp fever.

Unmistakably, the death of Luynes was a stroke of good fortune for France, though it left a serious power-vacuum in Paris. Into it, and out of his temporary disgrace, moved Richelieu – at the behest of a king disoriented by the loss of his favourite. With Luynes now dead, Louis became reconciled to his mother; and in 1622 her new favourite, the Bishop of Luçon, was made Cardinal Richelieu. Two years later, swallowing his pride, Louis called in the man he had previously viewed as a dangerous prelate 'ready to set fire to the four corners of the realm' and invited him to take over his government. This decision was to transform an unattractive and accident-prone princeling into a monarch with a claim to greatness – if only a greatness that lay in his remarkable willingness to entrust the running of the country almost entirely to his brilliant *premier ministre*. Richelieu was to declare that 'My first goal was the majesty of the King; the second was the greatness of the realm.' Historians such as Montesquieu, however, saw it differently: Richelieu had assigned the King the role of playing 'second fiddle in the realm and first in Europe'.

Armand Jean du Plessis de Richelieu was born in Paris in 1585 of noble family from Poitou. With his arched nose and thin lips, his goatee and military moustache, his pale complexion and slender build, he cut a distinguished figure that was to dominate the portraits of the epoch. Beneath the cool, reasoned exterior was a man of passion, occasionally capable of violent rage. France, as Richelieu saw it, was in a mess, but, ever the pragmatist, he eschewed grand designs in favour of a method. 'In politics,' he would say, 'one is impelled far more by the necessity of things than by a pre-established will.'

Richelieu's early programme operated on three fronts: to crush Huguenot power, to humble the 'Great Lords' among the French nobles, grown too rich and too powerful under the Regency, and to thwart the designs of Habsburg Austria. In the first of these, he was greatly aided by the folly of James I's favourite, the Duke of Buckingham. Buckingham precipitated an Anglo-French war, into which the key Huguenot stronghold of La Rochelle on the Bay of Biscay was unwillingly drawn. After suffering terrible privations, La Rochelle was starved out following a fourteen-month siege in 1627–8. Buckingham simply pulled out, abandoning his Huguenot allies to their fate. Acting with great moderation in the wake of this disaster for the Protestant cause, Richelieu directed Louis towards humanity, reconfirming the Edict of Nantes, depriving the Huguenots of their fortresses and their armies, but guaranteeing them liberty of conscience. As a result of this 'Peace of Grace', the Huguenots caused no real trouble for the government during the next few decades.

By way of humbling the nobles, the second prong of his strategy, Richelieu began by purging from the Conseil d'Etat, the chief governing council, all the ministers who opposed him. For many years without an heir, Louis was a natural object for conspiracy. At one time or another, his half-brothers, the Vendômes, the illegitimate sons of Henri IV, and his own brother, Gaston d'Orléans, six years younger, were all plotting against him and Richelieu. Gaston, until 1638 the presumptive heir to the throne, was an attractive but feckless libertine of no great intelligence, and in 1626 he became seriously embroiled in a plot to assassinate Richelieu. After a period of exile abroad, Gaston was back in France in 1632, now involved with the Duc de Montmorency in open rebellion in the Languedoc. Montmorency was wounded and captured, then executed. Given that he was the greatest nobleman of France outside the royal family itself, and had an outstanding record of service to the Crown, the sentence came as a profound shock, provoking many appeals for clemency. But, whereas Richelieu might have yielded, Louis showed himself remorselessly harsh in having the sentence carried out. 'One should not pity a man who is about to suffer his punishment,' he said, 'one should only pity him for having deserved it.'

From then on, Gaston was seen as a broken reed (at least until the troubled days of the Fronde under Louis XIV), the throne at last made secure when, seemingly almost in a fit of absent-mindedness while sheltering from a storm overnight in her apartment, Louis caused Anne to conceive an heir, who was born on 5 September 1638, almost twenty-three years after their marriage. Two years later a similar miracle produced a second son, Philippe. Gaston, Richelieu's bitter enemy, seemed to have lost all hope of succeeding to the throne.

In his third aim of humbling the Habsburgs, now grown so powerful through the aggrandizements of Charles V, Richelieu was largely successful in keeping out of the grisly Thirty Years War that ravaged Germany and the countries east of the Rhine. Even so, in 1636, Spanish armies invading from Holland almost reached the gates of Paris. Though subsequently this could be seen as a last effort of waning Spanish power, at the time there was serious alarm in the city, and Parisians were grateful yet again for the protective walls that Philippe Auguste and Charles V had given them, though anxious about their state of repair. 'Not a turret but would have come tumbling down at the sound of a roll of drums,' it was reported.

GOVERNANCE OF PARIS

Building astutely, and ruthlessly, on the absolutist foundations laid by Henri and Sully, Louis XIII and Richelieu steadily tightened the monarchy's grip on Paris. It was a tendency that would continue into the ill-fated Second Empire of Louis Napoleon. In the mother country of liberty, the instinct for authoritarianism is never far below the surface. Almost never before had the charge of *lèse-majesté* been made so frequently outside Paris; although there were many uprisings in the provinces, Paris remained curiously tranquil throughout the time of Richelieu. It was Richelieu's plain preference to govern via councils, rather than through favourites, but from the beginning of his ascendancy to the end, he ruled the city councils with a heavy hand – and the more powerful he grew the heavier that hand became. Louis himself could treat the Paris Parlement with downright brutality. On one chilling occasion he warned its First President, Guy Le Jay, of the limit of his powers: 'If you continue your schemes, I will clip your nails so close that your flesh will suffer from it.'

In the Paris of Henri IV, duelling had become all the rage among *galants*, often taking place in the Place Royale. Each year several hundred members of the gentry perished in duels. Now Richelieu showed himself ruthlessly determined to stamp out what, to him, was a particularly heinous sin. *Pour encourager les autres*, in June 1627 a well-known noble, the Comte de Montmorency-Bouteville, arrested for duelling, was refused a pardon and beheaded. This caused a major sensation.

Unlike his father, Louis was not dedicated to Paris; like his Valois antecedents, when not at the wars or involved in acts of repression in the provinces he was addicted to *la chasse*. Richelieu, on the other hand, spent as much time in Paris as he could, because that was where lay the fount of power, as well as the potential sources of revolt. During the two Richelieu decades, the geographical centre of gravity of Paris gradually but systematically moved westwards, away from the smells and congestion of the Marais. To the great coral-like entity of the Louvre, Louis added only a tiny accretion, the Pavillon de l'Horloge, and a stretch of the west wing of the Cour Carrée.

But Richelieu, always shrewd in matters of real estate, agglomerated a vast property that stretched from the back door of the Louvre in the south to the city wall in the north. Through the centre he built a long straight street (now, appropriately, the Rue Richelieu in the banking district of the 2nd arrondissement), and divided the expanses on either side into building lots. To the west of it, between 1633 and 1639, he had built for himself a sumptuous palace with eight elegant and classically regular courtyards, which Richelieu bequeathed to the King. Known initially as the Palais Cardinal, when the royal family moved in after Richelieu's death it gained the name it has held ever since, the Palais Royal. 'An entire city, built with pomp, seems to have arisen miraculously from an old ditch,' exclaimed Corneille, his praise possibly conditioned by the fact that he found there both a patron and a stage for his plays. The Palais Cardinal set a new standard, now in stone, of classical uniformity in Paris, though sadly little remains of the original design.

The shift in the religious balance following the death of Henri had resulted in a powerful Catholic renaissance. The clergy had regained respect and influence, and so had the Jesuits, who expanded everywhere in their role of educators. In the three decades after the assassination of 1610, on the Right Bank no fewer than eighteen new religious foundations had made their appearance (including the important seminary of Saint-Sulpice), with a similar number on the Left Bank. Many major churches were also begun at this time. On the Left Bank, to mark the birth of the Dauphin in 1638, Anne transformed the simple little monastery of Val-de-Grâce in the Rue Saint-Jacques into an imposing abbey, with a cupola in the new style, emulating those of Florence and Rome – though technical problems delayed completion of the great dome till 1665. Louis was much given to church building as a form of thanksgiving (he erected Notre-Dame des Victoires to celebrate the fall of La Rochelle), but his most outstanding and most enduring contribution to the architecture of Paris lay in the middle of the Seine, in the Île Saint-Louis.

Just upstream from the age-old Île de la Cité lay two small muddy islets, their use over the centuries indicated by the name Île aux Vaches. Henri IV had it in mind to join them together, build a dyke round them to keep the Seine out, and then develop the resulting island. His assassination brought the project to a halt, but Louis carried it forward under Henri's builder Christopher Marie, together with two financiers – Poulletier and Le Regrattier – all of whose names survive to this day on the Île. In return for its development, they were guaranteed rents from the houses over sixty years, a highly remunerative undertaking. For the first time an area of Paris was laid out on a grid system, thereby guaranteeing its survival from the subsequent attentions of Baron Haussmann. In 1618 the island was connected to the Right Bank by the Pont Marie (named after the architect, not – as might be thought given the piety of Louis and Anne – the Holy Virgin) and two years later to the Left Bank by the Pont de la Tournelle. The bridges were finished by 1645, the handsome *quais* by Louis' death in 1643. Within thirty years, the two mudbanks had been transformed into a beautiful city in miniature, a seventeenth-century jewel encapsulating in its streets of pot-bellied houses both uniformity and individualism. Many of the houses were designed by Le Vau, who understandably kept one of the best for himself. His masterpiece, at the east end of the island, unquestionably is the Hôtel Lambert, marking a new development in style as a private town house for the affluent individual rather than as a showpiece to impress the public. Here Voltaire, Chopin and – more recently – the actress Michèle Morgan later lived, and it is now a treasure trove belonging to Baron Guy de Rothschild – alas, now somewhat marred by the ugly modern block of the Institut du Monde Arabe that fills the horizon just across the river. From its inception, prostitutes from the Marais were banned from the Île, lending it (compared with the Place des Vosges) a somewhat sombre, almost puritan tranquillity. Somehow the Île remained aloof from most of the revolts that rocked Paris in the eighteenth and nineteenth centuries, and today the clamour of the city still passes it by.

Among the major projects envisaged by Henri IV, the grandiose scheme for the Place de France was abandoned by Richelieu as simply too ambitious. But the thirty-three-year reign of Louis XIII might have left more of a mark on Paris had he not been taken for a ride by unscrupulous speculators. Notable among these was a Louis Le Barbier, driven on by an admirable ambition to secure good matches for his daughters. Le Barbier undertook for Louis the colossal venture of demolishing Charles V's wall, bringing several new *faubourgs* into the city (five on the Left Bank alone), and then building a new protective wall. Richelieu was in a hurry to build the new wall on the Right Bank, not merely out of strategic considerations, but because the old one obscured the view from his Palais Cardinal. A contract was signed in October 1631, but the contractors, Pierre Pidou and Charles Froger, were as unreliable as Le Barbier – whose front-men they turned out to be. Virtually nothing was ever completed; Le Barbier died in 1641, a ruined man. Given the treatment meted out to the likes of Concini, he and his accomplices were lucky to escape with their lives.

ARTS AND LETTERS

Few Frenchmen today would deny that Richelieu's greatest cultural legacy to France lay not in bricks and mortar, but in the creation of the Académie Française to defend and enhance the purity of the French language. Founded in 1635 and consisting initially of nine men of letters with an average age of thirty-six, it was then followed in 1648 by the Académie Royale de Peinture et de Sculpture and in 1671 by the all-powerful Académie Royale d'Architecture, designed similarly to establish and maintain standards in building. Originally organizations without a home, the Académies had to wait for Cardinal Mazarin to commission for them the superb Institut de France complex (opened in 1688) with its glittering cupola and its two arms that seem to reach out to embrace the very heart of Paris from its eminence on the Left Bank of the Seine.

The civil war in France had brought art to a new low. In Paris the League attacked Renaissance art as heretical, so few young artists of talent were attracted to the capital. Henri IV was no connoisseur, and had no time to become one; Marie de Medici lacked the necessary taste, and commissioning Rubens did little to make of Paris a city attractive to artists. Fortunately Richelieu had both taste and the power to indulge it. He bought paintings and sculpture from Italy, and invited the portrait painter Philippe de Champaigne from Brussels. In 1635 he commissioned Nicolas Poussin to paint more of the light-hearted bacchanals and landscapes which had made his early reputation; Poussin, of Norman peasant stock, found money and fame in the capital, but not the technical encouragement he needed. In 1642, snubbing his rich but pretentious Paris patrons, he left France for the Rome that was always the source of his inspiration.

His fellow Norman, Pierre Corneille, the great dramatist adept in both comedy and tragedy, was set to work by Richelieu as one of his *cinq auteurs*, writing plays under the Cardinal's careful direction, some of which were performed before the King. In January 1637 he produced his heroic tragedy *Le Cid*, dealing with the conflict between sexual passion and honour – a milestone in the history of French drama. Corneille was notable for his belief in free will, in marked contrast to the theme of impotence conveyed in Greek classical tragedy, the tradition that was to be inherited by Racine.

Another figure of importance in French literature, a Norman like Poussin and Corneille, was the poet François de Malherbe. Henri IV brought him to Paris in 1605 as his official poet, and he remained in favour under Louis XIII and Richelieu. Renowned for his slowness in composition, he once spent three years writing stanzas on the death of a noble lady, so that when he came to present them the bereaved husband had already remarried – and died. Thus Malherbe left few verses to posterity, but what was important about him was the rigorous purity of his style and diction, and his clarity. He eschewed all Latinisms and foreign usage, in preference for common Parisian speech. This made him an important precursor of the Académie and what it was to stand for through the centuries. Though Henri had neither the instinct nor the time to be a patron of literature, no more than of painting, his own letters, passionate and forthright as they were, broke new ground as classics of their kind. In many ways one sees his short, glorious reign as having laid the essential groundwork in Paris on which his widow, son and grandson – and Richelieu – were all to build with such success, accomplishing a kind of nationalization of the French arts.

Finally there was the great essayist, Michel Eyquem de Montaigne, so much admired down the years for the freshness, vigour and gaiety of his language. One of the last of the great provincial writers, it was Montaigne who called the Paris of Henri IV 'la gloire de la France et l'un des plus nobles ornements du monde'. Justly, he was to have one of the grandest avenues in Paris named after him.

A NEW REGENT

The era of Louis XIII and Richelieu ended quite suddenly. At the last meeting of the two men, in Tarascon in 1642, both were so ill – the Cardinal's body eaten away with ulcers – that the King ordered their beds to be placed next to each other. It was a tearful leave-taking. Richelieu died in December that year. Five months later, Louis was also carried away, in May 1643 – apparently by tuberculosis, and amid no great mourning. Even so, it could reasonably be claimed that the Cardinal had made his master 'le plus grand roi du monde'.

For a third time, the French found themselves ruled by a woman regent, the Queen Mother, Anne. Louis XIV was not yet five years old. Once more things looked perilous for France. Yet within a week of the child King's accession a renewed Spanish advance upon Paris from the Low Countries was defeated, at Rocroi, by the twenty-two-year-old Duc d'Enghien, Prince de Condé (son of the troublesome but ineffectual would-be cuckold of Henri IV). One of the great military victories of French history, it was both an augury of what was to come and a hands-off warning to France's enemies. Ahead lay the age of the Roi Soleil, whose effulgence would have been impossible without the achievements of his grandfather Henri IV.

AGE THREE: 1643–1795

LOUIS XIV

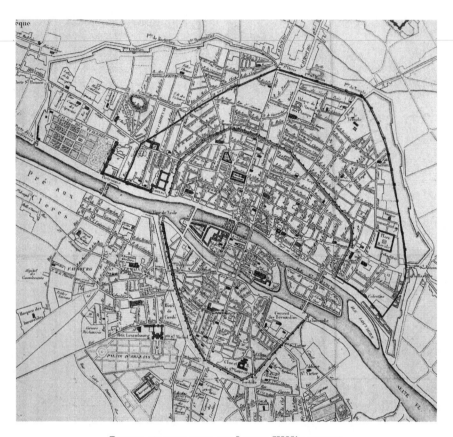

PARIS AT THE END OF LOUIS XIII'S REIGN

7

The Move to Versailles

The civil wars started in Paris just as they did in London, over
a little money.

Voltaire

MAZARIN AND THE FRONDE

On his accession, the four-year-old Louis went to live in the Louvre
with his mother Anne and his younger brother Philippe, before moving
into the Palais Royal. From the earliest days Louis loved playing there
with soldiers, a silver set having been made for him specially by a
goldsmith from Nancy. He even had his own miniature collection
of gold cannon drawn by fleas. As he grew older he would march
through the Palais Royal deafening bystanders with his drum, and later
still take to target practice on sparrows in the gardens with a small
arquebus.

With Richelieu dead, Anne called on his far less austere, Italian-born
secretary Jules Mazarin to be first minister. Rumours, unsubstantiated,
held that he also became the Queen Mother's lover. Aged forty, Cardinal
Mazarin was a highly cultivated man (though, according to Voltaire, he
never learned to pronounce French properly), a lover of opera and
drama, and he seemed unassuming and always smiling, flexible where
Richelieu had been ruthless. But he was to follow in much the same
pattern; and it was ironic that the two senior churchmen should both
be so unhesitant in resorting to the sword. Mazarin's reputation for
avarice made him few friends, while his lifestyle also rendered him
heavy-handed with taxation. In 1648 the little-loved *paulette* tax, first

levied by Sully, came up for renewal. The Paris Parlement protested vigorously.

Acting against the advice of Mazarin, Anne ordered the arrest of three of the leading troublemakers in Parlement. One was an elder called Pierre Broussel, who was immensely popular with Parisians. On learning of his arrest, Paris closed up shop and took to the streets. That night angry demonstrators forced Anne and Louis to take refuge in the Palais Royal, which was not nearly so formidable a bastion as the Louvre. The next morning some 1,200 barricades of chains, barrels and paving stones were thrown up across the capital. Mazarin prevailed upon Anne to give way, and Broussel was released. But the situation remained tense, with the Palais Royal highly vulnerable. On 13 September the royal family fled Paris for the Château de Rueil. It was an intolerable humiliation that must have made the most powerful impression on an impressionable young king. Meanwhile, his head swollen by his triumph at Rocroi, the Prince de Condé was making for Paris; and, in England, where Charles I was about to lose his head, a dangerous example in rebellion had been set.

In the words of Voltaire: 'The civil wars started in Paris just as they did in London, over a little money.' And what was beginning was indeed a civil war, the first since the early days of Henri of Navarre, and largely concentrated in and around Paris. The rebels now called themselves *frondeurs* – a *fronde* was a sling, which had been used to hurl pebbles through Mazarin's windows – and the Fronde indeed came more to resemble ill-disciplined small boys with catapults. The first of the successive uprisings, lasting from 1648 until 1649, was known as the 'Fronde de Parlement'; it contended for principles. The second, the 'Fronde des Princes', which lasted until 1653, was concerned chiefly with the rivalry of competing princes.

The Peace of Westphalia in October 1648, although it left Spain still at war with France, brought an end to the Thirty Years War. At the end of that month Anne deemed it safe to return to Paris, to await the arrival of the twenty-seven-year-old hero, the 'Grand Condé'. Now a duke six times over, Condé would surround Paris and cut off food supplies. But, with only 15,000 men, he realized (like Henri IV before him) that he was not strong enough to besiege the city. The Fronde won a first success with the capture of the Bastille, and once again the Queen Mother and the child King left Paris – this time for Saint-Germain-en-Laye, reduced to a state of penury by the exigencies of civil war. In March 1649, shocked by how matters had got out of hand in London with the execution of the King of England two months previously, the moderates of Parlement recoiled from further revolt and signed an agreement by which Parisians agreed to lay down their arms and give up the Bastille in return for an amnesty.

It was only a truce. Now France's other great – and ambitious – soldier entered the lists against the King. The Marshal Vicomte de Turenne, egged on by his mistress, a troublesome beauty called Geneviève de Longueville (once heard to admit, 'I don't enjoy innocent pleasures!'), into collusion with the Spaniards, marched in 1650 to within fifty kilometres of Paris. Meanwhile, Condé had shown himself to be so arrogant, to the point of endangering the monarchy, that Mazarin had had him arrested, together with two other princes. Condé snorted, 'So this is what I get for my services!' Elements of a Feydeau farce now took over, with rival princes popping in and out of closets and switching loyalties with abandon.

Paris was soon in a ferment again. In February 1651, Anne decided to leave Paris once more. But Louis' laying out of his boots and travelling suit sparked off murmurs in the city. The mob burst through the gates of the Palais Royal, demanding to see the infant King. It was a potentially ugly and certainly humiliating situation. Anne, however, played a remarkably cool hand, telling Louis of what was afoot and instructing him to feign sleep. An emissary of the mob, who had insisted on an audience with the King, was taken into the royal bedchamber – where he was greatly discountenanced to find a sleeping child.

Momentarily safe, Anne and the King remained precariously in Paris, more or less under house arrest at the Palais Royal by the *frondeurs*. Mazarin, however, decided it prudent to go into temporary exile near Cologne, having released Condé on the way. But he continued to direct Anne by letter from the Rhineland. Condé immediately joined the rebel forces in Paris and incited civil war throughout France. Skilfully Anne regained the loyalty of Turenne, the only general who could match Condé, and who – thoroughly disenchanted by Condé's self-serving pretensions – changed sides to lead the royal forces to a series of victories in the provinces. Facing defeat there, Condé decided to stake all on one last throw: he would seize Paris. In the wings Mazarin played a waiting game, assured that the Grand Condé could always be relied upon to thwart his own stratagems.

In September 1651, at thirteen Louis came of age. He rode to Parlement, which was sitting at the Palais de Justice, and there declared in resolute tones, '*Messieurs*, I have come to my Parlement to tell you that, following the law of the land, I intend to take over the government myself; and I hope by the goodness of God that it will be with piety and justice.' Writing to Mazarin a courtier praised the young King as having displayed 'the bearing and intelligence of a man of twenty-five'. The following October Louis made his formal state entry into Paris, and appointed Anne as his chief counsellor. But he made it plain that henceforth he in person would rule France and exact loyalty. In August he suspended Parlement and transferred it to Pontoise, whence it might operate in greater tranquillity than within the turbulent capital. Only fourteen counsellors of the Conseil d'Etat obeyed him; given all the circumstances and dangers, it was a courageous act for a young boy. Louis was learning rapidly the art of governing.

By this time, Paris had been reduced to a state of anarchy and misery – and hunger. Intermittently besieged by Condé and his squabbling fellow princes, cut off from outside supplies, starvation was constantly in attendance, with fears of a repetition of the horrors of 1590. The environs of the city were devastated by the warring factions. Murder, destruction of crops and pillage were the order of the day.

Four troublesome and chaotic years had passed by, in which Anne and Louis had been forced to leave Paris four times. Mazarin came back from Germany at the head of a small army of 7,000 men, wearing green ribbons to distinguish them from the yellowy-grey of Condé's men. Condé remained just outside Paris, in control but 'his power diminishing day by day and his army growing ever weaker', with his own arrogance undiminished and the war-weariness of the Parisian populace mounting. Unhelpful allies for him, too, were the hated Spanish troops who supported him – only recently bitter enemies whom the Parisians thought Henri IV had got rid of once and for all back in 1594. Heading the royal armies, the redoubtable Turenne now in June 1652, with 12,000 men to Condé's 6,000, led the King (currently resident in Saint-Denis) and his court towards his own capital.

On 4 July representatives of bourgeois and clergy gathered in the Hôtel de Ville to discuss the restoration of order. But their meeting ended in massacre, with at least a hundred killed and the building set on fire by Condé's rag-tag supporters. The smoke could be seen all over Paris. His cause thoroughly discredited, Condé crept out of the city. A week later Louis re-entered it, taking up residence not in the vulnerable Palais Royal, but in the ancient and much more easily defended bastion of the Louvre. Parlement renounced its claims to have a voice in political and financial affairs; in return Louis undertook to ensure that officeholders would get paid off. The rebellious grandees were guaranteed pensions and lands – provided they never tried to force their way into the Conseil d'Etat.

The Paris Fronde, both components of it, was finished (though it dragged on for another year in the provinces, and for several more in Normandy). Wisely, Louis promised a general amnesty; there was no unconditional surrender, and no savage reprisals. Condé was sentenced to death *in absentia*, but was pardoned in 1660; though, if ever a warlord deserved to lose his head or be locked up for ever in the Bastille, it was he – certainly this would have been his fate under earlier French monarchs. Later, back in favour, Condé was to win important battles against Louis' foreign enemies. To nobody's astonishment more than his own, in February 1653 Cardinal Mazarin was invited back, received by Louis 'as a father and by the people as a master', and entertained at what remained of the Hôtel de Ville 'amid the acclamations of the citizens'. The appreciative Italian flung money to the populace, but was said to have commented on 'the fickleness or rather the folly of the Parisians'.

Thus ended the last great revolutionary struggle in France before 1789. All authority would now reside in Louis alone. Witnessing his triumphal entry into Paris in 1652, the diarist John Evelyn, over from Commonwealth England, remarked with a touch of envy, 'The French are the only nation in Europe to idolize their sovereign.' Louis had won a notable victory, and would waste no time in capitalizing upon it. As Voltaire put it, the King 'found himself absolute master of a kingdom still shaken from the blows it had received, every branch of administration in disorder, but full of resources'. The country at large had never been more impoverished. Fields were covered in weeds and brambles, livestock slaughtered by marauding bands. There was nowhere enough to eat, and food had to be imported into the countryside from the royal granaries. Paris was a shambles, with murder and theft rampant. Yet the country, blessed as ever with Sully's *deux mamelles*, its combination of benign climate and fertile land, managed to survive.

Although on the first anniversary of July 1652 the now subservient Hôtel de Ville launched a grand festival celebrating the re-establishment of royal authority, henceforth Louis watched it like a hawk. In June 1654, he was belatedly crowned at Rheims. While out hunting in April 1655, he had word that Parlement was meeting without his knowledge. Galloping six kilometres, he entered the Palais de Justice in his riding boots to forbid the meeting to continue. Legend has it that, cracking his whip, he uttered the famous words, 'L'état, c'est moi.'

For the ensuing twenty-five years, he would be assiduous in avoiding both Parlement and the Hôtel de Ville – which he would always regard as the contentious focus of the Paris Fronde.

MARRIAGE AND INDEPENDENCE

Four years later, in 1659, Louis signed the Treaty of the Pyrenees, at last bringing to an end the wars with Spain, which had been France's principal enemy ever since the days of François I and Charles V more than a century and a half before. He sealed it with marriage to his cousin, the Infanta Maria Theresa, daughter of Philip IV of Spain. In exchange for an extravagant dowry of half a million gold écus, his bride renounced her rights to the Spanish throne. From now on, Spain was militarily out of the picture. At the same time, the menace of France's other hereditary enemy, England, was nullified by domestic turmoil: Cromwell dead, the Commonwealth about to pack its bags, and Charles II – who had spent his mature life as a humble refugee enjoying the hospitality of France – about to be restored as monarch without real power and without animosity to France. Thus Paris could look forward to the best part of a century of stability and prosperity, almost unrivalled in her long history. There would be wars, but they would be far off, incapable of disturbing Parisian life. There was nonetheless plenty of excitement in store for the capital.

The marriage of Louis and the Infanta was celebrated on the Franco-Spanish frontier at Saint-Jean-de-Luz. Louis then made his triumphal entry into Paris in August 1660. As pure *spectacle* Parisians had never seen anything quite like it. At the end of the Faubourg Saint-Antoine, near where only a few years previously the Fronde had fought its last battle, a vast throne was set up on a site henceforth known as the Place du Trône. Here Louis received all the official bodies of Paris filing past in homage. Then an immense procession escorted the young couple through numerous triumphal arches to the Louvre, past the Hôtel de Ville of unhappy memory. Looking down on them from glittering balconies were the Queen Mother Anne, the ageing Mazarin, the victorious Marshal Turenne – and a Mme Scarron, who, as Marquise de Maintenon, would eventually become Louis' last wife.

1. Norsemen besiege Paris, c. 885. Engraving after Alphonse de Neuville.

2. Héloïse and Abelard, from a fourteenth-century manuscript.

3. Philippe Auguste, 1165–1223.
Engraving by A. L. François
Sergent-Marceau.

4. Burning of the Templars;
Jacques de Molay curses
Philippe le Bel, 1314.

5. Fourteenth-century rioters pillage a Paris house, from the *Chronicle of France*.

6. Execution of Jacques Clément, assassin of Henri III. A similar fate awaited Ravaillac, assassin of Henri IV. Engraving from the school of Zacharias Dolendo, 1589.

7. *Scène Galante* at the Gates of Paris, detail showing Notre-Dame. Sixteenth-century French school.

8. Assassination of Henri IV, 14 May 1610. Engraving by Gaspar Bouttats.

9. Portrait of Molière by
Pierre Mignard.

10. Portrait of Racine by
Jean-Bàptiste Santerre.

11. Madame de Maintenon, with Ninon de Lenclos (centre) and André Le Nôtre, by Georgine Gérard, 1837.

12. Transporting the equestrian statue of Louis XIV to the Place Vendôme. Painting by René Antoine Houasse, 1699.

13. Distribution of
bread at the Louvre
during the food
shortage, 1709.

14. Demolition
of houses on the
Pont Notre-Dame
by Hubert Robert,
1786.

15. Clearing of old houses round
the Louvre. Watercolour by
Thomas Girtin, 1801–2.

16. Dominique-Vivant,
Baron Denon, of the Louvre.
Portrait by Robert Lefèvre,
1808.

17. Napoleon's unfortunate elephant, Place de la Bastille. Watercolour by Jean-Antoine Alavoine, c. 1810.

18. The Russian contingent entering Paris. English school, lithograph, 1814.

The cavalcade was accompanied by massed trumpet and drum fanfares, the trumpeters dressed in blue and silver, while twenty-four violins serenaded the King. Two young poets present that day – La Fontaine and Racine (aged only twenty-one) – wrote odes to commemorate the occasion. An estimated 100,000 Parisians saw their king that day; they would never be so close to him again, or indeed to any other French monarch.

Two years later, to celebrate the birth of his firstborn, Louis would mount another great *spectacle*. This time, evoking the days of Henri II and Louis XIII in the Place Royale, it was a *carrousel*, a great equestrian show with sumptuously attired horsemen vying with each other in a cross between a medieval tournament and a ballet. To mount it, a large space was cleared in front of the Tuileries Palace (the site of the Arc du Carrousel erected by Napoleon), and a vast amphitheatre built to house 15,000 spectators. Five teams of princes of the blood were fantastically dressed to represent Romans, Persians, Turks, Indians and Americans. The King himself took part, dressed as a Roman emperor (this was to become his favourite role) and wearing a sun on his shield with the inscription *Ut vidi vici* ('As I saw, I conquered'). The resplendent cavalcade traversed Paris twice, to the resounding acclaim of spectators on every rooftop. Here lay the beginnings of the myth of the Age of the Roi Soleil.

In February 1661, there was a serious fire at the Louvre, and Mazarin moved from his apartments in that palace to Vincennes. There, playing with his warblers and his monkey, he died the following March, aged only fifty-nine but prematurely exhausted. A grief-stricken Louis burst into tears; 'he loved me and I loved him,' he later said of this discreet and sagacious 'stepfather' – an admission he would make of no one else. For two hours after learning of the death of his loyal friend and guide he shut himself up alone; then he called in his first council. It is possible that he was also relieved. As he wrote in his memoirs, 'I felt my mind and courage soar ... I felt quite another man. I discovered in myself qualities I had never suspected.' Later he was heard to remark, 'La face du théâtre change' – or, as he put it to his entourage, 'In future I shall be my own prime minister.' Louis was now alone, and the sole ruler of France. With a population of eighteen million in 1660, compared with England's five million, Spain's six, Austria's six and Russia's fourteen million, his was substantially the largest country in Europe. And Paris, the largest capital, now had been getting on for half a million inhabitants.

FOUQUET

Much as Louis was addicted to *théâtre* and *spectacle*, woe betide any lesser mortal who might seem to try to upstage him, or even compete with him. Nicolas Fouquet, a vain, ostentatious and ambitious parvenu, had been Louis' minister superintendent of finance since 1653. Now aged forty-five, he had just built himself a magnificent mansion at Vaux-le-Vicomte, some forty kilometres south-east of Paris. His crest, still visible on that great unfinished pile, was a squirrel with the challenging motto *Quo non ascendet* ('How far will he not climb'). He had many friends in high places; it was reckoned that some 116 people owed their wealth or position to him. He had spent lavishly – and not unwisely – on the arts; in fact, between 1655 and 1660 Fouquet had virtually replaced the King as the nation's leading patron, employing a galaxy of the greatest French artists and writers. There had even been some talk that he would eventually succeed Mazarin as prime minister.

On the day after the Cardinal's death, however, Louis had appointed Mazarin's astute and incorruptible secretary, Jean-Baptiste Colbert, as Fouquet's assistant. Five months later, on 17 August 1661, Fouquet audaciously invited the King to a lavish gala at Vaux-le-Vicomte. The royal retinue was greeted by a tableau depicting a lion (the King) stepping on a serpent (which was Colbert's crest), while in the lion's paw a squirrel sat munching a nut. It was hardly diplomatic – nor was it politically adroit. Fouquet, however, had spared no expense in his attempt to flatter his monarch. The massive iron gates gleamed with freshly applied gilt; in the vast gardens laid down by André Le Nôtre 200 *jets d'eau* and fifty fountains spouted on either side of a main alley nearly a kilometre long. For the previous five years, some 18,000 workmen had toiled to produce this wonder of the modern age, eradicating three villages that had happened to be in the way. Certainly it trumped the modest royal hunting-lodge of the King's father out at Versailles, which Louis was currently doing up.

Inside the imposing mansion the royal party dined off a magnificent gold service which likewise must have made its impression on the King, who had had to sell off his plate to meet military expenditure. Following this feast, in an outdoor theatre lit with torches, Molière introduced his play *Les Fâcheux* ('The Bores'), written especially for the occasion. The King visibly enjoyed the play, which seemed to mock one of his more tiresome courtiers; but the whole episode outraged him. At various points in the evening, Louis came close to losing his temper – whispering to his mother, 'Madame, shall we make these people disgorge?' Anne had to restrain him from arresting Fouquet on the spot, prudently cautioning Louis, 'No, not in his house, not at an entertainment he is giving for you.'

'Luxe, insolent et audacieux' was, however, the damning impression of Fouquet that Louis took away with him from that disastrous evening. Less than three weeks later, just as he was arriving at a meeting in Nantes, Fouquet was arrested by the legendary D'Artagnan of *Three Musketeers* fame. He was heard to murmur, with supreme hubris, 'I thought I stood higher with the King than anyone in France.' His trial – before twenty-two judges – dragged on for the best part of three years. For France as a whole, the economy was in a terrible mess, so the prosecution of the mighty and arrogant Superintendent of Finance was extremely popular among the Paris mob. But most of the charges against Fouquet were disgracefully trumped up, at the King's instigation, and a fair trial was hardly possible. The affair did neither the regime nor Colbert (who had plotted against his boss) nor Louis much credit. Many in high positions in Paris, including one of the judges, Olivier d'Ormesson, were sympathetic to the defendant (d'Ormesson was ruined by the King as a result). La Fontaine composed some sympathetic verses, while the articulate and influential Mme de Sévigné expressed open admiration for Fouquet, among other things for his calmness during the protracted trial. Had it not been for such support the death sentence would almost certainly have been pronounced. As it was, on 17 November 1664, Fouquet was imprisoned for life. His doctor and personal valet broke down in court, and insisted on following him into prison. He was never to see his beloved, unfinished house again.

What was important for Paris were the consequences that the fall of Fouquet had for Louis – and for France. In the ruthlessness he displayed towards him, the King was motivated by his obsessive fear of conspiracies – by no means irrational, given the recent Fronde wars. But, shamelessly, as if re-enacting the story of Naboth's Vineyard, Louis grabbed the fallen man's architect Le Vau, his garden-designer Le Nôtre, his muralist Le Brun and his skilled artisans, and set them to work on Versailles – the seeds of whose greater glory lay in Fouquet's disastrous gala of August 1661. Moreover, as was abundantly confirmed after the trial, Louis would now rule supreme. Colbert, the bourgeois son of a draper from Rheims, would move into Fouquet's slot – but, brilliant administrator though he turned out to be, he would always be Louis' man. Henceforth, under the Roi Soleil, the government would be characterized by the three qualities of order, regularity and unity.

THE 'AFFAIRE DES POISONS'

To set the seal on Louis' lonely position at the summit of power, in 1666 his much loved mother, who had exerted so profound an influence over him in the early days, and all through the trials and tribulations of the Fronde, died. Louis wept unrestrainedly. Meanwhile, gossip in Paris had begun to focus more than ever on the King's mistresses. Louis had swiftly become sexually disenchanted with his plain Spanish bride, once she had given him an heir, and – in the way of French monarchs – had energetically set to acquiring beautiful young women from the court. First there came Louise de La Vallière, with whom Louis fell passionately in love almost simultaneously with the beginnings of his obsession with Versailles around 1661. Then, six years later, with poor Louise eventually forced to take flight to a convent, she was supplanted by the wily Athénaïs de Montespan. For a decade Athénaïs ruled unthreatened by any rival until the appearance at court of the tall blonde beauty Marie-Adélaïde de Fontanges, described by the arch-gossip Mme de Sévigné as being 'belle comme une ange, sotte comme un panier', and by the less bitchy as being 'far above everything that had been seen for a long time at Versailles, in addition to her height, her poise and the air about her capable of surprising and of charming a court as *galante* as her'. Louis rapidly seduced this young girl, a state of affairs which Athénaïs was determined to bring to an end. Between them the mistresses bore Louis a regiment of illegitimates (Montespan alone provided eight, while most of the Queen's children died), at the same time spawning the most intense jealousies and rivalries that were to culminate in the highly dangerous 'Affaire des Poisons'.

A series of sudden deaths among the eminent had caused Paris to succumb to near-hysterical rumours of poisoning. As early as 1670 suspicions had surrounded the death of 'Madame', Princess Henrietta of England, the sad youngest daughter of Charles I and first wife of the King's homosexual brother Philippe d'Orléans, 'Monsieur'. Sudden deaths proliferated, including those of the Comte de Soissons, the Duc de Savoie and Colbert. Allegations of black masses and witchcraft became linked with abortions and the purveyance of love-philtres to the rich and mighty – and with the poisoning of inconvenient relatives or rivals, or simply of disobliging associates.

Rumours became fact with the trial before the Paris law courts in 1676 of a noblewoman, no less a personage than Marie-Madeleine d'Aubray, the Marquise de Brinvilliers. Mme de Brinvilliers made a full confession: she had poisoned and killed her father, her two brothers and various patients in hospitals that she visited. She had also tried to poison her husband, in order to marry her lover, a Captain Sainte-Croix. But Sainte-Croix, 'who did not want a wife as malicious as himself', gave an antidote to the Marquis, 'such that, having been shuttled about five or six times in this way, first poisoned and then cured from poison, he remained alive', claimed Mme de Sévigné. Despite confessing all to her judges, Mme de Brinvilliers was put to 'la question ordinaire et extraordinaire à l'eau'. This was a most unpleasant form of torture which involved filling the stomach full to bursting with water, while leaving no external marks.

According to Mme de Sévigné, writing to her daughter in May 1676, in Paris at that time 'people are talking of nothing but the speeches and doings of the Brinvilliers woman ... everywhere we ask for details of what she says, what she does, what she eats, and how she sleeps'. Two months later La Brinvilliers was led to the scaffold at Notre-Dame, and the executioner cut off her head with a single blow of the axe – the merciful treatment accorded a noblewoman. Sévigné reported, almost with flippancy:

> Well, it's all over and done with, La Brinvilliers is in the air; her poor little body was thrown, after the execution, into a great big fire, and the cinders to the wind, such that we will breathe her in and, by the little spirits communicating through the air, some poisoned humour will take us all ...

Indeed, the 'Affaire des Poisons' was far from over. The trial and execution of Mme de Brinvilliers were soon to be seen as no more than an essential prologue to the sentences passed from 1679 to 1682.

Revelations derived from the Brinvilliers case set in motion a chain of investigations under the aegis of Louis' able chief of police in Paris, Nicolas-Gabriel de La Reynie, who established a Chambre Ardente especially to deal with the fresh poisoning charges. In March 1679, a woman called Mme Voisin was arrested, and was soon disclosing that she had been approached by the Duchesse de Bouillon 'for a little poison to kill off an old husband who is killing her with boredom'. The Comtesse de Soissons had asked Mme Voisin if she 'could bring back a lover who had left her'. Here there opened a whole new avenue of investigation – the supply of love-philtres, *cantharides* (also known as 'Spanish fly'). One name after another surfaced during these interrogations, and thus it was that between 7 April 1679 and 8 April 1682 there were no fewer than 210 interrogations before the Chambre Ardente, which decreed the arrest of 319 people, of whom 218 were incarcerated and interrogated a total of 865 times. Eighty-eight of these were brought to justice, leaving more than a hundred still to be judged when the business was brought to an abrupt halt.

One of the defendants who gave important evidence under duress was an unsavoury-sounding priest, the Abbé Guibourg, sacristan of Saint-Marcel Church in Saint-Denis, sixty years old, physically deformed and blind in one eye, who was a friend and accomplice of Mme Voisin. He admitted to having provided false certificates of marriage and to having passed books, love-powders, cards and dice 'under the chalice' during Mass. He described in repugnant detail how he had performed a Black Mass on several occasions – once on the belly of a woman on the ramparts of Saint-Denis, at two o'clock in the morning, with the apparent intention of invoking the devil 'in order to make a pact with him'. At her own trial the judge asked the Duchesse de Bouillon whether she had seen the devil and if so what he was like. She replied with spirit, 'Small, dark and ugly – just like you!' She was acquitted, but was then banished to the provinces.

A long procession of women of lesser rank went to the stake to be burned alive as witches. Finally, there arrived the day of execution of La Voisin herself, burned alive in February 1680 at the Place de Grève. Among an enormous range of confessions under torture, she had admitted to having incinerated more than 2,500 aborted children. On being brought to the stake, Mme Voisin pushed away both the crucifix and the confessor. Mme de Sévigné recorded:

> she was attached to the stake, seated and bound with iron, she was covered with straw. She swore a lot; she pushed back the straw five

or six times; finally the fire started to take, and she was lost from sight, and her ashes are in the air at the present moment.

So much for the death of Mme Voisin, notorious for her crimes and her impiety.

Sévigné went on to add, ominously: 'People believe that there will be greater episodes to follow which will take us by surprise.' Later, however, she corrected herself, predicting cryptically that nothing would now come of it – because 'there is a branch of the poisoning business which one can never reach'.

Indeed, with extraordinary suddenness, further prosecutions were suspended and the work of the Chambre Ardente terminated. Evidence, intertwined with rumour, kept bringing the investigations closer and closer to the King's most intimate entourage. First there were suggestions of a drive against sodomy, highly embarrassing to Monsieur and his circle. But most dangerous of all was the increasing mention of the name of Athénaïs de Montespan. Now thirty-eight, Montespan, to date the longest-reigning of Louis' mistresses and probably the most sexually adept of them all, had come to feel that she was losing way in the King's affections – a feeling reinforced by the arrival of Marie-Adélaïde de Fontanges. To hold him, she had – so it appeared – liberally fed him with aphrodisiacs, or love-philtres. The chief result, however, had been to give the King terrible headaches, which had gravely worried his doctors.

There were darker rumours too. During the latter stages of Mme Voisin's trial, her daughter had alleged that a woman, acting under her mother's orders, had performed many conjurations and ceremonies on behalf of Mme de Montespan, such as burning faggots and reading from a paper the lady's and the King's names. The incantation read:

Faggot, I burn you; it is not you that I am burning, it is the body, the soul, the spirit, the heart and the understanding of Louis de Bourbon, so that he will be able neither to come nor to go, neither to rest nor to sleep until he has done the will of so and so, naming the name of the said lady, and this forever more.

The priest Guibourg also claimed that it was for Montespan that his Black Masses had been said. Young Mlle Voisin went on to describe one occasion when 'a lady was placed naked upon a mattress, with her head hanging down and supported by a pillow on a chair propped upside down, her legs hanging, a napkin on her belly, and on the napkin a cross at the place of the stomach, the chalice on the belly'. The horrible details continued, with allegations of how Voisin's daughter, officiating at a Black Mass for Mme de Montespan, had taken:

> an infant apparently born before term, put him into a basin, cut his throat, spilled the blood into the cup and consecrated the blood with the host, brought the Mass to its finish, and had the entrails of the child taken away; the next day . . . the mother Voisin carried the blood and the host to be distilled into vials of glass which Mme de Montespan took away with her . . .

From this evidence, Montespan was clearly implicated, and indeed was the naked 'lady' at the Black Mass. She was further accused of attempting the murder by poison of Mlle de Fontanges, and even of attempting to murder the King himself by means of a poisoned petition delivered by her accomplice Voisin. All of these charges carried the death penalty. La Reynie's investigation then moved still closer, with the interrogation of Montespan's own sister-in-law, Mme de Vivonne. But Louis could not allow his mistress, a lover to whom he had been publicly attached for thirteen years, and who had been the mother of his legitimated bastards, to be *mis dans le bain* by the Chambre Ardente, tortured like the Marquise de Brinvilliers and the other riff-raff accused. Rather than face any more scandal, in 1682 he ordered Louis Boucherat, presiding over the Chambre Ardente, to put an end to its enquiries. For Louis in his middle years appearances were everything; never mind the unspeakable activities they covered up.

The last execution in the 'Affaire des Poisons', of a humble valet, took place on the Place de Grève in July 1682. Swiftly Louis had the trial proceedings burned. Yet, despite the suspension of the Chambre Ardente's investigations, the scandal continued. When Louvois, Colbert's dour successor, died in July 1691, his son claimed that he had been poisoned. Although the King's intervention had saved her from the possible horrors of 'examination', the reign of the powerful Machiavellian Athénaïs de Montespan was over. For appearance's sake, she was allowed to linger on at court in a marginal role for another ten years. Doubtless this was as much to keep her activities under close watch as for any pleasure of her; then she was bundled off to Saint-Joseph, the convent she had herself founded, where she resided for seventeen more years expiating her sins.

The austerely prim and devout ex-governess (to Mme de Montespan's children, there was the final shaft), Françoise Scarron, otherwise known as Mme de Maintenon, now moved in as the King's mistress – and stayed there for the rest of his reign. Her replacement of Montespan took place at almost the same time as the move to Versailles, and would profoundly affect the style and the mood there, as well as the overall direction of the King's life. Meanwhile, and given the degree of embarrassment which an abandoned Mme de Montespan might have caused the King in Paris, and given the suspicions bandied about in the capital, could it be that Louis XIV's escape to Versailles had an added immediacy directly linked to the scandal, the worst that was to rock Paris in the whole reign? It gave him every good reason to want to wash his hands of the whole affair, and move his entourage out to the wholesome pure air of Versailles.

DEPARTURE FOR VERSAILLES

On 6 May 1682, Louis XIV abandoned Paris for Versailles. It was slightly less than a century after his grandfather had fought so hard to gain mastery of his capital. That was the day Louis made the official announcement that, henceforth, the seat of the French government would be out at his former hunting-lodge, Versailles, twenty kilometres removed from the Louvre. In Nancy Mitford's words:

> [Louis] arrived there with some pomp, accompanied by his family, his ministers and the whole Court. The Court of France for ever in the country! The fashionable world was filled with dismay now that the long-expected blow had fallen. Not all the criticism was frivolous, however. For years Colbert had begged his master to abandon the project, for the obvious administrative reasons ...

The house was still far from ready, but the King – like any sensible houseowner – thought he would never get the workmen out unless he moved in himself. Jules Hardouin-Mansart was still at work finishing the Galerie des Glaces.

The rest of the accommodation, to provide lodgings for between 2,000 and 5,000 people, was austere to say the least. In many cases rooms had been chopped up into tiny units with no regard for the imposing façade, giving on to dismal little interior wells. But at least the

King himself and his descendants could feel safe there. Although they were virtually unguarded, over the coming century there would be only one half-hearted attempt at assassination.

Aged forty-four in 1682, Louis was at the peak of his powers. In 1661 his queen Maria Theresa had presented him with a son and heir, the Grand Dauphin, who showed promise of becoming a sound ruler and who in turn, later in that year of the move to Versailles, produced an heir, the Duc de Bourgogne. As we have seen, the King's mistresses, the Duchesse de La Vallière and the Marquise de Montespan, had provided a clutch of further children, several of whom had been legitimized. Thus the succession to the throne of France, only recently so shaky, now seemed assured. The King's own health was excellent; the territory of France seemed at last secure from external foes; and the nation seemed, rarely and miraculously, at peace with herself. Much of the work of Henri IV appeared to have reached fruition. His grandson could now, with some justification, call himself Louis le Grand (the title which the municipality of Paris had unctuously bestowed on him in 1678) and the Roi Soleil. He could afford a little personal extravagance in building a new country seat, but what had decided him to pull out of the capital for which Henri of Navarre had fought so ardently?

Like many of his Valois forebears, including François I, Louis preferred country to town. Already by 1665 he had taken to spending one day a week out at his father's modest hunting-lodge in the woodlands of Versailles. Yet it was not so much *la chasse* that drew him as peace and tranquillity; he needed space. And this was something rooted in the experiences of his early years, in his love of order in all things, as well as in the nature of Paris. Frankly, he disliked Paris; from 1670 until the end of his reign, he would grace the city with his presence only twenty-five times. But his hostility, and his move to Versailles, did Paris only limited harm. In the course of his long reign, the capital still managed to flourish.

8

A Building Boom

Let no one speak to me of anything small.

Bernini to Louis XIV, in 1665

COLBERT

The Fronde, the trial of Fouquet and the various 'Affaires des Poisons' had all been significant milestones on Louis XIV's road to Versailles, as he made his escape from his reasoned fear of plots against his person, as well as from the gossip that seethed in his turbulent capital. But what of his very considerable accomplishments in the city he was about to abandon? What was built, what was changed and what was destroyed during the first half of Louis' reign which ended with his decampment for Versailles in 1682?

By the end of his first ten years of personal rule, Louis XIV had launched what had been a virtually bankrupt country on a course of remarkable prosperity. Both in Paris and at Versailles his ambitious building programme from the 1660s onwards was predicated on three factors: the continuation of peace (or, at least, involvement in wars for the pursuit of *la Gloire* that could be won with little effort or expense); the brilliant policies of the man who succeeded the disgraced Fouquet, Jean-Baptiste Colbert; and the extraordinary inherited and inherent wealth of the country at large. Colbert was already forty-one when appointed assistant to Fouquet in 1661. His capacity for ruthlessness was displayed in the destruction of his boss; he was a teetotaller, icily cold and humourless, earning the nickname of the 'Man of Marble' or 'le Nord' (Mme de Sévigné's sobriquet). Of him the venerable Mazarin, in whose employ Colbert's career had started, was alleged to have said to the King shortly before his death, 'Sire, I owe you everything, but I believe I can repay some of my debt by giving you Colbert.' In fact it was a debt that he thereby discharged fully, and with interest.

A worthy successor to Sully, and in contrast to Fouquet, Colbert was immaculately honest. Into the administration of French finances he introduced a new precision and order, and was almost unique among Louis' sycophantic entourage in being able to confront the King over his extravagances and the use, or abuse, of royal power. After Mazarin and Fouquet, Louis would permit no one near him with the power of a prime minister; yet Colbert's influence over his two decades in office came to reach areas far beyond that of a superintendent of finance, not least in the centralization of the nation, France, upon the capital, Paris. Thanks to his early financial reforms, he rapidly achieved a surplus of receipts over expenditure. Nevertheless, and until the mid-eighteenth century, a large share of state revenue still came via such archaic practices, widely open to graft and sleaze, as the sale of offices and allowing 'tax farmers' to take their substantial cut of the revenue gleaned.

Under Colbert's regime, a kind of industrial revolution swept the country. Shipbuilding developed; the army was modernized and expanded; mines, foundries, mills and refineries thrived, as did the wool trade on the back of such prestige industries as Savonnerie carpets and France's superlative Gobelin tapestries. France, emulating the serious side of her pleasure-loving king, went earnestly to work; as Louis advised the heir who was never to succeed, 'Never forget that it is by work that a king rules.' The building boom in Paris was but one aspect of Colbert's far-reaching influence. When his restraining hand was removed from the treasury by death in 1683, it reinforced the impact on Paris of Louis' departure for Versailles.

While Paris expanded dramatically, becoming a city of 400,000, the rural population if anything declined. The seventeenth century was mostly a time of hardship and recession for the French peasantry; the weather was capricious, producing frequent years of terrible harvests, and agriculture had not matched the advances being achieved in England. In a bad year a village could easily lose between 10 and 20 per cent of its population. The price of land was such that the purchase of a holding large enough to support one family might cost a labourer the equivalent of a century's wages. Moreover, the peasantry found itself exploited, parasitically, by the state, the Church, landlords and bureaucrats alike. There were occasional popular revolts against taxation, and regular bread riots in provincial towns, yet because of the centralized power of Paris under the absolute monarchy they were never permitted to amount to anything – at least not for another hundred years. Paris and the provinces would continue to look at each other with mutual dislike, disdain and distrust.

One of the first projects in Paris to receive the attention of Colbert (in 1664 he had also become superintendent of buildings) was the construction of the Collège des Quatre Nations. For this purpose Mazarin had left in his will two million livres, earmarked to provide a Parisian education for sixty boys from the provinces. To find room for the Collège, the old Tour de Nesle from the time of Philippe le Bel, dominating as it did the Left Bank of the Seine, was demolished in 1663. In its place rose a superb piece of baroque designed by Le Vau, with the most magnificent library in Paris – later to become the home of the Académie Française (see p. 112). Appropriate to the origins of its benefactor, its curved façade – embracing an elliptical church within – was surmounted by a typically Italianate dome, which made it something rare in a city of square squares.

A far more daunting project, however, was the completion of the Louvre – that hardy perennial which claimed the resources of many rulers both before and after Louis. In 1661 fire had ravaged part of it, and Le Vau had been brought in to undertake restoration, with Le Brun painting his extravagant frescoes depicting the triumph of the chariot of Apollo, in a pointed and grandiose compliment to the Roi Soleil. The main priority was the construction of a grand façade to crown the courtyard to the east, the Cour Carrée of François I, more or less completed by 1659. Louis had his own very clear ideas on architecture, and placed a strong emphasis on the classical. So he invited from Rome Gian-Lorenzo Bernini whose Piazza of Saint Peter's had established him as the most famous architect of his day.

Aged sixty-six, Bernini brought with him all the arrogance of an Italian of the High Renaissance. Employing what was his idea of flattery, he told the most powerful king in Europe, 'inasmuch as you have not seen the buildings of Italy you have remarkably good taste'. At their first meeting in Saint-Germain, he said to Louis, 'I have seen, Sire, palaces of emperors and popes ... from Rome to Paris. But for a king of France ... we must construct something more magnificent ... Let no one speak to me of anything small!' This last was the kind of talk that appealed to Louis, and initially Bernini got on surprisingly well with him. Louis sat for him no fewer than thirteen times to produce the outstanding bust, probably the best likeness of the Roi Soleil ever achieved, which now graces Versailles.

But Bernini the architect was a different story. He contemptuously swept aside the sketches of his leading French contemporaries, terminating any argument by repeatedly quoting Michelangelo as the ultimate arbiter of good taste. His initial plans had to be modified, because the terraces and meridional flat roofs would not withstand the rain and snow of a Paris winter; the high pitches of the roofing genius François Mansart (great-uncle of the Louvre architect Hardouin-Mansart) were more suitable. Already, under construction just across the river, there was an example of glorious baroque in the shape of Le Vau's Collège des Quatre Nations. Not all the Paris establishment was enamoured of it, but Bernini was encouraged. For the Louvre he came up with an even grander baroque façade of imposing convex arcs. But it involved demolishing houses to the east, and crowding in upon the antique Church of Saint-Germain-l'Auxerrois, much beloved by Parisians. And the ever practical Colbert wondered where the servants would sleep, and how food was to be brought from the kitchens.

After a six-month sojourn, during which he modified his 'projects' for the Louvre several times and managed to offend almost everybody, Bernini was sent home laden with money, and his plans were discreetly dropped. Louis thought them just too florid for France's sober northern clime. In any case, his brief attention span was already beginning to switch to schemes for Versailles. Instead of the Italian, Claude Perrault was brought in to design a classical storeyed building with the façade of a great Roman temple imposed on it. Perrault, brother of the writer Charles, was by profession a doctor (described as spending his spare time in the dissection of camels), an amateur rather than a professional architect who had never designed a building in his life before. Nevertheless, his plans were at least as ambitious as Bernini's had been. For the façade's massive central pediment, topping a majestic colonnade of fifty-two tall Corinthian pillars, Perrault selected two immense monolithic blocks from the quarries in nearby Meudon. Each of these, around twenty metres long and nearly three metres in height, weighed so much that to hoist them in position a special machine on rollers had to be constructed – not unlike the methods used by the ancient Eygptians to build the pyramids.

Begun in 1667 and completed three years later, the massive façade introduced on to the Paris landscape the 'colossal' style of classical purism which was to be emulated by Napoleon with his construction of the Madeleine and its counterpart, the Chamber of Deputies, one and a half centuries later. It represented a complete break with the traditions of French architecture since Henri IV. But, as Louis' interest shifted, so the interior of the Louvre remained unfinished, embraced by scaffolding until 1755 – just in time for the Revolution. By then Perrault's grand façade had lost its point, as the whole centre of gravity of the city had moved westwards, to the Tuileries Palace and, beyond, to what was to become the Concorde. The edifice which had been so grandly conceived as an imposing front was to be left high and dry as little more than a glorified tradesmen's entrance, huddled about by insignificant houses. Between 1667 and 1680 Perrault went on to work at the long southern façade of the Louvre that bordered the Seine.

With Louis' departure for Versailles and his accompanying switch of interests, the Louvre fell on hard times. Between 1670 and 1672 the sum earmarked for expenditure on the palace fell by 80 per cent. The great building came to house a miscellany of temporary occupants. First there were artists setting up their studios in the deserted galleries, together with their hangers-on. Then came a diversity of dealers, prostitutes included, building shacks within the precincts, and stabling their horses in the Cour Carrée. Some of the squatters made off with panelling and pictures, and progressively the palace was allowed to fall into disrepair. Over the years of neglect the Louvre was also used as a granary and a printing works. By 1750, its state had become so bad that demolition was considered; there were suggestions of installing an opera or a royal library there, but all such projects ran aground on the rocks of finance. It was a sorry plight for so historic a building, on which such grandiose efforts had been lavished over the ages; and the Roi Soleil has much to answer for here. Finally the Convention, in 1793, with one of its few sensible decrees, saved the Louvre by opening the Grande Galerie to exhibit choice artefacts from the royal collections of the fallen monarch – including the *Mona Lisa*. But the Louvre had to wait for Napoleon before its salvation was assured.

THE BOULEVARDS AND THE DEVELOPING ARCHITECTURE

With the defeat of the Fronde, continuing peace and security at large had seemed to remove all direct military threat to Paris, and this now led Louis to undertake a still more sweeping alteration to the face of the city. With its population now bursting out of the confines of the old crumbling walls of Philippe Auguste and Charles V (which had become the dumping ground for all sorts of city rubbish and ordure), Louis decreed the levelling of the existing ramparts. In their place, he laid out long and straight promenades which came to be known as 'boulevards' – a corruption of the German word *Bollwerk*, meaning a bulwark or rampart. Agreeably lined with shady trees, the *grands boulevards* from their earliest days became favourite places of promenade, while wealthy Parisians built stately houses looking out on to them. The greatest of all the boulevards, of course, was the new Champs-Elysées, laid out by Le Nôtre – who had been 'liberated' from Vaux-le-Vicomte following the demise of Fouquet – from 1667 onwards. While it presented a magnificent vista leading to the Tuileries Palace, Le Nôtre's inspired work further shifted the centre of gravity of the Louvre westwards, and away from Perrault's grand façade.

Next, begun in 1671 (though not completed till the last years of Louis' reign, when military triumphs were wearing a bit thin), came the monumental edifice of the Hôtel des Invalides on the Left Bank, eventually topped by Jules Hardouin-Mansart's great dome.* At more than 100 metres high, it dwarfed Le Vau's dome for Mazarin's Collège upstream, and was the very apotheosis of baroque in Paris. Designed, generously, to house the old soldiers who would survive the wars that Louis was planning, construction of the Invalides was, uniquely, funded out of the army budget (indicating how much Louis was prepared to make available for military ventures). With its long avenues radiating out in all directions, which would find echoes in Versailles, the Invalides presented Parisians with the most exciting perspective yet seen in the city. Decorated only with helmets, prancing horses and other military para-

---

* Its restoration in 1934 required 250 tonnes of lead roofing, and 360,000 sheets of gold leaf.

phernalia, its rather austere frontage, 210 metres long, was a masterpiece of classical grandeur. The complex centres on Mansart's magnificent church, which in 1840 became the final resting place of France's greatest soldier, Napoleon.

Louis' *anciens combattants* were not entirely happy with the Invalides; they chafed at the harsh military discipline maintained there – not least the regulation that, if caught *in flagrante* with a woman of the town, the veteran and his lover were to be exposed together, much to the delight of the Parisians. When complaints about the soup escalated into a full-scale riot, Colbert's brutal successor, the Marquis de Louvois, did not hesitate to call in a firing squad.

Though the Invalides was built to house up to 7,000 pensioners, the last was admitted before the First World War, and since then it has housed various army offices and museums. In the aftermath of the First World War, captured Krupp cannon stood proudly in front of the façade; after the Second World War, these were replaced by two German Panzer tanks – until the new *entente cordiale* with the eastern neighbour prescribed their discreet withdrawal into the appropriate museum.

Among the other grand churches worked on in Louis' first flurry of construction in Paris was the displeasingly hideous Saint-Sulpice (just north of the Luxembourg Palace), with its seemingly incomplete and asymmetrical eggcup towers (for Victor Hugo, they evoked two enormous clarinets). As with other major churches, including Saint-Roch (a little north of the Louvre), work was suspended after the move to Versailles and not recommenced until the next century.

In 1671, as the last in a series of similar academies created by Mazarin and Colbert, the Académie Royale d'Architecture was founded, its first director François Blondel. A passionate enthusiast for the ancient, classical tradition (Palladio was one of his heroes), Blondel fortuitously praised Louis as a king who had at last given Parisian architects the opportunity to build enduring monuments that could compete with those of ancient times and that would enhance the reputation of the ruler. Thus, declared Blondel to his captive students, 'will architecture, restored by the French, appear in all its brilliance and all its glory'. Henceforth *la Gloire* and sheer *spectacle* were to be embraced as essential components of the style of the grander Parisian buildings.

Under Blondel, reinforced by the King's patronage and the new wealth of the era, an unprecedented classical harmony prevailed, offering uniformity and even standardization. Strict rules were laid down:

private dwellings had to be built of stone, instead of the fire-prone timber frames and lath and plaster of earlier ages;* they were forbidden by law to have first floors bulging out over the street, where carriages might collide with them; frontages could be no more than eight toises (15.6 metres) high; staircases were moved from the centre to the side, and kitchens transplanted from the wings to separate structures in the courtyard. Straight lines became the norm, irregular tiled roofs being replaced by a single roof of grey slate or lead. More ornate interiors were counterpointed by sober simplicity in exterior design.

External modesty was also a feature of the grand *hôtels particuliers* of the epoch (and indeed of later ones), where extensive private gardens and displays of conspicuous consumption within lay concealed from public gaze behind a sombre *porte-cochère* which gave on to the street. Typical of the finest of these is Mme de Sévigné's in the Marais, now the home of the Carnavalet Museum; only a little less grand was the Rue des Tournelles mansion built by Jules Mansart for Ninon de Lenclos. The Grand Siècle was to be also the age of the emancipation of the French bourgeoisie; Louis needed the money with which they had managed to enrich themselves. Perhaps as a consequence of the days of the Fronde, or of their own shady dealings, the Paris *financiers* had become obsessed by their own security. Affluent Paris was to become, and remain, a city as secret as any North African casbah. Meanwhile, over a relatively short space of time, a significant step had been taken towards the monochrome Paris of the nineteenth century. As was later remarked, Louis XIV inherited a city of brick and left it marble. But, with the disappearance of the warm brickwork panels of Henri IV and Louis XIII, as the Place Royale gave way to the bourgeois vulgarity of Vaux-le-Vicomte, architecturally what was gained did not always compensate for what was lost – at any rate in terms of colour and texture.

---

* The catastrophic Fire of London in 1666 had delivered a message well heeded by Colbert's and Louis' town-planners.

CLEANING UP

All the time the wealthy *financiers* and their mansions were moving steadily westwards away from the compressed and smelly confines of the Marais. Instead, new *faubourgs* like Saint-Germain were opening up to smart, bourgeois Paris. In terms of salubrity, the old centre of Paris had not come all that far from the stink and the plagues of black flies of the days of Philippe Auguste. As one of his last contributions to the city he was abandoning, in 1680 Louis – appalled by its 'thousand intolerable stenches' – petitioned to have water closets installed in the Louvre. During those years when building enthusiasm reigned, main thorough-fares were paved and streets were widened.

Colbert was to go down in the history of Paris as the city's 'greatest urbanist', second only to Louis Napoleon's Baron Haussmann. But Colbert's truly remarkable accomplishment was that his modernizing was carried out without the brutal demolitions of Haussmann which so ravaged the old Paris. Colbert dreamed of creating 'a new Rome' of obelisks, triumphal arches, a new royal palace – and a pyramid (at the western end of the Louvre, more than two centuries before I. M. Pei conceived his structure). Yet they were never completed. Apart from the odd Italianate domes of the Invalides, the Collège de France and the Church of Val-de-Grâce, in its overall aspect seventeenth-century Paris remained by and large a city of gothic spires. In the words of the great twentieth-century songster of the Seine, Charles Trenet, under Colbert 'Paris reste Paris.' Colbert deplored the expenditure on Versailles, which he regarded as 'an isolated, rural château', in no way fit for the headquarters of Europe's greatest king, and a distraction from the rebuilding of Paris. But one year after Louis' move to Versailles, Colbert was dead.

Foremost of the problems confronting Colbert were Paris's endemic, and linked, problems of drains and the provision of pure drinking water. Right in the heart of the city, the ancient Île de la Cité had no sewers, and its sewage flowed directly into the Seine through open gutters. Just opposite, on the Right Bank, up to 1666 butchers were still heaping all the slaughterhouse waste into the river; tanners and dyers continued to dump their evil-smelling effluents off the Quai de la Mégisserie; while from the new Île Saint-Louis' Pont Marie the scraps left by the poultry-dealers caused the area to be known as the 'Vallée de la Misère'.

Colbert issued every sort of ordinance banning the dumping of excrement on ramparts and in moats, and forbidding pollution of the Seine. Citizens were encouraged to report offenders, and personally bring them to jail. By 1676, a handsome new quay with a roadway eight metres wide had been constructed between the Louvre and the Saint-Antoine quarter to the east, thus clearing out an area of maximum pollution. Offending enterprises were relocated to the suburbs. But these efforts met with traditional resistance, with some of the tanneries and dyers moving upstream, so pollution was still preoccupying Parlement in 1697. To 'embellish the River Seine', in 1676, Louis had imported a large flock of white swans, but they took one look and flew back to their native Rouen. More successfully, many kilometres of covered sewer were installed under Colbert's orders, and fifteen new fountains brought pure water from safe sources twenty-five kilometres outside the city via the imposing new Aqueduct of Arcueil.

At the time of Louis' triumphal entry in 1660, there was no street lighting in Paris, apart from the odd lantern here and there. This made it by night, in the words of the critic Nicolas Boileau, more dangerous than a dark wood, and few law-abiding citizens would venture out after dark. Art students from the Academy were reluctant to return to their lodgings after 7 p.m. in winter, for fear of falling into the hands of armed bands. In 1667 Louis appointed Nicolas-Gabriel de La Reynie as chief of police, the first to hold this new office which removed responsibility for the policing of Paris from the hands of the city magistrates.* La Reynie, the closest thing to a mayor Paris had yet had, was an unqualified success, filling the job for over thirty years (he was later a central figure in the 'Affaire de Poisons': see Chapter 7). One of his first tasks was to provide Paris with a comprehensive system of street lighting, so that by the end of the seventeenth century the city could boast a total of 6,500 lamps on public streets. These consisted of groups of candles in a lantern, each one lit at dusk and burning till the small hours. Lighting up must have been a Herculean task. A visiting English doctor called Martin Lister noted heavy penalties meted out to any youth breaking the lanterns as a prank: 'he is sent forthwith to the Gallies; and there

---

*Under the regime of Louis XIV the all-embracing term 'police' meant much more; it covered, in effect, the whole civil administration of the city; thus La Reynie was in charge not only of law and order, but also of health and sanitation.

were three young Gentlemen of good Families who were in Prison for having done it in a Frolick . . .'

Lister was highly impressed by Louis' and La Reynie's achievements (in London, a parsimonious administration lit the lamps only on moonless nights), and soon every city in Europe would follow suit. Hand in hand with illumination, naturally, went fire precautions, and La Reynie also provided Paris with a fire-service, forerunners of the *sapeurs pompiers*. Although, initially, it relied on buckets, by the end of the century it was able to use a portable pump designed by an actor, François Dumouriez de Perier.

LOW LIFE AND HIGH LIFE

In 1673, Louis struck a medal to celebrate the triumph of the capital over crime. It may have been somewhat premature, but La Reynie's contributions to law and order, as well as to health, had already been quite breathtaking. When he took over, he found that – in the aftermath of the Fronde – the Châtelet, hitherto responsible for law and order, had fallen into a state of total decay. Whole sectors of the city were no-go areas ruled by thugs and armed beggars, or even by gangs of lackeys working for the affluent which lay in wait for unwary students. In the eleven *cours des miracles*, or ghettos – marginal quarters like that near the Church of Saint-Martin des Champs, Rue Saint-Honoré, Faubourg Saint-Marcel, Faubourg Saint-Germain and church of Saint-Roch – the guard (*le guet*) did not dare to enter. For the year 1642 alone, 342 murders took place during night hours on the streets of Paris, while in the aftermath of the Fronde social ills became much worse.

La Reynie strengthened the police force and brought in a range of new laws and ordinances to quell street violence in the city. There was a ban on bearing weapons at night, which even applied to 'men of quality' unless they had lanterns to make themselves readily identifiable; 'valets' were not even allowed to carry a baton or a stick. It was also forbidden to take arms into theatres (always places of potential disorder) or to gather outside in disorderly assemblies. Duelling was banned once again; beggars and vagabonds were ordered to leave the city by a certain deadline. Under La Reynie and his equally effective successor d'Argenson, there was an extensive codification of criminal and civil law the like of which would not be seen again until Napoleon.

For those sentenced to death, hanging was the normal mode of execution – except for nobles, who were still entitled to be beheaded; this privilege remained on the statute books until, as one historian puts it, in the 1790s 'French revolutionary terrorists extended that privilege to everyone'. As the fates of the wretched Brinvilliers and Voisin demonstrated, torture and burning at the stake were penalties still reserved for offenders such as poisoners. (Often the death sentence included a 'retentum', a secret provision for the executioner to strangle the condemned as he attached him to the stake – described as an *adoucissement* of the sentence.) Even in the years of the eighteenth-century Enlightenment, rascals like the engaging serial brigand Cartouche would be broken on the wheel, a hideous fate which he faced with exemplary courage; while his young nephew, sentenced to be suspended by his wrists for two hours on the Place de Grève, died in agony as onlookers mocked.

For less serious offences, there were the galleys – an archaic and harsh form of punishment that also provided the backbone of the French navy well after Louis XIV. Meanwhile, the much feared Bastille, where the average stay during Louis' reign was about sixteen months, had graduated into something like a luxury home for the rich in trouble. There some of the residents' 'rooms' resembled those in a good hotel. As early as 1670, prisoners were allowed to hang tapestries on the walls and to carpet the floor; in 1684 Louis donated a lending library to it. To be in the Bastille was no great shame, the identities of its inmates protected with the kind of secrecy to which Parisians attached so much importance. Regarded as a much worse fate, in the event of royal disfavour, was the terrible sentence of exile from Paris (later, from Versailles) to the miscreant's country estates, there to die of lingering boredom – the most dreadful condemnation for any Frenchman. Still worse, prostitutes would often be transhipped to the colonies, to Canada or Louisiana, to expiate their sins by incrementing the settlers' birthrate. Such was the immortalized end of Manon Lescaut, exiled to die in the unspeakable desert of Biloxi.

As with most urban societies, in the Paris of Louis XIV crime was closely linked with poverty. On the one hand, La Reynie strove, with some harshness, to get beggars and the poor in general off the streets and out of town. On the other hand, the compassionate side of Louis XIV led him to spend heavily on hospitals for the poor. The famous

Salpêtrière, once an arsenal on the eastern outskirts of Paris, now in the 13th arrondissement close to the Gare d'Austerlitz and still one of Paris's major hospitals, was one of his creations, initially filled with beggars, paupers and down-and-outs. Built around a magnificent basilica designed by the architect of the Invalides, Libéral Bruant, the Salpêtrière had the lofty objective of providing a charitable institution where 'all the poor would be gathered on clean premises, so as to be tended to, be educated and given an occupation'. Alas, these good intentions swiftly evaporated after 1682 as Louis left Paris and lost interest. The hospital failed to become economically viable, and could offer accommodation for only a fraction of the mendicant population, which was constantly augmented by beggars from the countryside. Appallingly overcrowded (at one time it had 10,000 inmates), the Salpêtrière also became a prison for prostitutes, and later, in the eighteenth century, it became Paris's principal lunatic asylum, a particularly dreadful place where the mentally deranged were chained to the walls. In September 1792, revolutionaries from the Faubourg Saint-Marcel set forth with the noble intent of liberating the prostitutes; but liquor got the better of them and instead they dragged out on to the street forty-five wretched madwomen and massacred them in a pointless orgy of killing.

Occasionally grain crises afflicted the country at large, and in the early 1660s Colbert found himself forced to import food from as far off as Poland. As always, in Paris it was the poor who came off worst. Vast quantities of free grain, *le blé du roi*, were distributed, with Louis even selling bread through the wall that surrounded the Tuileries Palace in order to break an alleged monopoly by the Parisian bakers. Fortunately for the capital, there were no food crises on a similar scale during the remaining years of the century, but hunger was never far removed for the city's underprivileged.

The observant Englishman Dr Lister, though not greatly concerned with the lot of 'the common people', noted that during Lent they 'feed much on White Kidney Beans' (presumably a kind of flageolet) which he had never come across in England, but with which he was 'well pleased'. Otherwise he found the average Parisian diet to consist chiefly of 'Bread and Herbs', the bread much coarser than country bread, supplemented by large quantities of red onions, garlic and sorrel. He added that Parisians 'delight in nothing so much as mushrooms', which he found grown liberally in fields in what is now the Rue de Vaugirard on the Left Bank. Paris introduced him to the *morille*, 'The first of that kind of Mushroom, that I remember ever to have seen'. But, always the good practitioner, he warned that many visitors fell sick from eating the wrong kind of mushroom: 'a sudden shortness of breath, and sometimes Vomitings, or went off in a Diarrhoea or Dysentery'. Most surprising is the variety of wines he found imported from considerable distances. Lister regularly drank wine from Languedoc, and even from Spain and Italy; he esteemed the 'Vin de Bonne' (Beaune), but considered both the red and white Saint-Laurence from southern Provence to be 'the most delicious Wine I have ever tasted in my life'.

Like contemporary Londoners, Parisians indulged a great deal in coffee, sugar, tea and chocolate. Perhaps not unexpectedly, Lister recorded how – compared with his earlier visits – Parisians 'are strangely altered in their Constitutions and Habit of Body; from lean and slender, they are become fat and corpulent, the Women especially: Which, in my Opinion, can proceed from nothing so much as the daily drinking of strong Liquors'. The King himself was said to have a gargantuan appetite. Though he eschewed chocolate, tea and coffee (in 1711 the death of one of the royal princesses was blamed on coffee), he had 'often' been observed to polish off 'four full dishes of different soups, an entire pheasant, a partridge, a large plate of salad, two large slices of ham, mutton in gravy and garlic, a plate of pastries and then, in addition, fruit and hard-boiled eggs'.

The table manners displayed by the Parisian bourgeois under Louis XIV, which generally reflected those of the court, are illuminatingly set out in a book dated 1671 by Antoine de Courtin, *Nouveau Traité de la civilité qui se pratique en France parmi les honnêtes gens*. During meals the men kept on their swords, cloaks and plumed hats (except when rising for the grace, and they were expected to doff their hats and bow each time Madame, the hostess, passed a plate). This must have been extremely inconvenient. Although the fork had been introduced into *la haute société* around 1600, it had not become universally accepted among the bourgeoisie; in *Le Bourgeois Gentilhomme*, Molière's popular satire on the vanity of the Parisian *nouveaux riches*, the rascally Comte Dorante mocks Mme la Marquise for serving the pretentious bourgeois M. Jourdain with her fingers. According to de Courtin it was proper etiquette to eat olives with a spoon rather than a fork; and oranges (which were served with the joint) had to be sliced sideways, not like an apple. 'There's nothing of worse breeding', he decreed, 'than to lick your fingers, your knife, your spoon or your fork; and nothing more unattractive than to clean and wipe the plate with your fingers' – unless it be 'to blow your nose on your napkin'. Most degrading of all, though, was to be caught 'trying to make off with fruit in your napkin, or your pocket, from the table of a person you wish to honour'. On the other hand, it was good form to sing with the dessert.

Thus, concludes the historian Georges Mongrédien in his engaging *La Vie quotidienne sous Louis XIV*, 'the most delicate nuances of courtesy mingled with the most slovenly behaviour'. This was the world in which the Galerie des Glaces and the fountains of Versailles coexisted with the open sewers of the Île de la Cité. So the *bon bourgeois* of seventeenth-century Paris could 'show that he belonged to a highly sophisticated social world, but one which had not yet succeeded in developing hygiene and comfort'.

CULTURE

The sense of security that the reign of Louis XIV brought allowed Parisians to enjoy their leisure. Apart from the periodic grand *spectacles* that were guaranteed to engage and distract, there was time to watch or to participate in games. Predecessor of our modern tennis, the *jeu de paume* – greatly favoured by the King – became immensely popular, with no fewer than 114 courts springing up in Paris. Less testing were skittles, *le mail* (which was to evolve into croquet); for women, there was shuttlecock. Above all, gambling – notably at Versailles – became all the rage. Harmless family entertainments such as *trictrac* and dominoes graduated into games like *piquet, lansquenet, pharaon* and *hoca* played for serious money. On Christmas Day 1678 (according to Mme de Sévigné), Mme de Montespan, the reigning mistress, lost 700,000 écus; on another occasion she lost 400,000 pistoles to the bank – but, possibly with the connivance of the banker, was able to win it all back. Inciting the court to take part in lotteries, Louis was all for gambling of every kind; the opiate of the nobles, it was one very simple way of 'domesticating' or taming them.

For a distraction, however, which many could take part in and enjoy, there was nothing quite to compare with the theatre or the opera. A flourishing of the arts usually requires a set of special conditions, rather as a pearl does. Could Shakespeare have produced what he did without the immense self-assurance of the Elizabethan world scene? The age of

Louis – at least in its earlier, pre-Versailles days – was also the age of
Racine, Molière and Boileau, and of Lully and Couperin. Possibly the
sombre tragedies of Racine could have flourished in the times of Henri
IV and Louis XIII, but almost certainly it required the sureties of the
reign of the Roi Soleil for a Molière to make such mock of human
frailties, manners and mannerisms. Could such hilarious farces, which
so effectively flayed contemporary social affectations, have been performed at any earlier time in French history? Would the *Fables* of La
Fontaine, with all their taunting scepticism, have fallen on such fertile
ground in previous ages? And what about the biting wit of La Rochefoucauld and his *Maxims*? Could they have appealed without the scepticism
which swept France in the wake of the religious wars of the previous
century – and which would form an important part of the philosophic
backdrop to 1789?

As in many things, the taste for the theatre filtered down from the
King, his passion for the stage – and his personal involvement in it –
rivalled only by his love for building. By the end of the seventeenth
century, it was reckoned that the Comédie Française could count
between 10,000 and 17,000 regular patrons. Educated women like Mme
de Sévigné would have gone to see every new piece as it appeared on
the boards, ten to twelve times a year (her *Letters* are peppered with
repeated allusions to contemporary drama). And so would the rowdy
denizens of the pit, the *parterre*, paying their few sous for the privilege
of standing in great discomfort – and sometimes danger – to whom even
the great Molière always had the adroitness to address his shafts.

The sizzling excitement of the theatre in Louis' Paris was not
confined to the stage, with the hubbub in the *parterres* regularly drowning out the players' lines. The early theatres of Paris were long and
narrow – like the tennis courts they moved into – and candle-lit, so that
there was not much division between audience and players, with the
former often leaping on to the stage. There were hilarious scenes straight
out of *opéra bouffe* when members of the cast had to make hurried and
undignified escapes from angry fans. Violence was never far off, with
the police frequently called in to restore order between rival claques.
On more than one occasion the King himself had to intervene to stop
audiences whistling at the actors. In 1668, even at Molière's theatre,
favoured with royal protection and the title of the Troupe du Roi, a body
of soldiery, who had tried to gain entry without paying, in a fury killed
the unfortunate doorkeeper with repeated sword-thrusts – even after
he had unbuckled and thrown them his own weapon. The cast were

threatened with the same fate, until the actor Béjart – made up as an old man for the play – mounted the stage and pleaded, '*Messieurs*, have pity on a poor old man of seventy-five who has but a few more days to live!'

Louis was the first of France's monarchs to offer consistent support for artists and writers. Though it was not quite sufficient to lure Poussin and Claude Lorrain back to France, patronage rested heavily in his hands, so that Racine was enticed away from the stage to be historiographer royal (as was Boileau, in the same year of 1677) – a distinguished but artistically sterile post which possibly destroyed his immense talent: after *Phèdre* Racine never wrote another tragedy. Molière, on the other hand, benefited greatly from Louis' favour. His company took up residence in Richelieu's old quarters of the Palais Royal, premises they shared with Scaramouche's Comédie Italienne. Here Paris was able to witness the flowering of Molière's wit: in *L'Avare* (about the destructive consequences of the pursuit of riches), *Le Misanthrope* (with its confrontation between coquetry and sincerity taken to excess), *Le Bourgeois Gentilhomme* (an attack on bourgeois pretensions), *Le Malade imaginaire* (which dissected hypochondria and medical quackery), and his most outrageously daring, *Tartuffe* (an assault on religious hypocrisy).

Probably only the King's backing saved Molière from serious trouble over *Tartuffe*, which became the most financially successful of all his works; even so, it was banned for five years, until 1669, and the playwright may have been fortunate not to be around after the rise of Mme de Maintenon and the Revocation of the Edict of Nantes (see Chapter 9). He died in 1673. It was said of him by one of his contemporaries that, rather than provoking belly-laughs, he had the unique knack of making his audience 'rire dans l'âme'. That is probably why he continues to appeal down the ages.

Then there was Jean Baptiste Lully, the ugly Italian – dirty, untidy, coarse, a heavy drinker who later became wholly debauched. But he was the father of French opera, and it was thanks to his genius that it had its first golden age. A typical Lully production, in 1672, would open with the inevitable prologue depicting the Sun (Louis, of course) defeating Envy and the Serpent (Holland, the current enemy). Lully was a dictator in his own realm, but everywhere was the guiding hand of the King. It was Louis himself who selected the dramatist Philippe Quinault to produce the libretti for Lully's operas.

The King's patronage could be patchy, and subject to whim. The great Corneille, for instance, was allowed to die a pauper in 1684, embittered by neglect and failure and by the success of his young rival, Racine. In 1697, the hugely successful Comédie Italienne was arbitrarily suppressed, without warning, after it had lampooned Mme de Maintenon. After this, in 1701, the iron grip of censorship descended on the theatre of Paris, to be reapplied at various times in subsequent French history.

Royal patronage was supplemented by the powerful Parisian ladies who ran influential salons, not least that of Mme de Scudéry. Here, in a house of the Marais, elegant women with pyramid-like headdresses and heavily powdered faces and men in their feathered hats would mount Madeleine de Scudéry's dark staircase every Saturday, to take part in her *ruelles*. One of the most coveted invitations of the epoch, the Scudéry salon cultivated refined conversation to excess, making it a salient and irresistible target for lampooning by Molière (in *Les Précieuses ridicules*). Madeleine herself, an early forebear of today's feminists, was a profilic writer of romantic novels, and several of her fans in the Académie (where she won a prize for eloquence) tried to have the ban on women lifted so that she could join the Immortels.*

Other than the theatre, the one great leisure function most appealing to *Parisiennes* of all ranks through the ages, and particularly at the time of Louis XIV, was the promenade. Lister could note with admiration how the easy turning circle of the carriages designed for the narrow streets also made for a much lower coach box than the English equivalent, thereby making it easier for the passengers to see and be seen. There being, especially compared with contemporary London, very few open green spaces – apart from Henri IV's Place Royale and Place Dauphine – the *promeneurs* all headed for the Tuileries and Marie de Medici's Cour de la Reine, which stretched all the way from the Louvre to the present Place de l'Alma.

Even here, broad as it was – it had a *rond-point* 100 metres wide in which a hundred carriages could easily turn – the thoroughfare could be crowded with an extraordinary density of traffic. Once Lister counted 'near 80 coaches' on the Cours de la Reine. To add to the excitement, into this elegant parade would often mingle *troupeaux* of cattle and sheep on their way to the markets of Les Halles. For Parisians, this great throng offered unmatched opportunities for romantic or more earthy

---

* Popular term for members of the Académie derived from its original seal, which bore the words 'À l'immortalité'.

encounters. For consummation of passing unions thus inaugurated, there was (as in later centuries) always the discreetly leafy Bois de Boulogne. Such pleasure-seeking was all very well, but an end to the revels of the *ancien régime* loomed.

9

Death of the *Ancien Régime*

Before being at court, I had never known boredom, but I have
since acquainted myself with it well.

Mme de Maintenon

WARS AND *LA GLOIRE*

The trouble with Louis XIV, as indeed with some other rulers of France
in succeeding centuries, lay in his addictive pursuit of *la Gloire*, that
most elusive of viragos. If only he had stuck to the pursuit of *la Gloire*
in the boudoir or in his building plans (both spheres in which he
excelled), all might have been well. But he was obsessed by the great
military exploits of the Caesars, of Charlemagne and his own grandfather, Henri IV. When he was a youth of eighteen campaigning during
the Fronde, he was complimented on being even younger than Henri IV
had been when he first went to war. 'But he achieved more than me,'
complained young Louis, adding, 'in future I hope to win a great name
for myself'. Twelve years later, he admitted, 'My dominant passion is
certainly love of glory.' By then, on the most slender of pretexts, he had
already fought a campaign, the War of Devolution, against his wife's
country, Spain. This engagement (conducted in 1667 by Turenne, almost
without battle) had acquired for him the key cities of Lille, Douai and
Tournai in Spanish Flanders. In the age of the moderate Montaigne,
glory had signified vanity and had been denounced as a vice, but to
Louis it represented the heights of human achievement. A cheap victory,
signed at Aix-la-Chapelle in 1668, only gave him a taste for more.

Colbert had long struggled valiantly to control Louis' financial excesses, but from 1671 until his death in 1683 he was fighting a losing battle against the King's evil genius, François-Michel Le Tellier, better known as the Marquis de Louvois, who between 1672 and 1689 was effectively foreign minister. To give Louvois due credit, from a disorganized mob at the time of Louis' coronation he had turned the French army into a first-class fighting machine, the most formidable in Europe. Even in time of peace, it came to number 150,000 men under arms – men whom Colbert could readily have used in divers projects to enrich the country. Louvois augmented the number of the barbarically atavistic galleys in the French navy from six to forty, each containing 200 wretches. Originally they were manned by criminals and Turks taken in the Barbary Wars. When the Turks were worn out, they were sold on in slavery in America – and substantially replaced, after the 1685 Revocation of the Edict of Nantes, by French Protestants caught attempting to emigrate illegally.

By 1670, as we have seen, France was the strongest power in Europe; Spain was enfeebled; Germany and Italy were parcelled out and divided; England, weakened by the years of Civil War, had on the throne a peace-loving Catholic monarch, Charles II, who was a personal friend of the King of France and indebted to him for financial support. With enduring peace seemingly at hand, France had no need of a vast army. As would have been the preference of Vauban, Europe's greatest genius at building fortresses – exquisite works of art in themselves – she could have put up ramparts on her north-eastern frontier and consolidated it bit by bit without resort to war. Vauban hated the bombardments of open cities in which Louvois revelled. But Louvois pushed towards war a monarch already bent upon *la Gloire*.

In 1672 Louis launched a carefully planned war of unprovoked aggression against the tiny but prosperous country of Holland. Though he had overt reasons for disliking the staunchly Protestant Dutch, he was largely motivated by naked greed. The proud Dutch, however, flooded their dykes and the war dragged on for seven years. Holland was ruined financially, but managed to keep her frontiers intact. A stray bullet cost the life of the great Turenne (at Salzbach, in 1675); more dangerously the war awoke to Louis' menacing ambitions the rest of Europe – and particularly England, where Holland's hero, William of Orange, was shortly to assume the throne. All it achieved for France, through the Treaty of Nijmegen, was the (temporary) acquisition of Lorraine and the definitive cession of the Franche-Comté – plus some magnificent paintings and tapestries of the Roi Soleil, astride a prancing horse, crossing the Rhine or besieging Maastricht. For Louis it was the apogee of *la Gloire*.

From now on, a new swagger entered into his pronouncements. Yet, within the next decade, it had brought all his neighbours (bar Switzerland) to unite against him under the alliance of the League of Augsburg. Pre-emptively, Louis marched across the Rhine, taking Cologne and with appalling brutality devastating the Palatinate. It was an excess that would be held against France by Germans for decades, if not centuries, to come – bearing with it the most poisonous of fruit. After another nine years of war, which had negated much of Colbert's good works in domestic development, under the Treaty of Ryswick (1697) Louis was forced to renounce virtually all his gains.

The glorious reign ended, ingloriously, in yet another war – the War of the Spanish Succession. This time it was one which Louis, ageing and tired of *la Gloire*, had not sought but had blundered into. For the first time since the Hundred Years War, England – now thoroughly stirred up by Louis – despatched a major force deep into the heart of the continent. Under the mighty Duke of Marlborough, defeat after humiliating defeat was inflicted on France: Blenheim, where Louis lost 30,000 out of an army of 50,000, and Gibraltar (both in 1704), Ramillies and Oudenarde (in 1706 and 1708). 'God seems to have forgotten all I have done for him,' grumbled Louis after Ramillies. In 1708 Lille was lost. The following year Nature entered the war on the side of the Alliance, imposing on France, and especially on Paris, the harshest winter on record; at Versailles bottles of liqueur, even in a room with a blazing fire, burst with the frost. To continue financing the war, Louis was forced to melt down his gold plate. Then came Malplaquet, where 11,000 Frenchmen died in the bloodiest battle of the age. Finally, as if there were no end to the punishments the Almighty would inflict on Louis for all his hubristic arrogance, there followed the terrible sequence of illnesses which would decimate his family and menace the succession.

At last, in 1712, when the victorious Allies were mustering to advance on Paris, and it looked as if the country was facing total defeat, possibly even the downfall of the monarchy, Marshal de Villars turned the tide with a brilliant sequence of victories at Denain and Douai. Within six weeks Villars had driven the invaders out of France, and an ailing Louis was able – just – to conclude an honourable peace at Utrecht in 1713. France and the monarchy were saved. Out of this conflict, however, came the foundations of the British Empire, and the economic ruin of all that Colbert had built up – with the value of the livre depreciated 25 per cent in the thirty years up to Utrecht.

PERSECUTING HUGUENOTS AND JANSENISTS

The rise of Mme de Maintenon, around the time of the move to Versailles, represented a fundamental change in the life of the hedonistic king. From now on Louis' prodigious sexual urges were to be kept closely in check, his Catholic conscience more rigorously activated. Born Françoise d'Aubigné, Mme de Maintenon had married a (very) minor poetaster called Paul Scarron, much older than herself and a cripple allegedly shaped like the letter Z – and a platonic admirer of the famous courtesan, Ninon de Lenclos. She was very different from all the previous women in the King's life, three years older than he, beyond the age of childbearing, and with some of the traditional qualities of the governess. Handsome, but certainly no beauty, she kept the King on the straight and narrow, with the emphasis on the narrow. Her piety was boundless, and she deplored the venality of Versailles. Late in life she would speak about her 'long struggle for the King's soul'. In return, the King referred to her as 'Your Solidity'. Whether they were ever married, morganatically, remains a mystery. Nevertheless, with her ascent a sharp change of mood became apparent. In 1683, the year after the move to Versailles, the Queen – Spanish Infanta to the end, dividing her time between her Spanish confessor and Spanish maid – died, in the arms of Mme de Maintenon. 'Poor woman,' was the King's immortal epitaph, 'it's the only time she has ever given me any trouble.' Though in Paris Ninon de Lenclos' court of love ('the triumph of vice conducted with wit', as Saint-Simon described it) continued to reign, at Versailles the Widow Scarron's power at court was now complete.

Influenced by Scarron, Louis decided on the fateful, if not fatal, step of the Revocation of the Edict of Nantes, in 1685. His desire to get rid once and for all of the Protestants stemmed from his passion for unity and order. For years he had been quietly oppressing them, but within the existing liberal laws laid down by his grandfather. Then, in the period just preceding the move to Versailles, he had begun to think of ways of converting all the Protestants. In 1681, Mme de Maintenon had rejoiced, 'If God preserve the King there will not be one Huguenot left twenty years hence.' Four years later came the Revocation.

Of all Louis' harsher policies, not even the wars affected Paris and Parisians quite so radically, and disastrously, as this. With enthusiasm Louvois added an extra note of horror to Louis' Revocation with his brutal *dragonnades*, armed raids accompanied by torture, pillage and scorched earth against Protestant dissenters in the provinces – Languedoc in particular. Within a matter of months of the Revocation, France's Protestants had been reduced by three-quarters; most had become Catholics; some had emigrated; others, alleged infringers of the law, had been sent to the galleys – the punishment for any Calvinist skilled worker trying to flee. The goods and property of Protestant families were confiscated, to further inhibit them from leaving the country. Wealth bequeathed to Protestant foundations was also to be confiscated and applied instead to the royal hospitals. The ensuing violence took place largely in the countryside, where Protestants were obliged to go to Mass and to take communion; those spitting out the host were condemned to be burned alive; others who refused the last rites on their deathbed had their corpses dragged about the street after their death.

If Languedoc bled cruelly, however, it was nothing compared to the catastrophic and lasting damage inflicted on the capital, Paris – even though she was never exposed to the worst atrocities committed in the provinces. There the ghosts of Saint Bartholomew's Night and the bitter siege of 1590 were still capable of casting their sombre shadows. Protestant numbers had already become reduced to perhaps 15,000, but these were the elite. Some of the most prestigious among the Huguenot nobility in Paris were now expedited to the Bastille, subject to a strict regime and freed only once they converted. Many of them died there. Among the Parisian Protestants were leading painters, sculptors, architects and court musicians, including Claude Le Jeune; there were *médailleurs* and *maîtres tapissiers*, such as the masters of the Gobelin factory; and there were leaders in finance, industry and science.

Many of these people fled the country after 1685. They included men like Christiaan Huygens, inventor of the pendulum clock and the first to derive the theory that the stars were in fact other suns, who returned to his native Holland. Silk-makers emigrated to England, glass-makers to Denmark, and 600 army officers departed to reinforce the ranks of France's enemies. At the Battle of the Boyne hundreds of French Huguenots fought in the ranks of William of Orange against the Irish Catholics. Many, later encouraged by Frederick the Great, ended up in

Prussia, their descendants leading the cohorts that would invade France in three successive wars from 1870 onwards. By 1700 between a third and a half of the population of Berlin was reckoned to be refugees from Louis' misguided religious strategy. This strategy also hardened Protestant opinion against him abroad: the League of Augsburg, uniting as it did France's enemies against her, was but one of the laden consequences.

The Huguenots were not the only religious body to feel the scourge of royal bigotry. The Jansenists were a gloomy sect founded by a Dutchman called Cornelius Jansen (1585–1638), who, becoming Bishop of Ypres, had sought a return to the simplicity and discipline of the early Christians. With ideas reminiscent of Calvin's, and believing in free will and predestination, the sect had their Paris headquarters in the convent of Port-Royal-des-Champs. In their austerity they often seemed holier than the Jesuits, which was to be a constant source of friction. Among the eminent supporters of Jansenism were Pascal and Racine, and it was at Port-Royal that La Rochefoucauld wrote his famous maxims. Blaise Pascal, who died in 1662 when he was only thirty-nine, was one of the stars in the firmament of the Roi Soleil. Son of a tax *fonctionnaire*, a frail genius racked by headaches and insomnia who never knew a day without pain, he wrote an essay on conic sections when he was sixteen and developed the first calculating machine while in his twenties. He was also credited with postulating a key philosophical question: 'Is Christianity primarily a religion of reason or a religion of love?' In 1655, after undergoing a mystical experience, he moved into the Port-Royal, where his niece worked. From here he published his masterpiece, the *Lettres provinciales*, a blistering Jansenist satire on the Jesuits.

Racine, who wrote a history of the Port-Royal, was deeply influenced by Jansenism as well, his conscience torn by its teachings. Perhaps rather feebly, and to show his *bonne volonté* in the court, as well as ingratiating himself with Mme de Maintenon, in his later years he wrote a play at her request for the girls' school she had founded for the under-educated daughters of French country squires. Called *Esther* and drawn from the Bible, the play was produced numerous times at Versailles in the winter of 1689. But this did nothing for the Jansenists. In 1709, Louis finally seized an opportunity to raze the Port-Royal convent to the ground, and – after a brief period of persecution – to disperse the nuns. Yet the controversy was to flare up again after his death, afflicting French religious life into the nineteenth century.

Much of religious thought and teaching in Louis' Paris continued to centre on the Sorbonne. Since its foundation it had expanded steadily: the Collège d'Harcourt (later Lycée Saint-Louis) in 1280; the Collège Cardinal Lemoine in 1302; the Collège de Navarre (later Ecole Polytechnique) in 1304; the Collège de Lombards (for Italian students) in 1333. By the end of the fifteenth century there were fifty-two separate colleges. In 1470, German technicians set up Paris's first printing press there. Through the years of the later Middle Ages and into the early Renaissance it had continued its reputation for rowdiness; the great poet François Villon, who was constantly in trouble, found refuge there. During the Hundred Years War it had fallen on hard times. But under the great Richelieu (who studied there, later became its Chancellor, and asked to be buried there) the Sorbonne experienced a new flowering and considerable expansion. Richelieu's architect Jacques Lemercier added its classical chapel. Louis XIV continued the work of Richelieu and sustained the Sorbonne, but did little to alter its curriculum, which up to the Revolution remained largely clerical in content.

PARIS NEGLECTED

As Louis fought his wars, progressively ever more disastrous, and threw his energies and the state's resources into developing Versailles, so Paris withered on the vine – not least, as we have observed, the abandoned Louvre.

Most of the new public works in Paris were now indivisibly associated with the personal glorification of the Roi Soleil, superb pieces of architecture though they undoubtedly were. There was the magnificent Place Vendôme, designed to be centred on a statue six metres high of a conquering monarch on horseback, in Roman costume but with a seventeenth-century wig. Unthinkable in the times of Philippe Auguste or Henri IV, the horse would supposedly be big enough to hold in its stomach twenty people around a table. (Fortunately, it was never built; in its place was erected the Vendôme Column, a shifting cast of latterday Caesars atop it.) Then there were the triumphal arches, Portes Saint-Denis and Saint-Martin, and the Place des Victoires, before 1686 one of the most dangerous areas of Paris – now home to twenty-first-century couturiers such as Kenzo. Here the centrepiece, a four-metre-high statue of the King standing in his coronation robes, depicted four chained women at its base, representing his subjected enemies. 'Gilded all over', it drew Martin Lister's intense disapproval:

> Close behind is the statue of Victoire, that is a female of vast size, with wings, holding a laurel crown over the head of the King and resting one foot upon a globe. Great exceptions are taken by artists to the gilding ... but what I chiefly dislike in this performance is the *great woman* perpetually at the king's back; which, instead of expressing victory, seems to act as an encumbrance, and to fatigue him with her company ... this woman is enough to give a man a surfeit ...

It was said that each king had his statue among those he most loved; Henri IV in the midst of the people on the Pont Neuf; Louis XIII among the tumultuous favourites of the Place Royale; while Louis XIV resided with the tax collectors in the Place des Victoires.

As already noted, Louis' excursions to Paris in his later years were few and far between. These were usually to dedicate one or other attribute of self-glorification. During this fallow period the most handsome addition to Paris architecture was the new Pont Royal, linking the Tuileries to the Left Bank. In her diary Mme de Sévigné recorded one day in February 1684 how its predecessor, the old Pont Rouge, 'had left for Saint-Cloud this morning' – yet another of the old wooden bridges washed away by the Seine in one of its moments of ferocity. Opened in 1689, its replacement, the elegant Pont Royal, remains one of the city's principal glories.

In the years 1689–97 war again exacerbated the plight of the poor. Then, in 1693, another disaster struck in the shape of a poor harvest, compounded by inefficient (and probably corrupt) means of storing grain. Paris hungered, grumbled and longed for peace. A new prayer, at once seditious and blasphemous, went the rounds: 'Our Father who art in Versailles, thy name is no longer hallowed; thy kingdom is diminished; thy will is no longer done on earth or on the waves. Give us our bread, which is lacking to us ...' But the prosperous city bourgeois maintained their girths, their riches out of sight of the poor, just as the coquetry which was symbolized by Ninon's Paris went unseen by Scarron's newly pious Versailles.

BOREDOM AT VERSAILLES

Meanwhile, radiating outwards from the person of the King, life went on at Versailles – where, even as late as May 1682, some 36,000 men and 6,000 horses were still toiling away in the great enterprise of construction. At the centre of everything was the King, *l'état* personified, surely the most courteous monarch there ever was, but demanding total obeisance and all-embracing loyalty. Surrounded by 10,000 courtiers, he lived virtually without a guard – there would only ever be one half-hearted attempt on his person. After a while, once the numbing grandeur of Versailles had begun to wear thin, the boredom must have been excruciating – ennui, that most pernicious and dreaded of all French diseases. Like Dante's Inferno, this ennui had its concentric circles. The worst, the outer circle, was to be out of favour with the King and sentenced to exile on one's own estates in the provinces; the unfortunate Chevalier de Bouillon, for one, was exiled in perpetuity for having been overheard daring to call the Roi Soleil 'an old country squire, living in the provinces with his aged mistress'. Then there was exile in Paris, still away from court; finally, the innermost circle of all, there was Versailles itself.

For a courtier with no taste for cards (which so often spelt financial ruin), for hunting or for gossip, it was a leaden existence – futile, wearisome and often demeaning. Life in *ce pays-ci*, as it was called, became bound by petty codes and customs, and meaningless rules: for instance, in chapel only princes of the blood were permitted to place their hassocks straight, the rest had to put theirs down at an irregular angle. Even the faithful Governess Scarron herself, so closely linked with that ennui, was once heard to complain, 'Before being at court, I had never known boredom, but I have since acquainted myself with it well.'

It was all part of Louis' essential apparatus of state. As Stendhal who, as a good Frenchman, also knew about ennui, wrote a century and a half later, 'The masterpiece of Louis XIV was to create such boredom out of exile.' Within its opiate embrace, Louis' nobles could no longer plot against him, and from it they could escape only to an outer circle of boredom. 'When one is wretched enough to be far from your Majesty one is not only unhappy but ridiculous,' wrote one such exile craving to come back into the cage. The French aristocracy, the ruling class, was reduced to impotence. But in the long term the concentration of so many courtiers at Versailles and the absentee-landlordism it engendered also proved the ruin of every element of local government in France.

After Louis' profane loves had been cleared out by the Governess Scarron, Versailles became even more boring. In 1686, a middle-aged Louis was operated on (amazingly, with success) for a painful anal fistula – his first real illness. Seven years later, he decided that – much as he loved doing so – he would ride to war no more. Following the marriage of Marie-Adélaïde of Savoy to his grandson, in 1697, the great ball of the reign took place in the Galerie des Glaces. Then, with the turn of the century and accumulating disasters, the dancing dwindled and finally ceased. Even Louis seemed to weary of the splendour and the tedium; to get away from the teeming crowds of the obsequious that he had himself created, he decided to build at Marly a small retreat where he could sometimes be alone. Shivering, Mme de Maintenon complained, 'Symmetry, symmetry, if I stay much longer here I shall become paralytic. Not a door or window will shut.'

Versailles rapidly became an old folk's home, as the young and fashionable steadily trickled off back to Paris. Humming with pleasure, life began to centre once more on the Palais Royal and Monsieur's libertine young son Philippe II d'Orléans, the future Regent. Nevertheless, in all things – except perhaps morals – Paris continued sedulously to ape Versailles.

THE END OF THE *GRAND SIÈCLE*

At the turn of the century, the Roi Soleil's family life had never seemed sunnier. He was the most favoured, as well as the most powerful, monarch on earth. In manners, style and the arts – in almost all things French – other nations tried to model themselves on France, and especially on the Paris which Louis had created, and then abandoned. French furniture and French porcelain were to be seen everywhere in the houses of the rich all over Europe. There was virtually a common

European civilization, which was French and aristocratic. French was, and remained, the international language of polite society. For Frederick II ('the Great') of Prussia, French became his language of choice.

Then, for Louis, the terrible sequence of reversals began. The bad omens were there the very year of the move to Versailles, with the death in labour of the Dauphine, as she gave birth to Louis' first grandson, the Duc de Bourgogne. Charmingly the quacks prescribed that a sheep be flayed alive in her room and the ailing Princess wrapped in its skin; the ladies-in-waiting were horrified; the Dauphine died in agony anyway. Then, in 1701, queer old Monsieur died of a stroke, supposedly brought on by a row with his elder brother. 'And so ended this year, 1701,' wrote Saint-Simon, 'and all the happiness of the King with it.' But worse was to come. The following year brought the disastrous War of the Spanish Succession – which Louis never wanted, but into which he was propelled by the diplomatic follies of his previous wars. Europe, refusing to accept a Bourbon prince on the throne of Spain (left heirless by the death of Louis' brother-in-law), which would have given France an impossible agglomeration of power, united against Louis. Marlborough marched to Blenheim and back, destroying French armies right, left and centre as he went. In 1706, a total eclipse of the sun seemed like a portent of the new chain of catastrophes that were about to engulf the Roi Soleil. The following year, Dutch scouts – eager to revenge past injuries – pushed almost to Versailles. Living from hour to hour, the court expected at any moment to have to evacuate to Chambord. Then came Marshal de Villars' miraculous, eleventh-hour counterstroke, liberating – by the end of 1712 – all of France.

In the meantime, however, fresh disasters befell France, and Louis personally. We have seen that the winter of 1709 brought perhaps the worst cold ever recorded; in Paris on 13 January the thermometer fell to minus 21.5 degrees Centigrade, and even sunny Provence registered temperatures of minus 16 degrees. Altogether France lost half of her livestock that winter; vines everywhere were killed. In Burgundy, children were reported living off boiled grass and roots; 'Some even crop the fields like sheep.' The Seine froze solid, and ice snapped the moorings of barges. The cold even killed Louis' confessor, Père La chaise, and a former royal mistress, the Princesse de Soubise, frozen to death in her palace. Impoverished by war, Louis was unable to pay for the 'King's bread' of past years that had sustained the poor of Paris – except by raising fresh taxes. On his way out wolf-hunting, the Dauphin found his way barred by ravenous women clamouring for food. Wolves once again roamed the provinces. Twenty-four thousand Parisians are recorded as having died that winter; and there were riots, with mobs setting off ominously for Versailles. Ugly rumours ran round that Mme de Maintenon was buying up wheat for her own use. Struggling against calamity, La Reynie's able successor d'Argenson declared prophetically, 'I foresee that the fires will soon burn in this capital and I fear they will be difficult to extinguish.' In the context, it seems miraculous that it would take another eighty years before the flames raged out of control.

Louis was plunged into depression, which even Mme de Maintenon was unable to dispel. 'Sometimes,' she recorded, 'he has a fit of crying that he cannot control, sometimes he is not well. He has no conversation.' But Louis' personal afflictions had hardly begun. In 1711, Monseigneur, the Dauphin, kept in semi-seclusion at Marly, where – infuriatingly – he 'stood in the corner whistling and tapping his snuffbox', caught smallpox and died. All Louis' hopes, and affections, now centred on his grandson, the new Dauphin, a serious young man of thirty who reflected the King's own capacity for hard work, and his twenty-five-year-old wife, Marie-Adélaïde of Savoy, whom Louis adored and whose charm and gaiety had brought new life to an ageing court. But in January 1712, while Louis was still in mourning for his son, Marie-Adélaïde caught measles; on 9 February she died. Ten days later, her husband succumbed to the same disease. In March – as the Allies were beginning to threaten Versailles – their five-year-old son Louis died too. Three dauphins within the year! Suspicions of poisoning once again raised their ugly head, with fingers pointed at Philippe, the new Duc d'Orléans, a libertine known to read Rabelais during Mass, and brought by the deaths closer to the throne. Panic swept the court, though Louis kept his head, murmuring piously to Villars, 'God punishes me, and I have deserved it. I shall suffer less in the next world.'

Darkness had descended on Versailles. After Marie-Adélaïde, there were no more balls or entertainments. Then, on 13 August 1715, the King felt a stabbing pain in his left leg; ten days later, despite prescriptions of massive doses of asses' milk, it turned black. Gangrene had set in. Louis sent for his heir, his five-year-old great-grandson, yet another Louis, and told him, '*Mignon*, you are going to be a great king.' Then he passed him this lapidary last testament: 'Try to remain at peace with your neighbours. I have loved war too much.' On 1 September the Roi Soleil was extinct, four days short of his seventy-seventh birthday, and having occupied the throne for seventy-two years and a quarter. 'His name cannot be uttered without respect, without linking it to an eternally memorable century,' wrote Voltaire in an excess of homage for so sceptical a critic. Yet later in his life Voltaire could remember seeing, as the great King was laid to rest, little tents set up along the road to Saint-Denis, along which the funeral cortège would pass, where 'people were drinking, singing and laughing'. The old monarch had begun to seem immortal, doggedly ruling over a nation that had become increasingly weary with the burdens he had imposed on it. The *grand siècle* was well and truly over; the bills would shortly be presented for payment.

ANOTHER REGENCY

Discreetly, Mme de Maintenon withdrew from Versailles, declaring that the King had died 'like a hero and a saint'. She lived out the remaining four years of her life in seclusion at nearby Saint-Cyr. The act of dying, she declared on her deathbed, was 'the least important event of my life'. At Versailles the atmosphere of gloom-bound piety she had done so much to create lingered on for a while, at least until the new child King, Louis XV, was old enough to take over. It was a melancholic place, haunted by phantoms and memories. On the accession of the Regent, Philippe, Duc d'Orléans, the court – and life itself – moved back to Paris, after an exile of thirty-three years. Once again, it became the true centre and soul of France, for the first time in almost a century.

The Regent took up his official residence in Richelieu's Palais Royal (where he had in fact been living for many a year), and with him came the seat of government. Philippe was aged forty-one at the time of his uncle's death, but he looked older. Debauchery and too many drunken evenings had taken their toll. His left arm had been smashed by a cannonball in the wars, and his eyesight had deteriorated to the point where he had to peer so closely at documents that his quill pen became entangled in his wig. He was less careful about his dress than he had once been, provoking Saint-Simon to quip that no one had less work to do than his Royal Highness's master of the wardrobe, except his confessor. Yet he remained a man of great charm and wit. He was voraciously well read, in literature as in philosophy, and was gifted with a remarkable memory. He was more compassionate and tolerant than most of his contemporaries, yet his reputation down the ages was that of a debauchee, philanderer and rake; he was rumoured to have seduced his own daughter and even to have poisoned the Dauphin – and perhaps the King too. He spent as much time as he could in the Palais Royal, wenching and debauching. Even his pious best friend, Saint-Simon, so disapproved of the raffish hangers-on at the Palais Royal that when the Roi Soleil was alive he agreed to meet Philippe only at court in Versailles, never in Paris. Politically, his principal handicap was that the Roi Soleil had not allowed him to play any part in public life, with the result that he was totally lacking in the knowledge that experience brings.

Yet the man with the daunting task of running the country in the wake of the Roi Soleil proved himself to be far more than just an ambitious, Rabelaisian profligate. He was as accomplished in the arts as he had been as a soldier in Louis XIV's battles; he encouraged Watteau and the melancholy gaiety of the *fête galante*, and he saw the point of Voltaire. A skilled diplomatist, he helped bring to an end Louis' wars, which were ruining France; he opened the prisons of Paris and liberated the galley slaves – one of the most dreadful abuses of human rights left over from the Middle Ages, encouraged and even augmented by Louis. In his efforts to educate the silent and reserved child King, Louis XV, he did his best, employing a light touch and encouraging him with the words, 'But are you not the master? I am here only to explain, propose, receive your orders and execute them.' The French economy was in terrible shape, and Philippe could also claim advanced and – to say the least – venturesome ideas on how to put it right. But here he came unstuck, with disastrous consequences for Paris that were to bring the Revolution a notch or two closer.

To the city he brought in John Law, an Edinburgh financier (and one of the few *Anglo-Saxons* to rate a major entry in *Le Petit Larousse*). Law introduced paper money, setting up in 1716 a 'General Bank' to discount commercial paper, which, in 1718, became the Royal Bank with the state as its principal shareholder. This was followed by an adventurous scheme to settle the wastes of Louisiana (named after Louis XIV; New Orleans, it should be noted, was named after the Regent, Philippe). Paris was hit by a febrile wave of speculation and optimism. Tourists and provincials, bent on getting rich quickly, crowded into the city. All went reasonably well, until greed – or prescience – persuaded the Prince de Conti to arrive, on 2 March, with three covered wagons, demanding gold from the bank in exchange for fourteen million shares. The following day, another eminent aristocrat, the Duc de Condé-Bourbon, a prince of the blood no less, rolled up insisting that he sell a further twenty-five million shares. The Regent was appalled: 'It appears, Monsieur, that you take pleasure in destroying in a moment that which we have had so much trouble in establishing ... What are you each going to do with such a great amount of money?'

Now, following after the grandees, nervous bourgeois speculators swamped the bank with their paper money, calling for gold and silver in payment. There was simply not enough to cover demand; the full vulnerability of 'Law's System' was exposed. The bubble burst, with terrible and far-reaching consequences. By May, an edict slashed the value of paper shares and notes by 50 per cent. The city was horror-struck. Commented Saint-Simon: 'every rich man thought himself ruined without resource, and every poor man saw himself a beggar'. Paris seethed; social discontent multiplied, developing into civil disorder, with murders and robberies rampant. In July, Law – recognized by the mob – narrowly escaped being lynched. On 9 December, excoriated by Parisians as 'that miserable Englishman' (though he was of course a Scot), Law resigned, retiring to die quietly in Venice nine years later, himself totally impoverished – not a swindler, but an honest and misguided optimist.

Typically, Paris seemed to shrug off the disaster with her habitual insouciance. Life returned to the gaiety expressed in the works of Watteau in his last years (he died in 1721), and then moved on to the frothy and equally unreal world of Fragonard. Nevertheless, Law and his 'System' had caused the monarchy to totter. The bourgeoisie, created and enriched by the Roi Soleil, had been ruined; worse, they had become dangerously disillusioned with a regime that had proved itself to be so flawed. It would take almost a hundred years, plus the genius of a Bonaparte, before a new and trustworthy Banque de France could be established.

Worn out by his debaucheries, and doubtless by the Law catastrophe, Philippe died in 1723 – in the arms of a mistress. A grisly story circulated that, at his post-mortem, one of his Great Danes jumped up and ate his heart.

LOUIS XV

On the death of the Regent, Philippe d'Orléans, Louis XV was still an immature child of thirteen. Whereas his illustrious great-grandfather had been hardened by the Fronde, the young King was brought up to know only cringing, flattery and licentiousness. Shortly after the Regent's death, he came across as 'a handsome young man, frail and gloomy, with the pretty face of a girl, unfeeling and cold'. He succeeded in being both timid and violent, an unfortunate combination – and secretive. Moving back to Versailles after the death of the Regent, he was to find himself more cut off from his people than any of his predecessors. He had no particular interest in literature or music or the arts – until Mme de Pompadour came along. At first, following Philippe, young Louis turned over the governance of France to Cardinal Fleury, described by one historian as 'an agreeable nobody'. Certainly the Cardinal was neither a Sully nor a Colbert, and – in the opinion of Saint-Simon – had 'not the slightest notion of anything when he took the helm'.

When Fleury died, aged eighty-eight, in 1742, the King allowed himself – and France – to be ruled by his mistresses, first Mme de Pompadour for two decades, then, after her demise, by the much hated vulgarian Mme du Barry. He had begun by affronting Spain with his change of marital intent, marrying in 1725 the daughter of the Polish claimant, Maria Leszczynska. Seldom addressing a word to her, Louis gave her ten children in ten years ('Always going to bed, always being brought to bed,' sighed the unhappy Queen). Wearing no cosmetics, and supposedly spending her time embroidering altar cloths, she bored Louis, and then closed her bedroom door to him when he was only thirty. He had affairs with four (de Nesle) sisters in a row. When the last, the Duchesse de Châteauroux, died – poison was rumoured – Louis, out hunting, picked up a woman of modest bourgeois birth but of considerable character unpromisingly called Mlle Poisson. Promoted Marquise de Pompadour, she too appears to have been frigid, keeping a hold on the King by supplying him with quantities of young girls – including, allegedly, her own daughter. The Parc-aux-Cerfs at Versailles – visited nightly by Louis for assignations arranged by Pompadour – gained an infamous reputation.

Here lies one twenty years a maid,
Fifteen a whore, and seven a procuress

was the epitaph the pamphleteers gave her when she died, aged forty-three and of natural causes, in 1764. Thanks to her interference in high policy, her extravagance and her wanton influence on the King, Pompadour died unmourned, despised by the court as a bourgeois but hated by the bourgeois of Paris as being in league with the tax collectors. Nevertheless, through her encouragement of the arts and architecture, France's cultural heritage owes more to her than it likes to admit. At Versailles the Petit Trianon, and in Paris the Ecole Militaire and the Place de la Concorde, all owe something to Mlle Poisson, as does Sèvres porcelain. Her place was taken by another of low birth, a pretty prostitute called Jeanne Bécu, later Comtesse du Barry. She was, so Louis confided to that great expert on the art of philandering, the Duc de Richelieu, 'The only woman in France who can make me forget that I am in my sixties.'

There was never to be a Mme de Maintenon who could bring Louis XV in his maturer years to a sense of gravitas. Although, with the highly developed sexual urges of the Bourbon clan, his amorous exploits were no more excessive than those of Henri IV or Louis XIV, his ineffectiveness as a ruler ensured that they were considered scandalous even in the century of de Sade and Choderlos de Laclos. With tragedy, post-Racine, dying as an art, the essential frivolity of the life and times of Louis XV is reflected in the dramas of Marivaux, perhaps especially when compared with those of Molière; while such serious talents as Voltaire, Rousseau, Montesquieu and the *encyclopédistes* – illustrious as they were – hardly lent support to a threatened dynasty. Painted by Pompadour's protégé Boucher ('His lovers are shepherds, but incapable of watching a flock,' complained the critics), life at Versailles grew ever more feckless, pointless and removed from the real world. Unfortunately, the court there was composed largely of absentee landlords seeking refuge from the mounting disfavour of their peasants, and allowing their estates to fall into rack and ruin. Unlike their English counterparts, they never travelled or made the 'grand tour', so their horizons became ever more narrow. More than a diversion, at Versailles sex became the principal occupation; it was acceptable, when princes of the blood like the Chartres dined out, for them to ask for the use of their hostess's bed during the meal. In contrast with Empress Maria Theresa's respected and austere court in Vienna, Louis' earned its reputation as the most corrupt in Europe, Mme du Barry symbolizing the completeness of its corruption.

In Paris the tenor of life at court was mirrored and embodied in the person of the wicked but brave and brilliant Armand, Duc de Richelieu, marshal of France and grand-nephew of the great Cardinal. Adept at climbing in and out of bedroom windows, he won fame by audaciously scaling the supposedly impregnable heights of Fort Saint-Philip at Mahon, on the isle of Minorca, thereby achieving the surrender of the British garrison. It was one of the few French successes in the Seven Years War (1756–63), and a victory famed both for the execution of the unfortunate British commander, Admiral Byng ('pour encourager les autres'), and for the invention, by Richelieu's enterprising cook, of Mahonaise sauce. Described at the time as being 'husband to all wives except his own', Richelieu married three times under three reigns and sired a child (illegitimate) in his eighties. Strolling round the Place Royale the Duc was given to reminiscing happily that he had slept with the lady of every single household. Through all his escapades, however, he was generally able to count on the support of the King, who described him as 'an old family acquaintance; they found him once under my mother's bed!' Aged ninety-two, still *en pleine vigueur*, he chose prudently to die one year before the Revolution.

For France, victories on the battlefield exonerate scandals; but Louis XV was a loser. Paying little heed to the last words of his predecessor, he likewise impoverished the country by his wars (though he hated battles), wars even more foolish and unsuccessful than those of Louis XIV. At first, blundering far into the eastern marches of Europe, Louis supported that new upstart, Frederick II of Prussia, then turned against him. In the first war (of the Austrian Succession), the French army found itself having to fight a terrible mid-winter retreat from Prague; in the second, it was roundly defeated by an embattled Frederick at Rossbach. In both conflicts Prussia emerged with net gains, pointers to the crushing defeats that German arms would inflict on France in the next two centuries. Worse still, in the course of the bitter Seven Years War, which was almost a first world war, France lost her empire in Canada (though, at the time, Voltaire scathingly wrote off this vast domain as 'quelques arpents de neige' – a few acres of snow), the Mississippi territory and India, while Britain gained hers. As French historians accept, the Peace of Paris signed in 1763 was one of the saddest in French history. About the only territorial acquisition of the reign was Corsica, where an important actor in the history of France was waiting to be born.

From being 'le bien-aimé' Louis progressively became France's most unpopular monarch. By the 1750s he had been forced to construct a 'Route de la Révolte' whereby he could travel from his Palais de Fontainebleau to Versailles without traversing turbulent Paris. In 1757, a half-mad servingman, Robert François Damiens, tried to assassinate him with a penknife. Only the King appeared to be astonished. 'Why try to kill me?' he asked. 'I have done no one any harm.' Few historians would agree. Damiens was put to death no less cruelly than Ravaillac, the successful assassin of the admirable Henri IV a century and a half previously. Tried by sixty judges and tortured judicially for several hours before his execution (despite the King's request that he should not be harmed), Damiens – like Ravaillac – was pulled limb from limb by four horses; but first his flesh was torn open by giant, red-hot pincers and molten lead poured into the wounds.

In May 1774, regretted by no one and horribly disfigured, Louis was carried off by smallpox. His burial was carried out in secrecy at Saint-Denis, for fear of the cortège being attacked by angry Parisians. With remarkable similarity to the end of Louis XIV, both the Dauphin and his wife had predeceased the King. So it was Louis' grandson who inherited, as the twenty-year-old Louis XVI – as popular as his predecessor had been unpopular. At least superficially, once again the barometer looked set fair.

NEW BOUNDARIES

The Paris of Louis XV and XVI was still a noisy, smelly city, the largest in Europe, and with her narrow streets still medieval in plan. Jean-Jacques Rousseau, habitually prejudiced towards the rustic, found it a city of 'small, dirty and stinking streets, ugly black houses, an air of filth, poverty, beggars, carters, sewing women, women hawking tisanes and old hats'. The writer Restif de la Bretonne agreed, providing a glimpse of what Paris was like on a wet night: water gushing from the housetops in torrents, the Rue Montmartre a river of filth.

Little or nothing was added to Parisian architecture during the Regency, or during the early years of Louis XV when continuing wars left little to spend. The Palais Bourbon, however, was erected in 1722–8 for a legitimized daughter of Louis XIV and Mme de Montespan, and there was intense building activity during the years 1758–88. Ten thousand new houses were erected, and a great deal of demolition carried out – as witness the superb records painted by Hubert Robert, the chronicler supreme of ruins. The old wooden houses encumbering bridges like the Pont Notre-Dame were pulled down. In 1786, a royal decree ordered that all the houses on the endangered Seine bridges should be removed – but the Revolution intervened before it could be complied with. A minimum width for new streets was fixed at 9.75 metres. A new wall, known as the 'Farmers General', twenty-five kilometres in length, enlarged the boundaries of the city to coincide with today's outer line of boulevards. It was completed just in time for the Revolution – for which its construction was in part responsible.

During the first half of the century Parisian architects and interior decorators flirted with the light-hearted frivolity of Italian and German rococo, of which Fontaine's and d'Ivry's ornate north and eastern frontages of the Palais Royal, and the resplendently ornate Salon de la Princesse by Germain Boffrand in the Marais' Hôtel de Soubise are superb examples. But on the whole Parisian architecture settled down into an elegant classicism, developed under Louis XIV and admired and copied throughout Europe. Behind this French classicism lay a body of architectural theory, fostered by the Académie Royale d'Architecture. Here Jacques-François Blondel (no relation, apparently, of his great namesake of Louis XIV's time) produced his prolific drawings. These show the typical townhouse which was to become the prototype of chic, bourgeois Paris when the Regent brought life back to the city on the death of Louis XIV. Private houses, often already divided into apartments, would rise from five floors to six, seven or even nine by the time of the Revolution.

Among the few new churches built was Soufflot's basilica to Sainte Geneviève, up above the Sorbonne, which – after the Revolution – was to become the vast, cold and empty dome of the Panthéon, resting place of the great and the good of France, including Victor Hugo, Rousseau, Voltaire, Zola and Jean Moulin. As already noted, Mme de Pompadour (who made her brother, de Marigny, Controller of Buildings) influenced the construction of the Ecole Militaire. Designed to accommodate 500 *gentilhommes* preparing for a military career and conveniently adjacent to Louis XIV's Invalides, the imposing Ecole occupied much of the hitherto empty Plain of Grenelle, and in front of it would be created an enormous open space, the Champ-de-Mars, where 25,000 men could manoeuvre (a feature of which Napoleon would make considerable use). But by far the most lasting architectural achievement of the century, one which also bore the stamp of Pompadour's influence, was the massive Place Louis XV. In 1748 the Peace of Aix-la-Chapelle, which ended the War of the Austrian Succession but did little else for France, was marked by the city elders of Paris with a statue in honour of Louis XV. The King generously offered a large open site belonging to the royal estates just west of the Tuileries Gardens.

From this concept, a competition, won by the distinguished architect Jacques-Ange Gabriel (who also designed the Ecole Militaire) and boosted by Mme de Pompadour, grew into an ambitious scheme of a colossal piazza surrounding the royal effigy. Almost as soon as it was erected, the statue of Louis 'le bien-aimé' as a Roman emperor on horseback had placards attached to it, damning the King's vices and his indifference to the plight of the poor; and it was to become the site of the guillotine that would shortly remove the head of his grandson. Begun in 1757, inaugurated in 1763 and completed in 1772, it was first known as Place Louis XV, then from 1792 as the Place de la Révolution, and from 1795 as the Place de la Concorde. The new piazza instantly altered the whole structure of Paris more definitively than anything else in its history. Soon to become the heart of the expanding city, it denoted the final end of the ascendancy of the Marais, the Louvre and the Palais Royal. Under Gabriel's scheme, a new axis was created running up the Rue Royale and the bridge, eventually named the Pont de la Concorde (begun in 1788, as the last major work before the deluge), linking it to the Left Bank. On the far side of the piazza, Gabriel built two imposing twin palaces, one of which was to house the Ministry of the Navy and the other the Hôtel Crillon. The inauguration of the Place, however, was hardly auspicious for the future of Parisian *circulation*: the transporter bringing the weighty statue of the King got stuck outside the Elysées Palace (built by the Comte d'Evreux in 1718 and subsequently purchased by Mme de Pompadour), giving Paris wags cause to jest, 'They will never get him past the Hôtel Pompadour.' Following the ceremony, the new Place was seized with a monumental traffic jam, because there was then no bridge between the Pont Royal and the Pont de Sèvres. Nevertheless, Gabriel's great achievement soon led to the creation of new residential districts around the Rue Saint-Honoré and further developed the once isolated Faubourg Saint-Germain on the Left Bank. Paris was marching decisively westward, but money was running out; at Versailles, Louis was forced to reduce his stable to 1,000 horses; in Paris Soufflot died in 1780, reputedly of a broken heart because his vast church up on Mont Sainte-Geneviève could not be completed.

At least in one respect, however, in the last days of the *ancien régime*, eyes were distracted from what was going on in Paris terrestrially to the air, where, on the very brink of revolution, was to be pioneered one of the modern world's greatest inventions: human flight. On 5 June 1783 the Montgolfier brothers sent up their first hot-air balloon; two months later a physicist, Jacques Charles, released from the Champ-de-Mars a more sophisticated device filled with hydrogen. He was watched by a tremendous crowd. Among them was Benjamin Franklin, recently arrived in Paris as American ambassador (following the Declaration of Independence in 1776) full of scientific knowledge and fresh revolutionary zeal, and who was to remark to those doubting the value of balloons, 'Of what use is the new-born baby?' Though Louis XVI had first suggested that two criminals under sentence of death be allowed to make the world's first manned flight, in fact it was to be made, on 21 November in the same year, by Pilâtre de Rozier and the Marquis d'Arlandes in a Montgolfier hot-air balloon, flying for twenty-five minutes at an altitude of 100 metres across an astounded city. (The intrepid de Rozier was killed two years later while trying to cross the English Channel – a feat which had already earned Jean-Pierre Blanchard £50 and a life pension from Louis XVI.) Less than a hundred years later the heroic Balloons of Paris, successors of the *montgolfières* (hot air) and the *charlières* (gas), were to capture the imagination of Parisians, and beyond, by establishing a tenuous lifeline to the outside world, during the siege by Moltke's Prussians. At the same time, on the ground attention was attracted by more spurious scientific practitioners such as the German Mesmer, offering 20,000 louis to make the universal cures of Mesmerism available to the world at large; and Count Cagliostro, a complete fraud who claimed possession of an Elixir of Life – and was finally exiled from Paris in 1786.

TO THE BRINK – AND OVER

By the time Louis XV died, he had – through his excesses, his extravagance and his incompetence in war – forfeited both at home and abroad
virtually all the respect that his great-grandfather had so painstakingly
built up for France a hundred years previously over the *grand siècle*. Yet
the new young King was acclaimed in Paris with a fervour such as had
greeted none of his Bourbon predecessors since Henri IV – despite his
appearance, and despite the bad auguries. Rather pathetically he proclaimed, 'I should like to be loved.' A thickset man with a puffy face not
brimming over with intelligence, and bulging myopic eyes, Louis XVI
was pious and chaste – unlike his predecessor – humanitarian by
instinct, well meaning but lethargic. His wife Marie Antoinette, justly or
unjustly, will always be renowned for her bovine Habsburg extravagance; if she didn't actually say 'Let them eat cake', she might as well
have done. At their prodigiously lavish wedding in May 1770, there
occurred an appalling disaster on the still incomplete Place Louis XV
which superstitious Parisians viewed as the most sinister of omens. A
stray rocket ignited a depot of fireworks intended for the celebrations,
and, in the ensuing fire and panic among onlookers trapped in the
narrow defile of Gabriel's Rue Royale, 133 were counted dead.

While Marie Antoinette and her ladies cavorted at Versailles, playing
at shepherdesses in her *hameau,* a phoney peasant hamlet constructed
in the park, real countrymen in the reign of Louis XVI were struggling
against the threat of constant hunger and worsening poverty. Nevertheless, in Paris as the *ancien régime* ground to the end which with
hindsight seems inevitable, there were great plans on the drawing board.
Paris would be surrounded with a new *grand boulevard*: there was to be
a new Place Royale that would fulfil Henri IV's unrealized scheme: all
the houses cluttering the Louvre and the Tuileries were to be removed;
the sinister Grand Châtelet was also to be demolished, and there were
even plans to demolish the Bastille and replace it with a large *place,*
notionally to be named after Louis XVI; streets were to be straightened,
the number of bridges and public fountains to be increased, the quays
embellished. The insanitary Hôtel Dieu was to be 'reformed', and the
cemeteries relocated from the centre of the city. Ironically, almost all

these projects were later to be carried out after the Revolution by Napoleon and Haussmann.

Yet, if looks and auguries were against Louis XVI, so too were circumstances, for his accession coincided with a prolonged period of economic stagnation. On the other hand, as with Tsarist Russia in 1914, it seems that in 1789 there was a widespread belief that a time of prosperity was at hand, coupled to an era of universal felicity. But, looking at the way the cards were stacked against him, one wonders whether a Philippe Auguste, a Henri IV, a Roi Soleil or even a Bonaparte could have averted – or diverted – the deluge that was building up. Equally, one is amazed that it hadn't burst on France a hundred years before. Inexorably the tide turned against the monarchy, which – though seemingly all-powerful still by the spring of 1789 – hastened its own end. The echoes of the recent American Revolution – won at such enormous financial cost to France, which had sent arms and men to support the rebels – were to militate against Louis, as did the gentle reasoning of the *philosophes* and *encyclopédistes* by their discrediting of the *ancien régime* in all its aspects. The new King was having to pay the bill for the wars and extravagances of both his predecessors, Louis XIV and Louis XV.

The winter of 1788–9 was a particularly severe one, with cold, hunger and discontent all linking hands against the government. In January 1789, Louis' hard-pressed director-general of finances, Jacques Necker, a Swiss banker, unable to cope with France's national debt of one billion livres, an unprecedented amount, sought a panacea in convoking a meeting of the Estates-General, a body that had not met since the time of Louis XIII's majority in 1614. There now took place the famous gathering in the Jeu de Paume, or indoor tennis court, so well depicted by David. The floodgates were now opening. The aristocracy had lost its influence; the bourgeoisie, already shaken to the core by the bursting of the Law bubble, now wanted something more than reform – though what that was it did not quite know until the Jacobins, a society of radicals, led the way. On 11 July, the King sacked Necker, and with him went the best hope of reform. Fearing national bankruptcy, the Bourse closed its doors. An empty exchequer and republican sentiment now combined.

Relentlessly, event followed on disastrous event. On 28 April, following a riot in a paper factory, the first shots had been fired in the wretched east-end Faubourg Saint-Antoine, where the final clashes of the Fronde had taken place against the young Louis XIV. What Carlyle categorized as the 'bestial dawning of the age of reason' achieved its symbolic moment with the storming of the Bastille by insurgents from the same turbulent *faubourg* on 14 July. This grim fortress, regarded as a symbol of royal authority, held no more than seven prisoners, one of whom had spent twenty-three years there and – blinded by the sun – emerged into daylight wondering whether Louis XV was still on the throne. A hundred of the insurgents were killed by fire from the Bastille. The mob went mad. The ancient fortress was seized, and demolished stone by stone, the Governor killed and his head stuck on a pike.

A terrible wave of violence now surged through the city, where dark forces were thrown up as if from the depths of the earth by some volcanic eruption, forces that would not finally be quelled until the advent of Napoleon. All the impassioned hatreds that had been storing up in Paris since the Roi Soleil now exploded. The day before, there had been a sinister foretaste of this with the pointless sacking of the convent of Saint-Lazare. Formerly a hospital for lepers, by the seventeenth century the convent had become headquarters for charitable undertakings. Even the fruit trees in its orchard were now chopped down, and ferocious women – precursors of the *tricoteuses* – killed and made off with all the chickens in its poultry farm. When the police arrived the following morning, they were just in time to rescue two old priests about to be hanged from nearby lamp posts. It was an unpleasant harbinger of what revolution would bring to Paris.

Returning that afternoon from his favourite pastime, *la chasse*, Louis enquired, 'Is this a rebellion?' 'No, Sire,' came the reply, 'it is a revolution.'

That October, rioters led by a troop of women marched on Versailles and hustled the royal family back to the Tuileries, where they remained virtual prisoners of the newly formed Paris Commune for the next three years. A revolutionary National Guard was created which would play a part in every uprising in Paris from 1789 to 1871, its arms forged in the sequestered precincts of Marie de Medici's princely Luxembourg Palace. On the night of 20 June the following year, disguised as a lackey, Louis XVI made his ill-organized and ill-fated flight eastwards from Paris, heading for Brussels, to seek refuge with the Allied forces that were menacing France. Turned back at Varennes, his doom was sealed. In June 1792, the Tuileries Palace was invaded and pillaged by the mob, who placed the symbol of revolution, a *bonnet rouge*, on the King's head and forced him to drink with them. Three months later, in a climax of revolutionary violence, a surge of promiscuous killing was unleashed in the September Massacres: more than 1,200 priestly or aristocratic prisoners, women and children included, were hacked to death. Paris seemed seized by a mindless and uncontrollable lust for blood. That December Louis, who was now being held with his family in the Tower of the Temple, was put on trial, to be guillotined on the Concorde on 21 January 1793, a few metres from the empty pedestal where the statue of his grandfather had once stood. After a risible trial, Marie Antoinette followed him to the scaffold on 16 October; 30,000 troops had to be deployed to keep order that day. Under mysterious circumstances never resolved, the ten-year-old Dauphin, in effect Louis XVII, was murdered in the Temple two years later.

Paris now disappeared into a dark cloud of terror and anarchy – in which Dr Guillotine's modern-minded invention accounted for 2,800 deaths in Paris alone, and for 14,000 in the provinces.

AGE FOUR: 1795–1815

NAPOLEON

PRE-REVOLUTIONARY PARIS OF 1789

10

Empire and Reform

Ah! Now I hear the bell of Notre-Dame; I like it much better
than the *canon d'alarme*!

A glazier on the Île Saint-Louis, in 1802

NEW DAWN, NEW MAN

In 1800, Paris greeted a new century, a new dawn, with optimism – and
hope. The years of anarchy and bloodshed were receding ever further
into the past. The Revolution was dead; but 'Vive la Révolution!'

Those terrible years, the *revanche* of the downtrodden proletariat of
Saint-Antoine against the Versailles of the Roi Soleil, had seen Paris
ravaged by mobs in 1789, the takeover of government by the Convention
in 1792, the execution of Louis XVI and Marie Antoinette the following
year, the establishment of the so-called Committee of Public Safety,
and the Terror of 1793–4. At the same time – miraculously – France's
revolutionary armies triumphed in the field against coalitions of her
external enemies. In July 1794, the Terror ended with the guillotining of
the dreadful 'sea-green incorruptible', François-Maximilien-Joseph de
Robespierre. Gradually extremism gave way to moderation, as the Directory replaced the Convention. Under the Directory, feeble and corrupt
as it was, reason and hope began to return to Paris. But the last decade
had brought the city only dismay and destruction. Nothing had been
built; on the contrary churches had been vandalized by the hundred,
their ancient statues decapitated. With the new century, however, Paris
had found a new master – a master who was brimming over with new
ideas.

Outside the Tuileries Palace on 19 February 1800, the thirty-year-old

General Napoleon Bonaparte jumped on to his horse to review the troops assembled on the terrace. He was watched and applauded by crowds gathered in the streets giving on to the Carrousel, at the windows of the houses and on the palace balconies. Paris was all agog, electric with an excitement mingled with curiosity and apprehension, to see the man of the moment who, until very recently, had been a relatively unknown young general, unimpressive in stature, who spoke imperfect French with a strong Corsican accent. Already an enormously successful commander in his twenties, Bonaparte on his return to Paris in 1797 had been acclaimed with full honours in the Luxembourg Palace by the Directory, its members clad in scarlet togas in emulation of ancient Rome. Every beautiful *Parisienne* had crowded into the court-yard, but, as a witness recorded, 'in spite of the luxury, the elegance of the women's clothes and the sumptuous costumes of the Directors, every eye was fixed on the spare, sallow, sickly-looking man in a simple coat, who appeared to fill all the space around him'. A few days later, Talleyrand, Napoleon's future foreign minister, had thrown a splendid ball for him, unrevolutionary in its extravagance.

Two years later, in 1799, Napoleon had hastened home from one of his less successful campaigns, in Egypt, to find himself swept into power with the coup of 18 Brumaire (9 November 1799 in the revolutionary calendar), replacing the corrupt and inefficient Directory as one of three consuls. The idea of joint consuls was taken from Roman practice, and, as sometimes happened under that empire, soon *le petit caporal* was to manoeuvre himself into the post of first consul for life – making himself *de facto* ruler of twenty-seven million Frenchmen. Although on the eve of the Brumaire coup Parisians had viewed Bonaparte with scant enthu-siasm 'as a man whom nobody likes, and everybody prefers', now two months later outside the Tuileries they were eager to set eyes on him. The face of their new first consul was as yet hardly familiar to Parisians – hence the crush – for, over the previous four years, he had spent a total of 1,174 days away from Paris. More familiar to the Parisian *beau monde* was the face of his beautiful Creole consort, the six-years-older Josephine de Beauharnais. Well known in society as the widow of a guillotined general, and mistress in turn of three Directors – Tallien, Gohier and Barras – she had married General Bonaparte while he was on leave in 1796; and had come close to being divorced for infidelity while he was away in Egypt.

Within a few weeks of the parade outside the Tuileries, the new First Consul was off to fight a fresh campaign, in Italy. Yet again a French ruler would succumb to the urge to interfere in Italian affairs in the pursuit of *la Gloire*. Though longing for peace, Parisians were able to persuade themselves that this new campaign was all the fault of *les perfides Anglais* and their Austrian henchmen, who had given France no rest since the execution of Louis XVI, and had recently formed another hostile coalition against her. Potentially outnumbered and in a highly dangerous position, in May Bonaparte pulled off one of his greatest and most daring ventures – marching an army across the Great Saint Bernard Pass to take a greatly superior Austrian army in the rear. Nevertheless, on 14 June, outside the small village of Marengo, the First Consul came perilously close to decisive defeat. The day was saved only by the unplanned arrival of General Desaix, acting against orders, who turned defeat into victory – but at the cost of his own life. Desaix became a Napoleonic hero, and henceforth Marengo (after whom he named his favourite white charger) held a unique place for Bonaparte in the annals of his battles. Milan was occupied, the Austrians accepted defeat, the Second Coalition collapsed, and France's new ruler returned to Paris in triumph, clad in all the laurels of *la Gloire*. For most of the next fifteen years his star would seem unassailable.

News of Marengo preceded him to Paris. The cannon thundering out proclaimed 'Italy is taken!' The city went wild with unaccustomed rejoicing. Here at last was a leader, able to assert French supremacy – and at a moderate cost in lives. Moreover, at home Napoleon promised to reverse the anarchy, destruction and decay left behind by a decade of revolutionaries. He wrote ahead to his brother Lucien that he was intending to arrive in Paris without warning. Still mistrustful of any kind of pomp and circumstance, he was averse to making a grand entry with a parade, instead creeping through the city gates almost stealthily at 2 a.m. on 2 July. But popular enthusiasm carried everything away, to his considerable surprise. On his arrival, a dense crowd converged on the Tuileries, and he had to show himself several times on the balcony 'amid a tempest of cries of joy'. The *défilé* lasted a whole day. At night almost every house in Paris was lit up. Over the two decades of Napoleon's astonishing career, similar parades and celebrations would mark his victories and his triumphs, the path of his rise and his fall; equally they would provide markers to his achievements for the often bedazzled, often nervous, capital.

THE LEGACY OF THE REVOLUTION

The whole of the Marengo campaign kept Bonaparte out of Paris for only fifty-seven days. It would give him nearly five years of peace, the longest in his career, which he could spend in Paris, devoting himself to restoring and reforming the social fabric of France. There was much to be done, mountains and pyramids to be moved. Inflation was rampant: shoes worth five livres in 1790 cost 200 in 1795, and 2,000 in 1797. The country – once more – was bankrupt, but imbued with the singular urge to reinvent herself.

Returning to France in 1800 after seven years' self-exile, the writer Chateaubriand had been dismayed by the ravages that he found inflicted by the Revolution, especially in its militant atheism: 'the ruinous castles, the belfries empty of bells, the graveyards with never a cross and the headless statues of saints'. At Saint-Denis, the resting place of French monarchs from time immemorial, tombs had been defaced, decapitated or totally destroyed, their royal contents sacrilegiously scattered. In Paris, though it was horribly vandalized, Notre-Dame had escaped by a whisker – scheduled for destruction, its stones had actually been put up for auction. Louis IX's priceless Sainte-Chapelle, profaned and used as a flour warehouse, and so dilapidated that it bore a sign proclaiming 'National property, for sale', had also survived. But a great many churches had been totally destroyed. In the centre of squares, pedestals stood bereft of their statues; almost the only monument left was that of the sombre Place de la Révolution (renamed Concorde only a few months after Robespierre's execution there). The façade of the Tuileries, which had once housed Robespierre and the dreaded Committee of Public Safety, was still marked with bullet holes, while the Church of Saint-Roch bore the more recent scars of General Bonaparte's own 'whiff of grapeshot' from 1795. The great houses of the nobility and the bourgeois had been pillaged, with barely a courtyard gate still left on its hinges. Walls had been brought down, and shacks built upon the girdle of market gardens. On both banks of the Seine Paris resembled one immense house-breakers' yard, combined with a no less enormous junk shop.

Although the massacres perpetrated on the Royalist Vendée far exceeded the Terror in Paris, the mess left behind by the revolutionary Commune would have daunted any lesser man than Napoleon. A worn, wrecked and exhausted city, Paris now smelt more of filthy mud and sewage than she had at the worst moments of the Middle Ages. There had after all been 'ten years of anarchy, sedition and laxity, during which no useful work had been undertaken, not a street had been cleaned, not a residence repaired, nothing improved or cleansed', as Sainte-Beuve wrote. There was a serious lack of clean water, a deficiency only partially offset by a few so-called 'purifying fountains' with which to fill buckets. Most Parisians, however, preferred to take their chances with the ever more polluted Seine. 'You are barbarians,' Stendhal castigated the post-revolutionary Parisians; 'your streets stink aloud; you can't take a step in them without being covered with black mud, which gives a disgusting appearance to the populace, forced to travel on foot. This comes of the absurd idea of turning your streets into a main sewer.' Walkers hugged the walls to avoid being run over in the squalid streets. Even in the more salubrious areas, armed robbers (some of them outlawed priests or noblemen forced into hiding) preyed on those spared by Robespierre and his allies, while as an ironic reminder of the levelling work of Madame Guillotine, *la Veuve*, in the Place de la Révolution there still stood a peeling pink cardboard statue of Liberty.

France after the Terror resembled a madman who had been subjected to excessive bleeding. Yet, in providing another example of Paris's miraculous capacity to recover from catastrophe, within only fourteen months of the dreadful Robespierre losing his sea-green head on the scaffold, the capital under the Directory had begun to explode in an amazing display of gaiety and frivolity – one of the most dissipated periods in the city's history. There might be hunger and riots in the rest of the country, but for now all Paris danced. The city was indeed seized by a kind of dance mania. Everywhere *bals publics* sprang up; by 1797 they totalled nearly 700, and there the waltz – recently imported from Germany – reigned. All classes joined in the craze, not least the young aristocrats who had ventured back and had come into inheritances earlier than if their fathers had not been guillotined. (Some of the relatives of the guillotined found it smart to wear round their necks a thin red ribbon; 'à la victime' as it was called.) It was even rumoured that that great survivor, Director Paul-Jean-François-Nicolas, Vicomte de Barras, had his two mistresses dance naked before him – Mme Tallien and Josephine de Beauharnais, the future Empress – in a scene made famous by the cartoon of Gillray.

Outside the dance halls, the Parisians' zest for living, for a revival of life itself, extended – even while the tocsins were still sounding the call to arms – to the Pavilion of Hanover, a popular meeting-place on the Boulevard des Italiens, where the children of Louis XIV by Mme de Montespan and, later, the incorrigible Duc de Richelieu had once lived. Here, amid the gaming tables and the stalls dispensing mouth-watering ice-creams, Thérèse Tallien, Josephine de Beauharnais and Barras all held forth, promoting the success of the Paris fashions of 1798–1800, for the benefit of the mistresses of men who had somehow enriched themselves and now crept out of their hiding places. The new modes represented an astounding rejection and throwing-off almost to excess of all the puritanism of the revolutionary years. The styles for women, Graeco-Roman imitations, were exaggeratedly high-waisted, as low cut as minimal decency would allow, and as gauzily transparent as possible (the diaphanous material would often be moistened with water). There were the *merveilleuses*, eccentrics dressed as classical beings – Ceres, Galathea or Diana – all with immense, imaginative and high unproletarian hats.

The *merveilleuses* would be escorted by the equally ridiculous *incroyables*, men whose aim, in sharp contrast, was often to appear as ragged and as uncouth as possible, or in deliberately over-length coats with leg-of-mutton sleeves, wide padded lapels, exaggerated cravats and 'coiffures *à la* Titus sprouting from empty heads'. Alternatively there were the elegant, Royalist *muscadins*, hair often set in tight curls, legs sheathed in fragile, flesh-coloured breeches that had to be changed several times in the course of an evening's dancing. They displayed black revers in mourning for the late King, and would sometimes carry a knobbly walking-stick – with which to 'hunt terrorists'. The *incroyables* would cheerfully walk about the Paris streets in white stockings, regardless of the mud; this represented, remarks one French historian, 'a great expense of effort to achieve a painful result'. Returning to Paris from self-exile in America, a former deputy of the revolutionary Constituent Assembly, Jean-Nicolas Démeunier, described in a letter to a friend how the *merveilleuses* and *incroyables* would 'talk about politics as they dance, and express their longing for the return of the monarchy as they eat ices or watch fireworks with affected boredom'.

Deeper down, however, the social topography of Paris, with the residual violence and hatreds left over from 1789, was little changed. In the eyes of a modern German historian, Johannes Willms, 'The Paris of the rich and the Paris of the poor grew into two separate cultural and political worlds, divided by a wall of fear and mistrust.' Here was to be the source of repeated turbulence and upheaval all through the next century and beyond.

THE PEACE OF AMIENS AND THE CONCORDAT

In March 1802, Napoleon concluded the Peace of Amiens with England. What the English, smarting from defeat, dismissively called 'the peace which passeth all understanding' heralded for both France and Napoleon a halcyon period. Alas, in the words of Winston Churchill, 'the tourist season was short'. During these thirteen months of peace, English tourists crossed the Channel in their tens of thousands to savour the abandoned joys of post-Directory Paris. With its 547,000 inhabitants to London's 960,000 at the turn of the century, Paris seemed to her British visitors a decrepit city, where cattle were still driven through the streets on their way to market – much as it had struck Dr Lister over a hundred years before. The tourists would have reacted with scepticism to Napoleon's declared ambition of 1798 to 'make Paris not only the most beautiful city that is in the world, the most beautiful that ever existed, but also the most beautiful that could ever exist'.

Nevertheless, for the English tourists swarming in, as the chestnuts along the Seine sprang into blossom that spring, it was all quite captivating: suddenly, it was *gai Paris*, 1801. They rejoiced at discovering in the Champs-Elysées Greek goddesses naked under their gauze dresses; they were titillated by the spectacle of Mme Hamelin sitting in a box at the theatre, her bare breasts outlined 'in a river of diamonds' – though the more puritanical among them wondered whether the recent storms and frosts on the vines had been sent as a punishment from the heavens for the indecency of the *Parisiennes'* dress.

The Parisians sometimes found their visitors unlovable and uncouth. At the opera in the stifling summer of 1802, two Englishmen in a box took off their coats to sit in shirtsleeves, and were roundly booed from the *parterre*, never exactly renowned for its chic, to the extent that the *commissaire de service* had to be summoned to remind them of continental niceties. But for all their disapproval of the visitors the Parisians swiftly began to ape English dress and styles, as dandies in black dress coats and shiny riding boots made their appearance on the boulevards.

Foreigners privileged to be invited to the First Consul's birthday celebrations were charmed by the graciousness and bonhomie with which he greeted them. Keen to respect the sensibilities of his English visitors, he arranged, on either side of his chimneypiece, busts of Fox and Nelson. His court was certainly a brilliant one – 'A newly born government', he told his secretary, 'must dazzle and astonish' – but, in contrast to the splendour of the generals and Mameluke orderlies who escorted him on parades, Napoleon's own uniform was notably simple, putting his visitors in mind of an English sea captain in undress. Could this really be the ogre who had lately terrorized all Europe? Among his own people, he had never been so popular as he was that year.

Very soon there were the first small signs of the clock being turned back on the Revolution. First Bonaparte abolished the savage Law of Hostages, which had made the illegal return of émigrés punishable by death, and he next proclaimed a general amnesty for virtually all categories of proscribed exiles. (He was keen to attract the support of the monarchists for his plans of continental conquest.) Within the first year of the Consulate alone, over 40,000 families were permitted to return. The *bonnet rouge* was removed from steeples; the titles 'Madame' or 'Mademoiselle' replaced the dreaded appellation of 'citoyenne'; the revolutionary calendar of ten months was discreetly dropped in favour of the old twelve months, so that '18 Brumaire, An VII' once more became 9 November 1799; and the good old pre-revolutionary festivals like Christmas and Easter once more returned to fashion. Dropping its revolutionary name, the former Place Royale now became (and remained for ever) the Place des Vosges – for the very good reason that that *département* had excelled itself in revenue contributions over the previous year. Churches ceased to be 'decadel temples', such as the Temple of Concord, of Genius or of Hymen, and resumed their former names. And in May 1802 Napoleon instituted the new award of the Légion d'Honneur: a new society, he reasoned, needed a new elite, an aristocracy not of birth but of merit. Boundless in his own ambition Napoleon derided it in others, remarking disdainfully of his own creation, the Légion, 'It is by such baubles that one leads men by the nose!' Under the Empire no fewer than 48,000 *rubans rouges* were distributed (including 1,200 to civilians). 'Hanging by a thread!' said the cynics, yet the Légion would remain a source of power and influence for republican regimes long after Napoleon's demise.

One of the most complex issues Bonaparte confronted as first consul, and which would take five years to sort out, was that of giving houses a rational street number. Hitherto there were none; the Revolution, with motives of state security, had tried but had ended in such a muddle that a certain Isaïe Carus, mentioned in a police report, was listed as residing at 1,087 Rue du Bac. Now Napoleon conceived the present-day system of odd and even numbers on alternate sides, with every street numbering from its position relative to the Seine.

Aware that piety was once more fashionable, Napoleon had the synagogues reopened and decreed that churches which had been wrecked during the Revolution were to be restored. In this last enterprise, it was not architectural values alone that prompted him. With the Revolution fading away, the final years of the century had been marked by a strong religious revival which progressed side by side with the new Romantic movement – a development encapsulated in Chateaubriand's work *Le Génie du Christianisme*. Sensitive to the new mood, Napoleon then erased the divisions that still prevailed in France by his Concordat with Pope Pius VII, signed in July 1801. All this was part and parcel of his somewhat cynical attitude to religion, a way of posing as the champion of Old Catholic France, a hero-leader who would restore her former values. As he warned visiting Vendéean leaders, 'I intend to re-establish religion, not for your sake but for mine.' Achieved after nine months of secret negotiations, a triumph of diplomacy for Bonaparte, the Concordat brought France back into the Roman Catholic fold (though the head of state retained the right to appoint bishops).

On Easter Day 1802, Napoleon sealed the new agreement with a grand Te Deum sung at Notre-Dame to celebrate the re-establishment of peace, which also came across as a powerful ceremony of atonement. It was the second of his extravaganzas since coming to power. After ten years' silence, the tenor bell in the cathedral tolled out to proclaim the new alliance between France and the Vatican. At 11 a.m., preceded by four regiments of cavalry, a procession of coaches rolled up, with grooms in the full livery of the *ancien régime*, bringing the three Consuls, ministers and the Corps Diplomatique. Bonaparte was received under the portico by the recently nominated Archbishop, the ancient Monseigneur de Belloy, and solemnly escorted up to the choir. It was duly noted that, of the grandees present, only the two defrocked priests, former Bishop Talleyrand and ex-priest Fouché (the Minister of Police), knew properly how to genuflect. There was some surprise when the military presented arms and the drums beat a salute. Commenting on the large number of troops and gendarmes drawn up around the cathedral, irreverent wits suggested that this was to prevent God the

Father from being burgled, while one general remarked afterwards that it had been 'A fine piece of church flummery! The only thing missing was the million men who gave their lives in order to destroy what you have just re-established!' Perhaps a more general Parisian view of the ceremony, however, was that of a glazier across on the Île Saint-Louis who was heard to exclaim, 'Ah! Now I hear the bell of Notre-Dame; I like it much better than the *canon d'alarme!*'

Napoleon and Josephine spent as much time as possible at the Château de Malmaison, only an hour's drive out of Paris (it takes rather longer now), where they could enjoy her roses, and the painting of them by the great Redouté. This brief period of peace was the happiest time of their lives, and the longest they would spend together: he had a better chance of keeping the voracious sexual appetite of the hot-blooded Creole under control; she could keep tabs on his passing infidelities.

Then they had the Tuileries. After a hundred days spent in Marie de Medici's Luxembourg, in the spring of 1800 they moved into Louis XVI's ill-starred Palace. It was soon abuzz with Napoleonic bees and Ns, replacing the languid fleurs-de-lys of the Bourbons on all embroideries, carpets and escutcheons. Only a few years previously, as a young captain in a ragged coat, Bonaparte had been accustomed to climbing the backstairs there to the Topographical Bureau of the Committee of Public Safety, the post procured for him by Barras. In 1800 there were still traces of dried blood in the corridors from the massacre of the Swiss Guards in 1792. Josephine had misgivings. 'I was never made for so much grandeur,' she confessed to her sister-in-law Hortense: 'I will never be happy here. I can feel the Queen's ghost asking what I am doing in her bed.' Napoleon was more robust, picking her up and carrying her off to the royal suite: 'Come on, little Creole, get into the bed of your masters!' He regarded residence in the Tuileries as an essential sign of the continuity of power, but he was realistic about his permanence there. 'It's not enough to be here,' he remarked to his old schoolfriend Louis Bourrienne, who had become his secretary; 'The problem will be to stay.'

By the end of the Peace of Amiens, Napoleon's authoritarian rule seemed to be comprehensively established, with all aspects of national life under his control. Yet a crucial element in the whole structure was missing: the continuity of succession. It was abundantly clear to all Paris that everything depended on the survival in power of this one remarkable being. As early as Christmas Eve 1800, six months after Marengo, the First Consul's mortality was brought dramatically home. On his way to a Haydn oratorio at the Opéra he had narrowly escaped death when a massive bomb hidden under straw in a wagon exploded in the Rue Saint-Nicaise. The blast destroyed the carriage in which Hortense and Napoleon's sister Caroline Bonaparte were being conveyed, killing one of the horses and splashing Hortense with blood. Fifty-two bystanders and part of the escort were killed or maimed. The sinister Fouché had two Chouans (Royalist guerrillas from the south-west) guillotined and almost a hundred former Jacobins deported. In true Parisian tradition, the executions of the guilty were watched by enormous crowds, thronging all the bridges and the quays on the route to the scaffold.

The explosion in the Rue Saint-Nicaise had some long-term consequences. In the first place, it strengthened the hand of Fouché, lending the regime the trappings of authoritarianism which it had not possessed before. Secondly, the structural damage caused to so many old buildings in the vicinity of the Louvre determined Napoleon to launch a major rebuilding programme. Thirdly, it focused the attention of the childless First Consul on the problems of his succession. At the beginning of 1804, two more plots against him would be uncovered in Paris; they were followed by one of the few mass guillotinings of Napoleon's rule, and one of the suspects, General Pichegru, was found strangled in prison. These three *attentats* would lead, in 1804, to Napoleon's greatest error of judgement – the murder of the Duc d'Enghien. One night in March 1804, the thirty-two-year-old d'Enghien (a totally harmless princeling, but one feared by Napoleon – doubtless egged on by Fouché – as a potentially dangerous claimant to the Bourbon throne) was kidnapped from his retreat in Germany by French cavalry. Spirited off to the Château de Vincennes, a week later, after a perfunctory court martial which produced no evidence against him, he was executed by firing squad, together with his inseparable dog, and buried in a grave which had been dug well in advance. It was, in the immortal phrase of Talleyrand, whose own hands were far from clean, 'worse than a crime, it was a blunder'.

CIVIL REFORMS

It was during these fleeting years of peace that Napoleon, acting with the speed and energy which he brought to his military operations, carried through the civil reforms that were to be his most durable achievements. He was, of course, helped by the radical changes already effected by the Revolution, which had got rid of all those institutions it considered to have outlived their usefulness. Even if Napoleon had never fought a battle, these reforms would still entitle him to acclaim as one of history's great rulers.

Impelled by the disastrous floods of the previous winter, which had left the Champs-Elysées partly submerged, Napoleon embarked on the reorganization of the quays of the Seine. He began in 1802 by ordering the construction of the Quai d'Orsay, which was eventually to stretch all the way to the Ecole Militaire. Ambitious plans for canals and reservoirs were drawn up, providing Paris with her modern water supply. Named the Musée Napoléon, the Louvre was completed in 1803 to display the Italian art treasures looted in the First Consul's recent campaigns. Before long there would come the grandiose architecture inspired by military conquests. There were also works of purely economic significance, like the Bourse and the giant Halle des Vins – intended to make Paris the main entrepôt for wine in northern Europe.

The list of construction work started is an impressive one, especially given how little time Napoleon was able to devote to the home front: the Rue de Rivoli, Rue de Castiglione, Rue Napoléon (later renamed Rue de la Paix), the Conseil d'Etat and the Cour des Comptes, four new bridges, the Madeleine transformed into a Temple of Victory with the portico of the Palais Bourbon, facing it across the Concorde, remodelled in matching Roman style. Everywhere new fountains and parks were constructed.

Napoleon's views on education, as expressed at a session of the Conseil d'Etat held at the Tuileries in 1804–5, were simply stated and non-revolutionary. 'Up to the present,' he declared,

> the only good education we have met with is that of the ecclesiastical bodies. I would rather see the children of the village in the hands

of a man who knows only his catechism, but whose principles are known to me, than of some half-baked man of learning who has no foundation for his morality and no fixed ideas.

In 1795 the Directory had introduced a new secular system of education, on to which stem, accepting the best and rejecting the worst, Napoleon grafted in 1802 one of the most favoured and long-lasting of all his reforms – the *lycées*, or state secondary schools. As with so many of his reforms, his intention at least in part was to provide a steady flow of military and administrative cadres essential to the Napoleonic machine. He also converted the high-grade Ecole Polytechnique, founded by the Convention in 1794, into a military college for gunners and engineers. He next set his seal on the Ecole Normale Supérieure, likewise initiated by the Convention and still today the breeding ground for French intellectual leaders.

Both the latter innovations were created within the embrace of the Sorbonne, which – like every other institution in Paris – swiftly felt the imprint of the new master. Under the Revolution the great University founded by Abelard had once more fallen on hard times. On account of its clerical orientations it had received rough treatment from the revolutionaries, who stole its marbles and left it to crumble. Suppressed, it remained empty until Napoleon took a hand in 1806, establishing the Académie de Paris and the Facultés des Lettres, des Sciences et de Théologie in its buildings. Once again the Sorbonne thrived – but only briefly. Then, as before, it was allowed to fall into decay. For the first part of the nineteenth century following the fall of the Empire, arguments continued on its rebuilding, but nothing was done until Haussmann came along.

Though the Directory had done something to improve France's political structure, between 1799 and 1804 her constitution was extensively remodelled by Napoleon, to the great advantage of his personal power of course. As it did in his military technique, rationalization drove his civil reforms. In February 1800, the various *départements* were placed under the charge of prefects; the following year the metric system was set up; and in 1802 a new national police force was raised. France was to become more tightly centralized on Paris than ever it had been under the Roi Soleil. Before Napoleon, France had been plagued by 360 separate local codes; he now began the prodigious labour of unifying them into one set. By 1804 the Code Civil (better known as the Code Napoléon) had been voted through the legislature. Though comprising over 2,000 articles, it took only four years to complete and is still for the most part in force. Typical both of his energy and of his personal interest in administrative reform, Napoleon attended no fewer than 57 of the 109 meetings devoted to it. Regulating virtually every function of life, the Code imposed *inter alia* the equal division of property among sons – thereby doing more than the Revolution had done to break up the big estates.

The precarious French economic and financial system also benefited from Napoleon's attention, accompanied by often ruthless measures. From the Revolution France emerged with a tax burden at least as great as at the end of the *ancien régime*, but the Directory had at least managed to straighten out some of the chaos of the nation's finances. Taxation had been thoroughly overhauled, with taxes restructured, and – for almost the first time – actually collected with pitiless efficiency. Fines were imposed on those who did not pay promptly, and even the workers were subject to taxes; thus both the Consulate and the Empire were able to benefit from these sweeping reforms. Bonaparte swiftly reduced the number of tax collectors from 200,000 to fewer than 6,000; at the same time, the yields doubled. The Banque de France was established in 1800, and given complete control over the national debt and the issue of paper money. Unemployment in Paris was kept to a low level, but labour was hard and the hours long. Outside Paris, in the countryside, the life of the average peasant was not much affected by either the Consulate or the Empire. The great roads built by Napoleon radiated out from Paris towards frontiers with distinct military purposes, but did little to bring rural France into contact with the modern world.

In general, however, both peasant and urban working classes seem to have been better fed than they were either before 1789 or after 1815 – partly thanks to strict government controls on corn exports and price levels – and they came to regard the Napoleonic era as one of relative prosperity. Napoleon claimed to have gained the allegiance of the working classes by 'bread and circuses', and certainly the appeal to native jingoism of great victories such as Marengo did much to alleviate dissatisfaction over any loss of civil or political liberties. But, as with most dictators, it would also mean that he had to keep on going, producing one triumph after another abroad.

A CORONATION

In December 1804, Napoleon mounted the greatest public entertainment that Paris had seen since the famous *spectacles* of Louis XIV – his coronation as emperor. It had not been entirely a good year: the abduction from Germany and summary execution of the Duc d'Enghien had lost him considerable goodwill at home and, together with his proclamation of the Empire on 18 May, had precipitated the Third Coalition against him. But now, by the ceremony on 2 December, Bonaparte – and his dynasty – would be confirmed in everlasting power.

Preparations had been going on for months. To the eternal credit of the about-to-be-Emperor, restoration work demanded by the Coronation had saved Notre-Dame (which had only recently been formally handed back to the Roman Catholic clergy) from the terrible ravages of the Revolution. With the declared intention of clearing the area round the cathedral for aesthetic reasons, so that it could be better seen, but also to allow access for the vast retinue of cavalry, troops and coaches designated for the Coronation, Napoleon had started to demolish many of the medieval houses that hemmed it in. A first instalment of his own grandiose schemes for rebuilding the city as 'the most beautiful that could ever exist', this began what Haussmann would complete under the Emperor's nephew. To get it all completed on time, from the summer of 1804 workmen had laboured all night by the light of torches. In the Concorde, a huge star had been erected on the exact spot where Louis XVI had been executed, and imposing *N*s surrounded by laurel wreaths were placed atop all the surrounding buildings.

To perform the ceremony, Napoleon – exploiting the new Concordat – had summoned or coerced Pope Pius VII all the way from Rome. It was an extraordinary display of arrogance for a ruler so recently under excommunication. In bitter cold at the end of November, Pontiff and future Emperor met on the road near Fontainebleau. Weary from his long journey, the Pope was obliged to descend from his carriage and stand in the mud to be received by Napoleon. He was then conducted into the inferior position in the imperial coach. Paris had never seen a pope before, and the frail, mild-mannered man made the most favourable of impressions. Even the hard-line Jacobins bowed their heads before him. Parisian vendors of rosaries did a roaring trade – one was said to have made a net profit of 40,000 francs in January 1805 alone.

On the morning of the Coronation, Napoleon once again kept his captive Pope waiting, chilly and apprehensive, before having him escorted from the Tuileries by four squadrons of dragoons and six carriage-loads of cardinals, bishops and priests; as someone noted, the last time so many clerics had been seen on that route they had been bundled into tumbrils. After waiting patiently in the cold, thousands of Parisians watched the Emperor's giant coach go past – on its roof the crown of Charlemagne, no less, supported by eagles. As church bells pealed and cannon sounded out in their hundreds, 8,000 outriders accompanied the procession, far outdoing even the excesses of Louis XIV. Some bystanders noted the eight horses now harnessed to the great coach, a number properly reserved exclusively for royalty. George Sand's father wrote to his wife, 'Goodbye to the Republic. Neither you nor I will miss it.' It was a view echoing that of many a Parisian.

Waiting at Notre-Dame were sixty bishops with their clergy, the Senate, the Legislative Body, the Conseil d'Etat, and ministers of the various European powers. Closest to the Emperor were generals mostly from plebeian backgrounds, some of whom had been Jacobins and regicides only the previous decade, now all bearing resounding titles: Grand Chamberlains, Grand Marshals, Grand Masters of the Hounds. In the west end of the cathedral, and opposite the altar, on a platform twenty-four steps high sat an immense throne. Here Napoleon, not the Pope, placed the imperial crown on his own head, as Josephine knelt before him. There were moments of dissonance, which threatened to introduce farce into a scene of high majesty. Between the altar and the throne, an altercation broke out between Josephine and the jealous sisters-in-law carrying her train, which momentarily arrested her procession. Chagrined by receiving only two tickets for the Coronation, David, the court painter, sought his revenge by painting himself into the ponderous formal tableau. On the return journey to the Tuileries, there was an unfortunate omen when the weighty crown toppled off the coach.

At this point, when he had taken to himself a concentration of power comparable only to that of the Roman Caesars, of Charlemagne and of the Holy Roman emperors, Napoleon was still only thirty-five. *Le petit caporal* or *le Tondu*, as the army fondly called him, was beginning to show just a few signs of filling out; his cheeks were plumper, the waistband of his breeches tauter, his skin sallower. Already he had been *cocu* by Josephine (and vice versa). Soon it would be time to do once again what he did best: to demonstrate to the world the military supremacy of France.

11

'The Most Beautiful City That Could Ever Exist'

If the Heavens had granted me another twenty years and some leisure, you would have looked in vain for the Old Paris...

Napoleon on Saint Helena

RETURN FROM AUSTERLITZ

The Peace of Amiens had reached the end of its short life in May 1803 when England, alarmed by Napoleon's naval activity, resumed her blockade of France. Napoleon was determined to invade England and assembled 177,000 men and more than 2,000 craft in the Channel ports, only to be frustrated repeatedly by adverse winds. When the new Third Coalition – in which Britain was joined by Russia, Austria, Sweden and Naples – menaced him from the east, the French Emperor acted decisively, even precipitately. On 1 October 1805, finally abandoning all thoughts of invading *perfide Albion*, Napoleon reversed direction and headed eastwards for the greatest military triumph of his career. It was one of his rare campaigns without a female consort. Never would he be more admired and worshipped by his soldiers than during this brief and dazzling operation. Nevertheless, he left an ill-humoured and extremely anxious Paris. In the Senate there had been little more than token enthusiasm when he explained the causes of the new war, laying the blame squarely on the Allies. Since the ending of the Peace of Amiens and of its accompanying boom, the French economy had nosedived. A poor harvest had made bread prices soar, and the national finances were soon in a mess once again, with the budget showing an immense deficit and taxes rising. All of this provoked something akin to panic on the Bourse. Thus it was absolutely imperative for Napoleon to win a swift and conclusive victory, otherwise the country would be in serious danger of bankruptcy. A call-up of 80,000 troops had done little to enhance his popularity in the capital. Leaving the Tuileries on his long march, the Emperor had been vexed by the unwonted lack of warmth towards him shown by the citizenry.

Yet, within the month, after marching through Germany at a prodigious speed, Napoleon at the head of the Grande Armée had trapped a whole Austrian army at Ulm and received its surrender. By 14 November he was entering Vienna in triumph. Two weeks later, brought to bay – so it seemed – far away in the heart of what is now the Czech Republic, he then turned and defeated the vastly superior combined forces of Austria and Russia. The Battle of Austerlitz, one of the most perfectly conceived and executed in the history of warfare – though an immensely risky affair – would always remain the jewel of all military jewels in Napoleon's crown.

But this was not how Paris saw it when the news came through on 26 November. The city was still in an ill humour. With such a hands-on ruler, anxiety was often rife during his absences on campaign, and Paris was never more nervous. Up to 1803, Napoleon had appeared to Frenchmen as a peacemaker, but thenceforth it was as the conqueror and founder of a new empire – a change of role that, as of 1805, was by no means to every Parisian's liking. Vienna was the first Allied capital ever to be occupied during all the wars of the previous decade, yet news of Napoleon's triumphal entry was greeted in Paris with a momentary *froideur*. What was Napoleon getting himself into? Unmistakably the hand of the police could be seen fomenting the 'spontaneous' joy in the streets, and 'inviting' householders to display all their lights. The rejoicing did not last long; and it would be dimmed by the news of the loss of Admiral Villeneuve's fleet at Trafalgar. But much more menacing in its immediacy was the awareness that the Banque Récamier had stopped payments. And what a terrifying predicament – the Grande Armée with the Emperor himself so many hundreds of kilometres from home, surrounded by powerful enemies in the heart of Europe!

Next, hardly pausing for breath, Napoleon was striking northward into Saxony, to defeat the combined forces of Prussia (which had belatedly joined the Allies against France in the Fourth Coalition) in another smashing, decisive victory at Jena. Then he was marching in triumph through a prostrate Berlin. Following this, in pursuit of the Russians, he was plunging eastwards into Poland, to Warsaw (where he was smitten by the beautiful Marie Walewska), and then finally – 1,600 kilometres from Paris – he fought the last two battles of the campaign, Eylau and Friedland, less tidy and far costlier victories than Austerlitz and Jena, but victories all the same. In July 1807, from a raft anchored midstream in the River Niemen, Napoleon received the defeated Tsar Alexander I of Russia in an elegant pavilion of striped canvas. On the 7th of that month, the Peace of Tilsit was concluded. It was Napoleon's finest achievement, and one of the greatest in the annals of France. 'One of the culminating points of modern history,' declared Napoleon's starry-eyed schoolfriend Bourrienne: 'the waters of the Niemen reflected the image of Napoleon at the height of his glory'. Pitt's Third Coalition had been rent asunder; Pitt, the arch-enemy, himself was dead, and, survey-ing from the raft in the Niemen the ruins of the rival empires, Napoleon could truly proclaim himself to be Master of All Europe. Everything was possible. But history is fickle. The next time Napoleon ventured on to the Niemen, just five years later, he would be *en route* to his first great defeat, and the beginning of his eclipse.

After the historic victory at Austerlitz, Napoleon was back in Paris at ten o'clock on the night of Sunday, 26 January 1806; within an hour he was issuing orders on how to resolve the bank crisis. He had been out of town for just 124 days, in which time he had smashed all his enemies – a true *Blitzkrieg* before its time. In the ensuing year, sixty-one days' absence would suffice to bring Prussia to her knees; while, by the time of the destruction of the Allies' Fourth Coalition and the conclusion of the Peace of Tilsit in July 1807, he would have been absent over the two years for a total of 306 days – the longest he would ever be away from the capital.

To commemorate the Grande Armée's military triumph at Austerlitz, and also as part of his 'bread and circuses' strategy of distracting uneasy Parisian minds with evidence of *la Gloire*, Napoleon projected a huge exposition of manufactures associating the arts of peace with the tri-umphs of war. (In the event, there was no such exhibition until 1819.) To keep the city's growing body of unemployed quiet, Napoleon set them to work digging a new canal – the Ourcq. Outside the Tuileries the Arc du Carrousel, a triumphal arch in the Roman style, was to be erected; in Louis XIV's Place Vendôme, a lofty column would be wrapped with the bronze of enemy cannon captured at Austerlitz. For the Grande Armée's heroes, a colossal banquet was offered by the city – to which Napoleon, with his extraordinary attention to detail, proposed adding 'a few bull-fights in the Spanish manner', a diversion which he thought would please the warriors. A vast camp was prepared at Meudon, designed to quarter the whole Grande Armée, only for Napoleon to decide that the Imperial Guard alone should be allowed to figure in the Parisian celebrations. But by this time Napoleon was at war with Prussia, so the Grande Armée headed east again, instead of marching through Paris.

When news of the next remarkable victory, at Jena, reached the capital, Parisians again reacted 'without over-excitement, like a well-behaved child'. Frochot, the Prefect of the Seine, was actually exhorted to do whatever he could to 'facilitate the explosion of [public] enthusiasm', possibly by encouraging 'dance resorts ordinarily frequented by the people on a Sunday, the *bastringues*, that is, to make them more attractive, better attended, gayer, more animated'. A deputation was sent by the Senate to Berlin, more to persuade Napoleon to make peace than to offer congratulations for Jena.

What continued to be much more immediately preoccupying to Parisians, during this period of astonishing events in faraway countries, was news in the autumn of 1805 of the collapse of the Banque Récamier, which had suspended withdrawals, thereby provoking a sequence of bankruptcies and bringing whole industries to a standstill. Anarchy imported by the zealots of the Revolution had caused capital to flee the city, and had destroyed the basis of commercial prosperity in Paris. This was being slowly rebuilt under the Consulate, but when the peace ended in 1803, and with it the tourist boom, Paris had experienced a tremendous inflation of prices, especially in luxuries; a woman's coiffure for a single evening, for instance, cost three times the tariff of a few years before. The Banque Récamier had been a rock-like institution – the elderly Jacques Récamier a pillar of respectability, his wife Juliette renowned for her salon and her sofa, a paragon of virtue (until she met Chateaubriand). Yet when Récamier pleaded for a modest government loan to bail out the bank, Napoleon was unmoved, writing from Austerlitz within days of his triumph there, 'Is it at a time like this that I must be obliged to make advances to men who got themselves involved in bad businesses?' and, more brutally, 'I am not the lover of Madame Récamier, not I, and I am not going to come to the help of *négociants* who keep up a house costing 600,000 francs a year.'

The Récamiers would survive – indeed recoup their fortune – but for a while it looked as if the whole of France was facing bankruptcy. As a result of the breakdown of commerce with England, businesses collapsed right and left, and Parisians tightened their belts. Unhelpfully, Napoleon told them to break their habit of colonial foodstuffs: 'Let your women take Swiss tea, it is just as good as the tea of the caravane, and chicory coffee is as healthy as Arabian coffee...!' And he warned the writer Mme de Staël and her coterie, 'Beware that I don't spot them wearing dresses of English material!' It was almost certainly only by the success of Napoleon's triumphs on distant battlefields like Austerlitz and Jena that serious disorder was averted in Paris.

THE PEACE OF TILSIT

The winter of 1806–7 continued just as difficult and dreary, with the English blockade affecting not only Paris but cities as far away as Lyons. In Paris, hardship was complicated by the prolonged absence on campaign of the court, aggravated by the knowledge that the Grande Armée was bogged down in the mud of Poland. Josephine, suffering pangs of jealousy when rumours reached her of Marie Walewska, thought of joining Napoleon in Warsaw, but he would have none of it. She had to stay in Paris. 'I want you to be gay and bring a little life into the capital,' he told her. But the spring of 1807 brought a renewal of confidence in Paris. The economy seemed to be turning the corner; and in Tilsit the Napoleonic apparatus went into top gear to ensure that the Emperor's victorious return to his capital would this time remain fixed in Parisian memories. There was in any case little doubt about the genuineness of the warmth now being displayed by Parisians.

On 27 July 1807, cannon thundering out from the Invalides announced that the Emperor had returned from the eastern front. Heralds clad in medieval costume and illuminated by torchlight proclaimed the treaty he had just concluded. The whole of Paris, and Saint-Cloud where he spent his first nights, were lit up with spontaneous illuminations. (Typically, one of Napoleon's first actions on reaching Saint-Cloud was to summon his architect to pursue his grandiose plans for a Temple de la Gloire at the Madeleine.) Official deputations flooded in from all over France and Europe. Military bands and spectators jammed the broad avenues, as the magnificent Imperial Guard made its triumphal entry. There were endless parades, balls and fêtes. In November, Paris laid on the celebrations for the Imperial Guard which had been called off the previous year. At the head of a glittering cavalcade, Marshal Bessières, hero of Austerlitz, magnificent on his charger, led the Guard into Paris via the Porte de la Villette and onward through the Arc de Triomphe du Carrousel, still hidden in scaffolding. That night a vast banquet was offered to all the soldiers of the Guard the length of the Champs-Elysées. The following day another grandiose fête was thrown by the Senate at the Luxembourg; alas – possibly an augury of the gods – icy rain and snow turned the occasion into a rout.

Perhaps the most brilliant of all Paris's celebrations of Tilsit was that marking the Emperor's birthday on 15 August. An extraordinary gaiety pervaded the streets, never to be seen again in Napoleon's day. Houses were hung with metres of calico inscribed with flowery and obsequious eulogies, and even vendors of thermometers turned poets for the occasion:

> I know not what genius will venture
> To sing a hero guided by victory.
> For my part, I could not make a thermometer
> Capable of marking the degree of his fame!

read the banner on one hardware shop. That day, in Notre-Dame, Napoleon declared, with hubristic grandeur, that everything 'comes from God. He has granted me great victories. I come in the premier capital of my Empire to render thanks to Providence for its gifts, and to recommend myself to your prayers and those of the clergy.' Fouché went over the top, declaring in a confidential note addressed to the Tuileries that 'Today's fête is really national. Foreigners have been able to compare the birthday of Napoleon to that of Saint Louis.'

Hubris, the device that destroyed the Greek heroes of ancient mythology – was it now to be the undoing of Napoleon? Emulating Louis XIV after the Peace of Nijmegen in 1678, the Emperor bestowed upon himself the title 'le Grand'. He gazed down on an empire which stretched from the Pyrenees to the Niemen, ruled over either by puppet sovereigns or by members of his clan promoted to unimaginable heights – an empire far greater than anything achieved by Louis XIV or Charlemagne. The Peace of Tilsit seemed to give him endless options. But would he take them? Would the Peace last, any more than the Peace of Amiens had? Older Parisians wondered where it would all end. Talleyrand, foreseeing what lay ahead, soon resigned in despair.

From Tilsit Napoleon had ordered the abolition of the inefficient city administration he had inherited from the Directory, doing away with the system of incompetent elected bodies. Instead Paris was to be administered by various *conseils d'administration*, possessed of immense powers, and all coming under the Minister of the Interior, who in turn represented the full authority of the Emperor. Most important of all was the special bureaucracy set up to co-ordinate the efforts of administrators, architects and engineers to carry out Napoleon's building plans. The Emperor tried to run Paris like an army, but it was not the kind of army to which he was accustomed, or which he could bend to his will.

It was characteristic of Napoleon that he had issued these orders from Tilsit. For all the bureaucracy he had created in Paris, one of the extraordinary features of the Napoleonic regime is that this highly centralized and increasingly autocratic state was in fact run from a tent or from a Polish château – or wherever Napoleon happened to be. Every day his minions in Paris would be bombarded by letters, orders and draft decrees. While he was in East Prussia preparing for the bitter Friedland campaign, an angry letter flew off to Fouché: 'I understand that the city of Paris is no longer illuminated ... those in charge are scoundrels.' In Tilsit, he would be fretting that the fountains in Paris weren't working properly or that Ourcq Canal wasn't completed; or he would be decreeing demolition of the old houses on the Pont Saint-Michel.

REBUILDING AROUND THE LOUVRE

Napoleon's plans for rebuilding the city which he, the Corsican, had inherited, and with which, as dictator, he was now free to do whatsoever he pleased, were no less grandiose than his ambitions for military conquest. The bomb explosion of Christmas Eve 1800 provided him with both a first incentive and a pretext such as his predecessors had lacked. He started by demolishing the forty-odd houses damaged by the blast, then went on to clear the whole area of the medieval buildings and narrow streets which cluttered up the approaches to the Louvre. The result was several elegant new streets, all named after Napoleonic triumphs, including the Rue de Castiglione, Rue des Pyramides, Rue de la Paix (changed from Rue Napoléon after the Restoration in 1814) and the Rue de Rivoli, as well as the open space of the Place du Carrousel fronting on to the Tuileries. To achieve all this he resorted to draconian measures to take over property, notably convents left ravaged by revolution, and to drive out house-owners with little recompense.

The Rue de Rivoli, which became the second-longest street in Paris (after Vaugirard) and one of the straightest, was intended to run all the way from the Place de la Bastille in the east to the Concorde. Though it represented the most imposing achievement in large-scale domestic housing since Henri IV's Place Dauphine, the only section actually completed (and that only partially) in Napoleon's day was the grandly arcaded stretch opposite the Louvre that one knows today, designed by the Emperor's two favourite artists, Percier and Fontaine. The strictest conditions were imposed on the new Rivoli units once completed: residents were not to use hammers; there were to be no butchers, bakers or anybody using an oven. As a result, by 1810 so few houses had been built that Napoleon was forced to grant special tax exemptions for twenty years for developers, extended the following year to thirty. Even though the original grand design was never completed, the seemingly endless perspective of the massive arcades and the continuous line of ironwork balconies above them today still presents an effect unrivalled anywhere else in the world, an example of the true grandeur of Paris.

In the cleared area opposite the Rivoli arcades, Napoleon laid down the stately north wing of the Louvre – though, like so much else, that too had to await completion at the hands of his nephew, Napoleon III. In preserving intact the old sections of the building and resisting the impulses of his architects to tear them down, Napoleon showed remarkably good architectural sense, explaining, 'One must leave to each of the sections the character of its century, while adopting for the new work a more economic style.' Most important was the establishment in the Louvre, from 1803 onwards, of Europe's biggest art gallery, to provide a permanent home for the many works of art he had stolen from the countries he had conquered and occupied.

To run this new Musée Napoléon for him, the Emperor found one of those extraordinary geniuses thrown up by an extraordinary epoch – Vivant Denon. Fifty-five years old, a former diplomat, chargé d'affaires in Naples, Denon was something of a roué (which appealed to Napoleon) and a considerable artist in his own right. Travelling with Napoleon on the abortive Egyptian expedition, he had returned with a remarkable portfolio of sketches, and thereafter accompanied Napoleon on almost all his campaigns, becoming famed as 'l'oeil de l'armée'. The notion of a gallery open to the public stemmed from the historically much maligned

Louis XVI. In the sixteenth and seventeenth centuries the royal collections had been kept for the private delectation of the court and of privileged visitors, and only in the middle of the eighteenth century had Marigny, brother of Mme de Pompadour, put forward the idea of opening the royal galleries. It was Louis XVI himself who suggested reuniting everything that the Crown possessed of 'beauty in painting and sculpture' under the name of 'museum' (a concept borrowed from England). Explained Denon, 'The French Republic, by its force, the superiority of its light and its artists, is the only country in the world which could provide an inviolable asylum to these masterpieces.'

Napoleon took a great interest – amounting to interference – in the museum named after him. On his return from Jena in September 1806, he was already complaining about the queues on a Saturday afternoon – with the result that opening hours on Saturday and Sunday were extended. He was also horrified to see the galleries with smoking stoves, to keep the *gardiens* warm: 'Get them out ... they will end up by burning my conquests!' Equally shocking was the lack of public lavatories, leading to the misuse of the galleries by the unhappy *gardiens*, who were paid a menial wage, one-tenth of what Denon received. It was hardly surprising that in 1810 thieves broke in to make off with some priceless tapestries.

In September 1802, the *Medici Venus* – 'The glory of Florence' – arrived at the Louvre after a journey of ten months. Rumbling across Europe, the heavy pieces of looted sculpture required special carriages drawn by up to fifteen pairs of oxen. The following March came the first convoy of loot from Naples. Napoleon's greed seems to have known no bounds; in 1810 he declared to a deeply embarrassed Canova, the great Florentine sculptor, 'Here are the principal works of art; only missing is the Farnese *Hercules*, but we shall have that also.' Deeply shocked, Canova replied, 'Let your Majesty at least leave something in Italy!' It was perhaps amazing that not more was ruined on the journey; describing in 1809 the looting of twenty masterpieces from Spain, Denon reported ominously, 'There has been more damage, due to negligence in the packing, of the first despatch of Italian primitives.' The arrivals from Italy continued until the end of the Empire; the last consignment, in December 1813, in fact never left Italy.

THE ARCS DE TRIOMPHE

Just about the only two *embellissements* that were planned and actually completed during the Empire were monuments to Napoleon's famous victory at Austerlitz: the Vendôme Column and the Arc du Carrousel. In imitation of Trajan's victory column in Rome and originally designed to bear a statue of Charlemagne, the new Vendôme Column was solemnly unveiled on 15 August 1810, marking the end of the most brilliant period of the whole reign. For many years it was to provide an illustrious symbol for old soldiers to rally at its base.

In the space gained by his demolitions round the Place du Carrousel, Napoleon planted his triumphal arch to commemorate Austerlitz. The *pièce de résistance* of the Carrousel comprised the famous horses looted from Venice by Napoleon during the first Italian campaign – originally made for a temple in ancient Corinth. Remarkably, the Carrousel had its first stone laid only eight months after the Battle of Austerlitz; it then remained clad in scaffolding for the next two years. Furious about the delay, Napoleon demanded of the Intendant-Général when the scaffolding was finally to be removed. The answer came, 'We are only waiting for the statue of your Majesty.' Napoleon flew into a terrifying rage: 'What statue are you talking about? – I never asked for one; nor did I order that my statue should be the principal subject of a monument raised by me, and at my expense, for the glory of the army which I had the honour to command.' He insisted that the chariot drawn by the four Venetian horses should remain empty. And so it did until Waterloo, when the horses were returned to Venice, and an allegorical figure representing the Restoration filled the empty chariot, as it does today. But Napoleon could not hide his disappointment. Compared with Louis XIV's triumphal arch at the Porte Saint-Denis, he thought the Carrousel was altogether too 'mesquin' (mean, or mediocre); he felt humiliated at not being able to rival the monument consecrated to the martial triumphs of his great predecessor and rival in *la Gloire.*

Hence the much more imposing monument, designed by Jean Chalgrin, on top of the hill at the Etoile (so called because it was already the hub of eight different roads), for all time to remain the most enduring and dominating symbol of Paris. The history of the Arc de Triomphe was to be a turbulent one, and its completion was beyond even the all-powerful Emperor's capacity. Although the first stone of the Arc was laid in August 1806, just before Napoleon set off for the Jena campaign, such was the immensity of its weight predicted by the engineers that foundations eight metres deep had to be dug. That year he admitted that the Arc 'would be a futile work which would have no kind of significance if it wasn't a means of encouraging architecture'. Typically, by now preoccupied with building a Louvre-sized palace for his infant son, the King of Rome (born in March 1811), Napoleon lost interest. Louis XVIII, inheriting the incomplete structure, contemplated razing it, but was persuaded to recommence work in 1823; it was finally unveiled by the last King of France, Louis-Philippe, in 1836. Even so it remains incomplete, as the discussion about what to place atop it, whether another chariot or an effigy of Napoleon standing on a pile of enemy arms or on a terrestrial globe, or a huge eagle, a statue of liberty or a gigantic star, was never resolved.

Rising up from the Champs-Elysées among open fields and vineyards, the Arc de Triomphe in Napoleon's imagination would be set off by two enormous lakes on either side of the Champs-Elysées, complete with boats. Among other unrealized fantasies for Paris was the Emperor's notion of a memorial at the Etoile in the shape of a monster elephant. What it represented – whether a symbol of power or Napoleon's covetous feelings for India – no one quite seems to know. Later the plan was to transfer it instead to the Place de la Bastille, and it was to be cast there, in 1811, in bronze from cannon captured from the Spanish insurgents. But the disastrous Iberian adventure failed to supply enough captured weapons to build an elephant on that scale, so instead it was fashioned out of wood and painted plaster. Under the Parisian weather the elephant gradually disintegrated, evolving into the home of thousands of rats and somehow symbolic of the decay of Empire. Coming upon it thirty years later, Victor Hugo, who hated all Bonapartes, latched on to the decrepit mammoth for a passage in *Les Misérables*:

> in this deserted and exposed corner of the Place, the large head of the colossus, its trunk, its tusks, its tower, its enormous rump, its four feet resembling columns, under a starlit night formed a frightening and terrible silhouette ... It was sombre, enigmatic and immense. It was some kind of potent phantom, visible and upright alongside the invisible spectre of the Bastille.

WATER

Strolling with his Minister of the Interior at Malmaison, Napoleon was said to have declared (when he was still First Consul), 'I want to do something really great and useful for Paris', to which Chaptal replied instantly, 'Give it water!' For a city on the brink of the industrial age, post-revolutionary Paris remained a disgrace, insofar as – even by 1807 – its 600,000 inhabitants had to make do with less than nine litres per head a day. By a decree of May 1806, Napoleon ordered the digging of nineteen new wells, and prescribed that by the following year fresh water was to flow through all the fountains of Paris, night and day. This was inspired by the powerful impression the fountains of Rome had made on him; Paris was to emulate Rome. But fountains were only part of the solution; where was the water to come from? Certainly not from the filthy Seine, where as late as 1811, after a ham fair in the city, some 450 kilos of rotting meat would be chucked into the river – by no means an isolated event. So Napoleon would bring fresh water to the city all the way from the River Ourcq, by a canal one hundred kilometres long. Digging started in 1802 and was supposed to be completed by the autumn of 1805, but there were repeated delays, partly thanks to the shortage of manpower caused by the insatiable demands of the Grande Armée. Finally, on 2 December 1808 – the anniversary of Austerlitz, of course – a momentous opening ceremony announced the arrival of the sweet waters of the Ourcq in the Bassin de la Villette. It would be some years, though, before any but the courtesans of the *beau monde* would be able to give up sharing a bath. Nevertheless, the opening of the Ourcq Canal was indeed a historic moment for Paris; Napoleon had succeeded where all previous rulers had failed. He also began constructing a modern sewer system, but here work lagged deplorably once his energetic hand was removed.

The most tangible part of Paris's water problem continued to be presented by the polluted and disease-ridden river running through its centre. The Pont Saint-Michel, originally built in 1387, had been destroyed several times, then rebuilt with thirty-two houses on it. Partly for aesthetic reasons, the Bourbon kings had hesitated to remove them; then their removal had been decreed in 1786, only for the Revolution to intervene. Finally demolition was ordered from Tilsit in 1807, Napoleon believing that the old houses spoiled the panorama down the river, but chiefly because of the pollution they caused to the waters below. Paris had long suffered from a serious shortage of bridges across the Seine, with ferries plying back and forth even from the Louvre; then, under the Consulate and Empire, four new bridges were laid down. All were to be toll bridges: five centimes for people on foot, ten for horseback and fifteen for a coach with one horse, twenty for a coach with two horses, two for a donkey.

Meanwhile, the Seine rolled on, encumbered with floating mills and boat wash-houses, and as filthy as ever. Undeterred, the nude bathers continued to plunge into it. One *Parisienne* recalled how a naked male had retrieved her hat which had blown into the river, apologizing chivalrously, 'Excuse me, Madame, for wearing no gloves!'

Another perennial problem posed by the sacred river was its inconvenient habit of overflowing its banks at unpredictable intervals. The *inondation* of 1801–2 had been the worst since 1740, and boats had to be used to circulate in a number of streets. As a result, Napoleon as First Consul instantly decided to construct the Quai d'Orsay, running without a break between the Pont Royal and Concorde – a scheme which had been on the drawing board ever since the reign of Louis XIV. It was where the famous barges were built for the invasion of England, and for a while there was little but an appalling mess, but the Quai was completed by 1806. In March 1808, Napoleon issued a decree to continue the quays from the Concorde all the way to the Ecole Militaire on the Left Bank. Three years later he built the short Quai Montebello opposite the Hôtel Dieu, in honour of his favourite marshal, killed at Aspern-Essling in 1809. By 1812, the length of the quays constructed over ten years reached 3,000 metres. Of the Emperor's many proud *embellissements*, the quays were the ones which evoked possibly the most praise for both efficacy and beauty.

DREAMS AND THEIR REALIZATION

Inevitably, many of Napoleon's grandiose projects – like those of Louis XIV before him – reflected that illusive commodity so precious to French hearts: *la Gloire*. The most imposing of all was the great imperial palace at Chaillot intended for the infant King of Rome. The site selected stood on what was later known as the Trocadéro heights, where the present hideous 1930s Chaillot complex stands, facing the Eiffel Tower. In Napoleon's time it was an idyllic corner of cottages and vineyards, where Catherine de Medici once had a country house. It was to be an 'imperial city', 'a Kremlin a hundred times more beautiful than Moscow's', and larger even than decaying Versailles. With his usual despatch Napoleon had work begin in May 1811 on what the architects, Fontaine and Percier, regarded as 'the vastest and most extraordinary work of our century' – a palace and park covering the whole area of today's Trocadéro, La Muette and Porte Maillot, or about half the present 16th arrondissement. Triple terraces would rise to it from the Seine, culminating in an immense colonnade with a frontage 400 metres long, and freely imitating Mansart at Versailles. In terms of what it could have meant for Paris as a whole, this display of true *folie de grandeur* was distinctly alarming. But just as 'Aiglon', King of Rome, would never rule, so Chaillot would never be built.

For the duration of the Empire Paris was described as resembling one vast building site. When the King of Württemberg was asked, on a visit in 1810, what he thought of Paris, he replied tersely, 'Fine, for a town that the architects have taken by assault!' Despite the endless bullying, the barrage of orders and decrees from the far-flung corners of Empire, works repeatedly fell behind. 'It required all my character, to write six, ten letters a day and go red with rage,' Napoleon admitted on Saint Helena. Sometimes he almost despaired and, as a man of the south, several times contemplated escaping altogether from the negative attitude of the Parisians to found an entirely new capital in Lyons, 'a habitation worthy of my rank and fortune'; he thought of calling it, modestly, 'Napoléonville'.

In all Napoleon's vast building schemes, the estimates would always be set too low; he would initiate projects on a staggering scale, but by the time of Waterloo few would have been completed. The civilian bureaucracy of Paris was to defeat even an emperor at the full height of his formidable powers. As a consequence, Napoleon, always so decisive in battle, showed himself often disastrously hesitant and pusillanimous in his *embellissement* campaign for Paris, repeatedly changing his mind and unable to concentrate his thoughts. At times he seemed all but overwhelmed by the architectural heritage of the Bourbons. An example was the muddle over the memorial to General Desaix, the fallen hero of Marengo. After ten years of indecision, a statue of Desaix was erected in the Place des Victoires, on the site where the Convention had removed the huge monument to Louis XIV. But when it was finally unveiled on 15 August 1810, Napoleon's birthday, Parisians were shocked to see the general, not clad as a warrior of Rome or Greece, but totally naked. Reacting to the city's sudden display of prudishness, the press announced that there were 'faults in the casting'. It was not just a sudden excess of *pudibonderie*, but generals, clad or nude, were also getting to be out of vogue in the city. Desaix was melted down; come the Restoration his bronze was recycled for the statue of Henri IV on the Pont Neuf.

The problem of Louis XIV's Versailles, too, showed Napoleon at his most indecisive. Left empty and dilapidated by the Revolution, the palace was considered by Napoleon as a home for the wounded; but then he changed his mind. The palace stayed empty. Exasperated, Napoleon demanded to know 'why the Revolution, which destroyed so much, hadn't demolished the château of Versailles? I wouldn't then have a misjudgement of Louis XIV, and an old, badly built château on my hands.' In 1813, when things were turning out badly for him, he was still grumbling: 'If I ever do anything to the façade of Versailles facing Paris I want it to be my architecture so it won't accord with the rest.' Fortunately, by that time he no longer had the option.

Although the boulevards remained piled up with building materials in imperial Paris, there continued to be an almost complete absence of pavements. The English in 1802 had been shocked by the narrowness and dirtiness of the streets, and the terrible noise of iron- and wooden-wheeled vehicles rolling over uneven *pavé*. But there was little improvement over the next dozen years. Malodorous gutters still ran down the centre, except in the new streets like Rivoli where they were finally channelled down each side. One night Caulaincourt, Napoleon's Master of the Horse, fell – carriage and all – into a huge pothole in the Place Vendôme.

Equally little advance was made in illumination of the city. Philippe Lebon, inventor of gas illumination, died mysteriously, stabbed in the Champs-Elysées, on the eve of the Emperor's Coronation. As a result, gas-lighting was never introduced in Napoleon's time. The 4,200 lights throughout Paris added up to rather fewer than at the time of Louis XIV a century and half previously. One writer described imperial Paris as 'not the City of Light but the city of candle ends'. Napoleon once wrote angrily to Fouché declaring that the non-lighting of Paris 'amounts to an embezzlement'. Hampered by the narrow streets, Paris's firefighting service was not much better. In 1808, the cornmarket was allowed to burn down through incompetence, but the worst disaster was to occur in 1810 – the conflagration in the ballroom at the Austrian Embassy, which horribly, and ominously, marred Napoleon's marriage to Marie Louise.

THE UNDERCLASS

Despite the efforts of Fouché, supported by all the trappings of a police state, lawlessness persisted in Paris. As the effects of the British blockade bit deeper, so smuggling became a major Parisian industry, and, with the involvement of army deserters and even senior officers, tended to be run like a military operation. Fake carriages with dummy passengers filled with 300 litres of cognac were employed to dupe the Customs and Excise, and a tunnel half a kilometre long was dug under the city *barrières*, to emerge beneath a convent. By 1808 the situation had become so bad that a ban was imposed on any construction work within a hundred metres of the city perimeter. In the Chaussée d'Antin, the smartest corner of Paris, the beautiful and virtuous Mme Récamier held her legendary salon. But within yards of the Chaussée thieves and pickpockets proliferated, making it at night virtually a no-go area. Among the victims in 1807 was David the painter, when a well-dressed individual pretending to be his servant extracted 18,000 francs from a bank, accompanied the bank clerk to David's nearby studio, then hit him over the head and made off with the money. Equally rapacious were the gambling dens around the Palais Royal, just as they had been under the most louche days of the Regent, the Duc d'Orléans.

Marvellously described in Balzac's *La Peau de chagrin*, men who had lost their fortune on the tables in a matter of hours would be conducted into a 'recovery' room, also known as the *salle des blessés*. Nearby was a gunsmith's selling pistols, also inhabited by a former priest. Thus, it was said, in a space of a few hours victims could 'be ruined, commit suicide, and pass to a better world with the help of religion'. When by imperial decree gambling houses were banned in 1806 throughout the country, Paris was left exempt – the tax collected from the Palais Royal was altogether too profitable to the government.

During the Consulate one of the plagues of Paris had been the multitude of beggars. One German visitor was profoundly 'moved by the horrible, endless begging in the streets ... in bad, dirty weather, when one cannot step too far away from the houses without ending up in a sea of sludge, or when one is in danger of falling under a wheel, one has to make one's way through long rows of beggars who cannot be avoided'. There were reported to be over 100,000 of these vagrants in 1802, and the figure did not decrease by the end of the Empire. Many were discharged old soldiers, reproaching civilians with their silent salutes. In 1809, the Paris police declared its intention of creating a large home for beggars outside Paris at Villers-Cotterets. But nothing was ever done. Similarly, as of 1806 the English press reckoned the number of prostitutes in Paris to be as high as 75,000. Allowing for the exaggeration of an impressionable and *perfide* enemy this was a considerable number.

Meanwhile much of the incidental robbery and violence on the streets of Paris was caused by licentious soldiery on leave, deserters or draft-dodgers. There were numerous ways of avoiding the call to arms, such as chopping off a finger or knocking out front teeth (without which a soldier could not tear open a musket cartridge), and it seems significant that, in 1806, the year of Jena, there were only 14,300 Parisians in military service out of a population of nearly 600,000. By 1810 the rate of desertions from the Grande Armée had become alarming, and many deserters had taken refuge among the criminal underclass in Paris. *Parisiennes* had been delighted by dashing cavalry officers bowing to them with their enormous plumes, and the handsome veterans would be applauded when they paraded on the Carrousel – but for the rest of the time the soldiery were the terror of Paris, recognized for their brutality towards inoffensive citizens. One soldier relieved himself over customers in an underground café, and when a waiter reproached him he was beaten up; at the door of the Senate, a young man was cut to pieces by an infantry sergeant for bumping against him; at Montrouge three soldiers disembowelled a stranger, on the ground that he had 'looked at them in an insulting manner'. Six soldiers raped a respectable woman at the Port-au-Blé, then threw her into the Seine. And so it went on.

Swollen by the deserters, the underclass of the Paris poor lived as miserably as ever under the *ancien régime*. There were areas of pronounced sordidness around the Hôtel Dieu, in the Faubourg Saint-Marceau and the 12th arrondissement where, in 1813, one-fifth of the population were listed as indigent. Conditions in these poorer *quartiers* were appalling. One contemporary observer wrote:

> The extreme overcrowding of residents in certain quarters, and the stench of the household animals blended with that of excrement, decaying animal cadavers and rotting food, all create extensive atmospheric pollution in which people live and eat. The fetid air is a visible haze that generally covers Paris and there are districts over which it is particularly thick.

Every worker had to possess a registration book, and anyone without was treated as a vagabond. Hours were harsh – builders worked from 6 a.m. to 7 p.m. in summer, with wages fixed at between three and five francs a day, and when it came to litigation it was the employer's word that was always accepted. Following a decree of 1806, strikers would be sent to prison (as were twenty-seven in that first year). Bakers were fortunate if they lived to the age of fifty. Nevertheless, the workers of Paris, Jingoes all through the Revolution, remained hawks from Marengo onwards – though they became increasingly apathetic towards politics.

As always, hand in hand with poverty marched disease. On a visit to the Hôtel Dieu in November 1801, Chaptal had been profoundly shocked by the lack of hygiene, the disorder and the dirt and dilapidation he found. He succeeded in persuading the Paris authorities to relocate elsewhere pregnant women and sick children, and above all the mad. Hitherto sick children of the working classes had been mixed in with adults in ordinary hospitals – greatly to their detriment, not least of their morals. Relaxation of morals under the Revolution had resulted in a galloping increase in venereal disease, euphemistically known as *les maladies honteuses*, and the 'progress of immorality' had demanded the creation of a special hospital in the vacant Capucin monastery in the Faubourg Saint-Jacques. At first called simply the Hospital of the Vénériens, then – later more delicately – the Hospital du Midi, the Vénériens had an enormous waiting-list. Yet by the end of the Empire great strides had been made in improving the medieval conditions in Paris hospitals. At the time of Napoleon's accession, there had been the three main establishments – the Hôtel Dieu, La Vérité and Saint-Louis; by the time of his fall, the capital counted no fewer than eleven hospitals with only modest charges. Orphanages had been founded and a special hospital for *enfants malades* opened in the Rue de Sèvres.

SALON LIFE

As has ever been the story of Paris from the days of Philippe Auguste onwards, alongside all this poverty and misery coexisted extreme affluence – despite the high reformist ambitions of the Empire. The old aristocracy – those who hadn't lost their heads – and the haute bourgeoisie had recouped their fortunes most miraculously; while a new class of nouveaux riches (which included the imperial family and its hangers-on) had arisen from the ashes of the Revolution with astonishing speed. Even the Récamiers, products and symbols of this revival, had somehow regained their fortunes following the bank crash of 1805.

From her legendary salon in the Chaussée d'Antin, once home of Louis XVI's ill-starred Minister of Finance, Necker, Juliette Récamier dispensed lavish hospitality. Daughter of a Lyons solicitor, financed by an elderly banker husband (whom she had married at sixteen) and closest (perhaps only) friend of Mme de Staël, she fashioned her house into a worldly shrine, its décor setting the standards of Empire style. Her great and serene beauty, which seemed to embody the period's ideal of feminine perfection, inspired many passions, none fulfilled until Chateaubriand came along and picked the lock.

'Mme Récamier has', wrote an impressionable German, 'such a thoroughly translucent skin that one can see the blood course through her veins ... her beautiful mouth, full of fine teeth, is always half open; she seems to find it quite natural that people like to look at her in the same position and pose for hours on end' – notably on the uncomfortable sofa to which she lent her name. Yet another dissatisfied customer of the great court painter, she rejected David's famous 1800 painting of her as a chilly vestal virgin, disliking the coarseness of the feet, and promptly placed a second order with one of his pupils – Baron Gérard.

David refused either to alter it or to release it from his studio; on his death, it went to the Louvre.

As well as setting the tone in salon life, dress and furnishings, Mme Récamier also played an important part in reviving the culinary arts in Paris. With the end of the Terror, there had been a proliferation of restaurants in Paris, opened by chefs of the *grands seigneurs* who had lost their jobs when their masters lost their heads. As early as 1798, there were an estimated 2,000 restaurateurs in the city, many of whom depended on the patronage of the Empress Josephine. There was Chez Noudet in the Palais Royal and not far from the Récamiers, which in 1813 cheered up Paris with the secrets of *brandades de morue* – the greatest gastronomic success of the time. Lower down the scale were the plentiful plebeian *bastringues* and *guinguettes*, outside the *barrières* where one could dance on grass lawns. Then there were the cafés, the most popular in the Palais Royal, but also much sought after was the Café de Paris, on the Pont Neuf where the old statue of Henri IV had stood. Then there was the unusual Café des Aveugles, with its orchestra composed entirely of blind musicians. Between six and nine in the evenings, Parisian bachelors would enjoy themselves in such cafés.

Under the Empire, eating times and habits changed. The old routine of *dîner* at 4 p.m. was abandoned by the chic for the more modern time of 7 p.m.; the old habit of singing with the dessert was deemed socially 'ridiculous' and was dropped. The *dîner* would usually finish at nine, though Napoleon himself, from military habit, found twenty minutes long enough for any repast (not dissimilar to his love-making, if reports are to be believed). There was no regular dining room in the Tuileries, so he would give orders each morning where the table was to be laid. Those, like Mme Récamier, keen on the *bonne table* would consult Grimond de la Reynière and his famed *Almanach des gourmands*. Here you could learn how to prepare a *gigot*; it had to be 'looked forward to like a lovers' first rendezvous, beaten as tender as a liar caught in the act, blonde as a German girl and bleeding like a Carib'. By 1812, however, when the *Almanach* closed down, all Paris was tightening its belt as, with the English blockade becoming ever more effective, gourmets found essential ingredients increasingly rare. Almost no rum, coffee, chocolate or sugar were coming in from the French West Indies. In common with ordinary Parisians, even imperial dignitaries were obliged to suspend a piece of sugar on a string from the ceiling, each member of the family allowed to dip it in their cup only briefly.

Despite the austerity imposed by war, imperial society was renowned for its parties, receptions and balls, which afforded varying degrees of pleasure to the *invités*. Starting at the top, Napoleon, characteristically, did everything on the grandest scale. There were five, and only five, imperial receptions mounted at the Hôtel de Ville attended by Napoleon, each a nightmare for the party planners. The first, two weeks after the Coronation, in December 1804, caused a major traffic jam with 6,000 coaches attempting to move. Even princes and marshals had to wait four to five hours before they could get away.

As soon as the Consulate became Empire there was a notable change in the style of *Parisienne* dress. Josephine led the way – but, as in all things, the orders came down from the top. For a while the daring Grecian nudity of the Directory prevailed, before Napoleon, the Mediterranean, let it be known that he wished to suppress 'this masquerade of gallantry'. He wanted women in general, not only of the court, to be less naked. Josephine's fun-loving friend Thérèse Tallien was ticked off for appearing as a particularly seductive, semi-clad Diana at the Opéra. Josephine was to provide the example with a 'relative severity in her attire'. Aided by her couturier Leroy, dresses under the Empire became heavier: 'sleeves short and puffed, the tunic falling straight, moulding the forms without stressing them'. These heavier dresses were also more expensive. A quite ordinary dress for the Empress would cost 3,000 francs – her bill for one year amounted to 143,314 francs, 10 centimes – and when her wardrobe was inventoried in 1809 it totalled 666 winter dresses, 230 summer ones and, *toujours la Créole*, only two pairs of knickers. An enormous amount of money was spent on rouge (3,000 francs a year for Josephine), because Napoleon hated pale women.

As for the men, dress had also sobered down considerably from the modes of the *incroyables*. In February 1805, a young Stendhal described himself as 'never so brilliant':

> I was wearing a black waistcoat, black silk breeches and stockings, with a cinnamon-bronze coat, a very well-tied cravat, a superb shirt-front. Never, I believe, was my ugliness more effaced by my general appearance ... I looked a very handsome man, after the style of Talma [the actor].

Thus attired, he could also have paraded passably down St James's without being taken for a French spy.

THEATRE AND CENSORSHIP

Once Napoleon had returned from Tilsit, it seemed as if he had begun to lose interest in some of the great institutions founded under the Consulate. To Fouché he declared that one newspaper – the official *Moniteur* – was quite sufficient, there was no need for others. When he came to power there had been over seventy papers in Paris; within a year these had been reduced to thirteen, all under strict censorship. Among other things, no caricatures of the ruler or his policies were permitted, a ban which accounted for the serious dearth in the cartoonist's art of the times. The once lively Paris press became uninformative and dull. Following Trafalgar, Stendhal's diaries reveal how little he was able to glean about political developments or commercial pressures in Europe from his reading of Paris journals. Censorship rapidly spread to books and plays as well, where any allusion to politics was forbidden. Fouché's spies were everywhere. All at court were required to report on each other, with suspects promptly arrested.

At the same time that Napoleon ordered the curtailment of newspapers, he instructed that the overall number of Paris theatres be reduced to eight. As a result, between fifteen and twenty *petits théâtres* were closed down. There were indeed too many in Paris, all struggling, but this ruthless measure also provided a means of controlling subversive propaganda on the stage.

Napoleon was passionately attached to the theatre and (to a lesser extent) the opera, but there was scarcely any other aspect of Parisian life in which he interfered more. From Milan in 1805, Napoleon told Fouché that he thought a new play about Henri IV was 'too close to the present day' even at two centuries' distance (clearly he viewed the assassination of Henri somewhat subjectively, in the light of the various recent plots against himself). He added, 'I think that you should prevent it, without showing your intervention.' In particular he objected to the words, in the heroic King's mouth, 'je tremble' on the ground that 'A sovereign may be afraid, but must never say so.'

The theatre attracted all classes of Parisian as an essential element of their daily pleasure. Geoffroy, the leading drama critic of the era, reckoned that – after the dead years of the Revolution – with the

Consulate the taste for the theatre had virtually grown into a *fureur*. With the curtain usually rising at 6 p.m., all performances were required to end around 9.30 – by police order, so as to make the journey home through darkened streets less menacing. In everything, the police presence – under the despised Prefect Dubois – made itself felt. By decree of 1806, no new play could be put on without the authority of the Minister. There were severe penalties for actors (and actresses) failing to clock in for a performance because of sudden laryngitis; they could be imprisoned, or confined in an abbey or convent. High-handed as such treatment may sound, the theatre managers had a point. Parisian *vedettes* of the time were notoriously undisciplined and would think little of taking a night off. Even Napoleon's favourite, the irresistible Mlle George, found herself in the summer of 1808 fined 3,000 francs for non-appearance, expelled from a number of societies and required to forfeit her pension rights.

A new stage morality was defined by Geoffroy: 'People are determined to have virtue on the stage, because there must be some somewhere.' Thus a dramatist must not introduce a woman deceiving her husband, nor a girl being seduced. Taste, always influenced from the top, was on the whole unreceptive to comedy. 'Our comedies serve no purpose [that is, no *political* purpose],' Napoleon once complained. 'On the other side of the Rhine they are not understood.' Beaumarchais' *Barbier de Séville* was widely applauded; Marivaux was just about acceptable; but Molière would be performed only 'when there is nothing better'. The great Corneille, neglected in the eighteenth century, was popular once more – because he was the favourite poet of the Emperor.

Nevertheless, as in the days of Louis XIV – and, indeed, as in many other epochs in the life of the Parisian theatre – it was the *parterre* that continued to wield the most effective powers of censorship. Out of six new plays produced between the summer of 1811 and December 1812 not one was allowed to succeed, thanks to the repeated interruption and barracking. The *parterre* would be quite different on Sundays, when it was populated by schoolboys. On weekdays, it would be far less good-humoured, turbulent and aggressive, even before the curtain went up. On one occasion, 'twenty hotheads' were recorded as climbing across the orchestra and on to the stage, demanding that Mme Duchesnois replace Mlle George in *Phèdre*. Eventually Fouché discovered the existence of a band of thirty or forty organized claques who would applaud or whistle to order, and threatened to refuse them entry to any theatre – or even to expel them from Paris.

The moment Napoleon arrived at a theatre there would be more or less unanimous applause. It gave him an opportunity to make contact with his public. But, almost immediately, the *parterre* would resume its liberty to demonstrate for or against the play, and on at least one occasion its hostility prevented the conclusion of a play even with the Emperor still in attendance. Once in the royal box, he could be seen lying full length on a sofa of velvet, arms and legs crossed. Standing behind him would be his attentive aide General Comte de Ségur, the Grand Chamberlain, in full uniform. Only seven weeks after Austerlitz, in January 1806, Napoleon's late arrival at the theatre caused the first scene to be played again. And once, at a command performance in 1803, there was an unscripted moment of comic-tragedy when a bat suddenly flew straight at Mlle George playing Hermione. 'Hermione' took instant refuge in the wings. The bat then swooped down on a terrified Josephine and her entourage in the imperial box.

The *vedettes* of the Napoleonic stage were as well known as the Napoleonic marshals, their varying merits, doings and foibles, and the scandals of their private lives, familiar to and discussed by the *parterre*. As the new age began, the Comédie Française found itself chronically short of dramatic talent; when re-formed in 1799, it had only one great tragic actress, Mlle Raucourt, who was already over forty and beginning to lose her looks. Two new *vedettes* arose in the shape of Mlle George (alias Josephine Weimer), renowned in equal parts for her acting, her beauty and her fierce temper, and Mlle Duchesnois. They became bitter enemies, and the *parterre* divided in support, like rival soccer fans.

Only fifteen at her début as Clytemnestra in November 1802, but already physically mature, Mlle George stunned Paris, and within a few months she had made her way to Napoleon's bed. On his third visit to the Comédie Française to watch her perform, as Emilie in Corneille's classic *Cinna*, Napoleon arrived late amid cries of 'Recommencez!' When Mlle George then came to the key line, 'Si j'ai séduit Cinna, j'en séduirai bien d'autres', the *parterre* exploded in tumultuous applause, rising to its feet with all heads turning towards the First Consul's box. According to Mlle George, it was later that same night that she succumbed: 'He undressed me little by little, and acted as my *femme de chambre* with so much gaiety, grace and decency that there was no resisting him.' The following morning the future Emperor thoughtfully helped her make the bed, 'witness of so much tenderness'.

Josephine was swiftly on the trail, however, on one occasion managing to catch the pair *in flagrante*. Napoleon, in the fervour of love-making, threw a faint. When he came to he found himself being cosseted by Josephine *en peignoir*, and young Mlle George stark naked. His fury was terrifying. In consequence, the liaison did not last long. Josephine revenged herself by announcing in the press that she was giving Mlle George's bitter rival, Mlle Duchesnois, an expensive coat for her next appearance in the role of *Phèdre*. 'He left me to become emperor,' sighed Mlle George. Her stage career was meteoric, both while the Empire lasted and afterwards, when new young talents like Victor Hugo came along. Meanwhile on the side she did indeed 'seduce many others' in the Empire *galère* – from Talleyrand and Murat to Lucien and Jérôme Bonaparte (the Emperor's brothers), and from the arch-enemies Tsar Alexander and the Duke of Wellington to Dumas *père*. Sadly, in her old age she was reduced to keeping the *chalets de nécessité* (public lavatories) at the Paris Exposition of 1855.

Yet, above all the warring actresses of the Empire, it was the great talent of François-Joseph Talma that reigned supreme. The son of a Parisian dentist who declined to follow his father's calling, Talma in the first decades of the century created the principal roles in all the famous tragedies of the day. He restored the reputation of tragedy in Paris, bringing in many lasting reforms in production and in method – such as less artificiality, less declamation. Skilful at adapting lines of the classics to contemporary events, he became a close intimate of Napoleon. Despite his tirades against 'tyrants', he was to be seen breakfasting regularly at the Tuileries with the Emperor.

Napoleon liked music and revelled in *spectacle*, but it is not certain how much he genuinely enjoyed opera – especially given the memories of the night so rudely spoiled for him by the bomb back in December 1800. But his interference was about the same as in the theatre. To Fouché he wrote from his campaign headquarters in 1807, 'I am very dissatisfied with the handling of the Opéra. Let Director Bonet know that matters of intrigue will not succeed with me . . . If it doesn't cease I will give them *une fanfare militaire* which will make them march with drums beating.' Immediately on his return to Paris Napoleon summoned the three curators of the Opéra to ask them what was happening.

The rickety state of the Paris Opéra evidently presented distinct physical dangers to dancers. At one performance, a 'machine' collapsed, throwing Mlle Aubery six metres from her throne, so that she suffered concussion and a broken leg. Acidly Napoleon would write from Eylau, in March 1807, in the middle of that bloody campaign, 'I see that the Mademoiselle Aubery affair occupies the Parisians more than all the losses that my army have suffered!' In 1808, Napoleon instructed his architect Fontaine to draw up 'a fine project' for a new home for the Opéra; it was to be 'a little like that of Milan'. He laid down the details, but noted somewhat casually that it could be 'located anywhere'. Work on the project, however, did not begin until 1813.

*

Readers of the novels of Jane Austen have often marvelled at how she could have lived through the Napoleonic era, have written so much, but have mentioned virtually nothing about the cataclysmic war that was taking place. But it becomes perhaps a little less remarkable when one considers how little life in Paris was affected by the war. There were the distractions of the new galleries in the Louvre, the new building works, the promenades, the theatre, the opera – and no serious press to report unpleasant realities from far-flung battlefields. Even the loss of the Grande Armée in the retreat from Moscow in 1812 hardly disturbed the rhythm of life in the capital. Only the actual appearance of Cossacks on the Champs-Elysées in 1814 could do that.

12

Downfall of an Empire

> Spring will bring Bonaparte back to us, with the swallows and
> the violets.
>
> Fouché, in 1814

IMPERIAL NUPTIALS

When life in Paris was interjected with tidings from far-flung battle-fronts, after Tilsit in 1807 they were rarely destined to bring great joy. From Madrid, where the 'Spanish Ulcer' was beginning its deadly work of sapping French strength, Napoleon returned to Paris in January 1809 to find morale disturbingly low. The economy was in a less healthy condition than when he had embarked on his Spanish adventure. The war represented a heavy financial burden, on top of the ever growing expense of keeping up his imperial splendour. The British blockade in particular was causing problems; once again *perfide Albion* was frustrating his ambitions at every turn. There was mounting resistance to conscription for the Spanish campaign, the first of Napoleon's military enterprises that had lacked the pretext of a foreign, royalist coalition united against revolutionary France. Desertion or self-mutilation was preferred by one in ten new recruits. 'Spontaneous' public enthusiasm, Fouché warned him, could no longer be depended on. The imperial family had also become markedly less popular, as their prodigious greed increased the overheads of the Empire. Napoleon understood the implications of all this, bluntly remarking to Fouché that 'This year is an inopportune time to shock public opinion by repudiating the popular Empress ... she is responsible for attaching a part of Paris society to me which would then leave me.' He would have to wait until he could achieve another triumph on the battlefield.

Meanwhile, in the east his once defeated enemies were moving again. On 13 April he departed Paris in haste for Vienna – attempting to leave before dawn, without telling Josephine. However, the about-to-be-abandoned Empress leaped out of bed and flew down to the courtyard in her bedroom slippers. 'Crying like a child, she threw herself into his carriage; she was so lightly dressed that his Majesty threw his fur-lined coat over her shoulders and then issued orders for her luggage to be sent on to her.' There followed another frantic excursion in pursuit of war together. Strasbourg was as far as she would be permitted to go this time. For Josephine it would be their last, poignant journey together. In a thoroughly despondent Paris the stock exchange tumbled. Plainly, the fate of the Empire, and of the Emperor, rested on the outcome of a single battle – more so than at any time since Marengo. But Wagram, in 1809, Napoleon's last victory, was so hard fought, so marginal, that it brought with it a sense only that 'we victors now know that we are mortal'.

When, following Wagram, the Peace of Vienna of that October was announced to theatre audiences it produced only modest enthusiasm. Consistent bad news was to follow as the Empire reached and passed its apogee. There were, of course, the usual *spectacles* to distract an uneasy populace. Then, once Josephine – with dignity – had permitted herself to be divorced, in 1810 came the grandiose nuptials of the Emperor and the nineteen-year-old Archduchess Marie Louise of Austria (in shedding the *bien-aimée* Josephine, reckoned the superstitious, he had shed his lucky star too). Politically, the new match was an act of great cynicism on both sides: in the words of André Maurois, Francis of Austria had 'sacrificed his Iphigenia in order to gain time; when the hour should strike, he would not scruple to dethrone the husband and take back the daughter'. For Napoleon, it was a matter of ensuring the continuation of his dynasty. Just five and a half years had passed since the historic ceremony in Notre-Dame, during which time Josephine had proved incapable of providing an heir. Whether driven by urgency or by Mediterranean virility, Napoleon had deflowered his new bride at Compiègne on her way to Paris, in advance of the official ceremony in the Tuileries. That day the route of the imperial cortège through the capital was lined with thousands of spectators. They seem to have been mostly curious, however, because – in contrast to the fallen Josephine – to Parisians Marie Louise's plump Teutonic face produced 'generally an unfavourable impression'. Manifestly ill at ease in the city which had murdered her aunt Marie Antoinette, the new Empress, moreover, never conquered the hearts of the French as had her predecessor.

For the marital grand *entrée*, a full-scale replica of the still unfinished Arc de Triomphe was created out of painted paper on a wooden framework. But there was an unfortunate omen when carpenters working on it went on strike. The Inspector-General of Police applied a stern hand, giving the carpenters four francs for what they had previously refused to do for eighteen, while six of them were thrown into jail. An even worse augury for the imperial marriage of Austria and France followed that July when a dreadful disaster overtook the Austrian Embassy at the ball celebrating the wedding. As the dancing began, a violent storm blew the curtains on to some candles. Fire took hold, and in moments there was chaos, with the hostess, Princess Schwarzenberg, and many others burned to death. Benjamin Constant's wife Charlotte, who was there, recorded the scene for him:

> ... I swear to you that I still think I'm living in a nightmare – a bare seven minutes covered the whole time from the moment we all started for the doors ... the flames reached out into the garden after us ... we heard the big mirrors cracking and the chandeliers crashing down ... and through it the screams of the wretched beings who were still inside.

Firemen who rushed to the scene turned out to be drunk, provoking from Napoleon his sole comment: 'I have discharged the colonel.'

On the night of 20 March 1811, a young Henri Beyle, better known as Stendhal, then a clerk at army headquarters in Paris, was abed with his girlfriend Angéline Bereyter when they were woken by the sudden, repeated booming of the cannon.

> We counted up to nineteen, when mad cheering broke out in the streets. We then realized that we had missed the first three salvos ... the cannon went on booming. It was a boy all right ... a young prince had been born. All around us people went wild with joy.

It was 'a grand and happy event', interjected Stendhal with unusual pomposity, while totting up, boastfully – in English – rather more personal statistics of his amatory prowess: 'I make that one or two every day, she five, sex [sic] and sometimes *neuf fois*.'

Marie Louise had indeed produced an heir, Napoleon II, the unhappy and short-lived 'Aiglon'. His father named him King of Rome, possibly in cynical remembrance of the defunct Holy Roman Empire which he had liquidated after Austerlitz. To Josephine he duly reported, 'My son is plump and well. He has my chest, my mouth and my eyes ... I hope he will fulfil his destiny.' It was news that must have been fairly agonizing for a discarded barren ex-Empress. In his journal, Stendhal went on to record his current disillusion: 'This capital of the greatest empire of modern times is used up for me, I have become blasé with regard to its pleasures ... Obviously I haven't the light, frivolous character necessary for enjoying Paris to the full.' He had by now come to look on the Parisians as 'a surly, fretful, envious people, in a perpetual state of dissatisfaction ... Even the pretty girls wore five or six wrinkles across their foreheads, etched in by envy.'

Stendhal's disillusion perhaps reflected something of the prevailing mood in the city. For all the natural relief that there was now an heir, spontaneous demonstrations of joy at the happy event were somewhat exaggerated by the police reports. In June there was an imposing ceremony for the christening of the King of Rome at Notre-Dame, but the crowds that turned out were described as being more curious than enthusiastic. Napoleon had hoped that the occasion would be first of a sequence of dynastic celebrations; in the event it was to prove the last party of Empire.

FAMINE

Within days of Napoleon's rejoicing at the birth of his heir, his two Councils of Commerce and Manufacturing presented to him some unpleasant home truths. Though, with the tightening of the British blockade, Paris had become the undisputed commercial centre of Europe, the problems that had shaken her in 1805 – still unresolved – emerged once more with increased force. Despite constantly raising taxes, Napoleon's treasury had run up a deficit of fifty million francs by the end of 1811. It forced him to issue a decree cancelling the arrears of pay owed to the soldiers who had died for him, thereby in effect cheating even the dead. Led by the Banque de France, the banks had got themselves enmeshed in a chain reaction of competitive discounting which the weaker brethren could not afford.

A first warning came with the fall of the important house of Lübeck, which had repercussions all over Europe. In February 1811 Mollien, the Finance Minister, could report that there were not twelve banks in Paris that remained truly sound. For each of the succeeding months of December 1810 to March 1811 there were more than forty business failures. Part of the trouble was a shortage of credit, and too many middlemen chasing too few goods. There were intermediaries selling goods they never possessed, without paying and without delivering. Speculation was rife; Talleyrand had no compunction about getting involved, and now some of the generals were too.

Much of the speculation concerned contraband run through the blockade, despite the penalties imposed by a despot increasingly enraged at the thwarting of his Continental System, by which – since 1807 – he had closed continental ports to Britain. There was a seizure of substantial American cargoes in Antwerp, with painful repercussions in Paris. But still the trade went on with the *commerçants* of Paris, despite the risks that they exposed themselves to, preferring to continue to offer their clientele contraband English goods. In the spring of 1811, a major consignment of contraband muslins and other fabrics was seized in the Rue Le Peletier, at the elegant heart of Paris. By June 1812, Mollien was daring to observe to Napoleon that 'Paris seems to have become the public market chosen by England to direct and consume all its transactions of currency.' The following week, driven over the brink by the double-dealing of his ally, Tsar Alexander, with the English arch-enemy, Napoleon recrossed the Niemen to invade Russia and teach the Tsar a lesson.

For the average Parisian, far worse than the renewed financial crisis was the *disette*, or famine, of 1811–12, brought about by a combination of native incompetence and the increasing rigour of the Royal Navy's blockade. Initially the harvest of 1811 promised to be excellent, then repeated thunderstorms caused serious damage, particularly in the Paris region. Administrators were caught out, because – although the harvest of 1811 was not demonstrably smaller than that of 1810 – they had allowed surpluses to run down. In Paris, the first signs of the dreaded *disette* were of boiled potatoes being sold around Les Halles instead of grain, and the sudden increase in the price of rice and vegetables. Shortages were exacerbated by provincials coming in to buy their bread from Paris, because it was of better quality there. Between 1811 and 1813, Napoleon summoned no fewer than fourteen conferences exclusively dealing with food supplies.

By the beginning of 1812 the price of bread was beginning to spiral upwards as the speculators got in on the act. A sack of flour fetching 93 francs in February (already an exceptional price) reached 115 by April. On 8 May, on the eve of his departure for Dresden, and Russia, Napoleon signed an important decree releasing stocks of flour to the Parisian millers. The reserves had all but run out.

Fortunately for Napoleon, and with the kind of luck that was now deserting his star, the harvest of 1812 turned out well, and that of the following year was abundant. The price of bread fell and normality returned – just in time to counterbalance, for a while, the sombre news of decisive defeat at Leipzig that was coming in from Germany.

RETREAT FROM MOSCOW

It was impossible for Napoleon to ignore the intensity and duration of the hardship that the *disette* had imposed on the Parisians. As the fateful 1812 campaign got under way, it was evident that the French nation, drawing on her revolutionary capital, could not for ever go on glorifying war for its own sake. Outside the army itself, always loyal to Napoleon, there was now little enough love for him in the country at large. Increasingly he had to rely on the terror of the omnipresent secret police, headed since 1810 by Fouché's even more thorough successor, General Savary, the kidnapper of the Duc d'Enghien. Soon after assuming office in Paris, Savary had imposed his stamp by executing two clerks in the Ministry of War for passing information to the Russians. As the Grande Armée headed for Moscow, Paris, recorded Laure, the vivacious wife of General Junot:

> presented a curious but melancholy spectacle. Husbands, sons, brothers and lovers were departing to join the army; while wives, mothers, sisters and mistresses either remained at home to weep, or sought amusement in Italy, Switzerland or the various watering-places of France.

Laure herself headed for Aix-les-Bains, where she listened to Talma recite from *The Tempest* in the middle of a storm, and then began a turbulent affair with the Marquis de Balincourt as her husband, increasingly demented, fought for his life on the Russian front.

So life continued in Paris, while the Grande Armée confronted failure outside Moscow and, in a terrible reverse, was forced to turn for home, struggling for its existence through the ice and snow of the great retreat. At last, on 20 December 1812, Laure Junot recalled, 'the cannon on the Invalides announced to the city of Paris that the Emperor had returned from Russia'. Three days later, lovesick and now abandoned by Balincourt, she tried to take an overdose of laudanum. The following January, Junot himself returned. In the place of the dashing young Governor of Paris who had left her a few short months before, 'there appeared a coarsened, aged man, walking with difficulty, bent and supported with a stick, dressed carelessly in a shabby greatcoat', his sanity overthrown by the vicissitudes of war. During the brief time he spent in Paris that dreadful winter, one colonel of the once indestructible Grande Armée found his family and friends:

> in general terror-stricken. The famous 29th Bulletin had informed France abruptly that the Grande Armée had been destroyed. The Emperor was invincible no longer. The campaign of 1813 was about to open ... people were shocked to see the Emperor entertaining at the Tuileries. It was an insult to public grief and revealed a cruel insensitivity to the victims. I shall always remember one of those dismal balls, at which I felt as if I were dancing on graves.

The mood in Paris darkened as the full horror of the Russian débâcle was brought home by the state of survivors like Junot – a preview of what was to come. In the words of Mlle Avrillon, who looked after the Empress's jewellery, 'we were all the more terrified ... because for twenty years so many uninterrupted successes had made us think reverses impossible'. The superstitious could not fail to note that the Russian campaign was the first which had been undertaken by the Emperor since his marriage with Marie Louise. There was a palpable, unspoken sense that Moscow heralded, as Talleyrand expressed it, 'the beginning of the end, and ... the end itself could not be far distant'.

THE BATTLE OF THE NATIONS

After Napoleon had sacrificed the whole of the Grande Armée in Russia in 1812, abandoning its shattered remnants as he scurried home to a disbelieving and restive Paris, this remarkable warlord had still been able to raise a fresh army to fight a new campaign in eastern Europe the following year. There, pitted against all Europe in the Battle of the Nations at Leipzig, he had suffered his first decisive defeat, in the bloodiest encounter Europe would know until 1914. Now his star – deprived of Josephine, whom the *grognards* (or grumblers, the veterans of the Grande Armée) deemed integral to it – had clearly turned against him. Nevertheless, he was still able to create new forces and fight one of his most brilliant campaigns, albeit a hopeless one, as the Allies surged across the frontiers of France and closed in on Paris in 1814. And he would repeat the miracle once more, in 1815, on his escape from Elba – until Waterloo finally removed his grip on France.

Up to almost the very last moment, even after the Allies had crossed the Rhine into France, Parisians continued to treat the war as a distant happening that could never immediately affect the capital. After all, Paris had not been entered by a foreign army since the unhappy days of Jeanne d'Arc in the fifteenth century; she had not been invested since Henri IV's siege in 1590; she had not experienced any warfare since the final flutter of the Fronde in 1652. On 1 February 1814, in the last of its *pièces de circonstances*, special heroic performances put on to celebrate contemporary events, the Théâtre National staged a patriotic show to evoke the fight of Charles Martel against the Saracens, and the 'Siege of Calais'; it was followed two weeks later by *Philippe Auguste à Bouvines*, just as 170,000 Austrians, Russians and Prussians were massing on the outskirts of Paris, and the city walls were about to fall. Then came brief moments of panic as reality set in. Out at the *barrières* there were screams of 'The Cossacks are coming! Shut all the shops!' Trees in the Bois de Boulogne were hastily cut down (as they would be again in 1870) to provide barricades against the Allied armies. Hospitals suddenly became overcrowded as wounded from the front straggled in, often finding doors barred against them. Shops emptied as speculators became hoarders, while hungry soldiers begged for bread in the streets.

Talleyrand, looking forward to the arrival of his new masters, the restored Bourbons, recorded 'grande incertitude'.

In the third week of March, Russian troops entered the east of Paris, on their third assault carrying the fortified redoubt which brave students of the Polytechnique had run up among the tombs of Père Lachaise, the new cemetery the Emperor had established only ten years previously. Abandoning Napoleon, Empress Marie Louise left for Blois, and then for Vienna. On 30 March Paris was subjected to cannonfire. Incredulous that things could come to this, the capital was not prepared for defence. As the Russians captured Montmartre, it was reported that the miller of the Moulin de la Gallette had been shot, his body bound to one of the sails of the famous *moulin*. After he and Marshal Mortier had fought hard at Romainville, Marmont, Duc de Ragusa, finally deserted his master and signed an armistice at two o'clock on the morning of the 31st.

The reaction of the Parisian on the street surprised observers, among them Napoleon's architect Fontaine: 'Who could have imagined that the actual event would resemble a festival that did not disturb public peace and order?' Cossacks clattered down the Champs-Elysées, and then encamped there. Their behaviour was far from immaculate – but, after what Moscow had suffered, it was surprising that it was not much worse.

On 6 April Napoleon signed his abdication, and departed for Elba, an exile that would last for less than a year. On a beautiful spring day, 31 March, the victorious Allies had marched into Paris led by the Red Cossacks of the Imperial Guard. It was a picturesque affair, almost on a par with the other triumphant *entrées* made by the deposed Emperor: heading it was Tsar Alexander, followed by the King of Prussia and then Prince Schwarzenberg, representing the Emperor of Austria. Their respective armies followed, green leaves in their shakos. Military grandees, bearing the white cockades of the Bourbons on their hats, pranced down on horseback to meet them, while various royalist gentry (including a returning Chateaubriand) appeared from nowhere to circulate among the crowds. By now thoroughly disenchanted with Paris and its inhabitants, a censorious Stendhal recorded the 'fickle delight' with which the Parisian crowd greeted its conquerors. The almost universal enthusiasm struck some as positively indecent. White handkerchiefs fluttered everywhere. 'The blue and red were trampled underfoot and the most rabid were those who had been the most Bonapartist ...' recorded Mme Chateaubriand. 'We women would cry "off with our heads!" were we to hear our neighbours do so.'

Then, on 4 May, came the restored Bourbon, Louis XVIII, returning to reclaim the nation lost by his decapitated brother and claiming that, 'by the grace of God', he had never ceased to be king. He entered Paris in an open carriage drawn by eight white horses; a Te Deum was sung at Notre-Dame, and the King was solemnly saluted by choirs, a concert and the release of a balloon decorated with white flags. At the other end of the Île, the statue of the first Bourbon, Henri IV, destroyed in the Revolution, was hastily resurrected in plaster on the Pont Neuf. It was all 'so like a party', remarked Mme de Coigny, 'that it is a pity it is a conquest', a sentiment that sums up the whole incongruous gala. Blücher lost a king's ransom of 1.5 million francs in one evening gaming in the ever receptive Palais Royal, and it was said that the Allied troops were spending more on pleasure than the reparations France had to pay to their governments. During those May days, Josephine, the former Empress, went riding with the gallant Tsar, caught a cold which turned into pneumonia and died – 'going', in the elegant words of her son Eugène, 'as gently and as sweetly to meet death as she had met life'.

By the Treaty of 30 May 1814, the Allied armies left Paris. After over twenty years of war, peace now seemed restored. But it was dreadful old Fouché who saw the truth, predicting for 1815 that 'Spring will bring Bonaparte back to us, with the swallows and the violets.'

THE ROAD TO SAINT HELENA

It proved to be a remarkably precise prophecy. All through the year that followed the withdrawal of the victorious Allies, Paris seethed with discontent. The streets swarmed with discharged and penniless veterans, while some 12,000 ex-officers on half-pay took to meeting in the cafés to lament 'the good old days' of the Empire. One after the other promises made by the new regime were seen to be broken, while in his tiny kingdom of Elba Napoleon – his own pension unpaid – paced up and down in anger and vengeful frustration and bided his time. Suddenly, it came one day in March 1815 when the Governor, his captor, took leave to visit his mistress on the Italian mainland. Napoleon landed back in the South of France, marching towards Paris, collecting new armies as he went, in the miracle known as the Hundred Days.

When he reached the capital, there took place yet another of those volte-faces that occur through French history, which amazed even Napoleon himself. 'They let me come back just as easily as they let the others go!' he exclaimed. Paris remained extraordinarily placid. About the worst upheaval took place in the Sorbonne, where no exams were set that winter and spring. At the Tuileries Palace, where seamstresses had been busy unpicking the Napoleonic bees from the carpets, replacing them reverently with hastily stuck-on fleurs-de-lys, the returned Chateaubriand gave the newly enthroned King a brave historian's advice – to remain and await the arrival of the usurper. Louis was more realistic. 'You would have me', he said, 'sit upon the curule chair [as the Roman senators did, awaiting the barbarians]. I don't feel like it.' The portly old King then clambered heavily into his coach and sped off to Ghent.

Paris, however, was not a cheerful place as Napoleon resumed control. Loud jubilation and songs from the immediate vicinity of the Tuileries contrasted sharply with the total darkness and silence prevailing in the outer districts. A new war threatened immediately as the Allies reassembled their forces. Spring never seemed to come, and it was an ominously grey and cold day as Napoleon reviewed his new armies on the Champ-de-Mars. It must have seemed, to Parisians, like a long hundred days as the Emperor set off with his reconstituted army to meet his fate at Waterloo.

Just as the first tidings of battle reaching Wellington in Brussels were bad, so false rumours arriving in Paris resulted – briefly – in 'extravagant rejoicing'. Government stocks rocketed, and 'a brilliant society' displayed itself once again in the Tuileries Gardens. Abruptly, however, the mood changed as the truth became apparent in the form of the last of Napoleon's great armies limping back to Paris, defeated. Instead of chic and busy shoppers, the Place Vendôme was filled with wounded men, groaning on straw at the foot of the soaring monument that depicted the zenith of all Bonaparte's past victories. Abandoning his army a third and final time, Napoleon hastened back to Paris. There, on 21 June, he called for Marie Walewska and their son Alexandre to say his last farewell, before going off into definitive exile. 'The mood was lugubrious,' recalled an aide. 'It was raining, the Emperor was burning state papers, and I was packing his personal effects.' Young Alexandre (who would become a minister under his father's nephew, Napoleon III) recorded that the Emperor took him in his arms, and 'a tear ran down his face'. The next day, the third anniversary of the launching of the march on Moscow, Napoleon abdicated a second time.

This year there was a sixteen-day siege as the Allies fought their way once more through the graves of Père Lachaise, as the Prussians stormed Issy, and as the National Guard put up a spirited resistance at the Barrière de Clichy in the north of the city. But as they reoccupied Paris, the Allies – after suffering further casualties – were in a far more sombre and less forgiving mood. Blücher's Prussians left a path of desolation on their route from Waterloo to Paris, a foretaste of what lay ahead in three subsequent German invasions; in Paris only Wellington's forceful personal intervention prevented Blücher from blowing up the Pont d'Iéna by way of erasing a permanent slight on Prussian arms. This time it was the turn of the triumphant British troops to bivouac in the Place de la Concorde. In the Bois they noted with disgust the wanton damage effected by Prussians in neighbouring encampments. 'Our camp was not remarkable for its courtesy towards them,' recorded Captain Gronow of the Grenadiers, with the best insular disdain. On the other hand, *Parisiennes* expressed shock on discovering that the Highlanders wore no *culottes* under their kilts.

The Allied sovereigns held swaggering parades on the Champ-de-Mars. French pride was shattered. Over the rest of the country a Royalist 'White Terror', comparable to the *épuration* which was to follow the Liberation of 1944, held sway. One Parisian eyewitness, Dr de la Sibouti, recalled that 'the Bois de Boulogne was laid bare, the statues of Luxembourg mutilated with sabre cuts; our hearths and homes were overrun by soldiers who spoke to us as masters. Such are the rites of war.' But, with generous objectivity, he went on to admit, 'Our own soldiers have probably abused them on more than one occasion.'

Nevertheless, for all the bitterness in the air, once again in her turbulent history Paris displayed her remarkable capacity to recover and live again as if little had happened. Captain Mercer of the Royal Horse Guards thought 'how strange it was that the French were so happy in their defeat...!' The wounded were cleared out of the Place Vendôme, which soon filled with beautiful women showing off their finest silks. On 8 July, the King returned; Chateaubriand witnessed those adept time-servers, Talleyrand and Fouché, welcoming him at Saint-Denis, while Wellington – amazed by the wild cheering – wondered whether it could possibly be the same Parisians cheering each time. In the Tuileries Palace, work at once recommenced on replacing the bees with fleurs-de-lys. At the Comédie Française, life began again as Mlle Mars (who had begun her career under the Revolution and would continue until 1841, after the last King had once more disappeared) resumed its traditions. In the Luxembourg Gardens the first bicycles (invented by a German) took part in a race; and there was a first session of the new Chamber of Deputies, imposed on the King by the Allied peace terms. The fearless Marshal Ney was shot, *pour décourager les autres*, it might have been said. But the French army, for all he had inflicted upon it, and no matter how often he had betrayed it, would never cease to revere the small man in the grey frock coat.

REPARATIONS AND RESTORATION

Considerably harsher than the terms offered by the Allies in 1814, the Treaty signed in November 1815 demanded 700 million francs in gold, eventually whittled down to 265 million. Compared with the fierce reparations that would be exacted on the defeated by the victors after the succeeding wars of 1870 and 1914–18, Paris escaped lightly. With a sense of honour which did England lasting credit, as well as setting the tone, the Duke of Wellington insisted on paying the market price for Pauline Borghese's sumptuous house on the Faubourg Saint-Honoré, for the site of the new British Embassy. His defeated foe would hardly have done the same in any of the conquered capitals he had occupied. What caused most distress in Paris, and was regarded (quite unfairly) as excessive vengefulness on the part of the occupiers, however, was the repatriation of the looted works of art in the Louvre, agreed as part of the terms of the peace settlement.

To undo the assiduity of Vivant Denon and gather up the master-pieces removed from Italy, from Rome Pope Pius VII sent Canova, the greatest sculptor of his day. It was a daunting, and in no way felicitous, commission. Andrew Robertson, the Scottish miniaturist whose visit to Paris coincided with Canova's, at first sight was agreeably 'surprised by the vivacity of Parisian night life, the cafés, the music, the dancing and the well-dressed people'. Rushing to the gallery of the Louvre after Waterloo, he saw 'the first and greatest productions of human genius', but was then shocked by 'the bare walls and frames where a number of the pictures had been taken away by the Allies and the original proprietors'. Blücher had been there before him. Sir Walter Scott, writing to his sister from Paris that autumn, was describing the Louvre as 'truly doleful to look at now, all the best statues are gone, and half the rest, the place full of dust, ropes, triangles, and pulleys, with boards, rollers etc'.

Faced with the dismantling of all he had achieved in the name of Napoleon, his life's work, Vivant Denon resigned, to die heartbroken in 1825, four years after his master, gazing out from his Left Bank house on the Quai Voltaire at his precious, ransacked Louvre across the Seine. Meanwhile Canova found himself virtually ostracized by the Paris art world as fellow artists such as Gros and Houdon cut him dead. But, worse than that, he found himself living in sheer *timore*, 'often afraid to go to his lodging there for fear of being murdered'. The job completed, he was delighted to leave occupied Paris for friendly London, which, following Waterloo, had taken over from Paris as the leading world capital of power and patronage. Even so, despite all the 'enforced redistributions' of 1815, the Louvre never lost its status as the world's greatest museum of art. As Denon predicted in a letter to Talleyrand of September 1815, 'We have already had some big losses, Monseigneur, but, with time, one could hope to recoup them. The gaps that exist will be filled in the long term.'

So, with the Congress of Vienna engineered by those astute statesmen Metternich and Talleyrand, after twenty years of war peace came finally to Europe. England withdrew to her island and her empire to prosper during a hundred years of Pax Britannica. Bonaparte, the disturber of Europe's equilibrium, was penned in at dank, wind-blown and termite-ridden Longwood on Saint Helena where he would die – possibly of arsenic poisoning, some continue to think – in 1821. Not till December 1840, on the anniversary of the Battle of Austerlitz, would his remains be brought back for interment under the great dome of the Invalides which Louis XIV had bequeathed to Paris. But for France, and Paris in particular, there would be little real tranquillity over the ensuing years. The country was financially, morally and physically in ruins. Estimates of her military dead alone range from 430,000 to 2,600,000. More insidiously still, the issues of the Great Revolution had never been properly resolved.

AGE FIVE: 1815–1871

THE COMMUNE

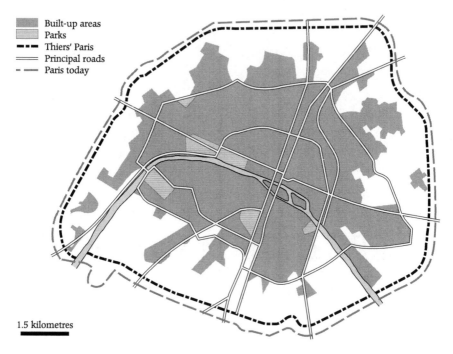

Built-up areas
Parks
Thiers' Paris
Principal roads
Paris today

1.5 kilometres

PARIS IN 1851 AT THE ACCESSION OF NAPOLEON III

13

Constitutional Monarchy
and Revolt

Parisians are like children; one constantly has to fill their
imagination, and if one cannot give them a victory in battle
every month, or a new constitution every year, then one has to
offer them daily some new building sites to visit, projects that
serve to beautify the city.

Comte de Rambuteau, *Mémoires*, p. 269

THE LAST BOURBONS

After the fervour and violent upheavals of the Napoleonic era, the years
1815 to 1870 offered a period of rest, readjustment and retrenchment
under the leadership successively of Louis XVIII, Charles X, Louis-
Philippe and Louis Napoleon. Or so it was on the surface, but underneath there were deep currents of discontent and disunity, waiting to
shake France and destroy more of Paris than either 1789 or any foreign
enemy had done. Returning to Paris during the Restoration, Stendhal
found a society 'profoundly ill at ease with itself'. Typical of the confusion of legitimacy and loyalties inherited by the new regime was the
varied fortune of the figure atop the mighty Vendôme Column. First, in
1818, the statue of Napoleon was removed, melted down and replaced
by a giant fleur-de-lys. Then, in 1833, Louis-Philippe – always keen to
oblige the prevailing mood – had the Emperor restored complete with
bicorne hat; but the statue displeased his nephew, Napoleon III, who
removed it to Les Invalides and replaced it with a copy of the original

figure. In 1871, the Commune revolutionaries – under the guidance of the painter Gustave Courbet – brought the whole column tumbling down. Finally, in 1875, Republican President McMahon had it restored with the present-day figure crowned in Caesarean laurels.

To have presided over, and healed, all the disarray left behind in 1815 France would have required an Henri IV. But Louis XVIII was certainly no Henri of Navarre; he was, so the people said, 'partly an old woman, partly a capon, partly a son of France, and partly a peasant'. He was homosexual, without a son, so obese and dropsy-ridden that eventually he had to be lifted in and out of his carriage. Aged beyond his sixty years, he would die after only nine years on the throne. But his instincts were not all bad. The politician-historian Guizot saw him as 'a moderate of the Old Regime and an eighteenth-century freethinker'.

Unfortunately, in his baggage train Louis brought with him a coterie of reactionary émigrés thirsting for vengeance after twenty-five years of exile and hardship, determined to put the clock back to the *ancien régime*, to Louis XIV if possible, and who gave rise to the famous epithet about the Bourbons having 'learned nothing and forgotten nothing'. Louis wanted to abide by the liberal 'Charter' modelled on English constitutional practice, which he had admired during his exile and been forced to accept on his return. But the émigré extremists, the 'Ultras', trampled it under foot, launching in the provinces a White Terror of threat and murder, with Royalist bands plundering, looting and settling old private scores. It was well said at the time, 'If you have not lived through 1815, you do not know what hatred is.'

Of the Ultras who surrounded him Louis remarked glumly, 'If these gentlemen had full freedom, they would end by purging me as well!' In Paris, the Pavillon de Marsan became the headquarters of reaction, and there the sons of the future Charles X, their wives, courtesans and bodyguards, all talked treason twenty-four hours a day. Plotting away against the regime too was the Charbonnerie, a secret society based on an Italian prototype; while the childless Louis' brother, and heir, the future Charles X – 'an émigré to his fingertips and a submissive bigot', in Guizot's eyes – also conspired against him. Then, in June 1820, and accompanied by revealingly little public emotion, the young Duc de Berry, nephew of Louis and third in succession to the throne, was assassinated by a 'a little weasel-faced mongrel', a fanatic called Louvel, motivated simply by 'hatred of the Bourbons'. The deed was seized upon by the Ultras as a welcome excuse to press for more power and a less liberal regime. Many of the harsher new laws passed reflected the pressures imposed on the regime; for instance, one 'on sacrilege' made theft of church vessels subject to the same penalty as parricide – the hand to be severed, and the head sliced off.

THE PROFILE OF RESTORATION PARIS

Compared with what preceded it under Napoleon and what was to follow under Baron Haussmann, during the years of the Restoration and of Louis-Philippe the profile of Paris changed but little. Its population had risen to over 700,000 (by 1844 it would reach one million, as more and more hopefuls flooded in from the provinces, enticed by the questionable blandishments of city life). These hordes were still crammed into a web of narrow, ill-paved and filthy streets. Among the few novelties was the Chapelle Expiatoire, built – first things first – for Parisians to atone for the murder of Louis XVI and his queen, on the exact place where they had originally been buried; and, with fine irony, the Rue Napoléon was renamed the Rue de la Paix. Uncompleted Napoleonic projects such as the Bourse – fundamental to the *enrichissez-vous* era on which Paris was about to embark – were completed. But lack of financial resources and of the absolutist power to project bold new commissions left its mark on the city. Stylistically, it was revived Louis XVI. New apartment buildings were lower and smaller, more spartan and utilitarian in style, with less spacious rooms. Most were swept aside by later and less ephemeral buildings. Many were erected, speculatively, at such high cost that they could be neither rented nor sold and the result left many houses empty. In the 1820s there were schemes launched to develop peripheral areas like the Batignolles on the Right Bank and Grenelle on the Left, which encouraged the speculators as wealth increased. Outside the old Octroi (customs) wall the delayed industrial revolution began implanting major manufacturing industries, years after London had done the same.

With more money came splendid galleries and covered passages constructed – by private speculators – around the Rue Vivienne and other Right Bank areas, for bourgeois shoppers to spend what was being accreted in the new counting houses constructed by financiers around Mme Récamier's Chaussée d'Antin. The aim of these opulent new arcades was not merely to 'protect the passer-by from the dangers of the streets; they had to hold him, enslave him, body and soul … he was supposed to feel so enchanted that he forgot everything: his wife, his children, the office, and dinner.' Heinrich Heine particularly enjoyed strolling through the Passage des Panoramas, though a contemporary German biographer observed that it was 'a place one avoids walking through in the evening if accompanied by a lady' – for here the elegant and affluent jostled shoulders, as they always had, with the underworld, pickpockets and tricksters, prostitutes and beggars.

Otherwise, little changed. The residential areas around the Louvre and Marais had fallen into decrepitude, and the revolutionary poor continued to exist, and seethe, in the Faubourg Saint-Antoine. By 1830, the western limit of the city was still the Place de la Concorde, while the Champs-Elysées continued to be bordered by ditches and hovels, with strange subterranean cabarets. An incomplete Arc de Triomphe stood in a forest glade, while the equally incomplete Madeleine rose out of a piece of *terrain vague* – though its unfinished beauty was to arouse the romantic sensibilities of Mrs Trollope, who on a moonlit night in 1835 thought this 'pale spectre of a Grecian temple … was the most beautiful object of art I ever looked at'. In place of Napoleon's decaying elephant monstrosity at the Bastille, Louis-Philippe erected the July Column, crowned by a statue with broken chains and a torch, as a symbol (unsuccessful) of reconciliation after the 1830 Revolution that brought him to power;* while that earlier symbol, the Concorde, was reorganized around the vast obelisk filched from Egypt (a suitably neutral device, politically).

As a consequence of the Revolution and the Napoleonic Wars the industrial revolution came late to Paris. By 1844, France still had only one-third as much railway line as Britain, and just over half as much as backward Prussia; the fastest mail-coach, carrying only four passengers in some discomfort, reached Bordeaux from Paris in forty-five hours, Lyons in forty-seven. Instead of appreciating its economic significance, many Parisians regarded the railway as an object of frivolity, with even the enlightened Adolphe Thiers remarking that a line from Paris to Saint-Germain would have amusement value only. When it was finally opened it reached no more than halfway. But in 1837 a momentous decision, unique in Europe, was taken to link Paris by rail with all the

---

* Within a year of its completion in 1840, it became a favourite jumping-off place for the unreconcilable and broken-hearted.

nation's frontiers. That same year – though it was considered too dangerous for King Louis-Philippe – Queen Amélie took the first train in Paris. Working girls could now go and dance in the Forest of Loges, once the favoured retreat of Diane de Poitiers, for only seventy-five centimes. The enterprise was backed by a banker from Vienna, James de Rothschild, who had arrived as Austrian consul-general in 1810, liked what he saw and swiftly become naturalized. Five years later those fearful for the King's safety found justification when a terrible accident occurred as an engine axle fractured on a fast train returning from Versailles. Of 700 Parisians who had been on a jaunt to see the fountains, 48 were killed and 110 injured.

Nevertheless, the railways continued to spread outward, with lines to Orléans and Rouen both opened in 1843, and it was soon possible to reach Calais from Paris in nine hours. At the same time, to accommodate the passengers a new form of architecture began to manifest itself in Paris – the *gare du chemin de fer*. Some, like the Gare Saint-Lazare, the city's first (built in 1836, and immortalized by the Impressionists), and the Gare d'Orsay (built in 1898, and one day to house those painters' works), were structures of considerable beauty in their own right.

As the money began to flow again, a whole new smart area began to be created south of the Champs-Elysées, around a country house which had once belonged to François I; so all the streets were given Renaissance names like Jean Goujon, Bayard, Cérisoles, Clément Marot and, of course, François I. But they were no safer at night than before. On the Left Bank, the Faubourg Saint-Germain ended just short of the Invalides, 'at a terrace and a ditch'. Emptied of its inhabitants by the Revolution, and with many of its grand houses still left vacant during the Napoleonic era, life now came slowly back to the *status quo ante* as the émigrés crept home during the Restoration. Once again, the stately *portes-cochères* of the Rue de Grenelle protected the same grand names – the Hôtels de Berwick, de Maurepas, de la Motte-Houdancourt, d'Harcourt, de la Salle, d'Avaray, de Lamoignon. The owners would be seen driving down the Rue du Bac, the principal artery linking the two banks, on their way to pay court at the Tuileries, or to the Opéra on Mondays, the Comédie Italienne on Thursdays.

Slowly the grandeur of the Left Bank became overshadowed in Saint-Germain by new breeds of Parisian – the Romantics and, further east, the Bohemians, the 'Mimis' freezing in their garrets in the Latin Quarter. One of the most important undertakings of the new regime was the Ecole des Beaux-Arts, set up in 1819 on the Quai Malaquais.

Swiftly it re-established Paris's pre-eminence in architectural education, attracting student architects from abroad, while the 'Beaux-Arts style' was to influence public building until as late as the First World War. Here the students laboured away in *ateliers*, cramped studios to which twenty or thirty of them would be attached, often directed by independent architects of distinction.

LIFE FOR THE POOR

One of the most remarkable features in all the history of France is the way in which, following two crushing nineteenth-century military disasters – Waterloo in 1815 and the capitulation to Prussia and the Commune of 1871 – each time there was an extraordinary blossoming in the gentler and more enduring works of humanity. It was almost as if they came in direct response to catastrophe on the military plane. Following 1871, it would be the burst of liberating colour and joy that was Impressionism; in 1815, it was the unique flowering of the great French novel, from Balzac and Hugo to Gautier, Flaubert and Daudet, from Dumas *père* and *fils* to Zola, Maupassant and Anatole France. Once the great dead hand of Napoleonic censorship was lifted from the arts, literature, and most especially the novel, began to flourish as never before. Founders of *romantisme*, the literature of revolt, artistic as well as political – Germaine de Staël (living just long enough to rejoice in the final fall of her arch-enemy), Chateaubriand, Stendhal and the poetic geniuses of Lamartine and Vigny – were followed closely by giants like Balzac (1799–1850) and later Hugo (1802–85).

Balzac and Hugo took it upon themselves, virtually for the first time, to tell of poverty in Paris, to describe what it was like to be really poor, in debt, pursued by the police, struggling to emerge from the underclass. The very stink of the Paris of the poor, the stale cabbage and untuned plumbing, with her hollow-cheeked, pale and sallow denizens, seeps out from Balzac's *Père Goriot* in this description of the *quartier* where Goriot himself, a once prosperous vermicelli merchant, lives in abject poverty:

> that illustrious valley of flaking plasterwork and gutters black with mud; a valley full of suffering that is real, and of joy that is often

false, where life is so hectic that it takes something quite extraordinary to produce feelings that last ... the houses are gloomy, the walls like a prison ... washed in that shade of yellow which so demeans all the houses in Paris ...

Balzac's preoccupation with the belief that 'wealth is virtue', and with the corruption that went hand in hand with it, was to run throughout his vast work, the *Comédie Humaine* and its ninety-odd novels and tales. Dumas *père* would echo the theme in *The Count of Monte Cristo*, portraying a society where everything – whether social standing or revenge – can be bought at a price. It would pick up speed during the bourgeois era of Louis-Philippe, reaching its apogee there, and on through the Paris of the Second Empire, finding revival under the Third Republic, and with echoes even down to the Paris of Pompidou, Giscard d'Estaing, Mitterrand and Chirac. As the Restoration took root, much of the positive social gains achieved during the Revolution and under Napoleon evaporated. Gradually as the gaps between Parisian classes widened, the poor becoming poorer, the rich becoming infinitely richer, it was not long before the politician-historian Guizot was codifying the principle of *enrichissez-vous* – with the unspoken rider, 'and leave politics to me'. During the early days of the Restoration, there were reckoned (by Eugène Sue) to be 30,000 thieves in Paris, their numbers swollen in the first instance by the thousands of impoverished ex-officers of the Grande Armée conducting dubious card games and ever on the lookout for an easy touch. Then came the fresh influx from the provinces. The immense pull of Paris at that time is well described by Balzac in *Le Cabinet des antiques* as:

a city that swallows up gifted individuals born everywhere in the kingdom, makes them part of its strange population, and dries out the intellectual capacities of the nation for its own benefit. The provinces themselves are responsible for the force that plunders them ... And as soon as a merchant has amassed a fortune, he thinks only of taking it to Paris, the city that thus comes to epitomize all of France.

Inevitably, living conditions became far worse in the fastest-growing sections of the city where the poorest people lived, while the baneful consequences of overcrowding cause Balzac's lawyer Derville in *Le Colonel Chabert* to exclaim, after listing all the variants of despicable human behaviour he has witnessed in the city, 'I shall move to the country with my wife; Paris frightens me.' A report by the *département* of the Seine in 1829 found that of 'the 224,000 households in Paris at least 136,000 must be described as being poor, and a further 32,000 households as living on the edge of poverty'. Within the areas where the over-populous *classes laborieuses* eked out a wretched existence, there was – initially – an ominous quietness; but all the time there was building up a new *classe dangereuse* that would one day erupt and spew out once again like lava into bourgeois Paris.

As before, these *quartiers* of the poor often lay cheek by jowl with those of the new rich. Behind the glitter of the Champs-Elysées and the *grands boulevards* marched rows of mean hovels, while a notable district for prostitutes lay between the elegant Avenue de l'Opéra and the Rue Richelieu. These 'unfortunates', as they were euphemistically called, proliferated; in the Palais Royal area their numbers were put at one for every sixty-three inhabitants, and in the Saint-Honoré *quartier* at one for every forty-two. The labyrinth of narrow streets, where vice and crime flourished, remained places of gloom and terror until the days of Haussmann, particularly at night – and in general the streets of Paris were just as squalid, malodorous and overcrowded as they always had been.

HEALTH AND HYGIENE

Under the Restoration and Louis-Philippe, health and hygiene in Paris lagged disgracefully, despite all Napoleon had done to improve the city's drains. If anything, with the surging population increase, the situation had worsened. There was no efficient, centralized means of collecting rubbish and filth, still deposited daily on the streets by the 224,000 households. One contemporary report describes how the dirt would:

> remain lying there for an indeterminate time ... Hardly has half of it been swept up when the rest is scattered in the gutters, blocking the water from draining away; it only disappears when strong rains flood the drains ...
>
> Bad gases and pestilential miasmas rise up to the place where the trash collects, not to mention that the sludge gets stuck between

the paving stones. But that is not all. A far worse and unhealthier stench streams from the underground sewers that benumbs passers-by, and forces residents to leave their houses.

Still running directly and untreated into the Seine, the sewage 'creates a swamp on the banks that pollutes the water used for washing or drinking by half the inhabitants of Paris'.

By comparison with Paris – even though the drains of Windsor would kill off Prince Albert – London was a sweet-smelling city. House-holds had a flush-sewage system working, while the Paris sewers still served mainly as street drains. Cesspools had to be emptied periodically, resulting in a disgusting and insalubrious smell. While Parisians would 'barely consume seven litres of water per day', according to Balzac, 'every citizen of London has the use of sixty-two litres'. Even by 1848 only 5,300 Parisian households were connected to the rudimentary and clogged-up sewage system, and would have to await Haussmann, and beyond, for better things.

Just outside the city things were worse. Up at Montfaucon (now in the 10th arrondissement), the former site of the hideous gibbets, fallen into disuse since the early seventeenth century, had become revolting knackers' yards and the depots of collected sewage. Out of them highly infectious streams trickled back down into the city and into her water reservoirs. From all this it was hardly surprising that, in 1832, Paris would be stricken with a major cholera epidemic, one of the worst in her history, its spread helped by the filthy streets. The first victim was claimed on 19 February; by 5 April there were 503 cases; on the 12th, as many as 1,020. The Opéra Comique was turned into an emergency hospital, and the hard-line Prime Minister, Casimir Périer, died of the disease, after visiting the Hôtel Dieu.

Day after day carts rattled through the disease-bearing streets piled high with corpses. Inevitably, the government was accused of having poisoned the wine supply and when the heir to Louis-Philippe's throne courageously visited the hospital wards he was denounced by the opposition for wanting to inspect the misery of the people. By the time the ravages of the epidemic were over, 18,402 Parisians had died. From a sociological point of view, the spread of its victims was pointed: in rich areas like the Chaussée d'Antin only eight per thousand succumbed, whereas in the poor districts such as the Hôtel de Ville fifty-three per thousand perished. Thus cholera was manifestly a disease of poverty and overcrowding. Clearly something radical had to be done.

In June 1833 a new, energetic Prefect of the Seine – Claude-Philibert Barthelot, Comte de Rambuteau – was appointed. But his plan for Paris was a continuation of Napoleon's *embellissement*, and little else. Stately monuments and beautiful public gardens, and some thirty new streets and a few bridges were built. But Rambuteau prided himself on being thrifty and, during most of his fifteen years in office, on average only 15 per cent of the total city expenditure went on the upkeep and improvement of the infrastructure. In September 1837, Balzac – incurably optimistic – wrote to his lover, Mme Hanska, 'In ten years we shall be clean, we shall no longer talk of the mud of Paris, and then we shall be so magnificent that Paris will truly be seen as a lady of the world, the first among queens, wreathed in walls.' But it was not to be. In 1849, Paris would be struck by yet another plague of cholera, this time claiming more than 19,000 victims.

BREAD AND CIRCUSES

For all the grimness of Restoration Paris, there was much to make life worth while and attractive – for most of the populace. The city began to throb with the innovations which science and the industrial revolution had to offer. Apart from the new invention of the bicycle, there was a new light vehicle called the fiacre, as one way of dealing with the problems of transport, and soon there were steamboats plying the Seine. There were medical advances like the first successful cataract operation (though it would have taken a brave man to risk it), performed by Dupuytren, chief surgeon in the Hôtel Dieu. The state of medicine was reflected in increasing longevity (for the better-off): Victor Hugo, Thiers and that veteran of revolutions, Lafayette, all lived into their eighties or late seventies. Then there was Jacques Daguerre with the novelty of his pivoted 'Diorama' – and, in 1838, the first photographs, or *daguerréotypes*. The first horse-drawn omnibus made its clip-clopping appearance on the clogged streets. And at last there was gas lighting (though a French invention, it was pioneered in London), accompanied in 1822 by the marvel of the vast gasometer in the Poissonnière district. As it gradually replaced flickering oil lamps the gentle glow of the gas lighting excitingly threw up the outline of a new city by

19. Paris coat of arms on the Hôtel de Ville. Motto: *Fluctuat nec mergitur*
(She is tossed on the waves but is not overwhelmed).

20. A lesson in theology at the Sorbonne. Illustration from the fifteenth-century
manuscript *Postilles sur le Pentateuch*.

21. Haymaking outside fifteenth-century Paris; Charles V's Louvre in the background. From *Les Très Riches Heures du Duc de Berry* by the Limbourg brothers.

22. Henri IV's Reine Margot. Portrait of Marguerite de Valois by François Clouet.

23. Henri IV before the walls of Paris, 1594. French school.

24. View from the Pont Neuf by Hendrick Mommers, 1668.

25. Louis XIV, with Louvois, Mansart and Le Nôtre at the *Machine de Marly*, Versailles in background, by Jean-Baptiste Martin, 1688.

26. Louis XIV inspects
Les Invalides, 26 August 1706,
by Pierre-Denis Martin.

27. Member of the
Directory, 1790.

28. *Parisienne* of the Directory period.

29. Napoleon and Josephine plan
the Coronation, 1804. Lithograph by
Jacques Onfray de Breville, 1910.

30. The consecration of the Emperor Napoleon and the coronation of the Empress Josephine, 2 December 1804, by Jacques Louis David – who painted himself in the balcony *ex post facto*.

31. Baron Haussmann, Napoleon III and Empress Eugénie visit builders at the Opéra.

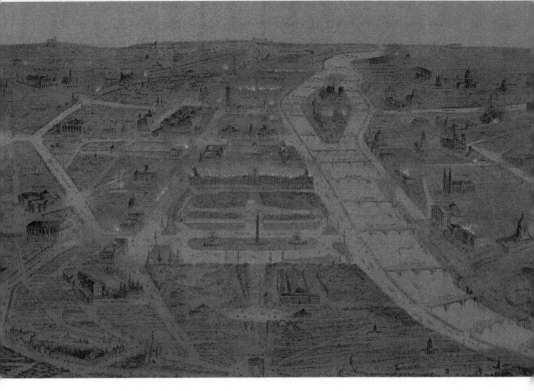

32. Paris burns under the Commune, May 1871, by H. Guesnu.

33. Terrace of the Café Wepler, Place Clichy. Lithograph by
François Henri Morisset, 1905.

34. *A Day at the Races* by
Maurice Taquoy, 1926.

35. De Gaulle supporters
march up the
Champs-Elysées,
30 May 1968. Photo by
Bruno Barbey.

night. It was also soft enough to mask most of the horrors of crime, poverty and filth, cladding the terrors of the night with a certain romantic charm.

Among the unchanging distractions that Paris life habitually offered, there was always the theatre – now returned to its old unfettered, unbridled rowdiness of pre-revolutionary days. In 1817, at the Comédie Française where Mlle Mars, alias Anne Boutet, resumed its great tradition, there was a reminder of the uninhibited days of Louis XIV when Ultras and leftists came to serious blows over a piece which, lampooning one faction, was cheered by the other. In the ensuing rumpus, a number of prominent citizens were injured. Thereafter theatre managers insisted that canes, umbrellas and other weapons be deposited at the door, giving rise to the present-day theatre cloakroom. Up on the unchic Boulevard du Temple the Théâtre des Funambules (literally, 'tightrope-walkers'), founded in 1816, achieved enormous popularity with its performances of mime, vaudeville and melodrama, playing to even noisier audiences, and with an always more financially precarious company. Here the great tragic clown Jean Deburau held sway as the lovelorn and pathetic Pierrot, ever hopeful but always disappointed. Deburau died in 1846 as tragically as he had lived, falling during a performance and dying of his injuries. But he and the Funambules were to live for ever in Carné's' immortal black-and-white film of a century later, *Les Enfants du paradis*, starring Jean-Louis Barrault.

Once more the comic opera, called 'the Italien' after the adjacent boulevard, also thrived – home of the new Romantic music. It was an epoch when concert-goers could hear Luigi Cherubini (Director of the Conservatoire de Paris), Frédéric Chopin, Franz Liszt and Hector Berlioz perform their works. Berlioz, who wrote his magical *Symphonie fantastique* for his Irish paramour while he was still only thirty – its lilting Romanticism offset by sombre reminders of the guillotine that seemed to typify the age – remained unacknowledged. He died in 1869, crushed by the critics at the apogee of the Second Empire, while lesser musicians like Offenbach carried off the laurels.

Parisians, declared Prefect Rambuteau, with just a touch of condescension:

> are like children; one constantly has to fill their imagination, and if one cannot give them a victory in battle every month, or a new constitution every year, then one has to offer them daily some new building sites to visit, projects that serve to beautify the city.

If Rambuteau was not up to the job of providing sufficient *embellissement* projects in the capital, neither were the variety of distractions and the great cultural efflorescence that had been offered by the Restoration sufficient to avert a renewal of that age-old Parisian disease, ennui, now apostrophized by the Romantic poet Lamartine. Not for the first time nor for the last, French regimes sought to divert dissatisfaction at home – growing by the year – by the pursuit of *la Gloire* abroad. Once it had been Italy, now it was Algeria.

In 1827, the Dey of Algiers lost his temper with the French Consul, Deval, struck him in the face with a fly-whisk and called him a 'wicked, faithless, idol-worshipping rascal'. Here was a perfect pretext for the increasingly unpopular government of Charles X to launch a foreign adventure. Though they waited for three years before avenging the terrible insult, in May 1830 a French expeditionary force landed on a beach at Sidi Ferruch, thirty kilometres west of Algiers, and began the annexation of the world's tenth-biggest nation, several times the size of France. It was under the liberal regime of Louis-Philippe rather than of Charles X that the often savage pacification of Algeria took place, but the adventure would not suffice to preserve the thrones of either.

Nonetheless, this most blatant example of 'bread and circuses' would help gain France 124 years of prosperity and power, but would end in eight years of hell that would bring down the Fourth Republic. The immediate benefits of the Algerian annexation were swift to arrive in the mother country: there were glamorous silk cloths, reaching even to provincial Rouen to help assuage the desperate ennui suffered by poor Emma Bovary; in Paris there was the can-can, the bizarre and shocking new dance first seen in the cholera year of 1832, and said to be based on something discovered in barbaric Algeria.

THE JULY MONARCHY

'La France s'ennuie!' In fact, most of France and most Frenchmen were reasonably contented with life under the restored monarchy. It was, once more, turbulent Paris where the trouble lay. There the reactionary Charles X had become progressively more unpopular, especially after he had expressed his intention of scrapping the Charter, to which the

Bourbon monarchy had pledged itself on returning to power. By the summer of 1830, this decision – added to economic recession and to an agricultural crisis on the scale of 1811 – was to prove catastrophic. In Paris there were once again soaring bread prices, wage cuts and unemployment; some 64,000 Parisians had no stable employment, signifying that they were dependent either on charity or on crime; while foreigners were horrified to discover four-year-olds working long hours in the mills. Soup kitchens reappeared on the streets, as they had in the early years of the Great Revolution. The warning signs were there, but no one noticed them.

In June Charles X issued four unconstitutional decrees which *inter alia* dissolved the Chamber of Deputies and suspended freedom of the press. Suddenly, on 26 July, a stiflingly hot day in Paris, the storm broke. A group of young people started a demonstration outside the Palais Royal. Within an hour a dense crowd had assembled in the gardens of the Palais. But they were driven away by the police, and by midnight all seemed calm. This calm, with its suggestion that the authorities were in control, proved fatal to the government. Charles X, relaxing out at Saint-Cloud, put Napoleon's veteran commander Marshal Marmont in charge. It was a foolish choice, because Parisians remembered him as the man who had surrendered the city to the enemy in 1814. On the 27th, the crowds were out again on the streets, this time setting up barricades near the Rue Saint-Honoré and around the Bourse. Several rioters were killed. Among the dead was a young woman shot down in the Rue Saint-Honoré with a stray bullet in the forehead. When a butcher's boy carried the corpse into the Place des Victoires, the spectacle aroused the crowd to calls for vengeance.

During the night fresh barricades were run up – this time in the eastern districts, the traditional haunts of revolution. Trees were felled, and workers from Saint-Antoine plundered gunsmiths for weapons and seized the Arsenal. On the morning of the 28th, headed by students of the Ecole Polytechnique, demonstrators peacefully occupied the Hôtel de Ville, unfurling the *tricolore* flag from its towers. Soon there were ominous indications that troops had begun to fraternize with the rebels. Elsewhere, on the Place de Grève and in the Rue Saint-Antoine, there was bitter fighting with numerous casualties. What had started as a minor revolt had exploded into a full-scale insurrection. Realizing that his troops were at a serious disadvantage fighting in the narrow streets, and receiving no clear instructions from Saint-Cloud, Marmont gave the order to withdraw from the inner city. The game was lost. But the fighting continued savagely on the 29th. Its centre moved westwards to the Louvre. A Swiss unit defending the Tuileries fled in panic, escaping from Paris via the Champs-Elysées. As it had done in 1792, the mob entered and sacked the Tuileries, getting hopelessly drunk in its copious cellars. The Archbishop's palace was also occupied, its furniture and rare books hurled into the Seine.

By the afternoon of the 29th, the insurgents – bewildered by the completeness of their success – found themselves in control of the whole city. Taking advantage of their momentary confusion, frightened liberal deputies began to react. Led by the young radical journalist Adolphe Thiers, they called for the abdication of Charles X. They eschewed the call of the left for a republic on the ground that it would expose France to 'terrible divisions'. Then they nominated Louis-Philippe, Duc d'Orléans, to assume the throne. Charles tried to save the dynasty by putting forward his grandson, the Duc de Bordeaux – as Henri V. But Paris would have none of it. Constitutional monarchy held no attractions for Charles. 'I would rather hew wood than be a king like the King of England!' he declared, before turning to the ever-at-hand Talleyrand and adding, 'I see no middle way between the throne and the scaffold.' The old cynic, who had seen it all, replied, 'Your Majesty forgets the post-chaise!' Charles took Talleyrand's advice, and the post-chaise – to dreaded England. He ended up in Gorizia (in Austrian-occupied northern Italy), where he died of cholera in 1836. 'Still another government', was Chateaubriand's acid comment, 'hurling itself down from the towers of Notre-Dame.'

As the last of the Bourbons took the road into exile, his departure was marked by one final note of absurdity. Charles' daughter-in-law, widow of the Duc de Berry, assassinated in Paris just after the Restoration, tried to regain the crown for her son; but it transpired that the virtuous widow, imprisoned in the citadel of Blaye, was in fact pregnant by an unknown lover. Her gambit ended in scandal and disrepute – and with it the long line of kings initiated by Henri IV 240 years previously.

Aged fifty-seven, Louis-Philippe was the great-great-grandson of the Regent to Louis XV, and his acceptability to both sides in 1830 stemmed largely from the fact that his father had been the duplicitous regicide Philippe Egalité – though apostasy had not sufficed to save his neck during the Terror. Louis-Philippe had been nominated for the post of Lieutenant-General of the Kingdom by both Charles X and the Commune* of Paris, and for the remainder of his eighteen-year rule between

* An improvised city assembly created in July 1789 after the fall of the Bastille, but

revolutions he would do his utmost to be all things to all sides. It was symbolic that the last King of France, the very antithesis of Louis XIV, accepted the crown not at Rheims but in the Palais Bourbon, as the politically elected ruler of 'the people'. Shorn of all mystical or inherited *droits*, the People's King had little more power than a British constitutional monarch.

From the first, Louis-Philippe played the role. He made his home in the Palais Royal – where his ancestor, the Regent, had once reigned – with a total absence of the pomp-and-circumstance of Versailles. He addressed workmen as 'my friends' and the National Guard as 'my comrades', and liked to stroll through the streets with a green umbrella under his arm, shaking hands promiscuously; at the least encouragement, he would appear on the balcony, obligingly brandishing the *tricolore* and lustily singing the Marseillaise. Heinrich Heine was somewhat shocked to learn that the King had two pairs of gloves for each occasion. When he shook hands 'with every spice merchant and artisan ... he wore a special dirty glove for that purpose, which he always took off and exchanged for a cleaner kid glove when he kept more elevated company and went to see the old aristocrats, his banker-ministers'.

As sumptuous carriages disappeared off the streets, Paris emulated the new royal family. The bourgeois at first revelled in their new monarch, in the peace and prosperity he signalled, and delightedly took up Guizot's exhortation of *enrichissez-vous*. Meanwhile the *classes laborieuses* of Paris had no such cause to celebrate; they – the poor and the revolutionaries of the Faubourg Saint-Antoine – felt that the bourgeois had once more cheated them out of their birthright, the rewards of insurrection, as indeed they had after the Great Revolution itself. The son of a regicide and regarded as a usurper by the legitimists, Louis-Philippe would always be highly vulnerable, for all his good intentions.

Within a year there was fresh trouble on the streets of Paris. In February 1831 riots broke out; in October there were further riots over Louis-Philippe's desire to drop the death penalty. The following year the cholera epidemic struck Paris, and fresh riots were provoked in June by the funeral of a cholera victim, General Lamarque, a revanchist demagogue. It was Lamarque's last words – 'I die regretting not having avenged France for the infamous treaties of 1815' – that unleashed the mobs. Half of Paris was taken over by some two or three thousand

---

deprived of most of its power under Napoleon's administrative reforms. Its name was to be borrowed for the insurrection of 1871 (see Chapter 15).

young insurgents, of whom one in ten were killed by cannonfire. Windows of the Foreigners' Club were broken, amid cries of 'Down with Louis-Philippe!' and 'He'll die on the scaffold like his father!' In April 1834 more riots brought about a shocking butchery by nervous troops of innocent civilians in the Marais' Rue Transnonain – to be fixed for ever in Parisian minds by Daumier's immortal cartoon of a man lying at the foot of his bed in nothing but nightcap and shirt.

In July 1835 a Corsican immigrant and extreme republican called Fieschi fired an infernal machine consisting of twenty-five musket barrels lashed together like organ tubes at Louis-Philippe's cortège as it rode slowly up the Boulevard du Temple. Fieschi's device exploded like the concentrated fire of a whole infantry platoon. The Minister of War, Napoleon I's veteran Marshal Mortier, dropped with a bullet through the head; thirteen others died, including a fourteen-year-old girl, and twenty-two were wounded. The King's horse was also hit, but he himself was untouched. He returned courageously to review the troops for two hours that afternoon, declaring 'C'est moi qui mène le fiacre!' Fieschi, horribly wounded by his own device, went to the guillotine – though he was the first French would-be regicide to be spared torture.

The King's courage under fire gained him some respite. In 1840, he sought new favour from the increasingly vocal Bonapartists by having the dead Emperor brought back to Paris and reinterred with great ceremony under Louis XIV's dome of the Invalides. Yet even this dramatic measure was not enough to save Louis-Philippe when the next storm came – in 1848.

YEAR OF REVOLUTION

Like that of 1968, the year 1848 was one of revolt and revolution across the board. In Europe, old political structures collapsed like houses of cards. Given the paucity of communications, what was remarkable was how swiftly revolution spread across Europe. 'There was', wrote a British historian, 'a sound of breaking glass in every continental capital west of the Russian frontier.' In Vienna even the seemingly immortal Metternich – who had given Europe its past three decades of peace – was deposed. By the end of 1848, except for Britain – where Prince Albert was able to sigh, 'we had our revolution yesterday, and it ended in rain' – there were to be dictators established in almost every country of Europe. The world had truly shifted on its axis.

It had all begun in Paris, in the last week of February. Once again, as during the last years of the Napoleonic era, there had been a prelude of poor harvests in 1846–7. On 22 February, a mass banquet, planned by the Opposition to give expression to Parisian discontent over government resistance to reform, was abruptly cancelled. The following afternoon fighting broke out at the Porte Saint-Martin and a number of people were killed. There were shouts of 'Down with Guizot!' – who, as successively Louis-Philippe's Minister for Foreign Affairs and Prime Minister, had been the virtual ruler of France for the past eight years. Stones were thrown at the Quai d'Orsay, railings ripped out at the Chamber of Deputies, and a highly reluctant Thiers seized and carried shoulder-high by demonstrators. Barricades began to appear on the Rue de Rivoli. Worst of all, there were cries of 'Vive la Réforme!' and 'Down with Guizot!' from the ranks of the National Guard, formed of middle-class Praetorians.

In alarm, the King jettisoned Guizot, but it was already too late. Near the elegant Boulevard des Capucines, the progress of 'a decidedly villainous-looking mob' singing revolutionary songs was blocked by the loyally Royalist 14th Battalion. When one of the rioters thrust his torch in the face of its commanding officer, a trigger-happy Corsican sergeant shot him dead. That single shot changed the course of French history. On hearing the shot, and thinking their chief threatened, the nervous soldiers fired a ragged volley into the crowd. Count Rodolphe Apponyi, an attaché at the Austrian Embassy, saw 'a hundred or more people laid low, stretched out, or rolling over another, shrieking and groaning'. News of the shooting raced through Paris. On his way back to his Embassy Apponyi observed an angry mob heading for the Tuileries.

There Louis-Philippe, horrified by events, had been advised by Thiers to retire to Saint-Cloud and assemble a force for retaking Paris. (It was advice Thiers would himself pursue twenty-three years later, when his time came in 1871.) The King refused; instead he called upon the unpopular Marshal Bugeaud, pacifier of Algeria, to take over command, only to order him to cease fire. The National Guard (on whose bourgeois units the government so crucially depended) went over to the insurgents, and as the sound of nearby firing reached the Tuileries on 24 February the old King abdicated in favour of his son, the Comte de Paris. He and Queen Amélie then left hurriedly through a side door in the Tuileries terrace. He who had once declared bravely, 'C'est moi qui mène le fiacre!' now left in one, just like his predecessor, for exile in England. With him, the last King of France, departed the thousand-year-old French monarchy.

Hardly had Louis-Philippe left than the mob invaded the Tuileries, just as they had done in the last days of Louis XVI. Though some looters were shot on the spot, women and children dressed themselves up in valuable tapestries; sofas and armchairs were flung out of the windows, portraits of the King were ripped to pieces, even Voltaire's bust was hurled down into the courtyard. The throne was carried in triumph through Paris, and set on fire at the foot of the July Column (which commemorated the July Days of 1830), while a great crowd danced round it. The Palais Royal was also sacked and gutted. A republic was proclaimed, as workers flocked to the Hôtel de Ville.

France, and Paris, were taken totally by surprise by the events of February 1848. With 350 dead over the three days, it was the least bloody uprising of the century. For many, the dominant bourgeoisie had become, as Tocqueville saw it, 'a small aristocracy, corrupt and vulgar, by which it seemed shameful to let oneself be ruled'. Few, probably, had really wanted Louis-Philippe to go. Says Tocqueville again, 'this time a regime was not overthrown, it was simply allowed to fall'. In truth, the monarchy had died out of sheer boredom, for 'lack of panache', in a uniquely French fashion. The good King had given France some of the happiest years in her history, but, as has been remarked, 'the French do not live on happiness'.

As the July Monarchy crumbled, so *romantisme* petered out. In its place came freedom of the press, freedom of assembly, universal suffrage and the right of every Parisian to join the National Guard. In Saint Petersburg, recalling what had followed 1792, a thoroughly alarmed Tsar shouted, 'Gentlemen, saddle your horses; France is a Republic!' In fact, the Second Republic was virtually doomed before it started. Once again the Parisian proletariat realized that – although, much more than in 1789, this had been a rising of the slums and the workers' districts – the new revolution had not been won by them. They emerged from it more abjectly poor, but more concentrated and more aware of their own strength than at any time before. These were conditions that remained highly favourable to revolt, and as early as June 1848 it broke out again in Paris – this time to be suppressed with far greater violence.

ENTER LOUIS NAPOLEON

In Paris the coming of the Republic was greeted with 'a carnival-like exuberance', according to Gustave Flaubert's sympathetic recollection, and 'enjoyment of a sort of camp life; nothing was more entertaining than this aspect of Paris during the first days'. But the mood swiftly changed as reality replaced fantasy. Unemployment in the capital spiralled up to the previously unheard-of total of 180,000. To bring matters to a head, the new (Republican) government, nominally of 'the people', dissolved the national workshop (*atelier*) scheme designed to provide work for the unemployed, on useless earthworks. From the *ateliers* left-wing political 'clubs' mushroomed throughout the city, their members studying with interest the revolts that had swept the rest of Europe – especially the heroic but futile Polish uprisings.

On 23 June, rioting began once more in Paris, and by the evening the whole eastern half of the city was in the hands of insurrectionists. Yet again the revolt was ill prepared, in effect a spontaneous insurrection against hunger and misery. But this time the government was ready for trouble. General Louis-Eugène Cavaignac, Minister of War and another successful pacifier in Algeria, had for some time been drawing up a battle plan against the 'Reds',* and was now invested with almost dictatorial powers. He spent a day bringing in 30,000 regular troops from outside the city, while the rebels constructed their barricades. The following day Cavaignac attacked, deploying his artillery without compunction against the barricades. The rebels fought back sullenly, without leaders, without cheers, and almost without hope. The killing was quite ruthless, but the battle continued for three days. When, most courageously, the Archbishop of Paris, Monsignor Affre, tried to intervene, he was mortally wounded.†

Killed, too, were no fewer than five of Cavaignac's generals, as well

---

* The Reds, as they were already called, embraced a wide range of revolutionaries that pre-dated Marxist Communists.

† The Archbishop of Paris died of wounds sustained on the barricades while attempting to mediate. A successor archbishop was taken hostage and executed by the Commune twenty-three years later.

as hundreds of unarmed civilians. Official figures – though these were almost certainly a gross underestimate – put the deaths at 914 among the government troops and 1,435 for the insurgents. A police commissioner counted fifteen large furniture vans piled high with corpses; many were 'shot while escaping', or summarily executed in the quarries of Montmartre or the Buttes-Chaumont in eastern Paris. The Rue Blanche reeked with rotting cadavers hastily interred in the Montmartre cemetery. The details of 11,616 Parisians captured after the 'June Days' were listed in the official records; thousands were arrested and transported to the colonies, or to Algeria, without trial. Flaubert provides a grim picture of one of the dungeons: 'Nine hundred men were there, crowded together in filth pell-mell, black with powder and clotted blood, shivering in fever and shouting in frenzy. Those who died were left to lie with the others.'

When it was all over, relieved bourgeois and dandies from the western arrondissements came out to inspect the havoc. From his exile in England, Louis-Philippe, recalling how few deaths had brought about his fall, commented with bitter irony that the Republic was lucky 'to be able to fire upon the people'. June 1848 had unleashed the most sanguinary fighting that had yet been seen on the streets of Paris. Yet the spectacle of a republic butchering its own supporters in a way that no French monarchy or empire could rival would be repeated, with even more hideous consequences, twenty-three years later under the Commune of Paris. The June Days had only created a new generation of embittered Parisians.

Following Cavaignac's intervention the military were indisputably masters of Paris, though the Second Republic limped on. There were elections for the presidency. A dark horse in the shape of Louis Napoleon Bonaparte, nephew of Napoleon I, emerged from exile and, backed by provinces and a middle class dismayed by recent events, won three-quarters of the total vote. This was, in fact, a massive vote against Paris. Louis Napoleon collected five and a half million votes to Cavaignac's million and a half; while Ledru-Rollin, the socialist candidate, polled only 370,000, and the poet Lamartine fewer than 8,000.

Louis Napoleon, remarked Thiers scathingly in private, was 'A *crétin* whom we will manage.' But this was soon to prove something of an exaggeration. While in exile in England, the new President of France had enrolled as a special constable during the London troubles. There he had studied carefully, at first hand, how an authoritarian figure like the Duke of Wellington could outflank the revolutionaries and bring to heel a great city. For the best part of two years, former Special Constable Bonaparte trod warily, and kept his counsel. On the evening of 1 December 1851, with great calm and betraying no emotion, he received guests at the Elysée, now the presidential palace, on the Faubourg Saint-Honoré. After the last guest had left, he opened a file labelled 'Rubicon' – obsessed, like his uncle, by the memory of Caesar. At dawn in a surprise coup, and under pretext of monarchist threats, his troops occupied key positions in Paris. It was the anniversary both of Austerlitz and of his uncle's coronation as emperor; again like his uncle, Louis Napoleon trusted in augury. In contrast to the revolts of 1848, fewer than 400 Parisians were killed. One of the dead was a courageous Deputy, Dr Baudin, who gained immortality by rashly climbing atop a barricade to proclaim, 'See how a man dies for twenty-five francs a day!'* and was promptly felled by three bullets. A further 26,000 'enemies of the regime' were later arrested and transported on the hulks. On 20 December, a plebiscite confirmed the latest Bonapartist coup by a huge majority of nearly seven and a half million to 650,000. A Te Deum was sung in Notre-Dame.

Twenty years later the French electorate would painfully agree with Thiers that Louis Napoleon was a *crétin* – though he had most certainly not proved 'manageable'. Meanwhile, however, the Second Empire had arrived.

---

* The daily wage of a Republican deputy.

14

The Second Empire

We ripped open the belly of old Paris, the neighbourhood of revolt and barricades, and cut a large opening through the almost impenetrable maze of alleys, piece by piece, and put in cross-streets whose continuations terminated the work.

Baron Haussmann, *Mémoires*, pp. 54–5

LOUIS NAPOLEON

On 2 December 1852, a year to the day after his coup, forty-seven years exactly since his uncle's famous victory at Austerlitz had welded together the First Empire, Louis Napoleon declared himself emperor, as Napoleon III.* So what did the Second Empire stand for? First and foremost, it pledged France to a return to the old Bonapartist ethos of authoritarian order, in contradistinction to the anarchic chaos of the short-lived Second Republic – yet it would end its days in a failed attempt to regain liberalism. To the envious world outside, it represented the summit of gaiety and frivolity, the music of Offenbach, the rediscovery of a joyous world in the unfettered splashes of Impressionist colour, and sexual liberation – yet, on its underside, there was decay, corruption and venereal disease. Through Prefect Haussmann old Paris would be reborn as an astonishing new city, but much that remained precious in the ancient capital was swept aside. For the bourgeoisie and the new rich, there would be an extension to the prosperity consolidated under Louis-Philippe; for the poor, however, there would be no improvement

---

* Napoleon II, the tragic son of Bonaparte and Marie Louise, died of tuberculosis, aged only twenty-two, in Vienna, a virtual prisoner of his Austrian grandfather.

in the misery of life. In foreign affairs, the Second Empire would offer self-determination of 'nationalities' abroad, but would end with a friendless France plunged into the worst military disaster of her long history – her proud capital starved, bombarded, humiliated and, finally, incendiarized by her own citizens.

Aged forty-three at the time of the 1851 coup, Louis Napoleon was the third son of Louis Bonaparte, briefly King of Holland, and – via his mother Hortense – also a grandson of Josephine. Twice he had made abortive attempts to overthrow Louis-Philippe. The second time, in 1840, he had been condemned to life imprisonment in the fortress of Ham near the Somme. But in 1846 he escaped to England, disguised as a mason called Badinguet – a nickname under which his enemies would thereafter constantly attack him. In his outward appearance, France's new ruler had none of the presence of his illustrious uncle. One who met him while in exile in England found 'a short, thickish, vulgar-looking man without the slightest resemblance to his imperial uncle or any intelligence in his countenance', while those who saw him enthroned in his full glory were disappointed to find a man with dull eyes, a long moustache and faintly absurd *impérial* goatee beard – the delight of caricaturists like Daumier who immortalized him as 'Ratapoil', a broken-down Quixote. To George Sand, who was disgusted by the bourgeois rapacity alongside so much misery that came to stigmatize his rule, he was a 'sleepwalker'.

Rarely has so controversial a character held so much power in Europe. He was bursting with contradictions: wild courage vied with timidity; astuteness with extraordinarily poor judgement; winning charm with boorishness; powerful reactionary instincts with progressiveness and humanity ahead of his time. Kindly writers dubbed him 'the Well-Intentioned'. But, whatever he intended for France, the end result was usually the opposite. In many ways, he was a very talented man, his reading during the years of imprisonment having made him much better educated than most of his peers. The trouble was that, for him, the time was always out of joint. His political legitimacy was questionable; to many he was simply the usurper (which indeed he was). Yet the ultimate catastrophe might have been averted had he not been confronted with two of the most adroit, and dangerous, statesmen of the nineteenth century, Cavour and Bismarck.

Having imposed an authoritarian regime on France, Louis Napoleon then set to work to create internal prosperity as one way of diverting minds from the loss of essential liberties. In the early years of the Second

Empire (exploiting the groundwork laid by Louis-Philippe) he had been strikingly successful, and prosperity had indeed become an acceptable substitute for the majority of Frenchmen. Over the short duration of the Second Empire, industrial production doubled and within only ten years foreign trade did the same. Quantities of gold cascaded into Paris from new mines in California and South Africa. The Bourse re-established itself as the biggest money market on the continent. Giant banking concerns like the Crédit Lyonnais and the Crédit Foncier were founded, the latter especially designed to stimulate Louis Napoleon's massive new building programme. In Paris there sprang up huge stores like M. Boucicaut's Maison du Bon Marché on the Left Bank. To women like Denise, Emile Zola's provincial heroine in *Au bonheur des dames*, these new emporia were indeed modern wonders of the world: 'Here, exposed to the street, right on the pavement, was a veritable landslide of cheap goods; the entrance was a temptation, with bargains that enticed passing customers.'

The national railway network increased from nothing in 1840 to 18,000 kilometres by 1870, so that all of a sudden the Riviera – formerly the haunt of only a few eccentric English at Cannes – became a Parisian resort. Paris was also now the country's largest inland port. Telegraph lines radiated out all over the country, and shipbuilding expanded as never before. The *enrichissez-vous* exhortation applied with even more force to the Second Empire. Men like M. Potin the grocer became millionaires overnight; and, as Alphonse Daudet's unhappy Nabab discovered, scandals and vicious intrigues could reduce them to nothing again just as quickly. Speculation raged, the contagion spreading to the summit of the establishment, with even the Emperor's most esteemed adviser, the Duc de Morny, heavily tainted.

Yet out of this frenzy a wealthy new bourgeoisie had arisen, installing itself solidly and comfortably in the châteaux from which its forebears had driven the aristocrats. As ostentatious as any European aristocracy and determined not to be driven out in its turn, the bourgeoisie was the chief political mainstay of the regime that was responsible for its good fortune – though it had little favourable to say of its benefactor. Never before had France as a whole been more prosperous, and in a very short time she had established herself as one of the world's leading industrial powers. Her population at the census of 1866 had grown to 37.5 million, but the most remarkable feature was the immense growth of the big cities, especially Paris, as a result of this industrialization. In the twenty years between 1831 and 1851 Paris alone grew in population from 786,000 to 1,053,000.

HAUSSMANN

'I want to be a second Augustus,' declared Louis Napoleon even before coming to power, 'because Augustus made Rome a city of marble.' One of the first steps he took after the coup of 1851 was to issue orders that all future work connected with the transformation of Paris would be sanctioned by simple decree. From then on he pursued the city's reconstruction with almost maniacal fervour. This was certainly the Second Empire's greatest surface achievement (in fact its one truly ineffaceable landmark). As an urban developer Louis Napoleon, for better or worse, ranks in Parisian history with Henri IV. In terms of scale alone he in his two decades of rule left far more of permanence behind him than his uncle, despite the immense powers wielded by Napoleon I. To a large extent it was Napoleon III who completed the unfinished grandiose designs of his uncle.

Between Emperor and master architect, there was an instant and almost total accord and identity of purpose. Georges-Eugène (later Baron) Haussmann had no training in architecture, but – a Protestant Alsatian with more than a streak of the German in his genes – he was really a highly efficient, ruthless and somewhat arrogant administrator, with a touch of financial wizardry. He was to describe himself, with painful accuracy, as having been chosen first and foremost 'as a demolition artist'. Aged forty when Louis Napoleon discovered him (he was then Prefect of the Var in the sleepy south), Haussmann was brought to Paris and installed as Prefect of the Seine. As such he found himself in a position of almost limitless power. With no mayor, as of yore the city council was appointed by the Prefect and its authority reduced to that of a municipal commission; while, as senior executive of the central government, the Prefect ruled over not only Paris but also all of her surrounding suburbs. In this role Haussmann was reinforced by Louis Napoleon's dictatorial decrees, which enabled him to expropriate at will properties and whole streets that were intended for development.

Financing, on a massive scale, was effected by a mix of private investment and huge public loans yielding at least 5 per cent. With both the
Bourse and industry supporting Louis Napoleon's coup, there was little
difficulty here.

During the first stage of the programme – the extension of Napoleon
I's Rue de Rivoli – expropriation so pushed up the value of property
bordering the development that Paris was able to finance part of her
costs virtually for nothing. Within two weeks of the December 1851 coup,
the city received a credit of over two million francs to clear, finally, the
slums between the Louvre and the Tuileries – one of the many undertakings which Napoleon I had failed to complete. Two days later a
further decree earmarked twenty-six million francs for the completion,
and extension, of the Louvre; in March 1852, a decree ordered the
construction of the Palais de l'Industrie on an empty space between
the Champs-Elysées and Marie de Medici's Cours de la Reine. In July,
the state conveyed to Paris what is now the Bois de Boulogne, lying well
outside the city limits – with the condition that she spent two million
francs developing it as a park, this being one of Louis Napoleon's hobby-
horses. Two weeks later came another decree laying down the Rue de
Rennes on the Left Bank.

Such was the breakneck speed of Louis Napoleon's and Haussmann's
programme. Once again Paris became one immense building site, of
mud, dust and rubble. The Hôtel de Ville was besieged – not by
insurgents this time, but by battalion-sized teams of masons and carpenters. The question remains, still hotly debated: was 'Haussmannization'
a net benefit for Paris, or the reverse? The financial cost was astronom-
ical. There were several priorities: functional – to clear the congestion of
old Paris; economic – to relieve the heavy pressure of rents; aesthetic –
to create a city beautiful in her grandeur and architectural unity; and
strategic – to lance the festering abscesses of the old city that had been,
from time immemorial, the lairs of assassins and rogues, such as the
Buttes-Chaumont, and of riot and revolution in the east of Paris. Largely
secondary were hygiene and social welfare – the amelioration of life for
the poor.

Like his illustrious and insatiably restless uncle, Louis Napoleon
was an unswervingly hands-on despot. And his technical know-how was
often superior. He was passionate, and knowledgeable, about the use of
industrial-age wrought iron and glass. 'I just want huge umbrellas,
nothing more!' he demanded of Victor Baltard when it came to reconstructing Les Halles. The result was seen not only in the new food

market, until its removal out to Rungis a century later, but also in Henri Labrouste's wondrously light and airy reading room in the (old) Bibliothèque Nationale with its delicate iron pillars, in the Rhinelander Jacques Hittorf's cathedral-like Gare du Nord and in the handsome remnants of Louis Napoleon's Marché du Temple. In marked contrast to Prince Albert in London, who so favoured the neo-gothic, Louis Napoleon disliked the gothic style; consequently it was little used in public buildings of the period. Windows in the new Hôtel Dieu would be pastiches of Henri IV rather than Abbé Suger. Perhaps fortunately for Paris – given the horrors, such as the Centre Pompidou, perpetrated on it by modern architects in the latter part of the twentieth century – both he and Haussmann believed in classical, traditional forms, restrainedly adapted to the new era.

Pressure to do something about the congestion of the streets of central Paris, already becoming an impossible problem back in the days of Philippe Auguste, had become as intense as it is in any modern city. In 1850, the Boulevard des Capucines carried 9,000 horses daily; by 1868, the figure had risen to 23,000. So, in the uncompromising language of Haussmann himself:

> We ripped open the belly of old Paris, the neighbourhood of revolt and barricades, and cut a large opening through the almost impenetrable maze of alleys, piece by piece, and put in cross-streets whose continuations terminated the work. Completion of the Rue de Turbigo finally helped eliminate the Rue Transnonain [scene of the unforgotten massacre of 1832] from the map of Paris.

In the centre of the city 20,000 houses were demolished and 40,000 new ones were built at an enormous cost (inflated by the arts of profiteers). At a stroke of the Baron's pen whole medieval *quartiers* that had resisted Henri IV, Louis XIV and XV, the Revolution and even Napoleon I were now destroyed. Great boulevards cut through the evil-smelling, chaotic alleys of old Paris, long and wide and straight as a die. The longest, Rue La Fayette, ran from the Chaussée d'Antin to La Villette for five kilometres without a single kink, and remains one of the city's main arteries unaltered (except for being *sens unique*) today. Other new creations, like the Boulevard de Sébastopol, the Avenue de Malakoff and the Pont de l'Alma (with its Herculean stone Zouaves that henceforth were to measure the level of the Seine in flood), drew their names from the Second Empire's (spurious) victories in the Crimea. With a minimum carriageway of twenty metres, the new streets were also substantially wider, while average building heights were also raised one storey.

The most radical impact of Haussmann was felt in the ancient, medieval heart of Paris, in the Île de la Cité. Here between 1841 and 1864 Eugène Viollet-le-Duc had been at work restoring and re-creating with considerable licence Notre-Dame, so ravaged by the Revolution – sometimes to good effect, sometimes not. Viollet-le-Duc capped his contribution to the great cathedral with a statue of himself up among the angels lining the roof, the only one with its eyes directed to heaven. Around Notre-Dame Haussmann now conducted a massacre as if an atomic bomb had exploded. Before him there had been clusters of 'mud-coloured houses, broken by a few worm-eaten window frames, which almost touched at the eaves, so narrow were the streets', wrote Eugène Sue in his *Mystères de Paris*. 'Black, filthy alleys led to steps even blacker and more filthy and so steep that one could only climb them with the help of a rope attached to the damp wall by iron brackets.'

It was all 'fearfully inconvenient and squalid' – and dangerous as well. In this area there lived, as late as 1856, some 14,000 people – many of them, according to Sue, 'released convicts, thieves, murderers'. As a young student Haussmann had frequently walked through these squalid streets, and knew them and their even more squalid denizens well. But there must also have been some medieval gems among the houses. All were now swept away. Instead, the Cité became a huge administrative centre, inhabited by law courts, lawyers and police. Few private houses survived there. Three major roads now traversed it, linked directly to the bridges. In front of Notre-Dame Haussmann created a vast open *parvis*, which opened up the prospect of the cathedral's magnificent façade and portico, but was open to fierce criticism on account of its excessive scale, and because it largely fulfilled the function of a police parade ground. Meanwhile, at the other end of the island, part of Henri IV's beautiful Place Dauphine was removed to be replaced with a pointlessly monumental staircase to the western aspect of the Palais de Justice.

On the Left Bank, in driving through the new Boulevard Saint-Germain Haussmann destroyed some of the magnificent *hôtels* that stood in his way – notably the birthplace (where number 188 Boulevard Saint-Germain now stands) of Louis XIV's Duc de Saint-Simon, whose family were among the earliest settlers in the *faubourg*. Further east, Haussmann's new road network encircled and sealed off the unhealthy and lawless slum that had grown up around the Mont Sainte-Geneviève.

Across the river, similarly ruthless treatment – but perhaps to better historic effect – was meted out to the clutter of houses between the Louvre and Tuileries, an area vividly described by Balzac, as of 1838, in *La Cousine Bette* as being:

> wrapped in the eternal shadow projected by the high galleries of the Louvre, blackened on this side by the northern wind ... One wonders who can live here, what must happen at night, when this alley turns into a haven for cutthroats, and when the vices of Paris, wrapped in the mantle of night, are given free rein.

At a cost of two million francs Louis Napoleon now managed to achieve that which not only his illustrious uncle, but also the long line of rulers from Philippe Auguste onwards, had failed to do: complete the Louvre. Continuing strictly in the style of his predecessor, he added the long galleries down the Rue de Rivoli and finished those Louis XIV had initiated along the Seine. The Louvre now became a massive entity, its outstretched arms linked at the western end by the Tuileries Palace, to create the greatest palace in the world, larger even than Philip II's sombre pile of the Escorial. Unforeseen by Louis Napoleon, it was also to be the apogee of the Louvre, given that a year after his fall the Tuileries Palace would be eradicated by Communard incendiaries.

Westwards from the Louvre, Paris with unprecedented speed began to reach out far beyond the Champs-Elysées. Likened by Flaubert to 'a river carrying on its current the bobbing manes of horses and the clothes and heads of men and women', the great avenue, lit by gas, for the first time became a respectable place in the hours of darkness. In Paris as a whole 32,000 gas lamps had replaced 15,000 oil lanterns by the time Haussmann departed. Whereas at the coming of the Second Empire, the Place de la Concorde was still the boundary of urban Paris, beyond it the voracious metropolis extended to embrace within it country villages like Chaillot and Auteuil (still regarded as 'just about the end of the world') in the south and the Place de Wagram in the north. In January 1860 the work began on demolishing the old Farmers General wall that encircled the city, and seven new arrondissements in and beyond the *faubourgs* were incorporated. In the half-century between 1806 and 1856, the population of the suburbs increased from 13,000 to 351,000 so that with one leap metropolitan Paris, now with a population approaching two million, spread out as far as the circle of protective forts that had been constructed by Thiers under Louis-Philippe.

Away from the centre, however, beyond the Arc de Triomphe, there still existed rural scenes; there were fields where the Trocadéro now stands, and windmills at Montmartre, while Passy had the air of an isolated village. The newly acquired space also allowed Louis Napoleon to indulge in the construction of parks for the people. If this was a ramification of 'bread and circuses', it was a totally beneficial one. In his beloved Bois de Boulogne, greatly influenced by his knowledge of Hyde Park, the Emperor himself did much of the landscaping, cutting new drives and creating artificial cascades. Leading to it was the most resplendent and most expensive of all the new thoroughfares, the Avenue de l'Impératrice, named after his Eugénie, not Josephine (it is now the Avenue Foch). At the other end of Paris, in the Buttes-Chaumont, another superb example of artistic landscape gardening was achieved. Still further out, the Bois de Vincennes – originally enclosed in 1183 by Philippe Auguste to house the animals presented to him by a conciliatory King of England – was also now laid out by Louis Napoleon as a spacious pleasure park. In 1848 Paris had only 19 hectares of parks; by 1870 the total was 1,800.

STYLE AND STRATEGY

For all Haussmann's massive public works, the salient feature of his new Paris was the apartment building. His standardized block, running for hundreds of unbroken metres down the new boulevards, was both an extrapolation of Napoleon I's Rue de Rivoli and a product of the new industrial age. An extraordinary degree of architectural unity was achieved by the continuous run of symmetrical wrought-iron balconies on the *piano nobile*, linking one building to another, as did a common cornice line which was there to reinforce the horizontal effect of a street's perspective. Pilasters linked the *piano nobile* with the floors above, while carved decoration of the external white limestone was otherwise minimal. The overall intent was that the visual impact should be that of the street rather than of the individual building. The austere appearance of the façade was softened by the trees lining the new, wider streets. Interior decor, however, would often be much more ornate. At street level, there would be a grand *porte-cochère* entrance through which carriages seldom passed.

In terms of planning regulations, little had been changed since those of 1783–4, and Haussmann annulled them with decrees of 1852 and 1859. By these, with health as well as aesthetic standards in mind, a lighting-angle formula of 45 degrees was established, so that on the new twenty-metre-wide streets a maximum height of twenty metres was now permitted, allowing insertion of another storey to provide six or seven floors. At the same time, because of rocketing ground values, deep sites were avoided – which meant that, unlike in Victorian London, Haussmann's apartments had few gardens, the streets few leafy squares.

The whole emphasis of a street of Haussmann apartment blocks, which remains the basic image still of Paris today, was one of bourgeois comfort. In his writings Proust describes what it was like to grow up as a child in 9 Boulevard Malesherbes, where the family of his successful doctor father enjoyed the luxuries of gas lighting, central heating from a coal furnace, running water, lavatories and a large bathroom, and a marble staircase with wrought-iron banisters. There were seven rooms (including Dr Proust's consulting rooms); and a fifteen-metre-long corridor separated the parents from the children's quarters, reeking of the eucalyptus fumigations for poor Marcel's asthma. On a middle-class physician's salary, the Prousts employed a live-in butler, chambermaid and cook. But Marcel deemed the family salon to be of 'an ugliness completely medical'.

With so much borrowed from the past, was there (leaving aside the new apartment blocks) any such thing as a Second Empire style? In church architecture, certainly, there was little to boast about: the Trinité was built in pseudo-Renaissance style; Saint-Augustin, crammed ingeniously into a narrow triangular space, was a Romano-Byzantine pastiche constructed around one of Baltard's iron frameworks. Perhaps the age is best epitomized by Charles Garnier's new Opéra, which in its florid magnificence symbolized the wealth of the day, its affection for the new rococo, with just a touch of vulgarity. However, because of its elaborateness, the most exotic decoration ever seen in Paris, it was not on stream for the Great Exposition of 1867, and in fact would only be opened eight years later, after the Empire had already fallen (when Garnier himself would even be made to pay for his seat).

For Haussmann aesthetics had been only one of several considerations. There was one further aim all-important to the precariously installed Emperor. In 1855 Queen Victoria came to Paris on an official visit, the first by an English monarch since Henry VI had been crowned at Notre-Dame in 1422. Cementing a brief period of *entente cordiale* that followed the joint Anglo-French effort in the Crimean War, Louis Napoleon had pushed the boat out and had laid down a special branch railway between the Gares du Nord and de l'Est, so as to make a better impression of the entry into Paris; he had flirted agreeably with the Widow of Windsor and had made her, she recorded, 'feel safe with him'. Exactly forty years after Waterloo, diplomacy persuaded her to genuflect over Napoleon's tomb, while the organ of the Invalides played God Save the Queen.

The Queen's sharp eye, however, had quickly noticed that her host had had the streets of Paris covered with macadam, 'to prevent the people from taking up the pavement as hitherto'. Later on, it would have been evident to any competent military observer what useful fields of fire Haussmann's long, straight streets provided, what opportunities to turn the flank of a barricade there were for troops debouching from their oblique intersections, and how easy the wide boulevards made it to convey riot-breaking squads from one end of Paris to another. In particular, evoking a century of Parisian insurrections, in the troublesome east end there was now the broad and straight Boulevard Voltaire to allow for speedy passage of troops between what is now the Place de la République and the Place de la Nation. At last, Haussmann felt assured, they had succeeded 'in cutting through the habitual storm-centres'. In the words of one French historian, Paris now was 'as strategically ordered as any battlefield'. In fact, however – and with what force will be seen later in the hideously destructive Communard revolution of 1871 – he had to a large extent achieved the defeat of his own purpose.

Henri de Rochefort, aristocrat turned revolutionary and most bitter opponent of Louis Napoleon's Second Empire, growled, 'Paris has been called France's head, but is now nothing but its legs.' By this he meant the legs of the underprivileged *classes laborieuses*. One of the major tragedies of Louis Napoleon's reign was that, however genuine he was in his desire to do something for the poor of Paris, the works of Haussmann were to have quite the opposite effect. Because of the escalation of rents in the newly developed *quartiers* – or because affordable accommodation had simply disappeared, as in the old Cité – the *classes laborieuses* were driven, eastwards and outwards, from the charmed city of the boulevards to crowded ghettos that were every bit as evil as those demolished in the centre. In a deeply suffering population, one inhabitant in every sixteen was living off public charity. One of these new slum shanty-towns would ironically become known as the 'Cité Dorée'. Meanwhile the bourgeoisie now represented a greater percentage of the inner-city population than ever before.

Thus Haussmannization had led to a kind of apartheid provoking sullen resentment. Far from piercing the traditional trouble-centres of Paris, Haussmann had just created new and much more threatening ones, in solidly proletarian and Red arrondissements such as Belleville and Ménilmontant, where in the latter days of the Empire no policeman would dare appear alone and where – as the Commune was to show – concentration of manpower had made the work of organizing a revolt easier than it had ever been. The consequences for Paris would be terrible, insofar as the bulk of the Communards who, in 1871, would destroy much of what the Prefect had not swept away in the city centre came from this expelled proletariat. Still, as in bygone ages, the areas which they now inhabited lacked proper sewerage, and the terrible stench of deprivation remained – as did the almost endemic diseases of typhoid (which, in 1865, accounted for 1,161 deaths) and tuberculosis, infant mortality and the curse of alcoholism. *L'eau à l'étage* was a luxury that only the affluent like the *famille* Proust could afford.

Controversy continues to surround the merits of Haussmann's new Paris. At the time it had its vigorous critics. The conservative Goncourt brothers said it made them think of 'some American Babylon of the future'; Gautier agreed: 'This is Philadelphia; it is Paris no longer!' (though he had never seen Philadelphia). George Sand, however, construed it a blessing to be able to walk without 'being forced every moment to consult the policeman on the street corner or the affable grocer'. Emile Zola, in his novel *Une Page d'amour*, tried hard to depict the great city as 'an enormous storm-tossed ocean, or a distant and alien Babylon', but in the end affection triumphed over distaste: 'I love the horizons of this big city with all my heart ... depending on whether a ray of sunshine brightens Paris, or a dull sky lets it dream, it resembles a joyful and melancholy poem. This is art, all around us. A living art, an art still unknown.'

MORAL TONE

Just as in England the Victorian social and moral code became forever attached to the name of the sovereign, so from the start Second Empire society had never shown itself more loyal than in its keenness to tread the paths laid down by its pleasure-loving Emperor. In the earliest days of the Second Empire, the *haut monde* were determined to revive the paradise of Louis XV. In the Forest of Fontainebleau courtesans went hunting with their lovers, dressed in the plumed hats and lace of that period. The *gratin* (the upper crust) too delightedly sought to escape from the bourgeois virtues of Louis-Philippe's regime.

If the Second Empire had an emblem, a cultural tone-setter, it had to be Jacques Offenbach, the German Jew from the Rhineland, who wrote no fewer than ninety infectiously gay and melodious operettas. Though his *La Belle Hélène* was intended as a satire on contemporary life, Second Empire critics exhibited the essential hypocrisy of the times by voicing their shock at the immorality of the ancients. Offenbach lingered on, almost forgotten, for nine years after the party that was the Second Empire came to its abrupt end. Symbolically, his *Tales of Hoffmann* (first performed just three months after his death), the *chef d'oeuvre* which he had spent years writing, was far more sombre in spirit than his previous works, reflecting the sense of morning-after that succeeded 1870–1.

In Paris nothing characterized the mood of the epoch more than those masked balls so cherished by Louis Napoleon, at which he delighted to appear as a Venetian noble of the seventeenth century. The masks allowed their wearers to enter a world of fantasy, the dazzling extravagance of the occasions themselves distracting the eye from disagreeable reality. Each ball was more sumptuous than the last, and throughout the reign those held at the Tuileries – far more fun than the entertainments offered by Napoleon I – took place with such regularity that they almost resembled a never-ending carnival.

As the fashions dictated, the women at these balls emphasized their bosoms to the limits of decency (and sometimes beyond): they were splendid, disturbing and voracious creatures. There was the nineteen-year-old Comtesse de Castiglione, Louis Napoleon's most delectable and dangerous mistress, a source of great trouble for his foreign policy. She once appeared at the Tuileries seductively dressed as a Queen of Hearts, which prompted from the Empress the lethal observation that 'her heart is a little low'. What went on in the antechambers to these entertainments the rest of Paris could easily guess, without needing to hear about Madame X, who had once returned to the ballroom with the Duc de Morny's Légion d'Honneur imprinted upon her cheek. Indeed the scene more often evoked Rubens than Watteau.

An unedifying hypocrisy ran through the Second Empire. Flaubert was prosecuted in 1857 for offending public morals with *Madame Bovary*, Manet was venomously attacked in the press for the 'immorality' of his *Olympia* and the *Déjeuner sur l'herbe*; and women smoking in the Tuileries Gardens were as liable to arrest as were young men bathing without a top at Trouville. Yet the moral tone of the Second Empire was far from elevated. Zola's *Nana* was its emblem, and its motto the rhetorical question from Offenbach's *La Belle Hélène*:

> Dis-moi, Vénus, quel plaisir trouves-tu
> À faire ainsi cascader la vertu?*

From top to bottom Paris was obsessed with love in all its varieties. In 1858 the Goncourts confided to their journal, with a slightly bemused air, 'Everybody talks about it all the time. It is something which seems to be extremely important and extremely absorbing.' Even in their own literary circle, where some of the foremost intellects of the day congregated, few evenings went by without someone like Sainte-Beuve discoursing on sex in an almost schoolboy vein.

The most notable of the *grandes horizontales*, 'La Païva', once asked Ponsard the playwright to write some lines in celebration of her grand new staircase (in which is now the Travellers' Club on the Champs-Elysées), and he came up with an adaptation from *Phèdre*: 'Ainsi que la vertu, le vice a ses degrés' (Vice, like virtue, has its steps both up and down). This was entirely true of the Second Empire, where everything was precisely ordered. Everyone had their place, their own step on the staircase. A married woman, forced to leave home when some indiscretion became known, could set herself up at one of several levels within the *demi-monde* without actually descending to prostitution. At the top of the social staircase, vast sums could change hands. Even Egyptian beys could be reduced to ruin in weeks. Louis Napoleon

---

* Tell me, Venus, what pleasure do you find
   In robbing me thus of my virtue?

himself reportedly bestowed on the Comtesse de Castiglione a pearl necklace worth 422,000 francs, and added 50,000 francs a month pin-money; while Lord Hertford, supposedly the most tight-fisted man in Paris, gave her a million for the joys of one night in which she promised to abandon herself to every known *volupté* (afterwards, it was said, she was confined to bed for three days). La Païva, who adopted the admirably punning motto of 'Qui paye y va' (Who pays, gets there), herself spent half a million francs a year on her table.

The *grandes horizontales* found their clients among the idle rich like the hero of Feuillet's *Monsieur de Camors* who gave this account of his day: 'I generally rise in the morning ... I go to the Bois, then to the club, and then to the Bois, and afterwards I return to the club ... In the evening if there's a first night anywhere I fly to it.' Every aspect of life in the Second Empire seemed devised for the greater convenience of these men. There was even a newspaper, the *Naïade*, printed on rubber so that dandies could read it while soaking in the bath. Later, as the fortunes of these idlers were dissipated in the same extravagant ways, they became known as *petits crevés*, for whose degenerate tastes there was nothing more amusing than a turkey dancing on a whitehot metal plate. They now took their pleasures, as did those lower down the social scale, among the semi-amateurs: the *comédiennes* – whom, it was said, the Bois de Boulogne 'devoured in quantity' – the *lorettes* (named after their territory around Notre-Dame de Lorette), the *grisettes* and the *cocodettes*. All these girls were available in large numbers at Mabille's, the celebrated dance-hall in today's chic Avenue Montaigne. Or, up in the 9th arrondissement, there was the new Folies Bergère, opened in 1858 – appropriately enough, next to a bedding shop called The Springy Mattress. Or there was the circus, which on opening night reminded the Goncourts of 'a stock exchange dealing in women's nights'.

For the Bohemians there were the *grenouillères* – free-spirited young women who flitted from garret to garret, such as the English art student who announced her attachment to 'free love and Courbet'. Still lower down the scale, there were the desperate children such as the little girl described by the Goncourts who had offered her fourteen-year-old sister, while 'her job was to breathe on the windows of the carriage so that the police could not see inside'. Finally, below stairs, for the working man of Paris there were innumerable cabarets where his handful of sous could buy him a low woman, or – more likely – render him blind drunk on raw spirit.

This depiction of rampant hedonism under the Second Empire

had its unsavoury underside. Syphilis was rife, and still more or less incurable. Many of the great men of the age were to die of it, among them de Maupassant, Jules Goncourt, Dumas *fils*, Baudelaire and Manet. Renoir once lamented that he could not be a true genius because he alone among his friends had not caught syphilis. This dreadful disease was symptomatic of the whole Second Empire: on the surface, all brightness and high spirits; beneath, darkness, decay and ultimately death.

With that facility the French sometimes have for attributing to an individual the failings of the nation at large, blame for the deficiencies and venality of the Second Empire was before very long laid upon the man at the top. In terms of morality, the Second Empire no doubt had a case. 'The example', as the Goncourts heard a guest declare at the salon of Princesse Mathilde (a cousin of the Emperor), 'comes from high up.' Almost the only characteristic Louis Napoleon shared with his exalted uncle was the notable sexual puissance of the Bonapartes. The interminable sequence of mistresses and paramours, which the chaste Eugénie found so hard to take, lasted as long as his health. The gossipy Princesse Mathilde claimed derisively, 'He chases the first petticoat he sees!'

Louis Napoleon most deserved the title of 'the Well-Meaning' for his attempts to improve the miserable lot of the Parisian working man. Here was perhaps the unhappiest paradox of his reign. It was the sector for which he strove hardest, yet when the crunch came the working class provided his most violent enemies. His far-reaching social reforms included establishing institutions of maternal welfare, societies of mutual assistance, workers' cities and homes for injured workers; he proposed shorter working hours and health legislation; and he got rid of the degrading prison hulks and granted the right to strike. The Emperor's personal contribution to charitable works was substantial, and in his efforts to ingratiate himself with the workers he even decreed that a new boulevard over the covered-in Saint-Martin canal should be named after a worker called Richard Lenoir. Many of Louis Napoleon's more progressive ideas, however, were stymied by the selfishness of the new bourgeoisie and the conservatism of the provinces (as so often in past and future Paris), circumstances which did not escape the attention of the *classes laborieuses* in the capital.

As much as anyone else Louis Napoleon was aware of the problems and the dangers. As he told the English politician Richard Cobden ominously, 'It is very difficult in France to make reforms; we make revolutions in France, not reforms.' Both economic and political problems had sharpened the workers' discontent. They alone, it seemed, had been excluded from the general prosperity. In Paris the average daily wage rose only 30 per cent during the Second Empire, while the cost of living rose 45 per cent and more. An unintended consequence of Haussmann's projects was that the rents of Parisian workers doubled over these years, so that by 1870 they swallowed one-third of the wage packet. Food could absorb another 60 per cent. Bourgeois chroniclers claimed that these workers did not like meat, but the reality is that it was too expensive for them. That is why in 1866 butchers started to sell cheap horsemeat, thus introducing a taste which four years later would be forced upon many more Parisians.

What life was actually like for a great many Parisians was powerfully evoked by the Goncourts. Jules' former mistress, a midwife called Maria, had gone to deliver a child at the upper end of the new Boulevard Magenta. There she found:

> a room where the planks that form the walls are coming apart and the floor is full of holes, through which rats are constantly appearing, rats which also come in whenever the door is opened, impudent poor men's rats which climb on to the table, carrying away whole hunks of bread, and worry the feet of the sleeping occupants ... The man, a costermonger, who has known better days, dead-drunk during his wife's labour. The woman, as drunk as her husband, lying on a straw mattress ... And during the delivery in this shanty, the wretched shanty of civilization, an organ-grinder's monkey, imitating and parodying the cries and angry oaths of the shrew in the throes of childbirth, piddling through a crack in the roof on to the snoring husband's back ...

It was not just the workers' physical conditions that made relations between the classes increasingly fraught. After all, in the industrial nineteenth century most workers still expected lives of poverty and misery. There were other sources of discontent under the Second Empire, philosophical and political, that at the time were harder to analyse. Workers began to fear that not only was employees' relative prosperity declining, but so was their ability to influence the development of the new industrial system, which was turning out increasingly to their disadvantage. Behind Parisian frustrations lay a particular, dangerous legacy. As already noted, after each of the three major uprisings within the past century – the Great Revolution of 1789, the July Days of 1830 and the February and June uprisings of 1848, the *classes laborieuses* of Paris had seen in retrospect that they had been swindled. It was their own blood that had flowed at the barricades, but each time it was the bourgeoisie who stole the advantage. So, seething out of sight in the ghettos created by Haussmann was an alarming build-up of hatred and resentment against the bourgeois men of property. Only three ingredients were required to spark off a new and more terrible explosion: weapons, organization and a diminution of the vigilant police state.

By 1870–1, all three would be in place, with the most appalling consequences for Paris.

APOGEE

Meanwhile, as Louis Napoleon's popularity ebbed away, discontent grew, and things were progressively going wrong abroad. In general the shadows were pressing in upon the Second Empire; so in 1867 Louis Napoleon threw its last and greatest party, what was to prove the grand finale of his 'bread and circuses' regime. To the astonishment of most of Paris, unlike its predecessor in 1855, which Queen Victoria had visited and which had opened a fortnight late while exhibits were still being uncrated, the Great Exposition of 1867 began precisely on time.

The heart of the exhibition, on the Champ-de-Mars, not far from where the Eiffel Tower stands today, was an enormous oval building of glass 482 metres long, set in a filigree of ironwork similar to the Crystal Palace in London. Inside this pavilion exhibits had been set out by all the leading countries of the new industrial era. 'There art elbowed industry,' wrote Théophile Gautier, 'white statues stood next to black machines, paintings hung side by side with rich fabrics from the Orient.' The pavilion was divided into seven regions, each representing a branch of human endeavour, where the exhibiting nations displayed their most recent achievements. It was the year that Lister introduced antisepsis, and Nobel invented dynamite. It was also the year that a German Jewish professor exiled in London published a fateful book entitled *Das Kapital.*

Above this extravaganza floated an unrecognized augury, a tethered balloon in which Nadar, the celebrated photographer, took visitors for flights over the exhibition grounds; while up and down the Seine new excursion boats with room for 150 passengers made their first journeys. They were called *bateaux-mouches*. There was something for everybody. Unsophisticated provincials crowded in to stare at the city women dressed in the new, svelte line with which the English couturier Worth had finally – that same year – ousted the crinoline with all its ample billows. From all over Paris the many ranks of the *demi-monde* also converged, the *cocodès* and *cocodettes, lorettes, grandes horizontales* and *petits crevés* parading past glowering men in black who peddled Bibles.

As the weeks passed, illustrious guests and visitors descended on Paris from all over the world. Among the guests came the Prince of Wales, delighting in the gay city he so relished. But the Tsar of Russia was the real guest of honour, because Louis Napoleon desired the security of an alliance with him against the perceptibly growing threat from Prussia – though it was King Wilhelm of Prussia himself and his giant Chancellor, Count Otto von Bismarck, whom everyone wanted to see. The old King set the edgy French at ease, and indeed seemed utterly relaxed himself. As someone was later to remark, he explored Paris as if intending to come back there one day. Even the fearsome Bismarck exuded bonhomie.

On 12 April the Emperor attended the première of Offenbach's *La Grande Duchesse de Gérolstein*, with Hortense Schneider in the title role. The opera depicted an amorous Grand Duchess of a joke German principality launching an unnecessary war because its Chancellor, Baron Puck, required a diversion from his domestic difficulties. The principality's armed forces were led by a joke German general called Boum. The joke was perhaps too obvious. When the Tsar came to see it, he and his party were said to have roared with unroyal laughter. Members of the French court were more interested in Bismarck's reaction, half fearing that they had gone too far. But the Iron Chancellor seemed to be enjoying himself more than anybody. Perhaps, one feels, his enjoyment really lay in some very secret joke of his own.

Parisians did not want this *féerique* dream of a Thousand and One Nights ever to end. The climax of it all came with a great military review at Longchamp of 31,000 troops. The Emperor arrived with an escort of Spahis on handsome black chargers, with the Tsar on his right and King Wilhelm on his left. The spectacular review ended with a massed cavalry charge of 10,000 cuirassiers who halted in perfect unison within five metres of the royal guests and saluted them with drawn sabres. Gravely the Tsar and the King of Prussia saluted their host, and bowed to the Empress Eugénie.

Louis Napoleon was especially keen to impress Tsar Alexander II. It was after all the uncle of this new Emperor of the French who had burned the Moscow of the Tsar's uncle, and memories of the Crimea were still raw. As they drove together from Longchamp, Alexander appeared to be in excellent humour. Then it all went terribly wrong. A young Polish patriot named Berezowski rushed from the crowd and fired a pistol at the Tsar. He missed, but the white gloves of the Tsarevich were spotted with blood from a wounded horse. The Tsar, shaken by this uncomfortable preview of the awful death that awaited him, was suddenly unfriendly. At a stroke Louis Napoleon's hopes for an accord with Russia seemed dashed.

But it was not until November that workers began the wearying labour of dismantling the Great Exposition, and the Seine was dark with barges queuing to carry away the detritus, the smashed papiermâché remains of the kiosks and pavilions. Before long the Champ-de-Mars was an empty field once more. A mood of after-the-ball-is-over settled on the city. To some it seemed that the exhibition had been the last hurrah of an imperial regime heading inexorably for destruction. There was no doubt that it had been a triumph: an astonishing fifteen million people had been to see it, three times the total its predecessor had attracted in 1855. But what had it done for the unemployed, for the creation of new prosperity or for France's international relations? Had the visiting foreigners merely acquired insight into French weaknesses and resentment of French triumphs? Comte Fleury's assessment – 'In any case, we had a devilish good time' – could be taken to apply as much to the Second Empire as to the exhibition alone. But the remark also sounds an elegiac note more easily detected in what Gautier said as he reflected on the Champ-de-Mars in grimmer circumstances three years later, when he felt that whole centuries had passed since 1867: 'C'était trop beau!'

As memories of the Great Exposition faded and the Empire hastened onward to oblivion, in the three years of life remaining to it the sounds of revelry were still heard. The masked balls carried on; in 1869 the last would be held, with Empress Eugénie splendidly, but ominously, attired as Marie Antoinette. Yet the worm was in the apple. The historian, with his potent instrument of hindsight, might wish, 'If only': if only Louis Napoleon had concentrated his energies on the expansion and embellishment of his capital. Instead, he would be drawn disastrously into foreign adventures, like other French rulers before him. In Italy, in an echo of French *Realpolitik* from Charles VIII down to Napoleon I, his meddling had cost him the support of the Church without winning the friendship of the King or Cavour. Similarly his ill-advised 'policy of nationalities' had led him courageously to back Polish independence, but at the same time – foolishly – it had earned him the hostility of the Tsar. In 1867 the collapse of his rash endeavour to found a new empire in Mexico, together with the humiliating execution of Maximilian Habsburg, cost him the chance of acquiring Austria as an ally, while earning him frowns from America and Britain. Suddenly there was a powerful Prussia, led by a Bismarck bent on trouble, facing an isolated France.

At home, things were no better. Under Louis Napoleon's authoritarian Empire, the government was to stand for cheap bread, great public works, holidays and leisure. The Emperor had genuinely wanted to be a good tyrant; but, alas, there is no such thing as a good tyrant. Under pressure from a dissatisfied public, in 1869 Louis Napoleon was forced to permit elections, and the successes of opposition Liberal candidates heralded the short-lived 'Liberal Empire'. As Tocqueville observes, the most dangerous moment for a dictatorship is when it first releases the brake. So it was to prove for Louis Napoleon. Paris in particular now became a stronghold of the Liberal opponents of the regime, and of protest. Meanwhile in 1869 there were also fateful investigations into Prefect Haussmann's finances. The following January he was sacked, and Paris was left without a strong hand on the wheel. The Emperor himself was a tired and sick man, with a large stone growing in his bladder. In the Tuileries acute nervousness reigned; the writer and friend of the regime Prosper Mérimée described the atmosphere as 'like that aroused by Mozart's music when the Commendatore is about to appear'. It looked as if the government, in time-honoured fashion, would be only too ready to seek the distraction of a foreign adventure. In the summer of 1870, it came.

That June, the newly appointed British Foreign Secretary Lord Granville gazed out with satisfaction on the world scene and claimed – with reason – that he could not discern 'a cloud in the sky'. In all his experience he had never known 'so great a lull in foreign affairs'. In Paris, Emperor Napoleon III's Prime Minister, Emile Ollivier, echoed Granville by declaring that 'at no period has the maintenance of peace seemed better assured'. Then, at the beginning of July 1870, a small cloud passed across the sun. For the previous two years the throne of Spain had been vacant, since the deposing of the unsatisfactory Queen Isabella. One of the possible candidates was a German princeling, Leopold of Hohenzollern-Sigmaringen. The idea of the Hohenzollern Candidacy had originated in Spain, but when Bismarck took it up Paris became alarmed. It was the thought of having German princes on the Pyrenees frontier as well as on the Rhine – though historians could have reminded French statesmen that, by filling the Spanish throne with a Bourbon prince less than two centuries previously, this kind of hegemony was almost exactly what Louis XIV had sought to impose on Europe.

So hostile was the response in France, egged on by inflammatory articles in the Paris press, that the Hohenzollern Candidacy was rapidly withdrawn. A relieved Lord Granville admonished the French government for the fierceness of its reaction, and the British press returned to such themes as Queen Victoria handing out prizes in Windsor Park. But in Paris hotheads were clamouring for a political success, and none was pushing harder than the Empress. Meanwhile, France's heavy-handed Foreign Secretary, the Duc de Gramont, began to goad the Prussians. It was not enough that the Hohenzollern Candidacy had been withdrawn, Prussia had to be put in her place. Accordingly, Gramont sent the French Ambassador in Berlin, Count Vincent Benedetti, to badger the King at Bad Ems, where he was taking the waters. Benedetti was received with the greatest courtesy by King Wilhelm, who had no desire (any more than his fellow German rulers) for war, observing that the unification of Germany would be 'the task of my grandson', not his.

This was not, however, the view of Bismarck, who was not at all prepared to wait two generations, and who judged that a war against France would help him to bond together the existing rather loose structure of the German federation into a unified nation – dominated, of course, by his native Prussia. But the *casus belli* would have to be chosen with the greatest care, so as to cast France in an unfavourable light among the other nations of Europe, and also with Prussia's own German allies. With the French now bent on pressing for diplomatic victories, Bismarck saw his chance. Irked by Benedetti's importuning at Bad Ems, the benign old King refused to give a guarantee that the Hohenzollern Candidacy would not be revived, and declined a request for a further audience. A telegram reporting on his interview was duly sent to Bismarck in Berlin. Without actually doctoring the text, as he has often been accused of doing, Bismarck sharpened the emphasis of the despatch before passing it to the Berlin press – and the world.

Even with Bismarck's editing, the famous Ems Telegram hardly seemed to constitute a *casus belli*. But the Chancellor had his ear well tuned to the prevailing tone in Paris. Frenzied crowds surged through the streets shouting 'À Berlin!' Simultaneously Zola's tragic courtesan

Nana was depicted as dying of her terrible disease, which to Zola personified the whole of Louis Napoleon's world: 'Venus was decomposing ... the room was empty. An enormous wave of desperation rose from the boulevard and made the curtain billow: "To Berlin! To Berlin! To Berlin!"' In one of the rashest claims in all military history, the French commander, Marshal Leboeuf, encouraged the hawks with his foolish declaration that the army was 'ready down to the last gaiter-button'. Now, with the publication of Bismarck's telegram, urged on by his Empress and Gramont, and fired by the ever shriller Paris press, Napoleon III took the plunge.

On 15 July, France declared war – in a state of exhilaration, recalling Napoleon I's resounding successes beyond the Rhine, and expecting a repeat performance in 1870. But, through Bismarck's cunning, she found herself at once branded a frivolous aggressor with neither friend nor ally. As the *Illustrated London News* declared, 'The Liberal Empire goes to war on a mere point of etiquette.' Within eighteen days of mobilization, Bismarck and his German allies were able to field an unheard-of force of 1,183,000 men. The German organization man, scourge of Europe over the next seventy-five years, had arrived. The laughter prompted by General Boum and the *Grand Duchess of Gérolstein* at the Great Exposition now seemed an awful misreading as Herr Krupp's terrifying great cannon, which he had exhibited in Paris just three years previously, moved to centre stage. In sharp contrast, scenes of dismal chaos accompanied French mobilization. 'Have arrived at Belfort,' telegraphed one desperate general. 'Can't find my brigade. Can't find the divisional commander. What shall I do? Don't know where my regiments are.' Over the first six weeks of war in the frontier provinces, disaster followed military disaster in swiftest succession.

On 1 September, a sick and defeated Napoleon III surrendered to King Wilhelm of Prussia at the head of his army in Sedan.

15

L'Année Terrible

It is in Paris that the beating of Europe's heart is felt. Paris is
the city of cities. Paris is the city of men. There has been an
Athens, there has been a Rome, and now there is a Paris ... Is
the nineteenth century to witness this frightful phenomenon?
A nation fallen from polity, to barbarism, abolishing the city
of nations; Germans extinguishing Paris ... Can you give this
spectacle to the world?

Victor Hugo, appeal to the Prussians, 9 September 1870

THE NEW REPUBLIC

On 3 September 1870 a stunned Paris received the news of the Emperor's
capitulation in Sedan with horror. 'What a sight,' recorded Edmond
Goncourt:*

the news of MacMahon's† defeat and the capture of the Emperor
spreading from group to group! Who can describe the consternation
written on every face, the sound of aimless steps pacing the streets
at random, the anxious conversations of shopkeepers and con-
cierges on their doorsteps ...

Then there is the menacing roar of the crowd, in which stupefaction had begun to give place to anger.

---

* Edmond was now writing alone, his beloved brother Jules having died painfully of
syphilis earlier in the summer.
† Duc de Magenta, general commanding the army at Sedan.

Almost immediately there followed a measure of delight – even in some bourgeois *quartiers*. Louis Napoleon and his Second Empire were gone for good. Like her two predecessors in the Tuileries, Empress Eugénie fled to England – from a side-door in the Palace, helped by her dentist. Thereupon the mob invaded the Tuileries Palace where they found pathetic signs of an unplanned departure: a toy sword half drawn on a bed, empty jewel-cases scattered on the floor, and on a table some pieces of bread and a half-devoured egg. As now seemed traditional in French revolutions, the mob quickly began obliterating all trace of the fallen regime. Just as at the outset of the Hundred Days the fleurs-de-lys had been scratched from the Tuileries carpets and replaced with Napoleonic bees, so now all the *N*s and imperial eagles were hacked away from the public buildings, and busts of the humbled Emperor rapturously flung into the Seine. At the main entrance of the Tuileries, late in the afternoon of 4 September, Goncourt saw scribbled in chalk the words 'Property of the People', while a young soldier held out his shako to the crowd and cried, 'For the army's wounded!'

With the sun shining and not a drop of blood shed, all Paris took to the streets to celebrate its most gratifying revolution. George Sand, now aged sixty-six, was jubilant: 'This is the third awakening; and it is beautiful beyond fancy ... Hail to thee, Republic! Thou art in worthy hands, and a great people will march under thy banner after a bloody expiation.' Standing by the Pont de la Concorde, Juliette Lambert observed a young worker in a red fez who had been singing the Marseillaise without a break for three hours while hanging on to one of the candelabra. Everyone seemed united by an irrational optimism, driven by the feeling that what had gone wrong before had all been the fault of the Emperor and his comprehensive mediocrity.

Meanwhile, the last vestiges of imperial society made their way to Brussels where they passed *en route* that most famous of all returning exiles, Victor Hugo, and his *ménage*. As he encountered the beaten remnants of the Sedan army, Hugo wept and remarked to his companions, 'I should have preferred never to return rather than see France so humiliated, to see France reduced to what she was under Louis XVIII!' In Paris, the end of the Empire was officially proclaimed, and a new Republic formed in the Hôtel de Ville – that symbol of Republicanism where the revolutionary municipal government of Paris had been created in 1789. It was assumed on the street that – now the Emperor and his bellicose regime were gone – the victorious Prussians would return home and leave France alone. Paris felt sure that Bismarck would promptly fall in with the bombastic appeal launched by Victor Hugo on 9 September:

> It is in Paris that the beating of Europe's heart is felt. Paris is the city of cities. Paris is the city of men. There has been an Athens, there has been a Rome, and now there is a Paris ... Is the nineteenth century to witness this frightful phenomenon? A nation fallen from polity, to barbarism, abolishing the city of nations; Germans extinguishing Paris ... Can you give this spectacle to the world?

Hugo was wasting his breath. Bismarck was not a man to be deterred by such a 'spectacle' – he had his own agenda. What the Parisians could not see in this hour of extraordinary rejoicing was the solid German phalanxes advancing ever closer, nor could they hear the German press at home shrieking for the destruction of 'the modern Babylon'. A bitter four months' siege now lay ahead, waged on the Parisian side with varying degrees of incompetence until late January 1871. At the Hôtel de Ville, the new government consisted of moderate Republicans – men like Favre, Ferry, Gambetta, Picard, Crémieux and Arago. Thiers declined office, but remained a powerful influence, while the post of president was handed to General Trochu, the lethargic and uninspiring Governor of Paris. Just as they had proved a thorny opposition to the left of Louis Napoleon, so now they found on their own left an explosive combination of revolutionaries. Here were sons and grandsons of those who had fought and died on the barricades of 1830, 1848 and 1851, such as Blanqui and Delescluze (professional revolutionaries who between them had spent many years in imperial jails), and Pyat and Flourens, supported by the embittered thousands who had been pushed into ghettos by Haussmann. Fulminating in the Red 'clubs' and gaining a powerful military presence by their participation in the National Guard militia, while proving a constant threat to the organized government, these revolutionaries were to press it to the end to fight the war *à outrance*. Under this pressure, with some reluctance Trochu and his team decided to continue the war. With an extraordinary degree of traditional arrogant self-assurance, Paris did so virtually without consulting the rest of France; once again she had decided on the country's behalf. It would be almost the last time.

As Paris settled down to resist the siege, a frenzy of activity engulfed the city. Troops that had survived the disasters of the first six weeks of war were encamped (while being reorganized by Generals Vinoy and Ducrot) on the Champ-de-Mars, where that now faraway memory, the

Great Exposition of three years previously, had once stood. Reinforced by territorial *mobiles* from the provinces, they totalled some 170,000. On top of this came the National Guard, expanded with indecent rapidity from 24,000 men at the outbreak of war eventually to number some 350,000; but it was to prove a liability – and a most dangerous one – in the course of the siege. In the centre of Paris, the Tuileries stables and gardens had been transformed into a vast artillery park. The Champ-de-Mars became a seething mass of troops – among whom Edmond Goncourt spotted pedlars selling paper and pencils for the poor devils to write out their wills. Meanwhile up at Montmartre, with grim prescience, common graves were dug to avert the spread of disease.

Nevertheless, the surest defence Paris had against the enemy swiftly closing in was the ring of forts constructed (with foresight?) by Thiers in 1840, against an invader who must then have seemed notional. The *enceinte* wall was ten metres high and divided into ninety-three bastions behind which ran a circular railway ferrying troops to the ramparts. It was a Maginot Line of its time, the principal defect being its age – which made it no longer proof against the plunging fire of which the monster cannons of Herr Krupp were now capable. On the other hand, its great advantage was its considerable circumference of some sixty kilometres. This would not only give the city room to breathe, and space to store essential supplies of food, fuel and ammunition, but it also meant that any investing army would be forced to occupy a contiguous front of approximately eighty kilometres against a possible break-out – which might require every spare soldier of the Prussian General von Moltke's enormous army. Meanwhile some 12,000 labourers set to work on reinforcing weak spots with improvised earthworks and laying land mines.

As in the days of Henri IV's siege, foodstuffs from the surrounding countryside streamed into Paris. Louis Napoleon's precious Bois de Boulogne became a sort of pastoral idyll. 'As far as ever the eye can reach,' wrote the Paris correspondent of the *Manchester Guardian,* 'over every open space, down the long, long avenue all the way to Longchamp itself, nothing but sheep, sheep, sheep! The South Downs themselves could not exhibit such a sea of wool.' In this Bois alone, there were herded an estimated 250,000 sheep, as well as 40,000 oxen, while an army of foresters now began cutting down the fine old trees in the Bois for fuel in the winter ahead. It seemed that, this time, in contrast to 1590, there was no way Paris could be starved into submission.

On 20 September, Uhlan cavalry from the two Prussian armies linked arms near Versailles, which surrendered without a shot. Paris was now effectively severed from the rest of France. For the first time since Henri IV's investment of Paris the city was encircled; in fact, it was the first time in modern history that a capital would be forced to endure a full-scale siege by a powerful and relentless enemy. The Crown Prince of Prussia positioned himself on a height overlooking the city and gazed down on the glittering gilt dome that held the remains of Prussia's one-time conqueror and arch-enemy. How close it must all have seemed! In the meantime, however, out in the provinces, taking their orders from the provisional government in Tours, new French armies were preparing for the day when, with the Paris garrison breaking out of the city, they could seize the occupying Prussians in a deadly vice. Now that Paris was menaced by the enemy, there was a new, tough mood of resistance at large in France. The question was, who was going to control and channel this will to fight; and how were operations to be co-ordinated between Paris and Tours now that the capital was totally cut off?

RESISTANCE

A possible answer to the second question was provided by the balloons of Paris – which were to constitute probably the most illustrious, most courageous and most inventive single episode of the siege. To most people today, the Siege of Paris prompts two main images: the eating of cats and rats by starving citizens, and the use of balloons. If the first epitomizes the depths a collapsing civilization can reach, the second symbolizes man's capacity for courage and resourcefulness in the face of adversity. The balloons of Paris would come close to being the nation's 'finest hour' of the whole war.

In Paris, seven balloons had been located, though most of them were in various states of disrepair. One of them, the *Neptune*, was sufficiently patched up, however, to be floated out of Paris on 23 September, over the heads of gaping Prussians. Its pilot Durouf landed safely at Evreux beyond the enemy's reach with 125 kilograms of despatches, after a three-hour flight. Four other balloons took off in quick succession, with (astonishingly enough) none of their crews being shot down, captured or otherwise coming to grief. The blockade seemed to have been broken, and a means of communicating with the provinces created.

Three days after Durouf's successful flight, the Minister of Posts in Paris set up a Balloon Post. Among the first to be invited to send a letter was the eighty-six-year-old daughter of the balloon's inventor, Mlle de Montgolfier. Balloons were soon taking off at a rate of two or three a week, usually from the foot of the Solferino Tower on top of Montmartre, or from outside the Gares du Nord or d'Orléans. Made of varnished cotton, because silk was unobtainable, and filled with highly explosive coal-gas, the balloons were capable of unpredictable motion in all three dimensions, none of which was controllable – in inexperienced hands they had a disagreeable habit of shooting suddenly up to six thousand feet, then falling back again to almost ground level.

To manufacture the balloons, Eugène Godard, veteran of some 800 flights, established an assembly line in the deserted Gare d'Orléans, while all over Paris small ancillary workshops laboured heroically. At the Gare du Nord, where the disused rails were rusted over, with grass growing between them, the finished balloons were varnished after being laid out, partially inflated, like rows of immense whales. In the station waiting-rooms teams of sailors were detailed to braid ropes and halliards. Gas for one balloon alone consumed the equivalent of seven tonnes of coal, out of Paris's total stocks of some 73,000 tonnes. For each satisfactory product, the factory received 4,000 francs (of which 300 were earmarked for the pilot), but there was a penalty clause imposing a fifty-franc fine for each day that delivery fell behind schedule. (In fact, the economics of the operation proved highly favourable to the government, since each balloon could carry 100,000 letters, bringing in a revenue of 20,000 francs.)

The most intractable problem was that the balloons offered only a one-way method of communication. Right up to the capitulation of Paris, balloonists were still trying to make the return journey into the capital, but none ever succeeded. It was the humble carrier-pigeon that was to prove the only means of breaking the blockade in reverse. A microphotography unit was set up in Tours, and there government despatches were reduced to a minute size, printed on feathery collodion membranes, so that one pigeon could carry up to 40,000 despatches, equivalent to the contents of a complete book. On reaching Paris, the despatches were projected by magic lantern, their contents transcribed by a battery of clerks. During the siege, 302 pigeons were sent off, of which 59 actually reached Paris. The remainder were taken by birds of prey, died of cold and hunger or ended up in Prussian pies. As a counter-measure, the Prussians imported falcons, which prompted one of the many imaginative Parisian 'inventors' to suggest that the pigeons be equipped with whistles to frighten off the predators. When the war finally ended, there was serious talk of rewarding the noble birds (which some compared to the saviour geese of Ancient Rome) by the incorporation of a pigeon in the city's coat of arms.

One of the earliest decisions the government took was to balloon a new plenipotentiary to the provisional government at Tours. The courageous Léon Gambetta, Minister of the Interior, volunteered for this adventure, and on 7 October he soared out of Paris in the *Armand Barbès*. But his bravery did not have quite the desired consequences. With Gambetta's intentions uncertain, and with a harsh winter beginning to close in, Trochu decided very late in the day to launch his major sortie from Paris, across the Marne to the south-east. Set for 29 November, it was designed to break the siege in co-ordination with an offensive by Gambetta's forces outside. But not until the 24th, only five days before the planned attack, was the despatch notifying Gambetta of it sent out aboard the *Ville d'Orléans*. The balloon took off under cover of darkness, shortly before midnight, and fifteen hours later landed – in Norway, 1,400 kilometres away. It was an astonishing voyage worthy of the imagination of Jules Verne, but it meant that the vital message reached Tours too late for Gambetta to co-ordinate his forces with Trochu's break-out. As a result, the supreme effort to free the city from the Prussian stranglehold collapsed. Morale in Paris plummeted, and hunger and bitter cold began to do their worst.

The *Ville d'Orléans*' trip was a rare failure. Altogether some sixty-five manned balloons left Paris during the siege. They carried 164 passengers, 381 pigeons, five dogs and nearly eleven tonnes of despatches, including approximately two and a half million letters, and only two balloonists died. The news they brought of Paris's continued resistance helped generate sympathy abroad for the French cause, as well as arousing hope in the provinces. But, above all, the knowledge that the city was not completely isolated from the outside world and that other French forces were still resisting the enemy somewhere in the provinces did a great deal to maintain Parisian morale. Though she was doomed, Paris could always point with pride to the epic of the balloons.

The balloon was not the only scientific development to preoccupy fertile Parisian minds during the siege. All kinds of inventions and ideas were put before the government, so that even before the Prussians got near to Paris it was obliged to set up a Comité Scientifique to handle this torrent of innovation. Most of the suggestions mixed science fiction with straightforward fantasy. One proposal was to poison the Seine where it left Paris; another was to set free the more dangerous animals from the zoo. But some of the 'inventions', though seemingly unworkable in 1870, have a certain familiarity today. There was the 'mobile rampart', a precursor of the tank (offered by an Italian engineer to Mayor Clemenceau of Montmartre, to whom as Premier of France in 1918 the tank would be a matter of national survival); there were gas shells that would give out 'suffocating vapours'; and there were 'pockets of Satan', filled with petroleum, which would explode over enemy positions, coating them with napalm-like fire. One modern-minded scientist conceived the idea of bombarding the Prussian lines with bottles containing smallpox germs. The search for new weapons led to a number of fatal accidents; one victim was the inventor of the hand-grenade, who blew himself up in his laboratory.

Some of the more eccentric schemes emerged from the Red clubs, and the most exotic of these were Jules Allix's *doigts prussiques*: pins dipped (appropriately enough) in prussic acid with which 'Amazons of the Seine' could defend their virtue. In October recruiting placards for the Amazons started to appear on walls all over Paris. These remarkable women were to be attired in black pantaloons with orange stripes, a black hooded blouse and a black képi with an orange band. Armed with a rifle and bearing a cartridge pouch slung across the shoulder, they were 'to defend the ramparts and the barricades, and to afford to the troops in the ranks of which they will be distributed all the domestic and fraternal services compatible with moral order and military discipline'. Allix explained the role of his *doigt prussique* as follows: 'The Prussian advances towards you – you put forth your hand, you prick him – he is dead, and you are pure and tranquil.' Unfortunately, although 15,000 women were said to have applied, this particular secret weapon was never put to use. The government, less concerned by the implications of the 'fraternal services' which the Amazons were to supply at the front than by the discovery that the organizers were apparently collecting enrolment 'fees', intervened.

In terms of military hardware, the greatest achievements lay in the manufacture of cannon, *mitrailleuses* and rifles during the siege, and for this the credit belongs to one man: Dorian, the Minister of Works. A peacetime industrialist, Dorian proved to be the most impressive member of the Trochu government, and the best of organizers. Under his direction, every available workshop and factory in Paris knuckled down to producing munitions; the Conservatoire des Arts et Métiers was turned into a giant cannon plant; and even along Napoleon's chic Rue de Rivoli the characteristic din of metalworkers came from basement windows where weapons were being forged. Shortages of raw materials were overcome by ingenious substitutes: steel was replaced by alloys of bronze and tin, there was discussion about exploiting that new rare metal, aluminium, and saltpetre for gunpowder was somehow extracted from old plaster. Even the bells of Saint-Denis Cathedral were melted down for cannon. As early as the end of September, Dorian's workshops were turning out 300,000 cartridges a day, and by the time the siege ended no fewer than 400 cannon had been manufactured in Paris.

Hardly less extraordinary was the means of financing the cannon, some 200 of which were subsidized through popular subscription launched by Victor Hugo. The inhabitants of the poorer, Red districts took the view that many of these had strictly speaking been bought by them, and their pride in the product of their sacrifices was understandably enormous. This was to become one of the immediate causes of civil war when the siege came to an end.

MORALE COLLAPSES

As the siege ground on, anger on the left was steadily mounting. The apparent ineptitude of Trochu and his bourgeois administration persuaded leaders of the Parisian proletariat, not entirely without reason, that they would rather do a deal with the Prussians than face a Dantonesque war to the finish – which might, incidentally, result in the destruction of Paris. Another bourgeois swindle at their expense seemed to be in the offing. 'The Prussians have been here a month and more and *nothing* has been done. Nothing but false reports,' grumbled a young Englishman, Charlie Carter, in a letter of October to his sister that echoed feelings widespread in Paris. A combination of boredom among the National Guard outposts on the ramparts, fiery rough red wine (which never ran out, even when Paris was down to her last rat) and effusions of scurrilous bombast from Félix Pyat's journal *Le Combat* fell on fertile ground inside the proliferating Red clubs. Precarious in its hold on power at the Hôtel de Ville, Trochu's team possessed none of the instruments of censorship, useful in wartime, that had been wielded by both Napoleons. Meanwhile, every utterance by the 'moderates' (equally not without reason) that the Reds inside the capital were as grave a menace as the Prussians outside was seized by them as a warning of what to expect. With the remarkable expansion of the National Guard, the power and weaponry of the Reds within it grew disproportionately.

At the end of October, after the failure of a major sortie at Le Bourget and the arrival of news of Marshal Bazaine's surrender at besieged Metz, angry Reds had actually broken into the Hôtel de Ville and temporarily seized control. There had been farcical and humiliating scenes as the swashbuckling Gustave Flourens, magnificently booted and spurred and wielding a massive Turkish scimitar, leaped on to the table, kicking over inkwells on a level with President Trochu's nose. Order was only restored by loyal troops suddenly appearing in the Hôtel de Ville via a secret subterranean passage from the nearby Napoleon Barracks, built for just such an eventuality. Ominously three of the Paris mayors – including Dr Clemenceau of Montmartre – had nevertheless declared themselves in favour of the 31 October revolt.

'The sufferings of Paris during the siege?' Edmond Goncourt wrote in his diary for 7 January 1871, within the bourgeois comfort of his house in the semi-detached village of Auteuil:

> A joke for two months. In the third month the joke went sour. Now nobody finds it funny any more, and we are moving fast towards starvation or, for the moment at least, towards an epidemic of gastritis. Half a pound of horsemeat, including the bones, which is two people's ration for three days, is lunch for an ordinary appetite.

The previous month Goncourt had noted, among his own circle, Gautier lamenting that he had to wear braces for the first time, 'his abdomen no longer supporting his trousers'. But, in terms of food, Goncourt and his friends were luckier than most. He continued, 'The greater part of Paris is living on coffee, wine and bread.' The failure of the Great Sortie at the end of November was to prove the turning point in the siege. Hitherto boredom had been the principal affliction; with the failure of the break-out and the sense that Paris was now on her own, morale began to collapse, and with the onset of serious winter, hunger and cold moved in. The hordes of cattle and sheep that in September had grazed in the Bois had long since gone. Fresh vegetables too were no longer to be had.

For one franc a day and at enormous risk to themselves, 'marauders' were sent out under the protection of *mobiles* to see what could be filched from no-man's land.

Early in October even bourgeois Paris had turned to horsemeat, first introduced by Parisian butchers four years before as low-cost food for the poor. As hunger tightened its grip, so many a splendid champion of the turf came to a well-spiced end in the casserole. Among them were two trotting horses presented by the Tsar to Louis Napoleon at the time of the Great Exposition, originally valued at 56,000 francs, now bought by a butcher for 800. It was in mid-November, however, that supplies of fresh meat were exhausted – and it was then that Parisians invented the exotic menus with which the siege will always be linked. The signs 'Feline and Canine Butchers' made their first appearance. To begin with, dog-loving Parisians objected fiercely to slaughtering domestic pets for human consumption, but soon necessity overcame their fastidiousness. By mid-December Henry Labouchère, the 'Besieged Resident' of the London *Daily News*, was telling his readers, 'I had a slice of spaniel the other day', adding that it made him 'feel like a cannibal'. A week later he reported that he had encountered a man who was fattening up a large cat which he planned to serve up on Christmas Day, 'surrounded with mice, like sausages'. Théophile Gautier claimed that cats and dogs in the city rapidly sensed their changed status:

> Soon the animals observed that man was regarding them in a strange manner and that, under the pretext of caressing them, his hand was feeling them like the fingers of a butcher, to ascertain the state of their embonpoint. More intellectual and more suspicious than dogs, the cats were the first to understand, and adopted the greatest prudence in their relations.

And then it was rats. Along with the carrier-pigeon, the rat was to become the most fabled animal of the Siege of Paris, and from December the National Guard spent much of its time engaged in vigorous rat-hunts. Even so, the number actually consumed was relatively few: according to one contemporary American calculation, only 300 rats were eaten during the whole siege, compared with 65,000 horses, 5,000 cats and 1,200 dogs. The elaborate sauces that were necessary to render them edible meant that rats were essentially a rich man's dish – hence the notorious menus of the Jockey Club, which featured such delicacies as *salmis de rats* and rat pie.

As the weeks passed, Parisian diets grew even more outlandish as the zoos started to offer up their animals. Victor Hugo was given some joints of bear, deer and antelope by the curator of the Jardin des Plantes, while kangaroo was on the menu at Goncourt's favourite haunt, Chez Brébant. The lions and tigers were thought too dangerous to kill, so they survived, as did the monkeys, apparently thanks to the Parisians' exaggerated Darwinian instincts. Otherwise no animal was safe. Unsurprisingly perhaps, opinions differed on the quality of these unusual dishes. After his meal of horse in November, a young Englishman called Tommy Bowles was so impressed he wrote, 'How people continue to eat pigs I can't imagine.' But by early January he was noting, 'I have now dined off camel, antelope, dog, donkey, mule and elephant, which I approve in the order in which I have written ... horse is really too disgusting, and it has a peculiar taste never to be forgotten.' His was not the only palate that became more discriminating: there was a significant variation in price between brewery and sewer rats, while Wickham Hoffman, a diplomat at the American Legation, declared a preference for light grey horses over black ones. Most butchers were only too ready to exploit the desperate shortages of meat (and they were justifiably loathed in consequence). A lamb offered to one British correspondent ironically proved to be a wolf.

No attempt was made by the government to control food distribution until it was much too late, and even then the steps taken were neither fair nor effective. To start with, price controls were imposed on certain staple foods, but these were inadequately enforced and were rapidly sidestepped by the growth of a flourishing black market. Meat rationing was introduced in mid-October, starting at 100 grams per person per day before being reduced eventually to 30 grams, but it covered none of the exotic meats described above. Restaurant customers were supposed to receive only one plate of meat, but this regulation was flouted wherever money spoke louder. Labouchère observed that 'in the expensive cafés of the Boulevards, feasts worthy of Lucullus are still served'. Nothing was ever done to oppose hoarding, and the provident bourgeoisie tended to live off private stocks which they had bought before the siege. The worst offenders were the speculators who released foodstuffs on to the market only when prices had soared. Some of them made a killing from beetroots bought in October at two centimes a piece and later sold for 1.75 francs.

Because it was more profitable to sell under the counter, but also because the inept distribution system meant that often their shops really were empty, traders would put up their shutters for long periods. This resulted in interminable food queues. Such a queue, one British correspondent wrote, was often 'more than a couple of hundred strong. Its outer edge towards the street was kept by armed Gardes Nationaux, who, patrolling like sheepdogs here and there, suppressed with difficulty the almost continual disputes.' For hours the unfortunate housewives would wait, often ending up empty-handed, burning with hatred equally for the petit bourgeois as represented by the ruthless butcher and for the rich bourgeois who could afford to buy without queuing. Pretty well the only effective rationing was accomplished by that most unfair instrument: price. The cost of most foodstuffs rocketed as the weeks passed. Compared with pre-war days, for example, the price of butter jumped by over one-third, and those of potatoes and rabbits had more than doubled. Oddly enough, there was never any shortage of wine or other alcohol. In the poorer districts of Paris drunkenness was never more pervasive, nor more pitiable. While the working-class women of Paris queued and hungered, the men got drunk on the barricades – all the while railing against the government.

BOMBARDMENT AND CAPITULATION

To the misery of hunger and cold, in a move aimed at ending the siege at the end of December, Bismarck and Moltke now added a new component of horror: the systematic bombardment of the civilian population. On the morning of the 27th, a French colonel and his wife were hosting a breakfast party for friends at the outpost of Avron, to the east of the city. All of a sudden, a Prussian shell burst right on top of them, killing six of the breakfasters instantly and seriously injuring the colonel. For the next two days Prussian heavy guns of a calibre hitherto unknown continued to hurl their huge shells down on Avron. On 5 January 1871, bombardment of Paris proper began. As Moltke put it with icy precision, 'an elevation of 30 degrees, by a peculiar contrivance, sent the shot into the heart of the city'. A small girl walking home from school near the Luxembourg was cut in two; six women in a food queue were killed; so was a *cantinière* of the National Guard while sleeping in her bed; in a bistro in the aptly named Rue de l'Enfer several drinkers were struck down.

Three or four hundred shells fell every day, at random and with no attempt to single out military targets. It marked the beginning of the Germanic technique of war by *Schrecklichkeit*. But, once the initial fear of the unknown had passed, indignation became the principal Parisian reaction – indignation that reached a peak on 11 January with the funeral of six little children all killed by the same shell. Then, in a manner comparable to the London Blitz of 1940, indignation was replaced by a surprising indifference to the indiscriminate shelling. Life went on as usual. House doors were left unlocked so that passers-by could take refuge from the shells. In the Louvre the Venus de Milo was crated up and stowed in a secret vault by the Prefect of Police himself; and piles of sandbags were stacked around the Arc de Triomphe and such treasures as the originals of the Chevaux de Marly (the fiery horses sculpted by Guillaume Coustou in 1740–5) on the Concorde. But soon the Prussians, under pressure from an outraged Europe, realized that the bombardment was proving a failure. The heavy guns (behemoths though they were by nineteenth-century standards) could not inflict that much serious damage. The humanitarian Crown Prince himself was beginning to oppose the bombardment. When he learned that Prussian shells had exploded among a Parisian church congregation, he exclaimed, 'Such a piece of news wrings my heart.'

Meanwhile, the Prussian court ensconced at Versailles had more immediate priorities. These were to have consequences that were much more far-reaching for European history than the disembowelling of innocent children in Paris by the terror-weapons of the new warfare. A large number of princes and princelings had gathered in Louis XIV's great château to participate in an event that was to bring Bismarck to the pinnacle of his life's ambitions. The big restaurant in the Hôtel des Réservoirs was full of food and wine and German voices. In a strange reversal of fortune, while the former Emperor of France sat dismally a prisoner in a provincial *Schloss* in Germany, his Empress in a depressing house in Kent, the King of Prussia took his afternoon tea in the Prefecture of Versailles, while Bismarck smoked, talked, drank and ate inexhaustibly in another, unpretentious, Versailles house as he planned the great day. At the nearby château, the proud lettering of the façade which dedicated it 'à toutes les gloires de la France' looked bleakly down on Prussian guns parked below. In the great staterooms where the Roi Soleil and Mme de Maintenon had paraded less than two centuries previously, German wounded lay in cots dominated by the rows of vast patriotic canvases proclaiming past French victories over their countrymen. From beyond Louis XIV's Rhine, court painters were being rushed to Versailles to record the historic event.

By 18 January the scene was set in the glittering Galerie des Glaces, where only a few years before Queen Victoria had danced with Louis Napoleon amid all the splendours of the Second Empire at its zenith. King Wilhelm I was to proclaim himself emperor of a Germany united over the corpse of a defunct French Empire. At twelve noon, recorded W. H. Russell of *The Times*:

> The boom of a gun far away rolls above the voices in the Court hailing the Emperor King. Then there is a hush of expectation, and then rich and sonorous rise the massive strains of the chorale chanted by the men of regimental bands assembled in a choir, as the King, bearing his helmet in his hand, and dressed in full uniform as a German general, stalked slowly up the long gallery, and, bowing to the clergy in front of the temporary altar opposite him, halted and dressed himself right and front, and then twirling his heavy moustache with his disengaged hand, surveyed the scene at each side of him.

This pleasing scene was multiplied in the great mirrors. Then the heavy figure of Bismarck, in the blue tunic and great boots of a Prussian cuirassier, stepped forward, holding his *Pickelhaube* by its spike, to proclaim the German Empire.

Bismarck at Versailles had triumphed over Louis XIV. Russell's very English comment on the extraordinary scene which had been enacted beneath a painting of Frenchmen whipping Germans was 'What a humorous jade Fortune is!' But, in besieged Paris, the humour was hardly evident, and Goncourt lamented prophetically, 'That really marks the end of the greatness of France.' Something of the old order of Europe died in the Galerie des Glaces. More than that, to the injury inflicted on France by the bombardment of *la ville lumière* an unforgettable insult had been added. In brutal combination, this injury and this insult would infuse into Franco-German relations for the next three-quarters of a century a terrible bitterness.

About the same time as the proclamation in the Galerie des Glaces, Trochu made one last, hopeless attempt to break the Prussian stranglehold. It was the turn of the National Guard, which had been so loud in its condemnation of the Hôtel de Ville's ineptitude and apathy. It attacked at Buzenval to the west of Paris, with half-trained troops debilitated by hunger and cold. Predictably, the result was a massacre.

Once again, on 22 January, furious Reds blaming the Trochu government launched an assault on the Hôtel de Ville. 'Civil war was a few metres away,' wrote Jules Favre. With Paris in a dreadful state, and faced now with this new spectre of an enemy within the walls, Trochu sent an emissary to Bismarck to ask for an armistice. The Iron Chancellor whistled a huntsman's air and remarked, 'Gentlemen, the kill!'

The hunt was over. The peace negotiations were painful, the Prussian terms savage. France lost Alsace and Lorraine, two of her fairest and richest provinces, and was required to pay a crippling indemnity of five billion francs, or more than seven times the total reparations demanded by the Allies in 1815 after twenty years of war in which French armies had devastated half the continent. But the term most hurtful to the pride of the defeated nation, and particularly to its half-starved and frozen capital, was Bismarck's insistence on a triumphal, symbolic march along the Champs-Elysées. It was brief, but sufficed to raise Parisian indignation to boiling point.

On the last night of February, all the customary nocturnal noises of Paris had fallen silent. The cafés emptied, and no fiacres rattled across the cobbles with late passengers. A few cavalry patrols moved silently through empty streets. As dawn came up blinds were drawn and windows shuttered. Early on Wednesday, 1 March, a lone German officer came riding down the Champs-Elysées with an escort of Uhlans. Behind him followed the rattle of kettle drums, with 30,000 German troops marching up an empty, silent avenue draped with black flags towards a sand-bagged Arc de Triomphe. Then, in the afternoon, they marched down again, wheeling into the Place de la Concorde as the music died away. Uniformed German sightseers at the Louvre were spotted by an angry crowd and pelted with coppers – a first instalment of reparations. There was more military music from the bivouacs in the Concorde that night. By the next morning, the last German had left. Paris's ordeal was over. But the insult lingered on. The city was enraged; patriotic Paris would have none of the treaty of shame; republican Paris would have none of the new Assembly created in the provinces; Paris, the capital, would not tolerate the government's decision to establish itself at Versailles, occupying billets only recently vacated by the Prussian conquerors. Revolutionaries of the left and patriots of the right found themselves united in anger, as a peace came which was no peace.

At last food, most of it from England, could be rushed into the devastated city. But Parisians were now in the grip of what physicians called 'obsidional fever', a sort of collective paranoia or mistrust. Psychologically, they were in no state to confront the humiliation of unprecedented defeat or of the harsh peace terms that came with it. The very appearance of the city, with most of the handsome trees on its boulevards cut down and many houses shattered by shellfire, was worlds away from the glittering Paris of 1867 – a contrast that did nothing for morale. In the streets men drifted aimlessly about, staring in desultory fashion into shop windows: regular troops and *mobiles* waiting to be sent back to their homes, National Guards with no employment, petits bourgeois with no trade. The scene, after months of confinement, terror and hunger, might seem peaceful enough. Yet, hidden away, a seething fury was ready to erupt into violence. This unhealthy condition required a leadership sensitive not just to the shifts in politics but also to the demands of psychology. Unfortunately the new government of France turned out to be as deficient in this respect as its predecessor had been in its handling of the war. At the end of February, Goncourt – though his own taste for work had at last returned – sensed that Paris was suffering 'under the most terrible of apprehensions, apprehension of the unknown'. More optimistically, an English commercial traveller, William Brown, living in Paris, wrote to his wife, 'it is all over now I feel sure, thank God', and spoke of 'the prospect of peace and business, the abundance of every kind of food, the beautiful Spring weather'. Nonetheless, it was certainly rash of Jules Ferry, on 5 March, confidently to telegraph from Paris to his colleague Jules Simon in Bordeaux, 'The city is entirely calm. The danger has passed.' It had not – far from it.

THE COMMUNE TAKES OVER

Capitulation to Bismarck confirmed the worst fears of the belligerent Parisian left that Thiers (who succeeded Trochu as president) and the new Republican Assembly were doing a deal with the enemy to restore the old imperial regime. The ingredients which were to spark off the Russian Revolution in 1917 – military humiliation, suppressed revolutionary fervour and deprivation – were all there. Missing only were the weapons. As the siege ended, however, Trochu's government had established safely up at Montmartre a guarded artillery park of some 200 cannon. Most of the guns bore National Guard numbers and had been paid for by public subscriptions during the siege. Then, at the end of February, detachments of the Guard seized the guns in a sudden *coup de main*. Efforts by loyal troops to regain them in March were not only repulsed but ended in the brutal lynching of two elderly generals – shot in a courtyard of Montmartre's Rue des Rosiers, amid scenes reminiscent of 1789 – and despite the efforts of Mayor Clemenceau. With dramatic suddenness, the seizure of the Montmartre guns shifted the whole balance of power in Paris – indeed in France as a whole.

Thiers now moved the army out of Paris – just as he had recommended Louis-Philippe to do in 1848 – to Versailles, which became the official seat of government. In Paris, the revolutionaries set up a rival regime, the Commune de Paris, inside the Hôtel de Ville. On 22 March, a counter-demonstration by unarmed conservative Friends of Order was broken up by gunfire in the Rue de la Paix, close to the present-day Ritz. A dozen were killed and many more wounded. The bridges between Paris and Versailles were now well and truly down. In Versailles Thiers regrouped his forces and prepared a second siege of Paris. In Paris, the Commune bickered, indulged in marginal social reforms – such as the abolition of night work in the bakeries – and squandered valuable time. For had the Communards promptly marched on Versailles, with their 200 cannon, they could almost certainly have defeated an army that had been largely disarmed by the Prussians. Karl Marx, who later made his name from his definitive work on the Commune, claimed this to have been one of its two cardinal errors (the other was its reluctance to seize the Bank of France): 'the defensive', he wrote, 'is the death of every armed rising; it is lost before it measures itself with its enemies'. This was an error that his future pupil, Lenin, born the previous year at Simbirsk, would not repeat when his time came.

Thus the insurgents had lost the initiative; and – with Prussian support – gradually Versailles was permitted to regain its badly shaken confidence. With what was more of a mob than an army, on 2 April, Palm Sunday, the Commune finally made a half-hearted move on Versailles. It was easily repulsed. One of the Guard's most flamboyant leaders, Gustave Flourens – who had led the insurgents into the Hôtel de Ville the previous October – was captured unarmed, and despatched with a single sabre blow. All the viciousness of civil war now appeared. Two days later, the Commune's Chief of Police and Procureur (a title with dread connotations from 1793), Raoul Rigault, ordered the taking of hostages. These were headed by no less a person than the Archbishop of Paris, Monseigneur Darboy. It was a deed by which Rigault's name would be longest remembered. During the interrogation of one of the imprisoned priests, a famous exchange ensued:

Rigault: What is your profession?
Priest: Servant of God.
Rigault: Where does your master live?
Priest: Everywhere.
Rigault (to a clerk): Take this down: X, describing himself servant of one called God, a vagrant.

Apart from being anti-religious, Red and left-wing, what really was the Commune? First of all, it was not, strictly speaking, 'Communist', having originated in 1789, when its precursor had been improvised simply to assume responsibility for administering Paris after the fall of the Bastille. With the extremists taking over in 1792 it was transformed into the Revolutionary Commune which forced the Assembly to dethrone Louis XVI. By default, it then found itself for a time the real government of France. Led by the violent Danton, on the one hand it firmly established the first French Republic, while on the other – with almost miraculous success – it chased the foreign Royalist invaders off French soil. The recollection of these two extraordinary achievements was what induced the Reds during the siege of Paris to reach back in history for the all-powerful amulet, the Commune. As one of its more significant leaders, Eugène Varlin (who was to be killed after being taken prisoner in the *semaine sanglante* of May), wrote to Bakunin, the Russian revolutionary, it wasn't a revolution they desired; they wanted only to set up a municipal council and defend the rights of Paris. In effect, the Commune was a kind of diffuse rallying point for all manner of social, political and philosophical grievances against the establishment – real or imagined. 'These people have good reason for fighting,' wrote Louis Rossel, one of its few impressive military commanders: 'they fight that their children may be less puny, less scrofulous, and less full of failings than themselves'.

There were the Jacobins, left-overs from the radical extremists of the Revolution of 1789, many of whom would have nothing to do with the Internationalists, or Socialists, on the Commune. Their leader was Charles Delescluze. His deeply eroded, tragic face still commanded support as well as sympathy, but at sixty-one he was prematurely worn out. There were the veterans of the barricades of 1848 and 1851 – and even of 1830. There were revolutionary feminists who belonged to the anarchist faction, such as the redoubtable *vierge rouge*, Louise Michel, who simply wanted Paris to rise 'in remembrance of its proud and heroic tradition'. 'Barbarian that I am,' she declared, 'I love cannon, the smell of powder, the machine-gun bullets in the air.' Like other Communards the *vierge rouge* was an illegitimate, the progeny of a French châtelain and his chambermaid. Then there were history's homeless Poles, including Dombrowski and Wroblewski, formidable fighters in the cause of freedom.

That outstanding British historian of France, Richard Cobb, was always struck by the mediocrity of the Communards: 'They were, above all, *des candides.* Never can leadership of a political movement have been so naive, so incoherent, and so incompetent.' Except for the horrible police chief Raoul Rigault, 'most were innocents who were not built for the scale of such tragic events'. The best one could say of the Commune was to define it as 'a tragic irrelevance, hopeless from the start, yet basically well intentioned, the brief spring of a Paris attempting to break away'. As events were to prove, however, the Commune was overwhelmed by the sheer diversity of aims arising out of the mishmash of personalities, ideologies and interests that it embraced.

After the April débâcle, military command of the Paris Commune devolved into the hands of the forty-seven-year-old Gustave-Paul Cluseret. A true soldier of fortune, he had graduated from the elitist military college Saint-Cyr, was wounded in the Crimea, then cashiered for 'irregularities' concerning army stores in Algeria. He found his way to America, enlisting as a volunteer on the side of the North during the Civil War before – startlingly – being promoted brigadier-general. 'Never', said Cluseret on taking over his undisciplined force, 'have I seen anything comparable to the anarchy of the National Guard ... It was perfect of its kind.' He appointed Rossel as his chief of staff, and the thirty-five-year-old Polish nobleman Jaroslaw Dombrowski as commandant of Paris. These were to prove the Commune's two ablest officers. But lacking was any kind of staffwork, or a proper commissariat. There seemed to be no effective chain of command: everybody gave orders, few obeyed them. And the Versaillais were closing in.

Already their guns were shelling central Paris, in a second bombardment just as indiscriminate towards the civil population as Moltke's had been. The courageous American Minister, Elihu Washburne, who stuck out both sieges, in May recorded shell splinters striking the US Legation near the Etoile 'within twenty feet of where I was writing'. Ironically, it was also the most staunchly bourgeois, anti-Communard parts of Paris that bore the brunt of government gunfire. Forming a tentative plan of campaign, Thiers' generals appreciated that the Achilles heel of the Communard defences lay at the Point du Jour, the extreme south-western tip of the city, close to where the Seine flows out towards Sèvres. It was here that his army would try to break in. Cluseret, summoning up a rare burst of energy, on 30 April marched out himself with 200 men to relieve Fort Issy; but, on his return to Paris, he found himself under arrest – charged with having sold himself to Versailles. Spymania was beginning to grip the city.

Cluseret's Chief of Staff, Rossel, now replaced him. Born of a Scottish mother, at twenty-six he had been promoted colonel of the engineers during the first siege, and was by far the most efficient soldier ever available to the Commune. Had he been in charge back in March, events might well have taken a different course. Now he ordered the rapid erection of a ring of barricades behind the city ramparts, those constructed by Thiers himself in the 1840s – a second line of defence in the event that MacMahon broke through the perimeter. But it was all too late. When he ordered a fresh attack to relieve Fort Issy, his battalion commanders evaporated. This was the last straw for Rossel, and on 8 May he sent in his resignation. For Fort Issy, having suffered over 500 dead and wounded, this also was the death-knell. Charles Delescluze, slowly dying of consumption, now took over.

Meanwhile as Thiers and his regulars looked more and more menacing, within the city the Communards – having seized the Archbishop – went from folly to irrelevant folly. Thiers' private house was spitefully demolished. In the Place Vendôme the great Column erected by Napoleon I to celebrate the victories of 1805 was brought crashing down. Its destruction now presented a final, futile gesture of contempt for the fallen Empire. (After the collapse of the Commune one of those held responsible, Gustave Courbet the painter, was condemned to pay for it, but took refuge in Switzerland.)

A CONCERT IN THE TUILERIES

On the sunny summer evening of Sunday, 21 May 1871, the self-elected Commune de Paris held a grandiose concert in the resplendent Tuileries Palace. Only the previous year it had been inhabited by the now deposed Emperor. No fewer than 1,500 musicians were engaged to take part.

As the Paris Commune enjoyed its last party, however, just outside the walls troops belonging to the legitimate government of Adolphe Thiers were waiting to enter the besieged city from Versailles. If ever there was a repeat of fiddling while Rome burned, this was it – though not even the most pessimistic apostle of gloom could possibly have foreseen that, within less than a week, much of the centre of Paris (including the historic and sumptuous Tuileries Palace itself) would lie in smoking ruins. Over 20,000 Parisians would have died in the grimmest blood-letting *la ville lumière* had ever known. The face of Paris, of France herself, and indeed the whole political philosophy of the West, would have been changed. Out of the grim *semaine sanglante*, Karl Marx would construct a cornerstone for his future doctrines, and an abyss of deep bitterness would be dug between the haves and have-nots of the nineteenth century. The savage street-by-street fighting would bequeath a legacy of a new style of warfare, and horror, to the twentieth century.

At the end of the concert that May evening, a Communard officer rose to announce, 'Citizens, Monsieur Thiers promised to enter Paris yesterday. Monsieur Thiers did not enter; he will not enter. Therefore I invite you here next Sunday, here at this same place.' At that very moment, however, in a scene more reminiscent of the Middle Ages if not of Greek mythology, Thiers' troops were actually entering the city through the Point du Jour gate, where a white flag had been spotted. Waving it was a civil engineer named Ducatel, who felt no love for the Commune and who had happened quite by chance to take his afternoon promenade near the battlements. He had been astonished to see that, around the Point du Jour, which had been heavily pounded by Thiers' cannon over the previous few days, there was not a single defender. It was not until Monday morning that most Parisians learned the news of the Versaillais' entry into the city. In the chic suburb of Auteuil, Dombrowski's forces had been taken completely by surprise. Sent out on reconnaissance, Assi, an incompetent early chairman of the Commune, was seized near the Trocadéro – the first of the Communard leaders to be captured.

By dawn on the 22nd, Marshal MacMahon had already poured 70,000 troops through five gaping breaches in the walls between the Portes of Passy and Saint-Cloud. They had been welcomed warmly in this predominantly bourgeois arrondissement, and 1,500 National Guards had surrendered. A frenzy of energy now belatedly gripped the Commune. At bayonet-point reluctant passers-by were forced to assist in the construction of barricades that should have been completed weeks before. 'If possible two or three trolleys, cabs or carts would form the foundation; all the apertures being filled with sand, the cubic paving stones from the road, sandbags, bricks or anything else,' reported Dr Powell, an English physician recently arrived in Paris.

On the Left Bank, Communards fought at Montparnasse Station until their ammunition ran out; their withdrawal was covered by a courageous singleton, who kept up a steady fire into the station from a one-man stronghold inside a newspaper kiosk. At the other end of the front, the Versailles troops were advancing rapidly towards Montmartre. Near the Madeleine, another English doctor, Alan Herbert, soon found himself a fascinated spectator of the Communard defence as, with mounting ferocity, Frenchmen killed Frenchmen:

> The first who fired was a grey-headed, grey-bearded old man, who was the most bloodthirsty old fellow I ever saw. He hounded the others on ... it was a horrible sight. They quarrelled as to ... whose turn it was to shoot and from time to time one heard such expressions as these: 'Oh, that caught him!' It was just like boys rabbit-shooting. I do not believe, however, they *killed* many.

As already noted, Haussmann's layout of the new Paris under Napoleon III had had as one of its objectives the provision of diagonal intersections so as to outflank barricades thrown up by revolutionaries. Now these proved highly effective for the regular troops to execute turning movements on the Communard defences. But about the only government advance on the Monday afternoon on the Right Bank had been to capture the garden of the British Embassy on the Faubourg Saint-Honoré. In their scattered little packets, the Communards were beginning to fight as never before – the fight of despair. As the front stabilized by nightfall on the 22nd, it lay roughly along a north–south axis, running from the Gare des Batignolles in the north, through the

Gare Saint-Lazare, the British Embassy, the Palais de l'Industrie (now the Grand Palais), across the Seine to the Chamber of Deputies, and up the Boulevard des Invalides to the Gare Montparnasse. Behind it, on the western side, one-third of Paris lay solidly in government hands.

Late that night, Dombrowski was brought under arrest to the Hôtel de Ville by the National Guard, for allegedly attempting to escape through the Prussian lines. He was the second of the Commune's few competent military commanders to fall.

PARIS BURNS

Dawn on Tuesday the 23rd broke on another glorious May day. The Versaillais Generals de Ladmirault and Clinchant were already assaulting the bastion of Montmartre from two directions. Up there, about the only Communard detachment which showed spirit was a squad of twenty-five women from the Women's Battalion, headed by the redoubtable Louise Michel, who had orders to blow up, if necessary, the Butte Montmartre. Now began the 'expiation' for which Thiers had called. Some forty-nine captured Communards were collected at random and summarily shot in the Rue des Rosiers, scene of the lynching of the two generals back in March. When the Madeleine was taken that day, Dr Herbert recorded:

> we saw the insurgents retreat from the different barricades and cross the Place. The troops then came in. A few scenes of horrid massacre and bloodshed, and then the streets were occupied by the regular troops ... I fear there is a very revengeful disposition amongst the regular troops, which is much to be regretted.

Garnier's still unfinished Opéra was soon hemmed in on three sides. Marine sharpshooters positioned in the top storey of the surrounding buildings directed a devastating fire down on to the Communards exposed behind their barricades. By 6 p.m., after both sides had suffered heavy losses, the Opéra was carried; and a soldier clambered up on to the statue of Apollo at its entrance and tore down the red flag. Near the Bibliothèque Nationale, Edmond Goncourt saw a Communard across the street killed by a bullet. His companion:

threw off his sword behind him, as if with scornful deliberation, bent down and tried to lift the dead man. The body was large and heavy and, like any inert object, evaded his efforts and rolled about in his arms from left to right. At last he raised it; and clutching it across his chest, he was carrying it away when a bullet, smashing his thigh, made the dead and the living spin in a hideous pirouette, collapsing one upon the other . . .

I retained in my ear for a long time the rending cries of a wounded soldier who had dragged himself to our door and whom the concierge, through a cowardly fear of compromising herself, refused to let in.

All through that Tuesday the 23rd, Paul-Antoine Brunel and his men had continued to hold out with extraordinary tenacity at the barricades in the Rue Royale and the Place de la Concorde. Turning movements from the direction of the Opéra were threatening their rear, and now deadly rifle-fire from sharpshooters on top of the high buildings along the Rue Royale mowed them down behind their barricades. Swiftly Brunel – justifying the nickname of 'The Burner' gained during the First Siege – ordered the firing of these buildings.

That evening, away in the darkness, Parisians saw the glow of a great fire. It looked as if the Tuileries Palace might be burning. Commander Jules Bergeret, one of the more incompetent Communard leaders who had just been released from a well-deserved spell in prison, had carried out a desperate action, dictated, apparently, more by vengefulness than by military necessity. Inside the Tuileries Palace, where only two days previously the last of the famous concerts had taken place, he stacked barrel after barrel of gunpowder. With a colossal roar the central dome housing the Salle des Maréchaux vanished in a conflagration that dwarfed any fireworks display laid on by either past Emperor.

By the night of the 24th, to Edwin Child lying low in the Marais of eastern Paris, 'it seemed literally as if the whole town was on fire and as if all the powers of hell were let loose'. The list of buildings already incendiarized was extensive: the Tuileries, a large part of the Palais Royal, the Palais de Justice, the Prefecture of Police and the Conseil d'Etat. Whole sections of streets including the Rue de Lille and much of the Rue de Rivoli were ablaze; so was the Ministry of Finance, housed in one wing of the Louvre, and the priceless treasures in the museum itself were gravely threatened. At Notre-Dame, which had escaped destruction by so narrow a margin during the Great Revolution, National Guards built up a large 'brazier' from chairs and pews; they were prevented just in time from setting it on fire. But the superb medieval building of the Hôtel de Ville, the focus of so much Parisian history from Philippe Auguste onwards, was also consigned to the flames, despite the protests of Delescluze.

Now there entered into the limelight *les pétroleuses*, daemonic maenads who allegedly crept about the city flinging petroleum-filled bottles into basement windows belonging to the bourgeoisie. 'Last night,' wrote another Briton in Paris on 25 May, Colonel John Stanley, 'three women were caught throwing small fire balls down the openings of cellars in the street. There was no doubt of it of course. Already smoke was coming from some of them. They were driven into a corner and shot then and there through the head.' Or were these women one of the grim myths that civil war produces? That night, too, the Communards committed their most infamous crime: the crude execution in an alley outside the prison of La Roquette of Monseigneur Darboy, the hostage Archbishop of Paris. Retribution was not long delayed in catching up with the Chief of Police responsible for his death, Raoul Rigault. The next day Rigault was seized on the Left Bank, at lodgings he shared under an assumed name with an actress, and he was shot in the head. For two days his body lay in the gutter, partly stripped by local women, and kicked and spat upon by passers-by.

On the evening of Thursday the 25th, as Commune resistance was beginning to crumble, Charles Delescluze decided that he would not 'submit to another defeat'. Dressed as always like an 1848 revolutionary in a top hat, black trousers, polished boots and frock coat, with a red sash tied round his waist, he set off towards an abandoned barricade. He was seen slowly to climb to the top, where he stood briefly before pitching forward on his face, felled by Versaillais rifle-fire. In defeat, the old Jacobin had achieved a measure of nobility denied to Emperor Napoleon III at Sedan. But the Commune was now leaderless.

Friday, 26 May was a day of savage killings on both sides, in which the battle became a ruthless mopping-up operation. Goncourt was moved to pity by one group of 400 Communard prisoners:

> The men had been split up into lines of seven or eight and tied to each other with string that cut into their wrists. They were just as they had been captured, most of them without hats or caps, and with their hair plastered down on their foreheads and faces by the fine rain that had been falling ever since this morning.

Many never reached prison camp in Versailles. Before the eyes of Alphonse Daudet:

> A large man, a true southerner, sweating, panting, had difficulty in keeping up. Two cavalrymen came up, attached tethers to each of his arms, around his body, and galloped. The man tries to run, but falls; he is dragged, a mass of bleeding flesh that emits a croaking sound; murmurs of pity from the crowd: 'Shoot him, and have done!' One of the troopers halts his horse, comes up and fires his carbine into the moaning and kicking parcel of meat. He is not dead ... the other trooper jumps from his horse, fires again. This time, that's it ...

One of the Versailles generals, the dashing Marquis de Gallifet, now secured for himself a reputation for barbarity that Paris would never forget. 'I am Gallifet,' he told prisoners. 'You people of Montmartre may think me cruel, but I am even crueller than you can imagine.' Twirling his moustaches, with his mistress on his arm, pointing out who should die and who should live, he is described as 'making caustic jests as he did so'. Troops under Gallifet's orders treated the captured Communards with particular brutality, many never surviving the journey to Versailles. The districts of Belleville and Ménilmontant alone were still wholly in Communard hands. Here, as at Warsaw and Leningrad in the Second World War, a whole population was now fighting for its life – not against a foreign army, but against its fellow countrymen. General Vinoy's regulars were approaching one of the last of the Commune's remaining strongholds: Père Lachaise Cemetery. Possessing what is still one of the best views of Paris, the vast cemetery dominated the whole smouldering city. There the last of the Communard defenders, firing from the cover of its elaborate family mausoleums, had to be winkled out gravestone by gravestone.

The next morning, 28 May, Thiers' army moved in for the kill. It was Whit Sunday. Within a few hours, there was only one Communard barricade left, on the Rue Ramponeau, where an unknown lone defender held off the attackers with a cool and undeviating accuracy. When he had expended his last cartridge, he strolled calmly away and disappeared. At La Roquette the unburied corpse of the murdered Archbishop had been discovered. That Whitsun morning, in revenge, the Versailles troops marched 147 of the captured Communards out to Père Lachaise and summarily shot them against a wall of the cemetery. Inside La Roquette, which held such grim memories for the hostages of the

Commune, some 1,900 prisoners are said to have been shot in two days, and at the Mazas prison another 400.

AFTERMATH

The last great siege of Paris was at an end. On 1 June, the London *Times* declared, 'Human nature shrinks in horror from the deeds that have been done in Paris … The wholesale executions inflicted by the Versailles soldiery, the triumph, the glee, the ribaldry of the "Party of Order" [Thiers' supporters] sicken the soul.' France herself was sickening of the slaughter. 'Let us kill no more, even murderers and incendiaries!' the *Paris-Journal* entreated on 2 June. 'Let us kill no more!'

Estimates of the numbers of Parisians slaughtered during the *semaine sanglante* vary wildly between 6,500 and 40,000. Reliable French historians today seem more or less agreed on a figure of between 20,000 and 25,000 – larger by far, even so, than the bloodletting of the Terror of 1793 in Paris. The Paris Commune itself was to remain a touchstone and a rallying point for the French left. Out of it would spring the Front Populaire of the 1930s, and the alliance of Socialists and Communists eventually to be presided over by François Mitterrand. For over a century, at each anniversary of the final massacre at Père Lachaise, the left would process in their thousands to lay wreaths at the cemetery's Mur des Fédérés.

The painter Auguste Renoir, who himself had narrowly escaped death at Communard hands, offered an eloquent epitaph to those terrible days: 'They were madmen, but they had in them that little flame which never dies.'

At the end of May 1871, Paris presented a dreadful sight. In the Place de la Concorde, the Tritons in the fountains were contorted into hideous shapes, the candelabras twisted, the statue of the city of Lille headless. Théophile Gautier noted the city's oppressive silence, and was particularly struck by the Rue de Lille, on the Left Bank, where his fellow author Prosper Mérimée had once lived: 'it seemed to be deserted throughout its length, like a street of Pompeii'. Of Mérimée's old house, only the walls still stood, his famous library reduced to ashes.

A silence of death reigned over these ruins; in the necropolises of Thebes or in the shafts of the Pyramids it was no more profound. No clatter of vehicles, no shouts of children, not even the song of a bird ... an incurable sadness invaded our souls.

Reaching Belleville, he was confronted by 'Empty streets. People drinking in cabarets, mute in a sinister fashion. The appearance of a quarter conquered, but not subjected.'

Even so, more of the city had survived than people might have imagined. The Venus de Milo was lifted reverently from the storage 'coffin' within the incendiarized Prefecture of Police, where she had been preserved since before the first siege. Gautier recorded how 'everybody leaned forward avidly to contemplate her. She still smiled, lying there so softly ... this vague and tender smile, her lips slightly apart as if all the better to breathe in life.' As she returned to the Louvre, it was like a symbol of the return of life to Paris herself. Indeed, normality was to be restored with remarkable speed. As early as 2 June, Elihu Washburne wrote of 'a marvellous change ... the smouldering fires have been extinguished and the tottering walls pulled down'. The couturier Worth purchased some of the rubble from the Tuileries to construct sham ruins in his garden, and the work of rebuilding Paris was soon under way. On 12 June Edwin Child wrote to his father, 'in about 6 months ... we shall wonder where all the fires took place'.

Once again France – and Paris – showed her extraordinary resilience. That summer omnibuses and fiacres were crowding the capital's streets again, *bateaux-mouches* were chugging up and down the Seine. The enterprising Thomas Cook was despatching hordes of English tourists to ogle at the 'ruins' of Paris. But some observers claimed that for a long time Parisians preferred to walk in the road rather than on the pavements – to avoid giving rise to the suspicion that they were *pétroleuses* intent on popping their incendiary packets through basement windows.

AGE SIX: 1871–1940

THE TREATY OF VERSAILLES

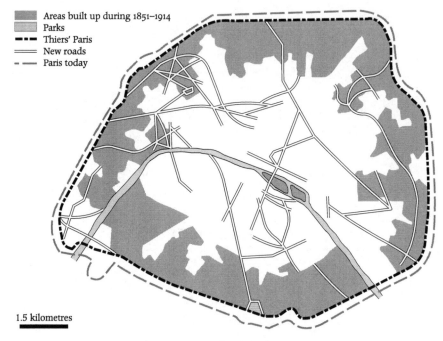

HAUSSMANN'S PARIS, 1851–1914

16

Belle Epoque

A great city is ... a work of art. It is a collective and complex art, it is true, but this makes it an even higher form of art.

Guillaume Chastenet to the Chamber of Deputies, in 1909

RECOVERY AND REVANCHISM

In November 1871, Edmond Goncourt recalled Flaubert repeating to him an observation that had been passed to him by a Chinese envoy in Paris: 'You are young, you Westerners, you have hardly any history to speak of ... It has always been like this ... The Siege and the Commune are everyday events for the human race.' To Goncourt this Mandarin vista helped place the inexplicable horrors of the past year in a sensible perspective. Once Paris had recovered, France herself was not far behind. After sketching dead Communards at the barricades, Manet was back at Boulogne painting *La Partie de Croquet.* Renoir and Degas came back to find studios in Paris; Monet and Pissarro returned from refuge in dank and foggy London. Suddenly, as if in reaction against the drabness and the horrors of the siege and the Commune, the Impressionists burst forth into a passionate blaze of colour, redolent with the love of simple, ordinary existence. They would be immortalizing with new life places like Courbevoie, Asnières, Gennevilliers, once front-line names during the two sieges, pleasant riverside villages which, in the coming century, would be swallowed up in industrial suburbs. Seurat would be painting his masterpiece of summer reveries on the Grande Jatte, the sand bar in the Seine which had so recently seen Trochu's National Guard charge across the river in its last, hopeless attempt to break the Prussian ring round Paris. The somnolent riverside villages of the Seine and Marne where Sisley had painted his early works, many within weekend-walking distance of the city, with their comfortable houses in ochre-coloured stone and fitted with green shutters – Champigny, Joinville, Epinay-sur-Orge, Bougival, Rueil, Issy – swiftly repaired the gaping holes left by war in roofs and walls, welcoming back the painters and the ambience of cheerfulness and leisure they brought with them. It all seemed like a symbolic regeneration comparable to the resurgence of literature that followed the cataclysm of 1815.

On the *quatorze juillet* 1873, the newly elected President, Marshal MacMahon, wounded and captured in the débâcle at Sedan only three years previously, reviewed a magnificent parade of the resurrected army on Longchamp racecourse. Eighteen months later, with all the pomp and circumstance of the fallen Empire, he would be opening Garnier's unfinished opera house, with its famous chandelier weighing six tonnes and its 2,156 seats. Together the two ceremonies proclaimed that France had come back to life again. Her industry blossomed in a new renaissance, this time based on firmer foundations than had existed under Louis Napoleon's Second Empire. Out of the ruins of Paris, the Hôtel de Ville was rebuilt with tremendous speed, a faithful image of its old, medieval self. Napoleon I took his place once more atop a resurrected Vendôme Column. Marking the final demise of the French monarchy, the all-too-evocative, blackened skeleton of the Tuileries Palace was obliterated, its singed debris sold off by auction. Sir Richard Wallace, that great British benefactor of Paris, presented the grateful city with eighty new drinking fountains. In 1874, Somerset Maugham was born at the British Embassy on Faubourg Saint-Honoré – part of the Embassy having been turned into a maternity ward after 1871, so as to enable British subjects born on French territory to evade conscription into a new French army eager to acquire fresh recruits.

Despite the upheaval of the lost war and the internecine violence of the Commune, it was soon evident that, in Paris, the rich had returned to being rich, and the poor remained poor – as ever. On the evenings of pay-day many would be found flocking to the nearest Mont de Piété to redeem their mattresses – the standard pledge of those below the poverty line. With the passing of Victor Hugo in 1885, the Parisian underclass found a new champion in Emile Zola, who in *L'Assommoir* portrayed deprivation and misery in terms of even darker realism.

Meanwhile, in the other, affluent Paris, the ever watchful Goncourt, passing by the Rue de la Paix in January 1872, noticed 'A blockage of private carriages'. He wondered 'who was the great personage whose door was beset by so many important people when I looked up above the carriage entrance and saw the name: Worth. Paris has not changed.' Just two years later, he would be recording a historic first encounter with an unknown fellow artist:

> Yesterday I spent the whole day in the studio of a strange painter called Degas ... Out of all the subjects in modern life he has chosen washerwomen and ballet-dancers. When you come to think of it, it is not a bad choice ... An original fellow, this Degas, sickly, neurotic ... Among all the artists I have met so far, he is the one who has best been able, in representing modern life, to catch the spirit of that life.

A short while later he would be recording conversation at the Café Riche with Flaubert, Zola, Turgenev and Daudet: 'We began with a long discussion on the special aptitudes of writers suffering from constipation and diarrhoea ...' Manifestly the priority of topics in literary circles had barely changed either.

To the astonishment of the world, the first half-billion of the five billion francs in reparations that France had to pay Germany were handed over just one month after the collapse of the Commune. The rest followed with a rapidity no European banker would have predicted. As early as September 1873 the crushing bill had been paid off, and the last German soldier removed from French soil. In 1872 the new Republican Assembly passed the first of the laws designed to restore the efficiency of France's humiliated army, and with it went a new spirit. Already by 15 June 1871, less than a month after the collapse of the Commune, the Rev. W. Gibson, an English Methodist clergyman who had spent ten years before the war trying to 'convert' the Parisians, was writing with gloomy foresight:

> ... I regret to find that the determination to seek to take their revenge sooner or later on Prussia is again manifesting itself among the Parisians ... Alas for France, and alas for the hope of the peace of Europe! ... Germany, when within the next few years she again encounters France in arms, will find her a very different foe from the France of 1870; and who knows but that before the end of this century there may be a similar triumph in Paris to that which is now being celebrated in Berlin? I vainly hoped that France would feel herself fairly beaten and be willing to accept her inferior position.

For the next forty-three years Frenchmen would ponder in silence Deputy Edgar Quinet's remark at the time of the debate on Bismarck's peace terms: 'the ceding of Alsace-Lorraine is nothing but war to perpetuity under the mask of peace'. This was approximately what Thiers had warned greedy Bismarck at the time. As long as Prussian soldiers stood guard the wrong side of Metz, not much more than 300 kilometres by straight, flat road from the capital, Paris would grieve and dream dangerously of *la revanche* – the dream that was 'never spoken, but never forgotten'.

In the summer of 1878, seven short years after the expiry of the Commune, Paris once more was host to the world at an international exhibition. Compared with the flamboyance of Louis Napoleon's Great Exposition of 1867, it was a rather muted affair, but it revealed a possibly more solid industrial achievement, showing to the world that *la ville lumière* was alive again, that France once more was an influence to be reckoned with on the international scene. Its main feature, facing the Champ-de-Mars where the exhibition was laid out, was an exotic oriental palace, of no particular relevance: the Trocadéro, constructed on the heights of Chaillot where Napoleon I had once projected that Brobdingnagian residence for his heir, the little King of Rome. The structure somehow managed to combine the functions of theatre, concert hall and water tower. But few Parisians had anything good to say about it; Goncourt was more interested in describing a dinner *chez* Zola, where they were offered 'Some grouse whose scented flesh Daudet compared to an old courtesan's flesh marinated in a bidet'.

Yet the national holiday, 30 June, marking the new Exposition Universelle turned into a spontaneous demonstration of French pride in Paris. For the first time since the Commune it was legal to fly the *tricolore*, and the brilliant display of flags lining the thronged streets persuaded both Manet and his younger colleague, the thirty-eight-year-old Monet, to paint the exhilarating scene from their studios (Monet rented a room off the Rue Saint-Denis just for the occasion).

The next *spectacle* to distract Paris was the funeral of Victor Hugo. There had already been a dummy-run, in 1881, when Paris went wild over the eightieth birthday of the old Titan, now become the idol of the 'people'. An estimated 600,000 Parisians had marched down the Avenue d'Eylau past his house, while with his grandchildren he spent the whole day at the open window, greeting the endless lines of well-wishers, and revelling in the mounds of flowers laid below in the street – thenceforth to become Avenue Victor Hugo.

When he died, on 22 May 1885, his body lay exposed to view under the Arc de Triomphe in a vast catafalque, upon a double platform clad in purple velvet that reached almost to the top of the arch, and guarded by twelve young poets, all through the night of the 31st. The next day the humble black hearse (which Hugo had specified), drawn by two horses, trundled through Paris before the eyes of two million Parisians, every head uncovered. The cortège halted at the Panthéon – Soufflot's great church, built on Louis XV's orders in 1764 in thanksgiving to Sainte Geneviève for his recovery from illness. Completed just in time for the Revolution to turn it into a mausoleum for famous men with the old Roman title of Panthéon, under the Restoration and Second Empire it had reverted to being a church, but on the occasion of Hugo's funeral the Third Republic once more returned it, now all draped in black, to its revolutionary function.

There was no doubting that Paris, still suffering from the terrible traumas of 1870–1, with no *grand homme* at the helm of government in the drably respectable Third Republic, needed a hero. But did Hugo – master of bombastic silliness during the siege, a champagne socialist of his time – quite deserve to lie among the best and greatest in the land? What about Balzac, Molière, Racine? Goncourt, in his treatment of the 'nation's sorrowful wake', was perhaps more realistic when reporting how, the night before, it had been:

> celebrated by a wholesale copulation, a priapic orgy, with all the prostitutes of Paris, on holiday from their brothels, coupling with all and sundry on the lawns of the Champs-Elysées – Republican marriages which the good-natured police treated with becoming respect!

The old roué himself would probably not have disapproved.

THREATS TO POLITICAL STABILITY

For the next three decades there would be at least a semblance of political stability – with three or four major blips, all of which had their focus on Paris. First there was the *affaire Boulanger*. In a momentary outburst of jingoism, it looked – in 1887 – alarmingly as if Paris might have found a new hero in the shape of General Georges Boulanger. When the dashing forty-nine-year-old Minister of War appeared, martially magnificent, at the *quatorze juillet* review at Longchamp, Parisians went mad with delight. Songs were heard in the street that seemed all too evocative of the summer of 1870:

> Regardez-le là-bas! Il nous sourit et passe:
> Il vient de délivrer la Lorraine et l'Alsace!

In Berlin, Bismarck's finger tightened on the trigger. Momentarily, the inflammatory Boulanger could have made himself master of Paris; but, fortunately for the peace of Europe, he lost his opportunity and – two years later – committed suicide on his mistress's grave. In Clemenceau's savage epitaph, he died 'as he had lived, like a subaltern'. The episode said something about the fragility of the Third Republic, the underlying power of revanchism and the continuing volatility of Paris – a time when there was Bonapartism without a Bonaparte.

Meanwhile, rumbling away in the background of French politics was the Panama Canal scandal, finally to explode in 1892. Ferdinand de Lesseps, the brilliant engineer and hero who had dug the Suez Canal, underestimated the costs of digging a similar canal across the Isthmus of Panama. To muzzle criticism, the Panama Company had paid money to newspapers and bought votes in the Chamber of Deputies. In 1892, the right-wing press – notably a wildly anti-Semitic paper, *La Libre Parole* – saw a political weapon and exploded a bombshell under the government. Baron Reinach, an eminent Jew who had acted as intermediary between the company and government Deputies, killed himself. In the ensuing investigations, only one politician (a former minister who confessed to having accepted 375,000 francs) was found guilty, but the mud bespattered a whole generation of French politicians. Even Clemenceau was compromised, and had to spend long years in the wilderness – years when France most needed his leadership.

Next to plague Paris came the apparently irrational Anarchist outrages. In the twenty years leading up to 1914, six heads of state were assassinated, culminating with Empress Elizabeth of Austria (1898), King Umberto I of Italy (1900) and US President McKinley (1901). Describing the pointlessness of the Anarchist cause, Barbara Tuchman says of their victims that 'not one could qualify as a tyrant. Their deaths were the gestures of desperate or deluded men to call attention to the Anarchist idea.' The first ruler to die (in 1881) was Tsar Alexander II. Here his *narodniki* assassins struck the wrong target, since of all the Russian autocrats he had done most to liberate the serfs, and his death was followed by a campaign of brutal repression.

In Paris the Anarchist scourge began (in the middle of the Panama scandal) with the bombings of houses of public figures by one Ravachol, alias François Claudius Königstein. Then a bomb was deposited, to coincide with a miners' strike in November 1892, in the mine company's office on the Avenue de l'Opéra. It exploded as an unfortunate *flic* was carrying it into the nearby police station, blowing him to pieces as well as five other *agents* in the room at the time. The following December, Auguste Vaillant exploded a bomb inside the Chamber of Deputies; it was intended to be a non-lethal protest, but in fact wounded several Deputies and led Vaillant to the guillotine. The week after his execution, another bomb exploded in the Café Terminus of the Gare Saint-Lazare, killing one and maiming twenty. The culprit, one Emile Henry, also proved to be the perpetrator of the bomb in the Avenue de l'Opéra, and was duly guillotined. Then, a month after Henry's execution (in May 1894) the Anarchists *en revanche* claimed their most eminent French victim when President Sadi Carnot was stabbed to death in Dijon by a young Italian worker.

Suddenly, however, the wave of Anarchist outrages, which was beginning to hold Paris in a grip of terror, ebbed as swiftly as it had begun. Meanwhile, in the backstreets and in Bohemia Ravachol briefly became something of a hero; a verb, *ravacholer,* meaning to 'wipe out an enemy', became current, while a song called 'La Ravachole' was sung to the tune of 'La Carmagnole', with the refrain:

> It will come, it will come
> Every bourgeois will have his bomb.

But if Ravachol's death had any lasting significance it surfaced, in 1895, a year after the last *attentat,* when Paris workers responded by creating the Confédération Geñérale du Travail (CGT) – the first time since the Commune that the prostrate city proletariat had dared raise its head to take collective action.

On 6 January 1895, Goncourt recorded in his diary how a friend of his, the painter Eugène Carrière, had been present at the Ecole Militaire when a very lonely figure, a slight, academic-looking officer called Alfred Dreyfus with rimless pince-nez, had had his epaulettes ceremoniously ripped off and been reduced to the ranks. Submerged in the crowd, Carrière studied 'some little boys up in the trees who, when Dreyfus arrived holding himself erect, shouted: "The swine!" and a few moments later, when he bowed his head: "The coward!"' To his great credit, even at that early stage and despite his own tendency towards anti-Semitism, Goncourt declared, 'I was not convinced of his guilt.' The Dreyfus Affair, or simply *l'affaire*, one of the most unpalatable episodes in all French history, for more than a decade focused the passions and attention of the entire country, averting its eyes from the clouds that were now gathering on the horizon. It was also peculiarly Parisian, in that Paris was where the central episodes were played out.

Dreyfus was a thirty-five-year-old French artillery captain, of a moderately prosperous Jewish family, but born in the Alsace seized by Germany when Dreyfus was still a child. Like many Alsatian Jews passionately attached to France, the Dreyfuses fled westwards, to escape Prussianism and likely conscription into the German army. This rise in the number of Jews in Paris had the usual effect of fanning anti-Semitism, aggravated by allegations emerging from the Panama Scandal. In October 1894, Dreyfus was confronted by a fellow officer, on the orders of the Chief of the French General Staff, with a *bordereau* – a memorandum – filched by a cleaner from the wastepaper basket of the German military attaché. It was alleged to have been written in Dreyfus' hand. The deadly *bordereau* contained some (fairly low-grade) intelligence about the firing mechanism of the latest French cannon. Dreyfus protested that it was a forgery, but no one believed him. After a mockery of a trial he was subjected to that most humiliating ceremony in front of troops drawn up on the parade ground of the Ecole Militaire, before being deported to the lethal Devil's Island, to serve out his sentence of life exile for espionage.

Terrible years went by before Colonel Picquart, an intelligence officer on the French General Staff, discovered that the *bordereau* was in fact a forgery. The real spy was revealed to be an unsavoury captain of Hungarian descent called Esterhazy, a man of many mistresses and many debts. Despite Picquart's powerful evidence, the French General Staff – closing ranks to conceal its previous blunder – refused to accept it, and Picquart himself was disgraced and sent to jail. In 1898 Emile Zola entered the lists. This writer of fiercely realistic novels, who was described by his friend Flaubert as 'A colossus with dirty feet, nevertheless a colossus', composed one of the most powerful pieces of journalism of all time – 'J'Accuse!' So powerful was the public emotion it whipped up that it made a retrial unavoidable – though Zola, too, went to prison for his pains.

'J'Accuse!', an open letter to the President of the Republic, dramatically crystallized opinion in Paris, forcing to the surface all manner of latent prejudices, submerged since the Great Revolution and well beyond – not least the anti-Semitism that had lurked since the days of Philippe le Bel. It forced Parisians to take sides: Dreyfus symbolized either the eternal Jewish traitor or the denial of justice. *L'affaire* was, in the words of Léon Blum, a future prime minister and a Jew himself, then in his twenties, 'A human crisis, less extended and less prolonged in time but no less violent than the French Revolution.' To an English visitor, 'Paris palpitated', and the same man sensed a lust for blood in the air. Divisions created by *l'affaire* ran all through Parisian society. At cafés 'Nationalists' and 'Revisionists' sat at different tables on opposite sides of the terraces; salons became polarized; Monet and Degas didn't speak for years; Clemenceau fought a duel with an outspoken anti-Semite; six out of seven Ministers of Defence resigned in the course of the scandal; while a President of the Republic died of a heart attack in the arms of his mistress, in the Elysée Palace.

From the point of view of contemporary European history, what had the most lethal impact were the divisions caused within the French army itself, only so recently recovering from its débâcle of 1870–1. When Dreyfus was finally cleared, but not till July 1906, the army leaders who had ranged themselves solidly against the wretched man sent the army several leagues further down the road of disrepute where Boulanger had first guided it. Also of significance was the fact that *l'affaire* coincided with the publication in France of the first effectively anti-military novels.

None of this went unnoticed across the Rhine in Kaiser Wilhelm's newly aggressive Germany, as internal conflict appeared to absorb all France's energies. Moreover, the passions fanned by the Dreyfus affair were to provide a kind of dress rehearsal for Paris politics in the 1930s.

TECHNOLOGY AND ARCHITECTURE

One additional effect of *l'affaire* and its attendant obsessiveness was to obscure from Parisians the very real material and technological advances being made in the last decades of the nineteenth century. Replacing gaslight, there was electricity (thanks to the 'Wizard of Menlo Park', Thomas Edison). There was the gramophone; there was the telephone (functioning by 1879, in Paris, about as efficiently as it would for the next century), which Goncourt observed in 1882 was 'the very latest thing, this leave-taking which cuts out all possibility of argument'; and there was a uniquely Parisian, Jules-Verne-like wonder, the *pneumatique*, whereby lovers could send each other *billets-doux* zipping through subterranean capsules delivered within an hour from one end of the city to another. There were horseless carriages, and in 1894 the first car race took place from Paris to Rouen, 123 kilometres. In 1885 Louis Pasteur in his Paris laboratory discovered a vaccine cure for rabies.

In 1895, Louis Lumière showed the first moving pictures.* One of his earliest 'Kinos', *Teasing the Gardener*, was a Monsieur-Hulot-like affair with a child stepping on a hose and getting soaked. Lumière himself, however, thought his invention 'a scientific curiosity with no commercial possibilities'. This may, however, have been said in the wake of the first major disaster of the infant industry, when 140 people died in a fire at a charity bazaar caused by Lumière's *cinématographe*. Rail networks proliferated and became faster; and there were more train crashes. The all-metal *vélocipède* became all the rage among *à la mode* Parisians. But, given what they had had to suffer over the previous six centuries and more, perhaps the greatest technological advance was one that was invisible to the eye – the new sewer system. Sketches of the times depict elegant ladies, genteelly holding their noses, being pulled along on a sightseeing carriage alongside the tumbling sewers under Paris.

Paris was becoming full of the new wonders of the world – not least its most visible symbol, the Eiffel Tower, designed to crown the 1889 Exposition. It was to mark the hundredth anniversary of the Revolution, but, more than that, it was to hail France's recovery and her spectacular entry into the modern world. Gustave Eiffel was an engineer of Alsatian origin, which fact perhaps helped gain popular support for his improbable project. His work on the construction of metal bridges and viaducts led him to propose for Paris what would then be the tallest building in the world – making France, he said, 'the only country with a 300 metre flagpole'. Eager to do anything to restore Paris's pre-1870 standing as world leader, the city fathers supported this extraordinary and risky

---

* There remains some controversy over whether he or Thomas Edison could properly claim to be the father of the moving picture. Edison's 'Kinetograph', patented in 1894, was an immobile, studio affair weighing 450 kilos; Lumière's *cinématographe*, hand-cranked and weighing less than nine kilos, could reasonably claim to be the first commercially viable projector.

venture. It would arise from the foot of the Champ-de-Mars, and look across and down upon the site intended for the King of Rome's vast palace. The technology was formidable: using two and a half million rivets, 300 steeplejacks working flat out would run it up in the space of two years; it would weigh only 7,000 tonnes in total, exerting a dead-weight pressure per square centimetre no greater than that of a man seated in a chair. It was intended to last for only twenty years, when its concession would expire, and it was saved from being dismantled in 1909 only because its huge radio antennae had become essential to the development of French radio telegraphy. But, predictably, some protests in the cultural community were violent. Gounod, Dumas *fils* and Garnier of Opéra fame were among fifty to sign a petition damning Eiffel's project as 'a monstrous construction', 'a hollow candlestick', or – worse – a 'solitary riddled *suppositoire*'. 'Metal asparagus' was another Parisian epithet. 'Le Douanier' Rousseau was one of the first artists to break ranks and treat it as a respectable subject for the canvas. But, as the alternative projects in the competition to commemorate the Revolution included a gigantic guillotine, fortunately Eiffel's design triumphed, at a modest cost of fifteen million francs.

On 31 March 1889, a sixty-strong party in top hats and tailcoats made the first official ascent – on foot. Prime Minister Tirard gave up at the first platform, and only Eiffel and ten others braved it to the top, where he had the Légion d'Honneur pinned to his breast. On the first platform, the 300 workmen still in overalls feasted and quaffed champagne. The critics were derisive once more when, on the day of the tower's inaug-uration, 7 May, none of the lifts worked. Nevertheless, 'le Tour Eiffel qui monte au ciel', in the words of the popular song, had arrived. Suicides and inventors of flying machines selected it as a jumping-off place (in 1964, a would-be suicide became the only one of 380 to survive after she landed on the roof of a car parked below).

Though the tower dominated the scene, beneath it a remarkable city had been built for the 1889 Exposition. To distract minds and hearts from France's territorial loss, the central theme was the colonial empire. Gazing at its minarets and domes with the same kind of superciliousness he had reserved for Louis Napoleon's grand show of two decades previously, Goncourt observed acidly, 'One can tell this Exhibition was going to be an Exhibition for dagoes.' Paris, he lamented, 'is no longer the Paris of old, but an open city to which all the robbers in the world, after making their fortune in business, come to eat poor food and rub against flesh which calls itself Parisian'.

If nothing else, the two Expos of 1878 and 1889 had once more re-established Paris as the world's leading host. Yet the Eiffel Tower and the exotic structures run up for 1889 gave a somewhat deceptively flamboyant picture of what in fact was being built in Paris. The departure of Haussmann, the collapse of the Second Empire and the chaos of the Commune brought to a halt public works and private buildings in the early 1870s. The great era of Haussmann was over, and nothing like it would ever be seen again in Paris. In the early 1880s, private building revived and even reached a peak that surpassed the previous boom of the 1860s. But, after 1870, under the Third Republic the city grew more slowly. By the early 1900s the rate of building permits had sunk to around 2,000 a year. Under Garnier, who became the doyen of architectural taste in the Ecole des Beaux-Arts, a greater freedom was afforded the architect until the end of the century. This was in marked contrast to the strictly controlled street uniformity imposed by Haussmann. Apartment houses grew taller and more motley in their exoticism and luxuriance. Glass and metal bow windows began to bulge out above the street. Briefly, very briefly, the craze for Art Nouveau seized the city, surviving mainly in the entrances to the new Métro stations commissioned at the end of the century. Paris borrowed from William Morris, while Manhattan borrowed from the Parisian apartment block. From a municipal commission set up in 1896 to re-examine building regulations, Louis Bonnier emerged as the high-priest of change and variety. Under his influence façades became more and more florid, often to the point of the ridiculous and the fantastical. Once again building regulations permitted structures to hang out over the street, as they had done before Louis XIV, making the new apartment blocks look top-heavy. Individualism and variety became everything. Haussmann would have rolled in his grave. Despite the demand for higher and higher buildings, though, Bonnier fortunately opposed the novelty of the American skyscraper as inappropriate.

Inevitably, the new century brought a reaction against Bonnier's architecture. By 1908, the government had intervened to reform building codes and protect the intrinsic beauty of Paris. An eminent member with a special interest in fine arts, Guillaume Chastenet, impressed the Chamber of Deputies with an appeal for a renewed urban aesthetic, declaring that 'A great city is ... a work of art. It is a collective and complex art, it is true, but this makes it an even higher form of art.' Once again the importance of harmony began to reassert itself. In the years up to the outbreak of the Great War, Paris's most notable new buildings included sumptuous grand hotels like the Astoria and Claridge (their architects were commissioned to build the Savoy and Claridge's in London) and great stations like the Gares de Lyons and d'Orsay. The latter, a superb piece of ornate architecture on any account, now marvellously converted into an art museum, managed discreetly to render itself compatible with the Louvre across the Seine. Nevertheless, economic recovery after 1870 never succeeded in generating a lasting architectural style.

The building developments – coupled with the soaring prices that always went with them – and improved communications within the city accounted for one of the most important migrations in Parisian history. The artists moved from the Left Bank's Latin Quarter, from Montparnasse to Montmartre. In almost every way Montmartre suited them better. The narrow irregular streets and low houses of what until recently had been a detached village, with windmills, vineyards and gardens, put on the map by the balloons of Paris flying from it during the siege, provided an exhilarating contrast to Haussmann's monumental, orderly and alienating Paris. An earlier generation led by Berlioz and writers like Murger, Nerval and Heine was replaced by Pissarro, Cézanne, Monet, Renoir and Toulouse-Lautrec, who were in turn succeeded by Van Gogh, Picasso, Braque, Matisse and Dufy, with the centenary year of 1900 acting as a kind of watershed. There in this sleepy village the artists and their favourite models such as Jeanne Avril, 'La Goulue' and Valentin-le-Désossé brought immortal fame to cafés and *bals musettes* such as the Moulin Rouge, the Moulin de la Galette, the Lapin Agile. Montmartre became something of a year-long carnival, where anyone abandoning bourgeois respectability could submerge his identity for a few hours, disappearing into an alluring milieu of Bohemians, prostitutes and criminals. For the artists it represented cheap and congenial living – with plenty of motifs to paint all round them. Slowly arising above them was the sugary white cupola of the Sacré-Coeur – the monument to reconciliation after the bloodletting of the Commune, loathed by some but painted by many others, and eventually to become as integral a part of the Paris skyline as its opposing pinnacle, the Eiffel Tower.

LA VIE DOUCE

The economic successes of the Third Republic during the 1880s and 1890s and right through to the outbreak of war in 1914 were enjoyed by a larger spectrum of Parisians than at any other time in history. Dubbed the Belle Epoque (or the 'Banquet Years' or the 'Miraculous Years'), it felt like a period that would last for ever. This age of excitement, of fear combined with optimistic expectation, saw the dawning of the consumer society in what one author called the *nivellement des jouissances*. By the end of the century this 'levelling of pleasures' found its blossoming in more than 200 *café-concerts, bal musettes, guinguettes* and *cabarets artistiques*. Sometimes called 'theatres of the poor', they offered a variety of inexpensive pleasures that drew not only the *classes laborieuses*; inevitably around the wealthy loafers and *badauds* circled the usual charivari of tarts, just as in Second Empire days. Even so, Edmond Goncourt recorded in 1881, 'According to a lecherous Englishman, the best place to pick up a woman in Paris is in the omnibus offices, and the remark is that of a foreigner who knows his Paris.' Ten years later he cited a friend's calculation that every year 80,000 tarts started work, but only about forty got to the top; these were 'all women born in the provinces' – because the *Parisiennes* had a 'mocking, ironical side to them which irritates the customer'.

As ever, hand in hand with sex went crimes of passion, duelling and murder. The first two categories were never punished with execution. Mme Caillaux, wife of a former prime minister, who marched into the office of Gaston Calmette, editor of *Le Figaro*, and emptied an entire pistol magazine into him for libelling her husband, was eventually acquitted. Duelling continued and right up to the 1920s, often over the flimsiest of provocations. In 1901 the gentle Debussy narrowly escaped a duel with an aggressive Maeterlinck over who should play his Mélisande. But for the more heinous offences the guillotine was always at the ready. Public executions continued outside La Roquette prison until 1899, and for long afterwards the five large stones on which had perched the guillotine were clearly visible.

Arriving at the Gare du Nord in 1873, George Moore was shocked by the 'haggard city' which greeted him, and the 'peculiar bleakness in the streets'. Writing of the same *quartier* a few years later in his uncompromising *L'Assommoir*, Zola observed that 'chests were hollow just from inhaling this air, where even gnats could not live, for lack of food'. But by the early years of the new century such was the general level of prosperity in the country at large that even the poor of Paris were able to benefit. During the Belle Epoque, life in France was wonderfully, unmistakably good. The phrase *la vie douce* could hardly convey what this meant – though the Germans' envious expression 'as content as a god in France' perhaps came closest. Never had there been so much for so many. It was an epoch seething with ideas and creativity. The bicycle and *le football* introduced new pleasures; the Orient Express and *wagons-lits* brought new and stranger places within range of Parisians. As Paris assumed once more her eminence as the world's centre of culture and pleasure, with every passing year it seemed increasingly impossible that the humiliation of 1870, let alone the Commune, had ever happened. National pride was further inflated by Louis Blériot's feat in 1909 of hopping across the Channel in an aeroplane.

In the country at large, the peasants were better clothed and fed than they had ever been; there was an abundance of good bread; consumption of wine and potatoes had increased by 50 per cent in the second half of the nineteenth century; consumption of meat, beer and cider by 100 per cent. Whereas the Third Republic had found a France in which French was a foreign language to half of its citizens, by 1913 a combination of communications such as roads, books, the press, posts and the telephone had welded together a remarkably united nation. In the realm of economics, marvels had been wrought, making France almost overnight, so it seemed, a great industrial power. After the British, French financiers were the bankers of the world. By 1913, France was producing 45,000 automobiles a year, making her the world leader. Between 1875 and 1913 a massive increase in state expenditure signified a proportionately large increase in social services. Her huge empire was flourishing and expanding. Yet, worryingly, France now had barely half the population of the new, vigorous German Empire, while in terms of overall commerce she had slipped behind both Britain and Germany.

By the summer of 1900, however, Paris was keen to give a party, celebrating the national resurrection and putting aside worries about Dreyfus, Germany and Alsace-Lorraine. Expo 1900 was to outshine even the exhibitions of 1867 and 1889. As they crossed the bridge which Louis XVI had begun and the Revolution had completed with stones from the demolished Bastille, visitors arriving on the Place de la Concorde were

greeted by a welcoming arch topped by an imposing Porte Monumen-
tale, oriental in its exoticism, more than a little over the top. At its
summit, instead of the conventional goddess of Progress or Enlightenment, stood a five-metre plaster-cast of *La Parisienne* by Paul Moreau-
Vauthier, with a massive bosom and a gown specially designed by
Paquin, welcoming the world with outstretched arms. Some thought it
represented the new influence that had been achieved by women under
the Third Republic. What was unmistakable, however, was its assertion
once more of the city's gender.

As a symbol of Expo 1900 much more imposing, as well as significant
in terms of contemporary political history, was the resplendent new
bridge, Pont Alexandre III, which linked the exhibition grounds on both
sides of the Seine. Today still the most dramatically magnificent bridge
in Paris, its cornerstone had been laid four years previously by President
Félix Faure and young Tsar Nicholas II in honour of the latter's tyranni-
cal father. Much more than just a bridge, its unique single span across
the river of over a hundred metres marked the new alliance so recently
forged (in 1894) between Republican France and a thoroughly repressive
Russia, which would bring with it fateful consequences before a decade
and a half of water had passed under it. At its inception, however,
visitors admired the decorations depicting the past glories of France on
each of its four monumental columns: on the Right Bank, France of the
Middle Ages faced modern France; while, on the Left Bank, France of the
Renaissance was paired with France of Louis XIV.

It was here, at one end of the bridge, that, on 14 April 1900, President
Loubet opened the exhibition. The site, on either bank of the Seine, was
so vast that it had to be linked by a *trottoir roulant,* in itself a wonder of
the modern world, powered by electricity whose ever expanding usage
was an underlying feature of the whole exhibition. The Palace of
Electricity, granted an appropriately dominant position and studded with
a galaxy of light bulbs, housed a mighty 3,000-horsepower steam gener-
ator produced by Germany's Siemens which, belching out smoke, lit and
powered the whole. (Climbing up the Eiffel Tower, Emile Zola took a
remarkable photograph of it, framed by the girders of that triumphant
edifice.) In contrast to previous exhibitions, offerings from the colossus
across the Rhine were pacific – great dynamos instead of monster
cannon. It was left to the host nation to show off her latest weapon, a
long-range gun by Schneider-Creusot. But Germany had to have the last
word: her model Hanseatic town boasted the highest spire in the
exhibition in its recreation of a gothic town hall.

On the Right Bank, at the foot of the Trocadéro, the emphasis was on colonization, a demonstration of whither France had diverted her energies since the loss of Alsace-Lorraine (at a time when Bismarck was murmuring pointedly, 'My map of Africa lies in Europe'). Opposite each other on the newly opened Avenue Alexandre III were the Petit Palais and the Grand Palais, specially run up for the exhibition, but as enduringly built as the Eiffel Tower, impressive marriages of glass and steel. Both Palais were dominated by French art, exhibiting more than 1,000 aritists. 'Paris', one critic proclaimed, 'has replaced Rome. The Foreigner, wherever his place of birth ... comes to Paris to seek his art training, and is content merely to visit Italy and its admirable "Past", now suffering the kiss of death.' Klimt, Picasso, Rouault and Rodin were all assembled in the same cross-section as Burne-Jones, mirroring the juxtapositions of medieval Paris and the Palais de l'Electricité, and presaging Cubism, Surrealism and Abstractionism. Monumental French sculptures filled the great hall of the Grand Palais, while larger-than-life Rodin proclaimed his pre-eminence by both exhibiting in the Decennial Exhibition and presenting a retrospective of 150 of his works in his own pavilion at the Place de l'Alma. (Monet remained aloof, holding a one-man show at Durand-Ruel ten days after the exhibition closed.)

That figure of *La Parisienne* which dominated the entrance to the 1900 Exposition was suggestive of just how far women had come in the Brave New Age. As Edith Wharton, embarking on a new life in the Rue de Varenne in 1906, observed with a touch of envy, 'as soon as a woman [of Paris] has personality, social circumstances permit her to make it felt'. But then Paris was eternally the woman's city. Even so the new century did seem to bring fresh horizons for women. There were women lawyers and women tennis players; there was Marie Laurencin with her soft pastel colours, perhaps the first woman to paint wholly as a woman; there was Marie Curie, the only woman to win the Nobel Prize twice, sharing both work and love in an idyllic marriage with Pierre, until he was killed in a senseless street accident, run over by a horse-drawn wagon. There was Misia with a plurality of husbands and lovers. And there was Colette, unhappily wed to the rascally Willy who grabbed all the credit for her 'Claudine' novels – she revenged herself in the arms of other women (notably the Marquise de Belboeuf, whose *cocu* husband came to blows with Willy during a pantomime in which Colette was performing). In the 1890s, the discovery of the poems of Sappho, coupled with publication of Pierre Louÿs' *Songs of Bilitis* (one of the great literary hoaxes of the time), demonstrated – to the advantage of many an appreciative *Parisienne* – that lesbianism had been respectable in classical times.

In 1904 women's daily working hours were reduced from eleven to ten; in 1907, a married woman was granted sole right to her earnings; in 1910, she was allowed eight weeks' unpaid maternity leave; and in 1913 a minimum salary was established for women working at home. Yet, curiously, the *Parisienne* pushed much less hard than her English sister to get the vote. There were perhaps better ways in which she could influence the political scene.

With all these changes and new openings inevitably came a dramatic change in dress. Women had to be physically mobile, to be able to clamber into a bus, or get into the new Métro, or into a *teuf-teuf*. The cumbersome bustle disappeared, and between 1900 and 1908 the 'Swan Bend' took over, based on a tight corset and a prominent bust and behind. Long tight-fitting skirts with leg-of-mutton sleeves entered the scene. Then the new designer Paul Poiret, operating from the Faubourg Saint-Honoré, launched into something like a resuscitated 'Empire' line – high waist, almost no bust, and no corset, straight and simple. The traditional S became an exclamation mark. The only concession to the extravagance of the past was the large, wide-brimmed hat topped with one huge plume. Nineteen-ten brought the hobble skirt, in which a woman could walk only by taking tiny steps – eventually made more practical with the addition of discreet pleats, or slits, at the side. Between 1908 and 1914 fashions, most inconsiderately, speeded up so that a girl could no longer get away with last summer's frock; and many a *Parisienne* would often change five times a day. With Poiret's new fashions came the first scent produced by a couturier: Le Fruit Défendu, smelling of peaches. And with the new fashions also came new, daring dances – the cakewalk and the tango, the latter forbidden to officers in uniform in Germany, but thriving in Proustian Paris.

DEEPENING THE DIVISIONS

On the whole Paris's salute to the new century was voted a triumph. Staying open until November, Expo 1900 attracted 50,860,801 visitors – fewer than expected, but still more than the entire population of the host nation. More fundamentally, it seemed to have launched the twentieth century with a new mood of hope, indeed a positive quest for joy, turning its back on what the Catholic polemicist Léon Bloy called 'the painful and abject nineteenth century'. In Paris, beyond the exhibition grounds, there were many signs of material progress. That July the first Métro opened, cutting the journey from Maillot to Vincennes from ninety minutes to twenty-five, and enlivening the Paris scene with its station entrances of pure Art Nouveau. Cars thronged the streets, many driven by chic, emancipated women in beekeeper-style veils to keep out the dust. Meanwhile, to demonstrate their own faith in the kind of future they were determined to obtain, including peace among all men, in October the Socialists held two huge congresses in the Salle Wagram under the aegis of the great Jean Jaurès.

Yet, if to France and her well-wishers Expo 1900 seemed to herald a century of human progress, to the Kaiser and the nervy sabre-rattlers of Berlin the magnificent Pont Alexandre III represented the Franco-Russian alliance of 1894, which in turn meant the encirclement of Germany – Berlin's great fear. Amid all the razzmatazz, one manifestation Germans would not have missed that summer was the sombre procession of men in black velvet suits, carrying flags of black crêpe through the Concorde, as they did every 14 July. Before the stone female figure of Strasbourg they made emotive speeches, followed by several minutes' silence, and then moved off chanting, 'Vous n'aurez pas l'Alsace et la Lorraine!'

If there was one aspect that changed immeasurably during the Belle Epoque, and in changing had changed life in Paris, it was the press. From the handful of journals under the Second Empire, numbers had multiplied. Opening in 1886, one new review, *La Vogue*, lasted only nine months, but in that time it managed to build up a circulation of 15,000. This expansion was good news for writers and artists, assured of a receptacle for their writings and of critiques for their *oeuvres*, but at the same time cut-throat competition led to a pursuit of sensation, *coûte que coûte*. A shortage of sensation at home led to virulence in foreign affairs, fuelling the flames of populist nationalism, with the consequences too horribly predictable as memories of the actual horrors of war faded with every passing year.

In the political arena, the years 1900–14 offered much for the Paris press to get its teeth into. First of all, the triumph of the Dreyfusards signalled a reaction back to militant anti-clericalism, hovering in the background ever since 1789. *L'affaire* brought the Radicals to the fore, with the right (which was seen closely to embrace both the Church and the army) as the enemy. In 1902, Emile Combes, a sixty-nine-year-old anti-clerical politician, came to power in Paris determined to complete the separation of Church and state in France. Possessed of all the prejudices of the small-town provincial, Combes legislated against 'unauthorized' religious orders (some of which had admittedly intervened in a most rashly improper fashion during the Dreyfus affair). Schools were closed, religious processions stopped. In the expropriations of nunneries and monasteries, wanton pillaging occurred. The army was finally called in to effect the expropriations, thereby confronting its officers with a grave issue of conscience. Typical was the case of a lieutenant-colonel who, on asking what his superior was going to do, was told 'I have 'flu,' whereupon, in a rage transcending rank, he seized his regimental commander fiercely, shouting, 'I suppose when the war comes you will have 'flu too!'

Combes' law exacerbated divisions within the army, to a large extent widening the same chasm dug by *l'affaire*. Worse still, as a consequence of Dreyfus, the responsibility for promotions had been transferred from the army commission to the Minister of War. The newly appointed, anti-clerical General André abused his power deplorably. Officers were set to spying on each other; the Grand Orient Lodge of the freemasons was used as an intelligence service to establish dossiers on their religious persuasions; promotion became more a matter of an officer's political views, and particularly to which church he went on Sundays, and how often, than of merit. Able officers like Foch, whose brother was a Jesuit, and de Castelnau – accompanied to the front in 1914 by his own private chaplain – would always be at a disadvantage. It was no coincidence that in 1911 the office of the new Chief of the General Staff fell to a general who ostentatiously ate meat on Good Friday.

L'affaire, Combes and André were followed by the most intense bout of Socialist-led anti-militarism that France had experienced since 1870. All politicians distrusted the General Staff. The repute of the army sank to its lowest ebb. In 1905, a new Act reduced military service to two years, and army effectives declined from 615,000 to 540,000. In Germany the new Kaiser with his bellicose moustaches noted all this, and waited.

THE ARTS

To muster and market the great burst of painting that followed on from the Impressionists, three years after the Exposition of 1900 closed its doors there opened in the basement of the Petit Palais the first of the Salons d'Automne. There was also the Salon des Indépendants, founded in 1884 by breakaways like Seurat, Signac and Redon. This had no selection committee, which explained how an unclassifiable primitive like the sweetly ingenuous 'Douanier' Rousseau found space on its walls. Rousseau was so loved by his eminent colleagues they gave him a special banquet in 1908, in the midst of which he engagingly fell asleep while a candle dripped wax unnoticed on his recumbent head. In contrast to Monet, Renoir and Cézanne, Vuillard and Bonnard took Impressionism indoors, as often as not to paint the comforts of an increasingly affluent bourgeois world.

This was not, however, the habitat which most of their colleagues knew. Matisse's miserable studio was so cold he had to work in overcoat and hat; Picasso's early lodgings in Montmartre, as described by his then mistress Fernande Olivier, consisted mainly of 'a mattress on four legs in one corner. A little rusty cast-iron stove with a yellow earthenware bowl on it which was used for washing ...' As late as 1907 Daniel-Henry Kahnweiler, one of a new breed of keen-eyed private dealers, could record, 'Nobody can imagine the poverty, the deplorable misery of those studios in the Rue Ravignan ... The wallpaper hung in tatters from the unplastered walls.' Yet it was then that he set eyes on the huge *Demoiselles d'Avignon*, one of the first examples of Cubism, and later to be worth several kings' ransoms.

In 1903, James Joyce wrote to thank his mother for a postal order of three shillings and fourpence, 'as I had been without food for 42 hours'. The previous year Trotsky had found an exiled Lenin living in straitened circumstances near the Parc Montsouris; Trotsky thought that Paris was 'like Odessa – but Odessa is better!' Among the painters up at Montmartre, Vlaminck played gypsy music on the violin to live; Derain worked as a professional boxer; while Van Dongen unloaded vegetables and sold newspapers. Picasso was saved from the gutter when a Catalan dealer, his first, paid him 150 francs a month – just enough to live on.

Then, in 1906, Ambroise Vollard paid him 2,000 francs for thirty canvases. Two years later Matisse was saved by a wealthy Russian entrepreneur, Sergei Schukine, who commissioned two large panels of dancers for his Moscow mansion, and subsequently bought no fewer than thirty-seven other canvases. It was fortunate for Matisse and others that such wealthy and discerning patrons existed – one of the more lastingly beneficial spin-offs of the highly questionable Franco-Russian alliance.

In the wake of the miraculous *richesse* of the Impressionists, Paris continued to be the epicentre of modern art. The immortal Cézanne died senselessly of hypothermia after being caught in a storm in 1906, aged sixty-seven, but close on the heels of his great legacy came the Nabis (derived from the Jewish word for prophet) movement of Sérusier, Bonnard and Vuillard. Then there was the scandalizing new group led by Matisse, which proudly assumed the pejorative nickname of Fauves: entering this world of flamboyant colour at the Salon d'Automne of 1905, a critic had exclaimed that it was 'Donatello au milieu des fauves' (Donatello in the wild beasts' den). Matisse, son of a grain-dealer from Flanders, Dufy, Vlaminck and Van Dongen were all northerners seeking refuge from greyness in the exuberant colours of the south, influenced by a Picasso just emerging from his exquisitely colourful Pink Period. To a romantic like Apollinaire, Matisse represented 'Instinct regained!' At all these exhibitions of the early 1900s, in sharpest contrast to the sedate *vernissages* of London and New York, viewers would give vent to the most powerful emotions, sometimes almost coming to blows in a manner more comparable to the Paris theatre through the ages.

There was no let-up. Once more led by Picasso, who by now was constantly administering shocks to the Paris art world, after Fauvism there arrived Cubism, pioneered by Cézanne in his last years. By 1911, the Cubists, having achieved recognition, had perhaps reached their pinnacle. That year a terrible, unthinkable blow struck: somebody stole the *Mona Lisa* off its wall in the Louvre. At first, Apollinaire was under suspicion; imprisoned briefly, he was plunged into deep depression, but the painting was found two years later, safe and sound in Florence, the theft having been carried out by a glazier working in the museum. It was a happy ending that lightened an increasingly gloomy scene. The greatest period of artistic creativity possibly since the Renaissance had passed its peak in Paris. It was somehow symptomatic of what was about to happen to Europe, to the world at large. Cubism, arm in arm with the dissonant themes of Stravinsky, would be succeeded by the violent nihilism of Italian Futurism, and by English Vorticism, its very name symbolic of the disaster just a year or two away.

In marked contrast to the Paris of a century previously, when Napoleon had contrived to whittle down the number of Paris theatres to a handful, there were now once again some forty-odd. Theatre life was as lively, and disputatious, as it ever had been. For those who, like Marcel Proust, didn't want to venture out, there was even an electrical device called the Théâtrophone, a subscriber service that enabled you to hear live music or a play. Listening to Debussy's *Pelléas et Mélisande*, Proust found that 'the scent of roses in the score is so strong that I have asthma whenever I hear it'.

In 1905 there was another efflorescence of drama in Paris. At the summit, Sarah Bernhardt reigned sublime, still after several decades at centre stage undistracted by her plethora of unsatisfactory love affairs – which critics would denounce from time to time. To confound them, in later years she would appear on stage recumbent in her famous coffin. Opening in time for Expo 1900, Bernhardt had managed to squeeze her fifty-five-year-old frame into a corseted uniform to appear as Rostand's tragic twenty-two-year-old hero in *L'Aiglon*, and, despite the absurdity of the casting, Paris loved every minute of its four hours. Her courage was boundless. While in Rio, playing *Tosca*, she bounced out of the net which was supposed to catch her in her death-plunge off the battlements, causing such damage to her right knee that she limped for the rest of her life. (Eventually, in 1915, the leg had to be amputated, and, ghoulishly, Barnum's circus offered $10,000 for the limb and the right to exhibit it.) But Bernhardt never gave up. Aged sixty-five she was playing a nineteen-year-old Jeanne d'Arc. Eventually she was awarded the Légion d'Honneur (like Dreyfus) – though not for acting, because an independent actress was still not considered 'respectable' in Paris.

During the Belle Epoque, opera and ballet audiences were as excitable as ever: the first night of *Pelléas et Mélisande* provoked something like a riot. One wag dubbed it *Pédéraste et Médisance*; another critic complained of waiting for 'a tune that never came. A succession of notes like the noise of the wind ... I prefer the wind.' Nevertheless, by Christmas 1906 *Pédéraste* would reach its fiftieth performance – every one of which had been attended by Maurice Ravel, while Romain Rolland rated it the most original opera ever written.

Two years later Diaghilev's Russian Ballet arrived, one of the most exciting and provocative events on the cultural scene of pre-war Paris, and a second major spin-off from the fateful Alliance sealed in 1894.

Since then everything Russian had been the rage in Paris, and from 1908 the ballet would return every year until 1914 put an end to it all. But, in a wonderfully Russian way, the Moscow bankers financing this important asset of the Alliance swiftly ran out of funds (or they disappeared into Grand Ducal pockets), a process accelerated by the incredible extravagance of the thirty-five-year-old Diaghilev's productions. As a result Parisian 'angels' found themselves picking up the tab.

At first Parisians were lukewarm in response to the Russian onslaught. Then suddenly they became seized by Fokine and Bakst, by the brilliantly exotic stage settings and by Nijinsky's acrobatics. Of *Schéhérazade* in the 1910–11 season, Proust – quite overcome – admitted, 'I never saw anything so beautiful.' Outrage and unbeatable publicity followed in the 1912 season when in *L'Après-midi d'un faune* Nijinsky chose to dance without a jockstrap. Shocked, Gaston Calmette, editor of *Le Figaro* – taking over the role of critic himself – condemned 'Gestures smacking of erotic bestiality and heavy shamelessness ... an ill-made beast, hideous from the front, even more hideous in profile'. Still more offensive to Parisian sensibilities was when Nijinsky in a Terpsichorean frenzy affected to masturbate into a nymph's abandoned scarf: 'a lecherous faun', thundered the soon-to-be assassinated Calmette, 'whose movements are filthy and bestial in their eroticism and his gestures as crude as they are indecent. That is all ... greeted by the boos it deserved.' The offending gesture was expunged, but audiences still flocked to the theatre.

Nineteen-thirteen brought to Paris Stravinsky, *The Rites of Spring* and more sensation. At the première, Gertrude Stein observed Apollinaire 'industriously kissing various important looking ladies' hands'. But 'No sooner did the music begin and the dancing than they began to hiss. The defendants began to applaud. We could hear nothing.' One young man became so excited that he beat rhythmically with his fists on the head of an American in the row in front of him, whose own emotion was so great that he claimed, 'I did not feel the blows for some time.' The conductor, Pierre Monteux, recalled that 'Everything available was tossed in our direction, but we continued to play on.' Amid the hubbub even the Théâtrophone broke down. Insults were exchanged. Ravel was called a 'sale Juif'. Eventually the row escalated into a full-scale riot, with the gendarmes forced to intervene – as in the days of Louis XIV. As much as anything what had, apparently, provoked the uproar was the 'barbarian' exaggeration of Stravinsky's music. Did the harsh clangour of Stravinsky seem to presage the violence that was about to engulf civilization?

More in tune with the happier mood of the Belle Epoque was the comic theatre of Georges Feydeau, that dashing figure of the boulevards. Speed – the speed of the era of electricity, telephone and motor car – was the essence of Feydeau's hilarious farces. Drawing on rich material from his own life, Feydeau's favourite prop was the bed, with people in it, hidden under it or behind it, his central figure the *cocu* husband. The backdrop to the contemporary Parisian scene was perhaps that, in the words of the young playwright Sacha Guitry, 'The burdens of marriage were too heavy to be borne by two people alone.' Meanwhile, there was Lumière's new-fangled Kino, still silent though accompanied by stirring music, but expanding its entertainment possibilities at ever increasing speed. With it would arrive the young Charlie Chaplin, starting aged twenty at the Folies Bergère in 1909, who, always deeply influenced by his early experience in Paris as Charlot, would delight Parisian audiences for many decades to come. By 1913 Paris already boasted thirty-seven cinemas; one of them, the Pathé, near the Invalides, ran to an orchestra of sixty and claimed to have the world's largest screen.

THE APPROACH OF WAR

Whether on stage or screen or in the cabarets, the message of that first decade and a half of the new century before the deluge was one of relentless optimism. Perhaps that was why Parisians had booed Stravinsky. Like Queen Victoria Paris was not interested in gloomy talk, and looked back at the men of the 1890s with something akin to pity, thinking how naive and lacking in subtlety they had been. Yet, for all the evidence of the march of technical progress, of perfectibility, there were occasional reminders that mankind had not yet tamed Nature – let alone himself. In January 1910 Paris was stricken with the worst floods in 150 years. Waters of the Seine came up to the famous Zouave's beard on the Pont de l'Alma, the standard flood measurement, and floating debris threatened to carry away the older bridges. Photographs of the time show a sailor sculling along Boulevard Haussmann towards Gare

Saint-Lazare. By 28 January, not a single pavement could be seen in the Île de la Cité, while the Île Saint-Louis was totally submerged. Bursting its banks, the Seine filled the courtyard of the Ecole des Beaux-Arts, and was five metres deep in the Quai d'Orsay station. Inhabitants near the Zoo were fearful that crocodiles would swim out of their pools and devour them. Sewers burst, looters appeared on the scene and 50,000 inhabitants fled their homes.

Even so, the prevailing mood – in Paris and nationally – was one of contentment. The Republic, writes André Maurois, 'was still Athenian'. It had 'no reason to be envious of Louis XIV's France, or of the France of the Renaissance; never had the country had greater renown or a more justifiable prestige ...' A nostalgia for *les neiges d'antan* would be summed up in 1913 with the appearance of the first instalment of Proust's monumental *À la recherche du temps perdu*. Yet, if ever there was a sign of the fragility, and hubris, inherent in human endeavours the previous year, 1912, was the year that the unsinkable *Titanic* sank. And in Europe there was the rumble, though seemingly distant, of wars in the Balkans.

As Europe hastened like lemmings towards a cliff, there is the sense of the inevitability of the forthcoming contest as when children pick sides at school. On the western side, most of the picking of teams had taken place in Paris. First, and perhaps most dangerous of all, in 1894 the Foreign Minister Théophile Delcassé – ever mindful of the loss of Alsace, and of how France had so foolishly gone to war in 1870 without a friend – had pioneered the 'defensive' Franco-Russian pact. From then till 1914 had grown the increasing popularity of all things Russian, from Diaghilev to Stravinsky. Germany, alarmed at potential enemies combining to west and east, lined up Austria, Bulgaria and later Turkey. Then, in 1903, the francophile Edward VII came over to charm a city still instinctively anti-England; the following year the *entente cordiale*, unnatural though it may have seemed to many a Frenchman and to many an Englishman, was signed. When fun-loving Edward died, Paris was draped in black, and cab-drivers tied crêpe bows on their whips. But on the international scene, to borrow the sombre words of Philip Guedalla,

> A dark resentment replaced the milder flavour of the old diplomatic rivalries, and a new bitterness was born of German inability to win a war with civilized restraint. But the great palace was still standing at Versailles; and in the Galerie des Glaces the mirrors waited on.

In 1905, and again in 1911, the Kaiser blundered into Morocco, stretching nerves in the Chancelleries of Europe and providing grist to the mill of Paris's Hun-eating nationalist press. In the Sorbonne, German experts like Charles Andler and Romain Rolland, striving for peace with kindred spirits across the Rhine, were progressively outgunned by the *Echo de Paris*, where Maurice Barrès damned Andler as a 'humanitarian anarchist', ready to 'betray' Alsace-Lorraine. One of Europe's best hopes of peace, the Socialist leader Jean Jaurès, son of a road-mender from the Tarn, bitterly opposed France's pact with a reactionary, feudal and unstable Russia, but hoped to defeat jingoism with an accord between French and German Socialists never to make war on each other. He firmly believed that, in the unspeakable event of war, German Socialists would tear up the railway lines rather than allow their brothers to go to war.

Events defeated him. Agadir, 1911, was the last straw, and the *joie de vivre* of the Belle Epoque gave way to deep distrust of Germany and her intentions. Three days before the outbreak of war, Jaurès himself was shot down in a café by a deranged young zealot, Raoul Villain. Even Proust began to deploy the label of the 'ugly German'. Among Parisians, there was a sudden last-minute attachment to the army, fanned by the jingoist press. In 1912, the restoration of military service to three years was greeted with remarkably good humour. In Paris – as opposed to the calmer provinces – war fever mounted, to the point where, after Agadir, even some sensible writers began to feel that war was not only thinkable, but perhaps actually desirable, in preference to the continuing tension – like a thunderstorm clearing away oppressively sultry weather. Declared Abel Bonnard, in *Figaro*, 'War refashions everything anew ... We must embrace it in all its savage poetry.' Even Apollinaire could write, apocalyptically, 'You are weary of this old world at last.'

17

The Great War

Is Paris ready to withstand a siege?

Adolphe Messimy, Minister of War, August 1914

AUGUST 1914

On 3 August 1914, Paris found herself at war again – in what men of that time, happily unable to see what lay ahead, would optimistically call the Great War, the War to End All Wars. Historians of the next generation would recognize it merely as the First World War, though their successors in future might well, imbued with all the powers of hindsight, come to see it more realistically as simply the first act in a second Thirty Years War.

The war would sweep away the age of prosperity and hope that all Europe had begun to enjoy, including backward Russia. Europe was about to enter a new Dark Age of unknowable duration, and for the next four years it was as if violence and destruction had become the sole arbiters in the world, with human leaders – so powerful and optimistic at the turn of the century – rendered impotent in the face of historical forces greater than anything they could have foreseen. On both sides there were many – and not just among the Kaiser's entourage in Berlin, or the sword-rattling revanchists of Paul Déroulède in Paris – who greeted the outbreak of war almost with relief, such had been the stresses and strains leading up to it in recent years.

Paul Claudel, Catholic mystic, diplomat and playwright, currently French consul in enemy Hamburg, was one of many young Europeans who saw war bringing adventure, even a kind of freedom: 'Freedom from one's job, from one's wife, from one's children, from a fixed place; adventure.' When Austria set the machine in motion by declaring war on Serbia, Louis Gillet, a brilliant young art historian, formerly a pacifist but now a lieutenant in an infantry regiment, saw an adventure of high altruism where it was 'beautiful to fight with pure hands and an innocent heart, to give one's life for divine justice'. To his mentor Romain Rolland, who had dedicated himself in vain to an understanding with Germany, he wrote, 'what an awakening ... Today we witness France's resurrection. Always the same: victory over Otho at Bouvines, Crusades, Cathedrals, Revolution, always we're the world's knights, God's paladins.' Within a matter of weeks half his battalion would be dead or wounded.

André Gide hastened back to Paris by the last available civilian train (as it went by he heard a railwayman shout, 'All aboard for Berlin! And what fun we'll have there!'), but, not being subject to conscription, three days into the war he anticipated adventure of a higher level: 'The wonderful behaviour of the government, of everyone, and of all France ... leaves room for every hope. One foresees the beginning of a new era: the United States of Europe bound by a treaty limiting their armaments.' Naturally, as to all Frenchmen now, the *sine qua non* of such a rosy future had to be the return of Alsace-Lorraine. Marcel Proust, however, right to the end, refused to believe in the prospect of war; it would be simply 'too frightful', he thought. He was much more concerned with finding a publisher for his very long novel, *À la recherche du temps perdu*. His chronic asthma disqualified him from military service. Instead he daydreamed of male bordels – having found himself pleasurably in one which he had mistaken for an air-raid shelter.

Outside Paris, in the provinces, reactions to the coming of war were distinctly more sombre. Yet even in brainwashed Paris there was little repetition of the wild, clamouring cries of 'A Berlin!' in that July of forty-four years previously. On 28 July 1914, the British Ambassador Lord Bertie recorded in his diary, 'There is much nervous excitement, but no popular demonstrations for war ...' Parisians, he noted, hoped that Britain would be the 'deciding factor' in keeping Germany out of the war. He told the Foreign Secretary Sir Edward Grey that if Britain should 'declare herself *solidaire* with France and Russia there will be no war'. Grey and the Asquith government – 'a house divided against itself, and they change their attitude day by day' in the opinion of Bertie – dithered. In execution of the Schlieffen Plan, Germany marched into and through Belgium, and on 4 August war became general. 'It will be a savage war,' Bertie noted prophetically from the Faubourg Saint-Honoré. Two days later, he recorded that Paris was rather 'like London would be on a Sunday in August. Very many shops are closed *pour cause de mobilisation.'*

Parisians, including many artists, were swift to join the colours. Braque and Derain rejoined their regiments and fought bravely at the front. Matisse came back to Paris from the south and did everything he could to enlist – but, at forty-five, was declared too old and was sent home. Raoul Dufy went to drive a van for the army postal service; Jean Cocteau, though classified unfit, became an ambulance driver for the Red Cross. Apollinaire, despite his Polish-Italian extraction, grateful for all that his adopted France had done for him, enlisted at thirty-four and, in the earliest days of the war, received a severe head wound from which he never properly recovered. Lieutenant Charles Péguy, aged forty-one, died in the very first days of the Marne, leading his company across an exposed beetroot field, to become almost beatified by his generation of artists. The twenty-eight-year-old Henri Alain-Fournier, whom peace had only allowed time to write his one great, mystical novel *Le Grand Meaulnes,* also fell in the early months of the war. Referring chiefly to the *gratin* and the privileged of Paris, Apollinaire complained that 'nearly everybody is running away'. Rodin and Debussy left for the provinces (but they were over-age anyway); Picasso, who was of course Spanish, drove his friends into Avignon station to join their regiments, and claimed, 'I never saw them again.' Romain Rolland remained in Switzerland, to continue to fight for peace; staying on in Paris, Marie Curie offered her medals to be melted down, and bought war bonds with her Nobel Prize money.

One of the few to try to dodge conscription was Gide's young publisher friend who had turned down Proust, Gaston Gallimard, who feigned illness until it induced real sickness and he was declared unfit for service. But in general few young Frenchmen stayed at home as *embusqués* (shirkers); the vast majority, with sober determination and a welling up of patriotism, joined the colours. Overnight the Gare de l'Est became the busiest and most crowded place in Paris, with a steady flow of soldiers marching towards it singing:

> C'est l'Alsace et la Lorraine . . .
> C'est l'Alsace qu'il nous faut!

Behind them rumbled batteries of the much vaunted *soixante-quinze,* with their long and narrow barrels the pride of the French army which was going to smash the enemy to the east. There were also many detachments of foreign volunteers marching under banners with such slogans as 'Greeks who love France', 'Romania rallies to the Mother of the Latin Races', 'Italy whose freedom was bought with French blood' and 'British volunteers for France'.

Among those to rush to the colours at the earliest possible moment were many members of the Dreyfus family, which had suffered so much at the hands of the army. Alfred's son Pierre fought in the first battles of 1914 as a corporal and ended the war a captain. The disgraced and rehabilitated Alfred himself, still in the army though aged fifty-five, repeatedly requested to be sent to the front and was finally permitted to take part as a gunner in the disastrous Nivelle Offensive of 1917.

Suddenly Paris was a deserted city. The streets were empty; there were no buses, only a few trams with women conductors. Theatres and cinemas were closed; cafés shut promptly at 8 p.m., restaurants at 9.30. At the Louvre, as in 1870, art treasures were crated up; iron shutters came down on many a shop. One merchant chalked up on his closed shop, 'Sleep peacefully, your mattress-maker is at the front!' Other shops promised to reopen in September – when it would all be over. On 20 August, Lord Bertie made a trip out to the Bois, which he found 'all so quiet and peaceful, and I thought of all the horrors going on in Belgium.' At night the beauty of *la ville lumière* was muted by the black-out, with Proust lamenting the quiet capital under the 'unchanged antique splendour of a moon cruelly, mysteriously serene, which poured the useless beauty of its light on monuments that were still intact'. Under moonlight, the Champs-Elysées, flooded with a blue-green sheen, seemed to some 'like a hallowed wood', while the silvery Seine took on a strange beauty all of its own. The night-time Paris defences were tested by sporadic raids of German planes (ironically called *Tauben* – or Doves), where Blériot had shown the way only five years previously. The *Tauben*, and later the weightier Zeppelins, would cause only pinpricks of damage and few casualties, but – as with Teutonic 'frightfulness' and terror weapons in earlier wars, as well as a later one – all the raids on Paris did was to stiffen resolve and make the war more terrible and more prolonged. How far it all seemed from the carefree days of the Belle Epoque!

Older Parisians, or those with a sense of history, who could recall the diet of rats in 1870, laid in extensive stocks of food. Everywhere in the city small workshops manufacturing weapons began to spring up, as they had in 1870. Meanwhile, at the beginning of August the painter

Maurice Vlaminck took a tram out to Porte Maillot on the western outskirts of the city, where he found that the Governor of Paris:

> had taken strong measures to defend the capital. A dozen or so big trees had been cut down and were laid across the Avenue de Neuilly with a view to stopping German cavalry; palisades and iron spikes set in timber were erected in the streets. As I looked at this improvised defence system I didn't know whether to laugh or cry.

But would the Kaiser's grey-clad hordes really arrive to besiege Paris again? What were their intentions? And what were the plans of the French General Staff?

MILITARY DISASTER

As the spectre of German militarism had grown more menacing from the Agadir Crisis of 1911 onwards, the damage caused in the French army by *l'affaire* and Emile Combes had been repaired with almost miraculous speed. Raymond Poincaré a staunch revanchist from Lorraine who would never allow himself to forget his childhood memories of *Pickelhauben* occupying his homeland, had been elected president, and the country was wholeheartedly behind him. When the Union Sacrée coalition was formed to prosecute the war, all politicians, even the left-wing pacifists, backed it in a display of loyalty and unity that had not been seen in France since Napoleon I (nor was it to be seen again in the Third, Fourth or even Fifth Republics). In 1914, the Chief of the Sûreté could remark confidently, 'The workers will not rise; they will follow the regimental bands.'

Morale had never been higher. The proportion of defectors on mobilization, previously expected to reach 13 per cent, in fact turned out to be less than 1.5 per cent, but an exaggerated notion pervaded the army of 1914 that the *furia francese*, the *élan vital* of the revolutionary and Napoleonic armies, would somehow suffice to repel and defeat the attacking Germans. 'You talk to us of heavy artillery. Thank God, we have none. The strength of the French army is in the lightness of its guns,' the General Staff told the Deputies in 1909. Thus, by August 1914, the whole French army possessed only 300 heavy guns, the Germans

3,500. The French were not overimpressed by the new, deadly machine gun either. In 1910, General Foch, then Commandant of the Staff College, was among those who had reckoned on a short, brutal conflict that would be over in weeks. Meanwhile, to ensure that the enemy should see them and be intimidated by their onrushing numbers, the infantry went to war in the blue *képis* and surcoats and red trousers of the nineteenth century, despising the Germans for changing to the less romantic, more practical, *Feldgrau*.

Under General Joseph Joffre, France's portly Commander-in-Chief, the French forces were committed to Plan XVII. This prescribed that, on the outbreak of war, four out of five armies, totalling 800,000 men, would surge forward – predictably – towards the lost territories, their objective the Rhine. Well informed of all this, the Germans wedded themselves to their Schlieffen Plan. Swinging down through neutral Belgium (the *casus belli* for Britain entering the war on France's side), the Germans planned a vast right hook which would sweep around behind Paris, and then pin the French armies that were attacking eastwards up against the Swiss frontier. Under Schlieffen's blueprint (drawn up some years before the war) Germany intended to knock France out in one mighty blow, before the Russian 'steamroller' could start rolling. Speed was essential, and there would be no room for any mistakes. Her plan was likened to a revolving door, and under their own Plan XVII the French army would add momentum to the door's rotation – thereby doing exactly what Schlieffen wanted. Fortunately for France, unfortunately for Germany, Schlieffen's successor, Moltke – nephew of the man who had crushed France in 1870, but possessing none of his military genius – tampered with the masterplan, weakening the impact of both the crucial right wing and the covering force facing the Russians.

As the grey-clad regiments advanced energetically through little Belgium and into France, aware of their strength and confident in the superiority of their race, young Frenchmen lusting for revenge were marching up at a rapid staccato pace. They ripped up the frontier posts in Alsace and sent them to be laid upon the grave of Déroulède. Then the enemy was located. The trumpeters sounded the call that sent a thrill more heady than wine through French veins:

> Y a la goutte à boire là-haut!
> Y a la goutte à boire!

All along the frontier the infantrymen in their red trousers, carrying heavy packs and long, unwieldy bayonets, broke into the double behind

their white-gloved officers. Many sang the Marseillaise. In the August
heat, the heavily encumbered French attacked in some sections from a
distance of nearly a kilometre from the enemy. Never had machine-
gunners had such a target. The French stubble-fields became transformed into gay carpets of red and blue. Splendid cuirassiers in glittering
breastplates from the age of Murat hurled their horses hopelessly at the
machine guns that were slaughtering the infantry. It was horrible, and
horribly predictable.

PARIS THREATENED – AGAIN

Throughout August it looked as if the Schlieffen Plan was going to work.
For days – due partly to stringent censorship, partly to *la bavure*
(administrative cock-up) and partly to the speed of the German advance,
Parisians were kept alarmingly in the dark about exactly where the
advancing Germans were, especially as the official bulletins kept reporting great French victories in the east. But when they started mentioning
the Somme Parisians began seriously to worry. Then came the tragic
cartloads of desperate refugees, anxiously interrogated by Parisians
about their provenance, each day arriving from villages that much closer
to the capital. Where were the German armies heading? As in 1870, it
had to be assumed – Paris.

Suddenly German outriders were popping up to capture the racing
stables at Chantilly, just forty kilometres north-east of Paris; one cavalry
detachment claimed it could see the Eiffel Tower. Railway stations to
the west and south were flooded with Parisians wanting to get out
before the enemy arrived. Those who stayed thronged to pray solemnly
at the shrine to Sainte Geneviève, entreating her to save Paris from the
new Huns, just as she had from their precursors under Attila. Something
akin to panic began to grip government offices in the city; according to
Adolphe Messimy, the Minister of War, it 'painted a livid mask of fear'
on the face of ministers. General Hirschauer, in charge of the city's
defence works, told him flatly that they were not ready to be manned.
The old 1870 fortifications were in a state of decay, and little had been
done to reactivate them since war began. On 13 August, Messimy called
in Hirschauer and told him to 'expect the German armies to be before

the walls of Paris in twelve days'. He added, 'Is Paris ready to withstand a siege?' Hirschauer responded with a clear 'No.' Worse still, two reserve divisions earmarked for the city's defence were now switched by Joffre to another threatened part of the front. Messimy rushed to the Elysée to see Poincaré and demand that the Military Governor of Paris – a role filled by the flaccid General Trochu back in 1870 – be replaced by a General Joseph Galliéni. Poincaré acceded.

It was an extraordinary, eleventh-hour appointment, prompted by despair, but out of it were to spring the most dramatic – and potentially doom-laden – hours in the whole history of Paris, and ultimately the nation's most decisive victory of 1914–18.

Galliéni was to prove an inspired, if unlikely, choice as the hero who was to save Paris – and France. He was aged sixty-five, retired from active service and already afflicted by the prostate cancer which would kill him two years later. As a twenty-one-year-old second lieutenant just out of Saint-Cyr, he had been captured at Sedan in 1870. An intellectual who studied contemporary military history (much against the trend of the time), he was an elegant, autocratic figure who carried himself like an officer on parade, tall and spare with pince-nez (like Dreyfus) and a bushy grey moustache. To Messimy on the night of his appointment he insisted that Paris could not be defended from within, as it had been in 1870: 'What do you give me to defend this immense place enclosing the heart and brain of France? A few territorial divisions and one fine division from Africa. That is nothing but a drop in the ocean.' Instead there would have to be a covering army of three active corps; otherwise he would not accept the post. Messimy thanked him effusively, shook Galliéni's hand several times, 'even kissing me', recalled Galliéni, and promised that he would do his best.

For the best part of two crucial weeks, however, Galliéni was left Commander of the Armies of Paris without an army. Meanwhile, the Germans were approaching ever closer, and, better informed than the general public, Galliéni and his staff learned with apprehension of the fate of the supposedly impregnable forts that protected the Belgian city of Liège. The German infantry having been repulsed several times with severe losses, General von Ludendorff now brought up a secret weapon, the immense 420mm Big Bertha mortars, developed in secret by Krupp over the previous four years and named after the formidable Krupp heiress – the heaviest siege guns yet deployed. At a range of eleven kilometres they projected a shell weighing over a tonne, with a delayed-action fuse enabling it to explode after penetration of a fort, however heavily protected it might be by thick concrete. Seeing one of the fat black monsters approach, pulled by thirty-six horses, a Belgian deputy for Liège described it as 'a piece of artillery so colossal that we could not believe our eyes ... It was the Belial of cannons.' Other Belgians thought they looked like 'overfed slugs'; but by 16 August all the 'impregnable' forts defending Belgium's biggest city had been reduced to rubble.

What havoc would these monster cannon wreak on *la ville lumière*! There were justifiable fears that whole quarters of the city would be pulverized by the gigantic shells.* The possibility of Paris falling, or being reduced to eating rats again – or being demolished – was urgently debated. There was no question of it being declared an open city. When, on 30 August, President Poincaré asked Galliéni how long Paris could hold out for, the cold answer came: 'Paris cannot hold out and you should make ready to leave as soon as possible.' Ministers, declared Galliéni, were 'no longer safe in the capital'. Already there was the danger of Uhlans penetrating and cutting the city off from the south. This time, it was argued, France was fighting as part of an alliance and it was the government's duty to remain in contact with the Allies, as well as with the rest of France. One new Socialist Minister, Jules Guesde, hotly attacked the bourgeois implications of the government leaving Paris, evoking recollections of the Commune of 1871:

> You want to open the gates to the enemy so Paris won't be pillaged.
> But on the day the Germans march through our streets there will
> be shots fired from every window in the working-class quarters. And
> then I will tell you what will happen: Paris will be burned!

That same evening – as if to underline matters – German *Tauben* struck at the Quai de Valmy, killing two people, then dropping leaflets to tell Parisians, 'There is nothing you can do but surrender', and warning them that the German army was at their gates, as it had been in 1870.

On 1 September, the eve of the anniversary of Sedan, the outlook for France appeared about as hopeless as it had in 1870. The next day, Galliéni sought out his new command, the Sixth Army. As he drove north to make contact with it, it became apparent how desperately late in the day it was when he passed refugees converging on Paris in flight

---

*In August 1944, as Paris was about to fall to the Allies, Hitler – determined to destroy Paris totally – ordered up an even bigger cannon, the giant 600mm Karl, firing a two-and-a-half-tonne shell, which had shattered the defences of Sebastopol earlier in the war. Fortunately, it did not arrive on the scene in time.

from oncoming Germans, their faces reflecting terror and despair. At Pontoise, just outside Paris to the north-west, where Monet and Renoir had once painted and where now the 61st and 62nd Divisions promised him by Joffre were coming in, all was in disorder, the troops bloody and tired. Inside the city, the Prefect of Police on whom he would have to depend for maintaining order had been in office only an hour. His predecessor had refused to stay behind, resigning 'for reasons of health'. Like most Parisians in the know, the American Ambassador Myron Herrick saw the 'terrible onslaught' of the Germans as being 'almost beyond resistance'. He himself had received a warning from the Germans that 'whole quarters' of Paris might be destroyed, and that he should leave the city. Determined to stay on, however, he promised Poincaré that he would protect the museums of Paris under the American flag (the US was then still neutral) as being 'in the custody of humanity at large'. He had his own courageous plan to save Paris from destruction: 'if the Germans reached the outskirts of the city, and demanded its surrender, [he would] go out and talk with their army commander, and, if possible, the Kaiser'.

That night the government left by train for Bordeaux, in the dark and in almost furtive secrecy. Galliéni took leave of the sacked Messimy's successor as Minister of War, the Socialist Etienne-Alexandre Millerand. He found him in an empty room, the contents of which had already been shipped off. The atmosphere was 'lugubrious'. Millerand's orders to Galliéni were to defend Paris *à outrance*. 'Do you understand, Monsieur le Ministre, the significance of the words *à outrance?*' asked Galliéni. He explained, 'They mean destruction, ruins, dynamiting bridges in the centre of the city.'

Millerand repeated, '*À outrance.*' It must have been a valediction of extraordinary poignancy, Galliéni recording that he felt 'pretty well persuaded, myself, that I was remaining to be killed'.

The next morning he issued a stand-and-die proclamation to Parisians:

ARMY OF PARIS, CITIZENS OF PARIS,
The members of the Government of the Republic have left Paris to give a new impetus to the national defence.
    I have received a mandate to defend Paris against the invader.
    This mandate I shall carry out to the end.
Paris, September 3, 1914
    Military Governor of Paris, Commander of the Army of Paris

Parisian reaction to the departure of the government was predictable. A parody of the Marseillaise made the rounds:

>   Aux gares, citoyens!
>   Montez dans les wagons!

Galliéni's commanders prepared orders to blow eighty bridges in the region, including those of Paris.

MIRACLE OF THE MARNE

Meanwhile, however, the 'miracle' so devoutly prayed for from Paris's protectress, Sainte Geneviève, had begun to take place. French Intelligence had received a satchel taken off the body of a German cavalry officer attached to General von Kluck's First Army. In it was a blood-stained map showing the lines of advance of that army swinging south-eastwards, and therefore away from the capital. Joffre and Galliéni immediately realized the significance of the move: as Kluck's army was on the right flank of the whole massive German wheeling movement it meant that the enveloping sweep was no longer going to take in Paris, but was to swing to the east in its endeavour to trap the French against the Swiss frontier. In its wider significance, it also in effect denoted the collapse of the whole German strategy, initiated by Moltke's pusillanimous tampering with the masterplan. In the east, unexpectedly, the Russians had been able to mount a powerful offensive which had taken most of East Prussia before Hindenburg and Ludendorff, Germany's most successful team in the war, had been able to smash it at Tannenberg. In the meantime, and in alarm at the Russian success, a timorous Moltke had despatched from the vital right flank in France forces essential to Kluck. This loss, plus troops already removed to reinforce the centre in France, meant that Kluck simply had insufficient men to carry out the great wheel west of Paris, while at the same time keeping in step with General von Bülow's Second Army on his left.

At their hastily created army headquarters in a girls' school just across from the Invalides, Galliéni's staff officers moved pins on the map and realized that here was an opportunity such as occurs in few generals' lifetimes. 'They offer us their flank! They offer us their flank!'

they exclaimed. Explaining the situation to Joffre, Galliéni pressed the elephantine Commander-in-Chief into turning the whole of his cumbersome great army around and launching an immediate combined offensive. Galliéni himself would unleash General Maunoury's only recently constituted Sixth Army into a forceful attack out of Paris, into Kluck's exposed flank. The omens were hardly good. The Sixth Army units had only just arrived, exhausted, after long forced marches. The whole of the seven armies under Joffre's command – including General French's small but heroic British Expeditionary Force – was also tired out after a month of retreats, dispiriting defeats and heavy casualties. On the other hand, Galliéni could note with satisfaction that the populace of Paris (those that hadn't already fled) were displaying 'calm and resolution'. The German army was exhausted; in the coming battle many German prisoners were actually taken asleep, unable to move another step. As of that first week of September, only the scent of victory, the shimmering vision of Paris in the near distance, kept them moving – as it had Napoleon's Grande Armée of a century earlier; and, seeing the state of fatigue of his own men, Kluck fatally convinced himself that the beaten enemy was in no condition to stage a come-back, or to turn itself about.

But 4 and 5 September were two more of the darkest days for the alliance. Up to this point Joffre had been prepared to sacrifice Paris, in marked contrast to Galliéni who remained convinced that the capital had to be defended – *à outrance*. In the previous ten days alone, France had lost the important cities of Lille, Valenciennes, Arras, Amiens, Cambrai, Laon and Soissons, as well as Rheims – where all the kings of France from Clovis to Louis XIV had been crowned – abandoned as an open city on 3 September. Kluck was already across the Seine south-east of Paris, and was still advancing. From his army's behaviour in neutral Belgium, it seemed quite clear to the French that the Kaiser would not spare Paris any more than Bismarck had. In London Allied leaders met to sign a pact binding each other not to make a separate peace. It was a measure of desperation and alarm. In Paris General Maunoury asked Galliéni, 'In case we should be overwhelmed, our line of retreat will be . . . ?' 'Nowhere,' was Galliéni's reply. To all his subordinate commanders he issued highly secret orders to list all resources in each district that had to be destroyed rather than fall into enemy hands. Even bridges in the heart of the city, like the sacred Pont Neuf, were to be blown up. A 'void' had to be left in front of the enemy – comparable to what Napoleon had found in Moscow in 1812 – in case the Germans should break through, he instructed General Hirschauer. The modern imagination quails before such a prospect, though it was one which, just thirty years later, the German commander in Paris in August 1944, General von Choltitz, would come close to facing.

That afternoon, after a passionate appeal to General French to turn the retreating British forces about, Joffre from his makeshift general headquarters near the battle-front issued the order that would ring down through history: 'We are going to fight on the Marne.' With his extraordinary capacity for calm (that rather unFrench characteristic) which was Joffre's signal contribution to victory, he then sat back to await results. On the 6th the great Allied counter-offensive began. The first blow came from Paris, with 60,000 men of General Maunoury's forces who had barely detrained rushed to the front. It was the famous 'Taxis of the Marne' that won the battle. Six hundred of the little red Renault taxis, so familiar to tourists, plied back and forth to the Ourcq battlefield only sixty kilometres distant. Each carrying five soldiers, they made the round-trip twice in the day, rushing up the reinforcements crucial to Maunoury's attack.

The immediate, tactical effect of this attack was to force Kluck to swing his flank westwards to meet the threat. As a result, a critical gap fifty kilometres wide opened up between his left and Bülow's Second Army. Into this gap marched French's battered army and the French Fifth Army. To their right, in command of a newly formed Ninth Army, the fiery General Foch, whose irrepressible passion for *l'attaque, toujours l'attaque* had proved an expensive liability in the lost Battle of the Frontiers, now came into his own with his famous order: 'Mon centre cède, ma droite recule, situation excellente. J'attaque!' But it was Galliéni and Paris that remain the true heroes of the Marne – Galliéni, the man whose *aperçu* turned defeat into a sparkling victory. After three days of battle, on 9 September Bülow ordered his army to fall back over the Marne. Two days later the retreat became general.

Sadly, exhaustion and the slowness of the attacking Allies prevented them from pressing their advantage to roll up the whole enemy front. For the next four grim years the front congealed into a line of static trench warfare reaching from the Channel to the Swiss frontier. But the 'Miracle of the Marne' provided a battered France with an immeasurable psychological victory. Germany had in fact lost the war, though it would take another four – or thirty – years to persuade her of this. But at what a cost for France: in the two weeks that the terrible Battle of the Frontiers lasted, she had lost over 300,000 men killed, wounded or missing, including 4,778 officers – representing no less than one-tenth of her total officer strength; while by the end of the first five months of the war in killed alone the French army had lost 300,000 men (or nearly a fifth more than Britain's total dead in the whole of the Second World War). France had also lost nearly 12 per cent of all her territory, comprising 16.3 per cent of her manufacturing capacity, 20.4 per cent of the wheat crop and 49.48 per cent of sugar-beet production, while nearly 900,000 hungry and destitute refugees had taken to the roads. Alsace-Lorraine remained firmly in enemy hands.

Nevertheless, Paris was saved. The government returned. Life slowly came back to a semblance of normality. The theatres reopened, though only for 'serious productions'; light entertainment still seemed somehow inappropriate to the now sombre mood of the country. Absinthe remained banned. As the country digested the disasters of August 1914 and then the Miracle of the Marne, and settled down to the dreadful battles of attrition of 1915, a feeling almost of smugness pervaded Paris. With details (not all of them substantiated) of German atrocities flooding in from Belgium and the occupied territories, there was a growing sense that 'France equalled Civilization, Germany, Barbarism.'

THE FRONT AND THE REAR

On 14 February 1916, Lord Bertie recorded, 'A big German attack is expected between Verdun and Rheims . . . The French are very confident. "Let them come," they say of the Germans, "So much the better. Let them all come."' This misplaced display of confidence heralded the beginning of the cruellest year of the war. Caught horribly unprepared at Verdun, France would suffer over 400,000 casualties; the Germans, attacking along a front only twenty-five kilometres in width, were to lose almost as many. In the ten months that it lasted, the Battle of Verdun was to gain grim repute as the worst battle in history. One more German miscalculation of enormous proportions, it would end in one of the most glorious victories in all France's history; yet its terrible cost would show her the way to defeat a generation later. Nineteen-sixteen was also, for Britain, the year of the Somme, the year when her new armies came of age in that dreadful blood-letting, on whose first day alone 60,000 young Britons and Empire troops would fall. The hero of the Marne, Galliéni, would retire and die; Joffre would be sacked – and so would his German opposite number, the chilly Falkenhayn, who had intended to 'bleed France white' at Verdun. Russia would launch her last offensive before succumbing to revolution. In Paris, Picasso's *Demoiselles d'Avignon* would be displayed for the first time; and the strange, nihilist new vogue called Dadaism would have its debut, perhaps marking the beginning of the end of one of the most fertile eras for the arts in the entire history of Paris.

By 1916 conditions of life behind the French lines stood roughly midway between those prevailing in Germany and those in Britain – which had still not mobilized her war effort to the same extent as France. While Germany was suffering privation under the Royal Navy's blockade, the French civilian population experienced few commodity shortages (the exception, of course, was in the occupied north-east). Coal was scarcest of all, some 40 per cent of French production having been lost after the German invasion of the Lille region, and Paris came to dread the onset of winter. But, despite the agricultural losses, food rationing never became a serious issue. In 1914, the making of croissants was forbidden, only to be allowed again five months later. In the autumn of 1915 the government took powers to requisition all cereal products at fixed prices, and the following year sugar, milk and eggs were brought within these provisions, but little use was made of them. As in the United States after Pearl Harbor, the authorities ordered a meatless day each week, though it was hardly enforced. Meanwhile, food-loving citizens might complain, but they exploited the black market so efficiently that throughout 1916 the food scarcity barely infringed on them. Not until 1917, when the U-boat campaign had reached its peak, was a Ministry of Food set up in Paris. Straight away it instructed butchers to close their shops for two days each week, banned bakers from selling fancy cakes, and at last with great reluctance started to distribute ration cards.

On the rare occasions when he was granted leave, the *permission-naire* from the slaughter at Verdun was inclined to head for Paris. Though it was only 250 kilometres away, visiting the capital was like crossing into another country, and to many a front-line *poilu** it seemed that Paris knew nothing whatever about the war. Indeed the official censor, nicknamed 'Anastasie', ensured that the truth about Verdun was

---

* *Poilus* (literally, the hairy ones) were the equivalent of the British 'Tommy' and the US 'doughboy', the private soldiers of the respective armies.

as far as possible kept out of the newspapers. The inherent liveliness of
Paris, always hard to subdue, had begun to break free from the constraints of the first part of the war so that, by mid-1916, it showed to a
battered world a façade of astonishing brilliance. To the weary *permis-
sionnaires* from Verdun it represented an invigorating exoticism. Rather
as London was to do in the 1940s, Paris seemed to have assembled every
uniform and race loyal to the Allied cause, with Moroccans, Senegalese,
Annamites and Malgaches mingling on the Champs-Elysées with cavalry
officers, Foreign Legionnaires, Highlanders, nurses and American flyers
from the volunteer Lafayette Squadron. The Opéra and the theatres had
reopened after the Marne. Crowds converged on the Folies Bergère to
see Mistinguett; Sarah Bernhardt, though now old and fading, devoted
her spare time from the theatre to her hospital for the wounded at the
Odéon; at the Opéra Comique *Manon* was playing, and in May, just
when the German army was unleashing its furious assault at Verdun,
the film *Salammbô* was given a glamorous première. But France's military predicament had not been forgotten. Patriotism surfaced in one
theatrical production after another: at the end of a show celebrating the
birth of Molière, Marthe Chenal came on wrapped in a *tricolore* to give
an ardent performance of the Marseillaise; and in the music halls most
nights the new favourites brought over by the British, 'Tipperary' and
'Roses of Picardy', and, of course, the now universally treasured 'Quand
Madelon', the 'Lili Marlene' of France in the Great War, were sung with
gusto.

In 1914 the art schools had a neglected air. The models had gone to
work in the munitions factories, and instead of students there were
elderly bourgeois looking for something to distract them. The ranks of
the creative arts were rapidly depleted, as we have seen. Yet somehow
the galleries of Paris were reopened and trading briskly, and publishers
had never sold so many books.

Those on leave from the trenches of Verdun regarded their country's
lively capital with mixed feelings. For Captain Delvert, a company
commander, the crowds of elegant women walking in the Bois de
Boulogne with their escorts reminded him sourly 'of a national holiday
or Longchamp Races ... It appears that the nation is suffering and that
all energies are being strained towards the goal of ultimate victory;
however this effort does not diminish the number of promenaders.'
It was with feelings of relief that Delvert returned to his regiment at
Verdun. In Henri Barbusse's great war novel, *Le Feu,* published that year,
1916, one of the characters comments bitterly while on leave, 'We are

divided into two foreign countries. The front, over there, where there is too much misery, and the rear, here, where there is too much contentment.'

For all the bravado of Paris, the war was inevitably giving rise to distortions and corruptions that by 1916 were rankling increasingly with the men at the front. There were the *embusqués*, who had continued to evade the war and the call-up, and the profiteers, who had already made large fortunes (and were speedily enriching the restaurateurs and the jewellers – as Captain Delvert noted). Even the meanest worker in a war factory was being paid a hundred sous a day, against the *poilu*'s five. As a result, inflation was accelerating; at the start of 1916, the cost-of-living index had hit 120 (July 1914 = 100), and by the end of the year it would be 135. The black market thrived, and occasionally the authorities had to beg citizens to stop hoarding gold. Expensive mistakes had been made at the outset of the war: agricultural production had been hampered by the number of peasants conscripted, and before long some had had to be sent back to the fields; the giant Renault motor works was shut down, apart from a small shop making stretchers (motor vehicles apparently being regarded as a luxury). But the economy somehow kept going, under what was mockingly called *système D*, a derivation from the verb *se débrouiller*, meaning 'to muddle through'. Less innocent than the disruptions caused by *système D* were the scandals such as that which came to light in 1916 of Hospital 27, where a dishonest doctor had been selling fake discharges from the army for several thousand francs each. The offenders escaped with trifling sentences, and it was widely believed that Deputies and even ministers had instituted a cover-up.

Despite her terrible losses and her suffering, France – like Germany – demonstrated an extraordinary solidarity. Giving powerful impetus to this solidarity was the Union Sacrée by which men of all political hues buried their differences in the interests of national unity. So the anti-militarist and crypto-anarchist Anatole France first tried to enlist, aged seventy, and then resumed his seat among the Conservatives of the Académie which he had abandoned shortly after the Dreyfus Affair; and the fiercely anti-clerical Clemenceau was seen to kiss an *abbé* on both cheeks.

Another great source of solidarity was the women of France. War had brought them, particularly the *Parisiennes*, an emancipation. When hostilities began they had hastened to become nurses, to take over the administrative tasks left by the men, and to work in the munitions factories. No doubt to start with, the women were attracted by the glamour of the nurse's uniform and by a desire for adventure; later, as those who had not lost a husband, lover or brother became fewer and fewer, their motives became more evidently selfless. Most of them had become *marraines* (or godmothers) to one or more soldiers, supplying them with everything from cheering letters to food parcels and woollies – and even with the highest service a woman can offer a man. It was no wonder that, as a source of inspiration, 'Quand Madelon' had almost replaced the Marseillaise.

MUTINY, CLEMENCEAU AND KRUPP

The winter of 1916–17 in Paris was, in the words of contemporaries, *un rude hiver* – bitterly cold. Luxuries and even some foodstuffs were in short supply. Propagandists made much of the 'glorious victory' at Verdun, where Fort Douaumont had finally been retaken in December, marking the end of the ten-month battle. The Germans had indeed been stopped, the only significant strategic defeat inflicted on them since the Miracle of the Marne, but at an almost suicidal cost. Even 'Anastasie' could not entirely conceal from Parisians the full extent of the casualties, unspeakable in themselves since caused almost entirely by the never-ending heavy artillery barrages. Too many *poilus* from Verdun had spent their *permissions* in Paris to keep it quiet. A serious malaise afflicted those in the know about the state of morale in the army. But here now was a brave new general, Nivelle, to replace the exhausted 'Papa' Joffre, and to introduce a new 'formula', heralding a new offensive. And, as the year wore on, most exhilarating for Parisian morale in the streets were the first contingents of American troops, who would surely win the war for the battered Allies, taking the place of the heroic 'Nijinskys' as, in the east, a broken Russia sued for peace. The advent of new money, as well as new soldiers, provoked fresh sparkle as in the cabarets nude women danced and posed on the stage for the Allies.

Alas, Nivelle's new formula led only to new disasters. Too much talked about in advance, it permitted Hindenburg and Ludendorff to dig in and prepare for it. On 16 April, the French infantry – exhilarated by all they had been promised – left their trenches on the Chemin des Dames with an *élan* unsurpassed in all their glorious history. By the following day, they had suffered something like 120,000 casualties. The Medical Services, seldom brilliant (in one hospital there were reported to be only four thermometers for 3,500 beds), were completely overwhelmed. In the rear areas, some 200 wounded assaulted a hospital train. Nivelle persisted with his offensive – but he had broken the French army. Men on leave waved red flags and sang revolutionary songs, imported from Russia. They beat up military police and railwaymen, and uncoupled engines to prevent trains leaving for the front. Interceding officers, including at least one general, were set upon.

On 3 May full-scale mutiny broke out. The 21st Division – which, significantly, had gone through some of the worst fighting at Verdun the previous year – was ordered into battle, but, to a man, it refused. The ringleaders were weeded out, summarily shot or sent to Devil's Island. But unit after unit followed the 21st, some of them the finest in the French army, and over 20,000 men deserted outright. Perhaps the most astonishing feature of the mutiny, however, was that no inkling of it was picked up by German Intelligence until order had been completely restored by the new chief, General Philippe Pétain, the Hero of Verdun. Indeed, almost to the end of the twentieth century, details remained veiled in secrecy. How many brave men were shot summarily can only be guessed, though accounts occasionally surfaced of whole units marched out to quiet sectors of the front and then deliberately shelled by their own artillery. Along with these draconian measures, Pétain – nicknamed 'le Médecin de l'Armée' – introduced relatively minor improvements in the French army which had been common to the British forces for most of the war.

In Paris throughout this grim period there abounded rumours that had previously been submerged of profiteering, conspiracy and treason, espionage and defeatism. Political leaders like Joseph Caillaux were contemplating a compromise peace; while more sinister were the activities of the out-and-out defeatists, ranged around the *Bonnet Rouge* newspaper and headed by Malvy, a former Minister of the Interior, and of the downright traitors who earned millions of francs from German sources for their work of demoralization. It was not until well into 1917 that the reckoning came: Malvy was sentenced to five years' banishment, the glamorous spy Mata Hari (possibly innocent, certainly insignificant) shot. Censors fought hard to suppress songs expressing disenchantment, pacifist sentiments, and socialist and revolutionary appeals. Meanwhile the *poilus'* war-weariness began to infect Parisian workers. For many of the more privileged denizens of Paris, however, life still continued much as before. Dining at the Ritz with other members of his coterie including Jean Cocteau, Proust watched the first great air-raid on Paris by heavy Gotha bombers. As the warning sirens sounded from the Eiffel Tower, Cocteau chirped, 'Someone's trod on the Eiffel Tower's toe, it's complaining.'

Politically, however, the situation in Paris was dire. The miraculous Union Sacrée collapsed, as the Socialists withdrew their support. There was one hope left: Clemenceau. The stormy petrel of French politics for over forty years, already a grown man and Mayor of Montmartre during the Siege and the Commune, leader of the Radicals, and now an old man of seventy-six, Clemenceau was in himself a kind of one-man committee of public safety. From now on the war would be waged relentlessly and ruthlessly: truly *à outrance*. In the inimitable words of Winston Churchill, 'The last desperate stroke had to be played. France had resolved to unbar the cage and let her tiger loose upon all foes, beyond the trenches or in her midst.' With the arrival of the old Tiger, assisted by Pétain and a redeemed Foch, and backed by the US Expeditionary Force commander General Pershing and his doughboys, everything began to change.

It was as well for France and the Alliance that there was a Clemenceau waiting in the wings at this juncture in history: 1918 was to see the most dangerous period of the war since 1914. German forces liberated from the east by the collapse of Russia enabled Ludendorff in March 1918 to launch a massive offensive aimed directly at Paris. Astutely Ludendorff struck at the hinge of the French and British armies, tearing a great hole in the British front through which his troops poured to the very gates of Amiens, and to Château Thierry, a hundred kilometres from Paris. Once again Paris lived under threat.

Then, on 24 March 1918, Lord Bertie recorded a new venture in Teutonic frightfulness. Explosions suddenly occurred in the middle of Paris, without warning and with no aircraft in the sky. Soon they were reckoned to be caused by shells from a super-long-range gun, firing from inside the German lines over 110 kilometres away. Once again, the genius of Herr Krupp had contributed a new hazard to civilization. The first shell landed in the east end, on the Quai de la Seine in the 19th arrondissement. Thereafter they followed at intervals of about half an hour. One shell landed on the Gare de l'Est, killing eight people and injuring another thirteen. 'Such a lovely day,' added Lord Bertie.

Like the relatively feeble Prussian cannon of 1870, the Paris Gun was a weapon of sheer terror, unjustified by any urge for retaliation. Clearly the Germans hoped that, coupled with the Ludendorff offensive, the continued bombardment would break the French will to resist. A masterpiece of German technical engineering, the Paris Gun was some thirty-five metres long and weighed 138 tonnes, but accuracy was extremely limited: although, wickedly, the gun was aimed at the Louvre, not a single shot hit this huge target. Even so, on Good Friday, 29 March, a shell struck the Church of Saint-Gervais during Mass. Seventy-five were killed outright and ninety injured, and many more died later. Ambassador Bertie noted that day, 'People are getting away from Paris as fast as there is train room for them.' Altogether Herr Krupp's little toy killed 256 Parisians, and wounded another 620. It would not affect the course of the war, but would certainly harden the peace terms. When the Armistice came, no trace was ever found of the great cannon, though even today pockmarks from the shell can be seen in the austere perpendicular columns of Saint-Gervais, which houses a small commemorative chapel to one of the First World War's least excusable atrocities.

Suddenly, and at long last, the fortunes of war swung round. By July the offensive power of Ludendorff's exhausted armies ran out of steam. With a regenerated Foch declaring 'Tout le monde à la bataille', and supported by fresh American troops, the Allied counter-strokes pushed forward all along the line. On 8 August, Haig's British army inflicted what Ludendorff admitted was 'the black day of the German army'. By early autumn the German line had been rolled back, out of France, out of the territory the Germans had held for the past four years – some of it for nearly fifty years.

ARMISTICE

At 11 a.m. on 11 November, all the guns ceased firing. The contrast in mood between the front and the rear in Paris spoke for all the differences that had progressively grown between the two disconnected worlds. 'Silent thankfulness' was how a correspondent of *The Times* described the prevailing sentiment among soldiers up on the line. Further back, 'amongst the troops in rest there is more jubilation'. But in Paris carnival reigned. The day had begun cold, misty and gloomy; then the bells started to toll, the celebratory cannon to fire, and with them the dancing

– and the crying. As the sun came out, Paris was gripped in a mad whirl of festivity. Civilians and soldiers of all nationalities poured out on to the Concorde, embracing each other, and singing 'Madelon! Madelon! Madelon!', 'Tipperary', 'Home, Sweet Home' and a new song recently imported from America, 'Over There'. There were rapturous demonstrations in front of the statue to the city of Strasbourg, still draped in black crêpe, and captured German guns were hauled up the Rue de Rivoli. But some of the densest crowds congregated around the Chamber of Deputies where Clemenceau was expected to speak. There, as the cannon continued to fire outside, the Tiger with the white walrus moustache, architect of victory, rose trembling and declaimed, 'Let us pay homage to our great dead, who have given us this victory!' The crowds grew and grew as peasants poured in from the countryside. In a display of inter-Allied amity that would barely see out the signing of the Peace Treaty, an American doughboy, a British Tommy and a French *poilu* were carried down the *grands boulevards* on the shoulders of the crowd. As the sunset produced a golden glow, Paris 'went charmingly off its head', recorded a *Times* correspondent. The climax came that evening as Marthe Chenal of the Opéra Comique, clad in a robe of red, white and blue and a black Alsatian cap, sang the Marseillaise to a wildly jubilant crowd from the steps of the Opéra.

But not everyone was cheering. Women, so many women, were dressed in deep mourning. Proust was lamenting the death of male lovers embodied in the person of 'Saint-Loup'; Jean Cocteau the death of his Jean Le Roy; while his friend and colleague Guillaume Apollinaire, who had never entirely recovered from his head wound in 1914, had died of 'flu just two days before the Armistice. Through the happy throngs rattled the hearses, spectres at the feast, bearing away victims of the worst epidemic of 'flu in history. Only in October victims in Paris had been dying at a rate of 350 a day; in the last week of October alone there had been 2,566 such deaths in Paris. Across the globe the deaths from 'flu were to total some forty million – or twice the number of war casualties. When the celebrants of Armistice Day in Paris paused to consider the costs in the grey light of the following day, they counted 1.4 million Frenchmen killed in action, the largest proportion of any of the combatant nations. Adding the civilian and 'flu deaths, France had lost 7 per cent of her population.

The carnival fever of Armistice Day was all too swiftly followed by a certain disillusion. For a long time, *la ville lumière* remained even darker than London. After all the wartime restrictions, the authorities were slow to get things going again. By the end of November Paris continued to look, and feel, as if she were still at war. Ration cards remained in force, restaurants and cafés closed early; homes and hotels were freezing from the continuing shortage of fuel. On to this scene there began to arrive VIPs and delegates for the forthcoming Peace Conference. There was King George V, and a swarm of American plenipotentiaries. The Hôtel Crillon was found to be too small for their 1,300-strong delegation, so Maxim's round the corner in the Rue Royale was annexed to it. Herbert Hoover, the food tsar who was still not yet forty-five, took over a whole block in the Avenue Montaigne; an unsmiling man, all the time he was in Paris he never once visited the theatre and rarely accepted an invitation to dinner. Acidly Jules Cambon, who had been nominated as one of France's five delegates to the conference and was dislodged from the commandeered Crillon, complained to his brother Paul, the Ambassador to London, that the foreigners were going 'to turn Paris into a bawdy-house'.

In sharp contrast to these visiting grandees came a sombre reminder of the suffering of the past four years in the shape of the returning prisoners-of-war, described by a French reporter as 'in the majority, no longer men but shadows clothed in torn rags, and so thin!' Their main receiving centre was in the Grand Palais of Exposition renown, which had been requisitioned as a hospital since 1914. The sight of these tattered and broken reminders of the war created in Paris a fresh rage for maximum reparations and indemnities from the defeated Germans.

It was perhaps hardly surprising that the post-Armistice Day cry in Paris was 'Plus jamais ça!'

18

The Phoney Peace

Paris is a bitch and ... one should not become infatuated with bitches, particularly when they have wit, imagination, experience and tradition behind their ruthlessness.

Robert McAlmon

PEACE-MAKING

'My work is finished,' observed an exhausted but triumphant Marshal Foch to Clemenceau on Armistice Day 1918; '... your work is beginning'. It was the understatement of the epoch; the work of drawing up a reasonable peace treaty with the crushed Germans would defeat all those involved in it, not least the old Tiger. Following the convergence on Paris of the swarms of diplomats and officialdom from all twenty-seven Allied countries, the serious work of drafting the treaty began in January 1919 – pointedly, with a meeting in the French Foreign Minister's private office in the Quai d'Orsay; pointedly because from beginning to end it was the French who would endeavour to direct and manipulate the negotiations. 'I never wanted to hold the Conference in his bloody capital,' Lloyd George complained later of his wartime ally, and – albeit in the gentler language of the campus – Woodrow Wilson would come to share roughly the same opinion. Lloyd George and Wilson's powerful adviser Colonel House would have preferred to stage the vital conference in a neutral city, such as Geneva, 'but the old man wept and protested so much that we gave way'. And, anyway, where else? After all it was France which had suffered most from the war, and had the greatest call for punishment of the enemy.

Passers-by gaped as Arabs in 'picturesque costume', Indian rajahs in

British khaki 'but with flowing native turbans', Japanese and Chinese, 'looking wise and saying nothing', all debouched on to the Concorde. But as the talks dragged on from week to week, month to month, Parisians' goodwill towards their former allies understandably evaporated. The new invaders were seen to commandeer scarce food and accommodation, and the best women. One French officer was soon telling Haig's liaison officer General Spears that 'he could not wait for the British and the Americans to get out of Paris so it could be a French city again'. On the other hand, Spears recorded US General Tasker Howard Bliss as grumbling that British policy seemed to be 'to bolster up for ever the decadent races [that is, the French] against the most efficient race in Europe [the Germans]'. Doubtless the outspoken General would not have kept such robust views to himself. Young Harold Nicolson, on the British Foreign Office team, 'gathered a vivid impression of the growing hatred of the French for the Americans. The latter have without doubt annoyed the Parisians ...' The US authorities, according to Nicolson, were finding it prudent to import their own military police: 'There have been some rough incidents.' As delegates would spend their weekends on tourist trips to the lunar landscape of the Somme battlefields, a bitter new song, 'Qui a gagné la guerre?', began to make the rounds.

The discouragingly swift turnaround in Pariso-American relations was not entirely surprising when one recalls how the most prominent figure of the moment was that of Thomas Woodrow Wilson, the name most inextricably bound up with the Treaty of Versailles, and consequently with its disastrous failure. The ascetic, unworldly Princeton professor from a stern Presbyterian background, who (France felt) never really understood the French (or maybe he understood them too well?), was indeed curiously out of sync with *la ville lumière*. His tendency to lecture from the height of a college podium was not well received by either of his peers, Clemenceau and Lloyd George, who both had a view that their nations too had been involved in a war to make the world safe for democracy. When it came to imposing the sweeping aphorisms of his 'Fourteen Points', Wilson was swiftly made to realize that it was rather easier to impart than to apply instruction. He was certainly no Talleyrand, nor was there any thought of inviting the Germans, as the Congress of Vienna had invited the defeated French, to attend the peace conference before the terms had been drawn up. His arrival in Paris on the morning of 14 December 1918, had been the greatest triumphal progress anyone had ever made there. The alarmingly dense crowds had pushed out into the street the files of troops lining the route taken by him and Clemenceau, so that at various points the presidential carriage could force its way through only with great difficulty.

The inequalities which war had imposed upon the peace-makers were apparent both within and without the Quai d'Orsay as winter slithered into spring. France had the biggest army in the world, but no money; the US had the money, but no accessible military force; Britain was somewhere in between, but increasingly anxious to withdraw back across the Channel again as soon as possible. While Germany was quite intact, the shattered skeletons of broken towns across the northern countryside of France glared reproachfully at the peace delegates. As they sojourned in Paris, leading the good life, the 1.4 million French dead breathed icily down the backs of their necks. Regular visits conveyed them to the ruins of Saint-Eustache, to be reminded of the outrage of that Good Friday of less than a year before. Paris and the Parisians would simply not allow their foreign guests to forget what France had suffered and lost. She had to have security, lasting security: frontiers in the ethnically German Rhineland, such as Louis le Grand had sought two and a half centuries previously, and Napoleon after him. The chant of 'Que l'Allemagne paye . . .' was constantly in the background.

By April 1919 none of the delegates meeting at the Quai d'Orsay were happy men. For all France's desperate pursuit of security at any price, Clemenceau – the man of '71 – had failed to gain for her a permanent frontier on the Rhine (instead he got a fifteen-year tenancy, which Adolf Hitler would promptly terminate) or annexation of the coal-rich Saar (though, throughout its entire history, the German-speaking Saar had been French for only twenty-three years). The Parisian press, as rabid as it had been in the run-up to war, launched savage and unrelenting personal attacks on Wilson and Lloyd George. As the wrangling dragged on, and the Allies went on demobilizing, it began to look as if soon the war would have to be fought again. Clemenceau stepped up the pressure to produce a treaty, any treaty. Whatever happened, it had to be signed and sealed by the Germans before the triumphal parade planned for the *quatorze juillet.*

Finally, and at the last minute, it was ready. The scene shifted from the Quai d'Orsay to Versailles. Why Versailles? Clemenceau, with his bitter recollections as mayor of Montmartre in 1871, claimed to believe that – if the Germans were to appear in force in Paris – there would be riot and revolution. Moreover, all the administrative machinery of the Allied Supreme War Council had been out there since the war years.

But, of far greater historical significance, was the pleasing congruence of making the enemy sign at the scene of his erstwhile great triumph, and France's appalling humiliation of that January of forty-eight winters previously. On 28 April the German delegation set off from Berlin to receive the terms that were to be imposed on them, headed by Count von Brockdorff-Rantzau from the Foreign Office. As their train reached the battlefields of northern France, the French *cheminots* – determined that the Germans should have the clearest view of the devastation the war had caused and be fully apprised of the hatred which awaited them – slowed it down to fifteen kilometres an hour. With icy correctness, a French colonel conducted them to the Hôtel des Reservoirs, selected because, in 1871, it was where the dejected French peace commission had resided while suing for peace with Bismarck.

On the evening of 7 May, when they read the terms set out in the 200-page document, with its 440 separate articles and 75,000 words, the Germans were rendered speechless. It was far worse than anything they had dreamed possible; the reparations alone would ruin their country, while most of her coalmines, Germany's principal underlying wealth, had been distributed among the Poles and the French. For the first time they began to speak of a *Diktat*: no German government could possibly accept it. Reactions among some of the Allied delegates echoed their sentiments. Young William C. Bullitt, who would return as US ambassador, resigned from the American delegation; in his note of resignation he declared forthrightly that he was 'going to lie on the sands of the Riviera and watch the world go to hell'. In Berlin, the Scheidemann government resigned. Foch ordered the remobilization of the French army, and fighting threatened to break out anew. In the joyous spring weather Paris was beset with depression, resignations and nervous breakdowns. Then the Germans, under their new Chancellor, Gustav Bauer, crumbled, as the Allies poised to march on Berlin.

On 28 June, a Saturday, the great hall in the Palace of Versailles was ready for the occasion it had been awaiting, like a sleeping princess, since Bismarck's triumphant Prussians had desecrated it by daring to crown an enemy emperor there. At the centre of the Galerie des Glaces, a horseshoe table had been set up for the plenipotentiaries; in front of it, 'like a guillotine', a small table for the signatures. In a 'harshly penetrating' voice, Clemenceau called out, 'Faîtes entrer les Allemands!' Once more the huge mirrors had Germans reflected in them; this time, in place of the triumphant princes and grandees of Prussia, they were two very ordinary little men in frock coats, Dr Müller and Dr Bell, 'isolated and pitiful'. From outside there came a crash of guns, announcing to Paris that the Second Treaty of Versailles – as Clemenceau dubbed it – had been signed. 'La séance est levée,' rasped Clemenceau, not a word more or less.

Whatever pity might have been felt for those two German delegates that day, historians would reflect that, had Britain and France lost, their punishment would have been no less harsh; the Treaty of Brest-Litovsk imposed by Germany on a prostrate Russia demonstrated that. To tidy and unforgetting French minds, Versailles 1919 may have represented a full circle from 1871; but in fact history would soon prove it to be only a half-circle, with the remainder to come twenty-one summers later. Wrote Winston Churchill, 'Victory was to be bought so dear as to be almost indistinguishable from defeat.'

CELEBRATIONS

This was, however, not how Parisians saw it in the immediate aftermath of Versailles. On the eve of the 14 July procession, an estimated 100,000 took up positions along the Champs-Elysées, their tone one of restrained jubilation. A temporary cenotaph occupied most of the huge vault of the Arc de Triomphe, its four sides each guarded by a figure of Victory, their wings made from the fabric of warplanes. On its plinth was the inscription 'Aux Morts pour la Patrie'. Throughout the night soldiers of the French army kept vigil with rifles reversed. As the dawn broke, spectators fortunate enough to have a place on the balconies high up on buildings flanking the Champs-Elysées could see, down the green line of the Avenue de la Grande Armée and all the way along the eight kilometres of the processional route, the fluttering flags and pennants of the Allied nations from a dense forest of white masts. On either side of the Rond Point was piled a small hill of captured German guns, crowned on one side by the Gallic cock of 1914, preening himself for the fight, and on the other by the victorious cock of 1918, crowing to the world.

Soon, for the first time since Bismarck's Prussians had paraded through it, military figures appeared under the Arc de Triomphe (the cenotaph had been moved aside at midnight). They were three young soldiers, dreadfully maimed by war, and trundled by nurses in invalid carriages. They were followed by more *grands mutilés* of all ranks, almost all with an eye or a limb missing. At a hobbling pace the column moved down the Champs-Elysées to the stands specially reserved for them, a party of 150 young Alsatian girls raining flowers down upon them.

After a lengthy pause in the procession, 'as if to permit us to breathe – or to dry our tears', there came *la Gloire* itself: a squadron of the splendid Gardes Républicaines rode through the sacred arch, and just forty metres behind them appeared Joffre and Foch. Then it was the Allies' turn. First, in alphabetical order, the Americans led by General Pershing. Next came the Belgians, then the British with Sir Douglas Haig at their head, and all the rest marching on the carpet of blossoms that had been flung before them. But, understandably, it was the weighty French contingent bringing up the rear of the parade for which the spectators had reserved their greatest enthusiasm. His austere face paler than ever, the Commander-in-Chief Marshal Pétain rode on a white horse ahead of wave after wave of *poilus*. For over an hour the French contingent marched past. Finally, nine of France's new assault tanks roared through the Arc de Triomphe. As the silence returned and the gilded cenotaph was hauled back under the arch, one onlooker reflected that 'a sight like this will never be seen again. Because there will never again be a war.'

LEFT-WING DISSENT

Throughout the night of 14 July 1919, revellers danced in the streets of a brightly lit Paris, so that it seemed to *The Times* like 'one vast ballroom'. But Americans who took part in these celebrations noticed that many women were dancing together, a symptom of France's shattering losses of manpower. Parisians that night must have hoped that peace would somehow return them to *la vie douce* of the pre-1914 Belle Epoque. Yet there was a spectre at the feast, called Communism. On the very day of the signature of the Peace Treaty, a Communist-led Métro and bus strike had paralysed the city. The government was being tough with these left-wing demonstrators, but its toughness was only making matters worse.

Meanwhile, worrying rumours were emanating from Washington

that President Wilson might not be able to persuade the American Congress to ratify the Peace Treaty which was supposed to guarantee France, once and for all, against the German threat. Four months later the rumours became reality.

For Parisians, however, it was the political constellation of the far left – Communists, Internationalists and extreme Socialists – that was attracting the most attention. In none other of the victorious nations had Russia's October Revolution aroused more fervent sympathy than among the workers of Paris – the home of revolution itself. The foundation in March 1919 of the Third International in Moscow had prompted the spiritual heirs of the martyred Communards to fan the flames of revolt – for which there was already abundant fuel on the French economic and social scene.

The post-war economy was indeed in a sorry state. France had spent a quarter of her national fortune during the war, and although with her customary recuperative genius she rapidly rebuilt her devastated industries and restored her agricultural production, it was her financial structure that had been most lastingly damaged. France had paid for the war by issuing paper money. Inflation soared as a result. By the Armistice the franc had lost nearly two-thirds of its value, exchanging at 26 to the pound sterling, and as early as the Victory Parade it had depreciated to 51 to the pound. By May 1926 its value had plummeted to 178 to the pound, and finally, only two months later, with a threatening mob pounding on the gates of the Palais Bourbon, to 220. Urged on by the revolutionary left, French workers had good reason to demand better conditions and higher wages to offset this inflation. National finances were further worsened by the additional millions of francs needed to fund the pensions of the host of ex-servicemen.

The post-war Minister of Finance, Louis-Lucien Klotz (according to Clemenceau 'the only Jew who knows nothing about money'), made it clear that he expected France's budgetary deficits to be redeemed by German reparations. But in 1923 Germany defaulted on her payments. France (unsupported by England) occupied the Ruhr in order to enforce payment, but she was soon obliged to withdraw, a humiliating setback to French power. While Britain and America were already emerging from the world slump, France remained in depression. Between 1928 and 1934, her industrial production fell by 17 per cent; between 1929 and 1936, average income slipped 30 per cent; and by the end of 1935 more than 800,000 were unemployed. So the nation's financial crisis ran on into the 1930s, bringing down government after government, making it impossible to achieve a consistent foreign policy, quite apart from a policy of reconciliation with Germany.

EXPANSION AND EXPATRIATES

By the 'hollow years' of the 1930s two-thirds of France's population lived in the towns and cities; forty years before, the figure had been exactly the reverse, with two-thirds living on the land. The explanation for this dramatic swing lay partly in the appalling losses suffered among the sons of the peasantry in 1914–18, partly also in the universal drift to the cities. Paris remained, as always, the principal magnet. Yet, although the outer *banlieues* expanded, the population of central Paris actually decreased, from nearly 3 million just after the war to just over 2.7 million by 1939 – not much more than it had been at the turn of the century. This reflected the serious lack of acceptable accommodation: more than half of the poorer young Parisians lived in one room or in a kitchen-bedroom, most of which had no toilet and no heating. It was not till around 1940 that most Parisian buildings had running water and drainage connected to a central sewer. How many centuries it had taken since the first endeavours of Philippe Auguste! The trouble was that, because of inhibiting legislation and stuffy building regulations imposed by successive post-1919 governments, there was little profit in building. Few private investors could afford the cost of constructing apartment blocks. Gone were the days of Haussmann. Instead speculators put their money into commercial property – and that bubble burst with the Depression. By 1939 the rate of dwelling construction had sunk from 6,470 storeys per year in 1914 to 400, with well over three-quarters dating from pre-1914.

In 1919, with the arrival of peace, the city of Paris had a unique opportunity for expansion. The line of Thiers' old walls and bastions, thirty-five kilometres in all, and so useful in 1870, was now rendered obsolete by the development of heavy cannon and bombers. Instead there would be the Maginot Line protecting France's eastern frontier. So this 'zone', representing a substantial proportion of the existing area of Paris, was purchased from the military, freeing it for immediate development. Demolition and construction began at once. Opened to private speculation, some 38,750 new dwelling units were run up, many lasting only a brief period. One critic described the result as a 'dense wall of mediocrity encircling the city'. Fresh slums and what were later to become known as *bidonvilles* sprang up, and the zone was infested with corruption and poverty. Indeed, at the Porte de Clignancourt (site of today's Marché aux Puces) forty-seven houses had to be demolished in 1921 because of an outbreak of bubonic plague. It became a terrible monument to the recently ended Great War. Building in the zone was not completed till the 1930s – though at the Liberation of 1944 the Allies still found something of an unoccupied desert there. Upon it de Gaulle's Fifth Republic would build the notorious 'Boulevard Périphérique', thereby girdling the city with a new impenetrable wall.

For the reasons already suggested, after 1919 most new building shifted towards the public sector, with a marked slowing – particularly in the 1930s – in the building of luxury apartments, now stark and become simply 'machines for living' with little that was decorative. Instead cinemas started to proliferate. The style of architecture changed, with a brief flash of inventiveness with the arrival of Art Deco in the mid-1920s – almost exclusively for the worse. It was perhaps just as well that there was a depression, with money short; otherwise the Swiss architect Le Corbusier might well have been able to refashion Paris in his own image. Le Corbusier had plans to destroy much of the centre of Paris on the Right Bank, replacing it with a grid of shoebox towers over 200 metres high. Perhaps for once Parisians had reason to thank the tangle of municipal building regulations descended from Bonnier's 1902 prescriptions.

In practical terms, the one enduring (though visually questionable) success Modernism in Paris could claim was the great Trocadéro complex built for the World Exposition of 1937, although some contemporaries with long memories thought the structure little better than the pseudo-oriental mishmash left over from the last Expo, which it replaced. A man called Freyssinet wanted to construct on Mont Valérien a tower 700 metres high, up which you could drive a car; instead, here, on the site designated by Napoleon for his Palace of the King of Rome, uncompromisingly angular structures (of the sort Mussolini was building in Rome and Stalin in Moscow) were dominated by the Soviet and German pavilions. Symbolic of their times, there an aggressive Nazi eagle glared across at the new Soviet Adam and Eve, striding optimistically towards an unrealizable future. Like the regimes they represented, both pavilions would disappear – though the central feature linking them would survive to house the new Modern Art Museum and the Museum of Man.

Meanwhile, as dwelling space dwindled in the centre of Paris, so the pollution and noise from automobile traffic grew ever worse, as the number of cars rose from 150,000 in 1922 to 500,000 in 1938. One Parisian lamented, 'C'est fini! the tranquillity of our streets, and the calm of promenading either on foot or in a carriage ... Paris belongs to the machines.'

In the harsh 1920s there was, however, one important faction of Parisian society which found life wonderfully good and *bon marché*: the expatriates, and especially Americans. In 1921 foreign residents of Paris comprised 5.3 per cent of the population; ten years later the figure had almost doubled, to 9.2 per cent – while foreigners also accounted for a quarter of all those arrested by the police. Oscar Wilde's Mrs Allonby observes that when good Americans die they go to Paris; but after 1919 even not-so-good Americans took off in droves for Paris. For $80 they could secure a ship berth; otherwise they could work their way 'shovelling out' in the holds of cattle boats; and the modest allowance in dollars would maintain an American in Paris for an indefinite period. The impulse generated was partly negative, an escape from the restrictive, puritan world that Prohibition under the Volstead Act had imposed on young Americans returning from the war. In Paris, by contrast, one was left free to lead one's private life, to swim – or sink. Many Americans had sampled the delights of the city when serving as Pershing's doughboys during the war and wanted to come back for more.

Paris also drew, once again, those of artistic bent as she had done in the days of Whistler, Henry James and Edith Wharton. The list was an imposing one: Gertrude Stein was already there, well established in her lair at Rue de Fleurus near the Luxembourg; then there were John Dos Passos, e.e. cummings, Stephen Vincent Benét, Archibald MacLeish, Louis Bromfield, Philip Barry, Robert Benchley and Dorothy Parker – not to mention F. Scott Fitzgerald and Ernest Hemingway. There was Sylvia Beach, famed founder of Shakespeare and Co., the English bookshop and gathering point near the Odéon – and brave publisher of Joyce's *Ulysses* and the *Life and Loves* of Frank Harris. Among itinerants, there was Cole Porter, with his nine cigarette cases and sixteen dressing gowns at 13 Rue Monsieur, his fibs (lapped up by Hollywood) about his wartime deeds in the Foreign Legion, his long-suffering wife Linda, and his *faiblesse* for lusty black men. Then there was the magical, tragic dancer

Isadora Duncan, broke and gallantly declaring that she didn't know where her next bottle of champagne was coming from, later strangled when her scarf became caught in the wheels of a car.

By 1927, there were said to be 15,000 Americans resident in Paris, but the real figure was estimated to be much more like 40,000. For watering holes, they tended to gravitate around the Dôme and the Coupole in Montparnasse – and the enchanting Closerie des Lilas, which thoughtfully installed for them a *bar américain* (though Hemingway gave it the cold shoulder for a while after the new management ordered the waiters, mostly Great War heroes, to shave off their military moustaches and don white jackets). Meanwhile, *bals* became *dancings* – to the deep shock of *académiciens*, guardians of the language.

> In Montmartre
> In Montmartre, everybody is playing a part

wrote Douglas Byng. Did the expatriate writers and artists (American and others) find the fulfilment that Paris seemed to promise them? If we believe Hemingway, in his first blush of love for Paris – and for his young bride Hadley – he for one was extremely poor, but happy. At 74 Rue du Cardinal Lemoine (then the centre of the rough Apache district and poor students' quarters in the Contrescarpe area of the 6th arrondissement), they rented in 1922 a tiny flat on the fourth floor. It had no running water and a malodorous stand-up toilet on the landing; in winter it was so cold that tangerines left on the table would freeze overnight.

On Hemingway's first meeting with the redoubtable Gertrude Stein she told him he had to 'either buy clothes or buy pictures ... It's that simple.' In fact, the Hemingways had money for neither clothes nor pictures; Ernest could not even afford to buy the books he needed from Sylvia Beach's Shakespeare & Co., so he borrowed them instead. Often having to skip on meals, his large frame suffered agonies from the aromas wafting out from Montparnasse *bistrots*. (James Joyce, who completed *Ulysses* across the way, at number 71 – though no plaque distinguishes it – frequently shared Hemingway's hunger.) In romantic vein, Hemingway wrote: 'If you are lucky enough to have lived in Paris as a young man, then wherever you go for the rest of your life, it stays with you, for Paris is a moveable feast.'

George Orwell, seriously impoverished in Paris in 1928, living in squalor at 6 Rue du Pot de Fer just round the corner from Hemingway's Rue du Cardinal Lemoine, could never afford such romantic musings.

His lodgings were not all that superior to those of his friend Boris where 'a long S-shaped train of bugs marched slowly across the wall above the bed'. The seventeen-hour day as a *plongeur* in a classy hotel kitchen was degrading. Deprived of any kind of luxury he compared himself to the wretched rickshaw men and their miserable horses in the Far East.

One American who made no bones about disliking Paris and the Parisians was Scott Fitzgerald. According to Hemingway, 'Since almost the only French he met regularly were waiters whom he did not understand, taxi drivers, garage employees and landlords, he had many opportunities to insult and abuse them.' Fitzgerald took to the bottle to the extent of terminally ruining a superb talent, and he blamed Paris – though ultimately he would recognize that 'I spoiled this city for myself. I didn't realize it, but the days came along one after another, and then two years were gone, and everything was gone, and I was gone.' Given the deadly combination of loneliness and satiety of pleasure that the city offered, young Americans coming to embrace her in the 1920s would have done well to heed the warning of poet Robert McAlmon: 'Paris is a bitch and ... one should not become infatuated with bitches, particularly when they have wit, imagination, experience and tradition behind their ruthlessness.' As Harold Stearns, racing reporter for the *Chicago Tribune*, observed, 'Paris does not reproach the person bent on going to the devil – it shrugs its shoulders and lets him go.' Occasionally Paris sat up and noticed, as when, in 1927, young Charles Lindbergh arrived after his record-breaking solo flight: Paris went wild and mobbed him and his midge-like *Spirit of St Louis*. Yet less than three months later Parisians were out on the streets booing America and Americans following the execution of Sacco and Vanzetti, the two Italian Anarchist immigrants whose fate aroused passions recalling the days of Dreyfus.

Stein dubbed her countrymen the 'lost generation'. Then came the crash of '29, and like butterflies in a storm they all vanished. Many of the expatriates, indeed, had to join the glum queue at the American Embassy for emergency funds to return home. The party was over. At the bottom end of the scale of those who did remain in Paris were the *chiens écrasés*, the tragic failures or the crossed in love, the *amputés de coeur* fished out of the relentless Seine.

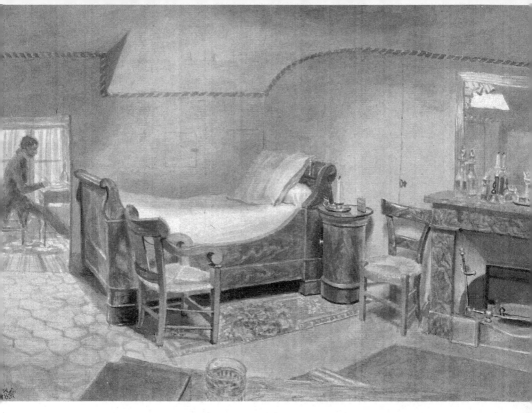

36. The *vie bohème*: an artist's attic, French school, c. 1830.

37. Burning Louis-Philippe's throne, 1848 Revolution.

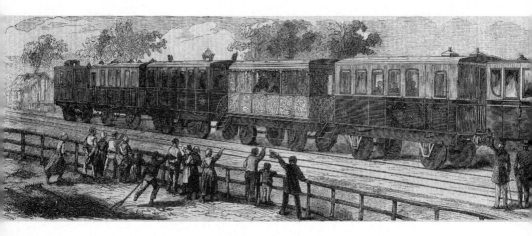

38. Napoleon III's new railway train, 1850s.

39. Communard barricade, Faubourg Saint-Antoine, March 1871.

40. (*opposite*) Gustave Eiffel at the top of his tower, 1889.

41. *Taxis of the Marne*, 1914, by André Hellé.

42. Allegory of the Armistice 1919, the Allies receive the defeated Germans, with Clemenceau, Lloyd George, Woodrow Wilson, and the diminutive Lawrence of Arabia by the side of Emir Feisal. Sketch by Augustus John, 1919.

43. Sarah Bernhardt,
as La Dame aux Camélias,
c. 1913.

44. Josephine Baker, and her
feathers, 1920s.

45. Edith Piaf, 1955.

46. Popular Front Demonstration, Mur des Fédérés, 1936. Photo by David Seymour.

47. Nazi occupation, Clichy, 1940; the German banner reads 'Wehrmacht Snack Bar'.

48. Liberation. In front of Notre-Dame, the crowd takes cover from enemy snipers, 26 August 1944.

49. The Generals' putsch, April 1961, Sherman tanks guarding the Assemblée.

50. *Les événements*, May 1968; a student HQ in the Sorbonne.
Photo by Guy le Querrec.

MUSIC AND SEX

The freedom that Paris offered in that heady false dawn of the 1920s held particularly true for black Americans. Many thousands had discovered Paris when serving as soldiers, and they relished the total lack of racial discrimination they found there: the bars and barriers that hemmed them in at home, stiff US army regulations forbidding fraternization with whites, magically fell away. For them Paris was instantly a land of opportunity, welcoming such famous artists as clarinettist Sidney Bechet and dancer Josephine Baker, who sailed for France with a party of two dozen other black musicians, singers and dancers in September 1925. Many black Americans stayed on and took root, notably the black exponents of *le jazz*. Parisians came in their droves to hear Bechet play 'Petite Fleur' at the Vieux Colombier. Paris was already jazz-mad. *Paris qui jazz* had been the title of a revue of 1920 at the Casino de Paris, a runaway success. There was 'A jazz band everywhere', in the words of a hit of that year. Every night at the Casino de Paris and the Folies Bergère was a sell-out, with Jean Cocteau describing a revue at the former as 'a kind of tamed catastrophe dancing on a hurricane of rhythms'.

In the upper-echelon music halls, Maurice Chevalier, the self-proclaimed ace French lover, epitomized the optimism of the jaunty, bright new era with his hit of 1921, his theme-song, 'Dans la vie faut pas s'en faire' (In life you mustn't worry), while for plebeian Paris Mistinguett, 'the little girl from Belleville' – still renowned for her legs, though in her fifties – brought the message of the humble *Parisienne* risen to golden success, of Paris recovered from the wounds of war. To the popular halls of the *faubourgs* a performer simply called Georgius (a.k.a. Georges Guibourg) and his troupe brought the same message of cocky revitalization. At both ends of the music-hall spectrum American song-and-dance, *le foxtrot*, was all the rage, and by 1926 one French columnist was reckoning that at most two out of ten songs performed were French.

It was on to this scene that the nineteen-year-old Josephine Baker, the lithe and sensual mulatto from St Louis, Missouri, exploded in 1925. Though so young, she was already well known on Broadway as a dancer with an ability to 'make her body do almost anything and to keep her eyes crossed at the same time'. At first, on arriving in Paris, she refused to dance bare-breasted; but when she did she created a sensation. On the stage of the small Théâtre des Champs-Elysées, where Nijinsky had once so stunned pre-war audiences by his abandoned dancing in *The Rites of Spring*, 'She made her entry entirely nude except for a pink flamingo feather between her limbs; she was being carried upside down and doing the splits on the shoulder of a black giant ... She was an unforgettable ebony statue.' After a moment's silence, the audience screamed. Here, recorded Janet Flanner, was 'a new model that to the French proved for the first time that black is beautiful ... she was the established new American star for Europe.'

What stunned the Parisian audience (apart from the few who judged her obscene) was her extraordinary energy. Every part of her body seemed to fly in a different direction. One critic was awed by 'her springing movements, a gushing stream of rhythm', while the more sophisticated had brought to mind Rousseau's apotheosis of the Noble Savage. The poet Anna de Noailles saw her as 'a pantheress with gold claws', a symbol of the most primitive sensuality. *Boulevardiers* became accustomed to seeing Josephine and her pet leopard Chiquita stalking, side by side, down the Champs-Elysées – two superb animals out of the same jungle – and they cheered her. Paris loved her style.

From the Théâtre des Champs-Elysées she moved up to the Folies Bergère, then at its peak of fame, where she electrified audiences by appearing out of the twilight, 'walking backwards on her hands and feet, arms and legs stiff, along the thick limb of a painted jungle tree and down the trunk, like a monkey. A white explorer was sleeping underneath ...' By the end of 1926 she had achieved a vogue unheard of for a foreign performer in Paris: 'There were Josephine Baker dolls, costumes, perfumes, pomades,' wrote Phyllis Rose (in *Jazz Cleopatra*); 'women's hair was slicked down like Josephine Baker, and to achieve this look, they could buy a product called "Bakerfix".' Coupled with Picasso's recent 'discovery' of African art, there was a sudden passion for everything black in Paris: 'black orchestras, black fêtes, black balls, exhibitions of black art'.

What truly stole Parisian hearts, however, was when Josephine took to song. The trilling tones come down the years, evoking that frenzied age of brief, elusive pleasure, that short period of illusion called Peace – the spirit of Paris in the 1920s and 1930s. Sung in a high-pitched warble, with an unashamedly Churchillian accent, her 'La Petite Tonkinoise' ('C'est moi qui suis sa petite ...') became the anthem by which everyone remembered the Paris of those years. But it was her nostalgic, highly emotive 'J'ai deux amours' ('mon pai-yee et Paree'), proclaiming her special bond with the city and sung a thousand times over, that seduced audiences and hard-boiled critics alike.

Josephine's love-life was as uninhibited and frenetic as her stage performances. She would dance over twelve hours a day, then make love all night; she had a legion of casual lovers, including the unstoppable writer and sexual braggart Georges Simenon. Her curiosity seemed boundless; reputedly she made love to the room-service waiter in the first Paris hotel she stayed at – to discover what French men were really like in bed. Of Parisian voyeurism she would remark scathingly, 'The white imagination sure is something when it comes to blacks!'

Apart from Josephine Baker, it was black American jazz that predominated in Paris in the 1920s. But there was one notable exception – the immortal George Gershwin. Visiting Paris for two months in 1928, like the typical young American tourist of the time, the thirty-year-old genius climbed the Eiffel Tower, visited Shakespeare & Co., played a duet with Stravinsky and heard *Rhapsody in Blue* massacred. Then, so taken by the traffic noises of Paris, he explored motor-accessory shops down the Avenue de la Grande Armée, squeezing all the bulb horns until settling on those suitable for the score that was running through his brain. The result, *An American in Paris*, one of his greatest compositions, spoke eloquently of the spark of vitality which his fellow countrymen had brought with them at the beginning of the decade.

With the return home of Gershwin, the crash of '29 and the decline in the 1930s in the popularity of Josephine Baker, the popular music of Paris tended to fall back more on its own resources. In jazz there was, for instance, 'Django' Reinhardt (born in Belgium of gypsy origins). But as the world outside grew more menacing, so Paris embraced a kind of schmaltzy nostalgia, looking inwards.

> Ah! qu'il était beau – mon village,
> Mon Paris, notre Paris
> On n'y parlait qu'un seul langage
> Ça suffisait pour être compris!

sang Lucien Boyer. There were songs of passionate love, fighting and death, the violence of the Apache, the wistful romanticism of Vincent Scotto's 'Sous les ponts de Paris'. There would be Charles Trenet, Jean Sablon – both of whom covered most of the century – and the short-lived, tragic 'little sparrow', Edith Piaf, with her fiercely sad lines. Then, as the Front Populaire became more self-confident, there would be increasingly militant songs about the class struggle. 'Tout va très bien, madame la marquise', with its mocking of the upper classes, made its mark everywhere.

The young composer Virgil Thomson summed up the motives for the American invasion of Paris in the 1920s in robustly down-to-earth terms: 'to get screwed, sharpen their wits and eat like kings for nothing'. In the first priority, Josephine Baker with her uninhibited, free-range sex life certainly set the pace. So too, as recorded in his *Tropic of Cancer* and other books, was the indefatigable Henry Miller. He put the allure of Paris in similar terms to Virgil Thomson:

> I understand then why it is that Paris attracts the tortured, the hallucinated, the great maniacs of love ... Here all boundaries fade away and the world reveals itself for the mad slaughter-house that it is ... An eternal city, Paris! ... The very navel of the world to which, like a blind and faltering idiot, one crawls back on hands and knees.

Operating an inventive triangular relationship with his wife June and that high-priestess of erotomania, Anaïs Nin, Henry Miller spent a great deal of his time in Paris on hands and knees, leaving virtually no fantasy or combination unexplored.

As has already been observed, Paris had a Sapphic subculture going back a good many years, at least as far as Pierre Louÿs' *Songs of Bilitis*. Early in the century Colette had thrown herself into the arms of the Marquise de Belboeuf. About the same time, a wealthy American, Natalie Barney, belonging to the pioneer generation of cultivated lesbian expatriates, had settled in Paris. According to Colette, Natalie boasted 'sea-blue eyes' and 'implacable teeth'. Her appetite for conquest, apparently, was extraordinary, far in excess of any straight male, even a Henry Miller or a Frank Harris. Keeping a neat little book of them all, she once recorded making eighteen rendezvous in a single night. Few of her female acquaintances, single or married, escaped those 'implacable teeth'. In and out they passed through the Greek temple at the bottom of Natalie's garden at 20 Rue Jacob, their path strewn with petals scattered by a small boy hidden out of sight, or she would test out neophytes at her favourite *pâtisserie*, Rumpelmayer's.

At the other end of the Sapphic spectrum was dumpy Gertrude Stein, rare among the expatriate lesbian patrons in being steadily monogamous to her faithful lover Alice B. Toklas. She told a sympathetic young Hemingway of her distaste for male homosexuals: 'they are disgusted with the act and are always changing partners and cannot be really happy'. In women, she declared, 'it is the opposite'. She was renowned for her strong views. Hemingway recalled that he could not remember her ever 'speaking so well of any writer who had not written favourably about her work', while her dislike of the author of *Ulysses* was such that 'if you brought up Joyce twice, you would not be invited back'. Fulcrum of the serious anglophone literary world in Paris, she vigorously bought works by the up-and-coming Picasso (he left a famous, much worked-over portrait of her), though Braque was to observe rather damningly that 'as an authority on the epoch it is safe to say she never went beyond the stage of tourist' and Matisse complained that she 'understood nothing about art'.

ESCAPIST ART AND LITERATURE

Escapism, of one form or another, was the name of the game throughout much of the 1920s and 1930s in Paris, of which sex – in its variety of contortions and distortions – was but one facet. Art was another. Born of the war, Dadaism was (fortunately) short-lived but was demonstrative of the move away from the happy realities of the Impressionists. In the late 1920s it was succeeded by Surrealism, the declared 'enemy of reason'. Pointedly it was spawned from a wartime hospital for shell-shocked *poilus* where the poets André Breton and Louis Aragon, both in their early twenties, had served as medical orderlies. Equally pointed, both founders of the new movement, which painters like Dali and Magritte were to take over, started life in the Communist Party. Surrealism stressed the priority of sexual freedom removed from religious constraints, and liberation of the unconscious. Symbolic, too, was the spectacle of Braque returning from the war with a turban of bandages covering his head wound. It was the horror of trenches which made many like them recoil from the traditional world that had taken the road to Verdun, embracing instead an idealist fantasy – just at the time, ironically, when Lenin and Stalin were perpetrating their worst excesses in southern Russia.

Geographically, too, the art scene had moved. From being the rural outpost that it had been pre-1914, Montmartre was now filled with apartment blocks, making it too expensive for struggling artists. Many, like Chagall (his work influenced by the bellowing of oxen in the nearby abattoir), moved back to form new ghettos in Montparnasse; only a Picasso, however, could afford to spend his honeymoon in the de luxe Hôtel Lutetia, on Boulevard Raspail. More the norm were artists like Brancusi and Soutine, working in the La Ruche (or 'beehive') studio complex in the 15th arrondissement. The studios were so narrow that tenants dubbed them coffins; they had neither heating nor running water. So great was the impoverished squalor in which Soutine worked that, when painting three stolen herrings, two rotted while he worked and a rat made off with the third.

In literature Dadaism and Surrealism were matched by the fairy-tale world of Cocteau and Giraudoux. Another form of escapism in the post-war era emphasized the humour of cuckoldry, a genre designed for the middle-aged male, known as *le démon de midi*, though there was compensation for their female opposite numbers in the form of bestsellers like Raymond Radiguet's brilliant novel *Le Diable au corps* (1923). But of much more profound significance for French literature in the late 1920s was the spate of anti-war literature that swept Europe. In Germany, Hitler had been swift to stifle such books as Remarque's *All Quiet on the Western Front*, but in France that particular novel had become a number-one bestseller, challenged only by the terrifying novel of Henri Barbusse, *Le Feu* (first published 1916, winning the Prix Goncourt, and selling 300,000 copies by the war's end). For France's Verdun generation, *Le Feu* provided an indelible reminder of what it had really been like, and for their juniors a nightmare fantasy the re-enactment of which had to be avoided at all costs. Wielding enormous intellectual influence were various anti-war associations formed by such giants of France's literary left wing as André Gide, Paul Eluard, Louis Aragon and Romain Rolland. Barbusse was the torch-bearer; when he died in 1935 more than 300,000 followed his coffin to Père Lachaise Cemetery.

Striking an altogether lighter note were the multitudinous novels about Inspector Maigret by Georges Simenon – 102 titles published between 1930 and 1972 – which succeeded so well in reflecting the humdrum life of the ordinary Parisian. Then there were the cheap romantic novels sold by the stack from newspaper vendors for between 25 centimes and 1 franc 75; and in a very special class of his own, Pagnol, with his tales of a Midi so very far from Parisian experience.

For all its philosophy of 'engagement', no form of literature set its face against reality more than the existentialism of young Jean-Paul

Sartre and his fellow hot-house inmates of the Café Flore in the later 1930s. In her autobiography, Sartre's mistress Simone de Beauvoir provides a frank account of the mind-set of French left-wing intellectuals. In the autumn of 1929 she felt she was living through a new Golden Age: 'Peace seemed finally assured; the expansion of the German Nazi party was a mere fringe phenomenon, without any serious significance ... It would not be long before colonialism folded up.' Of Hitler's coming to power in 1933, she writes: 'like everyone else on the French left, we watched these developments quite calmly'. In their film-going, this escapism, or detachment married to a dread of war, led Sartre and de Beauvoir to miss Jean Renoir's classic *La Grande Illusion* (1937) and to watch instead such American farces as *My Man Godfrey* and *Mr Deeds Goes to Town*.

Despite having given birth to the cinema, France got off to a slow start in the inter-war period. Of 430 films opening in Paris in 1934, less than a quarter were French and few survive. Spectacular exceptions were Abel Gance's eight-hour silent epic *Napoléon* of 1926 – which narrowly escaped the bin because of Gance's Pétainist sympathies in the Second World War – and Renoir's *La Grande Illusion*. If Gance's *tour de force* was possibly the most outstanding silent film ever made, *La Grande Illusion* comes close to being the greatest anti-war film. Its impact was such that, when the French prisoners-of-war sang the Marseillaise in one extraordinarily moving scene, Parisian audiences – regardless of political hue – also rose to their feet to sing.

THE RIGHT-WING LEAGUES

Soon after Hitler's occupation of the Rhineland in 1936, there were important elections in Paris. Jean-Paul Sartre for one refused to vote. 'The political aspirations of left-wing intellectuals made him shrug his shoulders,' Simone de Beauvoir explained. Yet, while regarding the French political scene with 'disengaged' aversion, de Beauvoir concedes at the same time that 'Sartre and I read every word' of the latest turn in what was known as the Stavisky scandal. This dichotomy characterized the attitudes of others far beyond the arid little circle of the Café Flore. The Third Republic was now shaken by a slew of corruption cases. First, in 1928, came the shocking arrest of Klotz, the former Minister of Finance whom Clemenceau had so despised, on charges of issuing dud cheques. The greatest outrage, however, was provoked by Serge Stavisky, the son of a Ukrainian Jewish dentist with extensive contacts among politicians, journalists and the judiciary. By 1933 his financial activities were being investigated, but a criminal case against him was postponed nineteen times. It so happened that the public prosecutor who was allowing Stavisky to remain free was the brother-in-law of the current Prime Minister, Camille Chautemps. All of a sudden Stavisky was found dead in a house in Chamonix where he had gone to ground with his mistress. Suicide was alleged, but he was popularly believed to have been shot by an eager *flic* – opportunely for Chautemps. Overnight Stavisky became the best-known name since Dreyfus – and once again there were ugly undertones of anti-Semitism.

On 27 January 1934, the Chautemps government fell, after an innings of just two months and four days. Over the previous eighteen months, there had been five different governments, but with virtually the same faces in each. From mid-1932 up to the outbreak of war in 1939 France's governments would total nineteen, including eleven different Premiers and eight Ministers of Finance. Just when the threat from Hitler's new Third Reich was reaching its peak, France lacked continuity in the direction of her affairs, her leaders regarded with increasing contempt by both ends of the political spectrum. A favourite insult hurled from Parisian taxis became 'Espèce de député!' The populace loathed the politicians, as did a progressively demoralized army; the politicians loathed each other. On 6 February 1934, passions overflowed in Paris – the start of something close to civil war in France. A group of right-wing, nationalist factions, which still clung to many of the illusions left over from the *quatorze juillet* of 1919 and were sickened by France's subsequent retreat from grandeur, united to march on the Chamber of Deputies.

Among the various right-wing 'leagues' were the Camelots du Roi, shocktroops of the monarchist, Catholic and anti-Semitic *Action Française* journal of Charles Maurras, which had spearheaded the campaign against Stavisky and his allies in the Radical Party. There were the violently anti-Communist Jeunesses Patriotes, who had taken on the role of Paul Déroulède's Ligue des Patriotes, set up to avenge the defeat of 1870; and there was Solidarité Française, funded by the perfumier François Coty, its members parading in a paramilitary uniform of black beret and blue shirt and chanting their slogan 'La France aux Français!'

The most articulate of the leagues was the Croix de Feu, founded in 1928 as an association of ex-soldiers decorated for bravery. Its leader, Colonel Casimir de la Rocque, had now dedicated himself to cleaning up the corrupt institutions of the Third Republic, and as a result the Croix de Feu acquired a political character, calling for 'Honesty' and 'Order' in public affairs. Although it was not strictly fascist (unlike some of the other leagues), it admired the efficiency and energy that Mussolini had instilled in Italian youth – and, as the scandals proliferated, it became more robustly anti-Republican.

Disgusted by the Stavisky scandal, de la Rocque combined with leaders of the other leagues to organize a march on the Assembly itself. On the morning of the 6th, *Action Française* appeared with inflammatory headlines: 'The thieves are barricading themselves in their cave. Against this abject regime, everyone in front of the Chamber of Deputies this evening.' That evening at about six o'clock the first shocktroops tried to break through police barriers erected on the Pont de la Concorde, throwing stones, bottles and lengths of lead piping; when mounted police charged them, they slashed the hocks of their horses with razors attached to walking-sticks. Inside the Chamber the new government, led by Edouard Daladier, was desperately manoeuvring to get a vote of confidence. By 7.30, the police were losing ground, and after three warnings had been given to the crowd they received the order to fire. Seven demonstrators were killed and many wounded. Though forced back as far as the Opéra, the crowd fought their way back on to the Concorde, whereupon the police opened fire a second time. It was midnight before the Deputies concluded that they were safe from a repetition of September 1870.

Of some 40,000 demonstrators, sixteen had been killed and more than 650 wounded; well over a thousand policemen had been injured. From his secret battle headquarters the following day Colonel de la Rocque declared, 'The Croix de Feu has surrounded the Chamber and forced the Deputies to flee.' This hardly accorded with the facts, but given the prevailing tensions it suddenly seemed – at least to the left – as if a new General Boulanger had emerged. Daladier now unexpectedly resigned. The former President Gaston Doumergue, aged seventy, took his place at the head of a national government and – to appease the *anciens combattants* of the right-wing leagues – the seventy-seven-year-old Marshal Pétain, Hero of Verdun, was appointed Minister of National Defence. It was the first time since 1871 that a Paris mob had brought about the collapse of a French government.

THE FRONT POPULAIRE

Shocked by the fall of Daladier, the entire left began to fear a right-wing *coup d'état* led by Colonel de la Rocque. On the morning of 9 February, the Communist *L'Humanité* summoned a mass meeting for that evening in the Place de la République, to demand the dissolution of both the Chamber and its opportunist allies, the right-wing leagues. That night two rival columns came towards each other near the République, one of Communists, the other of Jeunesses Socialistes, representing the two main left-wing parties, which had been at daggers drawn since falling out in 1920–1. At first a fight seemed inevitable. However, as the cry went up, 'We're not clashing, we're fraternizing ... we're all here to defend the Republic', the two groups mingled and shook hands, then marched onward together chanting 'Unity of action!' Three days later, the CGT trades union called a general strike in protest against the 'fascist peril', and, for the first time since it had broken away thirteen years before, the Communist CGTU collaborated fully. That day the new pact was sealed in blood when, among the old Communard strongholds of eastern Paris, three-cornered confrontations between strikers, right-wing troublemakers and the police led to four deaths.

These developments did nothing for national unity. After 6 February a right-wing *coup d'état* ceased to be a realistic possibility, while the left combined still more closely to put together a 'common front against fascism'. That July, the Socialist leader Léon Blum and the Communist Maurice Thorez signed a pact of unity, and by October *L'Humanité* was debating the advantages of a 'Front populaire contre le fascisme'. Meanwhile, France's economic plight was further enhancing the attractions of left-wing solidarity. On the *quatorze juillet* 1935, de la Rocque's Croix de Feu paraded smartly down the Champs-Elysées, but it was the left which got the upper hand. More than half a million Parisians gathered on the Bastille beneath giant red banners proclaiming 'Paix, Pain, Liberté!', and the Front Populaire was officially launched. Less than a year later, in May 1936, France went to the polls and the Front Populaire was swept into power. The Communists won seventy-two seats, having previously held only ten, but the Socialists, who gained another forty-nine seats, were the largest party, so it was Blum who formed a government. On

24 May some 400,000 Parisians congregated at the Mur des Fédérés to give thanks, amid cries of 'Vive le Front Populaire! Vive la Commune!' The left had achieved its greatest victory since 1871, but with Germany becoming ever more menacing, it was not at all clear what the new government should do.

For the workers of France the answer was increased pay, a forty-hour week with wages for forty-eight hours (or better) and holidays with pay. Otherwise they would strike. Three weeks after Blum's election, the Lavalette factory in north-west Paris and the Nieuport aircraft works at Issy in the south-west – building aeroplanes urgently needed by the French air force – were paralysed by strikes. These assumed a new form, *grèves sur le tas*, or sit-in strikes. The workers settled in, playing cards or *boules*, singing and dancing in an atmosphere reminiscent of the first heady days of the Commune. The whole of France was seized by this mood of mass escapism. Similar strikes paralysed the Farman aircraft works and the factories of Citroën, Renault, Gnome et Rhône, and Simca in the Paris area, almost all of them essential to the French armaments industry. By the beginning of June the number of strikers had reached 800,000 (eventually they were estimated to total two million), involving over 12,000 enterprises. Parisians started walking out to the factories on Sundays to watch the workers enjoying themselves among the idle machine-tools.

Events, by now thoroughly out of control, alarmed Blum. For him they represented a 'social explosion which slapped the government in the face', and he lost no time in preparing reforming legislation. Prices on the Bourse nose-dived, and some employers transferred their money abroad. In Paris, anti-Semitic emotions reawoken by Stavisky now focused on Blum himself, exacerbated by the influx of thousands of German and Austrian Jews fleeing Hitler. The ugly slogan 'Plutôt Hitler que Blum' began to make the rounds. Although at shop-floor level there were Communist agitators at work in the factories, the Front Populaire leaders seem to have been taken completely by surprise. Then on 8 June Blum signed the famous Matignon Agreement, granting French workers compulsory collective bargaining, annual paid holidays, a forty-hour week and an immediate general rise in wages of 7 to 15 per cent. Despite these extraordinary concessions, the strikes continued, until on the 11th Thorez intervened to admonish Parisian Communists, 'You must know when to end a strike!' Two days later, the workers abandoned their sit-in at Renault. That *quatorze juillet* the left celebrated its triumph in a mass meeting at the Bastille.

The Matignon Agreement, so Simone de Beauvoir recorded, 'filled us with joy'. Thanks to the fifteen days of paid holiday and the forty-hour week, 'couples on tandem bicycles could now be seen pedalling out of Paris every Saturday morning; they came back on Sunday evening with bunches of flowers and foliage tied to their handlebars'. Arcadian photographs appeared of workers thronging the beaches, picnicking and camping in the hitherto unfrequented countryside. 'Leisure! Leisure!' one newspaper rejoiced. Overnight life for hundreds of thousands of Parisians changed miraculously. A dramatic new interest in sports, notably football and cycling, took hold. Charles Trenet sang in 'La Route enchantée':

> Paris! Viens avec nous – tu verras
> Les joyeux matins et les grands chemins
> Où l'on marche à l'aventure
> Hiver comme été, toujours la nature, la route enchantée.

For the workers of Paris, underpaid and underprivileged for so long, it looked like paradise gained – all the unachieved dreams of the revolutions of the nineteenth century at last fulfilled. But could France afford it, with Hitler about to invade Austria and Czechoslovakia, and rearming at terrifying speed? Movingly, Léon Blum remarked, 'I had the feeling, in spite of everything, of having brought a lull, a vista, into their dark difficult lives ... we had given them hope.'

Yet the truth was that he had made the future of France more hopeless, as French industry continued to stagnate. Continuing to deceive herself militarily, France found the illusion of security behind her costly and theoretically impressive Maginot Line. When the Berlin-based American correspondent William L. Shirer visited Paris in October 1938 he found it:

> a frightful place, completely surrendered to defeatism with no inkling of what has happened to *France* ... Even the waiters, taxi-drivers, who used to be sound, are gushing about how wonderful it is that war has been avoided, that it would have been a crime, that they fought in one war and that was enough.

That, Shirer thought, 'would be okay if the Germans, who also fought in one war, felt the same way, but they don't'.

ON THE BRINK AGAIN

By 1939 the Front Populaire had brought the franc tumbling. Foreign crises were proliferating, effecting all sorts of contradictions in Paris. Closing the stable door after Hitler had completed his devouring of Czechoslovakia, in March Britain gave Poland a guarantee of her national integrity. After Mussolini had grabbed Albania, France joined Chamberlain in extending similar guarantees to Romania and Greece; but the Quai d'Orsay under the defeatist Georges Bonnet threatened to take the *Nouvelle Revue Française* to court the moment it attacked either Hitler or Mussolini. In May the pro-German pacifist Marcel Déat (who would come into his own the following year) published a powerful article entitled 'Do We Have to Die for Danzig?' – and *mourir pour Danzig* entered the Parisian vernacular. The previous summer the state visit to Paris by King George VI, patently an attempt to repeat the success of his grandfather and to bolster the *entente cordiale* – and French backbones – had been a notable success, largely through the irresistible charm of his francophone Queen. But still theatre audiences were heard to growl with disapproval when a stage character referred to the idea of the British and the French supporting each other, and by 1939 many a Parisian would freely admit to finding little to choose between British and Germans.

The 150th anniversary of the Great Revolution came and went with minimum fuss; certainly gazes were discreetly averted from any reference to the menaced *liberté* and *égalité* of the Czechs or Poles. There was much more interest in the thirty-second Tour de France, boycotted though it was by German and Italian riders. Even more in the forefront of the news, however, was the public guillotining on 17 June of a German serial killer, the handsome Eugene Weidmann. Affecting high moral disapproval, papers like *Paris-Match* and the *Petit Journal* revelled in accounts of the 'filthy spree' which had attended the decapitation at Versailles, with crowds – as in the times of Philippe le Bel – perched in trees and on rooftops with high expectation all through the preceding night – anything to escape from the nasty realities of the outside world of 1939. Within the fortnight a decree abolished public executions.

The fashions for 1939 prescribed a curious 'conjunction of Venus and Mars': 'clean cut and with a military air', but with flouncy petticoats and whalebone stays back in vogue again. In Paris that last summer season whirled by with an especial brilliance. The official receptions all seemed to be pervaded by a note of unreality, none more so than the July ball at the Polish Embassy. It seemed that, more than ever, the women had all been invited for their beauty as much as for their distinction, and the Ambassador, Lukasiewicz, aroused Parisian approval when he led his staff, barefooted, in a polonaise at three in the morning across the Embassy lawns.

Ten days later came the last *quatorze juillet* of the peace, evoking all the splendour and emotion of past ages: Foreign Legionnaires, Senegalese, cuirassiers in shining breastplates and a detachment of British Grenadiers in red tunics and bearskins to reassure Frenchmen of the reality of the *entente* – all under a drenching rain. Proclaimed by Daladier (premier since April 1938) as a 'fête of national unity', in fact it was a day of rival marches and counter-marches. Then three million Frenchmen headed for the mountains and beaches on paid holidays, many taking with them the new bestseller from America, *Autant en emporte le vent* (*Gone with the Wind*). President Lebrun retired to his home in Lorraine; Daladier spent his holiday on the yacht of a friend in the Mediterranean; Finance Minister Paul Reynaud went to Corsica, also on a friend's yacht. Even the Communist leaders departed insouciantly, Thorez to the Mediterranean and Duclos to the Pyrenees, as *L'Humanité* continued to call for a pact with Moscow. Something of an exception was Winston Churchill, who visited the Maginot Line – the hope of times to come. But, for the immediate future, there was little enough that offered encouragement. How radically the facts of life had changed since that *jour de gloire* of just twenty years before!

On 22 August news of the Nazi–Soviet Pact brought the holidays to a chilling end. Three days later reservists only recently released following the Munich mobilization were recalled. On 1 September, as *Je Suis Partout* ran a headline 'À bas la guerre, vive la France!', Hitler invaded Poland. Two days later France and Britain declared war on Germany. This time, a reversal of 1914, France was six hours behind her ally. Sartre began a letter to Simone de Beauvoir, 'C'est donc la connerie [idiocy] qui a triomphé.' More appositely Anatole de Monzie wrote in his diary, 'France at war does not believe in the war.' That said it all. The odds facing her were colossal. In marked contrast to either 1870 or 1914, a mood of resigned despondency settled on Paris, which gave way to deep pessimism as the new German *Blitzkrieg* smashed the valiant Poles within three weeks.

As if by some bizarre natural law governing the climate in years that preface a cataclysm, as in 1870 and 1914, the spring of 1940 was a beautiful one. Parisians relaxed in the *trottoir* cafés, listening to the strains of 'J'attendrai' and dreaming of the previous year's holidays. There were art shows in the Grand Palais, racing had resumed at Auteuil (it had been suspended on the outbreak of war) and soccer matches took place between Tommies and *poilus* in the suburbs. With Hitler apparently hesitating to attack the mighty Maginot Line, much of the fear of the previous winter had dissipated – to be replaced by the dread malady of ennui, particularly insidious within the dank casemates of the Line. The *poilus* of 1940 (according to Jean-Paul Sartre, who was one) took to looting vacated Alsatian farmhouses instead. Morale at the front during the *drôle du guerre* was low, but it was excellent in Paris. Films like Renoir's classic *La Règle du jeu*, deemed 'depressing, morbid and immoral', were banned, but the Casino de Paris had reopened with a sparkling new show, radiating optimism and unreality, with Josephine Baker and Maurice Chevalier. Traffic in the city was agreeably light; on the Rue de Rivoli you could buy flags of all nations – including a swastika, just in case. Paris had meatless days (though, in the Maginot Line, soldiers were consuming something like seven times the rations of the Wehrmacht), and sugarless days and liquorless days too; luxury chocolates were no longer available, and the *pâtisseries* closed three days a week (though inventive confectioners sold boxes of sweets shaped like gasmasks). But none of this made too much difference to Parisian gastronomy. Certainly few Parisians were hungry.

COLLAPSE

On 10 May Hitler struck in the west. The Dutch capitulated on the 14th, the Belgians two weeks later. By the 13th, the Panzers – striking through the supposedly impassable Ardennes – had pushed across the Meuse at Sedan, and were thrusting deep into France. Though this put them less than 200 kilometres from Paris, it was remarkable for how long nothing but disquieting rumours reached the capital. By and large, outside government circles, life therefore went on as usual. In good part the lack of alarm was because Paris had been spared the ruthless bombing that had flattened Warsaw and Rotterdam. The theatres remained open (at least until 20 May, the day the Panzers actually reached the Channel). The restaurants were full.

Operating out of the Hôtel Continental, the Censor was as all-powerful as twenty-five years previously. The 'official spokesman', a Colonel Thomas whose closely cropped hair, moustache and pince-nez reminded one British war correspondent of the unfortunate Dreyfus, had a staff of flinty women who wore small imitation scissors in their hats. On the 13th a few items of bad news got past Colonel Thomas, but not enough to arouse anxiety. On the 14th, Arthur Koestler, then a stateless refugee in France, picked up *L'Epoque* in a train and read the following declaration: 'The spirit of the heroic days of 1916 has returned; yesterday, in reconquering an outer fort of Sedan, our troops have shown a bravery worthy of the glorious days of Douaumont.' Shaken, he rushed to tell his friend Joliot-Curie, the scientist, 'They are at Sedan.' 'Sedan? You are dreaming . . . I did not know you were such a *paniquard.*' But when Koestler walked out into the street from Joliot-Curie's laboratory, he saw the latest edition of *Paris-Midi* with the words 'We Have Evacuated Sedan' splashed across the front page. 'That', recalled Koestler, 'was the moment when the chair under us broke down.'

It was not until the 16th, however, that alarm began to grow among Parisians. By then cars with number plates from areas ever closer to Paris were appearing in the city. Amid an atmosphere of incredulity mixed with panic, the two-month-old Reynaud government discussed leaving the capital, as in 1914. Then Reynaud's resolve hardened and he declared that they 'ought to remain in Paris, no matter how intense the bombing might be' – only to add, somewhat delphically, that the government 'should, however, take care not to fall into the enemy's hands'. Some Ministers – almost ignoring the approaching Wehrmacht – expressed the fear that, if Paris were abandoned, the Communists would seize power.

On the 16th, Winston Churchill, who had been Prime Minister for less than a week, flew to Paris to find out what was happening. There followed his historic meeting in the Quai d'Orsay, that same building where less than twenty years previously the victorious Allies had drafted the Peace Treaty for the defeated Germans to sign. Present were Reynaud, Daladier (now Minister of National Defence) and the French

Commander-in-Chief, General Maurice Gamelin. 'Everybody was standing,' Churchill recalled in his memoirs.

> At no time did we sit down around a table. Utter dejection was written on every face. In front of Gamelin on a student's easel was a map, about two yards square, with a black line purporting to show the Allied front. In this line there was drawn a small but sinister bulge at Sedan.

Churchill asked Gamelin: 'Where is the strategic reserve?' Then,

> breaking into French, which I used indifferently (in every sense): 'Où est la masse de manoeuvre?'
>
> General Gamelin turned to me and, with a shake of the head and a shrug, said: 'Aucune.'
>
> There was another long pause. Outside in the garden of the Quai d'Orsay clouds of smoke arose from large bonfires, and I saw from the window venerable officials pushing wheel-barrows of archives on to them.

It was 1914 all over again. But this time there was no Galliéni in Paris; and the French army was not the army of 1914.

Churchill returned to London grimly aware of what the future would hold. Reynaud, a brave little man surrounded by defeatists, spoke that night on the radio, admitting to the French public that the Germans had managed to create 'a broad pocket, south of the Meuse', but 'we filled in plenty [of such pockets] in 1918, as those of you who fought in the last war will not have forgotten!' Like French leaders before him, Reynaud led public prayers to Sainte Geneviève at Notre-Dame on 19 May and the following week the saviour saint's relics were borne through the streets in solemn procession. But in the meantime the city underwent one of the most startling transformations in its history – from maelstrom to mausoleum in a matter of days, with two-thirds of its residents departing in every manner of transport.

On 3 June, Paris was bombed for the first time. More than 250 civilians were killed. By the 8th, the sound of distant cannon had become almost continuous. For the third time in seventy years, Paris was a city under siege. 'The restaurants emptied,' said Alfred Fabre-Luce. 'The Ritz, abandoned by its last clients, resembled a palace in a spa on the day the baths closed down.' On the 10th, French radio announced, 'The Government is compelled to leave the capital for imperative military reasons. The Prime Minister is on his way to the armies.' At midnight, the car containing Reynaud and his newly appointed Under-Secretary for National Defence, a Brigadier-General Charles de Gaulle, left for the future seat of government at Tours. Behind them an endless stream of refugees poured out along the Boulevard Raspail. Ilya Ehrenburg, who – as a correspondent representing Hitler's Russian ally – remained in the city, watched as 'An old man laboriously pushed a handcart loaded with pillows on which huddled a small girl and a little dog that howled piteously.'

Up to now, the French government had been insisting in Gambetta-esque terms that it would fight in front of Paris and behind Paris, and as recently as that weekend it had announced that the capital had been placed 'in a state of defence'. Every fifty metres down the Champs-Elysées buses had been positioned diagonally in order to thwart German airborne troops. Then on the night of the 11th Gamelin's successor, General Maxime Weygand, declared Paris an 'open city'. That Paris should have capitulated without a struggle, while Warsaw, London, Leningrad and Stalingrad chose to face battle and be devastated, has ever since remained a contentious matter. But by 11 June there would have been little military advantage gained in fighting for Paris. Even so, her abandonment destroyed what was left of French morale. André Maurois recalls being warned, on 10 June, that Paris would not be defended: 'At that moment I knew everything was over. France deprived of Paris would become a body without a head. The war had been lost.'

As the German army reached the outskirts of Paris, rain fell on the city after the long weeks of blue skies – 'Göring's weather' the hard-pressed fighter pilots of the RAF called it. Early on the morning of 14 June, an officer on the staff of General von Küchler's Eighteenth Army, a Lieutenant-Colonel Dr Hans Speidel,* received two French officers who came under flag of truce to deliver up the capital. Hours later, units of the German 87th Infantry Division, led by an anti-tank gun detachment which went on to occupy the Hôtel de Ville and the Invalides, made a bloodless and orderly entry into a dazed Paris.

---

* Four years and a few weeks later, Speidel, now a lieutenant-general, was defending Paris against the Americans and Free French as Chief of Staff, Army Group B. After ending the war in a Gestapo prison camp, he returned to Paris in 1951 to negotiate the rearmament of Federal Germany. In 1957 he was in Paris again, as the first German Commander of Allied Land Forces in Europe.

AGE SEVEN: 1940–1969

DE GAULLE

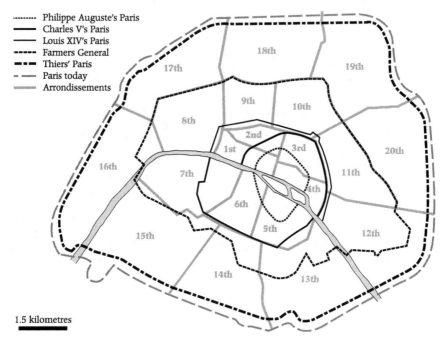

18th

17th

19th

9th

8th

10th

2nd

1st

3rd

16th

7th

11th

20th

4th

6th

5th

15th

12th

14th

13th

1.5 kilometres

THE DEVELOPMENT OF PARIS FROM PHILIPPE AUGUSTE TO THE PRESENT

19

The Occupation

For over four years, Paris had been on the conscience of the free world. Suddenly she became the loadstone as well. So long as the great city seemed to be asleep, captive and stupefied, everyone was agreed upon her formidable absence. But ... Paris was about to reappear. How many things could change!

Charles de Gaulle, *Mémoires de Guerre*, II, p. 289

SUMMER 1940

Paris now enters a dark night, the darkest, longest fifty months of all her long existence. Neither the Tsar's entry in 1815 nor the Prussians' in 1871 inflicted the humiliation – and the prolonged pain – that she would suffer between 1940 and 1944. The light of *la ville lumière* would truly be extinguished. Even with the euphoric moment of *la Libération* of August 1944 the darkness would not end. Out of the pit there would follow the bitter period of *épuration*, the savaging of one Frenchman, one group of Frenchmen, by another – a merciless civil conflict that would add thousands more victims to the large number of war casualties. Worse, it would leave wounds still very much unhealed two generations later. Over the first part of the scene two rival figures loom, facing each other like hostile queens on the chessboard: Marshal Pétain versus the man dubbed by Winston Churchill 'the Constable of France', Brigadier-General Charles de Gaulle. Though at first a brave but insignificant piece on the chessboard of war, the Constable would eventually triumph, bringing a certain order and opening the path to a grand *renouvellement* of France. Nevertheless, his epoch – his second coming –

too would end with one of the worst and most startling explosions Paris had yet seen: *les événements* of May 1968.

The principal victim – as well as the arena – of the Nazi Occupation was, of course, Paris. In August 1944 it was only by a hair's breadth that she would escape dreadful, if not total, destruction. The story of the Occupation is so unredeemingly terrible that an Anglo-Saxon historian writing about the glories of *la ville lumière* is faced with difficulties, when trying to encapsulate what is the unhappiest period in all her 2,000 years' history. How, anyway, can an Anglo-Saxon begin to comprehend the pressures and stresses imposed on both collaborators and members of the Resistance – we who, thank God, were never occupied? Does our lack of experience entitle us to pass the judgement: 'It couldn't have happened here'? I often wonder which of us would have been collaborators – the Drieu la Rochelles, the Brasillachs, or even a Sartre or a Cocteau? Or which of us would have joined the *maquis* in the Welsh mountains? What *might* we have done, especially in those early days of no hope, when Germany seemed certain to emerge triumphant? Smugly we think Drancy and the deportations of the Jews couldn't happen here, but can we be sure? Before consigning them to the lowest circle of *collabo* hell, it is also worth remembering that men like Céline and Darnand had all fought bravely in the First World War, before that pacificism which it generated led them to take the wrong turning. Even Pierre Laval at the post-war trial proved to be a man of laudable courage as he faced the inevitable death sentence. Events were just too big for them – including the old Marshal, at the head of it all in Vichy.

On 17 June 1940 William Shirer revisited Paris from a triumphant Berlin just three days after the German entry. He felt an ache in the pit of his stomach at the sight of the familiar but empty streets, which he had loved 'as you love a woman':

> I wished I had not come. My German companions were in high spirits.
> ... First shock: the streets are utterly deserted, the shops closed, the shutters down tight over all the windows. It was the emptiness that got you ... [All] had fled – the *patrons*, the *garçons*, the customers ...

Going round the Place de l'Opéra, he noted,

> For the first time in my life, no traffic tie-up here, no French cops shouting meaninglessly at cars hopelessly blocked. The façade of

the Opera House was hidden behind stacked sandbags. The Café de la Paix seemed to be just reopening. A lone *garçon* was bringing out some tables and chairs. German soldiers stood on the terrace grabbing them...

... I have a feeling that what we're seeing here in Paris is the complete breakdown of French society – a collapse of the army, of government, of the morale of the people. It is almost too tremendous to believe.

The following day, he observed there was already 'open fraternizing' between German troops and Parisians. He added that two newspapers had appeared the day before in Paris, *La Victoire* – 'as life's irony would have it' – and *Le Matin*: the latter 'has already begun to attack England, to blame England for France's predicament!'

Momentarily Hitler lost his nerve before Dunkirk and – in a profound error of judgement – issued his controversial 'halt order', which was to save the British Expeditionary Force. The 'Miracle of Dunkirk' came to pass, and 337,000 men (including 110,000 French) were evacuated by sea. For the Germans the campaign to conquer France now became largely a matter of marching, a pursuit down the highways. On 22 June France was forced to agree to a humiliating armistice. The brilliant six weeks' *Blitzkrieg* had cost the Germans no more than 27,074 killed. Contrary to the received image, the French army, or at least parts of it, had fought bravely, and had lost in killed alone 100,000 men. But one million prisoners-of-war had been taken, and they would remain in miserable conditions, sometimes exploited as slave labourers, in Germany for the next five years.

What was so shattering for Paris, and it was to set the tone for the ensuing four years of Occupation, was the sheer speed of the German takeover. It was the end of centuries of tradition: Paris the fortress had suddenly become the 'open city'. But life in the capital returned to a semblance of normality with parallel speed. The refugees began to come back. At the entry of the Germans, the Prefect of Police, Roger Langeron, reckoned that the total population had sunk to 700,000, or a quarter of its pre-war total. The fashionable western arrondissements were all but empty. Then, three weeks later, and under pressure from the Germans, some 300,000 returned. Exhaustion shows in photographs of a working-class family trudging home on foot, wheeling a worn-out grandmother in a child's pram. There were others who, in the privacy of their homes, found a way out rather than face what the future would bring; one of these was an eminent neurosurgeon who, having seen the Germans arrive on the Champs-Elysées, injected himself with strychnine.

Over the course of his ten-day visit that June, William Shirer noted a marked change. Where on the 17th he had recorded the streets 'utterly deserted', by the 23rd he found that the Rotonde and the Dôme restaurants in Montparnasse were:

> as jammed with crackpots as ever, and in front of us a large table full of middle-aged French women of the bourgeoisie, apparently recovering from their daze, because their anger was rising at the way the little *gamines* (*elles sont françaises, après tout!*) were picking up the German soldiers . . .

Another neutral American, Ambassador William C. Bullitt, who had walked out in disgust from the US delegation at Versailles in 1919, looked on with dismay as the German commanders moved into the Crillon just across the road from his Embassy. He sent one of his staff, Robert Murphy, over to the hotel to make contact with the new Kommandant of 'Gross Paris', General Bogislav von Stütnitz. There, in the Prince of Wales Suite, one of the Wehrmacht colonels turned out to be an old friend of Murphy's from pre-war days in Bavaria. Over the champagne Stütnitz declared cheerfully that the war would be over by the end of July – six weeks hence.

Almost immediately one of the city's most chic *bordels*, encouraged by the atmosphere of 'business as usual', put up a sign announcing that 'The house will reopen at three o'clock.' W. H. Smith on the Rue de Rivoli became a German bookshop. The theatres and cinemas opened their doors again; famous restaurants like Maxim's, the Grand Véfour and Fouquet's went on as before for their new clientele; racing resumed at Auteuil with the terraces crammed with binocular-bearing officers – the Kommandant taking over the President's box. *Haute couture* regained its former eminence, with Coco Chanel swiftly going to ground in the Ritz with a German officer, from which she seldom emerged until the war was over.

Under strict orders, the first Germans to arrive behaved well. On the Métro members of the Wehrmacht ostentatiously gave up their seats to women and old people, and there was a widely disseminated slogan, 'Have confidence in the German soldier.' Many Parisians were impressed: here was order brought of disorder. In their smart *Feldgrau* the occupiers looked like serious soldiers, unlike the demoralized rabble Parisians had seen passing through the city over previous weeks. There were comparisons, not always unspoken, with the Tommies who had sailed off and left France at Dunkirk, and with Woodrow Wilson's Americans, who had let France down so badly in 1919 and had not lifted a finger to help her this time. Within the month would come the shocking news that the Royal Navy had sunk the French fleet, with heavy loss of sailors' lives, at Mers-el-Kebir.

THE NEW MASTERS

Among the eminent visitors to Paris was Göring, who dined greedily at Maxim's; but before him there was Adolf Hitler himself, on Sunday, 23 June, on his way home from having danced a little jig of revenge outside the *wagons-lits* where the French surrender was signed in the clearing at Compiègne. He was accompanied by his favourite architect Albert Speer and the sculptor Arno Breker, a long-time resident of Paris, who planned the itinerary.

It was the triumphant Führer's first and last trip to the capital which he intended to be the second city of the Thousand Year Reich. Beginning at 6 a.m., in less than three hours he managed to 'do' the whole city. He paused to incline his head in silence at Napoleon's tomb and on the deserted steps of the Trocadéro to be photographed with the Eiffel Tower in the background. To Speer's disappointment, Hitler passed by the Louvre, the Sainte-Chapelle and even Notre-Dame, but on their way out of the city he made a bee-line for the Sacré-Coeur – which the Führer, with a rare display of taste, condemned as 'appalling'. At the Place Vauban behind the Invalides an angry Hitler ordered the immediate removal of the statue of the First World War General Mangin; he regarded it as an insulting reminder of the French occupation of the Ruhr in the 1920s. In the city which he wanted the future Berlin to emulate and indeed surpass, Hitler neither entered a private house nor stopped for a meal. Few recognized him, while the only Parisians he saw were a *gardien* at the Opéra (who suffered a heart attack), a newspaper vendor, a few *flics* and a handful of worshippers at the Sacré-Coeur. Breker heard him boast that he had taken it as his own responsibility 'to preserve undamaged this wonder of Western civilization. We have succeeded.' There is no evidence that any such order had ever been transmitted to the German army commanders, and – four years later as the Germans prepared to leave Paris – it would be a very different story.

As it was, the reality of the German occupation very soon became apparent. As a minor foretaste, the doomed statue of General Mangin was accompanied to destruction by the statues of such notables as Nurse Edith Cavell and Rouget de Lisle (composer of the Marseillaise). Other famous statues to disappear included those of Hugo, Zola, Villon, Berlioz and Desmoulins, while city officialdom had to strain itself to protect Henri IV on the Pont Neuf. By loudspeakers the inhabitants of Paris were warned, 'The German High Command will tolerate no act of hostility towards the occupation troops. All aggression, all sabotage will be punished by death.' Henceforth there would be a strict curfew from 9 p.m. to 5 a.m. each night. Thus were the ground rules laid. Already that first winter as rationing was imposed, suffering was to become intense as life became a constant hunt for fuel and food.

The new German administration established itself with astonishing rapidity and efficiency, even while the battle outside Paris still continued. Almost overnight there appeared outside the Opéra a maze of signs directing to various military *Abteilungen*, headquarters, units, hospitals, *Kinos*, hotels, recreation centres and every other kind of Wehrmacht function. (In the summer of 1944 there was even a helpful arrow pointing 'To the Normandy Front'.) Deprived of tourists, the main hotels were swiftly allocated: the Majestic on Avenue Kléber, in 1919 residence of the British peace delegation, became the headquarters of the High Command responsible for the whole of the Occupied Zone – that is, two-thirds of France, including all the northern provinces. The Claridge on the Champs-Elysées combined the police, economic and cultural administrations; the Lutetia on the Left Bank housed the Abwehr intelligence departments, the Crillon on the Concorde the sinister Sicherheitsdienst or SD; next door the navy moved, conveniently, into Gabriel's imposing Ministère de la Marine, while the Luftwaffe headed by Field Marshal Sperrle – who had Göring's eye for luxury – occupied Marie de Medici's Luxembourg. For their officers' club the Luftwaffe also occupied the choice address on the Faubourg Saint-Honoré which later became the American Residence; and the Kommandant and his staff took over the Meurice and part of the Crillon. Supreme insult, the Chamber of Deputies in the Palais Bourbon – where Daladier had stood up and declared war on Germany just nine months previously and which was now decked with swastikas – was requisitioned for the Kommandantur offices. The Gestapo moved in to 74 Avenue Foch and

9 Rue des Saussaies; as the Resistance developed, neighbours of these buildings would be kept awake at night by the screams emanating from their interrogation rooms. Soon there were more than a thousand Germans in the Majestic alone. Later in the war, when all available manpower was needed on the Russian Front, over 100,000 miscellaneous front-dodgers were dredged up from the fleshpots of Paris.

In addition to this top-heavy administration, each of the Nazi big-wigs – Göring, Ribbentrop, Goebbels, Rosenberg – found an excuse to set up their own *Verbindungs* office in the Capuan seductiveness of Paris. But throughout the Occupation one of the most influential Nazis in Paris was the German Ambassador, Otto Abetz, who operated out of the Hôtel de Beauharnais – with its Napoleonic associations – at 80 Rue de Lille. Aged only thirty-seven in 1940, Abetz was a remarkable man, by his own lights a genuine Francophile – married to a Frenchwoman – who had spent much time in pre-war France. He managed to convince Hitler that France, if treated considerately, might swiftly accept a subordinate place in the 'New Order'. His job in Paris was to work on 'elements receptive to conditioning favourably public opinion', and he was immensely successful, rapidly building up an extensive network of contacts. Few turned down his invitations. Illustrative of how fashionable Paris, the *gratin* and *le tout Paris* (café society), reacted to Abetz and the more *sortable* among the former enemy was Baron Elie de Rothschild's account of the parties given at his town mansion on the Avenue de Marigny while it was occupied by a Luftwaffe general. On returning from prison camp after the war Rothschild observed to the old family butler, Félix, that the house must have been very quiet during the Occupation. The butler replied, 'On the contrary, Monsieur Elie. There were receptions every evening.' 'But ... who came?' asked the astonished Rothschild. 'The same people, Monsieur Elie. The same as before the war.'

Least considerable, and generally unheeded, was the 'Embassy' of Pétain's Vichy regime, which governed the rump state of unoccupied France. Initially the Embassy was run from 27 Rue de Grenelle by Ambassador Léon Noël, but he was soon overridden by de Brinon, the personal representative of Pierre Laval (initially Pétain's deputy, from 1942 his Prime Minister), set up in style at the Matignon, residence of the premiers of France. The Vichy Embassy had derisory powers and little influence, and kept Vichy eminently ill-informed of what was happening in Paris. Although Abetz adroitly always showed it a smiling face, it earned the contempt of the German military as, under Laval's policy of total collaboration, Vichy became progressively the poodle of the occupiers.

Already in the summer of 1940, unseen and sinister matters were in hand. Under the mantle of Abetz, censorship in the shape of the 'Bernhard List' proscribed 150 books, which had to be removed from the libraries. Also under way was the requisitioning of Jewish houses in Paris and of the works of art contained in them, as well as those in Jewish-owned galleries. The Jeu de Paume became a huge depot for pillaged works of art on their way to Germany, Vivant Denon in reverse. Worse, many paintings – perhaps between 500 and 600 – deemed 'unfit for sale' were burned in the Louvre courtyard. These included works by 'decadents' like Miró. It has been estimated that by the end of the war some 20,000 works of art were conveyed to Germany. Many were destroyed in air-raids there or, for other reasons, were never subsequently recovered. That so many were located and returned safely to their owners after the war was largely due to the courage and tenacity of the *conservatrice* at the Jeu de Paume, Rose Valland, who managed to keep a discreet inventory of every item that passed out of the building.

THE *COLLABOS*

The line composed to celebrate the new staircase installed by the Second Empire's *grande horizontale* La Païva could well be applied to those who collaborated with the Nazis: 'Ainsi que la vertu, le vice a ses degrés' (see p. 275 above). While the German military instinctively tended to deal with the French right (not just the extreme right), Abetz's preference was for collaborators of the left, notably among the pre-war pacifists and those who believed that Versailles had given Germany a raw deal. From the first his wide network of French contacts included writers like Fernand de Brinon, Drieu la Rochelle and Jean Luchaire, a close friend from pre-war days, editor of *Le Matin*. Ambitious, and renowned for his expensive tastes, in July 1940 Luchaire declared to a fellow journalist, 'I shall be starting a big evening paper in Paris ... One must press on, my dear Jacques; one can't turn back in melancholy to a past that has been scrapped. We are young – we should not mourn but build ...' His 'building' led to the launch that November of *Les Nouveaux Temps*, which was to become the most influential of the collaborationist papers, financed by Laval and Abetz, and determinedly supportive of the Nazi line. Also at the top of the *collabo* staircase, each dedicated to the success of Germany but treated with initial coolness by Abetz, came Jacques Doriot and Marcel Déat, both left-wingers by origin.

Doriot had started life on the politburo of the Communist Party, then swung right to form the fascist Parti Populaire Français (PPF) and its journal *Le Cri du Peuple*. Déat had begun in Blum's Socialist party and was at one time regarded as Blum's successor. Violently opposed to France's entry into the war, he founded the journal *L'Oeuvre* and – in February 1941 – the Rassemblement National Populaire (RNP), which had its headquarters in the Faubourg Saint-Honoré at the former Seligman premises, requisitioned under the first takeovers of Jewish property. Doriot's PPF had a substantial proletarian base, but Déat's RNP was largely middle-aged and middle-class. Both parties embraced a large number of women among their membership.

Among the most anti-Semitic of the collaborationist press was *Au Pilori*, edited by Jean Drault, which in November 1942 was to come out with a leader urging that 'The Jewish question must be resolved immediately by the arrest and deportation of all Jews without exception.' Another eminent anti-Semite was the apocalyptic Céline, so obsessed by death and destruction that defeat and occupation, it has been said, 'fell short of his expectations'. Then there was the equally splenetic, extreme right-wing *Je Suis Partout*, now resumed after a deplorable pre-war record under Robert Brasillach and Lucien Rebatet. Briefly a prisoner-of-war, Brasillach was allowed back to Paris to take over the editorship of *Je Suis Partout*, whose circulation rose to an astonishing 300,000. He later explained himself in clearest terms:

> The German genius and I had an affair ... whether one likes it or not, we lived together. Whatever their outlook, during these years the French have all more or less been to bed with Germany, and whatever quarrels there were, the memory is sweet.

Could anything be less ambiguous?

All these *grands collaborateurs* at the top of the staircase of vice were wholeheartedly committed to the *deutsche Zukunft*, in the certain belief that Hitler was going to win (which, in summer 1940, looked a fair bet). They would pay a heavy price. Then came the French Communists, sullenly committed by the pact between Ribbentrop and Molotov the previous August to supporting the Germans. Until Hitler turned round and savaged the Soviet Union the following year, *L'Humanité* was allowed to thrive. Typical was its edition of 14 July: 'It is particularly comforting, in these times of misfortune, to see numerous Paris workers striking up friendliness with German soldiers . . . Bravo, comrades, *continuez.*' It was not surprising that this kind of exhortation to the 'comrades' encouraged them to come out into the open once more, like a lot of foolish mice, making it all the easier for the cat to pounce after 22 June 1941 when the Führer turned on Russia. At the other end of the social scale, and bent on getting on with the occupiers out of rather more selfish motives, came the *gratin* and *le tout Paris*, the frequenters of the former Rothschild house remarked on by the old butler, faithful in their infidelity. The arguments were exculpatory; the principle was 'business as usual' – to place a curb on Parisian social life would be less of a punishment to the Germans than to the *indigènes*.

Lower down the staircase of collaboration came the massed ranks of the petit bourgeoisie, the merchants, artisans and grocers, *bistrotiers* and restaurateurs – the majority of Parisians. They were significantly – and understandably – dependent on 'business as usual' as a matter of survival. Most often their relationship with the occupiers, as that of the Parisian in the street, would be one of icy correctness – one of cold stares, or of avoiding eye contact. The experience could be memorably painful to more sensitive young German soldiers finding themselves in Paris and simply wanting to be friendly, or preferably loved.

But a great many Germans found love and more among Parisians. As early as October 1943 some 85,000 illegitimate children had been fathered by Germans in France, and by the middle of the following year 80,000 Frenchwomen were claiming children's benefits from the military authorities, which French historians consider to have been 'only the tip of the iceberg'. The ordinary *collabo horizontale* perhaps deserves more sympathy from us now than she found at the time. The loss of two million French males sequestered in German prisoner-of-war camps or employed as slave labour represented a terrible deprivation to French womanhood; many of the occupying Wehrmacht were physically attractive and well behaved. But most of all, as the war dragged on and life became harsher and harsher in Paris, sleeping with a German often became the only way a woman could keep her children from starvation.

COLLABORATION OF INTELLECTUALS AND ARTISTS

Much harder to assess is the collaboration of the artists and intellectuals, particularly writers. On the assumption that the Germans would be in Paris indefinitely, *chef de ballet* Serge Lifar, Diaghilev's protégé, took the straightforward line that, at thirty-five in 1940, he should continue dancing as he would soon be too old to do it. Under his direction the ballet company of the Opéra opened with *Coppélia* on 28 August, little more than two months after the arrival of the Germans; the Opéra had opened four days before with, appropriately enough, *The Damnation of Faust.* But for whose benefit did Lifar mostly perform? Throughout the war more than a third of the seats (the best, naturally) at the Opéra Comique were reserved for Germans. With Mistinguett and Chevalier on the boards, the Casino de Paris reopened as early as 6 July – outside, a sign was posted prohibiting 'dogs and Jews'. Jean-Louis Barrault was to argue that continuing one's theatre work and ignoring the Germans was a positive attitude, and was all that could be done unless one were actively in the Resistance. The Paris theatre was soon back in full swing: by 1943 box-office receipts had attained a level three times what they had been in 1938.

For productive writers or journalists to continue in business meant rather more than just 'getting on'. To be published at all, they had to undertake the Faustian commitment of submitting their work for approval by the Nazi censors, which made each of them technically a collaborator. Moreover, as of September 1940 the association of French publishers signed an agreement with Abetz amounting to self-censorship. In exchange for suppressing works by Jews and 'subversives', the publishers were granted a margin of discretion in deciding what to publish and what to censor. The extent of literary collaboration was indicated by the statistic that on average 6,400 books were published in each of the four years of the Occupation. Indeed in 1943, at the height of the war, French publishers led the world with 9,348 titles, as against Britain's 6,705 and the USA's 8,320. (In the cinema, although initially Paris was flooded with German films, eventually the French industry overtook German production by turning out 225 full-length features and some 400 documentaries and cartoons; again all had to pass the censor.)

On the other hand, reading like a roll of honour was the Bernhard List of proscribed authors, whose number soon approached 8,000. These embraced a wide range of distinguished authors from Pierre Loti to Georges Duhamel and Henri Bordeaux, to André Malraux and (of course) Charles de Gaulle. What Parisians most wanted to read was pretty much as before the war: books on travel, novels, escapism. One of the most successful was Lucien Rebatet's *Les Décombres*, an outpouring of anti-Semitism and anti-republicanism which was nevertheless something of a literary masterpiece in its extraordinarily powerful evocation of the collapse of 1940. Published in 1942, it sold more than 60,000 copies.

Other well-known authors published under the Occupation included Cocteau, Simenon, Eluard, Queneau, Aragon, Marguerite Duras, Saint-Exupéry, Camus, de Beauvoir and Sartre. 'Politically,' Beauvoir complained, '... we found ourselves reduced to a position of impotence.' She and Sartre spent their time either gossiping at the Flore or bicycling in the countryside – apparently undisturbed by war or occupiers – while also freely publishing their works. Sartre's first play *Les Mouches* was staged in 1943 at the Théâtre de la Cité and was highly praised by the drama critic of the German *Pariser Zeitung*; and in June 1944, as the Allies were landing in Normandy, his best-known play *Huis clos*, with its famous line 'Hell is other people', opened in Paris. Alleged to be anti-German, the allegory was so subtle as to elude the notice of the censor. Later Camus parted company with Sartre, joining the Resistance to form the underground Combat. Sartre meanwhile joined the CNE (Comité National d'Ecrivains), largely dominated by Communists and fellow travellers, and acidly described by a modern historian as being 'less interested in resistance than in drawing up lists of other writers and journalists whom they would proscribe and silence after the war'.

But not all literary works which passed the German censor should be denigrated. Of lasting historical value, for instance, were the novels or memoirs of writers like Marcel Aymé and Emmanuel d'Astier de la Vigerie with their vivid descriptions of Paris under the Occupation, its almost beautiful emptiness and silence, free of dogs and traffic. To be a professional author like Jean Galtier-Boissière, who preferred to live in poverty selling second-hand books rather than undergo the indignity of submitting what he wrote for Nazi approval, required a special kind of courage. Meanwhile their rivals moved on up the literary ladder as their writings were snapped up by publishers who kept going throughout the war.

Perhaps closer to the norm was Colette, who had shown remarkable indifference to all the international crises of the pre-war period and who during the Occupation fell back on a philosophy of 'le sage repliement sur soi-même' – translatable, in less poetical terms, as lying low. She recalled the restrained attitude of her mother Sido in the face of the Prussian occupation of 1870 ('I went home and buried the good wine') and got on with her writing, publishing her fiction even in such pro-Vichy, anti-Semitic and anti-British organs as *Gringoire* and the committedly collaborationist *La Gerbe*. An apologist for Colette, Patrice Blank, who became a hero of the Resistance, regarded her as exemplifying:

> an unconsciousness shared by a large number of French artists. It was very widespread, and the excuse one heard most often was that the theatre should function 'normally' and the 'voice' of French culture should not be stifled. There were very few, and I underline very few, true *résistants*.

Similar principles applied to the art world. Many artists had fled Paris; Jews (swiftly excluded from exhibitions or galleries) wisely removed themselves to the US, as Chagall did. But just as many stayed. Braque lay low, yet happily received selected Germans in his studio and emerged to exhibit at the Salon d'Automne of 1943. Picasso – as a Spaniard, neutral – for all his outrage over the consequences of fascism that he had poured into his famous *Guernica* – was not averse to overtures and invitations from the occupiers. The various salons of winter and autumn were held as before, and as early as the end of 1940 the Orangerie in the Tuileries was showing an exhibition dedicated to Monet and Rodin. Even the private galleries and auction houses, like Drouot, managed to prosper, achieving higher and higher prices.

FIRST SUFFERINGS AND FIRST PROSCRIPTIONS

For many Parisians the winter of 1940–1 was one of a 'constant hunt for fuel and food', remembered as the worst of the war. The Nazi occupier was swift to plunder France to furnish his war machine and replenish German larders. With unforgiving suddenness the average daily intake of food was reduced to 1,300 calories per day. Invidious comparisons were made with the sieges of 1590 and 1870; certainly even at the darkest

moments of the First World War there had never been such privation. Bread (the Parisian's staple diet), sugar and noodles were rationed
in August 1940; butter, cheese, meat, coffee, pork and eggs followed in
October. Coffee was soon replaced by a revolting brew of acorns and
chickpeas, called *café national*. But possession of a ration card didn't
guarantee food. 'We have the tickets,' wrote Jean Guéhenno on 3 January
1941, 'but they don't permit one to obtain anything. The shops are
empty.' Parisians took to raising vast quantities of rabbits, even in their
apartments – the number reportedly rising to 400,000 at one point.

As much an enemy as hunger was the cold. With communications
still interrupted, only a minimum of fuel reached Paris during that
particularly cold winter of 1940–1. Worst of all was the plight of the
inactive – writers, teachers, artists, and unemployed, unable to keep
warm in their freezing habitations. Sunday, day of rest, was the day most
dreaded by the workers. The mortality rate soared. By 1941–2 it was 62
per cent over the 1938 level for the western areas of Paris, and revealingly
only 38 per cent up in the working-class districts of eastern Paris

For the less privileged Parisians there was not even the possibility of
driving into the countryside to fill their cars with food. There was no
petrol for civilians, and only 7,000 cars were actually licensed in Paris.
A vigilant *Feldgendarmerie* checked all traffic and permits; on Sundays
only Germans were allowed to drive at all. As a means of transportation
(apart from the key Métro, which kept running), bicycles took over.
Within the first three months of the Occupation 22,000 were reported
stolen in Paris. Then came the strange-looking vélo-taxis, often seen
propelled by an emaciated woman, with two strapping Germans and
their girlfriends in the cart-like trailer.

Apart from the poor, there was one particular section of Parisians
that, by definition, suffered worse than any other. No sooner had the
Occupation established itself than Jews were forbidden to stand in food
queues. By 27 September 1940, the German authorities had issued the
first *ordonnances* proscribing the Jews in France, the jaws of the deadly
trap which would close around them. Vichy followed suit with its own
statute a week later, defining what constituted a Jew. In Paris the Jews
then numbered some 150,000, or roughly half the total in France.

Life became progressively more difficult for the Jews of Paris as with
swift relentlessness new restrictions and proscriptions were imposed.
Property and business premises were requisitioned. Jewish professors
were forced to resign from the Sorbonne, as being hostile to the German
Reich. Jewish writers were prevented from publishing, Jewish artists

from exhibiting. Jews were forbidden to use public telephones. In September 1941 a massive exhibition was mounted in the Palais Berlitz on the Boulevard des Italiens entitled 'Le Juif et la France'. Designed to whip up anti-Semitism among Parisians, over 200,000 visited; there were no known protests, criticism or demonstrations against it. Then came the enforced wearing of the yellow star, the dreadful stigma of the east European ghetto under Hitler. Parisian reactions to it were mixed. Some Jews wearing it were insulted in the street, and children at school were mocked by their classmates. On the other hand, there were many cases of words of sympathy expressed in the Métro, one of the few places Jews could frequent, and there were a few brave examples of disgusted Parisian Gentiles actually volunteering to wear the yellow star themselves.

On 27 March 1942, the first of the deportations to Auschwitz took place. Out of 1,148, only 19 survived. Starting with the non-French Jews, themselves refugees from Nazi Europe, systematic *rafles* or round-ups had swept up the victims from all over Paris, herding them into temporary camps either at Drancy, a suburb close to Le Bourget, or inside the 'Vél d'Hiv', the huge cycling stadium inside the city on the Boulevard de Grenelle in the 15th arrondissement. Conditions were appalling in both. For the most part the French police and later the militia or *milice*, aiding the Gestapo in their dread work, acted with shocking brutality. A total of 76,000 Jews, possibly more unrecorded, were deported from France; the vast majority, some 67,000, passed via Drancy. Only about 2,500, or 3 per cent, survived.

THE TURN

By the winter of 1940–1 the Parisian honeymoon with the occupying Germans – insofar as there ever had been one – had begun to fade. In the world outside, the war continued. Britain had survived the Blitz, and in Egypt had severely mauled the Italian army. Churchill was defiant; de Gaulle was at his side, gradually rallying the Free French, who now began to seem like a serious force, even retaking from Vichy some of the French colonies in Africa. An incipient Resistance movement was raising its head in France, and even in Paris. In the capital that first bitter winter had shown the Nazis at their worst. In December the execution took place of the first Parisian, a harmless engineer called Jacques Bonsergent, involved in a minor scuffle with a drunken German soldier leaving a brasserie – in no way an act of resistance or of terrorism. Thrown into the prison of Cherche Midi he was sentenced to death, and executed at Vincennes on Christmas Eve. All Paris was profoundly shocked by the terse announcement of Bonsergent's death.

Then, in June 1941, an earth-shaking event occurred which, as well as changing the course of the war, profoundly affected French attitudes to it. Hitler invaded Russia. Frenchmen with a sense of history recalled the events of 1812, and remembered where his invasion had led Napoleon and the Grande Armée. Most immediately, the powerful French Communist Party from being an ally of Hitler became a bitter enemy. Automatically the *maquis* and the FFI (Free French of the Interior), backed and supplied by SOE (Special Operations Executive) from London, began to form a potent arm of resistance at the back of the Wehrmacht.

The first real demonstration of resistance, feeble though it might have been in the face of such overwhelming power, came from students of the Sorbonne on Armistice Day 1940. Following the arrest of a popular left-wing professor of atomic physics, a group placed a wreath in front of the statue of Clemenceau, on the Rond-Point of the Champs-Elysées, accompanied with a visiting card bearing the name of de Gaulle. By the end of the afternoon they were joined by other students, moving up to the Etoile with wreaths, singing the Marseillaise and chanting, 'De Gaulle! De Gaulle!' A number of the demonstrators were injured, and 123 arrests made.

The first real *réseau*, or Resistance network, was formed among ethnologists in the Trocadéro's Museum of Man. Inexperienced, imprudent and betrayed by *délateurs* (Frenchmen and women who denounced others to the German authorities), the *réseau* was tracked down before it could become much more effective than courageously producing an underground newspaper, *Résistance*. Between January and March 1941 eighteen arrests were made, one by one. The following February seven of the ethnologists were executed at Mont Valérien, the remainder deported.

The incredible courage and dedication required to set up and maintain a *réseau* in Paris should not be underestimated. Paris was not the *maquis* or the Massif Central, where members of the Resistance had at least some prospects of escape and regrouping. With no transportation, in the capital they had to rely almost exclusively on the Métro, always watched by the enemy. Under permanent surveillance and the ever present fear of *délation* by vigilant neighbours, constantly having to change their abode, and racked by hunger and fatigue, the agents lived their clandestine lives all too aware of what tortures awaited them if caught. Radio operators with their primitive and heavy apparatus were readily tracked down by sophisticated German detection vans. No less courageous, and especially vulnerable because of the immobility of their equipment, were the printers and photographers, who produced underground tracts as well as false documents by the million.

The invasion of Russia led, in April 1942, to the creation of the Communist-dominated FTP, or Francs-Tireurs et Partisans, which added a new ruthlessness to the savage cycle of assassination and sabotage against the German and Vichy French authorities, followed by the execution of innocent and uninvolved hostages taken at random. The Germans blamed everything on the Communists, hundreds of whom were executed at Mont Valérien, in the hopes that Parisians would become sickened by the killings. By the end of the war executions had reached 11,000, plus 5,000 (a third of them women) deported to the concentration camps.

After 1943, as the prospect of an Allied invasion of France grew closer, so – naturally – did the numbers of the Resistance swell, those joining late becoming sarcastically known as 'Résistants de la dernière minute'. At the same time the two rival groups, Communist and Gaullist, found themselves in mounting conflict with each other as they planned their post-victory agendas for takeover in France. The deadly spiral of anti-German *attentats* followed by ever more brutal reprisals continued. Progressively the *milice* took over from the Germans the odious work of repression and deportation, as every spare soldier was now required on the eastern front. Eventually even Pétain, from his isolation in Vichy, was sparked to complain to Laval on 6 August 1944 of the *milice*'s 'sinister action', given that 'proofs of collusion between the *milice* and the German police are daily provided'. Darnand, the *milice* boss, responded indignantly, 'And today, because the Americans stand at the gates of Paris, you start to tell me that I shall be the stain on the history of France? It is something which might have been thought of earlier.'

Meanwhile, for the simple Parisian, from 1943 onwards living conditions steadily worsened. In September, no meat reached Paris. The average ration sank to approximately 1,000 calories. To this deterioration was added the shock – to which, unlike London, Paris had hitherto been unaccustomed – of air-raids. In March 1941, the RAF had pounded the Renault works (now producing tanks for the Wehrmacht) at Boulogne-Billancourt, leaving 400 dead and 15,000 Paris civilians wounded in one raid. In August 1943 the La Chapelle workers' district in north-east Paris itself was hit, killing upwards of 4,000. The following month Renault was hit again; this time some of the targeting was so inaccurate that bombs fell in the 15th arrondissement, while only 10 per cent of the factory installations was destroyed. In sharp contrast to the acute anglophobia which the naval sinkings of Mers-el-Kebir in July 1940 had unleashed, the strength of support for the Anglo-American raids, despite the initial shock, shook both Vichy and the Germans. Relations between occupier and occupied worsened as, after 1943, all the Germans wanted from the French was labour, whereas before it had been willing support they were after. Electricity and gas cuts paralysed the city. In these last of the *années bleues* (so named because of the blue black-out covering the station entrances), an anxious silence pervaded the city, broken chiefly by the clackety-clack on the boulevards of the wooden shoes (there was no leather any more) worn by even the chicest *Parisienne*.

LIBERATION

As part of the Allied preparations for D-Day, an area round Montmartre was heavily bombed in April 1944, bringing the aged Marshal Pétain – who had celebrated his eighty-eighth birthday just three days previously – on his one and only visit to the capital to console the wounded. There was an enormous turnout around the Hôtel de Ville to welcome him (possibly some of the same people who would return to greet de Gaulle there four months later). Pathetically the old man declared his hope 'that I shall be able to come back soon to Paris, without being obliged to warn my guardians'. (In fact, on his next visit his 'guardians' would be in the uniform of Gaullist policemen, and he would be on trial for his life.) Pétain's adversary General de Gaulle was to write in his war memoirs:

> For over four years, Paris had been on the conscience of the free world. Suddenly she became the loadstone as well. So long as the

great city seemed to be asleep, captive and stupefied, everyone was agreed upon her formidable absence. But ... Paris was about to reappear. How many things could change!

The great race to liberate Paris and preserve her from destruction was now on.

For the Jewish survivors there was certainly no time to lose. That March, as Jean Cocteau was attending a chic opera soirée in Paris, Convoy Number 69 was preparing to leave Drancy; out of 1,501 (of whom 178 were under eighteen years old) all but 20 were to die at Auschwitz. And the trains for the Final Solution would keep on running up to the very last moment. One of the last Parisians to die was the Surrealist poet Robert Desnos, killed in Czechoslovakia in 1945 only days before his camp's deliverance by the Allies. In Paris, in the grim cellars of Vincennes and Mont Valérien the executions of members of the Resistance and hostages went on apace. Under pressure from the Germans, in March 1944 alone the Paris police made 4,746 arrests. But nobody, nothing, was under greater threat than *la ville lumière* herself now that Hitler, facing his own Wagnerian *Götterdämmerung,* had determined that Paris should go down with him and his Thousand-Year German Reich. Specific orders for destruction were sent to the German Kommandant, General von Choltitz – a reluctant, vacillating man, but still a Prussian officer with a rigid code of obedience, and, following the failed 20 July bomb plot against Hitler, fearful for his own skin and the safety of his family.

It was a question of whether the Allies could reach Paris before Choltitz and his SS underlings were compelled to begin pressing the plungers. The original plan of General Eisenhower, the Allied Commander-in-Chief, following the break-out from Normandy in early August was to bypass Paris, just as the Manstein Plan had done in 1940, and head full speed for Germany. It was a question of time, and petrol – Montgomery's and Patton's columns being severely limited by shortage of supplies, all of which still had to come ashore over the beaches of Normandy. Repeatedly de Gaulle begged Eisenhower to detach a column to liberate Paris. It was not just the destruction of the capital that de Gaulle feared. Echoing Weygand's obsession of June 1940 and even that of Adolphe Thiers seventy years previously, he was also deeply alarmed by the prospect of the Communists establishing a Red Commune in a destroyed city. His own FFI inside Paris were outmatched by the Communists, who he rightly feared had acquired predominance in all the organs of the Resistance. By now they were the best organized and often the most courageous troops on the inside. The danger was extreme, it being only a matter of weeks since the horrifying example of Warsaw, when General Bor-Komorowski's heroic Poles had risen in anticipation of the arrival of the Red Army. Warsaw had been viciously and systematically destroyed and 166,000 Poles slaughtered. The Red Army, halted on the wrong side of the Vistula, did not arrive till far too late. In the minds of all those planning the Liberation of Paris was the fate of Warsaw.

On 13 August Parisians heard the first sounds of distant gunfire to the west. Within a matter of days, a spontaneous uprising had begun in the city – beyond the control of either de Gaulle's headquarters in London or the approaching Allies. In command of the Communist forces was a thirty-six-year-old firebrand, 'Colonel Rol', Henri Tanguy, who had fought in the Spanish Civil War. Alarmingly he declared that 'Paris is worth 200,000 dead.' On the 15th the Communists brought the Paris railway workers out on strike. One strike followed another in lightning succession, effectively paralysing the city. For the first time during the whole period of German occupation the Métro stopped; electricity and gas failed; the cinemas closed – though, bizarrely, the theatres went on performing to the very last moment, by candlelight. Just as in 1871 euphoric young Parisians set to erecting hundreds of barricades throughout the city, though they would hardly be a match for Panzers.

Under constant pressure from Hitler in his East Prussian 'Wolf's Lair' (one of the Führer's last communications being the famous exhortation, 'Is Paris burning?'), Choltitz reluctantly but methodically began to prepare the demolition charges in such buildings as the Opéra and the Luxembourg. Trucks laden with naval torpedoes containing twelve tonnes of explosive crossed the city. Helpfully a local Luftwaffe general came to Choltitz offering to destroy the north-eastern end of the city, from Montmartre to the Buttes-Chaumont, in one long night of shuttle-bombing from Le Bourget airfield eight kilometres away. From the far reaches of the Reich a terrifying artillery piece, 'Karl', a giant 600 mm mortar, was sent on its way by Hitler to join in the destruction of the city, and the Führer talked of deluging the city with V-1 flying bombs.

On the 19th the police went on strike, allowing the Prefecture on the Île de la Cité to be taken over by the FFI, who turned it into a fortress. For the first time since 1940, Parisians saw the *tricolore* flutter above it. For the next five days the Prefecture held out as a focus of resistance as the Germans attacked it with every weapon in their arsenal. From his headquarters across the river in the Marais, de Gaulle's representative Alexandre Parodi, haunted by the image of a ravaged Warsaw, watched in alarm as Rol unleashed his premature uprising. Urgently he radioed de Gaulle to persuade Eisenhower to send troops to Paris immediately. Finally de Gaulle's entreaties won. Reluctantly, and with a superb sense of diplomatic imperatives, Eisenhower ordered General Bradley to despatch the French Second Armoured Division, under his subordinate General Leclerc, forthwith for Paris. Bradley was to have a back-up of units of the veteran US Fourth Division following close alongside Leclerc, just in case things went wrong or got out of hand. De Gaulle had meanwhile arrived at the recently liberated Château de Rambouillet, some fifty-five kilometres south-west of Paris. According to an aide, as he awaited Leclerc he took down from the library bookshelves a copy of Molière's *Le Bourgeois Gentilhomme*, to steady his nerves. To Leclerc he gave the order to move, adding, 'Go fast. We cannot have another Commune.'

General Bradley then learned, to his extreme annoyance, that Leclerc was already under way and planning to swing eastwards so as to enter Paris from the south, through the Porte d'Orléans – the route that Napoleon had followed in 1814 at the beginning of the Hundred Days, but contrary to the line of march laid down by Bradley's headquarters. French history books would henceforth be able to relate how Paris had been liberated by French forces, with a little Allied assistance. Nevertheless, the move on Paris was to prove barely in time. Inside the city Raoul Nordling, an inspired Swedish consul, had in the meantime managed to arrange a ceasefire with Choltitz. Even though it was soon broken, it almost certainly saved the men beleaguered in the Prefecture.

Under the ceasefire the German occupation forces began to pull out, accompanied by truckloads of loot. One officer was even seen trying to tear down the curtains at the Majestic and stuff them into his suitcase, to 'make a dress later on'. With them also left the leading *collabos*, to join Pétain and Laval – scooped up from the luxury of the Matignon – in semi-house arrest at the former Hohenzollern Schloss of Sigmaringen on the Danube. There, miserably, they sat out the remaining eight months of the war, treated with contempt by their Nazi 'liberators', waiting for the Allies and their inevitable fate. With their departure *Je Suis Partout* was rechristened by Parisian wits, *Je Suis Parti*.

LECLERC AND DE GAULLE

As fast as the German SS under Choltitz mined buildings, the *fifis* (nickname of the FFI) cut the wires. A truck full of naval torpedoes on its way to the Palais Bourbon was ambushed and blown up. At long last and just in time, as the defenders were running out of food and ammunition, on 24 August Leclerc's armour entered Paris. With the US 4th Division was an American major who later recalled 'fifteen solid miles of cheering, deliriously happy people waiting to shake your hand, to kiss you, to shower you with food and wine'. The almost hysterical welcome threatened to slow the advance. Meanwhile, inside the Kommandantur in the Meurice, Choltitz had received one more signal from Wehrmacht headquarters with the imperative question, 'Demolitions started?' He calmly finished his lunch, listened to the church bells outside proclaiming the arrival of the Allies, instructed his orderly to pack his grip for prisoner-of-war camp, and surrendered to Lieutenant Henri Karcher of Leclerc's division. Miraculously the ever-rickety Paris telephone system was still functioning, and Karcher was able to ring his stepfather in Auteuil with the news.

By the end of fighting on 27 August, the battle for Paris had cost Leclerc 71 killed and 225 wounded, though approximately 900 FFI had been killed, as well as some 600 civilian Parisians. German casualties as claimed by the FFI were 11,000 (somewhat larger than the forces actually under Choltitz's command) with fifty-seven tanks destroyed (compared with the four in fact at the Kommandant's disposal). That night US war correspondent Ernie Pyle recorded Paris's explosion of joy as 'the loveliest, brightest story of our time'.

The 26th of August was to be Charles de Gaulle's day: the day he had been waiting for since 18 June 1940 – possibly, indeed, the day for which fate had been preparing him since he fell wounded and a captive at Verdun in February 1916, but certainly the greatest of his entire life. After pacing impatiently up and down the great terrace at Rambouillet, he set off for Paris on the 25th, 'simultaneously gripped by emotion and filled with serenity'. He met his own son Philippe, then a naval ensign with Leclerc's division, on his way to the Palais Bourbon with a German major to accept the garrison's surrender. He expressed disapproval that

Colonel Rol's name should appear on the surrender document, alongside Leclerc's, then went to 'reoccupy' his old office at the Ministry of War in Rue Saint-Dominique. There he found nothing had changed since he and Paul Reynaud had left together on the night of 10 June 1940. At last he reached the Hôtel de Ville, on foot.

To the acute discomfort of the Allied planners, who had intended to keep control over the future French government at least in the short term, de Gaulle had stolen yet another march over them; and, indeed, over Colonel Rol's Communist cohorts, who had in fact done most of the fighting during Liberation week – albeit without de Gaulle's endorsement. Nobody in London or Washington had expected to see de Gaulle installed, and functioning, in Paris for some time. Yet there he was, digging in, and – as one senior US diplomat recognized, 'Nothing short of force was going to budge him out.' At the Hôtel de Ville de Gaulle told the euphoric members of his entourage, 'The enemy is shaken, but he is not beaten ... more than ever our national unity is a necessity ... War, unity, grandeur – that is my programme.' He then stepped out on to the balcony and made a brief speech to the mass of people who packed the square below. One of his most powerful, it was addressed anthropomorphically to the city at his feet:

> Paris! Paris outraged! Paris shattered! Paris martyred! But Paris *liberated*. Liberated by herself, liberated by her people, in concurrence with the armies of France, with the support and concurrence of the whole of France, of fighting France, the only France, the true France, eternal France.

Mention of Allied involvement in these great events was judiciously withheld. The crowd began to chant rhythmically 'De Gaulle! De Gaulle! De Gaulle!' One of the Communists was heard to remark, 'We've been had.' So, for that matter, had the General's Allies; and on that day was sealed the bid for independence and Gaullist pre-eminence that would be the source of many headaches in long years to come.

The next day, Saturday, 26 August, de Gaulle, wearing as always his uniform and *képi* of a simple brigadier-general, recognizable above all the crowds, his only decorations the Cross of Lorraine and the red-and-blue badge of the Free French, made his historic and solemn promenade down the Champs-Elysées. It had all the appearance of spontaneity, yet must have lain in de Gaulle's mind for many months. It began with his placing a wreath of red gladioli at the tomb of the Unknown Soldier at the Etoile. He relit the eternal flame, the first Frenchman to perform this sacred rite in freedom since 1940, then began the walk down the avenue which had been laid out by previous French rulers for just such an occasion. All the way down to the Concorde, rooftops and windows were crowded with cheering thousands, in a day of perfect sunshine.

The lofty, haughty, unsmiling figure dominated all around him. Behind him came the other Gaullist political notables who would resume trading under the flag of the Fourth Republic, and Generals Koenig, Juin and Leclerc who had led the Free French on the long route march from Africa and defeat. Behind came a mêlée of those who only so recently had been fighting to liberate Paris. It was an uneven mass; de Gaulle had specifically wanted to avoid anything resembling a formal military parade. Lining the streets were the battle-worn troops of Leclerc's division. This in itself was yet another source of antagonism with the American High Command, for Leclerc had been ordered to rejoin the march towards Germany, but de Gaulle had countermanded the order with the cool response: 'I loaned you Leclerc . . . I can perfectly well borrow him back for a few moments.' Pointedly none of the American troops of the US 4th Divison were invited to participate. Their time would come – but not for a few days.

De Gaulle's walk down the Champs-Elysées was a remarkably courageous, if not foolhardy, undertaking. Between him and Choltitz's withdrawing forces were only one US regiment and a combat team of Leclerc's division. Heavy fighting continued in the northern districts through the 27th; the city had not yet been cleared of enemy snipers, and there were many trigger-happy members of the FFI still at large. But this extraordinary man, on this extraordinary day, 'believed in the fortune of France' – as he had never ceased to do. As the procession debouched into the Concorde, the first shots rang out. Many of the crowd threw themselves down for cover, but de Gaulle walked straight on. An American sergeant, who admitted hiding behind his jeep and later 'felt ashamed', watched him keep on moving, standing 'very straight, standing tall for his country'.

Towards 4.30 in the afternoon, the entourage reached Notre-Dame for a Te Deum. Once more mysterious shots rang out, their provenance still a mystery to this day (though de Gaulle himself firmly blamed the Communists). Malcolm Muggeridge, then a British intelligence officer who had reached Paris late the previous night, witnessed the scene:

> The effect was fantastic. The huge congregation who had all been standing suddenly fell flat on their faces . . . There was a single

exception; one solitary figure, like a lonely giant. It was, of course, de Gaulle. Thenceforth, that was how I always saw him – towering and alone; the rest, prostrate.

The shooting confirmed de Gaulle in his intention to disarm the FFI and bring it under military discipline as soon as possible, and to assume 'the legitimate power' himself.

After 26 August 1944, remarked an American journalist with only slight exaggeration, 'De Gaulle had France in the palm of his hand.' With hindsight a historian today might also say that it was just as well. By his prompt intervention that month de Gaulle probably saved France from the murderous revolution that overtook Greece on liberation later that same year. He certainly forestalled a Communist takeover in Paris.

That night, as Paris indulged herself in an orgy of celebration, and priests (generally unheeded) distributed cautionary tracts to young *Parisiennes* – 'in the gaiety of the Liberation do not throw away your innocence. Think of your future family' – Hitler carried out one last act of futile vengeance. The commander of Luftflotte 3, who had earlier offered his services to Choltitz, launched from Le Bourget a valedictory raid of 150 planes on the east of the city. It was the heaviest air-raid Paris experienced during the entire war. Because of the celebrations, not a single anti-aircraft gun responded. Nearly a thousand Parisians were wounded, 214 killed, and the Halles aux Vins largely destroyed. It was a bitter reminder, amid all the rejoicing, that the war still continued. As de Gaulle watched the bombing from his old 1940 office in the Ministry of War, almost echoing Clemenceau in 1919, he sighed to an aide, '*Eh bien*, there you see – the war goes on. The hardest days are ahead. Our work has just begun.'

20

'I Was France'

How can you govern a country that has 246 varieties of cheese!

Charles de Gaulle, 1951

THE *ÉPURATION*

After all the humiliations, sorrow, dangers and deprivations of the Occupation, the three days of 24 to 26 August had provided Paris with an enormous catharsis. It would be pleasant to end the story of the Liberation on that heroic note, but its shadowy side now presented itself. In some ways what the French did to themselves after the Occupation was almost as painful as what the Germans had done to them during it. Even before the last Germans had left the city, the *épuration* began – in which vengeance was inextricably mixed with justice. The first victims, understandably, were the German troops themselves, often lynched or stood up against a wall when they emerged from their strongholds with hands raised. Then came the *collabos* – or the alleged *collabos*. The *épuration* took place all over France, but it was particularly far-reaching in Paris insofar as this was where collaboration had been most extensive and most visible. What especially struck Allied eyewitnesses was the ferocity with which women, the *collabos horizontales*, were treated. The shaving of heads, seen all over France, was perhaps the least indignity. Jean Cocteau records being shocked by the sight of one woman, 'completely naked', on the Avenue de la Grande Armée: 'they tore at her, they pushed her, they pulled her, they spat in her face. Her head had been shaven. She was covered in bruises and carried around her neck a placard: "I had my husband shot."'

Parisians prominent in the public eye such as writers, journalists, actors and artists were among the first to be affected, while industrialists who had worked for the Germans strangely seemed to escape. Cocteau's 'partner' Jean Marais swiftly seized the option of joining the army on 2 September, returning to take the lead in 1946 in Cocteau's *La Belle et la bête*. Cocteau remained, but was given a rough time. As early as 23 August Sacha Guitry was hustled out of his posh abode on the Champ-de-Mars by a posse of *fifis*, still in his yellow-flowered pyjamas and wearing a panama hat. He was taken to Drancy, which had been cleared of its surviving Jewish deportees, now transformed into a sifting centre for *collabos*. There he ran into his former wife, which entitled him to quip that 'One's mishaps never come singly!' The Vél d'Hiv, likewise of evil recent memory, had become a reception centre for all suspects arrested. One inmate recorded how, at Drancy, some 4,000 people were herded together for several days:

> at the mercy of forty FFI. These were commanded by a young chief of twenty-two, himself liberated from Drancy and animated with the single spirit of retaliation ...
>
> Numerous women have been violated. Many internees were woken up at night and beaten until blood flowed.

Many were held without charge or documentation. Finally in September de Gaulle himself intervened, appointing an inspector of prisons and internment camps, and gradually punishing excesses.

Nevertheless, the *épuration* continued. The dread word *délation* once again played its role as neighbour denounced neighbour, often merely to settle scores. All crimes and evils were, of course, heaped on the head of Vichy and the old Marshal, currently awaiting his fate in Sigmaringen. The beautiful Arletty, who had just made *Les Enfants du paradis*, deprived of her Luftwaffe lover and suite in the Ritz, was arrested in September, and grisly rumours ran through the city that her breasts had been cut off; almost certainly her head was shaven. But what was held against her was not so much that she had slept with a German senior officer as that she had dined with him at the Ritz when other Parisians went hungry. Occasionally the accused bit back with spirit, one *horizontale* declaring unashamedly, 'Mon cul est international, mais mon coeur est toujours français!' The mother of one seventeen-year-old complained, 'Why ever cut off her hair for it? ... She's just as willing to go to bed with the Americans!'

When in 1945 the surviving deportees began to trickle back from

German concentration camps – via the Hôtel Lutetia, which had so recently been the headquarters of the Abwehr – their appalling condition aroused another acute wave of anti-German and anti-*collabo* feelings. After the showing of newsfilms of the horrors of liberated Belsen, two jails were stormed and collaborators taken out and lynched. The trials of the *grands collabos* ground on through 1945 and 1946. Brasillach was shot; among the few leading writers who refused to sign a plea for clemency on his behalf were Sartre and de Beauvoir. In vain the noble Camus, who had taken up arms with the Resistance, begged for 'justice without hatred'. 'National indignity' (*dégradation nationale*) was a newly coined crime for which many thousands of *collabos* were imprisoned. Sentenced to life imprisonment, the rabid right-winger Charles Maurras insisted, 'C'est la revanche de Dreyfus!'

In the summer of 1945, in the Palais de Justice, began the trials of the leaders of Vichy, first of Pétain, then of Laval. To foreign observers, it seemed like a trial of Vichy itself as the French, who, denied access under the Occupation to anything that could be described as a newspaper, learned of its realities for the first time. Parisian feelings towards Pétain palpably tilted as the survivors from the death camps returned home, their emaciated appearance a powerful reminder of the iniquities committed in the name of Vichy. The old hero of Verdun, fallen into such disgrace, refused to speak in his defence. The only time when his face, according to an American journalist present, took on 'a marble mask of shame' was when the prosecution revealed the deportation of 120,000 Jews, of whom only 15,000 returned. The trial ended in August, the day after the end of the world war in which Pétain's Vichy had played so ignominious a part, with the Marshal disappearing for life into the fortress prison of the Île de Yeu in the Bay of Biscay. He died there, aged ninety-five, six years later. More of a disgraceful farce was the show-trial, beginning in October, of the hated Pierre Laval. It reminded some of 'a cross between an *auto-da-fé* and a tribunal during the Paris terror'. Screaming back at his prosecutors, Laval dominated the court, comporting himself with formidable courage up to the very moment when, barely resuscitated after taking cyanide, he died lashed to a chair before a firing squad at Fresnes Prison.

Meanwhile only a very subdued sympathy for the two leaders was voiced among the *gratin* of Paris who had so widely supported Vichy. Out of it all began to emerge the depressing truth that the Resistance had represented but a small minority, compared with the 'silent and massive acquiescence' of the rest of France. The real number of those killed in the course of the *épuration* has never been verified. It varies from a high of 105,000 for all France down to Robert Aron's estimate of only 30,000 to 40,000 – compared with 30,000 Frenchmen killed by the Germans and the *milice* during the Occupation. One more recent, French authority puts the figure at only 9,000 summary executions, most of them carried out before the Normandy landings, plus 767 death sentences carried out subsequently following lawful trials. The same author claims that the *épuration* in France was more 'moderate' than in Belgium, Holland, Norway and Denmark. The jury is still out, but in Paris alone there were 100,000 arrests. In lieu of prison, a quarter of all defendants in France were condemned to that new and lingering legal formula of *dégradation nationale*.

VICTORY IN EUROPE

As de Gaulle had warned on the night of 26 August, for Paris the war was not over. Though the Wehrmacht had retreated back across the Rhine – which prompted the over-optimistic to recall 1918 and assume that collapse would follow in short order – that December Field Marshal von Rundstedt struck back hard in the Ardennes. The Americans recoiled westwards, and to the French, all too mindful of 1940, momentarily it looked as if there might be a replay. There followed that first harsh winter of the Liberation, 1944–5. Gas and coal shortages meant that there was neither heating nor even cooking. For a family of three a week's ration came to half a pound of meat and three-fifths of a pound of butter. The irrepressible *chansonniers* produced a song entitled 'Sans beurre et sans brioches', a pun on the *brave* Bayard, 'le chevalier sans peur et sans reproche'. Even wine was rationed to three litres per adult per month. By the end of 1945, because of lack of fuel, it was further reduced to one litre a month, and not finally unrationed till mid-1948, though even then some of it was watered, or what the French call 'baptized', spoiling quickly.

Parisians began to grumble that things were even worse than they had been under the Occupation. Suddenly food cost still more – though, mysteriously, it was less on the black market. Largely through US military racketeers, the black market assumed giant proportions –

sometimes even the trucks disappeared into its maw along with the food they brought, threatening the Allied advance into Germany. There was nothing black-market cigarettes could not buy. To François Mauriac, government efforts against the black market resembled those of 'the child St Augustine saw on a beach who wanted to empty the sea with a shell'. Sensibly, the government gave up.

This time, unlike the aftermath of earlier national catastrophes which had laid France low, her recovery was agonizingly slow and halting. For once, *la France profonde* had lost her *richesse*. Bridges, roads, railways, industries had been ruined by war. The Germans had pulled out destroying crops and farms, as well as taking two-thirds of the country's trucks and railway rolling-stock. Between one and a half and two million buildings had been razed. There were still 800,000 skilled French factory workers serving as slave labour in Germany, another million or more remaining in the prisoner-of-war camps, plus the deport- ees. Altogether there were estimated to be four million more women than men in France as the war ended – many in mourning. Their wooden shoes continued to echo through empty streets like the sound of horses' hooves. In smart shop windows shoes were marked 'model' and were not for sale. Of luxuries there were none: Christmas-tree decorations that winter consisted of the aluminium foil dropped from Allied bombers to confuse German radar. Newspapers were reduced to a sheet or two. There was no petrol, except for doctors and taxi drivers (and except on the black market).

Even after the German surrender in May 1945, of true victory there was hardly a sign. It was indeed an exsanguinated Paris. Morally, four years of Occupation had left behind it a universal torpor; thousands of hours of queuing seemed to have killed something of the Parisian spirit. It was a glum city, restless, anxious, cantankerous and convalescent. Theatres were packed (partly for the warmth), but the shops and grocers still empty. VE-Day came and went with muted elation. Such enthusiasm as there was at the ending of the war in Europe was greatly tempered by the return of 300 women from Ravensbrück. They were met by General de Gaulle – who wept. Eleven had died *en route* from eastern Germany, and too much suffering showed in the survivors' faces and bodies.

Politically, there were continued grumbles of revolution in Paris among the Communists, who felt de Gaulle had cheated them in August. As the hot war moved, almost without break, into the Cold War, the situation remained tense. The Communist Party was convinced that it would soon be swept into power. Its boss, Maurice Thorez, who had spent the war conveniently in Moscow, having deserted from the French army in 1939, declared menacingly, 'We are in favour of revolution, tomorrow ... We are not going to help the capitalist regime to reform itself.' It set the scene for the Fourth Republic. In October 1945, France duly voted in a referendum to kill off the failed Third Republic, which had survived all of seventy-five turbulent years. Whereas the Third Republic had started off life so rich that, even after the depredations of the Franco-Prussian War, it easily paid off its debt to the enemy, the Fourth Republic was so poor that it had to begin by borrowing from America.

In the view of one observer, it was a bit like 'a woman with three hands, two left and one right' – the two left hands being constituted by the Socialists and the fearsomely powerful Communist Party, the right by the Catholic, moderate conservative Mouvement Républicain Populaire (MRP). In the relentless conflict between these rivals, 'whose simultaneous presence in goverment', said the veteran Léon Blum, 'is at once indispensable and impossible', consensus on any vital issue was rarely achieved. As de Gaulle pointed out, the old political life of the Third Republic had simply started up again. Governments came and went, twenty of them between 1945 and 1954: M. Pleven succeeded M. Queuille, who then replaced M. Pleven, who in turn was pushed out by M. Queuille – all in the space of thirteen months. When asked by an American senator what happened when French governments 'run out of horses', President Auriol replied, 'We go back to the original ones!' Thus were the old hacks of the Third Republic constantly recycled. For the next decade and a half, 'this absurd ballet' (as de Gaulle called it) would render government by political democracy all but impossible in France.

As de Gaulle had once declared with sublime modesty, 'I was France, the State, the government ... that moreover was why, finally, everyone obeyed me.' And, like Louis XIV and Napoleon I, he was determined there be no rivalry to the central authority of the state. But when he found that he would not, in fact, be 'obeyed' by the returning players from the Third Republic and that the authority of the government would constantly be challenged, in January 1946 (on the anniversary of Louis XVI's execution) he pulled out, into retirement. When asked what he intended to do, he replied laconically, 'J'attends!' Before embarking on the long wait, which would last twelve years, he left a stern New Year's Day warning: 'I predict you will bitterly regret having taken the road you have taken.' At the Palais Bourbon the Fourth Republic lurched on, from crisis to crisis, without him, steadily gaining the contempt of the public, just as its predecessor the Third had done. Illustrative of this contempt, the unpopular but piously named Premier André Marie, who survived just one month in the summer of 1948, had his brief regime rudely christened 'the government of the Immaculate Deception'.

FIRST SIGNS OF RECOVERY

Like a first swallow of spring, a small harbinger of recovery came in September 1945, with the return to Paris of the Windsors – plus their 134 pieces of luggage. One American journalist thought the lines on the Duke's face to be 'the result of too much sun, not too much thought'. Totally out of touch with the France they had fled in 1940, the Duchess remarked that 'Paris offered the most expensive discomfort she had ever known.' With them returned other distinguished émigré Parisians, such as Natalie Barney, back to her salon and Hellenic Temple in the Rue Jacob, while social revival in Paris revolved around the glittering Duff Coopers across the river at the British Residence.

Food shortages continued in Paris for at least two years after the war, hand in hand with a sense of gloom and a bitterly anti-German feeling. The winter of 1946–7 was, again, horribly cold, and Parisians shivered in unheated houses. There was constant fear of a Communist, Soviet-backed takeover. Nineteen-forty-seven was a year of endless strikes, with at one point three million workers out across the country. Then, suddenly, there was a reversal when in December Communist miners in the north derailed a train, killing sixteen people. As news reached Paris, the city was paralysed by strike action, the centre virtually in a state of siege, with armed police at every intersection. Revulsion was universal, and the derailment of the Paris–Tourcoing express was something of a turning point. 'We have had a brush with civil war and, given the possibility of Soviet intervention, with war itself,' so President Vincent Auriol wrote in the last pages of his diary for that year, but 'despite that France has begun her recovery'.

The following year, the creation of NATO gave military security to France, and Marshall Aid brought the beginnings of new prosperity. Fifty-three Paris theatres and five music halls had reopened and were going full blast; Josephine Baker had returned to the Folies Bergère. By 1949 rationing had ended; there were traffic jams in Paris and the first influx of American tourists since 1929; the franc was soaring, the dollar – overloaded by its generosity – sinking. Nevertheless, strikes continued endlessly to paralyse the French economy, and especially Paris. Year after year, the farmers and the middle classes, as well as the very rich, somehow avoided paying taxes with impunity. Inflation ran wild, resulting in a regular devaluation of the franc, and in 1951 spiralling prices and an overvalued currency had dragged exports down 20 per cent and pushed imports up 36 per cent. For years the French economy made practically no headway.

Britons could watch piously as France seemed to be strangling herself, but outside the popular gaze serious economic and industrial planning was under way. A number of outstanding civil servants were developing remarkable long-range schemes for the future. As early as December 1945, Jean Monnet and a small staff of brilliant men were at work contemplating what was to become the Schuman Coal and Steel Pool, the forerunner of the European Economic Community. For the first time in 150 years France was offering to assist the Germans, help them recreate their basic industries in conjunction with her own, so as to provide a new foundation for peace and prosperity in Europe. In June 1950 there was a first meeting, at the Quai d'Orsay's historic Salon de l'Horloge, of the European 'Six' – a six from which Britain was markedly absent.

Immediately after the war against Japan ended, an exhausted France found herself at war in Indo-China, her most precious colonial possession in the Far East, a war waged single-mindedly by that former assistant pastry-cook who had attended the Peace Conference of 1919 and had seen the mighty colonial powers in disarray there, Ho Chi Minh. Each year the *sale guerre* in the jungles consumed vast sums of money (twice as many dollars as the US gave France to pay for it) and class after class of Saint-Cyr officers (thousands more French lives than the US lost in Korea). The great General, who might just have brought it to a successful conclusion, de Lattre de Tassigny, died of cancer in 1952. He alone might have been intelligent enough to stave off the humiliating and decisive defeat which the French army was to suffer at Dien Bien Phu in May 1954. Catastrophe in Indo-China brought to power one of the ablest and most honest politicans of the Fourth Republic, the brilliant Sephardic Jew Pierre Mendès-France. In the face of determined opposition, with the usual unpleasant undertones of anti-Semitism on the right, Mendès-France was able to extricate France from the quagmire of Indo-China, handing on the baton to the US.

Then, within half a year of Dien Bien Phu, encouraged by France's defeat there, concerted revolt broke out in Algeria. There had already been uprisings to force France out of Tunisia and Morocco. However, established as an integral part of metropolitan France, Algeria was no mere colony, but the transcendent diamond in France's imperial diadem, with a million *pieds noirs* (as the colonists were called) settled there. Although at first little noticed in Paris, a combination of the war in Algeria and Mendès-France's unpopular attempts to wean Normandy school children from calvados on to milk and to alter the traditional drinking habits of France brought him down. The savage war struggled on for another seven and a half years, destroying the Fourth Republic, coming close to inflicting a military takeover in France, and bringing back de Gaulle as the only possible saviour. Meanwhile, as far as metropolitan France, and Paris in particular, was concerned, the conflicts in Indo-China and Algeria led to a sense of alienation among the troops not unlike that between the front and the rear in 1914–18. It was a sense of detachment that would rebound to hit de Gaulle – and metropolitan France – hard in the 1960s.

BIDONVILLES

During the Occupation, not surprisingly, all building and construction work in Paris came to an abrupt halt. About the only achievement was completion of a small stretch of the *autoroute de l'ouest* out at Saint-Cloud, which had been begun in 1935. Paris architects continued discussing the Porte Maillot development, and there were talks with Hitler's Albert Speer on the future plans for Berlin. Out of the immense destruction which had left so many of Europe's buildings damaged or destroyed, Paris mercifully had suffered relatively little. Nevertheless there was an acute housing shortage because of the flow of refugees from the devastated areas who reached Paris – and stuck. When the war ended, with neither funds nor material available, for ten years there was a virtual moratorium on any new work in Paris.

Those years constituted, architecturally, a dismal period in the history of Paris, for maintenance was deplorably neglected, old buildings like the Louvre left to crumble and be blackened by smoke and eroded by pollution. Slum areas and shanty towns continued to deteriorate alarmingly, and disgraceful *bidonvilles* sprang up in the areas once occupied by the old fortifications. The Chambre Syndicale de la Savonnerie revealed that in post-war Paris only 15 per cent of dwellings possessed bathrooms, and that soap consumption was the lowest in Europe – hence, concluded an American correspondent, 'the popularity of Eau-de-Cologne'. Even as late as 1954 the city authorities reported that 74 per cent of the capital's dwellings were 'substandard'.

Bringing the coldest weather in memory, the winter of 1954 also gave rise to a remarkable human phenomenon. So bitter was January that police found a woman frozen to death on the Boulevard de Sébastopol, an eviction notice clutched in her fist – a scene straight out of Balzac. The morgues were crammed with the frozen bodies of *clochards* whom even the hot air from the Métro grills could not warm. Appearing from nowhere, an unknown Jesuit priest calling himself the Abbé Pierre, a tiny bearded figure in his forties, the son of a wealthy Lyons silk manufacturer who had fought in the Resistance in the Vercors, seized the attention of all Paris. One evening, before the main feature, he leaped on to the stage of one of Paris's largest cinemas and pleaded, 'Mes amis, aidez-nous', before describing the misery of the poor in the *bidonvilles* out in the unseen suburbs of Saint-Denis and Nanterre. He struck a chord; within two weeks more than a billion francs poured in from all walks of life, including sentimental prostitutes. The directors of the Métro converted three unused stations into lodgings for the homeless; Abbé Pierre took to haunting the corridors of the National Assembly, until he persuaded the Minister of Housing Maurice Lemaire to accompany him into the slums where a child had recently died of cold, reducing Lemaire to tears and to admitting, 'It never occurred to me that we have such misery in France.' The Minister introduced a new bill to spend ten billion francs on low-cost housing. Then – typically of the Fourth Republic – the government fell, and nothing was done. Spring came, the poor disappeared from the Paris conscience, and so did Abbé Pierre.

The outstanding architectural monuments to the Fourth Republic were two great curved complexes of monotone concrete and windows, the UNESCO Building (completed in 1959), the largest building ever commissioned in Paris by an international body (but somewhat jerry-built), and the ORTF broadcasting centre (completed between 1956 and 1963) on the Right Bank, supposedly designed to resemble a gigantic electro-magnet. Conditioning all post-war city planning in Paris, as well as being its worst enemy, was the automobile. Turning the Concorde into a one-way *carrousel* and a ban on hooting were only first bites at the cherry. For years the city was heaved up as vast, sometimes seven-storey-deep car parks were burrowed under the Concorde, the Place Vendôme and almost everywhere else. There were violent protests as, in 1955, the magnificent chestnuts by the Place de l'Alma disappeared, then the riverside elms, victims of the new speedway down the Right Bank.

WRITERS AND ARTISTS

The end of the war led in Paris to an immense hunger for ideas, restricted only by an initial shortage of paper. The new writing based itself in Saint-Germain-des-Prés, and more specifically the bar of the Café Flore – which happened to be convenient to the residence of the great guru of Existentialism, Jean-Paul Sartre, and his consort Simone de Beauvoir. Holding forth with a torrent of sophistry in the smoke-filled rooms of the Flore, he never wanted for a captive audience of students, many of them American. De Beauvoir, sometimes known as *la grande sartreuse*, like a prim governess with her hair austerely tied back, was ever the better writer, breaking new feminist ground with her *Le Deuxième sexe* and providing valuable material for contemporary historians with her various books of memoirs and her criticism of the Algerian War in *La Force des choses* (1963).

Among the new writers of the 1950s whose books about the past war deeply shocked Parisians was Jean Dutourd, first of all with his flaying attack on the nastiness of the *petits collabos* in *Au bon beurre* (1952) and – three years later – with his *Les Taxis de la Marne*, which exalted heroism at the same time as it excoriated the debility of the 'men of '40'. A few months after the publication of *Au bon beurre* Parisian theatre-goers were agog with excitement at the first night of Samuel Beckett's *En attendant Godot* – even if many understood its cheerless message even less well than the philosophy of Sartre. Highly contemporary, but much more entertaining, was Raymond Queneau's irreverent bestseller of 1959, *Zazie dans le Métro*, featuring a horribly knowing child from the provinces, precociously aware of transvestism, lesbians, paedophilia and child prostitution, her one desire to travel on the Métro – which is of course on strike.

In the intensely hot August of 1954 the revered Colette died, and was given a public funeral in the Cour d'Honneur of the Palais Royal, paid for by the state – the highest posthumous honour attainable, and the first time it had ever been accorded to a woman. 'Pagan, sensuous, Dionysiac,' declaimed the Minister of Education in his funeral address, and all Paris mourned. Surrounded by her cats, her last few years had been spent being carried from place to place in a sedan chair, sometimes sending down to the Grand Véfour for a lark pie. 'What a beautiful life I've had,' she was recorded as remarking towards the end. 'It's a pity I didn't notice it sooner.' As Colette left the scene, so almost simultaneously a new female writer, aged only eighteen, arose to fill the gap – and take Paris by storm: Françoise Sagan, who was both a product of and a reaction against the Existentialist wave. Writing of *Bonjour tristesse*, her first novel, François Mauriac praised its literary merit but described its heroine as 'a charming little monster'.

Of the outstanding journalists of the 1950s and 1960s, there was of course Camus, who founded *Combat* as a Resistance organ during the war, to continue long afterwards as a national paper – with his rallying cry that it was required of his generation to rise 'up to the level of its despair'. There was also the vigorous young figure of Jean-Jacques Servan-Schreiber, who launched *L'Express*. Known popularly as J-J S-S, Servan-Schreiber headed the attack on French policy in Algeria, exposing the worst excesses of torture, before going on to attack the foe of American universal power in *Le Défi américain*. Also deserving of mention was that remarkable phenomenon, the Paris correspondent of the London *Evening Standard*, Sam White. With his gravelly voice, Australian prize-fighter's nose and generally dishevelled appearance, liberally covered with cigarette ash, Sam was central-casting for a tough foreign correspondent as played by Bogart.

In the world of painting, Picasso – forgiven his wartime career in Paris – went from strength to inventive strength (and from mistress to mistress), turning his hand to sculpture, fashioning marvellous bulls out of bits of old bicycles, broken urns and baskets. In 1949 he re-established both his pre-eminence and the claim of Paris once more to be the global art forum at an exhibition of sixty-four recent canvases. At the same time there was a retrospective of ninety works by Léger at the Modern

Art Museum. As Picasso cornered the market, so other fabled contemporaries left it: in 1954 Derain died, knocked off his bicycle at the age of seventy-four; Matisse went next, in November, aged eighty-four, followed, in 1955, by Léger, his funeral held under the auspices of the Communist Party, of which he (like Picasso) was a member, and by Utrillo – tragically alcoholic since the age of ten, much overrated as an original artist, but his canvases of a grey Montmartre still commanding the highest prices.

DISTRACTIONS

There was one branch of the arts in which Paris had always led the world, and did so again just as soon as wartime restrictions lifted – *haute couture*. To reclaim its ascendancy, the industry put on a remarkable exhibition even before the fighting ended, in the Louvre's Pavillon de Marsan at the end of March 1945, masterminded by Robert Ricci (son of Nina), Lucien Lelong, Christian Bérard, Dior, Patou, Carven and other great names. To beat shortages of materials the new designs that were going to sweep the post-war world were displayed on faceless, miniature dolls made of wire and looking like Surrealist sculptures. Some were even clad in silk underwear. In freezing attics, warming their hands over candles, an army of seamstresses and milliners had worked bravely and ceaselessly through the winter to produce the new clothes. To give it due importance the Garde Républicaine, *en grande tenue*, formed a guard of honour on the opening night. The exhibition was an immediate success: over 100,000 came to see it. Many could not possibly afford the dresses that would, eventually, be sold from the doll models, and had had nothing new to wear since 1939, but were drawn by this heroic statement that Paris's pre-eminence in beauty and luxury was once more alive after the grim Occupation years.

February 1947 saw Christian Dior, a newcomer – described as suffering from 'an almost desperate shyness augmented by a receding chin' – put on his first post-war show in the Avenue Montaigne. Such was the buzz about the show that some Parisians even tried to get in through the top of the house by ladder; it was that night that the New Look, with its tightened waists and ample skirts, was born, and Parisian *haute couture* was once more back on its rightful throne. Dior was followed by Givenchy, Balmain, Balenciaga, Courrèges, Saint-Laurent and others.

Not everyone instantly fell in behind these illustrious names, however. The fashionable Louise de Vilmorin, Duff Cooper's mistress, was heard to declare in Saint-Germain that fashion was 'a veneer foisted on naive women by despots. Give me sincere blue jeans!' Worse still, when Dior took his models to be photographed at the Rue Lepic market in a deprived area of Montmartre they were mobbed by angry stall-holders who tore their hair and tried to rip their expensive clothes off. Once more, it was a clear demonstration of the continued coexistence of two Parises – the rich and the poor. Following a fashion of a different kind, on the male side – as a kind of counterpart to London's teddy-boys and a protest against contemporary values – were the *zazous*, children of the affluent bourgeois with their long greasy hair and equally exaggerated jackets with high collars – sometimes set upon and beaten up by Communist or fascist youths.

The world of the fashion model was not always that far removed from that of the oldest profession, once more back with a swing following the Liberation – with barely a pause for the cropped hair to regrow. By the early 1950s the Paris vice squad estimated the number of working prostitutes at around 17,000; they ranged from the blowzy working man's whores plying their trade for a few francs in the Place de la Bastille to stunning girls who worked the bars along the Champs-Elysées. More discreet, and more distinguished, were the various *maisons de passe*, or *maisons de rendezvous*, such as was so devastatingly portrayed in Buñuel's 1966 film *Belle de Jour*, and catering to every taste and perversion. There clients would be entertained by dazzling young models or *jeunes filles biens* in quest of a little extra pocket money and some fun.

THE SECOND COMING

Beset by the unwinnable Algerian War, by the merry-go-round of collapsing governments which seemed finally to have run out of talent and by perennial strikes, the Fourth Republic stumbled on to its extinction. Nineteen-fifty-six began with the unhappy omens of the Eiffel Tower catching fire and Mistinguett dying, followed by the longest stretch of cold weather (colder than Moscow) since 1940, which caused a quarter of Paris traffic lights to freeze up. Fisticuffs broke out in the Assembly, and the year ended with the humiliation of Suez – with France, in Parisian eyes, let down by both Britain and the United States, marking a caesura of distrust of her *anglo-saxon* allies never quite to be repaired.

Then, as a last indication of the decay of political institutions, there was the short-lived phenomenon of Pierre Poujade, a thirty-five-year-old shopkeeper from the Lot. A powerful rabble-rouser who appealed to his audience by performing a kind of striptease on the platform, hurling off his jacket, pullover and finally his shirt as he warmed to his subject, Poujade created a grassroots political party out of the discontent of France's small shopkeepers. Unambiguously called UDCA – Union de Défense des Commerçants et Artisans – it had the unpleasantly thuggish and anti-Semitic tendencies of the extreme right, but it was suddenly swept into the Assembly on a wave of petit-bourgeois discontent with taxation and government generally. In the elections of January 1956 UDCA amazed Paris and Poujade himself by attracting nearly two and a half million votes, to win 53 seats, with the Communists at the other extreme increasing their share from 95 to 150. It was the worst defeat for the conventional parties of the centre since the Republic first saw the light of day – and until the 2002 flowering of Jean Marie Le Pen. But within the year the Poujadists in the Assembly, an undistinguished lot, began to disintegrate, and Poujade himself disappeared as swiftly as he had arrived; but Poujadism remained – in the English as well as the French vocabulary.

During the long years since his abrupt departure from politics in 1946, de Gaulle remained in the wilderness, fretting at Colombey-les-Deux-Eglises, more and more sickened by having to witness men of the circus of the Fourth Republic seemingly dedicated to reducing France to a third-rate power. Then, just as it had been war which had brought de Gaulle to the forefront in 1940 and again in 1944, so it was the war – the disastrous Algerian War – that brought him back again in May 1958. His return was precipitated by a crisis in Algiers, after the Fourth Republic had proved its inability to end the fighting in Algeria. Tempers had been rising among the military in Algiers since the beginning of 1958, and the last straw had come with the execution in Tunisia of three captured French soldiers, on charges of torture, rape and murder. Exasperated, the army staged a coup in Algiers, beginning on 13 May with the seizure of the Gouvernement-Général building where resided the organs of civil authority. The redoubtable General Massu formed a Committee of Public Safety – a sinister-sounding name to Parisians with a sense of history. A series of plots and counterplots, in Corsica and the mainland as well as in Algeria, thrust forward an apparently reluctant de Gaulle, aged sixty-seven. De Gaulle played hard to get, calculating sagely that to acquire a modicum of legitimacy he should step forward only when a clear majority of Frenchmen seemed to want him. Over several anxious days, Paris braced herself for a possible descent from the skies of the paras from Algeria, tough and hard-fighting men fed to the teeth with the tergiversations and pusillanimity of civilian politicians.

Finally, on 28 May, Premier Pflimlin resigned. De Gaulle, returning late to his hotel, told the concierge, 'Albert, j'ai gagné!' The left reacted violently, with a giant demonstration of perhaps half a million winding its way from the Place de la Nation to the Place de la République – though not nearly as violently as some had feared. President Coty intervened. De Gaulle agreed to form a government. Later he was to recall how at home that night 'above my house I watched the twilight descend on the last evening of a long solitude. What was this mysterious force that compelled me to tear myself away from it?'

On 1 June, for the first time since he had departed in January 1946, he presented himself to the Assembly, and was accepted. The Communist deputies thumped their desks and shouted, 'Le fascisme ne passera pas!' But within a short while 30 per cent of Communist electors had deserted the Party. (Bizarrely, industrialists and big business also opposed de Gaulle initially – on the ground that he stood for change.) Otherwise an audible sigh of relief descended on Paris. In September de Gaulle held a referendum to put to the nation his new constitution, which conferred formidable powers on the President. Sartre voiced the left's opposition to 'King Charles XI', declaring, 'I do not believe in God, but if in this plebiscite I had the duty of choosing between Him and the present incumbent, I would vote for God; He is more modest.' Nevertheless, de Gaulle won by a sweeping majority. After all the confusion of the last days of the Fourth Republic, the new authority and indeed majesty ushered in by him had the most immediate and galvanizing effect upon France as a whole.

In January the following year, shortly after his sixty-eighth birthday, de Gaulle became president. His only words to his predecessor, 'Au revoir, Monsieur Coty', seemed like a calculated snub to the Fourth Republic. The Fifth Republic, and the new Gaullist era, had begun. France's allies felt encouraged. In Paris, the Académie got on with life, vigorously debating the correct sex of the automobile.

ALGERIA MOVES TO PARIS

With de Gaulle, authority moved back from Algiers and her rebellious factions to Paris, which once more became the capital of France. And at the same time, and for the next four years, the war in Algeria moved to Paris. Promptly in June 1958, de Gaulle flew to Algeria where he stunned the *pieds noirs* with his 'Je vous ai compris' speech – though it soon became apparent that he had understood them not in quite the way they had hoped. Valuable time was wasted; the impetus lost. Soon disillusion was renewed on all sides as it became apparent that even Charles de Gaulle had no simple formula for ending the war. It was going to defeat him just as it had the men of the Fourth Republic. Meanwhile, as more and more conscripts returned to tell their families what was going on in Algeria, and reports of torture multiplied, so anti-war sentiment mounted in Paris – and with it the demonstrations. With uncharacteristic indecision de Gaulle let eighteen months run through his hands before coming out with any clear-cut new policy for Algeria, and his attempts to achieve a ceasefire with the FLN (Front de Libération Nationale) were rejected with a crushing snub. Meanwhile the 'ultras' or diehards among the *pieds noirs* of Algiers were becoming steadily more violent in their opposition to de Gaulle.

On 24 January 1960, there was a fresh eruption in Algiers which rocked Paris. Well-armed 'ultras' started building barricades, in the best Communard tradition; gendarmes were brought in to clear them and firing broke out. The result was six dead and twenty-four wounded among the demonstrators, but no fewer than fourteen dead and 123 wounded among the unfortunate gendarmes caught in a deadly cross-fire. For France it was the ugliest moment in the five-year-old war to date – Frenchmen were killing Frenchmen for the first time. The spectre of the 1940s, and, further back, of 1871, presented itself. Equally ominous was the spectacle of the elite paras manifestly siding with the demonstrators on the barricades. As Barricades Week dragged on, in Paris there was a grim sense that, once again, revolution was in the air.

Then on the evening of the 29th, the weather took a friendly hand: in Algiers the skies opened on the over-heated citizenry. That same night de Gaulle appeared on television across France, dressed – with deliberate effect – in the uniform with its two stars familiar to so many in the army who could recall 1940 and the historic promenade through Paris in August 1944. It was as a soldier as well as head of state that he ordered the army in Algeria to obey him and not to side with the insurrection. He ended on an imploring note: 'Finally, I speak to France. Well, my dear country, my old country, here we are together, once again, facing a harsh test.' Though saying nothing new, it was one of his finest speeches, a performance of tremendous power. De Gaulle won. Under an icy rain in Algiers the would-be insurgents broke up and went off home.

Yet 1960 was to offer increasingly little comfort to de Gaulle, bringing less support and fresh enemies, as it brought the FLN new allies, both in the outside world and within France herself. In a remarkable summer entente, the Communist and non-Communist trades unions joined together to plead for successful peace negotiations, with threats of a general strike 'as an answer to any insurrection or *coup d'état*'. Among Parisian youth the Algerian War was now dubbed 'The Hundred Years War'. The discovery of Jean-Paul Belmondo and the impact of the *nouvelle vague* French cinema – especially of Roger Vadim's *Les Liaisons danger-euses*, which seemed then as daring as it was embarrassing to the puritanical Gaullists – suggested which way domestic interests were turning. More and more articles were appearing in the press by young national servicemen returning from Algeria shocked by the 'immoral acts' in which they had been forced to participate, or had seen or heard about. Out of all this inflammation of liberal sentiment there emerged in September in Paris a powerful 'Manifesto of the 121', which incited French conscripts to desert. The 121 signatories were all celebrities, including Sartre, de Beauvoir, Françoise Sagan and Simone Signoret. At the same time the 'Jeanson Network' physically aided the underground activities of the FLN in France, running funds for it and helping FLN terrorists in hiding.

Over Easter 1961, there were more plastic bombs in Paris, killing six and wounding fifty; a bomb in the men's room of the Bourse injured thirty. Then, in April, came the gravest challenge to de Gaulle that the Algerian War was to bring. In Algiers on the 20th and 21st four disaffected senior generals raised the standard of revolt in the name of *Algérie française* – headed by a much respected airman, General Maurice Challe, and by the highly political and wily principal in the 1958 coup, General Raoul Salan. At a meeting of Cabinet ministers on the 22nd, de Gaulle predicted contemptuously that the putsch would be 'a matter of three days', adding a scathing aside about 'this army which, politically, always deludes itself'.

De Gaulle's premier, Michel Debré, issued somewhat hysterical instructions for 'citizens' to go to any airfields where the paras might be dropping, and 'convince the misled soldiers of their grave error'. Possibly the true hero of that day of utter stupefaction in Paris was Roger Frey, de Gaulle's Minister of the Interior. With great decisiveness, he arrested a general and several other conspirators *in flagrante*, thereby wrecking an organized attempt to march on the capital. To this end some 1,800 lightly equipped paras had been assembled in the Forest of Orléans, and another 400 in the Forest of Rambouillet. They were to combine with tank units from Rambouillet and to move in three columns on Paris, seizing the Elysée and other key points of the administration. But, having been made leaderless by their general's arrest, they received no orders until a detachment of gendarmes arrived and instructed them to disperse. Sheepishly, the powerful body of paras did as they were told.

On Sunday, 23 April, Paris was an eerie place to be. Decaying Sherman tanks left over from the Second World War clattered into position outside the Assembly and other government buildings – some of them having to be towed after breaking down. No air movement round the city was allowed; buses, the Métro and trains stopped running, and even the cinemas were shut. Only the cafés stayed open, and they were packed. Then, at eight o'clock that night de Gaulle addressed the nation on television. Wearing his brigadier's uniform once more, he spoke of his beloved army in revolt, of 'the nation defied, our strength shaken, our international prestige debased, our position and our role in Africa compromised. And by whom? *Hélas! Hélas! Hélas!* By men whose duty, honour and raison d'être it was to serve and to obey.' At last it was time to exert his personal authority: 'In the name of France, I order that all means, I repeat all means, be employed to block the road everywhere to those men ... I forbid every Frenchman, and above all every soldier, to execute any of their orders.'

In what became known as the 'Battle of the Transistors', an important essay in the power to influence via modern communications, all across Algeria French conscripts listened to de Gaulle's speech – and heeded him. The vast majority refused to go along with their rebellious colonels and generals, and the 1961 putsch was over. The elite Foreign Legion paras, the power behind the revolt, dynamited their barracks in Zeralda and marched out defiantly singing Piaf's 'Je ne regrette rien'. Challe, a thoroughly decent and honourable man, surrendered to French justice. He received a maximum sentence of fifteen years' imprisonment, and loss of his rank, decorations and pensions – ruined by a commitment which had been pressed on him to 'save the honour of the army', and which he had never really wanted. Salan disappeared into hiding in Algiers, to emerge as titular head of the OAS – the Organisation Armée Secrète – that would spread indiscriminate and senseless terror across Algeria, and soon import it to Paris. De Gaulle had won again – just. But the divisions and weaknesses which the Challe revolt had displayed within the French army meant that any prospect of *Algérie française* was now dead. De Gaulle was forced to negotiate with the FLN rebels, and not on his terms. In May 1961, the first talks took place at Evian on Lake Geneva; by July they had failed, with the FLN holding out for total capitulation by de Gaulle.

OAS

In the course of the war over thirty separate attempts were made on de Gaulle's life. On 8 September 1961, a disaffected young colonel, Jean-Marie Bastien-Thiry, carried out the most dramatic so far, exploding an enormous mine of plastic explosive and napalm at Pont-sur-Seine as de Gaulle's Citroën passed on his way home to Colombey. Over the six months, up to February 1962, that the principal OAS campaign in France lasted, it was to do as much as anything to incline the French towards de Gaulle's notion of an abrupt withdrawal from Algeria. Even without the activities of the OAS, a climate of violence had been growing in France, generated between the police and the Algerian community, a climate which in itself had been steadily arousing liberal hostility. This brutal sideshow resulted in sixteen policemen killed and forty-five wounded, most of them during August and September 1961.

In mid-October, 25,000 Algerian workers from the *bidonvilles* (incited by the FLN) gathered for a mass demonstration against the draconian curfew and other repressive measures imposed on them by the government. Though unarmed and largely pacific, the demonstrators were dispersed by the police with a level of violence that appalled Parisians. At the time it was rumoured that 'dozens of Algerians were thrown into the Seine and others were found hanged in the woods round Paris'; it now seems that the number of fatalities was close to 200. At the same time the deadly device of torture used by the French army in Algeria, the *gégène* or magneto, appeared in all its ugliness on the Parisian scene, and by January 1962 *France-Soir* was complaining that there was 'something wrong with justice', because indicted torturers were repeatedly escaping sentence.

Given their limited resources, and compared with the IRA or Palestinian suicide squads, the OAS were amateurs. Bombs, planted to hurt property rather than people, often did little damage. In November 1961 the largest explosion so far destroyed the Drugstore on the Champs-Elysées, infusing the pavement with the scent from its shattered stock. At the beginning of the following month a sinister one-eyed terrorist with the pseudonym Le Monocle, André Canal, who had settled in Algiers in 1940 and made a fortune out of sanitary equipment, took the lead in the Paris campaign – at the same time warring with other OAS factions. The Communist Party, as supporters of the FLN, came under fire. On 4 January 1962 the OAS machined-gunned French Communist Party headquarters in the Place Kossuth. Simultaneously, the homes of party functionaries were bombed. Later that month Le Monocle's gang perpetrated a 'festival of *plastique*', exploding eighteen bombs in a single night. The following week another thirteen bombs went off, to celebrate the second anniversary of Barricades Week. One of these, on 22 January, was detonated in the Quai d'Orsay, which killed one employee and wounded twelve others. Plans captured by the Paris police enabled them to prevent, just in time, the dynamiting of the Eiffel Tower and the setting off of another forty-eight bombs. But, apart from this, the police of metropolitan France seemed reluctant to arrest any of the terrorist leaders. By this time the French public was losing patience with the OAS.

The *plastiques* against writers and leaders of the left became more frequent and more inept. A bomb intended for Jean-Paul Sartre's apartment on the Rue Bonaparte was placed on the wrong floor; Sartre's front door was blown out, but the apartments on the floor above were destroyed. On the morning of 7 February, one of eleven bombings that day was inflicted on the Boulogne-sur-Seine home of André Malraux, de Gaulle's Minister of Culture. Malraux lived upstairs, and anyway was absent that day. The *plastique* was detonated on the ground floor, close to where the four-year-old Delphine Renard was playing with her dolls. Splinters of glass blinded her in one eye and badly disfigured her.[*]

---

[*] Three months later Le Monocle was arrested by the French police and charged with the Delphine Renard bombing. He was sentenced to death, but this was commuted to life imprisonment, and he was later amnestied.

Although this outrage against Delphine would have attracted little attention in contemporary Algiers, where maimings and killings were commonplace, it provoked uproar in Paris. The next day the left organized a demonstration at the Bastille. Although the Minister of the Interior, Roger Frey, refused to lift a ban on political gatherings, some 10,000 demonstrators assembled in an angry mood – as much against the authorities for allowing such atrocities to go unpunished as against the OAS. The police were nervous and, as so often in Paris, overreacted. After two or three hours of skirmishing, they suddenly charged without warning. In panic, a number of the demonstrators sought to escape down the stairs to the Charonne Métro station, but found the gates locked. The police now lost control of themselves, flinging demonstrators over the railings on to the heads of those penned in below, and following that up by pitching heavy iron tree-guards and marble-topped café tables down on them.

At the end of it all, eight demonstrators lay dead, including three women and a sixteen-year-old boy, and more than a hundred were injured (the police too suffered 140 casualties). On the following Tuesday, 13 February, a grim procession estimated at half a million strong followed the eight coffins to Père Lachaise Cemetery. In an excess of emotion, Simone de Beauvoir exclaimed in her diary, 'My God! How I hated the French!' The crisis in the Algerian War had been reached. *Algérie française* was dead – killed by the OAS.

The OAS broke up, the last *plastique* exploding in Paris in July 1963. Salan was captured in Algeria in April 1962 (and later narrowly escaped a death sentence). The last attempt against de Gaulle's life, and the one that came closest to success, took place in August 1962 at the Petit-Clamart, just outside Paris. An OAS band equipped with machine guns and led once again by Bastien-Thiry ambushed the President's car, with Mme de Gaulle in the back, missing them both by a hair's breadth, the bullets passing behind the General's head and in front of the head of his wife. Never losing his composure, de Gaulle the soldier criticized the would-be assassins as 'bad shots'. Bastien-Thiry was caught and executed, the first senior French officer to stand before a firing squad in many years. His death was to no avail. The second Evian talks had been concluded in March, with de Gaulle conceding everything to the FLN, including the recently discovered Algerian oil which France had fought so hard to keep. The *tricolore* was finally lowered in Algeria that summer. Amid tragic scenes one million *pieds noirs* left Algeria and the homes that had belonged to many of them for three generations. It was a miracle, owing almost entirely to the remarkable boom in the French economy under de Gaulle, that France was able to assimilate, almost overnight, so enormous an increment in her population. In independent Algeria, after brief intermissions of hope, the killings – now of Algerians by Algerians – would continue to the present day. In France the fiercely satirical, generally heartless magazine *Canard Enchaîné* took Parisians by surprise by printing in boldest letters, 'To de Gaulle, from his grateful country: once and for all, MERCI!'

REVIVAL

A century before, Napoleon III had described Algeria as 'a cannonball attached to the feet of France'. Now that the cannonball, unshackled, was allowed to roll away, France was 'free to look at France once more', as de Gaulle put it in 1960, and to 'marry her age'. Political reform followed political reform, with referendum upon referendum – until Parisians grew tired of having to troop to the polls yet again. In fact, there were few fronts on which de Gaulle was not attacking with determination and energy in his first six plenipotentiary months from June 1958. First and foremost there was the new constitution, involving a mountainous work of drafting and consultation. 'I considered it necessary', declared de Gaulle, 'for the government to derive not from parliament, in other words from the parties, but, over and above them, from a leader directly mandated by the nation as a whole and empowered to choose, to decide and to act.' The executive would be greatly strengthened, with many of the characteristics that had weakened the Third and Fourth Republics expunged from the body politic. For the first time in nearly a hundred years, France had a president vested with authority. The debilitating wrangling of the parties was a thing of the past, and so was any kind of political corruption. For the next few years under de Gaulle France enjoyed remarkable stability, unknown since the heyday of Louis Napoleon. Critics might grumble at de Gaulle's authoritarianism, that he was 'Charles XI' or a new Bonaparte, but he was never a self-serving despot or a would-be dictator. In his mystical references to 'une certaine idée de la France', if there was any viable affinity it was with Louis XIV, with his overriding pursuit of one thing: 'La grandeur de la France'. That was all that ever mattered to de Gaulle, and his every act was directed to that single end.

De Gaulle began to travel ever more widely, to remind the outside world of the sound of France's voice. It was a sound not always harmonious to the ears of her friends. The new year of peace, 1963, began with de Gaulle closing the door on Britain's entry into the European Economic Community, with some brutality towards his old wartime colleague and loyal advocate Harold Macmillan. No sooner had he dealt this blow to his *anglo-saxon* former ally than he was off to Germany, amazing everybody by his German when he declared 'Long live Franco-German friendship!' – and wooing a receptive Dr Adenauer, like him a product of the world pre-1914. In 1965, de Gaulle broke completely with NATO, explaining that France did not want to be drawn into any war not to her own liking. (From their Paris headquarters the departure ceremony of the fourteen NATO nations took place with admirable good humour, British army bands playing 'Charlie is my Darling' – a witty musical rebuke to the deliberately absent President de Gaulle.) The President embarked France upon her own go-it-alone, nuclear *force de frappe*. He recognized Mao's Peking, and in 1966 visited Khrushchev's Soviet Union, the first Western head of state ever to do so – to the consternation of *les Anglo-Saxons*. *The Times* observed that suddenly he seemed to be 'the only active revolutionary in Europe'.

'In the year of grace 1962,' de Gaulle was able to write in his memoirs, 'France's revival was in full flower. She had been threatened by civil war; bankruptcy had stared her in the face; the world had forgotten her voice. Now she was out of danger.' Indeed, so it seemed, with the ending of the Algerian War. Life began to resume its usual course. The Brittany farmers embarked upon an 'artichoke war', to the discomfort of Parisians. Academicians began to fret about the incursions of *franglais*. The title of the new Vadim-Bardot film, *Le Repos du guerrier*, seemed to characterize the era. The politician Debré was replaced at the Matignon by the banker Pompidou. France's gross national product rose by 6.8 per cent in the course of 1962. Free of the burden of Algeria, France's economy at last began to demonstrate a miraculous blossoming as a result of the thoughtful planting carried out during the latter years of the maligned Fourth Republic and the first four years of Gaullism. Entering its seventh year, in 1965, the Fifth Republic showed its sudden miraculous fiscal prosperity with official reserves reaching $5 billion – unequalled in all Europe except at the Bundesbank.

Nevertheless, in the sunshine of France's sudden climb to prosperity, the old shadows were not entirely banished. The serpent of Communism was still very much alive and wriggling in its opposition to de Gaulle and his *dirigiste* guidance of the economy. In October 1965 Paris was hit by a transport strike, with *L'Humanité* noting grandly, 'In Thursday's absence of traditional transportation, the workers took their cars to go to the factories.' It was surely the first time the Communist press had conceded that French workers were now paid well enough to own cars, rather than simply assembling them. Two years later, Paris was paralysed by what the media recorded as the greatest strike by the greatest number of workers France had ever known. Accompanied by slogans of 'Down with Pompidou!' and 'No Government by Decree!', it was not a strike for wages, but a purely political strike for purely political reasons. A hundred and fifty thousand workers paraded for three hours from the Bastille to the République. As one foreign correspondent observed, 'Only the sun and the moon continued their movements.'

The style with which de Gaulle conducted his presidential life at the Elysée, seated right in the heart of Paris, reflected the style of a highly personal government and his mystical notion of 'une certaine idée de la France'. Privately, neither de Gaulle nor his wife Yvonne was ever entirely happy there. Indeed, the General felt himself a prisoner. Life as head of state was entirely dedicated to the state. Excursions outside in Paris were few: to the dentist, to visit Marshal Juin dying in hospital. De Gaulle never dined in town, and after a while gave up his walks in the Bois de Boulogne, so as not to be besieged by the 'curious'.

BUILDING

As, under the impetus of de Gaulle's advent, all the economic and industrial plans laid under the Fourth Republic bore fruit, so too did the architecture of Paris, so long dormant, begin to burst into flower. Like the two Napoleons before him, de Gaulle showed considerable interest in plans for the city's development, frequently intervening. As with them, every proposition was subordinated to the one overriding question – did it promote *la grandeur de la France*? Like Napoleon I, de Gaulle looked forward to the day when a magnificent new Paris would become the wonder, if not the formal capital, of Europe. By 1962 population figures reached seven million for greater Paris, though the central city declined to 2.7 million from the 2.9 million of 1911. It was still overcrowded – with 353 people per hectare compared to 106 in London.

With his lofty objective in mind, de Gaulle made the inspired choice of appointing André Malraux as his Minister of Culture, a post he held until 1969 – charged with taking Paris in hand. Under this remarkable man, ten years younger than de Gaulle – writer and artist, philosopher, aesthete and man of action, fighter with the Republicans in Spain, convert from Communism; scourge of both left and right, and member of the Resistance, whose life resembled a novel that might have been written by Malraux himself – the stones of Paris came to life again. It was Malraux who was responsible for the *blanchissage* of Paris, for digging out the lower floor of the Louvre's Cour Carrée and returning it to its pristine glory, and restoring the Marais with the Place des Vosges, dilapidated almost to the point of total destruction, as its *pièce de résistance*. The cleaning of Paris by *blanchissage* transformed much of the capital. A secret anti-viral formula (made in Germany) was employed on the fabric of buildings, rubbed on like a paste, left to dry, then rinsed off with water. It was toothbrushing on a vast scale that filled Paris with workers in oilskins, just at the time when other buildings were being *plastiqué* by the OAS.

Work was also begun on the remarkable RER express underground system, capable of whisking Parisians on silent rubber wheels from Saint-Germain to the Etoile in four minutes during the rush hour, at 100 kilometres an hour. A giant hole – *le grand trou* – was built to create a new 'Forum' in the centre of Paris, for so many years encumbered by Les Halles, now translated out to Rungis on the way to Orly Airport. Under de Gaulle and his successors Paris grew dramatically upwards, as well as down into the bowels of the earth. Less felicitous were architectural scandals like the Tour Montparnasse (started 1959, but not finished till 1973), greatest urban project since Haussmann, and designed to be the highest skyscraper in all Europe, menacing the ascendancy of the Eiffel Tower and the Invalides. Then, opened in 1977, came Richard Rogers' Centre Pompidou, unhappy child of the first international competition ever held in Paris. There was the great and windy complex out at La Défense (where the last battle of the Siege of 1870–1 was fought and lost) and various other high-rise developments ringing Paris and threatening her historic skyline. Swallowing up ancient woodland like the Forest of Sénart, Paris built herself into the twentieth century. Of 300,000 new flats, one horrible dormitory complex was built in the form of a wriggling snake, nearly half a mile long. Meanwhile the old city centre changed, with Saint-Germain declared dead by the intelligentsia as bookshops were displaced by fashion boutiques or by trinket shops selling Limoges pillboxes topped with Jean-Paul Sartre's spectacles.

Almost more than any other city in the world, de Gaulle's Paris seemed to be dominated by cars. Art Buchwald of the *New York Herald Tribune* once complained that 'In New York or London taxis drive their clients towards their destination; in Paris, you accompany the *chauffeur* towards his garage or his restaurant.' Resentfully he reckoned that every day of his life he spent four hours in public transport. While huge holes continued to be burrowed to house the growing car population, the available street surface was only 10 per cent greater by the end of the 1960s than it had been in 1900. On the Champs-Elysées traffic moved at about the same speed it had when Henri IV was assassinated. Shortly after it was completed, at unimaginable cost, the *périphérique* girdling the city achieved an accident rate of one per kilometre per day. It was hardly any surprise that Paris should innovate a Western malady – road rage. Already by 1965 *les énervés du volant* – 'nervous wrecks at the wheel' – were being diagnosed: one dropped dead of a heart attack after a minor accident; another got out and assaulted an ambulance driver, causing a triple pile-up. Judges now began issuing automatic six-day jail sentences for such miscreants.

Then came François Mitterrand, whose hideous new 'people's opera' at the Bastille (begun in 1985) would dig as big a hole in Paris finances as any of those dug for dealing with the motor car. ('What is the difference between the people's opera and the *Titanic*?' went a joke at the time. Answer: 'The orchestra on the *Titanic* actually played.') A poll conducted among Parisians in 1990 ranked the Centre Georges Pompidou as the first monument they wished to see pulled down, the Bastille Opéra the second.

HUBRIS

During Malraux's years of power, many great art retrospectives were held in Paris: Delacroix's centenary; 'Douanier' Rousseau; and Picasso, vigorously alive, the war forgotten, eulogized in the Grand Palais in 1966 in a kind of monumental autobiography. In 1961 Braque turned eighty and was honoured with a special postage stamp; he died two years later and was accorded a spectacular send-off in front of a gleaming white Cour Carrée at the Louvre. In the salerooms a record price of seven million francs was paid for a Cézanne. Nineteen-sixty-five saw a massive exhibition of the 'hidden paintings' from Leningrad and Moscow with its breathtaking Matisses. By the following year, as the Vermeer exhibition in the Orangerie closed, still with huge queues, Janet Flanner was left gasping in the *New Yorker* that it was 'as if Paris were intoxicated with art and still could not satisfy her thirst'.

In the theatre the situation was perhaps a little less exciting. Ionesco, hitherto relatively unknown, had his first three-act play, *La Soif et la faim*, performed at the Comédie Française in 1966. Above the Odéon Jean-Louis Barrault created, in 'a broom cupboard', a minuscule hundred-seat theatre called the Petit Odéon. Jean Cocteau had died in 1963, and a year later Malraux was left grumbling that, whereas a century before some 3,000 people every evening went to the theatre, now three million sat at home watching television. 'You can put unimportant things on the screen,' he observed gloomily. 'Make no mistake about it, modern civilization is in the process of putting its immense resources at the service of what used to be called the Devil.'

Earlier in 1964 another powerful grumble was heard about French culture, on a theme close to the General's heart. Paris bookshops were filled with a wittily written book on a most serious subject by a professor of literature at the Sorbonne, René Etiemble – *Parlez-vous franglais?* It slated the insidious creeping into the sacred language of such barbaric usages of *les Anglo-Saxons* as *le weekend, le booking, le snack, le quick* and *un baby Scotch sur les rocks*. Not without reason, the learned professor complained that:

> Since the Liberation, our blood has become much diluted ... The vocabulary of the young generation that will be twenty years old in 1972 is already one-fourth composed of American words. At twenty these young people will not be able to read Molière, let alone Marcel Proust.

Apart from resolving the sex of the automobile, what was the Académie doing? Swiftly the fear of *franglais* had been followed up by the opening of the new American-style Drugstore in Saint-Germain, right opposite Sartre's fortress at the Flore. Throughout Paris there were more and more *snack bars, hamburgers*, novels in translation, and blue jeans on both sexes. And Ian Fleming's *Goldfinger* was to create something of a vogue in a city feeling once more that it was beginning to lack excitement.

Perhaps a more encouraging sign, however, that Paris was moving with the times was, in December 1962, the award of the Prix Goncourt to three women writers. Another historic turnaround was the fate of Stravinsky's *Rites of Spring*, so savagely attacked on its first performance half a century earlier. Not only did the new Maurice Béjart production in 1964 bring a Paris audience to its feet, applauding and shouting for half an hour, but three years later Malraux would select it, instead of Beethoven, as background music for a Gaullist rally. Meanwhile Paris was wildly excited at the rediscovery, on some musty shelf of the Bibliothèque Nationale, of the original MS of *Don Giovanni*. In 1964, Callas brought the house down with her *Tosca*; less enthralling was Paris's first subjection to music by Stockhausen. In the film world, during the early days of the Fifth Republic all Paris was seduced by the magical Brazilian rhythms of *Black Orpheus*; there was Truffaut's sombre, auto-biographical *Quatre cents coups*, and the no less traumatizing *Hiroshima mon amour*. Briefly the new Surrealist talent of Robbe-Grillet, exponent of the *nouveau roman*, became the toast of the town – and of the Cannes Film Festival. And of course there was Roger Vadim and the pouting Brigitte Bardot to make ageing blood vessels pound.

Josephine Baker returned; so did that venerable old trouper Maurice Chevalier, forgiven his wartime indiscretions. There was Yves Montand, usually clad in his workers' overalls, with his lachrymose 'Feuilles mortes'. But more heart-rending always was the tiny figure in the plain black dress of Edith Piaf, who had done so much to cloak a glum Paris in the 1940s with the warm light of 'La Vie en rose', going on to enchant the wide world beyond her Montmartre with 'Milord' and the paras' favourite, her tragic, autobiographical 'Je ne regrette rien':

> Farewell to love with its tremolo.
> I start again at *zéro* . . .

When Piaf died in 1963, within a few hours of her friend Cocteau, all Paris grieved. Forty thousand turned up to accompany her remains to her simple grave in Père Lachaise. Meanwhile women in Paris's oldest profession, who had always found a sympathetic friend in Piaf, were suffering a hard time under de Gaulle, doubtless influenced by the sternly moral 'Tante Yvonne'. Determined to clean up Paris, he reactiv-ated a draconian 330-year-old law which threatened, with the forfeiture of his property, any landlord who allowed prostitutes to work on his premises. Business was badly hit. On another level conventional morality was under siege by Mitterrand, in opposition, seizing on France's archaic attitudes to family planning and contraception, long a taboo subject, and making them political issues. With joy the Paris gossip columnists leaped on the young pro-Pill generation which was jeering at its Catholic opponents as *les lapinistes*, the rabbit clan, devoted to a culture of excessive fertility.

By the mid-1960s, despite all the material benefits that his regime had brought about, what de Gaulle dubbed the 'snarlers and grousers' were soon raising their voices in anticipation of the end of the Fifth Republic and an electoral replacement of the solitary ruler in the Elysée. Could it be that the General had served his purpose? that once again in its history France *s'ennuyait*? As he once acidly remarked, 'How can you govern a country that has 246 varieties of cheese!' The presidential elections of 1965 ended with de Gaulle gaining only 44 per cent of the votes, on a heavy poll. Humiliatingly for him, there had to be a second ballot. Ten and a half million votes had gone to the new star on the now united left, François Mitterrand, who had suddenly proved himself a most effective orator. The next political blow to de Gaulle came at the beginning of 1967 when his protégé, the brilliant young *énarque* economist Valéry Giscard d'Estaing, launched a new splinter Gaullist party. It had considerable success in the parliamentary elections, which reduced de Gaulle's majority to a dangerously small margin of just one seat. Yet still the barometer looked set fair. At his twice-yearly press conference in the Elysée in November 1966, de Gaulle was able to declare, 'We have nothing dramatic to say today. In contrast to the past, France right now is not living in any drama.' There was a certain smug, unspoken comparison to Lyndon Johnson's America, crippled as it was by the nightmare of Vietnam. At the press conference in November 1967, one correspondent dared enquire about *'après-Gaullisme'*. The seventy-seven-year-old President replied with considerable verve, 'Everything always has an end, and everyone eventually comes to a finish, though for the moment that is not the case ... *Après de Gaulle* might begin tonight, or in six months, or even a year,' he continued. 'However, if I wanted to make some people laugh and others groan, I could say that it might just as likely go on as it is now for ten years, or even fifteen. But, frankly, I don't think so.'

What a shock lay in store for him, and Paris, just a few brief months away.

21

Les Jours de Mai

One fighting speech from an old man of seventy-eight, and the
people of France rediscovered the sense of reality, petrol pumps
and holidays.

Raymond Aron, *The Elusive Revolution*, p. 157

PROBLEMS AT THE SORBONNE

The tremors started abroad, nevertheless it was in Paris – most unexpectedly – where the major eruption would take place. It was not, explained
the director of the Odéon theatre Jean-Louis Barrault, 'a French affair,
but a universal phenomenon. The lightning, in May, fell in Paris, that's
all. The storm, it seemed to me, came from afar, and continued to rumble
all round the world.' Call it sunspots or what you will, a kind of global
madness was to set its stamp on 1968, the year of violent student revolt
and of assassination. It determined the defeat of America in Vietnam
and the fall of de Gaulle in Paris. It also displayed the fissures that were
to bring the whole Soviet monolith toppling two decades later. Some of
those caught up in it likened 1968 to that other year of revolution, 1848,
when old political structures across Europe collapsed like the walls of
Jericho – not least in Paris, where that easy-going, liberal King, Louis-
Philippe, was brought down.

On 31 January 1968, the Vietnam peace talks that had been due
to begin shortly in Paris were pre-empted by the Viet Cong seizing
advantage of the traditional New Year's Tet celebrations to launch a
co-ordinated series of attacks on South Vietnamese cities. Initially the
American forces were taken by surprise, and the US Embassy in Saigon

was actually occupied by suicide squads for six hours. Large numbers of aircraft were destroyed on runways, and briefly it looked as if the Viet Cong had won. But the US forces reacted with vigour, recapturing the old capital of Hué and inflicting a clear-cut defeat on the Communists. None of this was seen in America, however, nor did Americans want to see it. A much greater impact was made by the filming of the public execution of a young Viet Cong suspect; while President Johnson's decision to send another 50,000 troops to Vietnam was taken as a sure sign that Tet had been a Communist victory. Campuses across the US burst into flame. It was the moment 'middle America' lost heart: the war in Vietnam seemed to be going nowhere. The following month America was stunned by the announcement that President Johnson, worn down by Vietnam and by anti-war protest, would not be a candidate in the 1968 presidential elections. Richard Nixon announced that he would run. Meanwhile Czechoslovakia saw the launch of the Prague Spring as Alexander Dubček astonished the world by relaxing press censorship and arresting the Chief of Police. For a few rapturous weeks it looked as if the Czechs would regain the freedom they had lost twenty years previously.

In Paris the year began with visual delight as the populace was enthralled by the Ingres Exhibition at the Grand Palais and its sensual *grandes odalisques,* their opulent expanses of flesh greeted as a welcome relief from a lean decade of abstract art. There was also a new Jacques Tati film, *Playtime,* topically chronicling a desperate and loony quest through the Montparnasse skyscraper, a cultured, nineteenth-century-minded Frenchman lost in twentieth-century imported architecture. It flopped. More successful as a protest against the same phenomenon was Servan-Schreiber's *Le Défi américain,* an immediate bestseller that proclaimed a dread of American cultural domination. This dread was echoed in Jean-Luc Godard's new film *Weekend,* its two unappealing lovers caught up in a nightmare world of traffic jams – rated by the critics as *le plus dingue,* the craziest Godard movie to date. Anti-Americanism was bolstered by noisy Vietnam demonstrations in Paris, sparked by the carnage at Hué – and given added point by the news of the assassination of Martin Luther King in Memphis, Tennessee. About the same time, in Germany, a left-wing student leader called Rudi Dutschke was shot in the head by a gunman claiming that he wished to emulate the King killing. Dutschke survived, but the shooting triggered off student riots across Germany. In Paris the Seine rose to flood level, once again. Premier Pompidou was able to declare comfortably that there was 'no opposition capable of overthrowing us, much less capable of replacing us'. On a more inspiring note was the exhibition of 'European Gothic', in the new, magnificently refurbished Pavillon de Flore of the Louvre. Aptly, in view of what lay just ahead, it focused Parisian minds on the glorious beginnings of Abelard's Sorbonne, in a spring of precocious sunshine.

Since Napoleon's reforms of a century and a half previously, the Sorbonne had largely reverted to its time-honoured slumbers. With his massacre of the Left Bank, Haussmann had begun the modernization of the University buildings, but it had taken to the end of the nineteenth century to complete in the form, ugly beyond belief, that existed until 1968. About the most exciting thing to happen there had been a major explosion accidentally set off in the Place de la Sorbonne in March 1869 by an inventor called M. Véron Fontaine, which killed Fontaine himself and six others and extensively damaged neighbouring buildings. In 1908, Mme Curie demonstrated in the Sorbonne laboratories the precursor of an even deadlier new form of explosive – radium – and became the first woman to lecture in its halls.

Then, sixty years later, in the glorious month of May 1968, the Sorbonne truly exploded.

It had all begun back in February at Nanterre, a new and particularly drab suburban campus of graffiti-covered concrete surrounded by mud. Started as an overflow for the overwhelmed Sorbonne, it already had more than 12,000 students in inadequate accommodation, with only 240 professors and assistant professors. There was a lack of warm food, and canteen queues could last an hour and a half, so there was plenty of time for revolutionary chat. On graduation students were faced with either no jobs, or dreary ones. Thus it was not unnatural that, if revolt were to break out in Paris, it should be at Nanterre. Against regulations, bored bourgeois youths established themselves in the same quarters as the girls. To call in the police to evacuate a student dormitory was clearly out of all proportion to the breach of collegiate discipline, but on 4 May Nanterre was placed in suspension. Helpfully the Gaullist Minister of Education told the residents there to take a cold bath.

With only a couple of hundred supporters, revolt was carried from Nanterre to the Sorbonne by a red-headed firebrand, Danny Cohn-Bendit, the son of affluent German Jews. The date coincided with the opening of the Vietnam peace conference, and it so happened that it was also the tenth anniversary of de Gaulle's return to power. Ten years of accumulated grievance were now suddenly poured on to the fires of student discontent.

The Sorbonne of that time seemed to have changed little since the age of Napoleon. On returning in 1955 to the Sorbonne's Faculty of Letters after twenty-seven years' absence at American and English universities, Raymond Aron was deeply shocked by what he found:

> What struck me most was the dinginess of the building and the institution. The chairs, in the tiny offices next to the lecture hall, could have come from the Flea Market. The rooms were grey, dirty, sad...
>
> ... The best students continued to take exams and their degrees without ever setting foot in the Sorbonne. The others were left to themselves, except for the help provided by the assistant. The professor, for the most part, did nothing but deliver lectures. My weekly schedule consisted of three hours...

By 1968 the Sorbonne had become bloated: with 130,000 students it was many times larger than Oxford and Cambridge put together.

In sum, with dreadful overcrowding in lecture halls, *mandarinisme* on the part of the teachers, a total lack of communication between them and their pupils, the absence of any form of pre-selection, over-centralization, excessive bureaucracy, the fossilization of the syllabus and the tyranny of endless examinations, the Paris students of May 1968 had a case. Egged on by their own professors, they then widened their target from establishing student power to turning university revolt into a social and political revolution.

LES ÉVÉNEMENTS

On the afternoon of Friday, 4 May, the head of the Sorbonne, Rector Jean Roche, called in the Paris police. It was an act that violated the sanctuary of the University, maintained over many centuries, and an unpardonable academic error. Roche requested that the police clear the University courtyard of a small, disputatious student meeting which, he feared, might lead to some incident of violence that could disturb the approaching spring examinations. The next day the police in their *paniers à salade* (armoured vans) moved in, closing the Sorbonne and arresting 500 students. Predictably, the traditionally heavy-handed CRS riot-police detachments overreacted, causing many hundreds of casualties. By a miracle, there were no deaths. Given the heat already generated on the Left Bank streets it is hard to imagine how far insurgent violence might have gone had only a few young students been mowed down by CRS bullets. The students took to the streets, supported by some professors and parents. Initially local inhabitants, espousing their cause, tended the wounded in their own homes in the Latin Quarter, assisted by women taxi drivers. By the Sunday morning, several of the arrested students had been sentenced to years in prison, without right of appeal. At this news the Sorbonne as a whole rose up in a sympathetic outburst of fury. Spreading across the river, students extinguished the flame on the Unknown Soldier's Tomb (it was alleged that Cohn-Bendit had urinated on it), organized a sit-in around it, and sang the Internationale.

What caught all foreign journalists by surprise in the early days of *les événements* was its sheer spontaneity. Students took possession of the Sorbonne buildings, brought in a piano, played and sang through the night and slept in the empty classrooms. Around the University and the Boul' Mich' they set to digging up the cube-shaped paving blocks, sawing down ancient plane trees and dragging up burned-out cars to construct barricades – much as their ancestors had done. With lightning speed an atmosphere of exultation and wild euphoria, evocative of the early days of the Commune, or of 1848, 1830 or even 1789, swept the area. 'Nous sommes chez nous!' the students kept chanting, as if that medieval section of old academic Paris were their property to defend – or to destroy. If a youth was found with tar on his fingers it was taken by the police as proof that he had been using paving blocks as ammunition or in a barricade, and he was hauled off to the police vans – a further ominous evocation of the final days of the Commune, when Communards with gunpowder-stained hands had been automatically taken aside and shot. To the deep disgust of academics like Aron and Druon, in the initial euphoria there were numerous cases of professors egging on students, with chemistry teachers even showing them how to make Molotov cocktails. Students were soon demanding to be part of the examination panels, and even to participate in the appointment of professors. New graffiti typifying the attitude towards discipline proclaimed, 'It is forbidden to forbid' and 'Never work', superimposed on such mystical Sartrean appeals for sexual liberation as 'I take my desires for reality, because I believe in the reality of desires.'

As the demands escalated, so with alarming swiftness what had started as a student protest edged towards full-scale political revolution, aimed at nothing less than the overthrow of the de Gaulle government. With the arrival of 13 May and the tenth anniversary of the Algiers coup that had brought the General to power, new slogans appeared, and not just on the Left Bank adjacent to the Sorbonne: 'Ten years, that's enough!' and 'De Gaulle to the museum!', while there were cries on the pavements of 'De Gaulle assassin!' As a reminder of 1848 there also reappeared the famous banner of 'La France s'ennuie!' In support of the students, the left organized an immense march, so dense that its head had reached its destination at Denfert-Rochereau before the end of the march, five kilometres distant at the other side of Paris, had managed to leave the Place de la République. Ominously the streets were empty of police. Students with armbands directed traffic on the Boul' Mich', while the government seemed in a state of shock, utterly paralysed, and caught totally unprepared. De Gaulle was in Romania, Premier Pompidou in Afghanistan. A further sign of the shift in public opinion came when the state radio and TV outfit, the ORTF, which for years had broadcast no anti-Gaullist criticism, now joined in the assault.

Meanwhile, at the same time as all this drama was taking place, only a short distance away negotiations were in process to try to achieve peace in Vietnam. Separated by the Seine, delegates of the South were boarded (at American expense) at the Hôtel Claridge on the Champs-Elysées, those from the North at the comfortably bourgeois Lutetia on Boulevard Raspail. Both residences bore the recent stigma of occidental defeat in wartime, while Ho Chi Minh's representatives at the Lutetia were almost within earshot of the revolt in the Latin Quarter. Certainly they would have smelled the tear gas. The two delegations met in the Majestic (also redolent of past memories), but delegates and journalists alike had the greatest difficulty in reaching it, because a general strike called by the left in support of the embattled students meant there were few taxis, half the normal number of buses and only a quarter of the usual Métro trains. It was perhaps hardly surprising if, reinforcing what Ho had himself witnessed in Paris in 1919 – and what the television screens showed them of US campuses in uproar – he and his fellow delegates from Hanoi returned to the Lutetia each evening increasingly persuaded of the imminent collapse of a West brought down by teenage rioters. The conference finally collapsed in the face of the intransigence of the North, a collapse that was to lead eventually to Communist victory. Could it have been other? Was the capital of Vietnam's old, vanquished oppressor the best site for so crucial a conference? If 'Danny the Red' failed at the Sorbonne, it might well be deemed that he had succeeded in Vietnam.

The strike spread like a brush fire in a heat-wave summer. By mid-May three million workers had come out on strike, and a week later the number had risen to ten million. Paris, like the government, was paralysed, with garbage piling up in the streets, no petrol in the pumps and food running short. The Banque de France itself went out on strike, as well as the engravers at the Mint, so banknotes were also running short. It seemed that the only success the Pompidou government could chalk up was preventing Cohn-Bendit from returning to Paris from Germany, where he had gone on a visit. The greatest turn of fortune for a beleaguered regime came, however, when students tried to spread the revolt to the big Renault works at Billancourt. Like the students at the Sorbonne, striking workers occupied the plant (as their fathers had done in 1936), but would not come out to join forces with the students. The age-old Marxist dream of workers and students marching hand in hand to the barricades was thus thwarted. The mighty Communist Party proved to be just as much off balance as the government, and the unions declined to follow the Sorbonne's lead. The Communists' aloofness owed a great deal to the bourgeois origins of the striking students – *les fils à papa* as they scathingly dubbed them. This time the schism was palpably more between generations than classes, between youth and its elders. The CGT even ordered that there be no interruption of electricity supplies. Bleating feebly about a new Front Populaire, the Communists lost their best chance since 1944 of seizing power in France – where, at one point in May, it seemed almost to be theirs for the asking.

As the clock ticked on and the situation in Paris worsened hourly, Parisians waited for de Gaulle to speak, to bring an end to the crisis – but nothing came. In the Assembly Mitterrand made political capital, proposing a caretaker government, and – in clear breach of the constitution – delivering an ultimatum that he would stand as a candidate for the presidency were the crisis not resolved within eighteen days. Pompidou continued to vacillate between repression and conciliation of the Latin Quarter, while in Romania de Gaulle was cheered by students whose Parisian opposite numbers were jeering and barracking him at home.

Evicted from the Sorbonne, students moved in on the nearby Odéon theatre. There, at first, they were welcomed with open arms by its director, the famous actor-manager Jean-Louis Barrault, and his partner the great Madeleine Renaud, the leading actress of her time. Barrault's enthusiasm swiftly waned. When he asked the visitors to stop smoking – explaining 'C'est un théâtre!' – he was ignored. The insurgents painted 'Ex-Odéon' across the safety-curtain and on the walls, and took over the stage, using it as a *tribune libre* where everybody could orate about their own problem, in a manner sharply evocative of the Commune.

The situation in the Odéon steadily worsened, with between 8,000 and 10,000 people a day surging through the corridors, on the stage and even onto the roof. By the 28th, the costume store had been broken into and, Barrault later wrote, 'delivered to veritable destruction, vandalism pure and simple ... Twenty years of work soiled, ravaged, annihilated ... This time, I burst out in sobs.' Barrault retreated to his quarters to read Rabelais. Eventually CRS in helmets surrounded the Odéon and liberated it. Three months later Barrault was sacked by Malraux's Ministry of Culture.

REACTION

Like Barrault, many other Parisians were now becoming disenchanted, if not positively alarmed, by the genie-in-the-bottle that had been released. Property and shops were at risk, and towards the end of May sympathy for the 'admirable youth' shifted towards revulsion. Thus it was that de Gaulle and Pompidou returned from their leisurely travels in the east to a swiftly worsening crisis. But still the government did virtually nothing to reverse the slide into chaos. During past moments of crisis, de Gaulle had told the nation that it could choose between him and chaos. Now, with growing unease, the French noted they still had him – yet they also had chaos. Paris was alive with rumours, but the most disturbing of these – in the last turbulent week of May – was that he had bolted. It looked like a repeat of what he had done in 1946, when, disgusted by French party politics, he had retreated to Colombey-les-Deux-Eglises, to (as he put it) *son village et son chagrin*.

The truth was that, in what seemed like panic, and without telling his Prime Minister, on Wednesday 29 May de Gaulle had indeed flown mysteriously out of Paris, eastwards. On learning of his departure,

Pompidou at first believed that the General was following in the foot-steps of Louis-Philippe. In fact he had headed for Baden-Baden – to get the support of General Massu and the French army in Germany – but he had departed in deep pessimism and with serious thoughts of resigning. He told Massu, 'I cannot fight against apathy, against the desire of a whole people to let itself break apart.' But the ever dependable Massu, reincarnation of a Napoleonic *grognard,* assured de Gaulle that the army would remain loyal, whatever. The deal was that de Gaulle would amnesty distinguished soldiers like Challe and Salan, currently languishing in jail for their roles in the 1961 putsch in Algiers, so that the army could be rehabilitated.

The following day de Gaulle returned to Paris, walking tall once more, to make the last powerful radio appeal of his career. A tremendous rallying cry, it came only just in time. The students were about to receive their first martyr, an innocent passer-by called Philippe Mathérion, killed by shrapnel from a CRS stun-grenade, but whose staunchly Gaullist parents managed to keep his death secret for long enough. A killing was possibly all that Paris needed to push her over the brink of revolu-tion. Using crude barrack-room language the President dismissed the students as *chie-en-lits* (shit-abeds), while in uncompromising terms he accused the Communists of seeking 'an international autocracy'. As Raymond Aron saw it, 'One fighting speech from an old man of seventy-eight, and the people of France rediscovered the sense of reality, petrol pumps and holidays.' It was to be the last time the old master of language and persuasion would be able to deploy his magic, the last time he would be able to intervene to save his country. But it worked.

That very same evening the Champs-Elysées filled with 100,000 pro-Gaullist counter-demonstrators, a sea of blue-white-red *tricolores* protest-ing against the red of anarchy and Communism, assembled with a spontaneity as remarkable as that with which *les événements* had broken out in the first place. The CRS emerged from their sinister black buses to clear the Sorbonne. There was one more nasty sideshow in the east end of Paris, where up at Belleville a savage fracas took place between Jews and Muslim migrant workers, apparently sparked partly by the Sorbonne revolt and partly by the first anniversary of Israel's Six-Day War of 1967. Several were killed, and fifty shops burned and looted. But by the beginning of June order had been restored, the strikes and stoppages ended.

Public gaze once more shifted to the Vietnam peace talks, still under way in Paris – and to the more heartening revolt of the students in

Prague. There they were rebelling to win freedoms long enjoyed by their Parisian counterparts. Then eyes were once more focused on America, where in June an art-loving actress shot and wounded Andy Warhol. Two days later in Los Angeles a twenty-four-year-old Palestinian, Sirhan Sirhan, shot dead Robert Kennedy, hours after he had won California's Democratic primary for the presidential election. In August Brezhnev's tanks crossed into Czechoslovakia, and Prague returned to the grip of a Moscow winter with censorship of the press reimposed.

Soon the bill for Paris's month of madness came in: 150 million francs, with more to follow, resulting – according to banker Georges Pompidou – in a 'slow haemorrhage' in the nation's finances. Devaluation of the franc became unavoidable. The opening item was for the re-laying in the streets around the Boul' Mich' of some one million stone paving blocks, prised up by the students to construct barricades. After a century and a half of insurrections and barricades, the city fathers finally took the wise decision to tar over the *pavé*, making it virtually inaccessible to future insurgents. The workers were placated by a huge wage boost of 10 to 14 per cent. But the invisible, long-term cost to Paris of 1968 was greater still: it was also the year when, influenced by *les événements*, the art market began to leave its traditional home for London and New York.

For the Sorbonne, a new law was hurriedly prepared by former premier Edgar Faure and adopted in November. The old University of 130,000 students, proven impossible to administer, was broken up into thirteen successors each of a maximum of 20,000, and efforts were made to avoid creating another Nanterre – an isolated university surrounded by *bidonvilles*. The reform was based on two principles, dear to General de Gaulle – participation and autonomy. These meant, in practice, that the dictatorial role of certain professors was abolished, and the control of the Ministry of Education in Paris removed. Faculty members henceforth had to live in the vicinity of the University, so as to provide a teacher–student relationship that had probably been lacking at the Sorbonne ever since the time of Abelard; and the *mandarins* were prevented from holding their University chairs virtually for life. The Napoleonic decree dating back to 1811 whereby the University was assured of being an 'asylum of safety' from the outside world was revoked. And students did not get the participation in University governance for which they had clamoured.

DE GAULLE GOES

The new year of 1969 opened as if nothing had happened in Paris the previous May. There was a token one-day national strike; then, in the theatre, the press galvanized itself to attack a blasphemous short play, *The Council of Love*, written by a Bavarian doctor, Oscar Panizza, who ended his life in a lunatic asylum. 'Stupid, boring, incongruous, obscene, repugnant, abject, ignoble, revolting, outrageous, offensive, filthy, vile, scandalous and deplorable' were the adjectives used by *Le Figaro*. Not even Nijinsky had attracted such damnation. Spring brought yet another referendum, the fifth of the Fifth Republic, as promised by de Gaulle the previous year. This time it related to a much discussed scheme to modernize and streamline the paralysing centralization of the country on Paris, which dated back to Louis XIV and beyond. It was not a major issue, but a thoroughly sensible measure, part of de Gaulle's programme for France 'marrying her age', and – as with past referendums – demanded simply a yes or a no at the polls. As usual it was put as a choice 'between progress and upheaval'. But France was bored with going to the polls, and – Paris in particular since the previous May – bored with de Gaulle.

On 10 April the General gave a television interview in which he abruptly declared that, if the referendum failed, he ought not to continue as head of state. The challenge was there. Three weeks later, on a poor turnout, the noes won by a narrow margin. Immediately de Gaulle packed up and departed from the Elysée, pausing only to shake hands with Colonel Laurent, commander of his palace military guard, and to issue the tersest of communiqués to an ungrateful people: 'I am ceasing to exercise my functions as President of the Republic. This decision takes effect from midnight tonight.' There was no constitutional reason whatsoever for him to resign, but over the past months he had been expressing pessimism and disillusion to his intimates: 'What's the point of all that I am doing? ... nothing has any importance.' After more than ten years in residence, one small *camionnette* sufficed to remove all the baggage of the General and his lady to Colombey-les-Deux-Eglises. De Gaulle's departure was in no way followed by the chaos he had so often predicted – though doubtless it would have been had he left the previous May. This in itself seemed almost like one more sign of disrespect from an ungrateful populace, who had turned on this ageing President just as they had turned on Pétain and Louis Napoleon before him. Seamlessly the apolitical Pompidou took over, moving into the Elysée. De Gaulle removed himself to storm-battered western Ireland. The following year he died. 'France is a widow,' declared the new President.

It was indeed the end of an epoch – an epoch which, through the person of de Gaulle, stretched back to the wars in Algeria and Indo-China, and to the Second World War, the Occupation, Liberation and *épuration*, and beyond to the turbulent, depressing 1930s and even to the First World War in which he himself had fallen wounded on the hideous battlefield of Verdun and been made a German prisoner-of-war. It marked the end of the most personal experiment in modern government that France has known since Napoleon Bonaparte grasped the crown imperial to place it on his head in Notre-Dame. On de Gaulle's departure the inevitable parallels were also drawn with Saint Louis and Philippe Auguste, but he had given his country a strong regime without ever falling for the institutional allure of fascism – whatever his foes on the left might say. He had, it could be claimed, saved the country of which he cherished that romantic, mystical 'certaine idée' once, twice, three times and more. He had changed the intangible map of Europe, and France's position in it; and – not least – he had helped bring Paris proudly into the modern world.

EPILOGUE

Death in Paris – The Père Lachaise Cemetery

Most of the cemeteries have long suffered from a condition of overcrowding. They can neither hold more corpses nor decompose those that are there. All decomposition takes place practically in the open. The ground has become a pitted black mire from the constant process of decay.

Prefect Frochot to Napoleon, 1801

As the city of light and life, Paris is also a city of the dead – her illustrious dead. Napoleon, Europe's most fearsome warlord since Genghis Khan and the Mongol hordes, left hecatombs of graves from Portugal to Moscow. Though brimming over with ideas for his *embellissement* of Paris for the living, as its civil administrator he had abruptly found himself faced with the urgent problem of creating space for the grateful dead of Paris. By the end of the eighteenth century the problem of burial inside the old city had become acute: within its cramped limits overpopulation of the dead presented an ever more difficult problem, more serious even than that of housing the living. In the pre-revolutionary capital, pretty well every parish had its own small cemetery, of which the largest, the Innocents, covered only 130 metres by 65. As these filled up, the corpses of the poorer classes were heaped into common graves, most of them many layers deep. Before long, terrible smells began to spread through the surrounding streets. When these common graves themselves reached bursting point, room for fresh bodies was created by disinterring the old bones and piling them up in hideous charnel houses near by.

One night in 1776, a shoemaker crossing the Innocents pitched into one of its open graves and was found dead there the next day. Four years later, the common grave at the Innocents subsided into the cellars of next-door houses, almost provoking the suffocation of their occupants. This was too much for Parisians gradually discovering the importance of hygiene. The Innocents was shut down, its mortal remains conveyed to the catacombs under Denfert-Rochereau on the Left Bank from which the stone for old Paris had been cut. This was, however, still not enough. It needed a revolutionary government to solve the problem, and under the new National Assembly all graveyards within the city walls were closed down in 1791. But, beyond that, not much was done.

Then, in 1801, Prefect Frochot brought the problem to the attention of the new First Consul. He reported:

> Most of the cemeteries have long suffered from a condition of overcrowding. They can neither hold more corpses nor decompose those that are there. All decomposition takes place practically in the open. The ground has become a pitted black mire from the constant process of decay.

Three years later Napoleon decreed the interment of all the Paris dead in three gigantic cemeteries to be laid out beyond the walls (a development that was not followed by London until 1842). The biggest was set up on property newly sold by a dispossessed landowner called Jacques Baron. The unfortunate Baron himself was among the first to be buried there. It came to be known, down through the ages and across the world, as Père Lachaise Cemetery. There it stands far from the bustle of the *grands boulevards*, in the centre of the unfashionable east end of Paris. Not many of the millions of tourists who descend upon the city each year seem to visit it; yet, one of the world's largest cemeteries, it contains probably more of France's past than any other forty-four hectares of her soil. Even for those uninterested in the stories of the army of eminent Frenchmen and women whose relics lie beneath its eccentric and extravagant slabs, in a city that grows more frenetic by the day Père Lachaise still provides an oasis of tranquillity from which some arresting and unusual views can be obtained. Yet it was also where the most brutal blood-letting in Parisian history took place. In it resides a whole history of Paris, indeed of France herself, in marble and stone.

Back in Philippe Auguste's twelfth century, the hill over which Père Lachaise now spreads was an agricultural smallholding owned by the Bishop of Paris. There he cultivated wheat, vegetables and grapes for his own wine press (handily close to Notre-Dame). In 1430 a rich spice-merchant, called Regnault de Wandonne, bought it and built himself a country house there, known as the Folie Regnault. Some 200 years later, the land was taken over by the Jesuits, who built a retreat there. Then, in 1675, one of their order, Père La Chaise, was appointed confessor to Louis XIV, and as a result of the Roi Soleil's generosity Père La Chaise's estate expanded and prospered. Soon the Mont Louis – as it was known for many years in honour of its benefactor – became a haunt of Paris's elegant courtesans, attracted as much by the prospect of encountering the King's influential confessor as by the excitement of the *fêtes galantes* held there. The Jesuits' domain evidently earned a powerfully hedonistic reputation, which persisted until long after Père La Chaise's death, at the age of eighty-five, in 1709. In 1762, with the downfall of the Jesuits, the estate was disposed of, and after passing through several hands it was bought by Jacques Baron. When the Revolution ruined him financially, Baron had to sell to the city of Paris.

From the heights of the Mont Louis, Père Lachaise Cemetery enjoys spectacular views over Paris – once the leaves have fallen from the trees. The visitor who stands by the chapel erected alongside the original manor of Louis XIV's confessor will be able to see the Panthéon, the Sacré-Coeur at Montmartre, the Eiffel Tower and the countryside beyond Meudon to the south-west. It was this eminence that led to Père Lachaise, three times in its history, becoming a battlefield – in 1814, 1815 and, its worst ordeal, during the bitter civil war of 1871, when the Paris Commune expired at the end of that blood-soaked May. On Whitsunday, 147 Communards were stood against a wall in the eastern corner of Père Lachaise and vengefully shot down. That wall, its bullet-scarred expanse graced by a simple commemorative plaque to the Communard martyrs, became a rallying-point for France's left wing. For more than a hundred years, every Whitsun marches would solemnly proceed to the Mur des Fédérés, as it is called – occasions that would often turn into political demonstrations on the controversies of the day.

Here, around the Mur des Fédérés, have congregated the tombs of some of France's proletarian heroes – Henri Barbusse, the leading anti-war novelist of the post-1918 generation; Picasso's friend Paul Eluard, the poet; Marcel Willard, the defender of Georgi Dimitrov, who was tried and acquitted of complicity in the Reichstag fire of 1933, later to become Prime Minister of Bulgaria. Near by a gleaming slab of black granite conceals the final resting place of Maurice Thorez, the influential and long-standing boss of France's Communist Party. Also in this section of Père Lachaise, which has become known as the Coin des Martyrs, are to be found various memorials to more recent examples of man's inhumanity to man. Plaques honouring young men of the Resistance murdered by the Gestapo are intermixed with grim monuments to the victims of the Nazi concentration camps. The courageous Frenchwomen who died at Ravensbrück are commemorated by a pair of manacled stone hands; Belsen by a group of emaciated figures in blackened bronze, looking with bitterness up at the heavens; and Mauthausen by a plain stone shaft inscribed with the chilling statistics of mass murder.

Between the opening of Père Lachaise on 21 May 1804 and the end of 1815, some 530 graves were sold; twenty years later 11,289 plots had been bought and embellished. Meanwhile, with consummate artistry, in 1810–11 Prefect Frochot had the existing skulls and bones from the old Paris cemeteries reinterred in elegant arrangements in the catacombs. Laid out like a modern grid-form metropolis, Père Lachaise has the feel of a town – truly, a city of the dead – with tidy paved and cobbled 'streets', complete with cast-iron signposts. By the 1820s it had become an international tourist attraction, featuring prominently in all guidebooks to Paris. As it expanded over the years, Père Lachaise came to embrace, in closest proximity, all the violent contrasts of Paris life. Not far from the Mur des Fédérés, on the very spot where the last Communard cannon fired its final round, there now stands a small chapel, built by the Municipality of Paris in memory of the man principally responsible for the defeat of the Commune – Adolphe Thiers. Also up by the Mur lie the bodies of Karl Marx's daughter Laura and her husband Paul Lafargue – who committed joint suicide in 1911; while near them is the painter Amedeo Modigliani, buried together with his lover Jeanne Hebuterne, who killed herself a few days after his painful death from meningitis.

In death democracy reigns. Close to the unadorned tombstone of Communist boss Thorez are massed the sumptuous vaults of the haute bourgeoisie, enemies of the French left. For while the scions of the pre-revolutionary nobility still tend to be interred (like Charles de Gaulle) in their own country parish churchyards, the remains of the bourgeois *deux cents familles* occupy a substantial part of Père Lachaise's forty-four hectares. In row after row stand the mausoleums carrying the hyphenated names of great banking, mercantile and industrial families. Together they present the greatest collection of architectural singularity in all Paris. Miniature pyramids rub shoulders with gothic chapels decorated with gargoyles and lacy pinnacles. A reduced Madeleine vies with what seems to be a replica of the Panthéon or a tiny Taj Mahal; another caprice is a pyramid supported by turtles and illustrating on its four sides an ibis, a bullock, a car and a sunburst, the whole *bombe surprise* topped by a giant egg. One imposing tomb was commissioned by a chess enthusiast to accommodate an additional thirty-one occupants – on the ground that the chessboard holds thirty-two pieces.

Over this labyrinth of extravagance rises the imperious alabaster tower erected by a tycoon, at least half as high as the obelisk in the Place de la Concorde. But few mausoleums are stranger than that inhabited by the Duc de Morny, Napoleon III's natural half-brother, great lover and statesman of the Second Empire, which seems to illustrate every known style from Rome to Armenia, with a hint of the Bogumil heretics of Bosnia, and is crowned by four protuberances shaped like public drinking fountains or giant golf-tees. The closest approximation to it, though on a larger scale, is the cemetery crematorium, with poignant rows of plaques registering the incineration of such and such an *inconnu* killed in the Allied air-raids of 1944. Once the site of a Muslim enclave set up by Napoleon III – who was vainly seeking friends – to please the Turks, it was designed as a grotesque copy of Istanbul's Aghia Sophia, its furnace spiralling up from four ersatz minarets. Père Lachaise today still exerts itself to attract the bones of Muslim oil potentates. Behind the crematorium lies Isadora Duncan, the American dancer of the 1920s strangled by her scarf in an open-top car; while just across the way is Marcel Proust, concealed in the bourgeois family tomb constructed in honour of his father's success as a professor of medicine.

From the imposing vulgarity of the nineteenth-century bourgeois repositories one turns almost with relief to the discreet imperial dignity of the tomb of Napoleon's favourite actor, Talma, and to the less lavish memorials to the great writers, painters, musicians, scientists, soldiers and explorers. It is here that reside the foremost historical treasures of Père Lachaise. But the whereabouts of these distinguished men and women, strewn across the cemetery, are often hard to locate; the tomb of Alphonse Daudet, for instance, lies almost entirely hidden between two bourgeois family crypts. The *gardiens* are helpful, although they sometimes seem to follow whims of their own. On my first visit, in the 1960s, it was Sarah Bernhardt I particularly wanted to find, but they insisted on marking my map with the name of Edith Piaf, then recently buried (together with her stuffed rabbit, squirrel and lion), to the accompaniment of thousands of mourning fans. On my next visit, Colette, under a simply marked pink stone, was the name pre-empting all others.

Some groups, such as the marshals of Napoleon (the most eminent French soldiers, Turenne, Foch and Bonaparte himself, are of course enshrined in the Invalides), are conveniently clustered together. Here in Père Lachaise, as might be expected – given its founder – one can find names evoking the martial glory of the Empire: Davout, Gouvion Saint-Cyr, Ney, Grouchy and Masséna; Nansouty and d'Hautpoul-Salette, commanders of the celebrated cavalry charge at Austerlitz; and General la Valette, married to a niece of Empress Josephine, and condemned to death by the second Restoration, but saved by his wife who switched clothes with him in prison. Though executed like Ney, Murat lies in a new crypt built by the family that flourishes to this day; here too is the no less ill-fated General Huchet de la Bedoyère, who helped Napoleon escape from Elba and who was executed after the Restoration the following year, aged only twenty-nine. Another illustrious name in the Napoleonic section is that of General Hugo, father of Victor – who resides, however, at the Panthéon, the highest honour Paris can accord her *grands hommes*.

Among the florid extravaganzas of the *deux cents familles* stand the more simple effigies of a M. and Mme Pigeon, laid out on their sarcophagus like two Plantagenet crusaders, side by side in bed beneath a stone sheet – a model of French bourgeois constancy. But the most famous as well as the cemetery's most senior incumbents are those doomed twelfth-century lovers Héloïse and Abelard. After many separations they lie together at last under an open gothic canopy (though whether the remains are really theirs has been questioned). Dating from 1701, an inscription composed by Héloïse's successor as Abbess of the Paraclete Convent speaks with a surprisingly tolerant sympathy of 'the love which had united their spirits during their lives, and which was conserved during their absence by the most tender and most spiritual letters'. Then there is Rachel Félix, the beautiful and impassioned actress of Louis-Philippe's reign, who exchanged the pithiest of love letters with the Prince de Joinville. After seeing her on stage, the Prince despatched his card to her: 'Where? When? How much?' Her equally concise response was, 'Your place. Tonight. Free.' Aptly enough, her tomb bears just the succinct inscription: 'Rachel'.

Just beyond the main gate and inscribed with equal modesty is the tomb of a more recent lover who paid the price in full: President of the Republic Félix Faure. In 1899 the screams of a woman in extreme distress were heard coming from the President's office. Orderlies who dashed to the rescue found a naked President of the Republic dead of a heart attack, his hand clutching with the fixity of muscles in spasm the hair of a sobbing redhead, in equal *déshabillé*. (Some visitors feel Faure's tomb is more deserving of the inscription accorded to the soldiers killed on the battlefield – *Mort en brave*.) A short distance away is the more recent grave of the pop singer Jim Morrison of the Doors, dead – mysteriously – at only twenty-eight. Here bands of devotees are likely to be found today rolling joints against a backdrop of Doors lyrics, declarations of love and paeans to drug use graffitied on to every surface within reach.

Right at the other end of Père Lachaise lies yet another penalized for the pursuit of illicit love: Oscar Wilde. In death poor Oscar underwent the same mutilation that Abelard suffered in life – a vandal emasculated the ugly Epstein angel that stands over his grave. Oscar's manhood was later restored, and protected by a glass cage. A sign in English and French now says: 'Do not deface this tomb; it is protected by law as an ancient monument and was restored in 1992.'

Near the outer wall lie the graves of two more recent literary partners, from the 1920s, in the 'Love that dare not speak its name' – Gertrude Stein, patroness of the Lost Generation, and her 'tiny, nimble and mustachioed' lover, Alice B. Toklas. Surprising, too, is the number of expatriates who – like Wilde – are buried in Père Lachaise. One is the renowned English roué and eccentric Lord Henry Seymour, founder of the exclusive Jockey Club but also one of the most popular figures with the Parisian proletariat of the mid-nineteenth century, who immortalized him with the jocularly appropriate sobriquet of 'Milord l'Arsouille' (roughly, Lord Crapulence or Ruffian). His favourite pastimes seem to have included shooting cigars out of the mouths of his servants with a rook rifle; putting itching powder in the clothes of his fencing master; and being boorishly rude to that unappealing last of the Bourbon monarchs, Charles X. He seems to have used his mistresses as sleeping potions. To one he wrote:

My dear Claire,
      Come to Sablonville at 9 a.m. John [the valet] will introduce you into my chamber. Sit near my bed and watch well over my slumbers. Your beautiful eyes will perform miracles, calming my long-disturbed sleep.
      Henry.

Milord l'Arsouille died miserably in the middle of a platonic affair, of anthrax. His half-brother, the fourth Marquess of Hertford, reputedly the richest and meanest man in Paris, also lies in the family vault at Père Lachaise; as does his natural son (it was a clan that went in for illegitimates), Richard Wallace, a man who did much to atone for the family shortcomings through his exceptional generosity to the needy during the Siege of Paris in 1870, later providing the city with drinking fountains for her poor which are still to this day known as 'Wallaces'. Two distinguished nineteenth-century British admirals also ended their careers in Père Lachaise: Sydney Smith, who inflicted upon Napoleon one of his earliest defeats at the Siege of Acre, but subsequently became an ardent Francophile, dying in Paris; and Alexander Cochrane, the officer responsible for burning down the White House during the War of 1812.

Scattered among the vaults of the *deux cents familles*, the various great representatives of the arts make an imposing list: Molière, La Fontaine, de Musset, the eccentric poet Gérard de Nerval, who trailed a tame lobster on a lead, and Honoré de Balzac. 'Friendship and glory are the only inhabitants of the tombs,' wrote Balzac; while he had his hero Rastignac bury the penniless Père Goriot among the ranks of wealthy bourgeois that fill the avenues of Père Lachaise. (*Père Goriot* ends with Rastignac looking down from the cemetery on the great city lying below and issuing his famous challenge: 'Paris, à nous deux maintenant!') Transferred from defunct cemeteries within the old walls, Molière and La Fontaine now rest side by side, in two unassumingly dignified caskets. Alfred de Musset, whom debauchery carried to Père Lachaise at the early age of forty-seven, was blackballed from Milord l'Arsouille's Jockey Club because his horsemanship was below standard; but on his death at least one of his ambitions was realized – that of having a birch tree planted to provide his grave with shade. Every summer evening de Musset's birch used to be lovingly watered by the *gardiens*, but eventually it had to be replaced. Alongside de Musset lies Prefect Georges-Eugène Haussmann, the Second Empire creator of modern Paris – so applauded by some but condemned by others for destroying the old centre of the city.

There are also the composers Bizet, Cherubini and Chopin (Maria Callas embarked on death here, but her ashes were later removed to be scattered on her beloved Aegean; Rossini, too, was transferred to his native Italy); and the painters Corot, Daumier, Géricault, David, Delacroix and Ingres. In contrast to de Musset's birch, fresh geraniums always seem to adorn the tomb of Chopin, renewed year in and year out by some anonymous admirers. Strangely enough the one person in Père

Lachaise to attract even more attention than Chopin is a celebrated medium of the Second Empire, Allan Kardec, whose Stonehenge-like monument is often festooned with flowers by believers – apparently in hopes of transferring to themselves his physical potency. Another contemporary of Kardec's with a special appeal for the fetishist is Victor Noir, a journalist shot down by an enraged Prince Napoleon in 1870, whose death provided a *cause célèbre* that made the Empire totter. The guidebook notes of Noir's darkened bronze effigy that: 'a certain part of the body shines brightly, thanks to the caresses of sterile women'. It is not entirely clear why a defunct journalist should be held capable of such wizardry. A less sought-after writer, but one who exacts the compassion of fellow strugglers in Père Lachaise, is the Abbé Delille. An Académicien at the age of thirty-four, Delille was forced by the Terror into exile, where he married his strong-minded governess. She used to lock him up until he had finished his quota of verse each day; the strain seems to have proved too much for his eyesight, and he died blind in 1813.

Among the great actors and actresses here, Sarah Bernhardt has an honoured resting place at Père Lachaise, while a less enlightened age denied poor Adrienne Lecouvreur (mistress to Marshal de Saxe) access to hallowed ground despite the protests of Voltaire, so she still lies interred beneath the intersection of the Rues de Bourgogne and de Grenelle on the Left Bank. Close to the 'Divine' Bernhardt lie together two more recent thespians, heart-throbs of mid-twentieth-century France – Yves Montand (born Ivo Livi) and Simone Signoret (born Simone Kaminker).

Interspersed among the famous, some tragic inscriptions catch the eye, such as that on the tomb of a bereaved family man to a deceased wife, mother and daughter: 'This tomb encloses, *hélas*, the three things which made the happiness of a father and a husband.'

Finally, there are the scientists and explorers: Champollion, the 'Father of Egyptology', who began deciphering the Rosetta Stone in 1822; Claude Chappe, the inventor of semaphore, who when his patent was contested flung himself into a sewer in 1805, aged forty-two; Antoine-Augustin Parmentier (1727–1813), the biochemist who introduced the potato to a reluctant France. Potatoes had previously been thought fit only for animals, but Parmentier was so persuasive that soldiers had to be called in to guard his own stocks; several new recipes were named after him, and his tombstone bears a bas-relief of potatoes and a chemistry still. The Parisian inventor of the gas-filled balloon, Professor Charles, appropriately lies in Père Lachaise. Also keeping company with the Professor is one of the earliest aviation casualties, Mme Blanchard, killed in 1819 on her sixty-seventh ascent, when she was accidentally brought down over Paris by a festive rocket.

Unless you have a family vault with a *concession perpetuelle*, it is difficult to obtain a lodging at Père Lachaise today. Plots can be 'leased' short-term, and after five years are cleared and relet, the remains deposited in a central ossuary. The cemetery is heavily overcrowded with some 10,000 tombs and the space was further reduced in 1874 when a tunnel of the Ceinture railway beneath it caved in, scattering corpses over the tracks; after that the whole section was emptied and turned into an avenue. Gaston Palewski, one of de Gaulle's most senior colleagues, confided to me in the 1960s that he had just applied for a shady plot, but had been told that he could only be placed on the waiting list and – to his great distress – could not even be guaranteed a site 'with a view over Paris'. On that same occasion, Nancy Mitford teased Palewski, her faithless lover, that she was sure that a space would be found, as 'Every once in a while they dig up the old bones, and then grind them up to make cosmetics for Chanel.'

The demand is only too understandable. Apart from the honour of sharing the last resting place of so many illustrious sons and daughters of France, it would be hard to conceive of a more agreeable place in which to be laid away than Père Lachaise, with its glorious views over Paris and its many tree-lined avenues. There used to be a bistro opposite, on the Rue du Repos, called Mieux Ici Qu'en Face. But that has itself passed on, and – with the exception of the melancholy reminders of the Coin des Martyrs – Death shows few signs of his sting in Père Lachaise today. For mothers and children and laughing couples, the cemetery has become something of a family park. Gossiping nursemaids tether their prams to the tomb railings, to stop their charges accelerating away off down the steep slopes; children climb gaily over the grandest crypts, as soon as the *gardiens'* backs are turned; and, just as Love and Death represent but two Janus faces of the same head, lovers sit heedlessly entwined on benches set in the sheltered alleys between the tombs – just as in the times of Père La Chaise himself the courtesans and gallants liked to travel out from seventeenth-century Paris to seek their pleasures on the Mont Louis.

*

Yet, for all the ephemeral human drama and sadness embraced in those shady avenues of Père Lachaise, rising above it all Paris lives on, grumbling but radiant, evolving but immutable – and eternal. Parisians may suffer perilously from ennui at regular intervals; but can Paris herself ever bore? Thoroughly female, at each age a particular woman or women, good or bad – Héloïse, a Reine Margot, a Ninon, a Josephine, a Païva, a Sarah Bernhardt or a Piaf – arises to delineate its passing features, but in the end there is always only one: Marianne herself.

Bibliography

Given that works on Napoleon are reputed to number some 600,000, books on Paris must easily run into seven figures. For any author to assemble anything like a complete bibliography would be a lifetime's task. Here, after a great amount of pruning, I have included books only that particularly aided me in writing this book.

GENERAL

Aulard, F. A., *Paris sous le Premier Empire: recueil des documents pour l'histoire de l'esprit public à Paris*. Paris, 1912.

Beevor, A. and Cooper, A., *Paris after the Liberation*. London, 1994.

Belloc, H., *Paris*. London, 1920.

Bidou, H., *Paris*. London, 1939.

Bredin, J.-D., *The Affair: The Case of Alfred Dreyfus*. New York, 1986.

Briggs, R., *Early Modern France, 1506–1715*. Oxford, 1977.

Castelot, A., *Paris the Turbulent City*. London, 1962.

Castries, Duc de, *The Lives of the Kings and Queens of France*. London, 1979.

Champigneulle, B., *Paris: architectures, sites et jardins*. Paris, 1973.

Clunn, H., *The Face of Paris: The Record of a Century's Changes and Developments*. London, 1933.

Cobb, R., *Promenades*. Oxford, 1980.

——— *The Streets of Paris*. London, 1980.

——— *Tour de France*. London, 1976.

Cole, R., *A Traveller's History of Paris*. Gloucester, 1944.

Couperie, P., *Paris through the Ages*. London, 1971.

Dark, S., *Paris*. London, 1926.

Dill, M., *Paris in Time*. New York, 1975.

Ehrlich, B., *Paris on the Seine*. London, 1962.

Evenson, N., *Paris: A Century of Change, 1878–1978*. New Haven, 1979.

Favier, J., *Nouvelle Histoire de Paris*. Paris, 1974.

Franklin, A., *La Vie privée d'autrefois*. Paris, 1973.

Gallienne, R. le, *From a Paris Garret*. London, 1943.

Hillairet, J., *Dictionnaire historique des rues de Paris* (2 vols). Paris, 1957–61.

Hofbauer, M. F., *Paris à travers les ages: aspects successifs des monuments et cartiers historiques de Paris depuis le troisième siècle jusqu'au même jour.* Paris, 1989.

Laffont, R., *Paris and its People.* Paris, 1958.

Landes, A. and S., *Paris Walks.* Washington DC, 1979.

Laver, J., *The Age of Illusion: Manners and Morals, 1750–1848.* London, 1972.

Lavisse, E., *Histoire de France jusqu'à la Révolution* (9 vols). Paris, 1901–11.

Lefrançois, P., *Paris à travers des siècles.* Paris, 1948.

Littlewood, I., *Paris: A Literary Companion.* London, 1987.

Magne, E., *Images de Paris sous Louis XIV.* Paris, 1948.

Maurois, A., *History of France.* Paris, 1949.

Michelet, J., *Histoire de France* (17 vols). Paris, 1901–11.

Morice, B., *Le Palais du Luxembourg et le destin des hommes.* Paris, 1971.

Neale, J. E., *The Age of Catherine de Medici.* London, 1943.

The Oxford Companion to French Literature, ed. P. Harvey and J. E. Heseltine. Oxford, 1959.

Peyrefitte, A., *The Trouble with France.* New York, 1981.

Polnay, P. de, *Aspects of Paris.* London, 1968.

Russell, J., *Paris.* London, 1983.

Salvadori, R., *Architect's Guide to Paris.* London, 1990.

Seignobos, C. (trans. C. A. Phillips), *A History of the French People.* Paris, 1939.

Seward, D., *The Bourbon Kings of France.* London, 1976.

Shennan, J., *France before the Revolution.* London, 1983.

Sue, E., *Les Mystères de Paris.* Paris, 1843.

Sutcliffe, A., *Paris: An Architectural History.* New Haven, 1993.

Tilly, C., *The Contentious French.* Cambridge, Mass., 1986.

Topolski, F., *Paris Lost.* London, 1973.

Vallois, T., *Round and About Paris* (3 vols). London, 1995–7.

Webster, P. and Powell, N., *St Germain des Prés.* London, 1984.

INTRODUCTION AND AGE ONE: 1180–1314

Baldwin, J. W., *Masters at Paris from 1179 to 1215: A Social Perspective in Renaissance and Renewal in the Twelfth Century*, ed. R. L. Benson and G. Constable. Cambridge, Mass., 1982.

Bjerken, M. P., *Medieval Paris.* New Jersey, 1937.

Boussard, J., *Nouvelle Histoire de Paris de la fin du siège de 885–886 à la mort de Philippe Auguste.* Paris, 1976.

Cazelles, R., *Nouvelle Histoire de Paris de la fin du règne de Philippe Auguste à la mort de Charles V 1223–1380.* Paris, 1972.

Champion, P., *La Vie de Paris au Moyen Age: l'avènement de Paris.* Paris, 1933.

Clanchy, M. T., *Abelard: A Medieval Life.* Oxford, 1997.

Davies, N., *Europe.* London, 1996.

Druon, M., *The Accursed Kings* (6 vols). London, 1956–61.

————— *The History of Paris from Caesar to Saint Louis.* London, 1969.

Duby, G., *Le Dimanche de Bouvines.* Paris, 1973.

Eco, U., *Art and Beauty in the Middle Ages.* Milan/New Haven, 1986.

Evans, J. (ed.), *The Flowering of the Middle Ages.* London, 1966.

Geremek, B., *The Margins of Society in Late Medieval Paris.* New York, 1987.

Gilson, E., *Heloise and Abelard.* Ann Arbor, Mich., 1960.

Hallam, E. H., *Capetian France.* London, 1980.

Holmes, U. T., *Daily Living in the Twelfth Century: Based on the Observations of Alexander Neckan in London and Paris.* Madison, Wis., 1952.

Jordan, W. C., *The French Monarchy and the Jews.* Philadelphia, 1989.

Lavisse, E. (ed.), *Histoire de France jusqu'à la Révolution* (vol. III, i and ii). Paris, 1901–11.

Le Breton, G., *Gesta Philippi Augusti, Philippidos* (2 vols). Paris, 1882–5.

Martineau, J., *Les Halles de Paris, des origines à 1789.* Paris, 1960.

Pope, A., 'Eloisa to Abelard' in *Poetical Works,* ed. H. Davis. Oxford, 1966.

Powicke, M., *The Thirteenth Century, 1216–1307.* Oxford, 1962.

Radice, B. (ed.), *The Letters of Abelard and Heloise.* London, 1974.

Ranum, O., *Paris in the Age of Absolutism.* New York, 1968.

Rashdall, H., *The Universities of Europe in the Middle Ages.* Oxford, 1936.

Russell, B., *History of Western Philosophy.* London, 1946.

Suger, Abbot, *Vie de Louis VI le Gros,* ed. H. Waquet. Paris, 1929.

Trevelyan, G. M., *A History of England.* London, 1926.

AGE TWO: 1314–1643

Babelon, J.-P., *Nouvelles Histoires de Paris.* Paris, 1986.

————— *Les Demeures parisiennes sous Henri IV et Louis XIII.* Paris, 1965.

Briggs, R., *Early Modern France, 1506–1715.* Oxford, 1977.

Champion, P., *Paris au temps des guerres de religion.* Paris, 1938.

Corneille, P., *Le Menteur.* 1st edn 1643; Paris, 2000.

Diefendorf, B., *Beneath the Cross.* Oxford, 1991.

Druon, M., *The Accursed Kings* (6 vols). London, 1956.

Duffy, E., *Saints and Sinners: A History of the Popes.* London, 1997.

Erlanger, G., *La Vie quotidienne sous Henri IV.* Paris, 1958.

Franklin, A., *Journal du Siège de Paris 1590.* Paris, 1876.

Fuller, J. F. C., *The Decisive Battles of the Western World* (vol. II). London, 1957.

Garrisson, J., *L'Edit de Nantes et sa révocation: histoire d'une intolérance.* Paris, 1985.

———— *Henri IV.* Paris, 1984.

———— *Marguerite de Valois.* Paris, 1994.

Greengrass, M., *France in the Age of Henri IV.* New York, 1984.

Lavisse, E. (ed.), *Histoire de France jusqu'à la Révolution* (vol. VI, i and ii). Paris, 1900–11.

L'Estoile, P. de, *Journal pour le règne de Henri IV.* Paris, 1943.

Mousnier, R. E., *The Assassination of Henri IV.* London, 1973.

Neale, J. E., *The Age of Catherine de Medici.* London, 1943.

Rabelais, F., *Pantagruel.* Paris, 1534–64.

Ranum, O., *Paris in the Age of Absolutism.* New York, 1968.

Sutherland, N. M., *The Massacre of St Bartholomew and the European Conflict, 1559–1572.* London, 1973.

Thompson, J. W., *The Wars of Religion in France, 1559–76.* New York, 1958.

Tuchman, B., *A Distant Mirror: the Calamitous Fourteenth Century.* New York, 1978.

Wolfe, M., *The Conversion of Henri IV: Politics, Power and Religious Belief in Early Modern France.* Cambridge, Mass., 1993.

Wood, J. B., *The King's Army: Warfare, Soldiers and Society during the French Wars of Religion, 1562–1576.* Oxford, 1996.

Ziegler, P., *The Black Death.* London, 1969.

AGE THREE: 1643–1795

Ashley, M., *Louis XIV and the Greatness of France.* London, 1946.

Belloc, H., *Paris.* London, 1920.

Briggs, R., *Early Modern France, 1506–1715.* Oxford, 1977.

Castelnau, J.-T. de, *Le Paris de Louis XIII, 1610–43.* Paris, 1929.

Cohen, E., *Ninon de Lenclos.* London, 1971.

Courteault, H., *La Fronde à Paris.* Paris, 1930.

Cronin, V., *Louis XIV.* London, 1964.

Crousaz-Cretet, Paul de, *Paris sous Louis XIV.* Paris, 1938.

Franklin, A., *La Vie de Paris sous Louis XIV: début de règne.* Paris, 1902.

Garrisson, J., *L'Edit de Nantes et sa révocation: histoire d'une intolérance.* Paris, 1985.

Gould, C., *Bernini in Paris.* London, 1981.

Isherwood, C., *Farce and Fantasy: Popular Entertainment in Eighteenth-Century Paris.* Oxford, 1986.

Jaurès, J., *Histoire socialiste de la Révolution Française* (vol. VI). Paris, 1972.

Lavedan, P., *Nouvelle Histoire de Paris: histoire de l'urbanisme de Paris.* Paris, 1975.

Laver, J., *The Age of Illusion: Manners and Morals, 1750–1848.* London, 1972.

Lavisse, E. (ed.), *Histoire de France jusqu'à la Révolution* (vols VII and VIII). Paris, 1900–11.

Lenôtre, G., *La Vie à Paris pendant la Révolution*. Paris, 1936.

Lister, M., *A Journey to Paris in the Year 1697*. Champaign, Ill., 1967.

Lough, J., *An Introduction to Seventeenth-Century France*. London, 1954.

Magne, E., *Images de Paris sous Louis XIV*. Paris, 1948.

—— *La Vie quotidienne sous Louis XIII*. Paris, 1964.

Mercier, S., *Paris pendant la Révolution, 1789–1798*. Paris, 1862.

Methirier, H., *Le Siècle de Louis XIII*. Paris, 1994.

Mitford, N., *Madame de Pompadour*. London, 1954.

—— *The Sun King*. London, 1976.

Mongrédien, G., *Madame de Montespan et L'Affaire des Poisons*. Paris, 1953.

—— *La Vie quotidienne sous Louis XIV*. Paris, 1948.

Pevitt, C., *Philippe Duc d'Orléans, Regent of France*. New York, 1997.

Ranum, O., *Paris in the Age of Absolutism*. New York, 1968.

Retz, Cardinal de (trans. P. Dovall), *Memoirs*. London, 1998.

Saint-Simon, Louis de Rouvroy, Duc de, *Mémoires* (8 vols). Paris, 1983–8.

Schama, S., *Citizens: A Chronicle of the French Revolution*. London, 1989.

Sévigné, Madame de, *Lettres*. London, 1927.

Sutcliffe, A., *Paris: An Architectural History*. New Haven, 1993.

Tapie, V.-L., *France in the Age of Louis XIII and Richelieu*. Cambridge, 1984.

Tilly, C., *The Contentious French*. Cambridge, Mass., 1986.

Tocqueville, A. de, *L'Ancien Régime*. Oxford, 1925.

Trout, A., *City on the Seine: Paris in the Time of Richelieu and Louis XIV*. London, 1966/New York, 1996.

Voltaire, F. M. A., *Le Siècle de Louis XIV*. Paris, 1947.

Wedgwood, C. V., *Richelieu and the French Monarchy*. Harmondsworth, 1978.

AGE FOUR: 1795–1815

Aulard, F. A., *Paris sous le Premier Empire: recueil des documents pour l'histoire de l'esprit public à Paris*. Paris, 1912.

Baudot, F., *Mémoire du Style Empire*. Paris, 1990.

Biver, M.-L., *Le Paris de Napoléon*. Paris, 1963.

Broglie, V. Duc de, *Souvenirs, 1785–1870* (4 vols). Paris, 1886.

Bruce, E., *Napoleon and Josephine: An Improbable Marriage*. London, 1995.

Chaptal, J.-A.-C., *Mes Souvenirs sur Napoléon*. Paris, 1893.

Chateaubriand, F. R., *Mémoires d'outre-tombe* (3 vols). Paris, 1951.

Cobb, R., *Paris and its Provinces, 1792–1802*. Oxford, 1975.

Dallas, G., *1815: The Roads to Waterloo*. London, 1996.

Denon, D.-V., *Correspondance*. Paris, 1999.

—— *L'Oeil de Napoléon* (catalogue). Paris (Louvre), 1999–2000.

Gallienne, R. le, *From a Paris Garret*. London, 1943.

George, Mlle, *A Favourite of Napoleon: Memoirs*, ed. P. Cheramy. London, 1909.

Horne, A., *How Far from Austerlitz? Napoleon, 1805–1815*. London, 1996.

Hugo, V., *Les Misérables* (2 vols). 1st edn 1862; trans. London, 1976.

Jack, B., *George Sand*. London, 1999.

Keats, J., *Stendhal*. London, 1994.

Laffont, R., *Paris and its People*. Paris, 1958.

Lanzac de Laborie, L. de, *Paris sous Napoléon* (8 vols). Paris, 1900–13.

Las Cases, E., *Le Mémorial de Sainte-Hélène*. Paris, 1951.

Lefebre, G., *Napoleon, 1807–15*. London, 1969.

May, G., *Stendhal and the Age of Napoleon*. New York, 1970.

Menuret de Chaume, J.-J., *Essais sur l'histoire médico-topographique de Paris*. Paris, 1804.

Reichardt, J. F., *Vertrauten Briefe aus Paris, Geschrieben in den Jahren 1802 und 1803* (3 vols). Hamburg, 1804.

Rémusat, C. de, *Mémoires de ma vie*. Paris, 1958.

Rice, H. C., *Thomas Jefferson's Paris*. Princeton, 1976.

Robiquet, J., *Daily Life in France under Napoleon*. London, 1962.

Shepherd, W., *Paris, 1802 and 1814*. London, 1814.

Sparrow, E., *Secret Service: British Agents in France, 1792–1815*. London, 1999.

Thiers, A., *Le Consulat et l'Empire*. Paris, 1932.

West, A., *Mortal Wounds*. London, 1975.

Willms, J., *Paris: Capital of Europe from the Revolution to the Belle Epoque*. New York, 1997.

AGE FIVE: 1815–1871

Alméras, H. d', *Les Mystères de Paris*. Paris, n.d.

——— *La Vie parisienne sous la Restauration*. Paris, 1958.

Alphonse, L., *De la salubrité de la ville de Paris*. Paris, 1826.

Apponyi, R., *Journal du Comte Rodolphe Apponyi*. Paris, 1926.

Baldick, R. (ed.), *Pages from the Goncourt Journal*. London, 1902.

Balzac, H. de, *La Comédie humaine* (12 vols). Paris, 1976–81.

——— *Le Père Goriot*. Paris, 1835; trans. Harmondsworth, 1951.

Baudelaire, C., *Les Fleurs du mal*. Paris, 1857.

Bidou, H., *Paris*. London, 1939.

Castries, Duc de, *The Lives of the Kings and Queens of France*. London, 1979.

Chastenet, J., *Une Epoque de contestation: la monarchie bourgeoise (1830–1848)*. Paris, 1976.

Child, Edwin, Private letters of Edwin Child (author's collection).

Cobb, R., *Tour de France*. London, 1976.

Dark, S., *Paris*. London, 1926.

Flaubert, G., *L'Education sentimentale*. Paris, 1864.

Fuchs, R. G., *Poor and Pregnant in Nineteenth-Century Paris*. New Brunswick, 1922.

Gautier, T., *Tableaux du Siège, Paris 1870–1871*. Paris, 1886.

Goncourt, E. and J. de, *Journal: mémoires de la vie littéraire*, ed. R. Ricutte (4 vols). Paris, 1958.

Guedalla, P., *The Hundred Years*. London, 1936.

Haussmann, G.-E., *Mémoires* (3 vols). Paris, 1894.

Heine, H., 'Französische Zustände', in *Sämtliche Schriften*. Munich, 1975.

Horne, A., *The Fall of Paris: The Siege and the Commune, 1870–71*. London, 1965.

────── *The Terrible Year: The Paris Commune 1871*. London, 1971.

Howarth, T. E. B., *Citizen King*. London, 1961.

Keats, J., *Stendhal*. London, 1994.

Laver, J., *The Age of Illusion: Manners and Morals, 1750–1848*. London, 1972.

Lewald, A., 'Ein Menschenleben', in *Gesammelte Schriften* (6 vols). Leipzig, 1844.

Luchet, A., *Nouveau Tableau de Paris*. Paris, 1935.

Rambuteau, C.-P. B., Comte de, *Mémoires du Comte de Rambuteau publiés par son petit-fils*. Paris, 1905.

Robb, G., *Victor Hugo*. London, 1997.

Sue, E., *Les Mystères de Paris*. Paris, 1843.

Sutcliffe, A., *Paris: An Architectural History*. New Haven, 1993.

Tombs, R., *The War against Paris, 1871*. Cambridge, 1981.

Willms, J., *Paris: Capital of Europe from the Revolution to the Belle Epoque*. New York, 1997.

Zola, E., *Une Page d'amour; les Rougon-Macquart* (5 vols). Paris, 1960.

AGE SIX: 1871–1940

Baldick, R. (ed.), *Pages from the Goncourt Journal*. London, 1902.

Bertie, Lord, *Diaries, 1914–18* (2 vols). London, 1924.

Boothe, C., *European Spring*. London, 1941.

Briggs, A., *Fins de Siècle*. London, 1996.

Burns, M., *Dreyfus: A Family Affair, 1789–1945*. London, 1992.

Bury, J. P. T., *France, 1914–1940*. London, 1949.

Churchill, W. S., *The Second World War* (vol. II). London, 1949.

Clemenceau, G., *Discours de guerre*. Paris, 1968.

Cobb, R., *French and Germans, Germans and French*. London, 1983.

────── *Promenades*. Oxford, 1980.

Cronin, V., *Paris, City of Light, 1919–1939*. London, 1994.

────── *Paris on the Eve, 1900–1914*. London, 1989.

Dallas, G., *1918: War and Peace*. London, 2000.

Donaldson, S., *Hemingway vs Fitzgerald: The Rise and Fall of a Literary Friendship*, London, 2000.

Du Camp, M., *Paris, ses organes, ses fonctions et sa vie dans la seconde moitié du XIXe siècle.* Paris, 1883–4.

Egremont, M., *Under Two Flags: The Life of Major-General Sir Edward Spears.* London, 1997.

Evenson, N., *Paris: A Century of Change, 1878–1978.* New Haven, 1979.

Fitzgerald, F. Scott, *The Letters of F. Scott Fitzgerald,* ed. A. Turnbull. London, 1963.

Flanner, J., *An American in Paris.* London, 1940.

——— *Paris was Yesterday.* New York, 1972.

Galliéni, Général, *Mémoires: défense de Paris, 25 Août–11 Septembre, 1914.* Paris, 1920.

Gaulle, C. de, *Mémoires de guerre.* Paris, 1956.

Gillet, L., *Correspondance avec Romain Rolland.* Paris, 1949.

Gosling, N., *Paris, 1900–1914: The Miraculous Years.* London, 1978.

Grayson, C. T., *Woodrow Wilson: An Intimate Memoir.* New York, 1940.

Guedalla, P., *The Hundred Years.* London, 1936.

Hankey, M., *The Supreme Control: At the Paris Peace Conference.* London, 1963.

Hausser, E., *Paris au jour le jour: les événements vus par la presse 1900–1919.* Paris, 1968.

Hemingway, E., *A Moveable Feast.* London, 1964.

Hirschauer, General, *Paris en état de défense.* Paris, 1927.

Hoover, H., *The Ordeal of Woodrow Wilson.* New York, 1958.

Horne, A., *The Fall of Paris: The Seige and the Commune 1870–1.* London, 1990.

——— *Price of Glory: Verdun, 1916.* London, 1962.

——— *To Lose a Battle: France, 1940.* London, 1969.

Jackson, J. H., *Clemenceau and the Third Republic.* London, 1946.

Junger, E., *Journal de guerre et d'Occupation, 1939–1948.* Paris, 1965.

Lanoux, A., *Paris in the Twenties.* New York, 1960.

Lavedan, E., *Nouvelle Histoire de Paris: histoire de l'urbanisme de Paris.* Paris, 1975.

Liddell Hart, B., *History of the World War, 1914–1918.* London, 1934.

Lloyd George, D., *Memoirs of the Peace Conference.* New Haven, 1939.

Mendès-France, P., *The Pursuit of Freedom.* London, 1956.

Miller, H., *Tropic of Cancer.* Paris, 1934.

Monzie, A. de, *Ci-Devant.* Paris, 1942.

Nicolson, H., *Peacemaking, 1919.* London, 1933.

Orwell, G., *Down and Out in Paris and London.* London, 1933.

Painter, G., *Marcel Proust: A Biography.* London, 1989.

Passos, J. Dos, *The Best Times: An Informal Memoire.* New York, 1966.

——— *Mr Wilson's War.* New York/London, 1963.

Poincaré R., *Memoirs* (4 vols). London, 1926.

Ponsonaillhe, C., *L'Exposition de Paris 1900 (Encyclopédie du Siècle).* Paris, 1900.

Proust, M., *À la recherche du temps perdu* (10 vols). Paris, 1922–7.

Pryce-Jones, D., *Paris in the Third Reich: A History of the German Occupation, 1940–1944.* London, 1981.

Radclyffe Hall, M., *The Well of Loneliness*. London, 1928.

Rearick, C., *The French in Love and War*. New Haven, 1997.

Rose, P., *Jazz Cleopatra: Josephine Baker and her Time*. London, 1990.

Rosenblum, R., Stevens, M. and Dumas, A., *1900: Art at the Crossroads*. London, 2000.

Shattuck, R., *The Banquet Years*. London, 1968.

Shirer, W. L., *Berlin Diary*. Paris, 1942.

Thurman, J., *Secrets of the Flesh: A Life of Colette*. New York, 1999.

Tuchman, B., *August 1914*. London, 1962.

―――― *The Proud Tower*. London, 1966.

Watt, R. M., *The Kings Depart*. New York, 1968.

Weber, E., *The Hollow Years: France in the 1930s*. London, 1995.

―――― *Peasants into Frenchmen*. London, 1977.

Wharton, E., *French Ways*. New York, 1919.

White, E., *Proust*. London, 1999.

Wiser, W., *The Crazy Years: Paris in the Twenties*. London, 1983.

Zeldin, T., *France, 1848–1945* (2 vols). Oxford, 1973–7.

Zweig, S., *The World of Yesterday*. London, 1943.

AGE SEVEN: 1940–1969

Amouroux, H., *La Grande Histoire des Français sous l'Occupation* (9 vols). Paris, 1988–91.

Ardagh, J., *The New French Revolution*. New York, 1968.

Aron, R., *The Elusive Revolution: Anatomy of a Student Revolt*. New York, 1969.

―――― *Histoire de la Libération de la France*. Paris, 1959.

―――― *Histoire de Vichy*. Paris, 1954.

―――― *Memoirs*. New York, 1990.

―――― *La Révolution introuvable*. Paris, 1968.

Barrault. J.-L., *Souvenirs pour demain*. Paris, 1972.

Beauvoir, S. de, *La Force de l'âge*. Paris, 1967.

Beevor, A. and Cooper, A., *Paris after the Liberation*. London, 1994.

Bizardel, Y., *Sous l'Occupation: souvenirs d'un conservateur de musée*. Paris, 1964.

Bourget, P., *Sur les murs de Paris, 1940–44*. Paris, 1959.

Brasillach, R., *Journal d'un homme occupé* (6 vols). Paris, 1964.

Chalendar, J. de, *Une Loi pour l'université*. Paris, 1970.

Cocteau, J., *Journal, 1942–1945*. Paris, 1989.

Cointet, J.-P., *Paris, '40–44*. Paris, 2001.

Collins, L. and Lapierre, D., *Is Paris Burning?* London, 1965.

Courtin, R., *De la clandestinité au pouvoir: journal de la Libération de Paris*. Paris, 1994.

Druon, M., *L'Avenir en désarroi*. Paris, 1968.

Dulong, C., *La Vie quotidienne à l'Elysée au temps de Charles de Gaulle*. Paris, 1974.

Elgey, G., *Histoire de la IVe République* (2 vols). Paris, 1965.

Evenson, N., *Paris: A Century of Change, 1878–1978*. New Haven, 1979.

Fenby, J., *On the Brink*. London, 1998.

Flanner, J., *An American in Paris*. London, 1940.

———— *Paris Journal, 1944–1965*. New York, 1965.

———— *Paris Journal, 1965–1970*. New York, 1970.

———— *Paris was Yesterday*. New York, 1972.

Galtier-Boissière, J., *Mon Journal pendant l'Occupation*. Paris, 1944.

Gaulle, C. de, *Mémoires de guerre* (2 vols). Paris, 1956.

———— *Memoirs of Hope*. London, 1971.

Gildea, R., *France since 1945*. Oxford, 1995.

Giles, F., *The Locust Years: The Story of the Fourth French Republic, 1946–1958*.
   London, 1991.

Gorce, P. de la, *The French Army*. London, 1963.

Gordon, D. A., 'World Reaction to the 1961 Paris Pogrom', unpublished paper.
   Sussex University, 1998.

Guéhenno, J., *Journal des Années Noires, 1940–1944*. Paris, 1947.

Horne, A., *The French Army in Politics, 1870–1970*. London, 1984.

———— *A Savage War of Peace: Algeria, 1954–1962*. London, 1977.

Junger, E., *Journal parisien*. Paris, 1980.

———— *Strahlungen*. Tübingen, 1949.

Karnow, S., *Paris in the Fifties*. New York, 1997.

Mauriac, F., *Journal* (5 vols). Paris, 1953.

Muggeridge, M., *Chronicles of Wasted Time: The Infernal Grove*. London, 1973.

Murphy, R., *Diplomat among Warriors*. London, 1964.

Nevin, T., *Ernest Junger and Germany: Into the Abyss*. London, 1977.

Ousby, I., *Occupation: The Ordeals of France, 1940–1944*. London, 1997.

Paxton, R., *Vichy France: Old Guard and New Order*. New York, 1981.

Pryce-Jones, D., *Paris in the Third Reich*. London, 1981.

Queneau, R., *Zazie dans le Métro*. Paris, 1959.

Ragache, G. and J.-R., *Des écrivains et des artistes sous l'Occupation*. Paris, 1988.

Rioux, J.-P., *The Fourth Republic, 1944–1958*. London, 1987.

Roberts, J. M., *History of the Twentieth Century*. London, 1976.

Schoenbrun, D., *Soldiers of the Night*. New York, 1980.

Shirer, W. L., *Berlin Diary*. Paris, 1942.

Thurman, J., *Secrets of the Flesh: A Life of Colette*. New York, 1999.

Tuilier, A., *Histoire de l'Université de Paris et de la Sorbonne*. Paris, 1994.

Vidal-Nacquet, P., *Torture: Cancer of Democracy*. London, 1963.

EPILOGUE: DEATH IN PARIS

Lanzac de Laborie, L. de, *Paris sous Napoléon* (8 vols). Paris, 1900–13.

Source Notes

The following source notes refer to works listed section by section in the Bibliography. I have found these texts outstandingly useful throughout: Bidou, Castelot, Clunn, Cobb (all the listed works), Couperie, Cronin (of the three listed, all provide outstandingly readable contributions to the history of Paris), Dark, Favier, Hillairet (the *Dictionnaire historique des rues de Paris* is a classic work of reference, and an inseparable companion), Hofbauer, Lavisse (though compiled a century ago, an admirable general history of France), Littlewood, Maurois (though written just after the Second World War, a well-balanced and colourful account that doesn't date), Sutcliffe (an excellent survey of the development of Paris architecture over the ages), Vallois (three volumes that provide an excellent guide arrondissement by arrondissement.

INTRODUCTION

page 9 'human genius' Maurois, p. 78

AGE ONE: 1180–1314

Particularly useful and to be recommended here: Baldwin, Druon, *Kings* and *Paris* (*The Accursed Kings* remains an enduring classic), Duby (one of France's leading experts on the Age of Philippe Auguste, sadly recently deceased), Geremek, Gilson, Holmes, Jordan, Lavisse, III, Radice.

21 *'rusé comme un renard'* Lavisse, III, i, 119 ff
45 *'chansons'* Maurois, 75
49 'great neurotics' Druon, *Paris*, 95
52 'a poor house' Holmes, 81
53 'All the organs' Druon, *Paris*, 99
58 'a bitter thing' Lavisse, III, ii, 183

AGE TWO: 1314–1643

Babelon, *Paris*, Briggs, Diefendorf, Garrisson, *Henri IV*, Greengrass, Lavisse, Ranum, Wolfe.

63 'heart of the kingdom' Druon, *Kings*, 11
66 'Those who were left' Ziegler, 83

69–70 'deep-rooted certainty' Maurois, 117, 112

74 'animal violence' ibid., 142–3

77 'not a woman' ibid., 164

79 'before Paris' Garrisson, 157

82 'Mistress, I am writing' ibid., 160

83 'no meat' Lavisse, VI, i, 322

91 'very wild place' Ranum, 19–20

98 'skin and bone' Lavisse, VI, ii, 129

101 'the entire populace' Greengrass, 251–3

102 'less astonishing' Maurois, 172–4

109 'clip your nails' ibid., 190

110 'An entire city' Corneille

Age Three: 1643–1795

Briggs, Cronin, *Louis XIV* (especially good on Fouquet), Mitford, *Sun*, Mongrédien, *Montespan* and *Vie* (especially on the 'Affaire des Poisons'), Pevitt, Ranum, Trout, Voltaire.

118 'The civil wars started' Voltaire, I, 64

127–30 'Well, it's all over' The execution of Brinvilliers and Voisin: Sévigné, 196, 240–1; Mongrédien, *Vie*, 201; Mongrédien, *Montespan*, 33, 75, 88

131 'with some pomp' Mitford, *Sun*, 95

139 Blondel Sutcliffe, 26

142 'he is sent forthwith' Lister, 25

146 'four full dishes' ibid., 148–68
'nothing of worse breeding' Mongrédien, *Montespan*, 97, 296

152 'My dominant passion' Cronin, *Louis XIV*, 189

159 'the statue of Victoire' Ranum, 284

160 'Before being at court' Mongrédien, *Vie*, 20

165 'are you not the master?' Pevitt, 300

Age Four: 1795–1815

Out of a gigantic bibliography: Dallas, Horne, *Austerlitz* (inevitably I drew some material from my own two books on Napoleon), Lanzac de Laborie, Robiquet, Willms.

De Laborie provided me with one of the great finds of this book. Its eight volumes were published between 1900 and 1913, only for the onset of the First World War to leave the sequence unfinished. I came across a copy, its pages still uncut, in the London Library. It is a marvellously well-researched work, amusing and packed with marginal information about Napoleon's Paris.

184 'ruinous castles' Horne, *Austerlitz*, 18

185 'You are barbarians' Robiquet, 63

186 'talk about politics' Willms, 94, n. 234
'The Paris of the rich' ibid., 96

190 'church flummery!' Robiquet, 46

196 'Goodbye to the Republic' Jack, 22

201 'without over-excitement' Laborie, III, 57–61
'I am not the lover' ibid., VI, 34, 37

202 warned the writer Mme de Staël, ibid., VI, 42

203 'comes from God' Lefebre, 7
'Today's fête' Laborie, III, 11

205 'One must leave' ibid., II, 170

206 'The French Republic' ibid., VIII, 234–5

207 'What statue' ibid., II, 180–2

208 decrepit mammoth Hugo, 179

211 King of Württemberg Laborie, II, 290
'Napoléonville' ibid., 91, 191

212 Versailles ibid., 191–2

214 'be ruined' Robiquet, 174
'endless begging' Reichardt, I, 25

215 'extreme overcrowding' Willms, 118

216 impressionable German Reichardt, I, 227ff

217 prepare a *gigot* Robiquet, 95

219 'je tremble' Laborie, VII, 207–8

220 'People are determined' ibid., 147ff

222 'I am very dissatisfied' ibid., VIII, 10, 16–17
Mlle Aubery ibid., 16–17

224 'the popular Empress' Horne, *Austerlitz*, 257

225 'Crying like a child' Bruce, 436
'Iphigenia' Maurois, 339

226 'I swear to you' West, 186
'We counted' Horne, *Austerlitz*, 292

227 'I have become blasé' Keats, 126

230 'in general terror-stricken' Bruce, 463–4

232 'We women' Maurois, 342

233 Mme de Coigny Laffont, 172

235 'Bois de Boulogne' Gallienne, 77

236 'well-dressed people' Denon, *L'Oeil*, 11
'bare walls' ibid.

237 'some big losses' Denon, *Correspondance*, 3518

AGE FIVE: 1815–1871

Balzac, Chastenet, Flaubert, Gautier, Goncourt, Haussmann, Horne, *Fall* (inevitably I have drawn on my own *The Fall of Paris* for material on both the Second

Empire and the Siege and the Commune of 1870–1), Sutcliffe (especially for analysis of the impact of Haussmann), Willms.

242 'a submissive bigot' Maurois, 357–62

244 'a place one avoids' Lewald, VI, 57

  'pale spectre' Bidou, 354

246 'that illustrious valley' Balzac, *Père Goriot*, 1–3, 8, 14

248 'remain lying there' Alphonse, 8ff

251 'are like children' Rambuteau, 269

254 'the post-chaise' Laver, 174

  'hurling itself down' Dark, 115

255 'a special dirty glove' Willms, 200

256 'breaking glass' Guedalla, 54

258 'a small aristocracy' Willms, 243

259 'a carnival-like exuberance' Flaubert, 325

260 'Nine hundred men' ibid.

263 'vulgar-looking man' Horne, *Fall*, 20

267 'We ripped open' Haussmann, 54ff

269 'bobbing manes' Vallois, I, 10

279 'art elbowed' Horne, *Fall*, 4

285 'MacMahon's defeat' Baldick, 169

287 'Europe's heart' Horne, *Fall*, 73

295 'the animals observed' ibid., 178

301 'it is all over' ibid., 266

303 'your profession?' ibid., 337

304 '*des candides*' Cobb, *Tour*, 128–31

308 'we saw the insurgents' Horne, *Fall*, 381, 383

310 Communard prisoners ibid., 405–7

313 'A silence of death' ibid., 420

Age Six: 1871–1940

Baldick, Cronin, *Eve* and *City*, Dallas, *1918*, Flanner, *American* and *Yesterday*, Pryce-Jones (a valuable British contribution to the story of the Occupation), Rose (for details of the entrancing Josephine Baker), Shattuck, Thurman (an outstanding recent biography of Colette).

317 'You are young' Baldick, 193–5

319 'painter called Degas' ibid., 206

  'I regret' Horne, *Fall*, 427

321 'wholesale copulation' Baldick, 307

323 '"The swine!"' ibid., 398

337 'Nobody can imagine' Gosling, 70, 112

340 'an ill-made beast' Cronin, *Eve*, 250

342 'was still Athenian' Maurois, 470
'A dark resentment' Guedalla, 138

343 'You are weary' Laffont, 244

345 'beautiful to fight' Gillet, 289, 299
'much nervous excitement' Bertie, I, 3–11

348 'strong measures' Cronin, *Eve*, 442

352 'Paris will be burned!' Tuchman, *August*, 374

353 'destruction, ruins' Galliéni, 59–64

359–60 'two foreign countries' Horne, *Price*, 190

364 'People are getting away' Bertie, II, 291

368 'a vivid impression' Dallas, *1918*, 348

378 'Paris is a bitch' Wiser, 66

380 'entirely nude' Flanner, *Yesterday*, xx
'Josephine Baker' Rose, 97ff

381 'qu'il était beau!' Rearick, 94

382 'I understand' Miller, 148, 166

390 'Paris! Viens avec nous' Weber, *Hollow*, 161
'a frightful place' Shirer, 125

395 'la masse de manoeuvre' Churchill, II, 42

396 'France deprived of Paris' Horne, *Lose*, 562

AGE SEVEN: 1940–1969

Aron, *Elusive*, Beevor and Cooper (excellent on the immediate aftermath of the Second World War), Collins and Lapierre (still reads well), Dulong (an engaging account of life in the Elysée under de Gaulle), Flanner (all four works), Giles.

400 'I wished I had not come' Shirer, 321–4

407 'The German genius and I' Pryce-Jones, 62

410 'a position of impotence' ibid., 168

411 'an unconsciousness shared' Thurman, 444

416 'For over four years' de Gaulle, *Guerre*, II, 289

421 'Paris outraged!' ibid., 308

422 'The effect was fantastic' Muggeridge, 211–12

425 'forty FFI' Courtin, 57, 66, 74

442 '*Hélas! Hélas! Hélas!*' Flanner, *1944–1965*, 479; Horne, *Savage*, 455

451 'Since the Liberation' Flanner, *1944–1965*, 275

453 'Everything always has an end' Flanner, *1965–1970*, 211

454 'One fighting speech' Aron, *Elusive*, 157
'a French affair' Barrault, 51

457 'What struck me most' Aron, *Elusive*, 232

464 'I am ceasing' Dulong, 229

EPILOGUE: DEATH IN PARIS

467 'Most of the cemeteries' Laborie, III, 368

Index

Index

extracts reading groups competitions books new events discounts extracts reading groups extracts discounts events competitions books new books reading groups events extracts discounts events new books extracts titles new reading groups interviews events extracts new books events discounts new books events reading groups books interviews new extracts events new discounts extracts discounts

www.panmacmillan.com

extracts events reading groups competitions books extracts new books